AND BOOK TRAINING PACKAGE AVAILABLE

ExamSim

Experience realistic, simulated exams on your own computer with Osborne's interactive ExamSim software. This computer-based test engine offers both standard and adaptive test modes, knowledge-based and product simulation questions like those found on the real exams, and review tools that help you study more efficiently. Intuitive controls allow you to move easily through the program: mark difficult or unanswered questions for further review and skip ahead, then assess your performance at the end.

Knowledge-based questions present challenging material in a multiple-choice format. Answer treatments not only explain why the correct options are right, they also tell you why the incorrect answers were wrong.

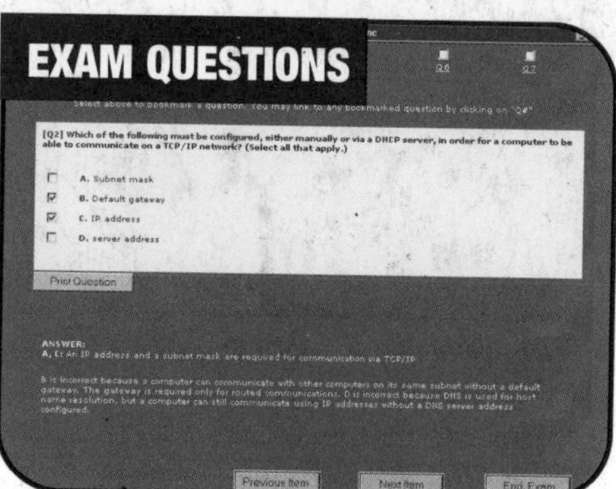

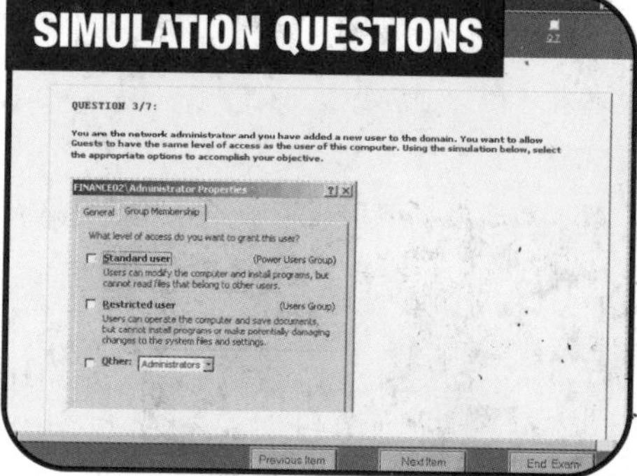

Realistic Windows 2000 product **Simulation Questions** test the skills you need to pass the exam—these questions look and feel like the simulation questions on the actual exam!

Additional CD-ROM Features

- Complete hyperlinked **e-book** for easy information access and self-paced study

- **DriveTime** audio tracks offer concise review of key exam topics for in the car or on the go!

System Requirements:

A PC running Internet Explorer version 5 or higher

Detailed **Score Reports** provide score analysis and history to chart your progress and focus your st[u]

MCSE Windows 2000 Network Administration Study Guide

(Exam 70-216)

MCSE Windows 2000 Network Administration Study Guide

(Exam 70-216)

Syngress Media, Inc.

Osborne McGraw-Hill

Berkeley New York St. Louis San Francisco Auckland Bogotá Hamburg London Madrid Mexico City
Milan Montreal New Delhi Panama City Paris São Paulo Singapore Sydney Tokyo Toronto

Osborne McGraw-Hill
2600 Tenth Street
Berkeley, California 94710
U.S.A.

For information on translations or book distributors outside the U.S.A., or to arrange bulk purchase discounts for sales promotions, premiums, or fund-raisers, please contact Osborne/**McGraw-Hill** at the above address.

MCSE Windows 2000 Network Administration Study Guide (Exam 70-216)

234567890 AGM AGM 0198765432109

Book p/n 0-07-212381-8 and CD p/n 0-07-212382-6
parts of ISBN 0-07-212383-4

Publisher
Brandon A. Nordin

Associate Publisher and Editor-in-Chief
Scott Rogers

Acquisitions Editor
Gareth Hancock

Associate Acquisitions Editor
Timothy Green

Editorial Management
Syngress Media, Inc.

Project Editors
Jennifer Malnick
Julie Smalley

Editorial Assistant
Tara Davis

Series Editors
Dr. Thomas W. Shinder
Debra Littlejohn Shinder

Technical Editor
James Truscott

Copy Editor
Beth Roberts

Proofreader
Caroll Proffitt

Indexer
Jack Lewis

Computer Designers
Jim Kussow
Lauren McCarthy
Roberta Steele

Illustrators
Michael T. Mueller
Robert Hansen
Beth Young

Series Design
Roberta Steele

Cover Design
Greg Scott

This book was published with Corel VENTURA™ Publisher.

FOREWORD

From Global Knowledge

At Global Knowledge we strive to support the multiplicity of learning styles required by our students to achieve success as technical professionals. In this series of books, it is our intention to offer the reader a valuable tool for successful completion of the MCSE Windows 2000 Certification exams.

As the world's largest IT training company, Global Knowledge is uniquely positioned to offer these books. The expertise gained each year from providing instructor-led training to hundreds of thousands of students worldwide has been captured in book form to enhance your learning experience. We hope that the quality of these books demonstrates our commitment to your lifelong learning success. Whether you choose to learn through the written word, computer-based training, Web delivery, or instructor-led training, Global Knowledge is committed to providing you the very best in each of those categories. For those of you who know Global Knowledge, or those of you who have just found us for the first time, our goal is to be your lifelong competency partner.

Thank you for the opportunity to serve you. We look forward to serving your needs again in the future.

Warmest regards,

Duncan Anderson
President and Chief Operating Officer, Global Knowledge

The Global Knowledge Advantage

Global Knowledge has a global delivery system for its products and services. The company has 28 subsidiaries, and offers its programs through a total of 60+ locations. No other vendor can provide consistent services across a geographic area this large. Global Knowledge is the largest independent information technology education provider, offering programs on a variety of platforms. This enables our multi-platform and multi-national customers to obtain all of their programs from a single vendor. The company has developed the unique Competus™ Framework software tool and methodology which can quickly reconfigure courseware to the proficiency level of a student on an interactive basis. Combined with self-paced and on-line programs, this technology can reduce the time required for training by prescribing content in only the deficient skills areas. The company has fully automated every aspect of the education process, from registration and follow-up, to "just-in-time" production of courseware. Global Knowledge Network through its Enterprise Services Consultancy, can customize programs and products to suit the needs of an individual customer.

Global Knowledge Classroom Education Programs

The backbone of our delivery options is classroom-based education. Our modern, well-equipped facilities staffed with the finest instructors offer programs in a wide variety of information technology topics, many of which lead to professional certifications.

Custom Learning Solutions

This delivery option has been created for companies and governments that value customized learning solutions. For them, our consultancy-based approach of developing targeted education solutions is most effective at helping them meet specific objectives.

Self-Paced and Multimedia Products

This delivery option offers self-paced program titles in interactive CD-ROM, videotape and audio tape programs. In addition, we offer custom development of interactive multimedia courseware to customers and partners. Call us at 1-888-427-4228.

Electronic Delivery of Training

Our network-based training service delivers efficient competency-based, interactive training via the World Wide Web and organizational intranets. This leading-edge delivery option provides a custom learning path and "just-in-time" training for maximum convenience to students.

ARG

American Research Group (ARG), a wholly-owned subsidiary of Global Knowledge, one of the largest worldwide training partners of Cisco Systems, offers a wide range of internetworking, LAN/WAN, Bay Networks, FORE Systems, IBM, and UNIX courses. ARG offers hands on network training in both instructor-led classes and self-paced PC-based training.

Global Knowledge Courses Available

Network Fundamentals

- Understanding Computer Networks
- Telecommunications Fundamentals I
- Telecommunications Fundamentals II
- Understanding Networking Fundamentals
- Implementing Computer Telephony Integration
- Introduction to Voice Over IP
- Introduction to Wide Area Networking
- Cabling Voice and Data Networks
- Introduction to LAN/WAN protocols
- Virtual Private Networks
- ATM Essentials

Network Security & Management

- Troubleshooting TCP/IP Networks
- Network Management
- Network Troubleshooting
- IP Address Management
- Network Security Administration
- Web Security
- Implementing UNIX Security
- Managing Cisco Network Security
- Windows NT 4.0 Security

IT Professional Skills

- Project Management for IT Professionals
- Advanced Project Management for IT Professionals
- Survival Skills for the New IT Manager
- Making IT Teams Work

LAN/WAN Internetworking

- Frame Relay Internetworking
- Implementing T1/T3 Services
- Understanding Digital Subscriber Line (xDSL)
- Internetworking with Routers and Switches
- Advanced Routing and Switching
- Multi-Layer Switching and Wire-Speed Routing
- Internetworking with TCP/IP
- ATM Internetworking
- OSPF Design and Configuration
- Border Gateway Protocol (BGP) Configuration

Authorized Vendor Training

Cisco Systems

- Introduction to Cisco Router Configuration
- Advanced Cisco Router Configuration
- Installation and Maintenance of Cisco Routers
- Cisco Internetwork Troubleshooting
- Cisco Internetwork Design
- Cisco Routers and LAN Switches
- Catalyst 5000 Series Configuration
- Cisco LAN Switch Configuration
- Managing Cisco Switched Internetworks
- Configuring, Monitoring, and Troubleshooting Dial-Up Services
- Cisco AS5200 Installation and Configuration
- Cisco Campus ATM Solutions

Bay Networks

- Bay Networks Accelerated Router Configuration
- Bay Networks Advanced IP Routing
- Bay Networks Hub Connectivity
- Bay Networks Accelar 1xxx Installation and Basic Configuration
- Bay Networks Centillion Switching

FORE Systems

- FORE ATM Enterprise Core Products
- FORE ATM Enterprise Edge Products
- FORE ATM Theory
- FORE LAN Certification

Operating Systems & Programming

Microsoft

- Introduction to Windows NT
- Microsoft Networking Essentials
- Windows NT 4.0 Workstation
- Windows NT 4.0 Server
- Advanced Windows NT 4.0 Server
- Windows NT Networking with TCP/IP
- Introduction to Microsoft Web Tools
- Windows NT Troubleshooting
- Windows Registry Configuration

UNIX

- UNIX Level I
- UNIX Level II
- Essentials of UNIX and NT Integration

Programming

- Introduction to JavaScript
- Java Programming
- PERL Programming
- Advanced PERL with CGI for the Web

Web Site Management & Development

- Building a Web Site
- Web Site Management and Performance
- Web Development Fundamentals

High Speed Networking

- Essentials of Wide Area Networking
- Integrating ISDN
- Fiber Optic Network Design
- Fiber Optic Network Installation
- Migrating to High Performance Ethernet

DIGITAL UNIX

- UNIX Utilities and Commands
- DIGITAL UNIX v4.0 System Administration
- DIGITAL UNIX v4.0 (TCP/IP) Network Management
- AdvFS, LSM, and RAID Configuration and Management
- DIGITAL UNIX TruCluster Software Configuration and Management
- UNIX Shell Programming Featuring Kornshell
- DIGITAL UNIX v4.0 Security Management
- DIGITAL UNIX v4.0 Performance Management
- DIGITAL UNIX v4.0 Intervals Overview

DIGITAL OpenVMS

- OpenVMS Skills for Users
- OpenVMS System and Network Node Management I
- OpenVMS System and Network Node Management II
- OpenVMS System and Network Node Management III
- OpenVMS System and Network Node Operations
- OpenVMS for Programmers
- OpenVMS System Troubleshooting for Systems Managers
- Configuring and Managing Complex VMScluster Systems
- Utilizing OpenVMS Features from C
- OpenVMS Performance Management
- Managing DEC TCP/IP Services for OpenVMS
- Programming in C

Hardware Courses

- AlphaServer 1000/1000A Installation, Configuration and Maintenance
- AlphaServer 2100 Server Maintenance
- AlphaServer 4100, Troubleshooting Techniques and Problem Solving

ABOUT THE CONTRIBUTORS

About Syngress Media

Syngress Media creates books and software for Information Technology professionals seeking skill enhancement and career advancement. Its products are designed to comply with vendor and industry standard course curricula, and are optimized for certification exam preparation. You can contact Syngress via the Web at www.syngress.com.

Contributors

Carol Bailey (MCSE+I). Based in London, Carol has over ten years of experience in networking, and currently has more than a dozen Microsoft exams to her name. She is a Sennior Technical Consultant working for Metascybe Systems Ltd., a company that specializes in PC software communications, offering their own connectivity products in addition to project work and consultancy for a diverse customer base. Working for a Microsoft Solutions Provider has provided Carol with a wide range of technical opportunities. Her work includes supporting the in-house networking services as well as all aspects of external customer support and consultancy.

Chris O. Broomes (MCSE, MCP+I, MCT, CCDA). A 1995 graduate of Temple University, Chris has over 7 years of networking experience. He started his career as a consultant at Temple University, and has worked with organizations such as Morgan, Lewis & Bockius, Temple University Dental School, and Dynamic Technologies, Inc. Currently, Chris is a Network Administrator in Philadelphia, PA, at EXE Technologies, Inc., a global provider of business-to-business e-fulfillment solutions. Chris resides in Lansdowne, PA, with his wife, Keisha, and son, Jared Christopher.

Matt Lind is a network security consultant who specializes in firewalls and intrusion detection. He and his beautiful wife Ronna live in Atlanta with their three perfect daughters Blake, Jordan, and Lauren.

Debra Littlejohn Shinder (MCSE, MCP+I, MCT) is an instructor in the AATP program at Eastfield College, Dallas County Community College District, where she has taught since 1992. She is Webmaster for the cities of Seagoville and Sunnyvale, Texas, as well as the family Web site at www.shinder.net. She and her husband,

Dr. Thomas W. Shinder, provide consulting and technical support services to Dallas-area organizations. She is also the proud mom of a daughter, Kristen, who is currently serving in the U.S. Navy in Italy, and a son, Kris, who is a high school chess champion. Deb has been a writer for most her life, and has published numerous articles in both technical and nontechnical fields. She can be contacted at deb@shinder.net.

Thomas W. Shinder, M.D. (MCSE, MCP+I, MCT) is a technology trainer and consultant in the Dallas-Ft. Worth metroplex. Dr. Shinder has consulted with major firms, including Xerox, Lucent Technologies, and FINA Oil, assisting in the development and implementation of IP-based communications strategies. Dr. Shinder attended medical school at the University of Illinois in Chicago, and trained in neurology at the Oregon Health Sciences Center in Portland, Oregon. His fascination with interneuronal communication ultimately melded with his interest in internetworking and led him to focus on systems engineering. Tom works passionately with his beloved wife, Deb Shinder, to design elegant and cost-efficient solutions for small and medium-sized businesses based on Windows NT/2000 platforms.

Technical Editor

James Truscott (MCSE, MCP+I) is an instructor in the MCSE program at Eastfield College and the Dallas County Community College District. He is also Senior Instructor for the Cowell Corporation and is teaching the Windows 2000 track for CLC Corporation in Dallas, Texas.

He is the Webmaster for Cowell Corporation in Richardson, Texas, and does consulting services for several Dallas-based businesses. His passion for computers started back in the 1960's when he was a programmer for Bell Telephone. One of his current projects includes developing Web sites for his students.

Series Editors

Thomas W. Shinder, M.D. (MCSE, MCP+I, MCT) is a technology trainer and consultant in the Dallas-Ft. Worth metroplex. Dr. Shinder has consulted with major firms, including Xerox, Lucent Technologies, and FINA Oil, assisting in the development and implementation of IP-based communications strategies. Dr. Shinder attended medical school at the University of Illinois in Chicago, and trained in neurology at the Oregon Health Sciences Center in Portland, Oregon. His fascination with interneuronal communication ultimately melded with his interest in internetworking and led him to focus on systems engineering. Tom works passionately with his beloved wife, Deb Shinder, to design elegant and cost-efficient solutions for small and medium-sized businesses based on Windows NT/2000 platforms.

Debra Littlejohn Shinder (MCSE, MCP+I, MCT) is an instructor in the AATP program at Eastfield College, Dallas County Community College District, where she has taught since 1992. She is Webmaster for the cities of Seagoville and Sunnyvale, Texas, as well as the family Web site at www.shinder.net. She and her husband, Dr. Thomas W. Shinder, provide consulting and technical support services to Dallas area organizations. She is also the proud mom of a daughter, Kristen, who is currently serving in the U.S. Navy in Italy, and a son, Kris, who is a high school chess champion. Deb has been a writer for most her life, and has published numerous articles in both technical and nontechnical fields. She can be contacted at deb@shinder.net.

ACKNOWLEDGMENTS

We would like to thank the following people:

- Richard Kristof of Global Knowledge for championing the series and providing access to some great people and information.
- All the incredibly hard-working folks at Osborne/McGraw-Hill: Brandon Nordin, Scott Rogers, Gareth Hancock, and Tim Green for their help in launching a great series and being solid team players. In addition, Tara Davis and Jenny Malnick for their help in fine-tuning the book.
- Monica Kilwine at Microsoft Corp., for being patient and diligent in answering all our questions.

CONTENTS AT A GLANCE

CONTENTS

PREFACE

This book's primary objective is to help you prepare for the MCSE Implementing and Administering a Windows 2000 Network Infrastructure exam under the new Windows 2000 certification track. As the Microsoft program transitions from Windows NT 4.0, it will become increasingly important that current and aspiring IT professionals have multiple resources available to assist them in increasing their knowledge and building their skills.

At the time of publication, all the exam objectives have been posted on the Microsoft Web site and the beta exam process has been completed. Microsoft has announced its commitment to measuring real-world skills. This book is designed with that premise in mind; its authors have practical experience in the field, using the Windows 2000 operating systems in hands-on situations, and have followed the development of the product since early beta versions.

Because the focus of the exams is on application and understanding, as opposed to memorization of facts, no book by itself can fully prepare you to obtain a passing score. It is essential that you work with the software to enhance your proficiency. Toward that end, this book includes many practical step-by-step exercises in each chapter that are designed to give you hands-on practice as well as guide you in truly learning Microsoft Windows 2000 Network Administration, not just learning *about* it.

In This Book

This book is organized in such a way as to serve as an in-depth review for the MCSE Implementing and Administering a Windows 2000 Network Infrastructure exam for both experienced Windows NT professionals and newcomers to Microsoft networking technologies. Each chapter covers a major aspect of the exam, with an emphasis on the "why" as well as the "how to" of working with and supporting Windows 2000 as a network administrator or engineer.

On the CD

The CD-ROM contains the CertTrainer software. CertTrainer comes complete with ExamSim, Skill Assessment tests, CertCam movie clips, the e-book (electronic version of the book), and Drive Time. CertTrainer is easy to install on any Windows 98/NT/2000 computer and must be installed to access these features. You may, however, browse the e-book direct from the CD without installation. For more information on the CD-ROM, please see Appendix A.

In Every Chapter

We've created a set of chapter components that call your attention to important items, reinforce important points, and provide helpful exam-taking hints. Take a look at what you'll find in every chapter:

- Every chapter begins with the **Certification Objectives**—what you need to know in order to pass the section on the exam dealing with the chapter topic. The Objective headings identify the objectives within the chapter, so you'll always know an objective when you see it!

- **Exam Watch** notes call attention to information about, and potential pitfalls in, the exam. These helpful hints are written by authors who have taken the exams and received their certification—who better to tell you what to worry about? They know what you're about to go through!
- **Practice Exercises** are interspersed throughout the chapters. These are step-by-step exercises that allow you to get the hands-on experience you need in order to pass the exams. They help you master skills that are likely to be an area of focus on the exam. Don't just read through the exercises; they are hands-on practice that you should be comfortable completing. Learning by doing is an effective way to increase your competency with a product. The practical exercises will be very helpful for any simulation exercises you may encounter on the MCSE Implementing and Administering a Windows 2000 Network Infrastructure exam.

- The **CertCam** icon that appears in many of the exercises indicates that those particular exercise steps are presented in .avi format on the accompanying

CD-ROM. These .avi clips walk you step-by-step through various system configurations and are narrated by Thomas W. Shinder, M.D., MCSE.

- **On The Job** notes describe the issues that come up most often in real-world settings. They provide a valuable perspective on certification- and product-related topics. They point out common mistakes and address questions that have arisen from on the job discussions and experience.
- **From The Classroom** sidebars describe the issues that come up most often in the training classroom setting. These sidebars highlight some of the most common and confusing problems that students encounter when taking a live Windows 2000 training course. You can get a leg up on those difficult-to-understand subjects by focusing extra attention on these sidebars.
- **Scenario and Solution** sections lay out potential problems and solutions in a quick-to-read format:

SCENARIO & SOLUTION	
Is Active Directory scalable?	Yes! Unlike the Windows NT security database, which is limited to approximately 40,000 objects, Active Directory supports literally millions of objects.
Is Active Directory compatible with other LDAP directory services?	Yes! Active Directory can share information with other directory services that support LDAP versions 2 and 3, such as Novell's NDS.

- The **Certification Summary** is a succinct review of the chapter and a restatement of salient points regarding the exam.

✓

- The **Two-Minute Drill** at the end of every chapter is a checklist of the main points of the chapter. It can be used for last-minute review.

- The **Self Test** offers questions similar to those found on the certification exams. The answers to these questions, as well as explanations of the answers, can be found at the end of each chapter. By taking the Self Test after completing each chapter, you'll reinforce what you've learned from that chapter while becoming familiar with the structure of the exam questions.

- The **Lab Question** at the end of the Self Test section offers a unique and challenging question format that requires you to understand multiple chapter concepts to answer correctly. These questions are more complex, and more comprehensive than the other questions, as they test your ability to take all the knowledge you have gained from reading the chapter and apply it to complicated, real-world situations. These questions are aimed to be more difficult than what you will find on the exam. If you can answer these questions, you have proved you know the subject!

The Global Knowledge Web Site

Check out the Web site. Global Knowledge invites you to become an active member of the Access Global Web site. This site is an online mall and an information repository that you'll find invaluable. You can access many types of products to assist you in your preparation for the exams, and you'll be able to participate in forums, online discussions, and threaded discussions. No other book brings you unlimited access to such a resource. You'll find more information about this site in Appendix B.

Some Pointers

Once you've finished reading this book, set aside some time to do a thorough review. You might want to return to the book several times and make use of all the methods it offers for reviewing the material:

1. *Reread all the Two-Minute Drills*, or have someone quiz you. You also can use the drills as a way to do a quick cram before the exam. You might want to make some flash cards out of 3 × 5 index cards that have the Two-Minute Drill material on them.
2. *Reread all the Exam Watch notes.* Remember that these notes are written by authors who have taken the exam and passed. They know what you should expect—and what you should be on the lookout for.
3. *Review all the Scenario & Solutions sections* for quick problem solving.
4. *Retake the Self Tests.* Taking the tests right after you've read the chapter is a good idea, because the questions help reinforce what you've just learned.

However, it's an even better idea to go back later and do all the questions in the book in one sitting. Pretend that you're taking the live exam. (When you go through the questions the first time, you should mark your answers on a separate piece of paper. That way, you can run through the questions as many times as you need to until you feel comfortable with the material.)

5. *Complete the Exercises.* Did you do the exercises when you read through each chapter? If not, do them! These exercises are designed to cover exam topics, and there's no better way to get to know this material than by practicing. Be sure you understand why you are performing each step in each exercise. If there is something you are not clear on, reread that section in the chapter.

INTRODUCTION

MCSE Certification

This book is designed to help you pass the MCSE Implementing and Administering a Windows 2000 Network Infrastructure exam. At the time this book was written, the exam objectives for the exam were posted on the Microsoft Web site, and the beta exams had been completed. We wrote this book to give you a complete and incisive review of all the important topics that are targeted for the exam. The information contained here will provide you with the required foundation of knowledge that will not only allow you to succeed in passing the MCSE Implementing and Administering a Windows 2000 Network Infrastructure exam, but will also make you a better Microsoft Certified Systems Engineer.

The nature of the Information Technology industry is changing rapidly, and the requirements and specifications for certification can change just as quickly without notice. Microsoft expects you to visit their Website at **http://www.microsoft.com/mcp/certstep/mcse.htm** regularly to get the most up-to-date information on the entire MCSE program.

TABLE i-1 Windows 2000 Certification Track

Core Exams		
Candidates Who Have *Not* Already Passed Windows NT 4.0 Exams All 4 of the Following Core Exams Required:	**OR**	**Candidates Who Have Passed three Windows NT 4.0 Exams (Exams 70-067, 70-068, and 70-073) Instead of the four Core Exams on Left, You May Take:**
Exam 70-210: Installing, Configuring and Administering Microsoft® Windows® 2000 Professional		**Exam 70-240**: Microsoft® Windows® 2000 Accelerated Exam for MCPs Certified on Microsoft® Windows NT® 4.0 The accelerated exam will be available until December 31, 2001. It covers the core competencies of exams **70-210, 70-215, 70-216, and 70-217.**

TABLE i-1 Windows 2000 Certification Track *(continued)*

Core Exams
Exam 70-215: Installing, Configuring and Administering Microsoft® Windows® 2000 Server
Exam 70-216: Implementing and Administering a Microsoft® Windows® 2000 Network Infrastructure
Exam 70-217: Implementing and Administering a Microsoft® Windows® 2000 Directory Services Infrastructure
PLUS – All Candidates – 1 of the Following Core Exams Required:
***Exam 70-219**: Designing a Microsoft® Windows® 2000 Directory Services Infrastructure
***Exam 70-220**: Designing Security for a Microsoft® Windows® 2000 Network
***Exam 70-221**: Designing a Microsoft® Windows® 2000 Network Infrastructure
PLUS – All Candidates – 2 Elective Exams Required:
Any current MCSE electives when the Windows 2000 exams listed above are released in their live versions. **Electives scheduled for retirement will not be considered current.** Selected third-party certifications that focus on interoperability will be accepted as an alternative to one elective exam.
***Exam 70-219**: Designing a Microsoft® Windows® 2000 Directory Services Infrastructure
***Exam 70-220**: Designing Security for a Microsoft® Windows® 2000 Network
***Exam 70-221**: Designing a Microsoft® Windows® 2000 Network Infrastructure
Exam 70-222: Upgrading from Microsoft® Windows® NT 4.0 to Microsoft® Windows® 2000

*Note that some of the Windows 2000 core exams can be used as elective exams as well. An exam that is used to meet the design requirement cannot also count as an elective. Each exam can only be counted once in the Windows 2000 Certification.

Let's look at two scenarios. The first applies to the person who has already taken the Windows NT 4.0 Server (70-067), Windows NT 4.0 Workstation (70-073), and Windows NT 4.0 Server in the Enterprise (70-068) exams. The second scenario covers the situation of the person who has not completed those Windows NT 4.0 exams and would like to concentrate ONLY on Windows 2000.

In the first scenario, you have the option of taking all four Windows 2000 core exams, or you can take the Windows 2000 Accelerated Exam for MCPs if you have already passed exams 70-067, 70-068, and 70-073. (Note that you must have passed those specific exams to qualify for the Accelerated Exam; if you have fulfilled your NT 4.0 MCSE requirements by passing the Windows 95 or Windows 98 exam as your client operating system option, and did not take the NT Workstation Exam, you don't qualify.)

After completing the core requirements, either by passing the four core exams or the one Accelerated exam, you must pass a "design" exam. The design exams include Designing a Microsoft Windows 2000 Directory Services Infrastructure (70-219), Designing Security for Microsoft Windows 2000 Network (70-220), and Designing a Microsoft Windows 2000 Network Infrastructure (70-221). One design exam is REQUIRED.

You also must pass two exams from the list of electives. However, you cannot use the design exam that you took as an elective. Each exam can only count once toward certification. This includes any of the MCSE electives that are current when the Windows 2000 exams are released. In summary, you would take a total of at least two more exams, the upgrade exam, and the design exam. Any additional exams would be dependent on which electives the candidate may have already completed.

In the second scenario, if you have not completed, and do not plan to complete the Core Windows NT 4.0 exams, you must pass the four core Windows 2000 exams, one design exam, and two elective exams. Again, no exam can be counted twice. In this case, you must pass a total of seven exams to obtain the Windows 2000 MCSE certification.

How to Take a Microsoft Certification Exam

If you have taken a Microsoft Certification exam before, we have some good news and some bad news. The good news is that the new testing formats will be a true measure of your ability and knowledge. Microsoft has "raised the bar" for its Windows 2000 certification exams. If you are an expert in the Windows 2000 operating system, and can troubleshoot and engineer efficient, cost effective solutions using Windows 2000, you will have no difficulty with the new exams.

The bad news is that if you have used resources such as "brain-dumps," boot-camps, or exam specific practice tests as your only method of test preparation, you will undoubtedly fail your Windows 2000 exams. The new Windows 2000 MCSE exams will test your knowledge, and your ability to apply that knowledge in more sophisticated and accurate ways than was expected for the MCSE exams for Windows NT 4.0.

In the Windows 2000 exams, Microsoft will use a variety of testing formats that include product simulations, adaptive testing, drag-and-drop matching, and possibly even "fill in the blank" questions (also called "free response" questions). The test-taking process will measure the examinee's fundamental knowledge of the Windows 2000 operating system rather than the ability to memorize a few facts and then answer a few simple multiple-choice questions.

In addition, the "pool" of questions for each exam will significantly increase. The greater number of questions combined with the adaptive testing techniques will enhance the validity and security of the certification process.

We will begin by looking at the purpose, focus, and structure of Microsoft certification tests, and examine the effect that these factors have on the kinds of questions you will face on your certification exams. We will define the structure of exam questions and investigate some common formats. Next, we will present a strategy for answering these questions. Finally, we will give some specific guidelines on what you should do on the day of your test.

Why Vendor Certification?

The Microsoft Certified Professional program, like the certification programs from Cisco, Novell, Oracle, and other software vendors, is maintained for the ultimate purpose of increasing the corporation's profits. A successful vendor certification program accomplishes this goal by helping to create a pool of experts in a company's software and by "branding" these experts so companies using the software can identify them.

We know that vendor certification has become increasingly popular in the last few years because it helps employers find qualified workers and because it helps software vendors like Microsoft sell their products. But why vendor certification rather than a more traditional approach like a college degree in computer science? A college education is a broadening and enriching experience, but a degree in computer science does not prepare students for most jobs in the IT industry.

A common truism in our business states that "If you are out of the IT industry for three years and want to return, you have to start over." The problem, of course, is *timeliness;* if a first-year student learns about a specific computer program, it probably will no longer be in wide use when he or she graduates. Although some colleges are trying to integrate Microsoft certification into their curriculum, the problem is not really a flaw in higher education, but a characteristic of the IT industry. Computer software is changing so rapidly that a four-year college just can't keep up.

A marked characteristic of the Microsoft certification program is an emphasis on performing specific job tasks rather than merely gathering knowledge. It may come as a shock, but most potential employers do not care how much you know about the theory of operating systems, networking, or database design. As one IT manager put it, "I don't really care what my employees know about the theory of our network. We don't need someone to sit at a desk and think about it. We need people who can actually do something to make it work better."

You should not think that this attitude is some kind of anti-intellectual revolt against "book learning." Knowledge is a necessary prerequisite, but it is not enough. More than one company has hired a computer science graduate as a network administrator, only to learn that the new employee has no idea how to add users, assign permissions, or perform the other day-to-day tasks necessary to maintain a network. This brings us to the second major characteristic of Microsoft certification that affects the questions you must be prepared to answer. In addition to timeliness, Microsoft certification is also job-task oriented.

The timeliness of Microsoft's certification program is obvious and is inherent in the fact that you will be tested on current versions of software in wide use today. The job task orientation of Microsoft certification is almost as obvious, but testing real-world job skills using a computer-based test is not easy.

Computerized Testing

Considering the popularity of Microsoft certification, and the fact that certification candidates are spread around the world, the only practical way to administer tests for the certification program is through Sylvan Prometric or Vue testing centers, which operate internationally. Sylvan Prometric and Vue provide proctor testing services for Microsoft, Oracle, Novell, Lotus, and the A+ computer technician certification. Although the IT industry accounts for much of Sylvan's revenue, the company provides services for a number of other businesses and organizations, such as FAA pre-flight pilot tests. Historically, several hundred questions were developed for a new Microsoft certification exam. The Windows 2000 MCSE exam pool is expected to contain hundreds of new questions. Microsoft is aware that many new MCSE candidates have been able to access information on test questions via the Internet or other resources. The company is very concerned about maintaining the MCSE as a "premium" certification. The significant increase in the number of test questions, together with stronger enforcement of the NDA (Non-disclosure agreement), will ensure that a higher standard for certification is attained.

Microsoft treats the test-building process very seriously. Test questions are first reviewed by a number of subject matter experts for technical accuracy and then are presented in a beta test. Taking the beta test may require several hours, due to the large number of questions. After a few weeks, Microsoft Certification uses the statistical feedback from Sylvan to check the performance of the beta questions. The beta test group for the Windows 2000 certification series included MCTs, MCSEs, and members of Microsoft's rapid deployment partners groups. Because the exams will be normalized based on this population, you can be sure that the passing scores will be difficult to achieve without detailed product knowledge.

Questions are discarded if most test takers get them right (too easy) or wrong (too difficult), and a number of other statistical measures are taken of each question. Although the scope of our discussion precludes a rigorous treatment of question analysis, you should be aware that Microsoft and other vendors spend a great deal of time and effort making sure their exam questions are valid.

The questions that survive statistical analysis form the pool of questions for the final certification exam.

Test Structure

The questions in a Microsoft form test will not be equally weighted. From what we can tell, different questions are given a value based on the level of difficulty. You will get more credit for getting a difficult question correct than if you got an easy one correct. Because the questions are weighted differently, and because the exams will likely use the adapter method of testing, your score will not bear any relationship to how many questions you answered correctly.

Microsoft has implemented *adaptive* testing. When an adaptive test begins, the candidate is first given a level-three question. If it is answered correctly, a question from the next higher level is presented, and an incorrect response results in a question from the next lower level. When 15 to 20 questions have been answered in this manner, the scoring algorithm is able to predict, with a high degree of statistical certainty, whether the candidate would pass or fail if all the questions in the form were answered. When the required degree of certainty is attained, the test ends and the candidate receives a pass/fail grade.

Adaptive testing has some definite advantages for everyone involved in the certification process. Adaptive tests allow Sylvan Prometric or Vue to deliver more tests with the same resources, as certification candidates often are in and out in 30 minutes or less. For candidates, the "fatigue factor" is reduced due to the shortened testing time. For Microsoft, adaptive testing means that fewer test questions are exposed to each candidate, and this can enhance the security, and therefore the overall validity, of certification tests.

One possible problem you may have with adaptive testing is that you are not allowed to mark and revisit questions. Since the adaptive algorithm is interactive, and all questions but the first are selected on the basis of your response to the previous question, it is not possible to skip a particular question or change an answer.

Question Types

Computerized test questions can be presented in a number of ways. Some of the possible formats are used on Microsoft certification exam, and some are not.

True/False

We are all familiar with True/False questions, but because of the inherent 50-percent chance of guessing the correct answer, you will not see questions of this type on Microsoft certification exams.

Multiple Choice

The majority of Microsoft certification questions are in the multiple-choice format, with either a single correct answer or multiple correct answers. One interesting variation on multiple-choice questions with multiple correct answers is whether or not the candidate is told how many answers are correct.

EXAMPLE:

Which two files can be altered to configure the MS-DOS environment? (Choose two.)

Or

Which files can be altered to configure the MS-DOS environment? (Choose all that apply.)

You may see both variations on Microsoft certification exams, but the trend seems to be toward the first type, where candidates are told explicitly how many answers are correct. Questions of the "choose all that apply" variety are more difficult and can be merely confusing.

Graphical Questions

One or more graphical elements are sometimes used as exhibits to help present or clarify an exam question. These elements may take the form of a network diagram, pictures of networking components, or screen shots from the software on which you are being tested. It is often easier to present the concepts required for a complex performance-based scenario with a graphic than with words.

Test questions known as *hotspots* actually incorporate graphics as part of the answer. These questions ask the certification candidate to click on a location or graphical element to answer the question. For example, you might be shown the diagram of a network and asked to click on an appropriate location for a router. The answer is correct if the candidate clicks within the *hotspot* that defines the correct location.

Free Response Questions

Another kind of question you sometimes see on Microsoft certification exams requires a *free response* or type-in answer. An example of this type of question might present a TCP/IP network scenario and ask the candidate to calculate and enter the correct subnet mask in dotted decimal notation.

Simulation Questions

Simulation questions provide a method for Microsoft to test how familiar the test taker is with the actual product interface and the candidate's ability to quickly implement a task using the interface. These questions will present an actual Windows 2000 interface that you must work with to solve a problem or implement a solution. If you are familiar with the product, you will be able to answer these questions quickly, and they will be the easiest questions on the exam. However, if you are not accustomed to working with Windows 2000, these questions will be difficult for you to answer. This is why actual hands-on practice with Windows 2000 is so important!

Knowledge-Based and Performance-Based Questions

Microsoft Certification develops a blueprint for each Microsoft certification exam with input from subject matter experts. This blueprint defines the content areas and objectives for each test, and each test question is created to test a specific objective. The basic information from the examination blueprint can be found on Microsoft's Web site in the Exam Prep Guide for each test.

Psychometricians (psychologists who specialize in designing and analyzing tests) categorize test questions as knowledge-based or performance-based. As the names imply, knowledge-based questions are designed to test knowledge, while performance-based questions are designed to test performance.

Some objectives demand a knowledge-based question. For example, objectives that use verbs like *list* and *identify* tend to test only what you know, not what you can do.

EXAMPLE:

Which two files can be altered to configure the MS-DOS environment? (Choose two.)

A. COMMAND.COM

B. AUTOEXEC.BAT

C. IO.SYS

D. CONFIG.SYS

Correct answers: B, D

Other objectives use action verbs like *install, configure,* and *troubleshoot* to define job tasks. These objectives can often be tested with either a knowledge-based question or a performance-based question.

EXAMPLE:

Objective: Configure an MS-DOS installation appropriately using the PATH statement in AUTOEXEC.BAT.

Knowledge-based question:

What is the correct syntax to set a path to the D: directory in AUTOEXEC.BAT?

A. SET PATH EQUAL TO D:

B. PATH D:

C. SETPATH D:

D. D:EQUALS PATH

Correct answer: B

Performance-based question:

Your company uses several DOS accounting applications that access a group of common utility programs. What is the best strategy for configuring the computers in the accounting department so that the accounting applications will always be able to access the utility programs?

A. Store all the utilities on a single floppy disk and make a copy of the disk for each computer in the accounting department.

B. Copy all the utilities to a directory on the C: drive of each computer in the accounting department and add a PATH statement pointing to this directory in the AUTOEXEC.BAT files.

C. Copy all the utilities to all application directories on each computer in the accounting department.

D. Place all the utilities in the C: directory on each computer, because the C: directory is automatically included in the PATH statement when AUTOEXEC.BAT is executed.

Correct answer: B

Even in this simple example, the superiority of the performance-based question is obvious. Whereas the knowledge-based question asks for a single fact, the performance-based question presents a real-life situation and requires that you make a decision based on this scenario. Thus, performance-based questions give more bang (validity) for the test author's buck (individual question).

Testing Job Performance

We have said that Microsoft certification focuses on timeliness and the ability to perform job tasks. We have also introduced the concept of performance-based questions, but even performance-based multiple-choice questions do not really measure performance. Another strategy is needed to test job skills.

Given unlimited resources, it is not difficult to test job skills. In an ideal world, Microsoft would fly MCP candidates to Redmond, place them in a controlled environment with a team of experts, and ask them to plan, install, maintain, and troubleshoot a Windows network. In a few days at most, the experts could reach a valid decision as to whether each candidate should or should not be granted MCDBA or MCSE status. Needless to say, this is not likely to happen.

Closer to reality, another way to test performance is by using the actual software and creating a testing program to present tasks and automatically grade a candidate's performance when the tasks are completed. This *cooperative* approach would be practical in some testing situations, but the same test that is presented to MCP candidates in Boston must also be available in Bahrain and Botswana. The most workable solution for measuring performance in today's testing environment is a *simulation* program. When the program is launched during a test, the candidate sees a simulation of the actual software that looks, and behaves, just like the real thing.

When the testing software presents a task, the simulation program is launched and the candidate performs the required task. The testing software then grades the candidate's performance on the required task and moves to the next question. Microsoft has introduced simulation questions on the certification exam for Internet Information Server 4.0. Simulation questions provide many advantages over other testing methodologies, and simulations are expected to become increasingly important in the Microsoft certification program. For example, studies have shown that there is test and the ability to perform the actual job tasks. Thus, simulations enhance the validity of the certification process.

Another truly wonderful benefit of simulations is in the area of test security. It is just not possible to cheat on a simulation question. In fact, you will be told exactly what tasks you are expected to perform on the test. How can a certification candidate cheat? By learning to perform the tasks? What a concept!

Study Strategies

There are appropriate ways to study for the different types of questions you will see on a Microsoft certification exam.

Knowledge-Based Questions

Knowledge-based questions require that you memorize facts. There are hundreds of facts inherent in every content area of every Microsoft certification exam. There are several keys to memorizing facts:

- **Repetition** The more times your brain is exposed to a fact, the more likely you are to remember it.
- **Association** Connecting facts within a logical framework makes them easier to remember.
- **Motor Association** It is often easier to remember something if you write it down or perform some other physical act, like clicking on a practice test answer.

We have said that the emphasis of Microsoft certification is job performance, and that there are very few knowledge-based questions on Microsoft certification exams. Why should you waste a lot of time learning filenames, IP address formulas, and other minutiae? Read on.

Performance-Based Questions

Most of the questions you will face on a Microsoft certification exam are performance-based scenario questions. We have discussed the superiority of these questions over simple knowledge-based questions, but you should remember that the job task orientation of Microsoft certification extends the knowledge you need to pass the exams; it does not replace this knowledge. Therefore, the first step in preparing for scenario questions is to absorb as many facts relating to the exam content areas as you can. In other words, go back to the previous section and follow the steps to prepare for an exam composed of knowledge-based questions.

The second step is to familiarize yourself with the format of the questions you are likely to see on the exam. You can do this by answering the questions in this study guide, by using Microsoft assessment tests, or by using practice tests on the included CD-ROM. The day of your test is not the time to be surprised by the construction of Microsoft exam questions.

At best, performance-based scenario questions really do test certification candidates at a higher cognitive level than knowledge-based questions. At worst, these questions can test your reading comprehension and test-taking ability rather than your ability to use Microsoft products. Be sure to get in the habit of reading the question carefully to determine what is being asked.

The third step in preparing for Microsoft scenario questions is to adopt the following attitude: Multiple-choice questions aren't really performance-based. It is all a cruel lie. These scenario questions are just knowledge-based questions with a story wrapped around them.

To answer a scenario question, you have to sift through the story to the underlying facts of the situation and apply your knowledge to determine the correct answer. This may sound silly at first, but the process we go through in solving real-life problems is quite similar. The key concept is that every scenario question (and every real-life problem) has a fact at its center, and if we can identify that fact, we can answer the question.

Simulations

Simulation questions really do measure your ability to perform job tasks. You must be able to perform the specified tasks. There are two ways to prepare for simulation questions:

1. Get experience with the actual software. If you have the resources, this is a great way to prepare for simulation questions.
2. Use the practice test on this books accompanying CD-ROM, as it contains simulation questions similar to those you will find on the Microsoft exam. This approach has the added advantage of grading your efforts. You can find additional practice tests at www.syngress.com and www.osborne.com.

Signing Up

Signing up to take a Microsoft certification exam is easy. Sylvan Prometric or Vue operators in each country can schedule tests at any testing center. There are, however, a few things you should know:

1. If you call Sylvan Prometric or Vue during a busy time, get a cup of coffee first, because you may be in for a long wait. The exam providers do an excellent job, but everyone in the world seems to want to sign up for a test on Monday morning.
2. You will need your social security number or some other unique identifier to sign up for a test, so have it at hand.
3. Pay for your test by credit card if at all possible. This makes things easier, and you can even schedule tests for the same day you call, if space is available at your local testing center.
4. Know the number and title of the test you want to take before you call. This is not essential, and the Sylvan operators will help you if they can. Having this information in advance, however, speeds up and improves the accuracy of the registration process.

Taking the Test

Teachers have always told you not to try to cram for exams because it does no good. If you are faced with a knowledge-based test requiring only that you regurgitate facts, cramming can mean the difference between passing and failing. This is not the case, however, with Microsoft certification exams. If you don't know it the night before, don't bother to stay up and cram.

Instead, create a schedule and stick to it. Plan your study time carefully, and do not schedule your test until you think you are ready to succeed. Follow these guidelines on the day of your exam:

1. Get a good night's sleep. The scenario questions you will face on a Microsoft certification exam require a clear head.
2. Remember to take two forms of identification—at least one with a picture. A driver's license with your picture and social security or credit card is acceptable.
3. Leave home in time to arrive at your testing center a few minutes early. It is not a good idea to feel rushed as you begin your exam.
4. Do not spend too much time on any one question. You cannot mark and revisit questions on an adaptive test, so you must do your best on each question as you go.
5. If you do not know the answer to a question, try to eliminate the obviously wrong answers and guess from the rest. If you can eliminate two out of four options, you have a 50-percent chance of guessing the correct answer.
6. For scenario questions, follow the steps we outlined earlier. Read the question carefully and try to identify the facts at the center of the story.

Finally, we would advise anyone attempting to earn Microsoft MCDBA and MCSE certification to adopt a philosophical attitude. The Windows 2000 MCSE will be the most difficult MCSE ever offered. The questions will be at a higher cognitive level than seen on all previous MCSE exams. Therefore, even if you are the kind of person who never fails a test, you are likely to fail at least one Windows 2000 certification test somewhere along the way. Do not get discouraged. Microsoft wants to ensure the value of your certification. Moreover, it will attempt to do so by keeping the standard as high as possible. If Microsoft certification were easy to obtain, more people would have it, and it would not be so respected and so valuable to your future in the IT industry.

MCSE

MICROSOFT CERTIFIED SYSTEMS ENGINEER

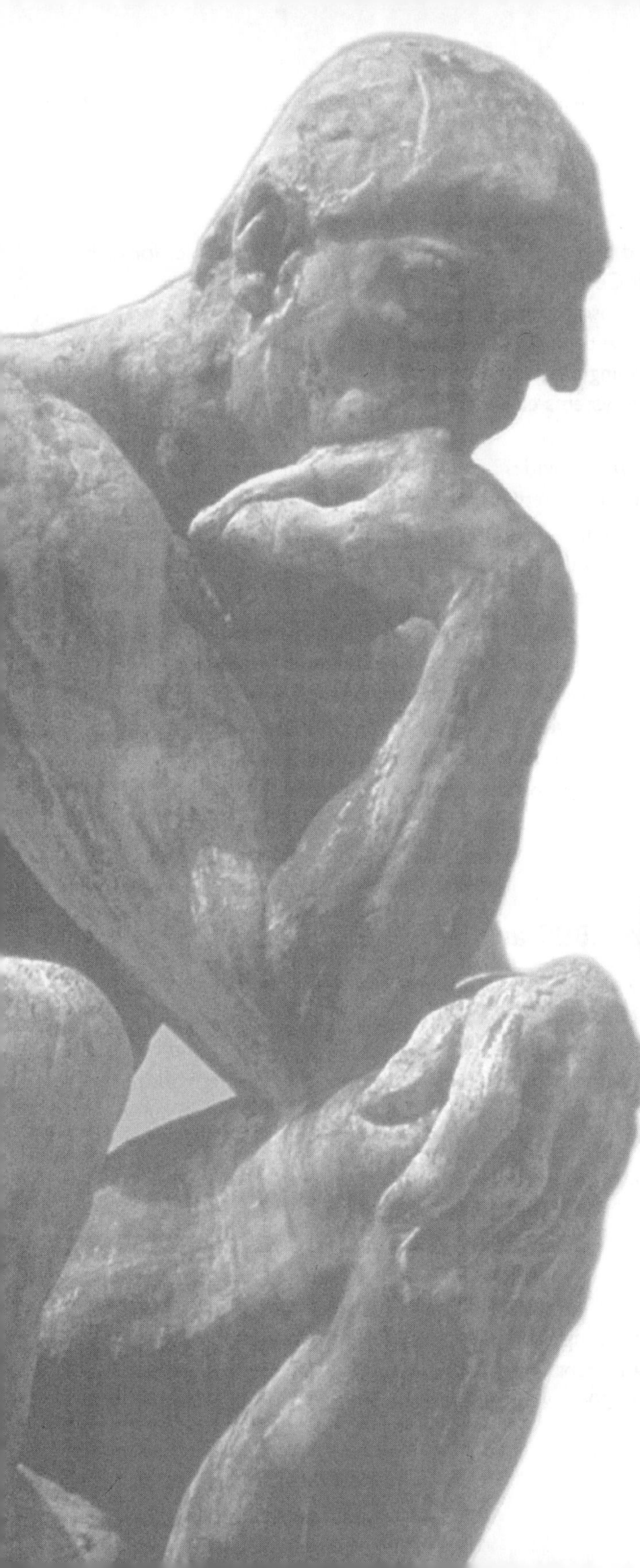

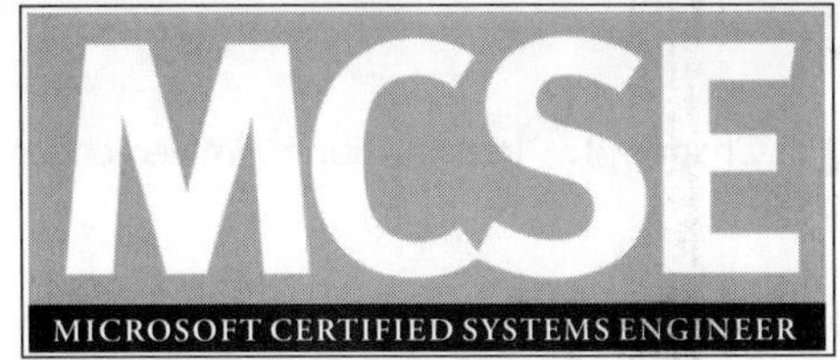

1

Introduction to Implementing and Administering a Windows 2000 Network

CERTIFICATION OBJECTIVES

1.01	What Is a Network Infrastructure
1.02	Overview of Exam 70-216
1.03	What We'll Cover in this Book
1.04	Networking Terminology
1.05	For "Newbies" and "Old Pros"
✓	Two-Minute Drill
Q&A	Self Test

Welcome to Windows 2000 and one of Microsoft's most important core topics for the Windows 2000 Microsoft Certified Systems Engineer (MCSE) certification track. Networking is what Microsoft's new operating system—and computing in general—is all about today. Understanding how to build, use, maintain, and troubleshoot the network infrastructure is essential to performing the duties of an administrator, and must be mastered in order to obtain certification as a systems engineer.

Knowledge of NT networking provides a good foundation for studying for this exam, but it's not enough. Although networking fundamentals remain the same at the physical level, administration of a Windows 2000 network requires many skills that were not required of an NT 4.0 administrator. With new features such as Active Directory, and a new emphasis on topics that were only touched on lightly, such as DNS, Windows 2000 is changing the world of networking and the way administrators perform common tasks. To understand and troubleshoot the new operating system, you *must* first have a thorough understanding of basic TCP/IP concepts such as Domain Name Services (DNS), the Dynamic Host Configuration Protocol (DHCP), Routing and Remote Access Services (RRAS) including Network Address Translation (NAT), the Windows Internet Name Service (WINS), Certificate Services, and the TCP/IP and NWLink protocol suites upon which modern networks are based.

Correlation Between Windows 2000 and NT 4.0 Exams

It might be tempting to try to draw a correlation between the NT 4.0 core exams and the new Windows 2000 core exams. In so doing, you might conclude that Exam 70-216, the core exam that covers implementation and administration of a Windows 2000 network infrastructure, is a replacement for the old Networking Essentials exam (70-058). However, the Windows 2000 Networking Infrastructure exam goes far beyond the basic networking terminology and concepts covered by the Networking Essentials exam.

Target Audience

Microsoft's stated "target audience" for this exam is somewhat different from the intended audience for the Networking Essentials exam (70-058), for which Microsoft lists no prerequisites on the exam preparation Web page. There has been a lot of talk, with the advent of the Windows 2000 certification track, about Microsoft's desire to "raise the bar" and restore the MCSE to the status of a "premium" certification. This is reflected in the suggested prerequisites.

Experienced Networking Professionals

According to the Microsoft Web site and documentation, exam candidates are presumed to be networking personnel operating in medium-to-very-large computing environments with a minimum of a year's experience in administering and implementing Windows networking components and supporting 200 or more users in five or more physical locations. It is also presumed that the exam taker is familiar with typical network services and applications, such as file and print sharing, databases, messaging services, proxy and/or firewalls, dial-in remote access servers, Web hosting, and desktop management and control.

What If You're New to Networking?

The above does not mean that if you don't have on-the-job experience as a network administrator you won't be able to pass the Windows 2000 exams. It does mean that if you don't meet the description of the exam's "target audience," you will need to study harder, and in particular you will need to get more hands-on practice in working with the products.

This book contains a large number of practical exercises that walk you through the steps of procedures common to working network professionals. In order to really understand the concepts and skills covered by the exam, it is essential that you do more than read through the exercises—you must work through them on a Windows 2000 computer. This can be done on a relatively simple home network, and we highly recommend that you consider setting up a two- or three-system lab if you don't have access to a network on the job or in a classroom situation. The cost of doing so is an investment that can quickly pay for itself in terms of time saved in obtaining the certification.

CERTIFICATION OBJECTIVE 1.01

What Is a Network Infrastructure?

Infrastructure is a big word that can be used to describe many things. It is often used to refer to the basic facilities, services, and installations necessary for a community or a society to function (such as roads, communications systems, water and sewer services, electrical power lines, and so forth.). The dictionary gives the following broad definition:

An underlying base or foundation of an organization or system.

From this, we can extrapolate that the infrastructure of a computer network consists of the basic components upon which it is built. We could further divide these into two subcategories:

- Those making up the *physical* infrastructure (the machines themselves, the cables and network interface cards, and hubs and routers)
- Those making up the *logical* infrastructure (the networking protocols, the DNS namespace and services, the IP addressing scheme and DHCP strategy, the remote access services, security protocols)

The first category is hardware-related, while the second is dependent on software components and their configuration.

New Focus on the Logical Infrastructure

The old Networking Essentials exam in the Windows NT 4.0 certification track focused primarily (although not exclusively) on the physical infrastructure. That exam was more knowledge-based than skills-based, and many questions measured the ability to recognize or recite such factual information as the layer of the OSI networking model at which specific protocols and connectivity devices operate, the number of bytes in a fixed-length ATM cell, or the number of nodes allowed on a segment in a particular type of network. Exam candidates were required to identify specifications of the Institute of Electrical and Electronics Engineers (IEEE) by specification number, name the characteristics of various wide area networking (WAN) technologies, and differentiate between common networking topologies, media access methods, and architectures.

The Windows 2000 core networking exam, Implementing and Administering a Windows 2000 Network Infrastructure, is focused almost entirely on the logical infrastructure. This doesn't mean Microsoft no longer believes a network administrator needs to know about hardware issues; rather, it appears to presume two things:

- The Windows 2000 exam candidate has prior networking experience and is already familiar with physical issues.
- The typical Windows 2000 exam candidate will be working in a company that has a medium-to-very-large network, and in this environment there is more likely to be a division between the personnel who do actual administrative tasks and the technicians who care for the hardware.

Components of the Logical Infrastructure

The physical infrastructure is, for many, easier to understand because its components are tangible; you can see and touch them. The logical infrastructure is more abstract and includes the following, which are covered in Exam 70-216:

- Network Protocols
- IP Addressing Schemes
- Name Resolution Services
- Remote Access
- Routing and Network Address Translation
- The Security Infrastructure (Certificate Services)

Networking Protocols

An important component of the logical foundation of a group of networked computers is the protocol(s) those computers use to communicate.

A protocol is a set of rules, or a standardized order of procedures, that the networking components of the systems follow when they transmit data over the network. There are physical layer protocols, which consist of specifications or standards governing the hardware components, and there are numerous other protocols that operate at higher layers of the networking model. But the term "network protocol" is usually used to refer to the network and transport layer protocols (often part of a protocol "stack" or "suite") used for communication over a local area network (LAN).

Although Windows 2000, like Windows NT and the Windows 9*x* operating systems, supports other LAN protocols such as NWLink (a Microsoft implementation of Novell's IPX/SPX protocol stack) and NetBEUI (a simple, fast, low-overhead protocol used primarily in small, nonrouted networks), the "protocol stack of choice" for Windows 2000 networks is, not coincidentally, the set of protocols upon which the global Internet is based—the Transmission Control Protocol/Internet Protocol, or TCP/IP suite of protocols.

Networking Models In order to fully understand how networking protocols function, you should be familiar with some of the popular networking models that describe the networking architecture and serve as the framework for standardization of the steps involved in network communications. The Open Systems Interconnection, or OSI model has become a common reference point for discussion of network protocols and connection devices.

The OSI model uses seven layers or levels to represent the communications process. This layered approach provides a logical division of responsibility, where each layer handles prescribed functions. The OSI model is used as a broad guideline for describing the network communications process. Not all protocol implementations map directly to the OSI model, but it serves as a good starting point for gaining a general understanding of how data is transferred across a network.

Figure 1-1 shows a graphical representation of the OSI networking model, from the "top down."

Communication takes place between corresponding layers on the Sending and Receiving computers. The data that is created by a user application (such as an e-mail message) enters the network communication process at the Application layer, and travels down the levels, with each layer adding header information that will be processed by its corresponding layer on the other side. At the Physical layer, the data is turned into electrical impulses, pulses of light, or radio signals (depending on the physical media being used) and sent out over the cable or over the air to the destination computer. When it arrives there, the networking components on that system process the data in the opposite order, finally delivering it (with the intervening headers stripped off) to the user application program (such as the recipient's e-mail program) at that end.

FIGURE 1-1

The seven layers of the Open Systems Interconnection model

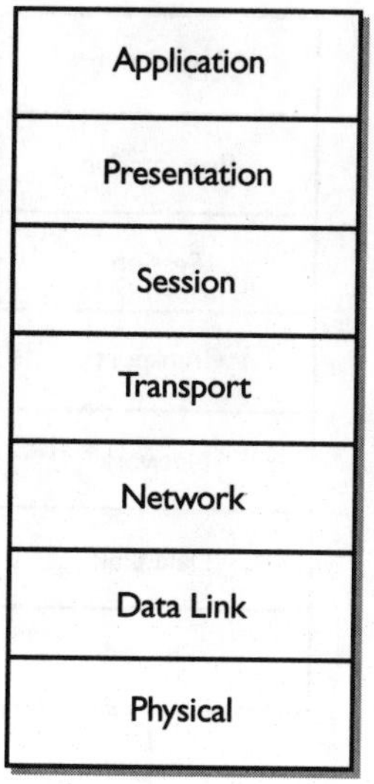

Application
Presentation
Session
Transport
Network
Data Link
Physical

Note that the Data Link layer as represented in the original implementation of the OSI model was later divided into two sublayers:

- Logical Link Control (LLC)
- Media Access Control (MAC)

Figure 1-2 shows how this process works.

The model is important to understanding protocols, because in a protocol stack such as TCP/IP, different protocols work at different layers, in conjunction with one another. We will discuss the separate functions of TCP, UDP, and IP a little later in this chapter.

The OSI model is not the only networking model in use. If you do much study of TCP/IP, you will also encounter the DoD (Department of Defense) model, and Microsoft has developed its own Windows networking model that intersperses layers called "boundary layers" representing open standards with vendor-specific components of its networking software.

OSI is an international standard, however, and Microsoft exams have traditionally required some knowledge of its structure and which protocols operate at which levels.

FIGURE 1-2

Communication occurs between corresponding layers of the OSI model

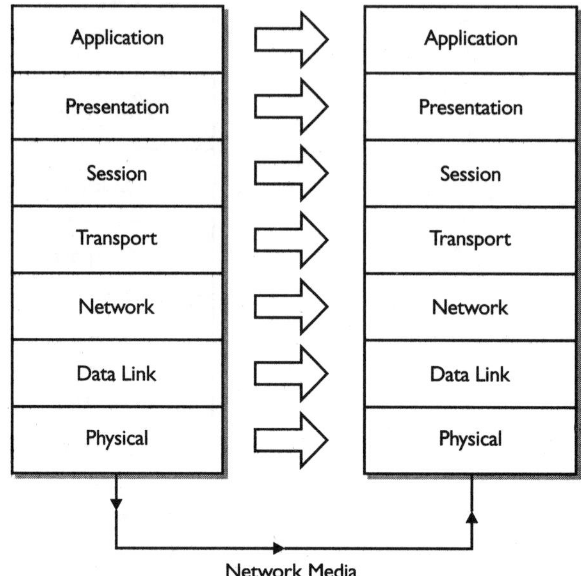

Why TCP/IP? The TCP/IP protocol suite is the current standard for large networks, up to and including the Internet itself. Although it is slower and requires more resource overhead than other common network/transport protocol stacks, it has the advantages of being easily routable and compatible with most platforms and operating systems. Using the TCP/IP protocols to connect to the Internet, a computer user in Los Angeles using a Windows system can communicate with someone in London using a Macintosh or someone in Tokyo using a Sun Solaris workstation. TCP/IP is the common "language" that makes it possible.

It would be difficult for an administrator to find a network environment today in which knowledge of TCP/IP is not required. Even Novell's NetWare server operating system, which for a long time relied on the IPX/SPX protocol stack for communications, has with the debut of NetWare 5.0 included support for "pure IP."

TCP/IP was originally designed for use on the ARPAnet, the predecessor of the Internet. The U.S. Department of Defense, in conjunction with major universities, developed the nation-wide system (which then was extended throughout the world) to provide highly reliable, redundant communications links that could withstand even a nuclear war. TCP/IP has also survived efforts to replace it with other protocols, most notably the OSI suite.

Because of its continuing popularity and its role as a foundation of communications on large (and more and more small) networks today, TCP/IP is an essential topic of study for an aspiring MCSE. The Windows NT 3.51 and 4.0 certification tracks included an elective exam devoted to TCP/IP. The Windows 2000 track does not. This is not because a mastery of TCP/IP is less important in the new certification track; rather, it is because it has become so much more important that the fundamentals of TCP/IP are now incorporated into the required core exams. A thorough understanding of TCP/IP and those topics formerly included in the TCP/IP exam material (DNS, WINS, DHCP) is required to pass the Networking Infrastructure exams (both the core 70-216 and the elective Designing a Windows 2000 Network Infrastructure, Exam 70-221).

exam Watch

Because Microsoft is focusing on the mastery of practical skills in the Windows 2000 exams, and because some exams may contain interactive simulations, it is imperative that you be intimately familiar with such processes as configuring and modifying TCP/IP properties.

Microsoft has made installation and configuration of TCP/IP and other supported protocols a relatively painless procedure, but there is still quite a bit of information that you will need to know in order to properly configure the TCP/IP stack on a Windows 2000 computer, including the following:

- The IP address that will be used by the computer (see the following section on IP address schemes) *or* that the computer will use the Dynamic Host Configuration Protocol (DHCP) to obtain an IP address—in which case, there must be a DHCP server on the network.
- The subnet mask, which determines which part of the IP address represents the network ID and which part represents the host ID.
- The default gateway(s), if the network is routed. You can configure multiple default gateways for each network interface in Windows 2000, although only one will be used (however, the others serve as "backup" gateways in case the first gateway is unavailable).

- The IP address of a DNS server that will be contacted to resolve fully qualified domain names (FQDNs) to IP addresses. Windows 2000 is far more dependent on DNS than was Windows NT, and in a network with a Windows 2000 domain controller using Active Directory, DNS is *not* an optional component.
- The IP address of a WINS server that will be contacted to resolve NetBIOS names to IP addresses. In a "pure" Windows 2000 environment, NetBIOS over TCP/IP (NetBT) can be disabled and WINS can be decommissioned; however, many networks will still need WINS for "downlevel" clients and application software that uses NetBIOS.

Note that much of this information, in addition to just the IP address, can be assigned by a DHCP server if the computer is configured to be a DHCP client.

Figure 1-3 shows the TCP/IP properties sheet for a Windows 2000 computer, where TCP/IP related settings are configured.

FIGURE 1-3

The Windows 2000 Internet Protocol (TCP/IP) Properties Sheet

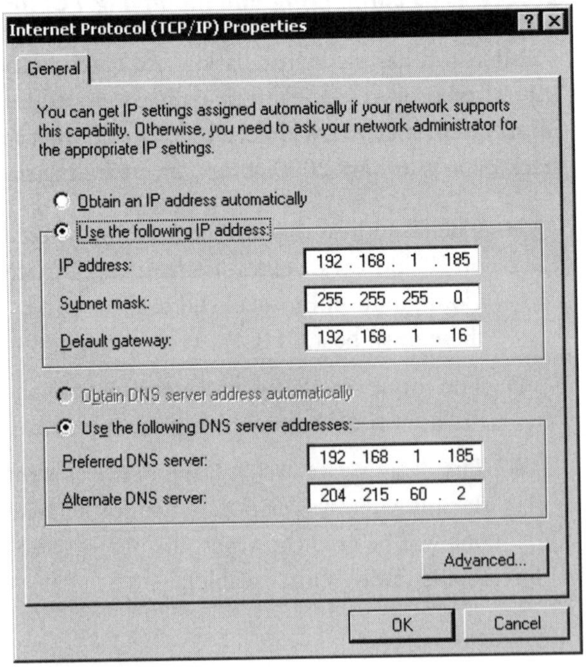

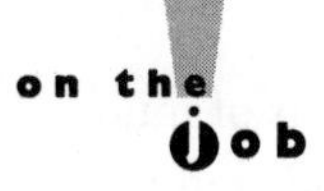

Although TCP/IP is Windows 2000's default protocol and is necessary for Internet connectivity, in the business world there are sometimes reasons to use a different protocol stack for LAN communications. One of these is heightened security. If you have internal computers that don't need Internet connectivity (for instance, the workstations in a department that deals with highly sensitive data), you may wish to run that part of the internal network on IPX/SPX. Then even if those computers are also connected to a server that has both TCP/IP and IPX/SPX running, outsiders using TCP/IP will not be able to access the internal systems whose only protocol is IPX/SPX (NWLink).

TCP/IP Components For the Networking Infrastructure exam, it will be important that you recognize the roles played by the major TCP/IP protocols that work at the Transport and Network layers of the networking model to get data packets to the proper destination in a reliable manner. These include TCP and UDP (the User Datagram Protocol) at the Transport layer, and IP at the Network layer:

- **Transmission Control Protocol (TCP)** The "mission" of TCP is to ensure reliable transfer of data. TCP is called a "connection-oriented" protocol because it establishes a virtual connection between the sending and receiving computers before sending data. A connection-oriented protocol such as TCP offers better error control, but its higher overhead means a loss of performance. TCP is also known as a "reliable" protocol because it requires an acknowledgment that the data sent was in fact received. If no acknowledgment (referred to as an ACK) arrives, TCP re-sends that data packet.
- **User Datagram Protocol (UDP)** Like TCP, UDP works at the Transport layer of the OSI model. Unlike TCP, it is a "connectionless" protocol, which means that although it suffers in the reliability department, it is faster because it is unhampered by error-checking duties. UDP is used for messages that don't require high levels of reliability.
- **Internet Protocol (IP)** At the Network layer, IP is responsible for actually getting the data packets to the correct destination. You could think of IP as the "navigational" protocol, since it maps out the route that will be taken over the network from sending to receiving computer. IP uses logical, assigned IP addresses (see *IP Addressing Schemes* later in the chapter) to perform both simple and complex routing functions.

TCP/IP Application Layer Protocols The TCP/IP suite consists of much more than just TCP/UDP and IP. There is a whole collection of Application layer protocols as well as utilities that can be used for monitoring, troubleshooting, and information gathering. You will need to know the functions of these, including:

- **File Transfer Protocol (FTP)** The File Transfer Protocol is used for copying files from one computer to another. Windows 2000 includes both a command-line FTP client program and the FTP server service that is installed as part of Internet Information Server 5.0. The Trivial File Transfer Protocol (TFTP) is a connectionless version.
- **Simple Network Management Protocol (SNMP)** The Simple Network Management Protocol provides a way to gather statistical information. An SNMP management system makes requests of an SNMP agent, and the information is stored in a Management Information Base (MIB). The MIB is a database that holds information about a networked computer (for example, how much hard disk space is available).
- **Telnet** Telnet is a TCP/IP-based service that allows users to log on to, run character-mode applications, and view files on a remote computer. Windows 2000 Server includes both Telnet server and Telnet client software.
- **Simple Mail Transfer Protocol (SMTP)** The Simple Mail Transfer Protocol is used for sending e-mail on the Internet. SMTP is a simple ASCII protocol and is non-vendor specific.
- **HyperText Transfer Protocol (HTTP)** The HyperText Transfer Protocol is perhaps the most familiar of the Application layer protocols, since it is used on the World Wide Web—the most popular of Internet services. HTTP is the protocol that allow computers to exchange files in various formats (text, graphic images, sound, video, and other multimedia files) via client software called a Web browser. A computer running a Web server program, such as Microsoft's Internet Information Server, stores files in HyperText Markup Language (HTML) format that can be accessed by the client browser. These HTML "pages" often contain hyperlinks for quickly and automatically connecting to other files on the Internet, on an intranet, or on the local machine.
- **Network News Transfer Protocol (NNTP)** The Network News Transfer Protocol is used for managing messages posted to private and public

newsgroups. NNTP servers provide for storage of newsgroup posts that can be downloaded by client software called a newsreader. Windows 2000 Server includes an NNTP server with IIS, and Outlook Explorer version 5, which is part of the Internet Explorer software included with Windows 2000, provides both an e-mail client and a newsreader.

TCP/IP Utilities The following are some of the handy command-line utilities included with the Windows 2000 TCP/IP suite:

- **IPCONFIG** Used to gather information about the TCP/IP configuration on the computer. Typing IPCONFIG at the command line will display the computer's IP address, subnet mask, and default gateway. Adding the /all switch will display additional information such as the host name, MAC address, node type, and much more.
- **NETSTAT** Used to display protocol statistics and current TCP/IP network connections.
- **NBTSTAT** Used to display the local NetBIOS name table, a table of NetBIOS names registered by local applications, and the NetBIOS name cache, a local cache listing of NetBIOS computer names that have been resolved to IP addresses.
- **NSLOOKUP** Used to check records, domain host aliases, domain host services, and operating system information by querying DNS servers.
- **ROUTE** Used to display or make modifications to the local routing table.
- **TRACERT** Used to trace the route a packet takes to a destination.
- **PING and PATHPING** Used to verify configurations and test IP connectivity by name or IP address. PATHPING combines features of PING and TRACERT with added functionality, and is used to trace the route a packet takes to a destination and display information on packet losses for each router in the path. PATHPING can also be used to troubleshoot Quality of Service (QoS) connectivity.
- **ARP** Used to display and modify the Address Resolution Protocol (ARP) cache.

IP Addressing Schemes

In addition to the protocols themselves, another important component of the infrastructure of a TCP/IP-based network is the addressing scheme used by IP to ensure that data transmissions reach the proper destination.

Version 4 of the Internet Protocol (IPv4), the current implementation, uses 32-bit binary addresses, which are expressed in most cases as their equivalent in "dotted decimal," the familiar four-octet format (such as 192.168.1.45). This is also sometimes referred to as "dotted quad" because there are four groups of digits separated by dots.

IP Address Assignment Address assignment—both manual assignment in which an administrator individually configures the TCP/IP properties of each computer on the network and automatic addressing methods such as DHCP and NAT—must be understood and mastered in order to work with TCP/IP. An administrator also needs to understand the "internals" of IP, how the logical addresses assigned at this level are mapped to the physical (Media Access Control) addresses that are ultimately used to get the data to its intended destination.

This means you need to know about protocols such as ARP (the Address Resolution Protocol) and RARP (Reverse ARP) and how they work.

Windows 2000 includes some new features that pertain to IP addressing, as well. Automatic Private IP Addressing (APIPA), which allows a DHCP client computer that is unable to find a DHCP server to assign itself a temporary address, and the auto addressing used by Internet Connection Sharing (ICS) are likely to be subjects of exam questions as well.

You should also be aware of the differences between "classful" and "classless" IP addressing, and know the default subnet masks for the common network classes, as shown in the following reference.

SCENARIO & SOLUTION	
Which default mask should I use for a Class A network?	255.0.0.0
Which default mask should I use for a Class B network?	255.255.0.0
Which default mask should I use for a Class C network?	255.255.255.0

FROM THE CLASSROOM

IP Addresses vs. Media Access Control Addresses

Don't confuse the IP address, used at the Network layer by IP, with the Media Access Control address used to identify each network interface at the lower levels of the OSI model. The IP address is a "logical" address, assigned by the network administrator. It bears no direct relation to the network interface card's "physical" address (often referred to as the MAC address because it is used at the Media Access Control sublayer of the OSI's Data Link layer). Changing a computer's (or more precisely, an individual NIC's) IP address is a software function. If you have administrative privileges, it's as simple as clicking the mouse a few times to open the proper dialog box and typing in a new number (the hardest part is knowing what number to type in). The MAC address, on the other hand, is hard-coded into the chip on the network card in the typical Ethernet network. Some network cards provide for a way to change the MAC address via jumper settings or software configuration, but this is not usual and you are limited to only a few possible settings.

—Debra Littlejohn Shinder, MCSE, MCP+I, MCT

DHCP The Dynamic Host Configuration Protocol (DHCP), derived from BOOTP, allows a server computer configured to be a DHCP server to automatically assign IP addresses from a specified pool to client machines that are configured to be DHCP clients.

The Windows 2000 implementation of DHCP includes new functionality, such as integration with DNS, better logging, the ability to create multicast scopes, detection of "rogue" (unauthorized) Windows 2000 DHCP servers, and support for automatic client configuration via APIPA.

IP Subnetting An important (and, both for network newbies and many experienced administrators, difficult) part of IP addressing is subnetting. This is the art and science of properly dividing a network into smaller connected IP networks (subnets), using a 32-bit number called the subnet mask to indicate the network ID.

exam Watch

Although some study guides and instructors may tell you that all you need to do to pass the IP subnetting portion of the Microsoft exams is to memorize tables defining subnet masks based on number of network and/or host IDs, there is no way to truly understand subnetting without learning to work with binary. Being able to convert dotted decimal addresses and masks to binary and then calculate and perform common operations such as ANDing on the binary digits will give you a big edge in answering subnetting questions on the exams. Not only will you be able to determine the correct answer, you'll know why it's correct.

The binary (base two) numbering system may seem confusing if you've never worked with anything but our common base ten system. However, you'll find that it's really pretty simple once you know the "tricks." In binary, there are only two digits: 0 and 1. This is particularly appropriate for computer calculations because it's easy to represent these two digits as electrical impulses or pulses of light—if the current or light is off, that's a 0, and if it's on, that's a one. This is the basis of digital signaling and is also called *discrete state* signaling.

Using this system, every possible number in our familiar base ten system can be represented by the 0s and 1s. Converting binary to decimal is not difficult, and is a necessary skill for learning IP subnetting, because the "real" numbers that the computer works with (and that you should work with in order to understand the process) are binary, but the software converts them to the "dotted decimal" format for entry into properties boxes.

Of course, the easiest way to covert decimal to binary or vice versa is to use the Windows calculator in scientific mode (choose "Scientific" from the View menu). Just check the "dec" radio button and enter the number in decimal, then click on the "bin" radio button, and tada! As if by magic, you have the binary equivalent.

exam Watch

Microsoft certification exams generally make the Windows calculator available for your use in performing these calculations; however, it is a good idea to know how to convert binary to decimal without the calculator.

The problem with using the calculator is that if you don't really understand how binary is converted to decimal, you may be confused by the calculator's results. For instance, when you convert the decimal 1 to binary, the result is 1. Let's say you are converting the last (rightmost) octet in the IP address 192.168.1.1 to binary.

You know that an octet has eight digits, but the calculator only displays one. Do you put seven zeros before or after the 1? If you know how to do the conversion manually, it's obvious.

We have eight binary digits, and each of them represents a decimal value, beginning with the rightmost digit and working our way back to the leftmost. Note that the rightmost digits are sometimes referred to as the low order bits, and the leftmost as the high order bits.

Each bit that is "turned on" (that is, shows a 1 instead of a 0) represents the value of that bit as shown in Figure 1-4. As you can see, the value increases by a power of 2 as you move from right to left. A bit that is "off" (represented by a 0) counts as 0. All we have to do then is add up the values of the bits that are "on."

You can use this simple formula to convert an octet in binary form, such as 10111001, to decimal. To do so, start at the right and look at which digits are turned on. We see that the bits represented by ones have decimal values of 1, 8, 16, 32, and 128. If we add up those values, we get a total of 185 for the octet, which matches with the value we get when we use the scientific calculator to convert 10111001 to decimal.

Another way of seeing how this is done when you're first learning how to convert to binary is to "line" up the numbers in three columns like this:

128 × 1 = 128

64 × 0 = 0

32 × 1 = 32

16 × 1 = 16

8 × 1 = 8

4 × 0 = 0

2 × 0 = 0

1 × 1 = 1

Then add up the number in the last column, which in this case is 185.

FIGURE 1-4

The value of each bit in an octet

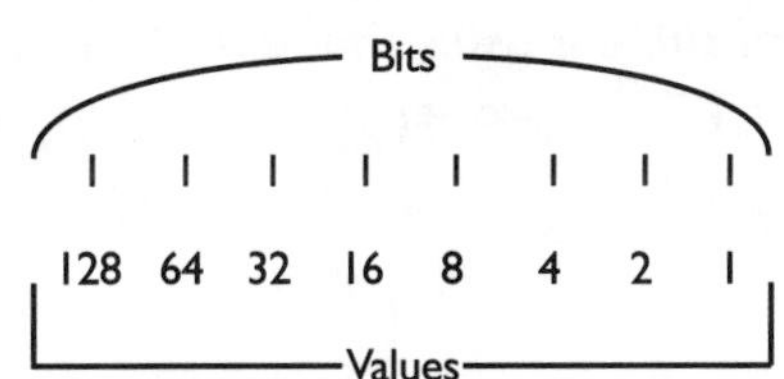

If all bits in an octet are "off," the decimal value is 0, and if all are "on," the value (total of 1, 2, 4, 8, 16, 32, 64, and 128) is 255.

The intricacies of subnet masking with be covered in chapter 6, "Installing, Configuring, Managing, Monitoring, and Troubleshooting Network Protocols."

Name Resolution Services

Another very important component of a networking infrastructure is name resolution. Why is this important? Because computers and humans are inherently different. The machines can only recognize and work with numbers (and only binary numbers, at that). To your computer, another system on the network with which it communicates is identified by numbers. We human beings are more comfortable if we can use "friendly names" to identify computers, Web sites, and other network resources that we wish to access.

A good example of this occurs when you browse the Web. If you want to access Microsoft's Web site, you type **www.microsoft.com** into your browser's URL box. Imagine having to remember, instead, the IP address 207.46.130.14—or worse yet, the binary form of that: 11001111 00101110 10000010 00001110—and having to type that in each time you wanted to go to the Microsoft site.

Well, without some form of name resolution, we would be stuck with keeping track of at least the dotted decimal version of all those Web sites. Incidences of Web addiction might decrease, but it would certainly make for a more frustrating user experience. Name resolution services, such as the Domain Name System service (DNS) and the Windows Internet Name Service (WINS), allow you to use friendlier names while they take over the task of getting those names converted into an IP address that the computer can use.

on the Job

One of the most common problems that network support personnel are called on to deal with is the case of the user whose Web browser "doesn't work"; that is, he or she isn't able to access Web pages by typing the URL into the address box. If you find that the browser will bring up the Web site when you type in its IP address instead of the "friendly name," you can be almost certain the culprit is a DNS problem. Either the DNS server is down, or if the client machine is using manual IP addressing, there is no DNS server address set in its TCP/IP properties.

DNS and WINS servers are machines that maintain databases matching up names to IP addresses, and accept queries from other machines on the network that need this information. Think of them as similar to the directory assistance service provided by your phone company; if you know the person's name but not his phone number, you call up and query directory assistance and then you can connect directly (by calling) to the person with whom you want to communicate.

DNS and WINS work similarly, but deal with different types of names. DNS resolves *fully qualified domain names* (also referred to as FQDNs) to IP addresses. These are the "dotted" or hierarchically structured names such as those used for Web sites. WINS resolves NetBIOS names, used by Windows operating systems prior to Windows 2000 and by many applications, to IP addresses. These are "flat" names, such as COMPUTER12 (the same computer's DNS name might be computer12.mydomain.com).

DNS The certification exams will expect you to know not only the theory behind DNS, but—because the Windows 2000 exams are performance-based—how to install and configure a DNS server and how to set up DNS clients, as well as how to troubleshoot problems that occur in the DNS name resolution process.

exam Watch

The DNS in Windows 2000 is dynamic (thus the term Dynamic DNS or DDNS). Unlike the DNS service in Windows NT 4.0, which had to be manually updated, the Windows 2000 DDNS database supports a new specification to the DNS standard for dynamic update. This permits hosts that store name information in DNS to dynamically register and update their records in zones maintained by DNS servers that can accept and process dynamic update messages.

In Windows 2000, DNS can be integrated with the Active Directory, making for more efficient replication of the DNS records. The certification exam is likely to focus heavily on planning the DNS namespace for a Windows 2000 network, and you will be expected to know how to monitor and troubleshoot the DNS service, and how DNS interacts with such new features as Network Address Translation (NAT).

You will also need to understand how a DNS server deployment is planned and implemented, and the different types of DNS servers. The following scenario and solution is a handy summarization of the server types and how you would use each in real world networking situations.

SCENARIO & SOLUTION	
What is the function of the primary DNS server?	The primary read/write copy of the DNS zone file is located on the primary DNS server. This server is known as "authoritative" for the domain or domains contained in the zone file it hosts.
What role does the secondary DNS server play?	The secondary DNS server contains a copy of the zone database file that is stored on the primary. You should have a secondary DNS server for fault tolerance. It also provides load balancing functionality so the query load can be distributed among multiple DNS servers.
What is a caching-only server and why would I need one?	The caching-only DNS server doesn't contain any zone information; it only stores (caches) the results of previous queries it has issued. You might want to place a caching-only server on the other side of a slow WAN link, since they don't generate zone transfer traffic.
What are forwarder and slave servers for?	A DNS forwarder accepts requests to resolve host names from another DNS server. A forwarder can be used to protect your internal DNS server from access by Internet users. Slave servers are a special type of forwarder, which is configured not to attempt to resolve the host name on its own.

WINS Despite the fact that Windows 2000 provides for the eventual decommissioning of WINS and disabling of NetBIOS, Microsoft obviously has not counted WINS out yet. In fact, many improvements have been made to the service in Windows 2000. Because in the "real world," the majority of networks will still be using NetBIOS for some time to come, the Networking Infrastructure exam will expect you to know how to configure WINS servers and clients, how WINS replication works, and how to use the MMC to manage the service.

Enhancements to WINS in Windows 2000 include

- **Persistent connections** Now you can configure each WINS server to maintain a persistent connection with one or more of its replication partners. This will increase the speed of replication and do away with the overhead involved in opening and terminating connections.

- **Manual tombstoning** Windows 2000 allows you to manually mark a record to eventually be deleted (this is called *tombstoning*). The tombstone state of the record replicates to other WINS servers, and this prevents any replicated copies of the deleted records from reappearing at the same server where they were originally deleted.
- **Better management utility** WINS is now managed through the MMC. This provides you with a powerful and more user-friendly environment that can be customized for better efficiency. The new MMC-based utilities are easier to use and operate more predictably, as they follow a common design.
- **Easier configuration of features** Several of the WINS features from earlier versions of Windows NT Server that required editing of the Registry to configure can now be configured more easily and directly. These include the ability to block records by a specific owner or WINS replication partner (formerly known as Persona Non Grata), or allow override of static mappings (formerly known as Migrate On/Off).
- **Better filtering and search of records** Improved filtering features and new search functions allow you to locate records more easily, by displaying only those that fit the criteria you specify.
- **Dynamic record deletion and multi-select** The WINS MMC snap-in allows you to point, click, and delete one or more WINS static or dynamic entries. (In NT, you had to use command-based utilities, such as Winscl.exe, to accomplish this). Windows 2000 also makes it possible to delete records that use names based on nonalphanumeric characters.
- **Record verification and version number validation** You can now check the consistency of names stored and replicated on your WINS servers quickly and easily. Record verification compares the IP addresses returned by a NetBIOS name query of different WINS servers. Version number validation examines the owner address-to-version number mapping tables.
- **Export** Using the Export feature, you can place WINS data in a comma-delimited text file and then export this file to Microsoft Excel or similar programs for analysis and reporting purposes.
- **More and better fault tolerance for clients** WINS clients running Windows 2000 or Windows 98 can now specify more than two WINS servers (up to a maximum of 12 addresses) per interface. This provides fault tolerance, as the extra WINS server addresses are used only if the primary and secondary WINS servers fail to respond.

- **Dynamic reinsertion of client names** WINS clients in Windows 2000 don't have to be restarted after they use WINS to force reinsertion and update of local NetBIOS names. There is a new option available in the Nbstat command, –RR, that provides the means of doing this. The –RR option can also be used with WINS clients that are running Windows NT 4.0, updated to Service Pack 4 or later.
- **Read-only feature on the WINS console** You can add members to a special group, the WINS Users group, which is automatically added when WINS is installed, and provide read-only access in the WINS console to WINS-related information on the server for members of the group. This way you can allow non-administrators to view WINS-related information, but they cannot make changes.
- **Command-line WINS administration tools** Although Windows 2000 Server includes a full graphical user interface for managing WINS servers, there is also a fully equivalent WINS command-line based tool for those who prefer to work at the command line.
- **Better WINS database engine** WINS in Windows 2000 uses the same performance-enhanced database engine technology that is used in Active Directory.

Remote Access

The remote access service is another very important component of the Windows 2000 networking infrastructure. Remote access is becoming a more and more common way of connecting to the enterprise network, as well as being used by home users and small businesses to connect to an Internet Service Provider (ISP) to gain access to Internet resources.

A remote access connection most typically uses common telephone lines and modems to establish a temporary, dial-in connection to a server. Windows 2000 also supports a second type of RAS connection, via virtual private networking (VPN). A remote access *node* (a node is a computer or device on the network) is able to function in the same way as a computer that is physically cabled to the network onsite, except that the connection will generally be slower. Windows 2000's RRAS (Routing and Remote Access Services) provides for a robust and easy-to-use remote access server service, as well as the ability to function as an RAS client.

For the exam, you will need to understand the basic concepts of remote access, and be familiar with the WAN protocols used to establish a remote link. The same network/transport protocols used on your LAN (TCP/IP, IPX/SPX, NetBEUI) can be used with RAS, but another protocol, which operates at the Data Link layer, is required for the wide area part of the connection. Windows 2000 supports the same two WAN link protocols (also sometimes referred to as "line protocols") as Windows NT 4.0:

- **PPP** The Point to Point Protocol (PPP) can be used by a Windows 2000 machine acting as an RAS client or by a Windows 2000 remote access server. PPP is the most popular of the wide area link protocols, and supports encryption, compression, and dynamic IP address assignment.
- **SLIP** The Serial Line Interface Protocol (SLIP) is an older WAN link protocol that does not support encryption or compression, and requires a manually configured static IP address. It can be used only on the Windows 2000 RAS client, and is used now primarily to connect to remote servers running the UNIX operating system.

exam watch

Be sure that, for the exam, you know the two supported WAN link protocols and the features and functions of each, as well as the two types of RAS connections supported by Windows 2000.

Because the Windows 2000 exams are performance-based, you will also be expected to know the procedural steps in creating and configuring a dial-up or VPN connection. This is done through the Network and Dialup Connections applet, accessed via Settings from the Start menu. As with many other configuration processes, Windows 2000 provides you with a wizard that walks you through the steps of setting up your new connection.

IP Routing

Routing refers to the process of forwarding computer communications traffic along the pathways of an internetwork (a network of networks). A computer set up to support routing receives transmitted messages and forwards them to their correct destinations over the most efficient available route, even if many routes are possible. The distance traveled from one router to the next is called a hop, and at each router, the destination IP address on the packet is compared to the routing table, and the best route is used to decide the endpoint of the next hop.

Fast, efficient, reliable routing of data is at the heart of all large networks, up to and including the global Internet.

IP routing can be done by specialized dedicated devices called routers, or by a computer whose operating system supports IP forwarding. Windows 2000 is designed to function as an IP (or IPX) router.

exam Watch

A router is also often referred to as a gateway. When an exam question mentions the "default gateway," it means the router (or computer functioning as a router) that serves as the "way out" of the network or subnet for sending of data to other networks. A network interface can have only one active default gateway at a time, although multiple gateways can be configured in Windows 2000 for fault tolerance purposes. Be aware that the term "gateway" is also used to refer to software that translates between protocols and connects networks of different types, such as connecting a Windows PC network to an IBM mainframe (SNA gateway) or to a NetWare network (Gateway Services for NetWare).

Be aware for exam purposes that there are two basic types of routing: static and dynamic.

Static Routing *Static routing* requires that an administrator manually construct a routing table, which contains the pathways to outside networks.

You should know how to use the ROUTE utility at the command line to view the routing table and manually add, delete, and modify routing table entries. Be familiar with the switches shown in Table 1-1.

TABLE 1-1 Switches and Commands Used with the ROUTE Utility

Switch or Command	Action	Comments
-f	Clears all gateway entries from the routing table.	Can be used with other commands to clear the table before invoking the action of the other command.
-p	Creates a persistent route.	Is used with the ADD command. Causes the entry to stay in the table when the computer is restarted.

TABLE 1-1 Switches and Commands Used with the ROUTE Utility *(continued)*

Switch or Command	Action	Comments
PRINT	Prints the route.	
ADD	Adds a route to the table.	
DELETE	Removes a route from the table.	
CHANGE	Allows you to modify a route that is already in the table.	
destination	Identifies the host computer that is the destination address.	
MASK	Signals the netmask value as the next entry.	
netmask	Identifies the subnet mask.	Default is 255.255.255.255.
gateway	Identifies the IP address of the gateway.	
interface	Identifies the interface number for the route.	
METRIC	Sets the cost for the destination.	By default, cost per hop is 1 but this can be modified.

Dynamic Routing *Dynamic routing* uses routing protocols such as the Routing Information Protocol (RIP) or Open Shortest Path First (OSPF) to allow routers to communicate with one another and automatically, dynamically update their routing tables without human intervention.

You should know that Windows 2000 supports the following routing protocols:

- RIPv1
- RIPv2
- OSPF

RIP is known as a *distance vector protocol.* This means that it has a maximum path length of 15 hops. If a packet must pass through more than 15 routers (gateways) to reach its destination, RIP considers the destination "unreachable." Another drawback of these protocols is that they are vulnerable to routing loops. RIP and the other distance vector protocols were designed for use in moderately sized networks, not for huge internetworks. However, RIP is a well-established standard and offers many advantages over static routing. Link state protocols are more efficient, and scale better than distance vector protocols, but they are also more complex.

OSPF belongs to a different group, the *link state protocols.* This type of protocol maps the network and updates the mapping database (called the link state database) whenever any changes are made to the network. Link state protocols are more efficient but more complex than distance vector protocols.

The Microsoft exams will expect you to know the differences between these protocol types, and how to add and configure the protocols. This is done through the Routing and Remote Access management console, as shown in Figure 1-5.

Configuring both static routing tables and the dynamic routing protocols will be covered in more detail in chapter 9, "Installing, Configuring, Managing, Monitoring, and Troubleshooting IP Routing."

The Security Infrastructure

Network security is a big concern to almost all network administrators today, in light of the growing popularity of "hack attacks" from outsiders, the increasing computer savvy of employees at all levels, and the amount and types of data that are stored on networked systems. Trade secrets, confidential client information, and other sensitive

FIGURE 1-5

Routing protocols are added and configured through the RRAS console

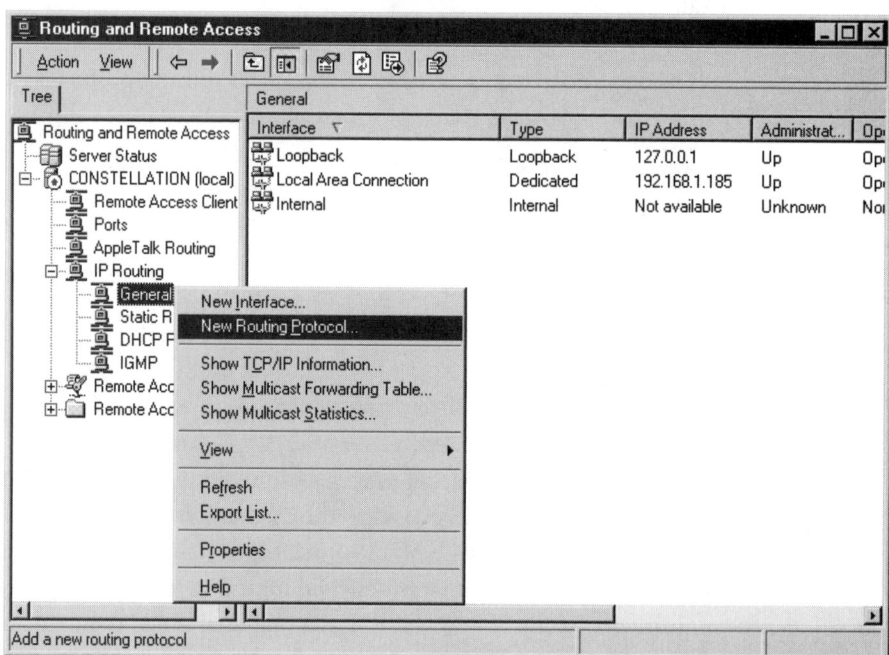

information lives on the hard disks of company networks and must be protected from both malicious and accidental access by unauthorized persons.

Microsoft has made many improvements to the security components in Windows 2000. In fact, security is such an integral factor in many of the new features, such as Active Directory and RRAS, that it is difficult to define it separately.

Windows 2000 security features include the following:

- Kerberos authentication
- IP Security (IPSec)
- Much improved policy management (Group Policy)
- Enhanced certificate services
- Encrypting File System (EFS)
- Secondary Logon
- Security Configuration Toolset
- Smart card support

Although the security-related topics will be covered in depth in the elective Exam 70-220, Designing Security for a Microsoft Windows 2000 Network, you will be expected to know about some of the basic security options for the Networking Infrastructure exam.

Exam 70-216 specifically covers topics pertaining to Certificate Services and installation and configuration of Certification Authority. You should get hands-on practice in setting up CA and issuing and revoking certificates prior to taking this exam.

CERTIFICATION OBJECTIVE 1.02

Overview of Exam 70-216

For a list of the learning objectives for Exam 70-216, see the Microsoft Web site at www.microsoft.com/mcp/exam/stat/SP70-216.htm . The objectives are somewhat broad, and you'll note that they are performance-based. This does not mean that you don't need to know any of the theory behind the concepts being tested. It does mean that *only* knowing the theory, without having ever put it into practice by working with the operating system, will make it difficult or even impossible for you to pass the exam.

The objectives are divided into logical categories that include all the general topics discussed earlier. More specifically:

- **DNS** For the DNS exam objective, you will need to be familiar with the installation procedure, how to configure the service, best practices for managing DNS/DDNS in a Windows 2000 network, how to monitor DNS performance, and basic troubleshooting of common DNS problems. Specifically, you'll need to know what a root server is and how to configure one, the function of zones and how they are configured (including for dynamic updates), how to set up the DNS client computer, and how to configure a DNS server to be caching-only. You'll also need to know how to implement a delegated DNS zone and how to manually create resource records.
- **DHCP** In relation to DHCP, you must be familiar with installation, configuration, management, monitoring, and troubleshooting principles. You should pay particular attention to installing the DHCP Server Service, and practice creating and managing scopes, superscopes, and multicast scopes. You will need to know how DHCP is integrated with DNS and be able to authorize a DHCP server in Active Directory.
- **RAS** For the Remote Access Services (RAS) portion of the exam, you'll need to know how to configure inbound connections and how to set remote access policies and configure profiles. You should also focus on configuring multilink connections and how to set up a virtual private network (VPN). Finally, you should know how DHCP is integrated with RRAS.
- **Network Protocols** Expect TCP/IP to be an important part of this exam, now that there is no separate exam on the topic. You should know how to install and configure it, how to configure TCP/IP packet filtering, and how to manage and monitor network traffic using Network Monitor and other tools. Be sure you understand the fundamentals of protocol security and have hands-on practice in enabling IPSec and configuring it for both transport and tunnel modes, as well as customizing IPSec policies and rules and managing and monitoring it. Also in relation to networking protocols, familiarize yourself with the installation and configuration of NWLink (IPX/SPX).

- **WINS** Even though WINS may be "on the way out," it is still very much alive and well in the first release of Windows 2000, and likely to be the subject of at least a few exam questions. So be sure you know how to install, configure, and troubleshoot WINS, and pay particular attention to WINS replication, management, and monitoring.
- **Routing** Windows 2000 can function as an IP router, and for the exam, you'll need to know how to configure static routes as well as the dynamic routing protocols in RRAS. Know how to implement demand-dial routing, and how to monitor and manage both border routing and internal routing.
- **ICS and NAT** Internet Connection Sharing and Network Address Translation are new features in Windows 2000 that are sure to come up in exam questions. You should know the difference between ICS (built into both Windows 2000 Professional and Server) and NAT (available only with the Server products), and how to install and configure both.
- **Security** Security is a major concern and has been the focus of many new Windows 2000 features. In fact, there is an elective exam that deals exclusively with security issues. For the Networking Infrastructure exam, you need to be familiar with the Windows 2000 Certificate services, and know how to install and configure Certificate Authority (CA), issue and revoke certificates, and remove the Encrypting File System (EFS) recovery keys.

exam Watch

Although much of the knowledge and skill you may have gained from working with NT in the past is transferable to Windows 2000, it is imperative that you not make assumptions that similar tasks are accomplished in the same way in Windows 2000. Nothing substitutes for hands-on experience using the operating system.

CERTIFICATION OBJECTIVE 1.03

What We'll Cover in This Book

Each of the exam topics covered in the 70-216 list of objectives will be addressed in this book. However, we will go beyond the basic "how to" aspect, even though the certification objectives are written almost exclusively as performance-based statements. We know that in order to really understand what you're doing, you need to know the theory behind it. If you have many long years of on-the-job experience working with NT, *and* have worked a great deal with extra add-on software and third-party products, you may already be familiar with the concepts behind these task-oriented objectives. Otherwise, it will benefit you to read the explanatory text carefully as well as performing the exercises in each chapter.

Knowledge

In the beginning of each chapter, we will try to provide you with a foundation of knowledge upon which conceptual comprehension and practices skills can be built. This includes definitions of new terms, explanations of processes, and discussion of relationships between components.

Topic Tie-ins

We will cross reference subjects that appear elsewhere in the book that tie in to the topic of the chapter and/or that will aid you in understanding the material to be presented in the chapter.

Concepts

In addition to basic knowledge-based information such as definitions and relationships, we will provide an overview of the concepts behind the skills-based exercises. For example, setting up a WINS server involves a skill set. The *concept* of WINS—resolution of NetBIOS names to IP addresses and why this needs to be done—is not absolutely necessary in order to perform the task, but will certainly be helpful to you in making configuration decisions.

The authors will attempt to make all abstract concepts as easy to understand as possible, using analogies and graphical illustrations.

Practical Skills

The heart of Windows 2000 exam preparation is development of practical skills—the ability not just to know about the operating system, but also to use it to perform common network administration tasks. The exams are performance-based, as is obvious from the wording of the exam objectives, almost all of which use action verbs such as "configure, install, monitor, troubleshoot, manage, create, remove, implement" and the like.

More so than with the NT exams, it is imperative that you do the practical exercises in each chapter, experiment with various settings and options, and get hands-on experience in performing the tasks about which you read.

Many of the exam questions will be relatively simple for those who have worked with the product, and almost impossible to answer for someone who hasn't gone through the processes themselves. In this book, we attempt to simulate the Windows 2000 working environment as much as possible by liberal use of screenshots and detailed descriptions of what to expect in response to particular actions or commands; however, there is no substitute for *doing it yourself.*

CERTIFICATION OBJECTIVE 1.04

Networking Terminology

For those who are beginning their study of Windows 2000 with little exposure to real-life networking, one of the most important (and perhaps most tedious) tasks is to "learn the language" of computer networking. At times, as you read through the study material, you may feel as if you're floating in a sea of acronyms and unfamiliar words.

In this book, our policy is to spell out all acronyms in full the first time they appear, and to define new terms within the text whenever possible. However, what's a well-known term to a networking professional may be "new" to you, and in a book this size, trying to flip back through the pages to find the first occurrence of a word could be a time-consuming process.

We suggest that you make liberal use of the Glossary. If you run across a word or term whose meaning you're not sure of, and that's not obvious from the context, don't just skim over it and hope it will be clarified later. Taking the time to look it up may seem to slow down your study, but it's one of the best ways to ensure that you remember the meaning later.

"Double Meanings"

Don't despair if you find that definitions are not always absolutely consistent from one source to the next. Within the computer industry and even within the more narrowly defined networking world, there are many subspecialty areas that have their own brand of jargon.

For example, you may hear the word "segment" used to describe a length of cable, or the computers that are connected to a length of backbone cable. You will hear the same word used, in discussions of TCP/IP, to describe the "chunks" into which data is broken down to be transmitted across the network. Likewise, "cell" means one thing in the context of wireless communications, and something else when discussing ATM technology.

The following scenario and solution lists some of these more confusing "double meanings" that you are likely to encounter in your studies of networking infrastructure fundamentals.

SCENARIO & SOLUTION	
What is a segment?	In discussions of the physical networking infrastructure, "segment" usually refers to a length of cable, or the portion of the network connected to a length of backbone cable between repeaters. In TCP/IP terminology, "segment" is the term used to describe the chunk of data sent by TCP over the network (roughly equivalent to the usage of "packet" or "frame").
I see the acronyms DN, DNM, DNS, and DDNS? What does it all mean and what, if any, is the relationship between them?	DN, in Active Directory parlance, stands for Distinguished Name, an LDAP way of uniquely identifying an object. A DNM is a Domain Naming Master, one of the operations masters roles played by domain controllers in a Windows 2000 network. DNS is Domain Name System, used to map fully qualified domain names to IP addresses. Dynamic DNS is the enhanced version used in Windows 2000. In the Networking Infrastructure exam, this last is the one you are more likely to encounter. The only relationship is their common status as components of Windows 2000. DNS will be familiar to NT 4.0 administrators; the others may not be.
What does PVC mean?	In discussing the physical networking infrastructure, PVC refers to polyvinyl chloride, the material out of which standard Ethernet cable is made. In discussions of networking concepts, PVC is used to mean Permanent Virtual Circuit, referring to a network pathway in which all packets follow the same route (as opposed to a switched virtual circuit).

SCENARIO & SOLUTION	
Why does the word "gateway" seem to have two different meanings?	"Gateway" is used in networking to refer to a router or a computer functioning as one, the "way out" of the network or subnet, to get to another network. The word "gateway" is also used in regard to software that connects a system using one protocol to a system using a different protocol, such as the Systems Network Architecture (SNA) software that allows a PC LAN to connect to an IBM mainframe, or the Gateway Services for NetWare used to provide a way for Microsoft clients to go through a Windows NT or Windows 2000 server to access files on a Novell file server.
What's the difference between OSI, ISO, and IOS?	OSI stands for Open Systems Interconnection and is used in all standard basic networking texts and classes in regard to the OSI layered networking model. The ISO is the organization that created this and other international standards; its name is the International Organization for Standardization and its short form, ISO, is not really an acronym but a derivative of a Greek word. IOS is the dedicated operating system used by Cisco routers.

CERTIFICATION OBJECTIVE 1.05

For "Newbies" and "Old Pros"

For those who are new to the world of networking, this chapter will contain a section that provides background information that, although not specifically covered by the Windows 2000 exam objectives, is essential to understanding the chapter topic(s). And for experienced administrators, there will be special tips for NT pros, pointing out the areas in which Windows 2000 differs (subtly or drastically) from its predecessor, and warning you of common pitfalls that you may encounter in making the transition to Microsoft's new way of doing things.

For Networking Newbies

If you are new to computer networking, we recommend that you take a course or study a good book in basic networking concepts. Even if you are following the Windows 2000 MCSE certification track, it would benefit you to study one of the NT 4.0 Networking Essentials study guides and/or take the Windows 2000 Network and Operating Systems Essentials course.

You will find that familiarizing yourself with basic networking concepts—such as physical topologies, characteristics of different cable and other media types, the popular networking architectures such as Ethernet, AppleTalk, and Token Ring, and often-referenced networking standards and models such as the OSI, DoD, and Windows models and the IEEE 802 specifications—will benefit you in many ways. Not only will the knowledge provide a solid foundation for the material you will be studying in the process of obtaining Microsoft certification, but most employers will expect you, as an MCP or MCSE, to recognize these fundamental concepts.

The very best investment a networking neophyte can make, though, is that of building your own network from the ground up. Even a simple two-computer thinnet network will give you a taste of the challenges faced by Enterprise pros in the field, and many of the setup, maintenance, and troubleshooting scenarios associated with large production networks can be simulated on a smaller scale with a small home network.

There are a number of excellent books, as well as numerous Web resources, available to guide you through the challenging experience of getting those first two computers to "talk" to one another.

For NT Pros

If you are already certified and/or experienced in NT 4.0, you may be able to skip some parts of this book that provide basic information about protocols and services with which you are already familiar. But don't skip too much! Windows 2000 is built on the NT kernel and you will find much in the new operating system that feels like "home"—but you will also discover, as you delve deeper, that there are many fundamental changes, even to "old friends" like DNS and WINS.

NT professionals will need to guard against the possibility that your experience and mastery of the earlier operating system will be your biggest enemy on the Windows 2000 certification exams. Expect questions that try to "trick" you by providing solutions that *would* have been correct if you were using NT, which measure whether you're aware of the differences between the two operating systems (just as there were traditionally questions on the NT certification exams that used a test-taker's experience with Windows 9*x* against him in the same way).

We certainly don't advise NT pros to "forget everything you ever knew" about network operating systems, but we do encourage you not only to study Windows 2000, but to actually use it on a day-to-day basis. If possible, upgrade your primary workstation to Windows 2000 Professional so that the slightly different ways of performing routine tasks, the subtle differences in the interface, become second nature to you. And work with Windows 2000 Server or Advanced Server—on the job, at home, or in the classroom. It's in the server products that the real differences between NT and Windows 2000 show themselves.

Your NT experience can put you a step ahead of the networking newcomers—*if* you remember not to make too many assumptions (generally a good policy to follow in all areas of life).

CERTIFICATION SUMMARY

This chapter has provided a brief introduction to the Windows 2000 certification exam process in general and an overview of the objectives of Exam 70-216, Implementing and Administering a Microsoft Windows 2000 Networking Infrastructure, in particular.

We have discussed some very fundamental concepts of Microsoft networking, such as IP addressing, name resolution, remote access, and security. We have also discussed those specific topics that are the focus of the Networking Infrastructure exam, such as DNS/DDNS, WINS, IP routing, TCP/IP, DHCP, NAT, and Windows 2000 certificate services.

We briefly touched on the importance of mastering common networking terminology, and provided examples of a few common cases of acronyms or terms that may have unclear or dual meanings.

In closing, we addressed the special needs of the two very different audiences who are likely to use this book: the networking novice who is beginning his or her career with the study of Windows 2000, and the networking professional who has experience working in the field with, and may already be certified in, other network operating systems.

TWO-MINUTE DRILL

What Is a Network Infrastructure?

- Microsoft's "target audience" for the Windows 2000 exams consists of networking professionals with at least one year's experience; this does not mean you can't pass the exams without that experience, but it does mean you will need to do more hands-on practice with the operating system.
- The Windows 2000 exams will involve questions that require a higher cognitive level to arrive at the correct solution; most questions will be performance-based rather than purely knowledge-based.
- A computer network has both a physical and a logical infrastructure. The former consists of hardware components; the latter is software-based and includes protocols and services upon which network communications depend. Exam 70-216 focuses on the components of the logical infrastructure.
- The TCP/IP protocol suite, on which most of today's medium-to-large networks (including the Internet) run, is an important component of the logical networking infrastructure, and a good understanding of how it works will be essential to passing the exam.
- Name resolution is an important component of the infrastructure because it allows "friendly" host names or NetBIOS names to be mapped to IP addresses (and the latter is used by the networking protocol for one computer to communicate with another).
- The Domain Name Service, DNS, maps fully qualified domain names to IP addresses. The Windows 2000 implementation, Dynamic DNS (DDNS) is an essential component of Windows 2000 networks and is likely to be the subject of one or more questions on Exam 70-216.
- The Windows Internet Naming Service (WINS) resolves NetBIOS names to IP addresses. Although WINS plays a lesser role in Windows 2000 networks, Microsoft has made several significant improvements to the service, and the exam will require that you know how to install, configure, manage, monitor, and troubleshoot the service, with a focus on WINS replication issues.

- The Dynamic Host Configuration Protocol (DHCP) is used for automatic assignment of IP addresses. Windows 2000's implementation of DHCP is integrated with DNS, and the ability to install, configure, monitor, and troubleshoot DHCP will be essential skills for passing the Networking Infrastructure exam.
- Remote access services in Windows 2000 include the ability to act as both a remote client (using PPP or SLIP) and a remote server (supporting PPP only). Connections can be dial-up or via virtual private networking (VPN), and you should know how to create and configure inbound connections, set up policies and profiles, and utilize multilink capabilities.
- IPSec is a new security feature in Windows 2000 that provides end-to-end security of IP packets (including over a VPN connection, if the L2TP tunneling protocol is used). You will need to know how to configure, customize, and monitor IPSec for the exam.
- IP routing is fundamental to any medium to large networking environment, and you will need to know, for Exam 70-216, how to install and configure dynamic routing protocols, as well as how to enter static routes in the routing table. You also need to understand the difference between border and internal routers.
- Network Address Translation (NAT), a new feature to Windows 2000, allows for the sharing of one Internet connection (or other WAN connection) with other computers on the LAN by mapping private IP addresses to one or more public registered address(es). The exam will expect you to be familiar with installation and configuration of both Internet Connection Sharing (ICS) that is included in both Windows 2000 Professional and Server, and the more full-featured form, called simply NAT, available only in the server products.
- One of many security features included in Windows 2000 is its certificate services. For the exam, you will need to know how to install and configure Certificate Authority and how to issue and revoke certificates.

SELF TEST

The following questions will help you measure your understanding of the material presented in this chapter. Read all of the choices carefully, as there may be more than one correct answer. Choose all correct answers for each question.

What Is a Network Infrastructure?

1. Which of the following is the network/transport protocol stack used on most medium and large networks today?

   A. IPX/SPX

   B. NetBEUI/NetBIOS

   C. TCP/IP

   D. DNS/DDNS

2. Which of the following is true of the Dynamic Host Configuration Protocol? (Select all that apply.)

   A. It has been replaced by APIPA in Windows 2000.

   B. It is used to automatically assign IP addresses.

   C. It is derived from BOOTP.

   D. It is a name resolution service.

3. Which of the following is the term used to refer to the IP address of the router or computer functioning as a router?

   A. The Subnet Mask

   B. The Default Gateway

   C. The Network ID

   D. The host ID

4. "A set of rules, or a standardized order of procedures, that the networking components of the systems follow when they transmit data over the network" is the definition of which of the following?

   A. Protocol

   B. Media

   C. Standards

   D. Models

5. Which of the following is a sublayer of the Data Link layer of the OSI networking model? (Select all that apply.)

   A. Presentation sublayer

   B. Media Access Control sublayer

   C. Network interface sublayer

   D. Logical Link Control sublayer

6. Which of the following pieces of information is required to manually configure the TCP/IP properties of a Windows 2000 client computer's network interface on a routed network? (Select all that apply.)

   A. The IP address assigned to the NIC

   B. The IP address of the Windows 2000 domain controller

   C. The default gateway address

   D. The subnet mask

7. Which of the following is the correct default subnet mask for a Class B network?

   A. 255.255.255.255

   B. 255.255.255.0

   C. 255.255.0.0

   D. 255.0.0.0

8. Which of the following is a "connectionless" protocol that operates at the Transport layer of the OSI model?

   A. UDP

   B. TCP

   C. IP

   D. FTP

9. Which of the following is a dynamic routing protocol supported by Windows 2000? (Select all that apply.)

   A. OSPF

   B. IOS

   C. RRAS

   D. RIP

10. Which of the following is a reason to have a secondary DNS server? (Select all that apply.)
    A. DNS servers work only in pairs.
    B. It provides fault tolerance.
    C. It is used for load balancing.
    D. You cannot have a secondary DNS server.

11. Which of the following is a "connection-oriented" protocol that operates at the Transport layer of the OSI model?
    A. UDP
    B. FTP
    C. IP
    D. TCP

12. The term "gateway" is used to refer to which of the following? (Select all that apply.)
    A. A router
    B. A bridge
    C. Software that translates between different protocols
    D. A device that connects different cable types

13. Which of the following is the TCP/IP utility that is used to display the local NetBIOS name table, a table of NetBIOS names registered by local applications, and the NetBIOS name cache, a local cache listing of NetBIOS computer names that have been resolved to IP addresses?
    A. NETSTAT
    B. NBTSTAT
    C. IPCONFIG
    D. TRACERT

14. Which of the following is true of the binary numbering system? (Select all that apply.)
    A. It uses both alpha and numeric characters.
    B. It is a base ten system.
    C. It is a base two system.
    D. It uses 0s and 1s, which are referred to as "bits."

15. Which of the following is a TCP/IP-based service that allows users to log on to, run character-mode applications, and view files on a remote computer?

    A. FTP

    B. Telnet

    C. HTTP

    D. RAS

SELF TEST ANSWERS

What Is a Network Infrastructure?

1. ☑ **C**. TCP/IP is the protocol of the global Internet and is used by most medium and large (and many small) LANS.
☒ **A**, **B**, and **D** are incorrect. IPX/SPX is the protocol stack traditionally used with Novell NetWare networks (although NetWare version 5.0 can run on pure IP). NetBEUI is a protocol used in small workgroups that do not need routing capabilities. NetBIOS is the API on which NetBEUI is based. The Domain Name System, DNS, and its Dynamic version as implemented in Windows 2000, DDNS, are name resolution services, not network/transport protocols.

2. ☑ **B**, **C**. DHCP is used to automatically assign IP addresses to computers configured as DHCP clients.
☒ **A** is incorrect. APIPA works in conjunction with DHCP, to allow DHCP clients who can't find a DHCP server to assign themselves addresses. **D** is incorrect because DHCP does not resolve names.

3. ☑ **B**. The address of the router that is used as the "way out" of the network (to send packets to remote networks) is referred to as the default gateway.
☒ **A** is incorrect because a subnet mask is a 32-bit number that identifies which part of an IP address indicates the network ID. **C** is incorrect because the network ID is that part of an IP address that identifies the network or subnet. **D** is incorrect because the host ID is that part of the IP address that identifies the individual computer, or host, on the network.

4. ☑ **A**. This is the definition of "protocol" in the context of computer networking.
☒ **B** is incorrect because media refers to the cable, airwaves, or other way in which messages are transmitted. **C** is incorrect because standards refer to established criteria followed by vendors, programmers, etc. to ensure compatibility between systems, programs, and components. **D** is incorrect because models, in networking context, are representations (usually graphical) of a process based on a set of standards.

5. ☑ **B**, **D**. The MAC and LLC sublayers make up the Data Link layer of the OSI model.
☒ **A** is incorrect because the Presentation layer is an independent layer in the OSI model, not a sublayer. **C** is incorrect because the Network Interface layer is a part of the Department of Defense (DoD) model, not part of the OSI model.

6. ☑ **A**, **C**, **D**. The IP address of the NIC whose TCP/IP properties are being configured and the subnet mask are always required for manual configuration. A default gateway address is required if the network is routed.

☒ **B** is incorrect because you do not need to enter the IP address of the domain controller when you configure a client computer's TCP/IP properties.

7. ☑ **C**. In a Class B network that is not subnetted, two octets are "masked" to represent the network ID, and the other two are unmasked to represent the Host ID.
☒ **A** is incorrect because 255.255.255.255 does not represent a valid default subnet mask for any of the network classes. **B** is incorrect because 255.255.255.0 is the default subnet mask for a Class C network. **D** is incorrect because 255.0.0.0 is the default subnet mask for a Class A network.

8. ☑ **A**. The User Datagram Protocol (UDP) is the TCP/IP stack's connectionless transport protocol, which is faster (but less reliable) than TCP.
☒ **B** is incorrect because although TCP operates at the Transport layer, it is a connection-oriented protocol. **C** is incorrect because although IP is connectionless, it operates at the Network layer of the OSI model. **D** is incorrect because FTP is an application layer protocol.

9. ☑ **A, D**. Open Shortest Path First and the Routing Information Protocol are both dynamic routing protocols included in the Windows 2000 router component.
☒ **B** is incorrect because IOS is the Cisco Systems operating system used by Cisco routers. **C** is incorrect because RRAS is the Routing and Remote Access Service.

10. ☑ **B, C**. A secondary DNS server has a copy of the zone file, which provides fault tolerance in case the primary DNS server goes down. It also is used for load balancing to take some of the burden of queries off the primary server.
☒ **A** is incorrect because a single DNS server can work by itself. **D** is incorrect because you can—but are not required to—have a secondary DNS server.

11. ☑ **D**. TCP, the Transmission Control Protocol, operates at the Transport layer of the OSI networking model and is "connection-oriented."
☒ **A** is incorrect because although the User Datagram Protocol operates at the Transport layer, it is a "connectionless" protocol. **B** is incorrect because FTP is an application layer protocol, and **C** is incorrect because IP operates at the Network layer.

12. ☑ **A, C**. Routers are referred to as "gateways," and the router to which packets going outside the local subnet are sent is referred to as the "default gateway." Software programs such as SNA and GSNW that translate between protocols to connect different types of networks are also called gateways.
☒ **B** is incorrect because a bridge does not offer a "way out" of the network and is not called a gateway. **D** is incorrect because a device that merely connects different cable types does not subnet the network and is not referred to as a gateway.

13. ☑ **B.** NBTSTAT displays NetBIOS information; the "NBT" stands for "NetBIOS over TCP/IP.
☒ A is incorrect because NETSTAT is used to display protocol statistics and current TCP/IP connections. **C** is incorrect because IPCONFIG is used to display general information about the TCP/IP configuration, such as IP address, subnet mask, and default gateway. **D** is incorrect because TRACERT is used to trace the route of a packet.

14. ☑ **C, D.** Binary is a base two system that uses the two digits 0 and 1 for all calculations. The digits are referred to as "bits."
☒ **A** is incorrect because it is the hexadecimal system that uses alpha and numeric characters. **B** is incorrect because it is the decimal system that is a base ten system.

15. ☑ **B.** Telnet is the TCP/IP Application layer protocol that allows users to view files and run programs on a remote computer (but does not allow uploading or downloading of files).
☒ **A** is incorrect because FTP is a service that allows users to upload files to or download files from an FTP server using FTP client software. **C** is incorrect because HTTP is the Hypertext Transfer Protocol used to access pages on the World Wide Web. **D** is incorrect because Remote Access Service (RAS) is used to establish a dial-up or VPN connection to another computer.

MCSE

MICROSOFT CERTIFIED SYSTEMS ENGINEER

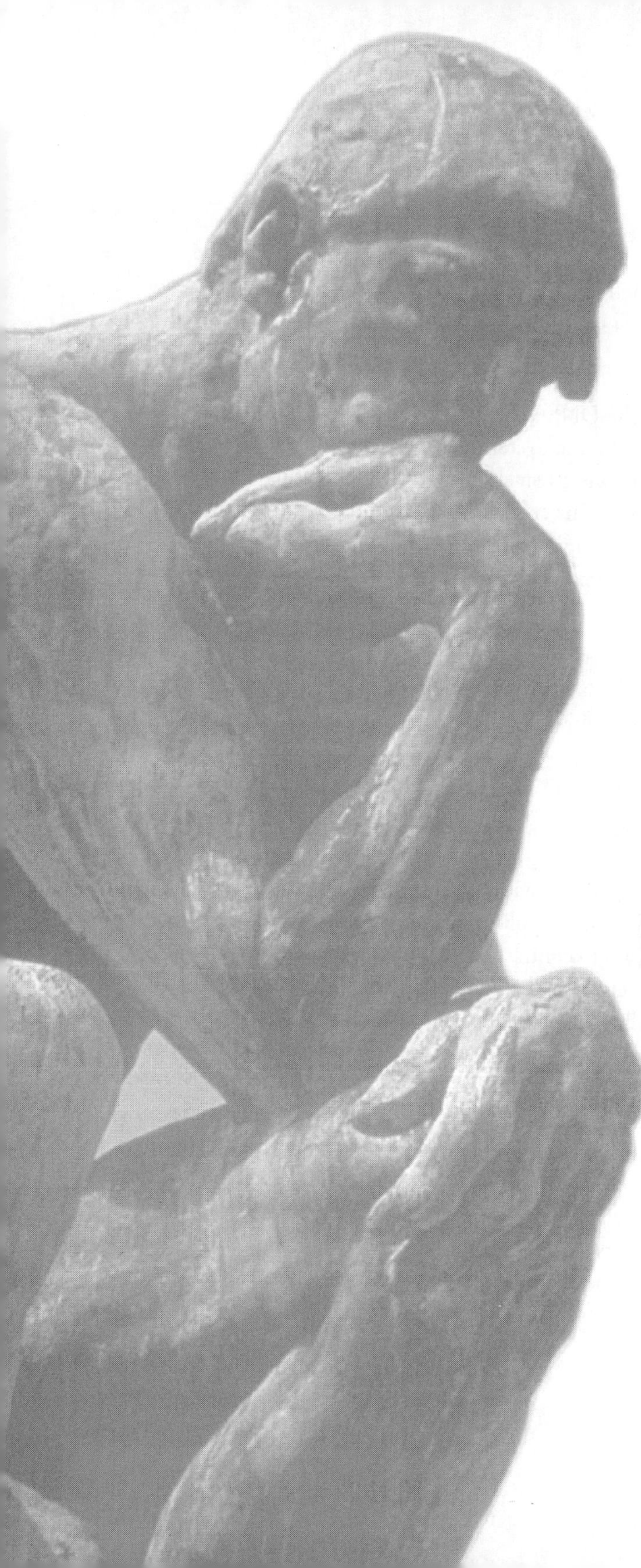

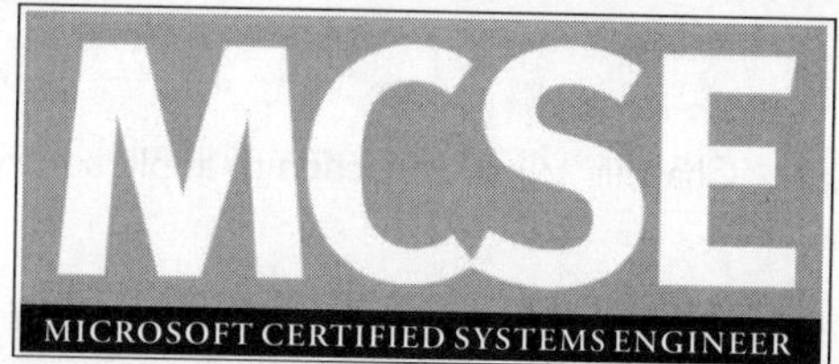

2

The Domain Naming System: Introductory Concepts and Procedures

CERTIFICATION OBJECTIVES

In this chapter we will examine some of the basic concepts and procedures involved with managing and maintaining a Domain Name System (DNS) and DNS Server for your organization. In Windows 2000, the DNS becomes the primary name system and domain locator for your network clients.

Here we will examine how the DNS is constructed and how objects are placed and located within the Domain Name System. We will also look at how to fit your organization into the DNS, and what you should do about creating a meaningful and functional DNS solution for your company. After you are comfortable with these basic DNS concepts, we will build on your knowledge and explore more advanced DNS principles in the next chapter.

CERTIFICATION OBJECTIVE 2.01

The Domain Naming System: Introductory Concepts and Procedures

The Domain Naming System (DNS) provides a solution to the problem of host naming and host name resolution for WinSock applications. In order to understand some of the key concepts of DNS, it is helpful to contrast DNS with another commonly used naming system on Microsoft Networks, the NetBIOS naming scheme.

Prior to Windows 2000, all Microsoft networks used NetBIOS as their primary naming scheme and method of identifying machines and services on the network. NetBIOS was initially designed as a monolithic transport protocol for IBM by Sytek in 1983. Since then, the NetBIOS command set has been integrated as a Session layer interface for other protocols, including its most common implementation: NetBEUI (NetBIOS Extended User Interface).

NetBIOS was designed for small, single-segment LANs. NetBIOS protocols are *broadcast based.* NetBIOS clients can find other network clients by using NetBIOS broadcast messages to identify the destination computer's hardware address. Once the hardware address is known, a session can be established with the destination computer (Figure 2-1).

FIGURE 2-1 A NetBIOS broadcast to resolve a NetBIOS name to a MAC address

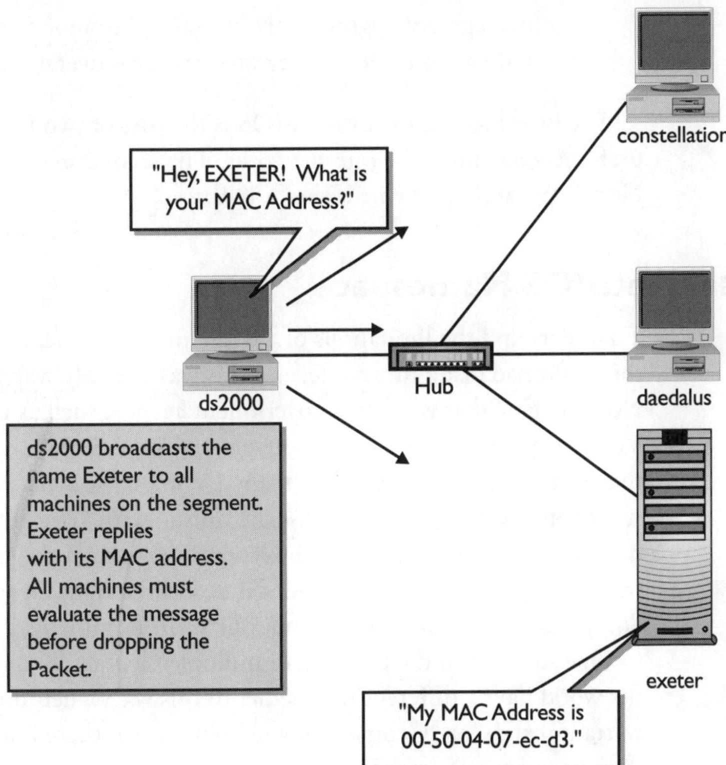

While the broadcast method worked well for small departmental LANs that occupied a single segment, this method of identifying other computers on Ethernet (broadcast-based) networks became problematic for several reasons:

- As the number of computers on a network segment increased, so the did the volume of broadcast traffic.
- NetBIOS-based protocols (NetBEUI) have no mechanism that allows them to include routing information. Routing instructions were not included in the NetBIOS frame specification.
- Even if a mechanism is employed to allow NetBIOS messages to be routed (such as overlaying NetBIOS over another, routable protocol), routers do not, by default, forward NetBIOS broadcasts. Forwarding broadcast traffic

across segments significantly increases the amount of network volume and would have a profound negative effect on overall network performance.

The broadcast nature of NetBIOS is the first of two factors that limit its usefulness on enterprise internetworks. The second major problem with the NetBIOS naming scheme is that it is *flat.*

The Flat NetBIOS Namespace

To understand the limitations of a flat naming scheme, imagine that everyone in the world had just a first name, and this was the only way people were identified. Now imagine that you run a government agency, such as the Department of Motor Vehicles. Each person in your state gets a driver's license. How many Georges are there? How many Carols? How many Debbies? How many Harrys? When an officer stops you and checks your license, he calls in with "I've got George here, do you have any priors on him?" Which George? Yes, one of the Georges out there has a warrant, but the officer has no idea if he has the right George sitting in front of him. So, he just arrests you and lets the courts sort it out later.

One solution to the problem of multiple Georges is to require that everyone in the world have a different first name. In this way, when the officer calls up for a warrant search for "George," he will know that if there is a warrant out for George, then he just got his man!

How would you coordinate the naming of everyone in the world (or at least in your country or state) so that everyone's name was different? And what would happen if some people didn't want to comply and decided that they wanted to name their child with a name that had already been used?

It would be virtually impossible to coordinate the naming of individuals so that everyone had a different name. And even if you were to implement such as system, some people would defy it and name their child with a name that was the same as one already in use. This would cause confusion in the naming structure for the people or the world, and the possibility would exist that a communication meant for one individual would be directed to the other person with the same name.

This is an example of the limitation of a flat namespace. The NetBIOS namespace is a flat namespace. This means that every computer on the network must have a different name. If two computers on a NetBIOS network have the same name, messages could be mistakenly forwarded to a computer that was not the intended destination.

The NetBIOS and WinSock Interfaces

DNS solves these problems because it does not use a flat naming structure. It uses a *hierarchical* naming system, much like how we use a system of First Name, Middle Name, and Last Name to aid in naming and identifying each other. Before we go into the details of the DNS namespace, we should discuss how applications access the network protocols and, specifically, how they interact with the TCP/IP protocol.

Network-enabled applications for Microsoft operating systems interact with the TCP/IP protocol stack via one of two Session layer interfaces: The *Windows Sockets (WinSock)* interface, or the *NetBIOS interface.*

These interfaces solve a key problem in name resolution on TCP/IP-based networks. Programs written to the NetBIOS interface treat the destination computer name as the "endpoint" for communications. NetBIOS applications only care about the name of the destination computer in order to establish a session with that machine. However, the TCP/IP protocol stack, including the Transmission Control Protocol and the Internet Protocol, has no awareness of NetBIOS computer names, and really doesn't care about them at all.

NetBIOS over TCP/IP or NetBT

In order to resolve this situation, NetBIOS applications interface with the TCP/IP protocol stack via the NetBIOS interface, which is implemented as *NetBIOS over TCP/IP*, or *NetBT.* When a request for a network resource is passed from a NetBIOS application down to the Application layer of the TCP/IP protocol stack, it interfaces with NetBT. It is at this point that the NetBIOS name is translated, or *resolved*, to an IP address. Once the NetBIOS name of the destination computer is resolved to a NetBIOS name, the request can be passed down the TCP/IP protocol stack. Figure 2-2 shows you how the process works.

The Windows Sockets (WinSock) Interface

Programs that were specifically written for TCP/IP-based networks use the WinSock interface. These programs, however, do not require a name for the destination computer in order to establish a session with it. All they require is a destination IP address in order to connect with the destination host.

While your computer may have little problem with the voluminous numbers of IP addresses out there for the servers we connect to, humans have a different opinion about remembering long lists of numbers. Think about the servers that you frequent

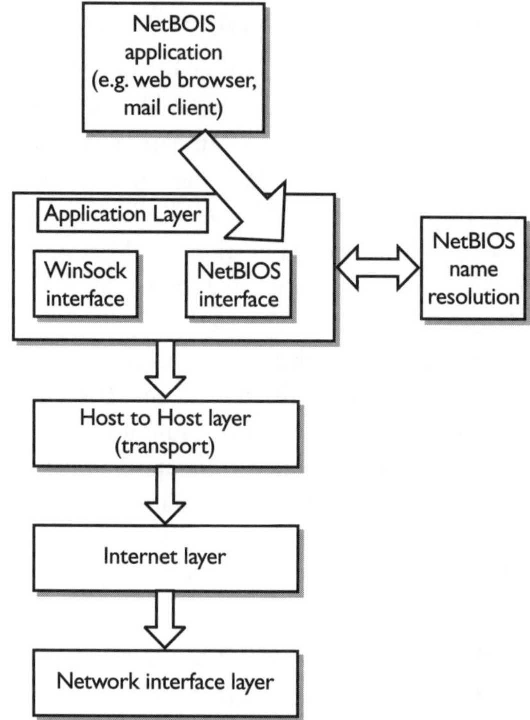

FIGURE 2-2

A NetBIOS communication moving down the protocol stack

on a regular basis: microsoft.com, zdnet.com, cnet.com, syngress.com, shinder.net, and a host of others. Do you know the IP addresses of those Web servers to which you connect regularly? Do you care to know all those IP addresses? Are you already unhappy that you have to remember 10-digit phone numbers and therefore bought a Windows CE pocket PC in order to handle the added complexity?

All but the most "alpha" of geeks find remembering computer names much easier than remembering numbers. So, while WinSock applications do not require a computer or host name to establish a session with a destination computer, they can employ a mechanism to do so. This is the process of *host name resolution.*

The Bottom Line on the Difference between NetBIOS and WinSock

Remember, NetBIOS-based programs must have the NetBIOS name translated or resolved to an IP address before a session can be established with a destination computer, while WinSock programs can use host names rather than IP addresses, but that this is not required. Host names represent a convenience only.

This is an important distinction because until Windows 2000, all the core networking components of Windows operating systems were NetBIOS based. That is why so much time has been devoted to the subject of NetBIOS name resolution in the past. Windows 2000 does not depend on NetBIOS names for the vast majority of its networking subsystems, and uses DNS host names instead. We will see the implications of these changes as we move through this chapter.

on the job

Windows 2000 machines can work with NetBIOS eliminated from its TCP/IP protocol stack. However, you must be sure that none of your applications requires the NetBIOS interface. The only way to know for sure if it is safe to eliminate NetBIOS is to test all your applications with NetBIOS disabled on a test network. Randomly eliminating NetBIOS can be hazardous to your heath!

The DNS Namespace

As you learned earlier, the DNS namespace is hierarchical rather than flat. Because of its hierarchical nature, you can have multiple computers with the same name on the same network and not have problems with misdirected messages. This is in contrast to the NetBIOS flat naming scheme, where you cannot have two computers on the same network with the same name.

The DNS namespace has at its top the *root domain.* The root domain is often represented either as a dot (".") or an empty space (" "). While the latter usage is technically correct, you won't get any questions wrong on the test if you use a dot instead.

Just under the root domain are the *top-level* domain names. Examples of the top-level domain names include .com, .net, .org, and .edu. Organizations that seek to have an Internet presence will obtain a domain name that is a member of one of the top-level domain names.

Each top-level domain is intended for a specific type of organization (although for the most part, it is a voluntary action to seek a top-level domain that represents your company best). For example, a commercial, profit-seeking entity would fit with the .com domain, an educational institution with the .edu domain, and a United States Federal Government institution with the .gov domain. Table 2-1 includes a list of top-level domain names and their intended memberships.

TABLE 2-1 Top-Level Domain Names

Top-Level Domain Name	Description	Examples
.com	The .com domain is meant for commercial, profit-making organizations. If your company is a for-profit entity, it would seek membership in the .com domain.	microsoft.com syngress.com osborne.com
.edu	The .edu domain is reserved for educational institutions. In the past, all educational institutions could gain membership to the .edu domain, but now only colleges and universities are allowed in the .edu domain.	mit.edu dcccd.edu berkeley.edu cornell.edu
.gov	United States Federal Government agencies are assigned membership to .gov domains.	whitehouse.gov irs.gov faa.gov
.int	International organizations are assigned to the .int domain.	nato.int
.mil	Various Branches of the United States Military establishment are assigned to the .mil domain.	ddn.mil navy.mil
.net	The .net domain was originally designed to include members that were part of the networking infrastructure on the Internet. However, competition for popular .com names has led to a wide variety of organizations belonging to the .net domain.	nsf.net dallas.net shinder.net tacteam.net
.org	Only nonprofit organizations belong to the .org domain.	ama.org ana.org

For an organization to have a place in the domain namespace that is separate and distinct from all other organizations, they must obtain a *second-level* domain name. It is the second-level domain name that distinguishes your organization from all others on the Internet. Examples of second-level domains are microsoft.com, osborne.com, and syngress.com.

A graphical view of the DNS hierarchy appears in Figure 2-3.

Note that at each level of the domain name hierarchy, all names must be different. For example, there cannot be two .com domains, there cannot be two .org domains, and there cannot be two microsoft.com domains. However, names can be repeated as long as they are not located at the same level in the hierarchy.

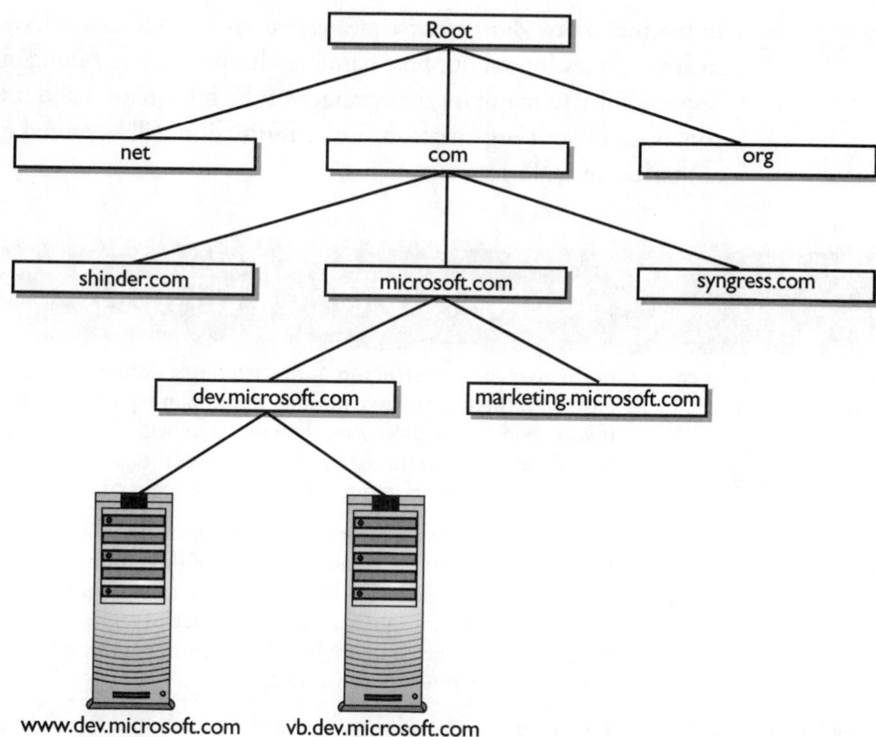

FIGURE 2-3 The Domain Naming System (DNS)

This explains how we can have an untold number of servers on the Internet with the name "www".

The root, top-level, and second-level domains are the only centrally managed aspects of DNS. In order to register your second-level domain, you must contact a domain registrar. In the past, the only organization that had the authority to register second-level domain names in the United States was Network Solutions Incorporated (or NSI, which you can find at www.nsi.com). However, NSI's monopoly over the domain registration business is no longer extant, and now a number of different organizations have the authority to register your second-level domain names.

You, as the DNS administrator for your organization, are responsible for all domains underneath your second-level domain name. You can partition your organization's namespace under the second-level domain however you want. You will also be responsible for maintaining at least two DNS servers that are *authoritative* for your second-level domain if you will be making resources available to Internet users. *Authoritative* means that your DNS servers have the authority to answer questions about host name resolutions for your domain. It will be your responsibility to maintain the accuracy of the information about the resources contained in your organization. This information will be stored on your authoritative DNS servers.

SCENARIO & SOLUTION	
How much does it cost to register a domain name?	In the past the cost structure for registering a domain name was simple. However, there are a large number of domain registrars from which to choose. If you choose to register your domain name with Network Solutions, Inc., you should expect to spend $70.00 for your initial registration, which is good for two years. After that, you must renew your registration.
Am I limited on the number of domain names that I can register?	At present, there is no limit on the number of domains you can register at once. However, there are some moves to control the number of domains that can be registered to a single individual at the same time in order to prevent "domain squatting." Domain squatting is the practice of registering a domain name in the hope that some company will buy it from you for a large sum of cash. This practice is very much frowned upon.
How long do I get to keep my domain name?	If you register with NSI, your initial registration is typically good for two years. They have recently made available a program where you can register your domain name for up to 10 years. Check www.nsi.com for details on registration.
What happens if I let my domain name registration expire?	If you allow your domain name registration to expire, it will become available to anyone who wishes to use it. In addition, your DNS server addresses will be dropped from the zone database and users will no longer be able to contact your public servers using FQDNs. In addition, a competitor or domain squatter may purchase your domain name if you let the registration expire. It is very important that you keep track of your domain name expiration dates for this reason.

Domain and Host Name Specifications

Every computer participating in the DNS namespace is a member of a domain. In order to understand the usefulness of the hierarchical nature of the DNS namespace, you should understand what a fully qualified domain name (FQDN) is and how they are used.

Fully Qualified Domain Names, or FQDNs

An FQDN represents a particular machine's location in the DNS namespace. By using the FQDN, you are able to pinpoint the machine's location in the domain namespace. A FQDN is the combination of a machine's *host* name, which is the computer name of the machine, and its domain membership name. For example, if you are running a company called widgets, you may have obtained the second-level domain name widgets.com. If you run a Web server for widgets.com, you probably will want to name it "www" so that users will be able to locate it easily at www.widgets.com.

exam Watch

Be aware that the www in the FQDN www.widgets.com does not represent a type of service identifier. The www is the host name of the machine. Many students believe that the www or ftp or mail labels at the beginning of an FQDN represent some type of identifier for the Application layer protocol to be used in the communication. These host names are used extensively on the Internet and on intranets to make identifying machines easier.

The FQDN contains two elements: a *label* that includes a domain or host name, and periods ("dots"). Each label is separated by a dot. Each label can contain up to 63 *bytes.* Note that we specify the length of a label by the number of bytes it uses, rather than the number of characters. This is because the Windows 2000 DNS Server supports *UTF-8* characters. Unlike the 8-bit (1 byte) ASCII characters that you usually work with, a single UTF-8 character can consume more than 8 bits per character. The entire FQDN must be less than or equal to 255 bytes.

exam Watch

A recent initiative introduced by domain registrars may allow for individual labels to be as long as 255 characters. However, most WinSock applications will not support labels of this length. Be careful on the exam if you are confronted with an excessively long label in an FQDN.

Think of the FQDN as an address. For example, consider the addresses 123 Main Street, Dallas, TX, and 123 Hitt Street, Dallas, TX. The street and city name would be comparable to the domain name, and the house number would be similar to the host name. Note that we are able to have two homes with the same house address (123) because these homes are located on different streets. In the same fashion, we are able to have machines with the same host names on the Internet, because they "live" in different domains.

Recently, the 63-byte limitation has been increased to over 200 bytes by the domain registrars. However, you must be careful when using domain or host names that exceed the 63-byte limit, because WinSock applications are often hard-coded not to accept more than that number of bytes per label in the FQDN.

Legal and UTF-8 Characters Standard DNS Servers support the label naming conventions as prescribed in RFCs 952 and 1123. These naming conventions state that legal characters for domain names include the following:

- A–Z
- a–z
- 0–9
- The dash (-)

Note that the underscore is *not* supported. This is important for you to remember, because many NetBIOS naming schemes unfortunately included the underscore character for the naming of machines on Microsoft networks prior to Windows 2000. If you choose to upgrade computers to Windows 2000 that have established NetBIOS names, Windows 2000 will replace the underscore character with a dash.

The Windows 2000 DNS Server supports an expanded character set that you can use when creating host and domain names. The *UTF-8* (UTF stands for *Unicode Character Set Transformation Format*) character set is a "superset" of the US-ASCII character set, and is a "translation" of the *UCS-2 (Unicode)* character set. The UTF-8 character set supports the characters used in virtually all known human languages. This makes the Windows 2000 DNS Server a truly universal DNS solution. RFC 2044 includes the specifications for supporting the UTF-8 character set for DNS servers.

If you do plan to implement the extended UTF-8 character set, you must be careful that you only employ Windows 2000 or other DNS servers that support UTF-8 naming. If a Windows 2000 Server has zones that include resource records with UTF-8 names and it tries a zone transfer with a downlevel DNS server that does not support this character set, the zone transfer will most likely fail. Also, be aware that many WinSock applications do not recognize these characters and will not be able to access hosts or domains that include the UTF-8 character set.

SCENARIO & SOLUTION	
I have heard that a fully qualified domain name must include a "dot" at the end. However, I never have to type this dot in order to access machines via their host name. Why is that?	They are right. A truly fully qualified domain name must include the trailing period. If it does not, then it is considered an unqualified domain name. However, most user applications (sometimes referred to as *user agents)* will automatically place the period for you when you enter the FQDN in the address line.
Do I have to name my Web server "www"? Do I have to name my ftp server "ftp" and my mail server "mail"?	You do not have to use www, ftp, or mail for your servers that deliver those services. Those host names are used conventionally to help denote the service provided on a particular server. However, you can use any host name you like, even when they are providing network services such as ftp, Web, and mail services.
What do you mean by "bytes" in a label? I thought that we used characters to figure out how long a label could be.	Since RFC 2181 allows any binary character string to be used for FQDN labels, it is better think about the size of the label, rather than the number of characters. This is especially the case when you are using the UTF-8 character set, where some characters will require more than 8 bits (1 byte).
How do I know if my WinSock application will support UTF-8 characters and labels longer than 63 bytes?	Compatibility is always an issue when upgrading to a new operating system. In order to know if your WinSock application supports the extended character set, you can contact the developer, or better, test your application yourself to see if they are compatible.

Planning Domain Names for an Organization

Before implementing a DNS naming scheme for your organization, you need to consider the following:

1. Is your organization using DNS now for intranet communication?
2. Does your organization have an Internet presence?
3. Does your organization already have a registered domain name?
4. Does your organization use the same domain name for internal and Internet resources?
5. Does you organization use different domain names for intranet and Internet resources?

If your organization plans to have an Internet presence, and plans to be connected to the Internet, you need to consider whether you want to use the same domain name both internally and externally, or if you want to use different domain names for your internal resources and your Internet resources.

on the Job

When planning your domain names you must take into account what DNS services are already deployed in your organization. Many companies have a significant DNS infrastructure already in place. Typically, these companies are using various forms of UNIX DNS servers, and the DNS administrators are UNIX and not Microsoft trained. In order to fully optimize your domain, you must work closely with the UNIX administrators, which can often be a challenge. Make it part of your upgrade plan to wine and dine your UNIX DNS admins.

Using the Same Domain Name for Both Intranet and Internet Resources

Using the same domain name for both your internal corporate resources and your Internet resources seems attractive at first—all machines are members of the same domain, and users don't have to remember different domain names based on whether a resource is internal or external.

However, there are some problems with this arrangement. In order to protect your DNS zone data from intruders, you must not keep any information about your internal resources on a DNS server that is accessible from the Internet. Therefore, you are going to need to maintain two different DNS zone databases for the single domain (we will discuss zones in a little bit). One of the zones will track your internal resources, and one of the zones will be responsible for resources that are accessible from the Internet. This means extra administrative effort on your part and can seriously cut into your "water-cooler" time.

Implementing the Same Domain Name for Internal and External Resources Another thing you must do when implementing the same domain name for internal and external resources is to mirror the external resources internally. For example, imagine that tacteam.net used the same domain name for its intranet- and Internet-located resources. We have Web servers for our intranet that employees use to access personnel information and other corporate inside information. We also have Web servers that we want to use to make information available to users who want information about us on the Internet.

We want to use the same host name for these servers in order to reduce the number of help desk calls from users who believe every Web server must be called "www". The problem is that when we use the same domain name for both the internal and external resources, the request for www.tacteam.net will resolve to a single computer, which we want to have available to Internet users.

However, we do not want Internet users to be able to access the confidential corporate information, and it would be unwise to place that information on an external Web server. But we still want our internal users to have access to the information that is located on the external Web server.

The solution is to mirror the Internet resources internally, and create a separate DNS zone database that is used for internal users. When a user issues a query for www.tacteam.net from within the intranet, it will be resolved from the internal DNS server that contains the internal zone database file. When an Internet user tries to access www.tacteam.net, it will sends its DNS query to the Internet DNS server, which will reply with the IP address of the external DNS server. Figure 2-4 shows how this arrangement works.

Using the same domain name for your internal and external resources is the option you are usually presented with when you are working with a company that already has an established Internet presence and has been using DNS for internal resources for some time. It's also a decision that is often made by someone other than you; therefore, you are presented with the situation and it's your job to implement it.

Using Different Domain Names for Intranet and Internet Resources

If your company is connected, or planning to connect, to the Internet you can choose to use different domain names for the internal and external resources maintained by the company. This makes life a lot easier because you don't have to worry about keeping different zone databases for the same domain name as you would have to do when you are using the same domain name for internal and external resources.

When you use different domain names, you pick an easy-to-remember, intuitive name for your external domain. If your company's name were Widgets Inc., then you would want a name like widgets.com. For your internal resources you should pick a related name, such as widgetscorp.com. Now, when users want to connect to internal resources they use the widgetscorp.com domain servers, and when they want to connect to external resources they use the widgets.com domain servers. Figure 2-5 demonstrates this easier-to-manage arrangement.

FIGURE 2-4 Mirroring external resources internally

Internet located resources are mirrored on the internal web server. Separate DNS zone database files are maintained for Internet and intranet resources. Internal clients will use the internal DNS server, and Internet clients will use the External DNS Server.

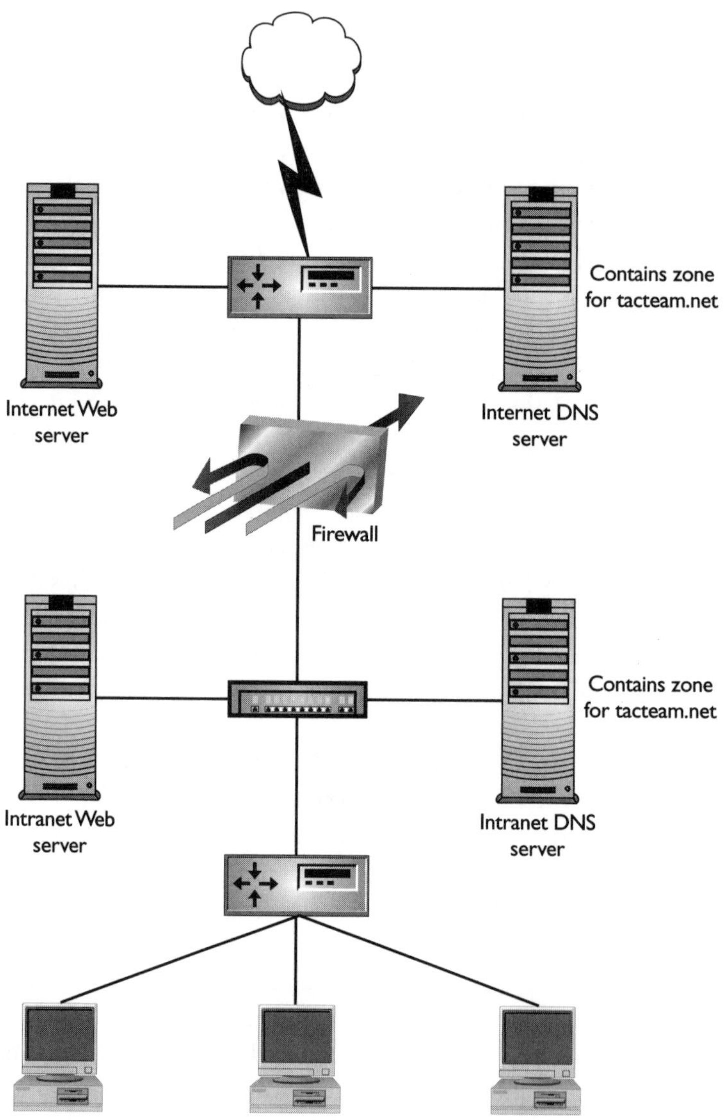

FIGURE 2-5 Maintaining intranet and Internet resources using different domain names

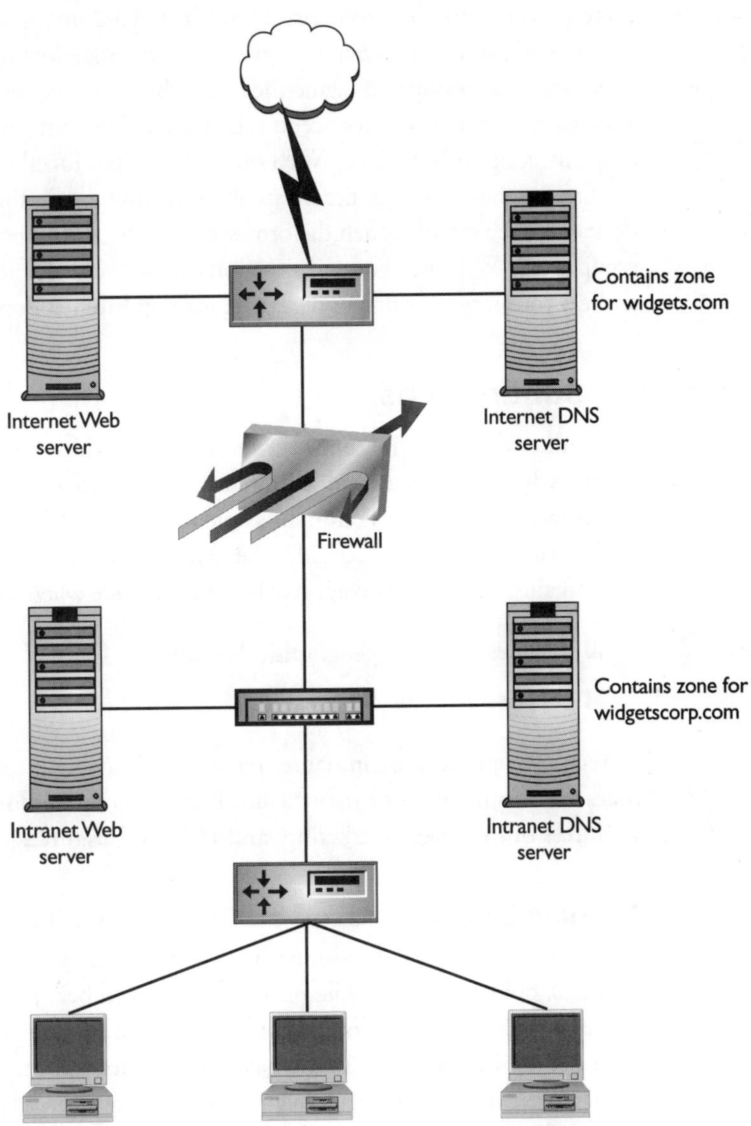
Using different domain names simplifies DNS zone management. While separate zone files are maintained for internal and external resources, they are for different domains and therefore easier to identify.
Contains zone for widgets.com
Internet Web server
Internet DNS server
Firewall
Contains zone for widgetscorp.com
Intranet Web server
Intranet DNS server

Since your internal domain is not accessible from the Internet, there will be no delegation record of your internal domain name on any Internet servers. This means there is no requirement to register your internal domain name.

However, you might want to register your internal domain name in order to avoid confusion. For example, imagine the boss, who isn't very computer literate, goes to a big meeting where a major account is at stake. He wants to impress the other people at the meeting with the fancy Web site you have put together for you internal domain. He fires up the browser in the meeting room and types in the URL for *your internal* domain's Web server. When the browser connects, lo and behold, it's your major competitor's Web site! This sad situation can be avoided if you spend a few dollars and get your internal domain registered with an Internet domain registrar.

Naming Your Subdomains

Remember that only the root, top-level, and second-level domains are managed centrally for Internet accessible domains. The DNS administrator of the organization manages any domains below the second-level domains.

Therefore, you have to consider the naming scheme you want to use for your subdomains. There are two approaches you can take when naming your subdomains:

- Names based on geographical location
- Names based on business unit

Examples of subdomain names based on business unit include sales.stuff.com, marketing.stuff.com, or hr.stuff.com. Each of these subdomains would contain the resources of the Sales, Marketing, and Human Resources divisions, respectively.

Naming Domains Based on Business Units

There are some problems with naming your domains based on business units. Since business, political, and sociological influences can bear heavily on the existence and names of business units, you might find yourself in a pinch when these units change their names. For example, in the past, the business unit that was responsible for managing employees was called "personnel." However, as people have become more commoditized, the name changed to "Human Resources" (I suppose this helps to differentiate them from the physical plant). If this trend continues, it's likely that today's "Human Resources" will turn into tomorrow's "Organic Assets." When

FROM THE CLASSROOM

Understanding the Domain Concept

The domain concept is often difficult for students to understand. This is even more so when students have just learned about the Windows NT 4.0 domain model and try to reconcile Windows NT 4.0 domains or Windows 2000 domains with DNS domains.

Windows NT 4.0 and Windows 2000 domains represent a unified security model. The Windows domain concept centralizes the location of security accounts for a group of users and computers that are members of the Windows domain. You might think of a Windows domain as being like a country. Each country has it own laws and rules, and members of each country participate in a similar security plan in order to protect its borders.

In contrast to the Windows NT 4.0 and Windows 2000 domain model, the DNS domain model is used to merely place resources in a hierarchical structure, which makes it easier to *find* computers located anywhere in the world. The process of *finding* these computers involves, at a minimum, the resolution of their host name and IP address. Note that this has *nothing* to do with any type of security model. The DNS is designed primarily as a Directory Service, and not a security service.

Yet, the Windows 2000 domain names are *based on* DNS domain names. This allows for easier integration of Windows 2000 security domain naming with the DNS. However, you are *not required* to use the same names for your Windows 2000 security domain names and your Windows 2000 DNS domain names. Creating such a schism would be foolish, and you would never do that!

The DNS Server Service is unquestionably one of the most important network services in use in Windows 2000 networks. It has supplanted the NetBIOS services used for computer naming and service location. DNS allows Windows 2000 systems to be easily integrated with your Internet presence. If you are to become a Windows 2000 *expert* you *must* be a DNS expert.

—Thomas W. Shinder, M.D., MCSE, MCP+I, MCT

that change comes around, you would have to change the entire domain name and reassign all the resources belonging to that domain, which is neither a pleasant nor easy task.

Naming Domains Based on Geography

A better alternative is to use geographical considerations when naming your subdomains. This is because geography is less likely to change than business units. If you want to make your life as easy as possible, you should keep your geographical designations as general as possible.

For example, use the subdomain names west.stuff.com, east.stuff.com, north.stuff.com, south.stuff.com, europe.stuff.com, and the like. This is in contrast to using losangeles.stuff.com, boston.stuff.com, fargo.stuff.com, and dallas.stuff.com. A location might change from Dallas to Houston, but you would not need to change the domain name, since the organization's employees would consider both Dallas and Houston "south."

Since Windows 2000 now uses DNS domain names rather than NetBIOS names for its Domain Security model, you might still have need for more granular control over resources based on business units. Since this is likely to be the case, you can create organizational units (OUs) within the appropriate domain that you can use to fine-tune permissions and other parameters using a Group Policy applied to that OU.

Root Name Servers

Something you'll need to understand for the Microsoft Exams is what a *root* name server is and why we care. We've already covered the idea of the Internet root name servers, which represent the top of the Internet DNS hierarchy. Your organization will also have a root name server, which is the DNS server that has authority for your second-level domain.

The concept of the root name server for your organization is important, because a root name server for your Windows 2000 domain must be in place before you can install Active Directory. If you don't have a root name server in place when you install the Active Directory, you can install one during the Active Directory installation process. The root name server is authoritative for your second-level domains, and may contain *delegations* for your subdomains. A delegation is a way of informing DNS clients of what DNS server or servers are authoritative for your subdomains. We will talk more about delegating authority for your subdomains later in the chapter.

exam Watch

Root name servers are those that are authoritative for the top of the domain tree, and provide a starting place for referrals to all subdomains of the root.

SCENARIO & SOLUTION	
I am having problems with my DNS clients not being able to resolve Internet names when using my DNS server. What might be the problem here?	When you install the Windows 2000 DNS Server, you may see an entry for ".". Delete that entry and your lookups will use the Internet root servers rather than treating your second-level domain as the root of the DNS namespace.
What if I decide to keep the same domain name for both my internal and external client and don't keep separate DNS databases? Will bad things happen?	You never know when bad things are going to happen. However, if you choose to use the same DNS zone database for your internal and external resources, you must place the zone information in a location that is available to Internet users. When that information is available on the open Internet, malicious individuals can access the information about your internal namespace. With this information, they can "focus" their hacking attempts on servers that seem "most interesting." Placing information about your internal namespace is considered a very bad security practice. If you value your job, don't do this.
I am installing a Windows 2000 DNS Server for our organization, but our organization already uses a UNIX server for DNS services. Do I need to create a second domain for my Windows 2000 domain?	The Windows 2000 computers require a DNS server that supports SRV records. The UNIX DNS server may support these records. If it does not, you may want to consider creating a subdomain, such as win2k.subdomain.com, for your Windows computers that require SRV records for service location and domain registration.

Zones of Authority

The domain namespace is a conceptual entity; you can't reach out and grab something in the domain namespace. The DNS is just a structure you use to categorize and track the machines by host name on a network. In order to make the DNS something that we can work with, you must have a way of storing the information in the DNS. The actual information about domains and what they contain is stored in a file called a *zone database* file. These are physical files that are stored on the DNS server in a folder on the DNS server's hard disk. The location of these zone files on disk is:

```
%systemroot%\system32\dns
```

In this section we will focus on *standard* zones. This is to differentiate them from *Active Directory integrated* zones. We will cover Active Directory integrated zones later in the chapter.

There are two types of zones we need to create:

- Forward lookup zones
- Reverse lookup zones

We'll focus on forward lookup zones first, and then discuss the utility and requirements of reverse lookup zones.

Forward Lookup Zones

Forward lookup zones are used to provide a mechanism to resolve host names to IP addresses for DNS clients. A forward lookup zone will contain what are known as *resource records.* These resource records contain the actual information about the resources available in the zone.

The Difference Between Zones and Domains It is important to realize that zones are not the same as domains. A zone can contain records for multiple domains, as long as those domains are *contiguous.*

For example, let's look at the microsoft.com domain. Microsoft will likely have subdomains to track its resources at various locations. Suppose that Microsoft has a West coast domain and an East coast domain that go by the names of west.microsoft.com and east.microsoft.com. Microsoft also owns the msn.com domain, and msn.com might have a subdomain called mail.microsoft.com.

Figure 2-6 depicts both domains in the domain namespace.

Notice in the figure that the microsoft.com domains are contiguous with each other, in that they all "touch" microsoft.com. The msn.com and the mail.msn.com domains are contiguous because they "touch" each other as well. However, the microsoft.com and the msn.com domains do *not* touch each other. Therefore, the msn.com domains and the microsoft.com domains cannot be members of the same zone because they are not contiguous.

Zones Allow for Delegation of Responsibility for Maintaining Zone Resources Zones also provide a method to delegate responsibility for maintaining the zone database. For example, suppose we have a company called TACteam, Inc. The

FIGURE 2-6

Contiguous and noncontiguous domains

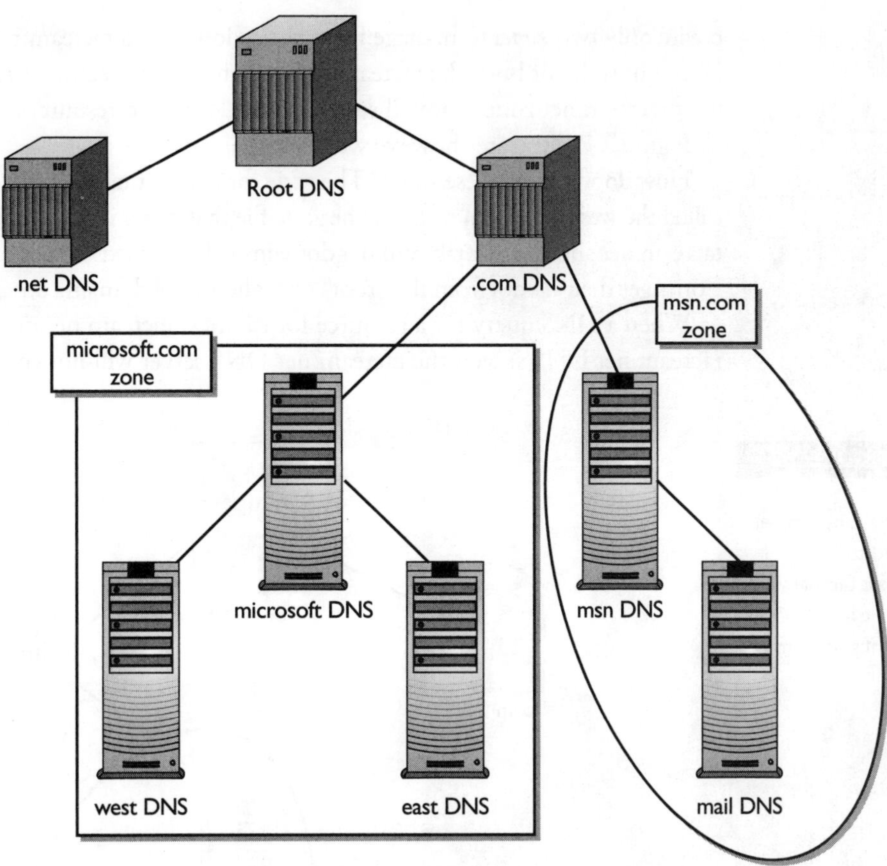

company uses the domain name tacteam.net. TACteam has offices in San Francisco, Dallas, and Boston. The main office is in Dallas, where there are several experienced administrators who can manage the DNS database for the Dallas resources. The San Francisco office also has several experienced administrators onsite who can reliably manage the zone database for their local resources.

The Boston location has mainly sales, marketing, and development staff, and while they are very good at what they do, they are not experienced DNS administrators. Therefore, we would be very wary of assigning responsibility to anyone in Boston for maintaining the DNS zone database for the Boston location.

The Dallas site's resources will be contained in the tacteam.net domain. The San Francisco resources will be maintained in the west.tacteam.net domain, and the Boston resources will be stored in the east.tacteam.net domain. However, we will create only two *zones* to manage these three domains: a tacteam.net zone that will be responsible for both the tacteam.net and the east.tacteam.net resources, and the west.tacteam.net zone that will store the San Francisco resources.

Figure 2-7 illustrates how we would set this up.

How do we name these zones? The zone for the west.tacteam.net domain will be called the west.tacteam.net zone. The zone file that stores information for both the tacteam.net and the east.tacteam.net domains will be called the tacteam.net zone. Zones get their names from the "root" or highest-level domain contained in that zone.

When a DNS query for a resource for the west.tacteam.net domain arrives at the tacteam.net DNS server, the tacteam.net DNS server will not contain a zone file

FIGURE 2-7

The tacteam.net and the west.tacteam.net zone configurations

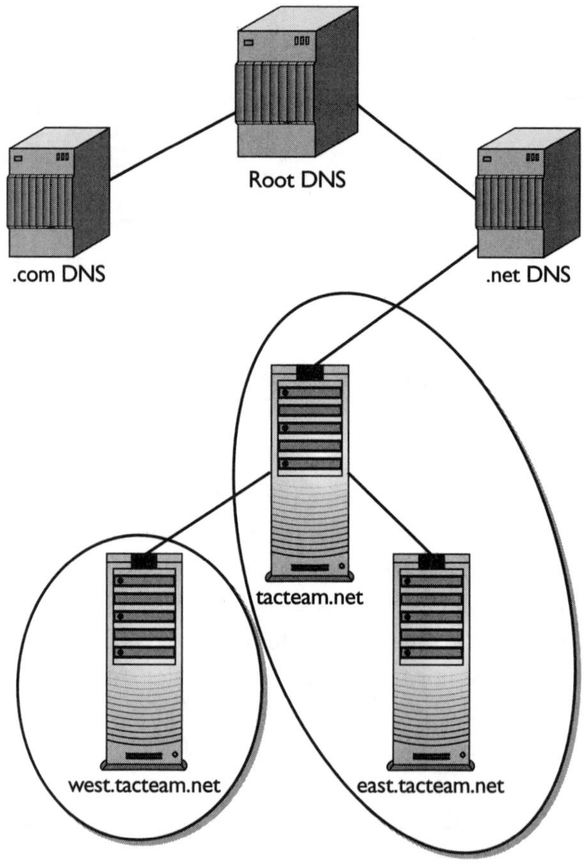

that can answer DNS queries. However, the tacteam.net DNS server will contain a *delegation* that will point to the west.tacteam.net DNS server so the query can be directed to the correct server for resolution.

exam Watch

Be sure you know the difference between zones and domains. The terms tend to be used interchangeably in various texts and in conversations. Know that a zone can contain multiple contiguous domains, and that a single DNS server can host multiple zones.

Reverse Lookup Zones

While forward lookup zones allow DNS clients to resolve a host name to an IP address, a reverse lookup zone allows the DNS client to do the opposite: resolve an IP address to a host name.

For example, you know the IP address of the destination computer, such as 192.168.1.3, but you want to know the host name assigned to that computer. In order to accomplish the task, the DNS client would use the reverse lookup zone for the Network ID in the request.

Reverse lookups are not something that can be easily accomplished using forward lookup zones. Think of forward lookup zones as something similar to a phone book. A phone book is indexed using people's last names. If you want to find a phone number quickly, you just go to the letter of the alphabet for his or her last name, and then go down the alphabetical list until you find the name. The phone number is right next to the person's name. What if we already knew the phone number, and wanted to find out whose name goes with that phone number? Since the phone book is indexed using names, our only alternative would be to look at *every* phone number in the book. If we start at the beginning, we can hope to be lucky and find that it's one in the front of the book.

This clearly isn't a very efficient method to search the IP address "namespace." At one time, "inverse lookups" were used to trawl the IP address space, but these were very limited because they searched forward lookup zones in a manner similar to what we talked about, searching the "phone book" from the beginning. As we have seen, this is very time consuming and inefficient.

The in-addr.arpa Domain To solve the problem, a new domain was created, called the *in-addr.arpa* domain. The in-addr.arpa domain indexes host names based on Network IDs and makes reverse lookups much more efficient and speedy.

You can create reverse lookup zones easily using the Windows 2000 DNS Management Console. Just right-click on your computer name in the console, and select New Zone. That will start up the New Zone wizard that walks you through the process of creating new zones, either forward or reverse lookup. The wizard will ask what type of zone you want to create, and you will select Reverse Lookup Zone rather than Forward Lookup Zone. The wizard will ask for the Network ID and automatically create a zone database file based on your answers.

Note the construction of the reverse lookup zone database file, which you can find in the DNS folder, which is a subfolder of the system32 folder in the system root directory. The name of the file is the network ID in reverse with the .dns file extension appended to it. For example, if you created a reverse lookup zone for 192.168.1.0, the name of the reverse lookup zone would be 1.168.192.in-addr.arpa.dns. This is because queries are examined and executed from right to left, just as they are with forward lookup zones.

Reverse lookup zones are especially helpful if your organization is using inventory or security software that depends on reverse lookups to identify the host names of the IP addresses they discover.

exam watch

Although Microsoft says that you do not have to create reverse lookup zones, you should always do so in order to prevent "Server not Found" errors. You will see this when performing an nslookup query. The first thing nslookup does is a reverse lookup for the host name of the DNS server. If you don't have a reverse lookup zone and a Pointer (PTR) record for the DNS server, you will get timeout errors. A good rule of thumb is to create your reverse lookup zones first, and then your forward lookup zones. In this way, the reverse lookup zones will be available when you create Host (A) records and want the wizard to create the PTR records automatically.

EXERCISE 2-1

Installing the Windows 2000 DNS Server

In this exercise you will install the Windows 2000 DNS Server. You can actually install the Windows 2000 DNS during operating system installation, or after the operating system has been installed.

If you intend to install the Windows 2000 Active Directory, you will be required to install the DNS Server at that time if there are no other Windows 2000 domain controllers online for that domain. In this exercise we will install the Windows 2000 DNS Service on a member server running Windows 2000 Advanced Server.

Warning: Do not install a Windows 2000 DNS Server on a live, production network unless you first contact your network administrator and confirm that this will not create problems with your existing network infrastructure.

1. Log on as Administrator to the Windows 2000 Advanced Server.
2. Open the Control Panel and open the Add/Remove Programs applet. You should see something similar to what appears in the following illustration.

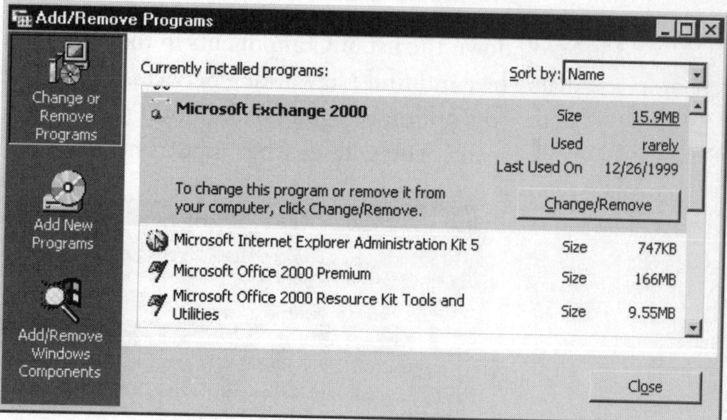

3. Click the Add/Remove Windows Components icon on the left side of the Add/Remove Programs dialog box. You will see what appears next.

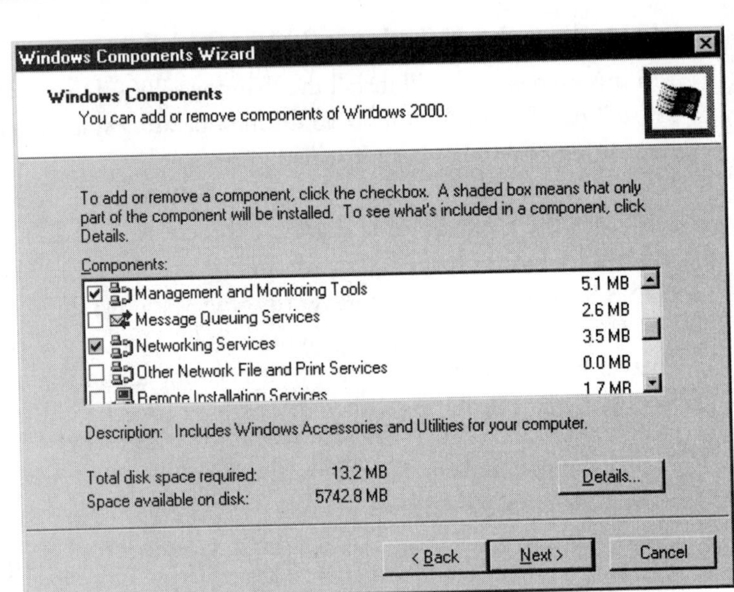

4. Scroll down the list of Components in the Windows Components Wizard dialog box and find Networking Services. Click once on Networking Services so that the option is highlighted, but do not click on the check box. Next, click Details. You will see what appears next.

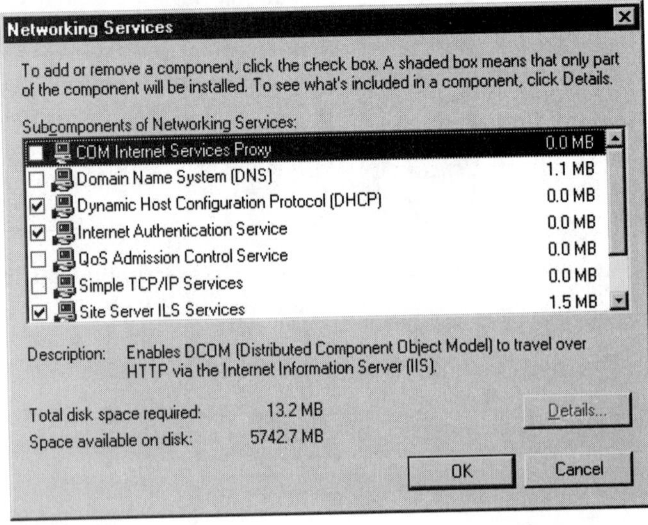

5. In the Networking Services dialog box, place a check mark in the Domain Name System (DNS) check box. Then click OK.
6. You are returned to the Windows Components Wizard dialog box. Click Next.
7. You may encounter the Insert Disk dialog box, which asks you to insert the Windows 2000 Advanced Server CD-ROM into your CD-ROM drive. You can either insert the CD-ROM into the drive, or click OK and point the wizard to a network share point. Click OK after pointing the wizard in the right direction.
8. When the wizard completes, you will see the Completing the Windows Components Wizard dialog box. Click Finish to complete the installation.

Now that the Windows 2000 DNS Server is installed, we can begin the task of creating zones. In the next exercise, you will create a forward lookup zone.

EXERCISE 2-2

Creating a Forward Lookup Zone

After the DNS Server is installed, several changes are made to your system. These include

- Adding the DNS Management Console to the Administrative Tools menu
- Adding the %systemroot%\system32\dns directory to your boot partition
- Adding numerous counters to your System Monitor

Right after you install the DNS Server, there are no zones yet installed on that server. In this exercise, you will create a primary zone for tacteam.net.

1. Log on as Administrator.
2. From the Start menu, open the Administrative Tools menu, and then click on DNS. After clicking on DNS, the DNS Console will open, and should look like the following illustration. Click any "+" signs you see in the left pane in order to expand all nodes.

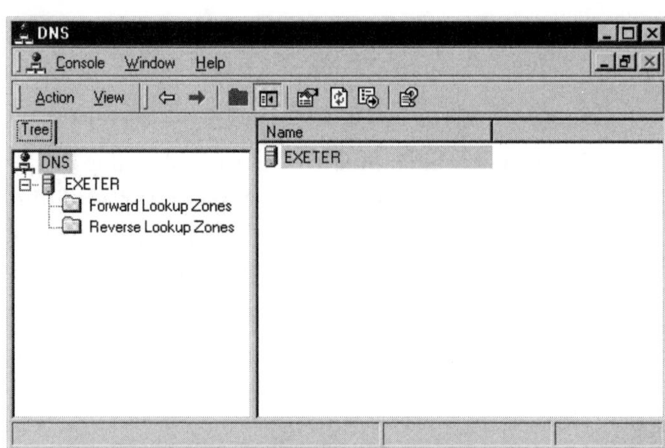

3. Right-click on Forward Lookup Zones and select New Zone. This will start the New Zone Wizard and you first see the Welcome dialog box. Click Next to move from the Welcome dialog box. You will see the Zone Type dialog box as shown next.

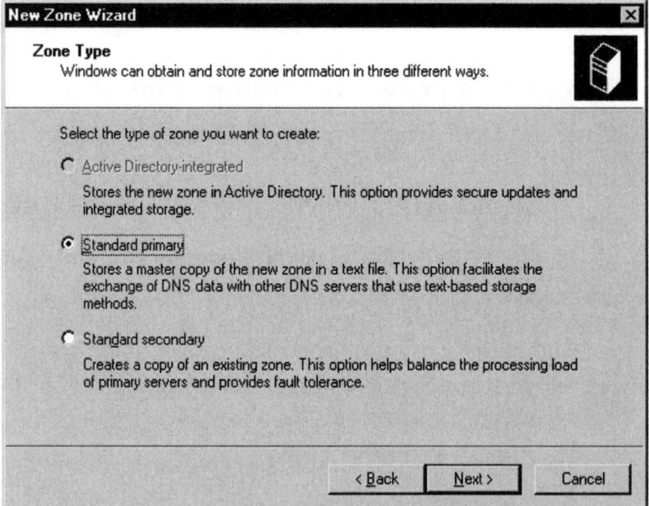

4. Note that in the Zone Type dialog box the Active Directory-integrated Option is grayed out. This option is only available on domain controllers,

and we are creating this zone on a member server. Later in the chapter we will see how to create an Active Directory integrated zone on a domain controller. Select Standard Primary and click Next.

5. You should now be at the Zone Name dialog box. Type **tacteam.net** in the text box provided. You should see what appears in the following illustration. Notice that you do not need to type the complete FQDN, as the trailing period is assumed in this case. Then click Next.

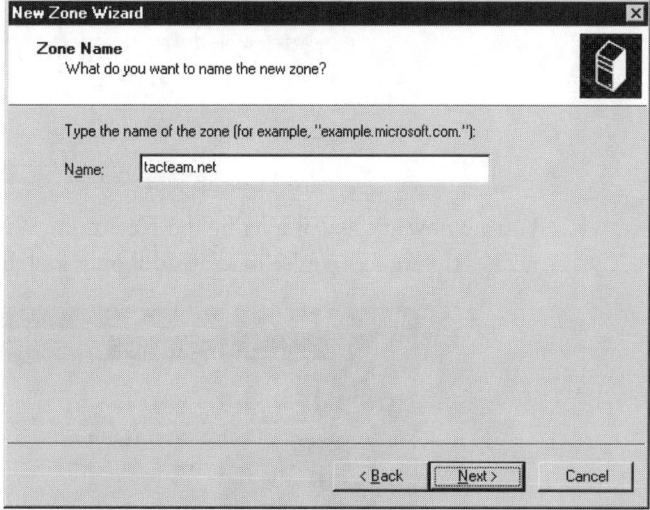

6. In the Zone File dialog box, select "Create a new file with this file name." The wizard lists in the text box the name of the zone with the .dns extension appended to it. If you wanted to create a new zone on your Windows 2000 DNS Server using a zone file from another Windows 2000 DNS Server, you could place that file in the %systemroot%\system32\dns folder and then type the name of the file in the "Use this existing file" text box. Note that you must first copy the file to the proper location before you can type the name in the text box. You should now see what appears in the following illustration. Click Next.

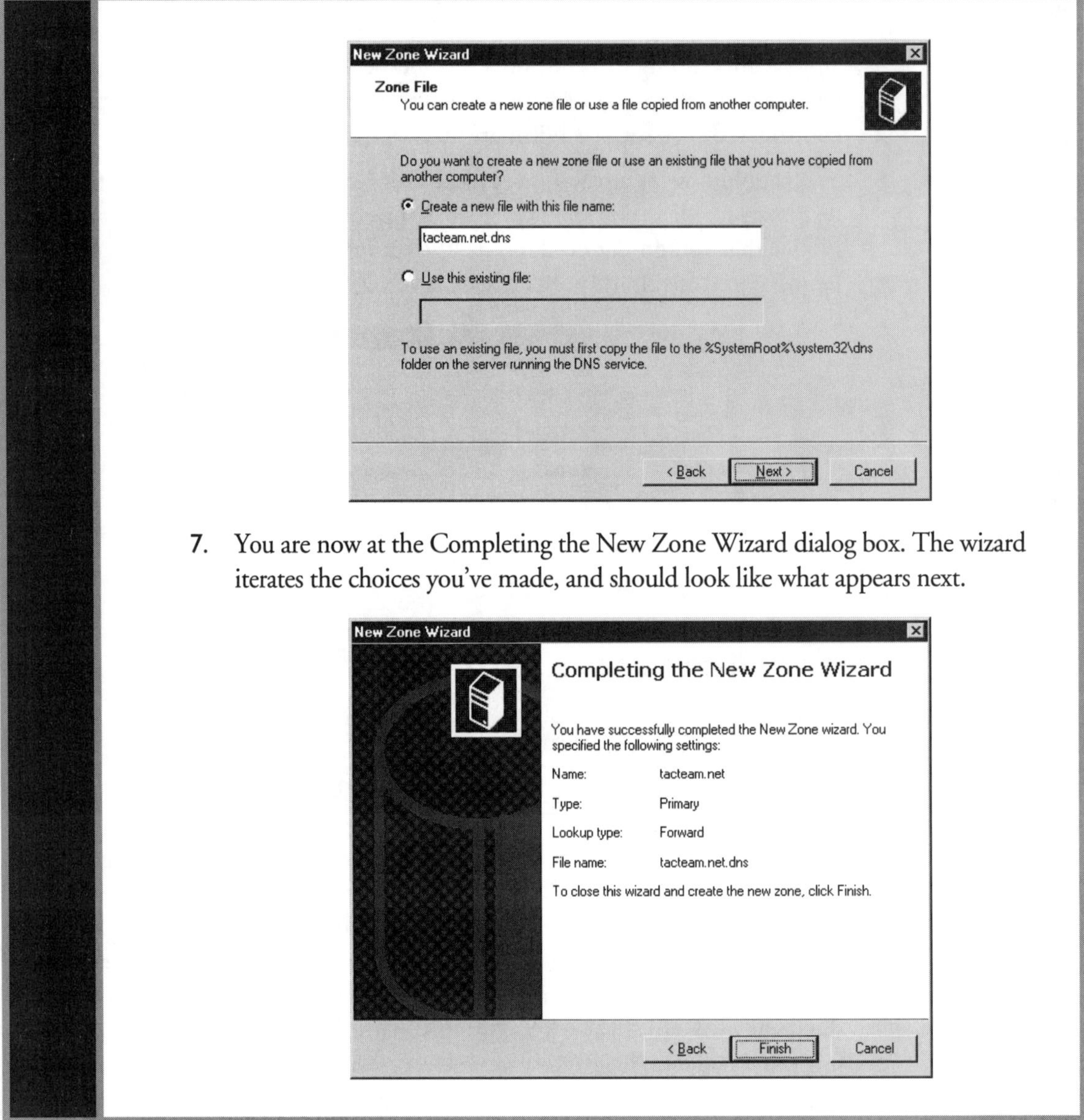

7. You are now at the Completing the New Zone Wizard dialog box. The wizard iterates the choices you've made, and should look like what appears next.

8. Click Finish to create the new zone.
9. Return to the DNS console and expand all nodes. You should see what appears in the following illustration.

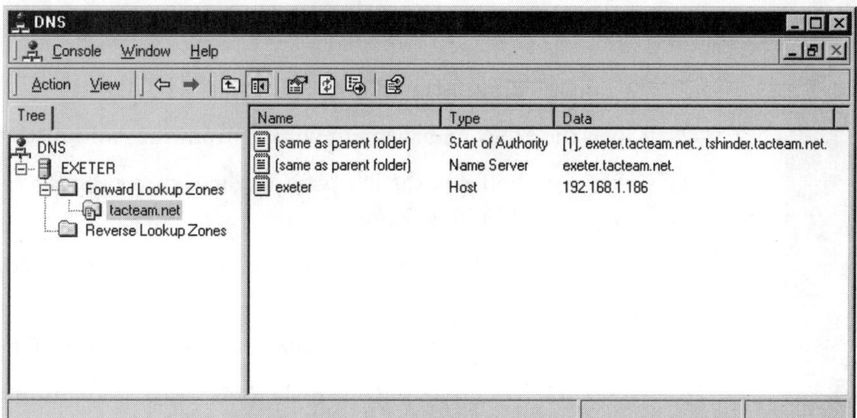

10. Close the DNS management console.

Note that after the zone is created, three resource records are created automatically:

- A Start of Authority resource record for the tacteam.net zone
- A Name Server (NS) record indicating the name of the server authoritative for the zone
- A Host (A) address record for the server that is authoritative for the zone

Now that you have created a forward lookup zone, you can move to the next step. In the next exercise, you will create a reverse lookup zone so that you can perform reverse queries against the DNS server.

Warning! Do not create new zones on a DNS server on your live, production network without first informing your network administrator and receiving confirmation that this will not create disruptions to your current network infrastructure.

EXERCISE 2-3

Creating a Reverse Lookup Zone

In this exercise you will create a reverse lookup zone for the Network ID 192.168.1.0. This will allow you to perform reverse lookups for all hosts that have registered Pointer (PTR) records in the reverse lookup zone. Later we will create a PTR record for the authoritative server for the zone in order to avoid error messages.

1. Log on as Administrator.
2. Open the DNS management console from the Administrative Tools menu.
3. Expand all nodes in the left pane. Right-click on the Reverse Lookup Zones node and select New Zone.
4. This starts the New Zone wizard and you are at the Welcome dialog box. Click Next.
5. In the Zone Type dialog box, select Standard Primary. Click Next.
6. In the Reverse Lookup Zone dialog box, select the option button for Network ID:, and then type **192.168.1** in the text box just below that. You should see what appears in the following illustration. Note the "Reverse lookup zone name:" option and the name that appears grayed out in the background. This will be the name of the zone based on what you typed in the Network ID text box. If you wish to choose another name for the reverse lookup zone, you can select this other option and type in the name of the reverse lookup zone file name you wish to use. Click Next.

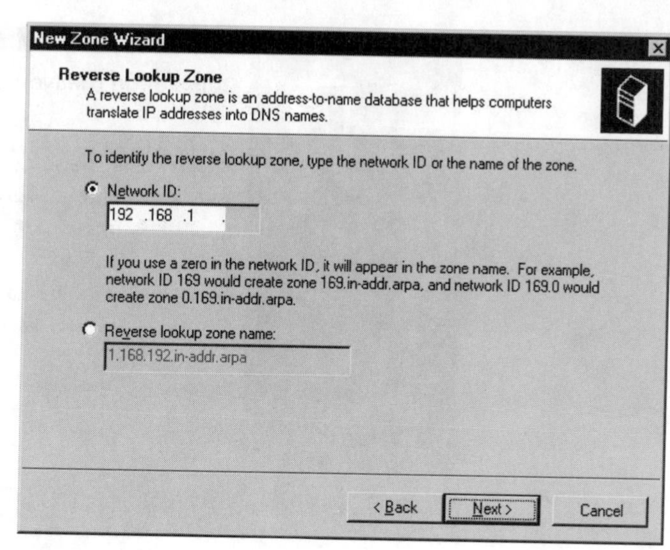

7. In the Zone File dialog box, select the "Create a new file with this file name" option button and accept the default zone name. Observe that the zone name is the Network ID in reverse with the in-addr.arpa domain name and .dns file extension appended to it. Click Next.
8. In the Completing the New Zone Wizard dialog box, read over the settings that the wizard will use to create the new zone. If they are correct, click Finish. If you need to make a correction, you can click Back and make corrections. You should see what appears next.

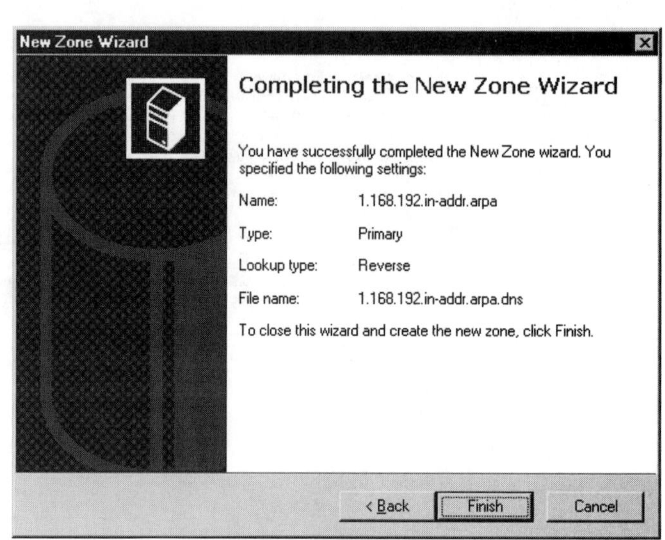

9. Expand all nodes in the left pane. Click on the 192.168.1.x Subnet node in the left pane. Notice that two resource records have been automatically created.
   ∧ A Start of Authority resource record for the zone
   ≠ A Name Server (NS) resource record for the zone
10. Close the DNS management console.

Warning! Do not create new zones on a DNS server on your live, production network without first informing your network administrator and receiving confirmation that this will not create disruptions to your current network infrastructure.

In the next section you will learn more about resource records. Resource records are used to populate the zones that you have just created. At the end of the resource records section you will add some resource records to these zones.

Resource Records

We have established at this point that the DNS server is actually a database server. Like all databases, it contains a file where the data is stored, which in this case is the zone database file. The database itself must be filled with data in the form of a record. If you are familiar with database design, then you know that a record is typically represented as a single row in a table. In order for us to add new rows or records to our DNS zone database file, we add *resource records.*

The resource record contains data about the resources contained in the domain. The resource record that you'll use most is the A, or Host Address, record. This record contains the host name to IP address mappings that most DNS clients will ask for when seeking to resolve a host name to an IP address.

The zone database can also contain information other than just simple host name to IP address mappings. Table 2-2 provides a list of some of the more commonly used resource records that are used to populate the DNS zone database files.

When we add a specific host to a domain, we add an A record. If we have a mail server, we would add that server's name and IP address with an MX record. A single computer can have multiple records of different types. For example, your Web server's host name on the Internet would most likely be named "www". However, internally you may want to refer to it by another name, such as "bigserver". You would enter an A record for "bigserver" and then create a CNAME record for "www". Both records would map to the same IP address.

In order to populate your reverse lookup zones, you use the Pointer (PTR) records. A Pointer record contains the IP address to host name mappings required to answer reverse lookup requests.

on the Job

Even though the Windows 2000 DNS Server supports Dynamic DNS updates, in a large established organization you are likely to need to add a good number of static records to the DNS database. The Windows 2000 DNS Server allows you to easily keep track of in spreadsheet or database format the resource record information stored in your zone databases. Just right-click the zone of interest and select the "Export list" command to save the information in a delimited text file that can be imported to Excel or Access databases.

TABLE 2-2 Important Resource Record Types

Resource Record Type	Name	Description
SOA	Start of Authority	The SOA identifies which DNS server is authoritative for the data within a domain. The first record in any zone file is the SOA.
NS	Name Server	An NS record lists the DNS servers that can return authoritative answers for the domain. This includes the Primary DNS server for the zone, and any other DNS servers to which you delegate authority for the zone. The NS record is also used to direct DNS client requests to other DNS servers when the server is not authoritative for a zone. For example, when you issue a query for the microsoft.com domain, the .com domain DNS server is not authoritative for the microsoft.com domain. However, an NS record is contained on the .com DNS server that can return a referral answer to the requesting client, which will direct it to the microsoft.com DNS server.
A	Address (or Host)	The Address record contains the host name to IP address mapping for the particular host. The majority of the records in the zone will be A address records.
SRV	Service	The SRV record provides information about available services on a particular host. This is similar to the "service identifier" (the hidden 16th character) in NetBIOS environments. If a particular host is looking for a server to authenticate against, it will check for a SRV record to find an authenticating host. SRV records are particularly important in Windows 2000 domains. Since the DNS server is now the primary domain locator for Windows 2000 clients, the appropriate SRV records must be contained on the DNS server to inform Windows 2000 clients of the location of a Windows 2000 domain controller that can authenticate a log on request.

TABLE 2-2 Important Resource Record Types *(continued)*

Resource Record Type	Name	Description
CNAME	Canonical Name	This is an alias for a computer with an existing A Address record. For example, if you have a computer called "bigserver" that is going to be your Web server, you could create a CNAME for it, such as "www". It is important to note that you must have an A record for the host that you intend to create the alias for, since the CNAME record requests that you include the host name of the computer for which you wish to create the alias.
MX	Mail Exchanger	Identifies the preferred mail servers on the network. If you have several mail servers, an order of precedence will be run. Note that the MX record has similar requirements to the CNAME record. You must have an existing A record for the machine that you wish to create a MX record for.
HINFO	Host Information	HINFO records provide information about the DNS server itself. Information about the CPU and operating system on the host can be included in the HINFO record. This information is used by application protocols such as FTP that can use special procedures when communicating between computers of the same CPU and OS type (RFC 1035).
PTR	Pointer	The Pointer record is created to allow for reverse lookups. Reverse lookups are valuable when doing security analysis and checking authenticity of source domains for e-mail.

EXERCISE 2-4

Adding Host Records to a Forward Lookup Zone

In this exercise you will add a Host (A) Address record to the forward lookup zone.

1. Open the DNS console from the Start menu.
2. Right-click on the tacteam.net zone in the left pane, and select New Host.
3. You should see what appeared in the previous illustration. In the Name text box, type **Daedalus**. In the IP address text box, type **192.168.1.3**. Place a check mark in the "Create associated pointer (PTR) record" check box. You should see what appears in the following illustration. Click Add Host. After clicking Add Host, you will see a dialog box that says "The host record daedalus.tacteam.net was successfully created." Note that in the Name text box you do not need to add the entire FQDN, just the host name. The domain name listed in the Location box will be appended to the host name you have typed in. Click OK to close the confirmation dialog box, and then click Done to close the New Host dialog box.

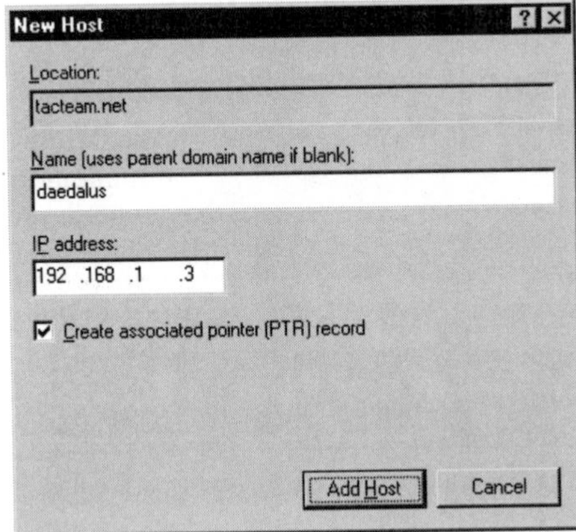

4. You are returned to the DNS console, which should look similar to the following illustration. The Host record for daedalus should appear in the right pane. Click on the 192.168.1.x Subnet node in the left pane.

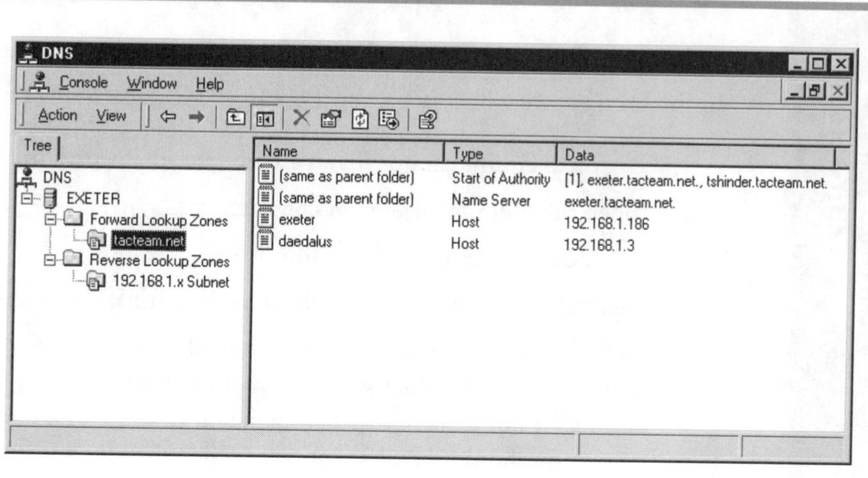

5. You see what appears in the next illustration. Notice that a Pointer record was added automatically for daedalus. If you do not see the added record, right-click anywhere in the right pane and click Refresh. This will update the display and you'll see the new record appear. Sometimes even after a refresh, you will not see the Pointer record appear. This is usually the case when you try to update the Pointer record; be sure to always Refresh to be sure that the record is indeed updated.

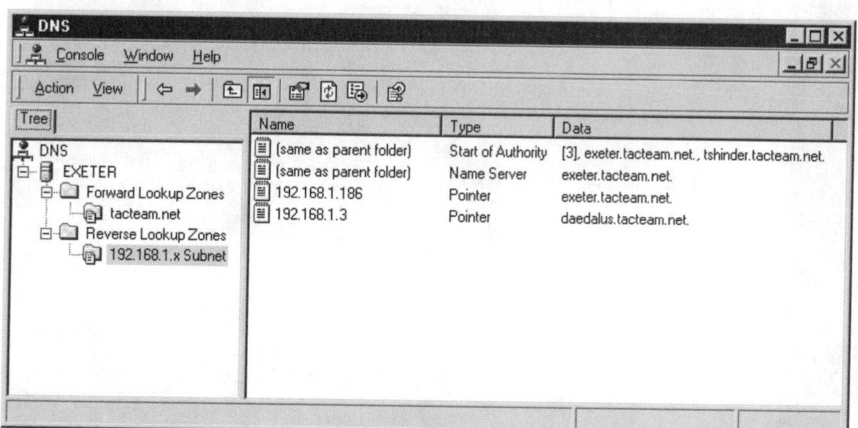

6. Close the DNS management console.

In the next exercise you will learn how to add a Pointer (PTR) record to a reverse lookup zone.

EXERCISE 2-5

Adding a Pointer Record to a Reverse Lookup Zone

In this exercise, we will create a new Pointer (PTR) record in a reverse lookup zone.

1. Log on as Administrator if you are not already logged on as such.
2. Open the DNS management console.
3. Expand all nodes in the left pane.
4. Right-click on 192.168.1.x Subnet in the left pane and select New Pointer.
5. In the "Host IP number" text box, type the Host ID **36**. In the "Host name" text box, type **blobalocity.tacteam.net** (in this instance, you can choose to include or not include the trailing period to the FQDN, it will work either way). You should see what appears in the following illustration. Click OK. The record should appear in the right pane. If it does not appear, right-click anywhere in the right pane and select Refresh.

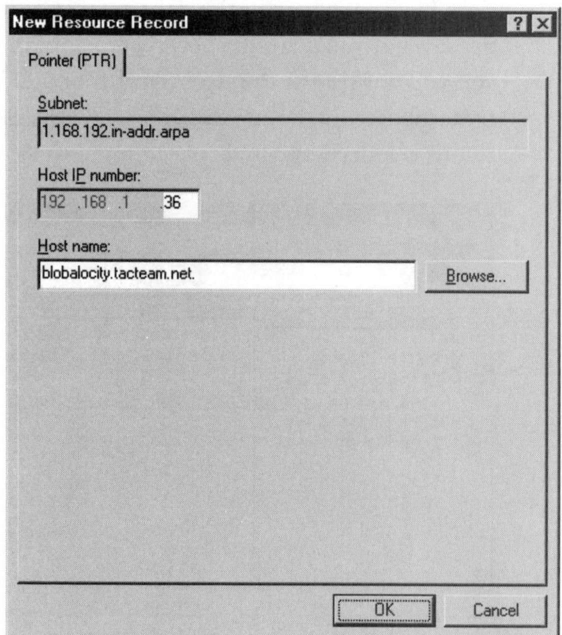

6. Close the DNS management console.

Zone Delegation

Zone delegation provides a way for you to distribute responsibility for zone database management, and provides a measure of load balancing for DNS servers. When you create a delegation for a zone, you are "passing the buck" to another DNS server to answer DNS queries for a particular zone. Zones can be delegated to Secondary DNS servers or Primaries.

In the earlier example, we talked about tacteam.net and how we distributed responsibility for its domains into two zones: the west.tacteam.net zone and the tacteam.net zone. Recall that the west.tacteam.net zone included the resource records for machines located in San Francisco, and the tacteam.net zone contained resource records for machines located in both Dallas and Boston.

You might be wondering at this point, "what DNS server actually answers the queries for these zones?" What we would like to do is have a machine located in San Francisco answer queries for the west.tacteam.net zone, and have machines in Dallas answer queries for the tacteam.net zone. In this way, the machines in Dallas don't have to answer all the queries for the entire tacteam.net domain and its subdomains.

Creating Delegations

The way we accomplish the goal is to create a delegation on a DNS server that is authoritative for the tacteam.net zone. You can create a delegation by making an NS record for the DNS server that is authoritative for the tacteam.net zone. In the present example, this delegation would point DNS clients to a DNS server in San Francisco that is authoritative for the west.tacteam.net zone.

You can create delegations for any domain for which a particular server is authoritative. For example, imagine for a moment that you are the DNS administrator for the .com domain. You do not want to be responsible for maintaining the zone database files for all the subdomains of the .com domain because that would be a monumental task. It would also put quite a bit of stress on your DNS servers. In order to distribute the responsibility for maintaining all the subdomains of the .com domain, you create *delegations* for each of those subdomains.

You would create a delegation, which includes an NS Record, for microsoft.com, syngress.com, osborne.com, and all the other .coms out there. When a DNS query is received by the .com DNS servers for one of these domains, the delegation record (NS resource record) will point the DNS client to the correct IP address of the DNS server authoritative for the zone.

In the example of tacteam.net, the .net DNS server will include a delegation record for the tacteam.net server, and the tacteam.net server will contain a delegation for the west.tacteam.net DNS server in San Francisco. The DNS server in San Francisco, which contains the resource records for the west.tacteam.net zone, will then be able to answer the DNS query authoritatively.

Glue Records

In Windows NT 4.0 when you created an NS record, the only information you had to include was the FQDN of the machine to be included in the referral. This lead to problems because in order to resolve the name of the machine noted in the delegation record, you had to have a Host (A) Address record to allow for the forward lookup.

This Host (A) Address record is referred to as a *glue record.* It's called a glue record because it associates the host name in the NS record with an IP address of the machine noted in the NS record. It glues together the name server's host name and IP address in this way.

Whenever you split your domains into subdomains, you must include on all parent domains delegation information, which will include NS records for authoritative servers and their corresponding glue records. This could be thought of as a form of a *lame delegation.* Technically, a lame delegation is when the NS record points to a server that does not contain a zone database file relevant to the zone being referred to.

The Windows 2000 DNS Server includes a *Delegation Wizard.* The Delegation Wizard will walk you through the process of creating delegations for your domains and subdomains. This takes a lot of the guesswork out of the process of creating NS records and delegations. In fact, if you try to manually add an NS record via the "Add New Record" command in the DNS console, you will find that you are not provided that option. In order to add an NS record, you will *have* to use the Delegation Wizard. You still may need to add your glue records manually.

on the Job

If you have problems with the GUI interface, you can always edit the zone database file directly with a text editor. Be sure to stop the DNS Server Service before making these changes. Be aware that manually editing the zone database file can cause errors if you do not follow the data-formatting conventions correctly. This may cause the zone to not load. It is best to stick with either the GUI or manually editing the cache.dns file and not switch between the two.

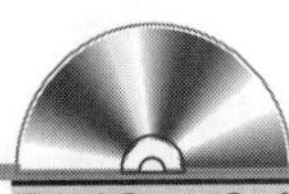

EXERCISE 2-6

Creating a Delegation Using the Delegation Wizard

In this exercise, we will create a delegation for the west.tacteam.net zone at one of our servers that is authoritative for the tacteam.net zone in Dallas. It will point to a DNS server in San Francisco.

1. Log on as Administrator if you have not already done so.
2. Open the DNS management console and expand all nodes in the left pane.
3. Right-click on the tacteam.net zone and select New Delegation.
4. This starts the New Delegation Wizard Welcome dialog box. Click Next.
5. In the Delegated Domain Name dialog box, type **west**. You should see what appears in the following illustration. Note that the fully qualified domain name is filled in automatically when you type the name of the subdomain in the text box above it. Click Next.

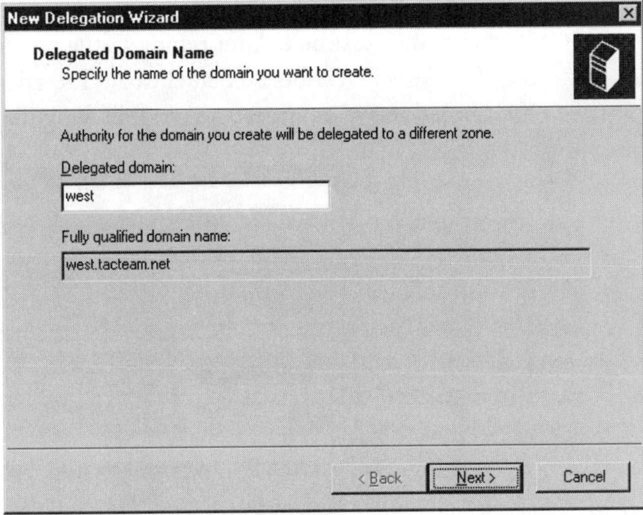

6. In the Name Servers dialog box you will need to add the name and the IP address of the DNS server that will answer authoritatively for the domain. Click Add as shown next.

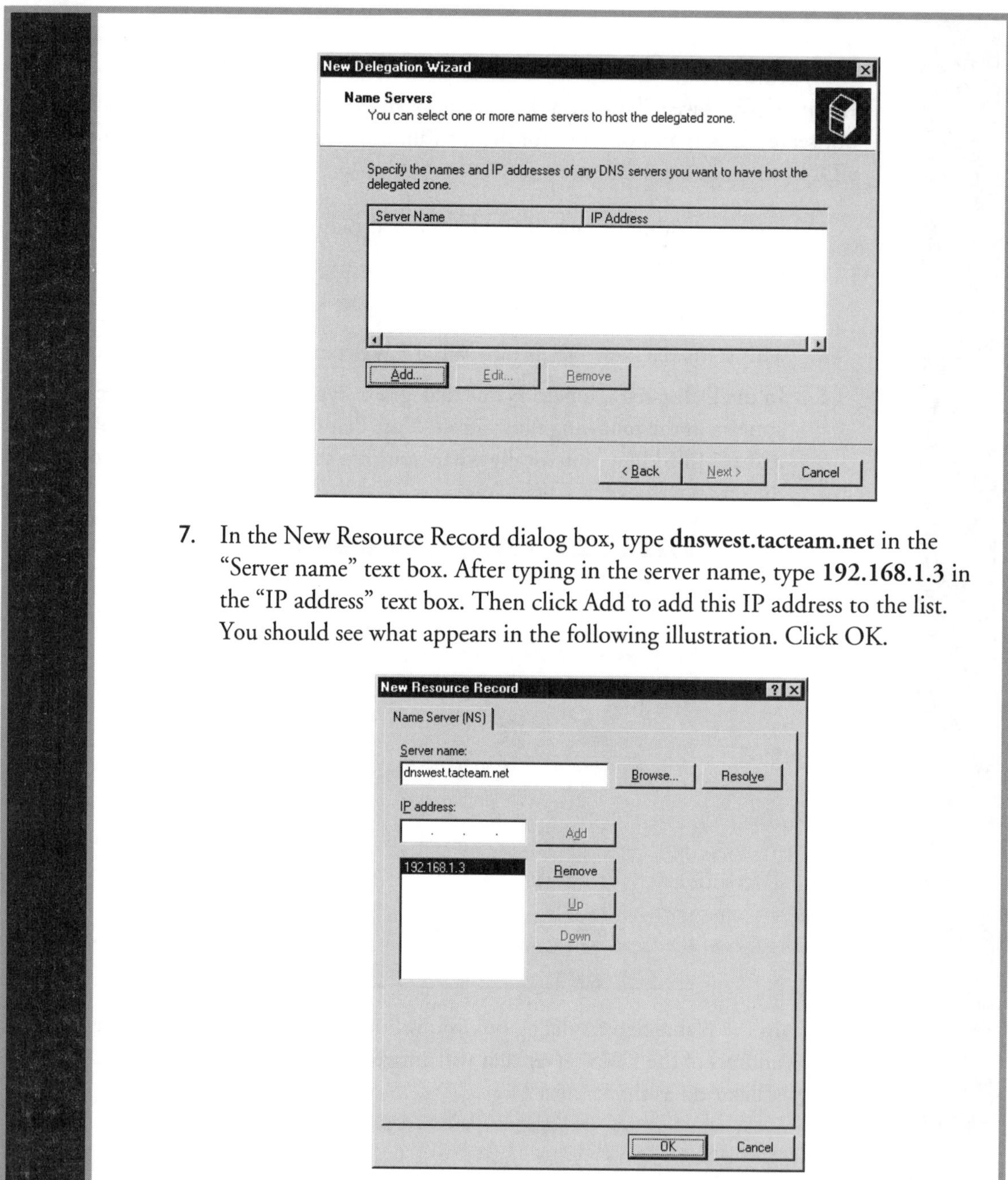

7. In the New Resource Record dialog box, type **dnswest.tacteam.net** in the "Server name" text box. After typing in the server name, type **192.168.1.3** in the "IP address" text box. Then click Add to add this IP address to the list. You should see what appears in the following illustration. Click OK.

8. You are returned to the Name Servers dialog box and dnswest.tacteam.net appears in the list of name servers that will host the delegated domain. Click Next.
9. Confirm the information presented to you by the wizard. Your information should look like that in the following illustration. Click Finish after confirming the information.

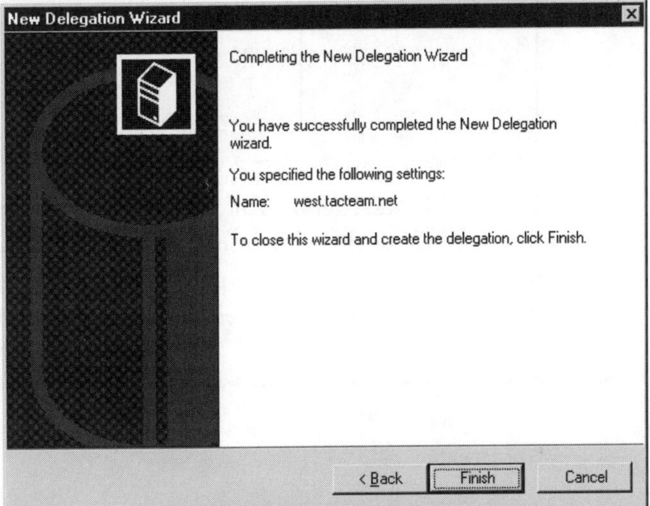

10. When you return to the DNS console, be sure that all nodes in the left pane are expanded. Under the tacteam.net zone, you will see the west zone. Note the icon is gray compared to the yellow folder icon for the tacteam.net zone. This indicates that the west.tacteam.net zone is a delegated zone. You should see what appears next.

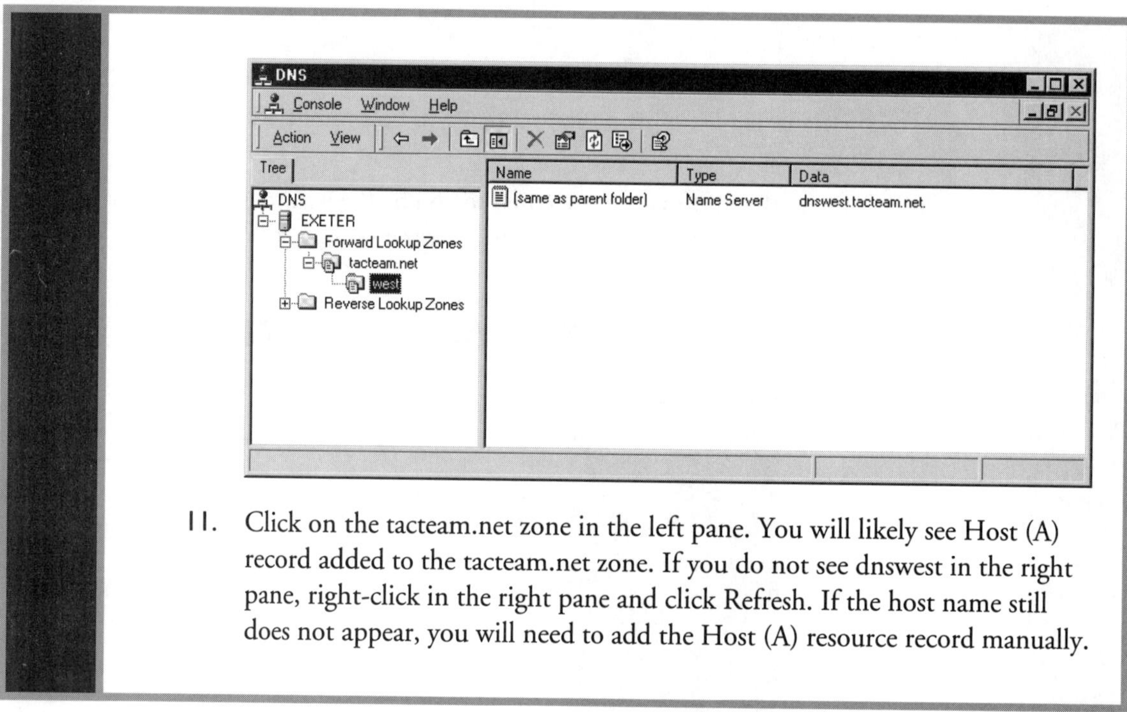

11. Click on the tacteam.net zone in the left pane. You will likely see Host (A) record added to the tacteam.net zone. If you do not see dnswest in the right pane, right-click in the right pane and click Refresh. If the host name still does not appear, you will need to add the Host (A) resource record manually.

Warning! Do not create new resource records on a DNS server on your live, production network without first informing your network administrator and receiving confirmation that this will not create disruptions to your current network infrastructure.

The DNS management console still has some bugs to work out, so if things do not work quite right the first time, try again. We'll see another example of problems with the console later in the chapter.

Zone Transfer

In order to provide a measure of fault tolerance for the DNS zone database, the DNS was designed to have at least *two* DNS servers responsible for answering queries for each zone. As you will learn more about later, Standard zones support

Primary and Secondary DNS zone types. A *Standard Primary zone* is the only read/write copy of the zone database file. A *Standard Secondary zone* is a read-only copy of the zone database file. The Primary and Secondary zones are contained on Primary and Secondary DNS servers for those zones. In order to copy the Primary zone file to the Secondary DNS server, a process of *zone transfer* is used.

Methods of Zone Transfer

The zone transfer process can be considered a "pull" operation. This is because the Secondary DNS server initiates the zone transfer process. The Secondary DNS server will initiate a zone transfer when:

- A Primary DNS server sends a "notify" message to the Secondary DNS server informing it that there has been a change to the zone database.
- The Secondary DNS server boots up.
- The Secondary DNS server's *Refresh Interval* has expired.

These are depicted in Figure 2-8.

The Secondary DNS server initiates the actual zone transfer. When the Secondary sends a "pull" request to the Primary DNS server, the first record the Primary DNS server sends is the *Start of Authority (SOA)* record. The SOA record is always the first record created on a DNS server authoritative for any particular zone.

The SOA record contains information about the *Refresh Interval.* The Secondary waits the amount of time specified by the Refresh Interval before asking for another update to its zone database file. The Refresh Interval determines how often the Primary DNS server for the zone updates the zone database on the Secondary.

When you create a new zone, it has a *serial number* of 1. Each time a change is made to the zone database on the Primary DNS server, the serial number is incremented by 1. Each time the Primary updates the Secondary's zone file, the Secondary's zone serial number is updated to match the serial number of the Primary's zone database as of the time of the zone transfer.

The serial number is included in the SOA Record sent by the Primary DNS server when the Secondary initiates the zone transfer. The Secondary examines the serial number in the SOA record and compares it to the serial number of its own zone file. If the Primary DNS server's serial number is larger, the Secondary sends one of two types of queries that begin the zone transfer process.

FIGURE 2-8

Zone transfer methods

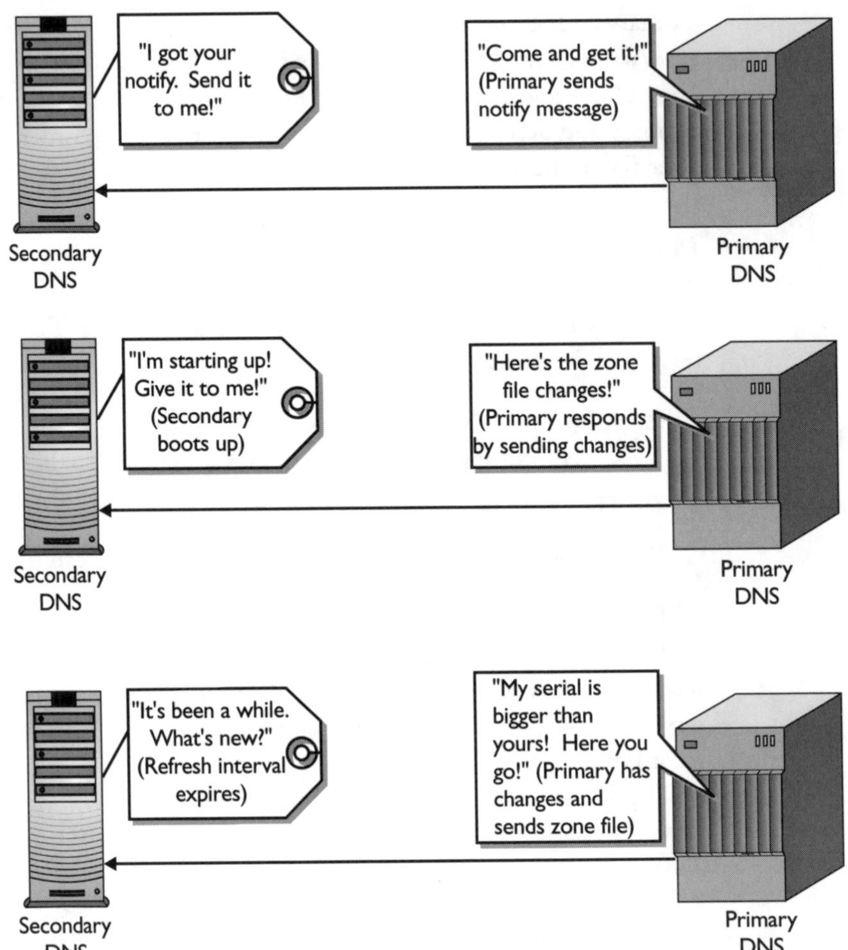

Types of Zone Transfer

Windows 2000 DNS Server supports two types of zone transfer, depending on what type of query request is sent to it from the Secondary DNS server:

- Entire Zone Transfer (AXFR)
- Incremental Zone Transfer (IXFR)

AXFR Queries Secondary DNS servers that only support the AXFR query type will receive a copy of the *entire* zone database file during the zone transfer process. The

Windows NT 4.0 DNS Server is only capable of asking for a copy of the zone database file via an AXFR request, and therefore always receives the entire zone database, regardless of how many changes have been made to the database since the last time it queried the Primary DNS Server for changes in the DNS zone database file.

IXFR Queries Windows 2000 Secondary servers are able to include in their requests information about the serial number of the zone database they currently own. These servers are able to issue IXFR queries, which allow for *incremental* zone transfers. During an incremental zone transfer, only records that have changed since the last zone transfer are sent to the Secondary DNS server. Sending only the records that have been changed saves bandwidth during the zone transfer process.

Windows 2000 DNS Servers Can Respond to Both AXFR and IXFR Requests

A Windows 2000 DNS Server is able to respond to both AXFR and IXFR queries. In addition, a Windows 2000 DNS Server that is acting as a Secondary can send both AXFR and IXFR queries. This allows the Windows 2000 DNS Server to be flexible in networks that have a mix of Windows 2000 and downlevel DNS servers.

There are times when the Primary will send the *entire* zone database in spite of receiving an IXFR request. These circumstances include

- The sum of the changes is larger than the entire zone.
- The age of the Secondary's zone database exceeds the number of changes tracked in the Primary's change log.
- The DNS server doesn't know what to do with an IXFR request.

In the first situation, it would make no sense to send the changes if the number of changes exceeds the number of records in the entire zone database file. To do so would waste bandwidth needlessly. The second situation is comparable to the change log that is kept by Windows NT 4.0 domain controllers that is used to determine which records in the SAM database need to be sent to the backup domain controllers (BDCs). If the Secondary has a zone with a serial number out of range of those being tracked in the Primary's change log, then the entire zone file will be sent to ensure the integrity of zones on the Secondary. The third situation is seen when a Windows 2000 Secondary sends an IXFR to a downlevel Primary, such as a Windows NT 4.0 DNS Server. In this case, the Windows NT 4.0 Primary will send the entire zone database file.

exam Watch

Be sure you know which DNS servers support which types of zone transfers. Remember that a Windows 2000 DNS Server can respond to either AXFR or IXFR queries from downlevel servers such as the Windows NT 4.0 DNS Server.

Masters, Secondaries, and Slaves

Understanding the relationships between servers transferring zone databases and what to call them can get confusing. It's important here to make some critical distinctions.

The server that is transferring the zone file to another server is called the *Master* server. The server receiving the zone files can be called either a *Slave* server or a *Secondary* server. It is preferred to refer to the machine receiving the zone file as a secondary, because the term *Slave DNS server* has another meaning that refers to an inability to perform recursion for DNS clients.

Another thing to know is that a Primary DNS server can also act as a Secondary for another zone. For example, dns.shinder.net is the Primary DNS server for the shinder.net zone. There is a Secondary for the shinder.net zone named dns1.shinder.net. We can make dns1.shinder.net a Secondary for the shinder.net zone. We have another DNS server that is the Primary for the tacteam.net zone named dns.tacteam.net. We want it to be a Secondary for the shinder.net zone. When dns1.shinder.net transfers the zone database for the shinder.net zone to dns.tacteam.net, dns1.shinder.net then becomes the Master for the zone transfer (Figure 2-9).

The Retry Interval

At times the Primary will not be available when the Secondary sends its pull request. To deal with this inevitable situation, the Start of Authority (SOA) record includes information about a *Retry Interval*. The Retry Interval defines the period of time the Secondary should wait until sending another pull request message. The Secondary will continue to retry the zone transfer until it is successful in contacting the Primary for its zone.

on the Job

When setting the Retry Interval, remember to make it shorter than the Refresh Interval. Otherwise, there's no sense in even setting a Retry Interval, since it will retry anyhow during the new Refresh.

FIGURE 2-9 How Secondaries can become Masters

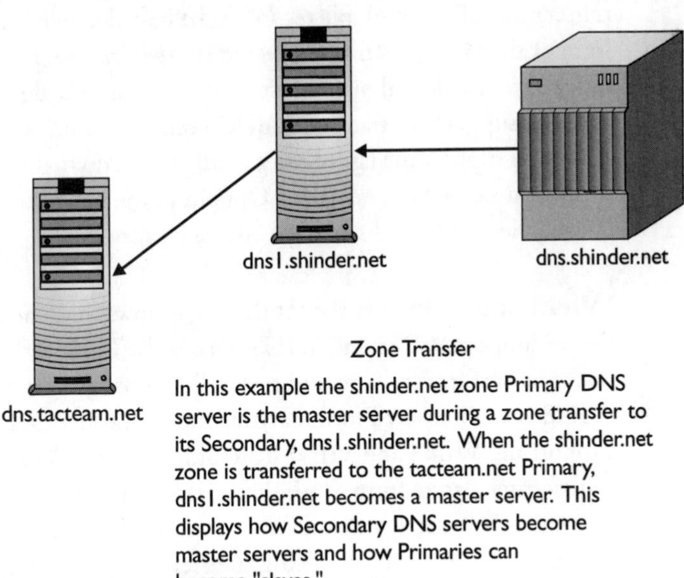

Masters and Secondaries
dns1.shinder.net
dns.shinder.net
dns.tacteam.net
Zone Transfer
In this example the shinder.net zone Primary DNS server is the master server during a zone transfer to its Secondary, dns1.shinder.net. When the shinder.net zone is transferred to the tacteam.net Primary, dns1.shinder.net becomes a master server. This displays how Secondary DNS servers become master servers and how Primaries can become "slaves."

Compatibility of DNS Server Versions

If you are running a mixed DNS environment that includes both Windows 2000 and downlevel DNS servers (BIND and Windows NT 4.0), then there are some issues you will need to address to minimize problems you might encounter.

Incremental Zone Transfers Some downlevel DNS servers do not support incremental zone transfer. They cannot issue an IXFR query to the Master server. Downlevel DNS servers only issue AXFR queries. However, as mentioned earlier, the Windows 2000 DNS Server is able to respond to downlevel clients' AXFR requests. The major issue you will need to deal with here is that of bandwidth consumption. If you have planned your DNS replication topology around the benefits of incremental zone transfers, you may want to make some changes to your DNS server network if you have Secondaries that do not support IXFR.

Fast Transfers The Windows 2000 DNS Server supports a method of zone transfer that allows multiple records to be included in a single message. This compressed form of zone file transfer is referred to as a *fast transfer*. Not all DNS servers support the fast transfer mode, although most of the popular ones do. One popular DNS server that does not support fast transfers is BIND versions before 4.9.4. Subsequent versions of BIND do support the fast transfer mode. If you do maintain BIND versions lower than 4.9.4, you can use the Advanced Options in the DNS server to indicate you have BIND Secondaries, and this disables the fast transfer mode.

WINS and WINS-R Records Windows 2000 and Windows NT 4.0 DNS Server support WINS and WINS-R records. These resource records allow a DNS server to perform forward and reverse lookups by referring to a WINS server. Since WINS is a Microsoft Proprietary technology, other DNS implementations do not support the WINS and WINS-R resource records. This may cause problems when transferring a zone from a Windows 2000 Primary to a third-party Secondary. If you have DNS servers that do not support WINS and WINS-R records, you can prevent these records from being transferred by selecting the check box for "do not replicate this record" in the WINS and WINS-R tabs in the appropriate forward and reverse lookup zones.

exam Watch

The Windows 2000 DNS Server supports WINS lookups. If you enable WINS lookups, the DNS server will query a WINS server with the host name portion of the FQDN. If the WINS server responds positively, the DNS server will reply with the host name and IP address combination. Be aware the FQDN returned via a WINS lookup can be misleading. We will go into detail regarding the hazards of WINS lookups in the Network Design Study Guide.

Third-Party Transfers to Windows 2000 DNS Servers If you have third-party DNS servers that act as Primaries for Secondary Windows 2000 DNS Servers, you may run into a situation where the third-party products support resource record types that are not supported by Windows 2000 DNS Servers. When the Windows 2000 machine receives record types that it does not support, it will drop the record and continue with the zone transfer process.

Table 2-3 sums up the compatibility issues you may run into when running in a mixed DNS server environment.

TABLE 2-3 Comparison of Support Features Among Popular DNS Servers

Feature	Windows 2000	Windows NT 4.0	BIND 8.2	BIND 8.1.2	BIND 4.9.7
SRV records	Yes	Yes (with SP4)	Yes	Yes	Yes
Dynamic Update	Yes	No	Yes	Yes	No
Secure Dynamic Update (GSS-TSIG)	Yes	No	No	No	No
WINS/WINS-R	Yes	Yes	No	No	No
Fast Transfer	Yes	Yes	Yes	Yes	Yes
IXFR	Yes	No	Yes	No	No
UTF-8	Yes	No	No	No	No

Be sure to check out this table when implementing a Windows 2000 DNS Server in a mixed environment. This is especially important if you are introducing Windows 2000 DNS into an established DNS environment where UNIX DNS servers are already deployed. It is extremely important that you work closely with the UNIX DNS administrators during all phases of your Windows 2000 DNS deployment.

CERTIFICATION SUMMARY

The Domain Naming System (DNS) provides for a more robust method of naming network resource than the NetBIOS naming scheme. NetBIOS uses a flat name space, and no two machines on a network can use the same NetBIOS name. The DNS allows for a hierarchical namespace where machines can use the same name as long as they live in different levels of the hierarchy.

The DNS uses fully qualified domain names (FQDNs) to identify hosts on the network. An FQDN is a combination of a host name and that host's domain name. Requests for network resources via an FQDN are passed through the WinSock interface, while requests for NetBIOS resources are passed through the NetBIOS interface.

NetBIOS applications use the NetBIOS name as the endpoint of communication. TCP/IP uses the destination IP address and Port number (socket) as the endpoint of communication. In order to allow NetBIOS applications to work on a TCP/IP network, a method must be available to resolve NetBIOS names to IP addresses. This is the primary function of NetBT or NetBIOS over TCP/IP.

WinSock applications do not require a host name to connect to a network resource. All that is required is an IP address. However, host names are easier to remember than IP addresses; therefore, a method must be in place to resolve host names to IP addresses. DNS servers provide this function.

When planning domain names for your organization, it is better to use geographical naming schemes rather than business unit-based naming schemes. The geographical approach tends to be more stable and makes the DNS administrator's life easier.

A DNS zone represents the physical component of the DNS. A DNS zone file contains information about domains and network resources contained within the domain. Remember that a single zone can contain multiple contiguous domains, and that a single DNS server can support multiple zones.

The two basic zone types are forward lookup zones and reverse lookup zones. A forward lookup zone resolves host names to IP addresses, and a reverse lookup zone resolves IP addresses to host names. Reverse lookup zones are not required, but are recommended. Reverse lookup zones use a special domain referred to as *in-addr.arpa.*

The zone file is a database file. The type of record added to the zone database is referred to as a resource record. These resource records populate the zone database and provide information about the resources contained within each zone and domain within the zone.

The DNS is a distributed database. You can take advantage of the distributed nature of the DNS by delegating responsibility among various servers for answering questions for a zone or group of zones. This is known as zone delegation. Secondary DNS servers are used to answer queries for a zone in order to take some of the load off a Primary DNS server.

Standard zones consist of single Primary and multiple Secondary DNS servers. The Primary DNS server contains the only read/write copy of the zone database file, while Secondaries contain read-only copies of the file. The Secondaries provide for both load balancing and fault tolerance for the zone.

Copies of the zone database file are placed on the Secondaries via zone transfer. When a zone is transferred from a Primary to a Secondary, either an AXFR or IXFR query initiates the process. Downlevel DNS servers such as the Windows NT 4.0 server can only issue AXFR queries. When the AXFR query is used, the entire zone is transferred. Windows 2000 DNS Servers support the IXFR query, which causes only the changed elements of the zone to be transferred.

Windows 2000 DNS Servers are RFC compliant. However, in a mixed DNS environment, not all DNS servers will support the same DNS options. Be sure in any mixed DNS environment that you check zone transfer compatibility among different DNS server implementations.

TWO-MINUTE DRILL

The Domain Naming System: Introductory Concepts and Procedures

- The NetBIOS namespace is flat.
- The DNS namespace is hierarchical.
- NetBIOS applications use NetBT or NetBIOS over TCP/IP in order to work correctly on TCP/IP-based networks.
- NetBIOS applications use the NetBIOS Session layer interface, while WinSock applications use the WinSock interface.
- A fully qualified domain name (FQDN)is a combination of the host name and the host's domain location.
- An unqualified domain name does not contain the entire domain path.
- Windows 2000 DNS Servers support UTF-8 character encoding, which allows you to use virtually any binary string in naming your domains.
- It is best to name your subdomains based on geographical consideration rather than business units, because geography is more stable.
- Information about domains and network resources is stored in zone database files.
- A single DNS server can contain multiple zone database files.
- A single zone can contain multiple domains.
- A forward lookup zone resolves host names to IP addresses.
- A reverse lookup zone resolves IP addresses to host names and uses the special in-addr.arpa domain to store its resource records.
- Resource records are used to populate the zone database file, which is used to located and define network resources contained within the zone.
- Zone delegation is used to distribute the responsibility for answering queries for a particular zone. You can also use zone delegation to distribute the responsibility for maintaining different parts of the domain namespace.

- ❑ Zone transfer is the process of transferring the zone database file from one DNS server to another. Standard zones transfer the zone file from Master servers to Secondary servers.
- ❑ The only read/write copy of the zone database file is stored on a Primary DNS server. Secondary DNS servers contain read-only copies.
- ❑ Zone transfers can be either complete or incremental. Downlevel DNS servers such as Windows NT 4.0 support only complete zones transfers, while the Windows 2000 DNS Server supports both incremental and complete zone transfers.
- ❑ The Windows 2000 DNS Server is RFC compliant, but not all features are supported by all DNS servers. In a mixed DNS environment, always check for features compatibility between various implementations of DNS.

SELF TEST

The following questions will help you measure your understanding of the material presented in this chapter. Read all of the choices carefully, as there may be more than one correct answer. Choose all correct answers for each question.

The Domain Naming System: Introductory Concepts and Procedures

1. You have a mixed operating system environment that includes Windows NT 4.0 Workstations, Windows NT 4.0 Servers, Windows 95 and Windows 98 machines, Sun Servers, and SCO UNIX Workstations. All these machines will need access to Web servers on your intranet and on the Internet. Which service will you need to install in order to allow for name resolution for all these operating systems?

A. WINS

B. DNS

C. DHCP

D. LDAP

2. Your corporation plans to install Internet Information Server 5.0 to provide Web hosting for your intranet. The DNS host name of the computer you will install IIS 5.0 on is *iis-srv-001-daltx.tacteam.net* and it already has a Host (A) address record in the zone database file. What resource records could you use to make it easier for users to access this server that will host both Web and FTP sites?

A. Host (A) Address record

B. MX record

C. PTR record

D. CNAME record

3. You are planning a TCP/IP-based Windows 2000 network. What service should you install to allow host name resolution on your network?

A. NNTP

B. RIPv2

C. DNS

D. RIS

4. After installing a Primary DNS server for a Windows 2000 Standard zone, you decide you should have some fault tolerance built into your corporate DNS solution. What kind of DNS servers can you implement in order to provide both fault tolerance and load balancing of host name resolution for your network?

A. A Secondary DNS server

B. A DNS Forwarder

C. A Zone Infrastructure server

D. A second Primary DNS server for the zone

5. You work in an organization that has more than 7,000 computers. The network has been upgraded to all Windows 2000 Professional or Windows 2000 Server computers. DNS is the only name resolution service on your network, as NetBIOS is no longer required and your WINS servers have been decommissioned. Users are allowed to share desktop resources with each other. What would you do to enable efficient name resolution while making your life as easy as possible?

A. Create a centralized LMHOSTS file and tell users to point to it.

B. Create a HOSTS file and have each user install it on his computer.

C. Allow your DNS server to accept Dynamic updates from all DNS clients in the organization.

D. Configure the DNS servers to perform WINS Lookups.

6. Your network has 5,000 Windows 95 clients and 3,500 Windows 98 clients. What services would you install to resolve fully qualified domain names to IP addresses?

A. DNS

B. L2TP/IPSec

C. QoS

D. OSPF

7. What is the name of the file your root server uses to resolve fully qualified domain names for which it has no authority?

A. cache.dns

B. domain.dns

C. HOSTS.dns

D. domain.in-addr.arpa

8. Which of the following are limitations of the UTF-8 character set when used on your Windows 2000 Server installation?

   A. You are limited to using single-byte characters for your domain names.

   B. Third-party Secondary DNS servers may experience errors when a zone containing UTF-8 characters is transferred to them from a Windows 2000 DNS Server.

   C. Many applications do not support the UTF-8 character set, and therefore cannot resolve domain names containing these characters.

   D. A Windows 2000 Active Directory Domain Name cannot exceed 63 bytes.

9. Your company has a registered domain name that is *company.com.* You use the company.com domain name for your Internet resources. You are upgrading your network to Windows 2000 and you need to use a domain name for your internal resources. You decide to take the easy way out and choose to use different domain names for your internal and Internet resources. Your internal domain name is abccompany.com. A week later, your boss tells you that you're fired! What did you do or not do to deserve such a punishment?

   A. You failed to create a delegation on the company.com DNS server for the abccompany.com DNS server.

   B. You forgot to copy the zone database from the Internet DNS server to the internal DNS server.

   C. You didn't include resource records for the company.com domain in your abccompany.com zone database file.

   D. You failed to register the internal domain name with a domain registrar.

10. You are the DNS administrator for your company. Your Windows 2000 domain name for your intranet is fastbytes.com. You want to create a domain called slowbytes.com and store that information in the same zone file. However, when you attempt to do so in the DNS management console, you find that you cannot. What is the problem?

    A. This is related to a bug in the DNS management console.

    B. You must first create a delegation for the slowbytes.com domain in the fastbytes.com domain before you can create the slowbytes.com domain in the fastbytes.com zone.

    C. You cannot include noncontiguous domains in a single zone file.

    D. A Secondary DNS server must be created for the slowbytes.com domain before creating it in the fastbytes.com zone.

11. You have been called to troubleshoot a problem with a company's DNS server setup. The administrator at the facility created a delegation for one of their subdomains, but when users

try to resolve host names for that subdomain using this DNS server, the queries fail. What is the most likely reason for the failures?

A. There is no HOSTS file on the machine.

B. You must restart the computer before the delegation will work properly.

C. The DNS cache must be flushed before the delegation will work properly.

D. There is no Host (A) record for the machine named in the NS record for the delegation.

12. How does the Secondary DNS server know when to start a zone transfer?

A. If the serial number for the zone on the Primary is larger than the serial number for the zone on the Secondary, then the Secondary DNS server will initiate a zone transfer.

B. A zone transfer begins automatically after the Refresh Interval has expired.

C. The Secondary will start the zone transfer after the Expiration Interval has expired.

D. The Primary DNS server sends an AXFR or IXFR query to the Secondary. If the Secondary DNS server's serial number is smaller than the Primary's, then the Primary will send the zone database to the Secondary.

13. The type of query a Secondary DNS server sends where only the changed records are sent back to the Secondary DNS Server is called:

A. RDP Query

B. CMAK Query

C. RSS Query

D. IXFR

14. A Master DNS server is:

A. The DNS server in charge of all the other DNS servers in an Active Directory domain

B. A DNS server that has seized the PDC emulator role

C. A DNS server containing a zone database file that will be copied to another DNS server

D. A DNS server that cannot perform recursive queries

15. You are working with a new company. This company wants to use Windows 2000 Servers and Windows 2000 Professional workstations. The name of the company is Syberlite, Inc. Syberlite is located in Galveston, Texas, and they have branch offices in Santa Monica, California; Laramie, Wyoming; and Carson City, Nevada. It is your job to design a domain-naming scheme for the company. What factors would you take into account when creating your naming scheme?

A. Will the company have an intranet or Internet presence?

B. Will the company be using fast transfer to zone transfer from Primary to Secondary DNS servers?

C. Will the company use the same or different domain names when creating an internal and external namespace?

D. Are your desired domain names already registered with a domain registrar?

16. After creating your domain-naming scheme for Syberlite, Inc, you need to decide how to delegate your zones. Do you want to manage all the zones yourself? Can you delegate responsibility for some of the subdomains to other administrators and have them manage their own zone? What is involved with creating a new zone for your subdomains? What are some of the factors involved with domain delegation and creating a new delegation?

A. Personnel at a delegated zone must be able to expertly manage the zone database for their domain.

B. You need to create a delegation using the Zone Delegation Wizard on the DNS server in the zone immediately above the delegation zone in the DNS tree.

C. A glue record must be in place to resolve the name contained in the delegation.

D. Delegations can only be created for Active Directory integrated zones.

17. What Session layer interface do NetBIOS programs use on a TCP/IP-based network?

A. WinSock

B. Microsoft SMB Redirector

C. CSNW

D. NetBT

18. Which of the following are correctly matched up?

A. NetBIOS: The domain that represents the top of the domain hierarchy for a given network. This domain may represent the root of an organization's domain naming scheme or that of the Internet DNS.

B. SOA: A record maintained on a DNS server that is authoritative for a given zone. Secondary DNS servers will first query for this record before initiating a zone transfer.

C. Zones: Where the actual information about the resources available for a given domain or set of domains is stored.

D. Root Domain: Formerly a monolithic transport protocol, now implemented as a Session layer interface in a variety of protocols for programs written to this specification

19. You are trying to investigate a problem with a DNS server located at another site. You are using the nslookup program to do this. The name of the zone you are interested in troubleshooting is tacteam.net. When you type **nslookup –ds `tacteam.net`** at the command line, you see that a number of other domain names were appended to the query, and it seems as if the query was treated like an unqualified request. However, ultimately you are able to get an answer. Why is this the case?

A. A Host (A) record was entered into the tacteam.net zone files for a machine named "tacteam.net".

B. The request for tacteam.net was not fully qualified and was treated as an unqualified request.

C. There is no entry for the tacteam.net domain on the destination computer.

D. All of the above.

20. You get a call from a user that he is unable to connect to one of your intranet Web servers. He tells you that when he types in **www.corpwebserver.com**, he receives an error message. While you still have him on the phone, you ask him to type **http://192.168.1.68** in the address bar of his Web browser. After he types in the IP address, he is able to receive the default Web page on the server. What is the most likely reason why he wasn't able to connect to the server using the FQDN?

A. The user lied about the problem in the first place, and had no problem connecting to the Web server using the FQDN.

B. There was no record in the WINS database for this server.

C. The DNS server requires Web requests to use Dynamic DNS updates.

D. The Host (A) address record on the DNS server had the incorrect IP address for www in the corpwebserver.com domain.

LAB QUESTION

In this lab you must perform the following steps. If you perform the steps correctly, everything will work. If you do not, it will not work.

The goal of the exercise is for you to configure a new zone, and then create a host record in that zone. You will add a resource record for a machine named "www" in your zone, and then perform an nslookup to confirm that both forward and reverse lookup work correctly.

1. Log on as Administrator if you have not already done so.
2. Go to your Network Properties dialog box for your network adapter, and change the DNS server to your own machine.
3. Open the DNS console and create a new Standard Primary zone called "practice.net".
4. In the practice.net zone, create a Host (A) record for machine "www".
5. Create a reverse lookup zone so that a reverse lookup can be performed on the IP address of the www.practice.net computer.
6. Open a command prompt and type: **nslookup www.practice.net.** (Include the trailing period when using nslookup) and press Enter.
7. After succeeding with the forward lookup, perform a reverse lookup by typing **prompt:nslookup <IP_address_of_www.practice.net>** at the command and press ENTER. (Note that you do not need to include a trailing period when doing a reverse lookup.)

SELF TEST ANSWERS

The Domain Naming System: Introductory Concepts and Procedures

1. ☑ **B.** DNS provides a platform-independent method to resolve host names to IP addresses. The Windows 2000 DNS Server can be used by virtually any host operating system that requires host name resolution.
   ☒ **A** is incorrect because WINS servers resolve NetBIOS names to IP addresses, not host names. Windows 2000 DNS Server can be configured to query WINS servers for name resolution by sending the host name portion of the FQDN to the WINS server. **C** is incorrect because a DHCP server assigns IP addressing information to DHCP clients, and does not resolve host names. A DHCP server can be configured to dynamic update a DDNS server with both the DHCP client's Host (A) and Pointer (PTR) information. **D** is incorrect because LDAP (Lightweight Directory Access Protocol) is a communication protocol designed for use on TCP/IP networks. It defines how an LDAP directory client can access a directory server, and how the client can perform directory operations and share directory data. Queries to the Active Directory are sent via LDAP.

2. ☑ **D.** A CNAME record allows you to create aliases for machines that already have an existing Host (A) address records CNAME records are commonly used to provide a means of identifying machines by the services they offer, rather than their primary host name. Common examples include using CNAME records to provide host name resolution to www, ftp, mail, and news. CNAME records also make it easier to reassign the IP address of the server without having to change the IP address on multiple resource records.
   ☒ **A** is incorrect because the Host (A) record does not provide for aliasing. However, you could add a Host (A) record for each of the names you would use the CNAME records you might otherwise create. However, if the IP address of the machine were to change, you would have to make the change on each Host (A) record, rather than a single Host (A). **C** is incorrect because the Pointer (PTR) record is used only in reverse lookup zones and provides for IP address to host name resolution. **B** is incorrect because the MX record is used to identify mail exchangers (mail servers) on the network. The MX record does not provide for server aliasing.

3. ☑ **C.** DNS servers can resolve host names to IP addresses and IP addresses to host names.
   ☒ **B** is incorrect. RIPv2 is a routing protocol that can be installed via the Routing and Remote Access Console. **A** is incorrect. NNTP (Network News Transfer Protocol) is used to transmit information to and from newsgroup servers. **D** is also incorrect. RIS (Remote Installation Services) is a service new to Windows 2000 that allows you to install Windows 2000 Professional remotely over the network.

4. ☑ **A.** A Secondary DNS provides for both load balancing and fault tolerance for the zone. A Secondary DNS server contains a read-only copy of the zone database file, while a Primary DNS server contains a read/write copy of the zone file.
   ☒ **B** is incorrect because a DNS Forwarder is a DNS server that receives DNS queries from another DNS server and returns the result back to the DNS server that issued the query. **C** is incorrect because there is no such thing as a Zone Infrastructure server. There is such a thing as an Infrastructure Master, which is one of the five Operations Masters in Windows 2000 domains. The Infrastructure Master is responsible for updating the group-to-user references whenever the members of groups are renamed or changed. At any time, there can be only one domain controller acting as the infrastructure master in each domain. **D** is incorrect because Standard zones can have only a single Primary DNS server. Active Directory integrated zones are multimaster and support multiple Primary DNS zones.

5. ☑ **C.** When NetBIOS is disabled on all machines on the network, the only method of name resolution is host name resolution. Therefore, all names will be resolved using DNS servers. You could create host records for each machine on the network, but this would be a very time consuming task, and you would have a tough time keeping track of machines that receive IP addresses dynamic via DHCP (if DHCP is enabled on the network). In this environment, where users are allowed to share their desktop resources with each other, the users must have a mechanism in place that will allow their WinSock applications to resolve host names to IP addresses. The easiest route here is to enable Dynamic Updates to your DNS zones so all machines automatically update the DNS zone database.
   ☒ **A** is incorrect because asking users to do anything is unwise at best and disastrous at worst. In addition, the LMHOSTS file is used to resolve NetBIOS names to IP addresses. However, an LMHOSTS file can be used during the host name resolution sequence if the other methods have failed. **B** is incorrect because you do not want users doing anything with their computers other than the work they've been assigned. In addition, it suffers the same limitations as the HOSTS file. **D** is incorrect because you have disabled NetBIOS on all the machines on the network, and therefore you have no need for WINS servers. Even if there were WINS servers installed, there would be no registrations, since there are no NetBIOS WINS clients on the network.

6. ☑ **A.** A DNS server can resolve both fully qualified domain names and unqualified domain names from DNS clients from virtually any operating system.
   ☒ **B** is incorrect because L2TP (Layer 2 Tunneling Protocol) is a tunneling protocol. IPSec (IP Security) is a security protocol that allows for host-to-host security and is used on TCP/IP-based networks. L2TP and IPSec are often used together to provide for extremely secure tunneling over public networks such as the Internet. **C** is incorrect. QoS (Quality of

Service) allows you to manipulate bandwidth available for hosts and applications and allows prioritization of bandwidth. B is also incorrect. OSPF (Open Shortest Path First) is a routing protocol that is more efficient and less bandwidth intensive than the other routing protocols supported by Windows 2000, which include RIP versions 1 and 2.

7. ☑ **A.** The cache.dns file is used by DNS servers as the first point of departure when resolving host names for domains for which it has no authority. If you wish to resolve Internet host names, the cache.dns file must contain the names and IP addresses of the Internet Root servers. If you do not wish to connect to the Internet and only need to connect to intranet domains, the cache.dns file should contain the names of DNS servers that are authoritative for the top level of your intranet domain name.

☒ **B, C,** and **D** are incorrect because those files do not exist.

8. ☑ **B, C, D. B** is correct. While the UTF-8 character set allows you to use names and characters in virtually almost all known languages, many third-party DNS servers do not support this extended character set. There may be errors encountered during zone transfer from Windows 2000 DNS Servers that utilize UTF-8 characters in their domain names. **C** is correct. Most WinSock applications built for the Windows platform do not support these characters, and therefore will not be able to resolve host names that contain them. **D** is correct. Although we did not cover this in the main text, you will find buried deep in the errata of the Windows 2000 Server resource kit a notation that Windows 2000 Active Directory domain names must not exceed 63 bytes. The wizard included in the dcpromo.exe program will prevent you from doing so.

☒ **A** is incorrect. UTF-8 characters are not limited to one byte per character, as is US-ASCII.

9. ☑ **D.** The problem was that the company CEO went to a meeting and tried to show the other participants in the meeting your internal corporate Web page. Because your internal corporate Web page is on the intranet, he is not able to access it from any external network, but the CEO isn't very technically inclined. When he tried to connect to the intranet Web site, he typed in the URL for the Web site like he does when he's at work. However, when he did so, it connected to your company's major competitor's Web site! It turned out that your competitor found out that you didn't register your internal domain name, and decided that they would register it themselves. You should have spent the $35 to register the name.

☒ **A** is incorrect. You do not need a delegation to your intranet domain. You want your intranet resources to be totally unavailable to Internet users. **B** is incorrect because you do not need a copy of the external DNS server's zone database file on your intranet. Internal requests for your Internet resources can be resolved using the Internet Root servers as the starting point for iterative queries to resolve your external domain's IP address. **C** is incorrect because you don't need to include resource records for *your external* domain on your internal DNS server.

10. ☑ C. Only contiguous domains can be contained in a single zone. Although a single zone file can contain numerous domains, all the domains must be contiguous.
☒ **B** is incorrect because even if you were to create a record to point to a DNS server authoritative for the slowbytes.com domain in the fastbytes.com zone, you still could not include the slowbytes.com domain in the fastbytes.com zone. **A** is incorrect because this behavior is not bug related, but a function of DNS itself. **D** is incorrect because creating a Secondary DNS server would not allow you to include noncontiguous domains in the same zone. In addition, you must create a Primary zone before you can create a Secondary zone.

11. ☑ D. When an NS record is created for the delegation, only the target machines' host name is included in the delegation record. In order to complete the delegation, a Host (A) address record must be included in order to resolve the name listed in the delegation record. This Host (A) record is sometimes referred to as a "glue" record.
☒ **A** is incorrect because HOSTS files are used to resolve host names to IP addresses and are not required for a delegation to work. However, you *could* use an entry in the HOSTS file, rather than a Host (A) address record, to resolve the name in the delegation, but this would not be an efficient or intelligent solution. **B** is incorrect because you do not need to restart the computer in order for the delegation record to be usable for DNS queries. You may want to restart the DNS server or reload the zone, depending on your experience with your particular machine. **C** is incorrect because you do not need to flush the DNS cache in order for the delegation to work properly.

12. ☑ A. The zone transfers process begins with the Secondary DNS server sending a Start of Authority query to the Primary DNS server. The Primary's SOA record contains the serial number on its zone database file. If the serial number for the zone on the Primary DNS server is larger than the serial on the Secondary, the Secondary DNS server will send either an AXFR or IXFR query, depending on the operating system running on the Secondary.
☒ **B** is incorrect because the Refresh Interval determines how long a Secondary should wait to try again if it was unsuccessful in an attempt to query its Primary for an SOA record. **C** is incorrect because the Expiration Interval is the period of time that the Secondary is totally unable to contact the Primary. If the Secondary is unable to contact the Primary for the period of time noted in the Expiration Interval, the Secondary will no longer answer queries for that zone. **D** is incorrect because the Primary does not send the SOA query to the Secondary. The Secondary always begins the zone transfer process by issuing the SOA query. You can configure a Primary to send a "Notify" message to a Secondary, after which the Secondary sends the SOA query. But the Primary will never send an SOA query to a Secondary.

13. ☑ **D.** The IXFR query allows only the records that have changed since the last zone transfer to be copied to the Secondary DNS server during subsequent zone transfers. In order for an IXFR query to take place, the Secondary DNS server must be able to issue them, and the Primary must be able to respond to them. Some DNS servers, such as the Windows NT 4.0 DNS Server, cannot issue or respond to IXFR queries. When these downlevel DNS servers receive an IXFR query, they drop it. Windows 2000 DNS Server can respond to both IXFR and AXFR queries. The AXFR query causes the entire zone database to be sent when changes have occurred since the last zone transfer.
☒ **A** is incorrect. The RDP (Remote Desktop Protocol) is used by Terminal Servers and Clients to communicate with each other during a terminal session. **B** is incorrect. CMAK stands for Connection Manager Administration Kit and is used to create dial-up interfaces for RAS users. **C** is also incorrect. RSS stands for Remote Storage Services and is not involved with the zone transfer process.

14. ☑ **C.** The definition of a Master DNS server is any DNS server that has a copy of the zone database file that it will send to another DNS server. A Master DNS server can be a Primary server sending the zone file to a Secondary, or it can be a Secondary sending the file to another Secondary.
☒ **B** is incorrect. The PDC emulator role has nothing to do with the DNS. When your Windows 2000 domain is running in mixed mode, the PDC emulator acts as a Windows NT primary domain controller. It processes password changes from clients and replicates updates to the BDCs. At any time, there can be only one domain controller acting as the PDC emulator in each domain in the forest. **A** is incorrect because there is no server role in Windows 2000 that places a DNS server "in charge" of other DNS servers. **D** is incorrect because a DNS server that cannot answer queries is sometimes referred to as a "Slave" server, if it is configured to use a forwarder.

15. ☑ **A, B, C, D. A** is correct because one of the first things you must do before creating a domain naming scheme for the company is to determine whether the company plans to maintain an Internet presence in addition to using DNS on the intranet. **B** is correct because fast transfers are used to compress the data in the zone transfer, and are not related to the process of developing a Domain Naming Scheme. Fast transfers can be problematic when you have BIND Secondaries that do not support the fast transfer method of zone compression. **C** is correct because if you use the same domain name for your internal and external resources, you will have to mirror the external resources internally and maintain two different copies of the DNS database with the same zone names. **D** is correct because you will not be able to use a domain name that is already in use on the Internet. You should also not use a domain name that has been registered to someone else on your intranet in order to avoid misunderstandings.

16. ☑ **A, B, C. A** is correct because zones should be delegated only to locations where there are experienced personnel who can reliably maintain the integrity and accuracy of the records in the zone database file. **B** is correct because you must use the New Zone Wizard in the DNS management console to create a new delegation. Unlike the DNS server in Windows NT 4.0, you cannot use the wizard to create an NS record to manually create a delegation. You can, however, edit the zone file directly using a text editor and add the NS record yourself. **C** is correct because a glue record, which is a Host (A) record for the DNS server authoritative for the new zone, must be in place to resolve the name of the server noted in the NS record.
☒ **D** is incorrect because you can delegate both Active Directory integrated and Standard zones.

17. ☑ **D.** NetBT (NetBIOS over TCP/IP) allows programs written to the NetBIOS Session layer interface to function correctly on TCP/IP networks. The primary job of NetBT is to resolve NetBIOS names to IP addresses so that the request for network resources can be passed down the TCP/IP protocol stack.
☒ **B** is incorrect because the SMB redirector allows machines to request network resources on Microsoft networks using any protocol. When network resources are requested, the request is "redirected" away from the local file system to the network computer. **C** is incorrect because CSNW (Client Service for NetWare) is used as a redirector to access resources that are located on NetWare servers, which use the NetWare Core Protocol as their file sharing protocol. **A** is incorrect because the WinSock interface is used by programs that are native TCP/IP programs, not NetBIOS programs.

18. ☑ **B, C. B** is correct because the Start of Authority Record is the first record in a zone indicating that it is a Primary zone. The SOA record contains information regarding the serial number for the zone, and who is responsible for the zone. In addition, the Refresh, Retry, and Expiration Intervals are included in the SOA record. **C** is correct because while the DNS is a conceptual entity that allows for a hierarchical naming system, the actual domains and resources are contained in zones and zone database files.
☒ **A** is incorrect because NetBIOS is a Session layer interface that allows programs written to the NetBIOS interface to communicate with the network protocols. **D** is incorrect because a root domain represents the top of a domain hierarchy. The Internet root domain consists of 13 root servers that contain referrals for the top-level domains. DNS servers not connected to the Internet would contain root domains specific for their organizations.

19. ☑ **B.** Most WinSock applications used in the Windows environment automatically place the trailing periods to the FQDN entered into the text boxes via the GUI interface. However, the nslookup program does not assume that there is a trailing period. Therefore, when a request for tacteam.net is send via nslookup, it is treated as an unqualified request. When an unqualified request is issued from a user agent (WinSock Program), a domain name is appended to the request, depending on how the client machine has been configured.
☒ A is incorrect because you cannot enter a host name that includes a period via the GUI interfaces on the DNS management console. In addition, periods are considered delimiters between labels, and it is assumed that the leftmost label represents a host name within a domain. C is incorrect because there must be entries for tacteam.net on the destination DNS server, since the query was ultimately answered.

20. ☑ **D.** It is most likely that the IP address was typed incorrectly when entering the Host (A) address record into the zone database file.
☒ A is incorrect because while users may at times feel the need to stretch the truth so that they will not be blamed for problems, its not the most likely answer. You should always take what users tell you as true, unless you can demonstrate otherwise. **B** is incorrect because this situation relates to host name resolution, and the WINS server provides NetBIOS name resolution. However, if the destination machine's NetBIOS name was "www", then the NetBIOS name resolution sequence could potentially be an issue. But, this is not the most likely answer. **C** is incorrect because requests for host name resolution for Web servers do not use the Dynamic Update Protocol; they only send DNS queries to the DNS server.

LAB ANSWER

If you have any problems with this exercise, please visit the Web site and we'll see if we can figure out what happened.

MCSE

MICROSOFT CERTIFIED SYSTEMS ENGINEER

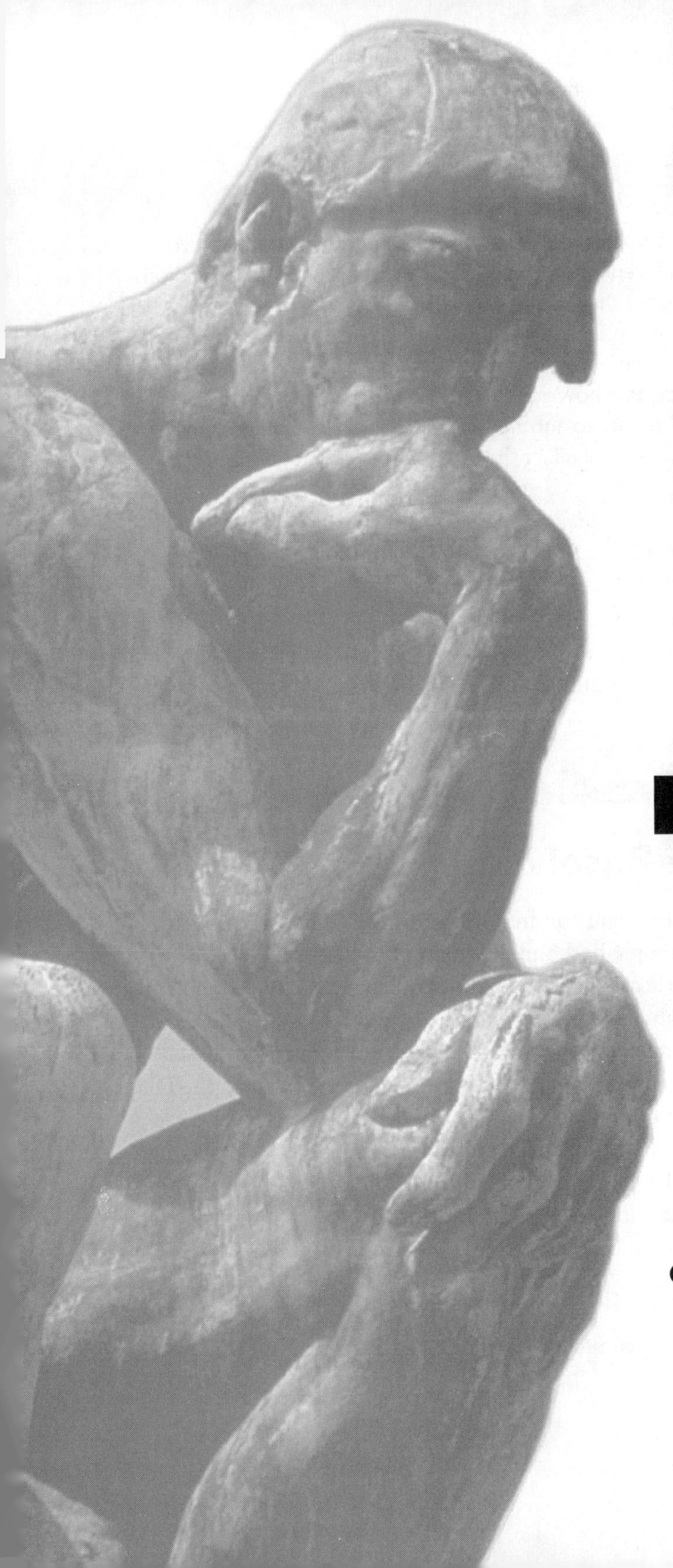

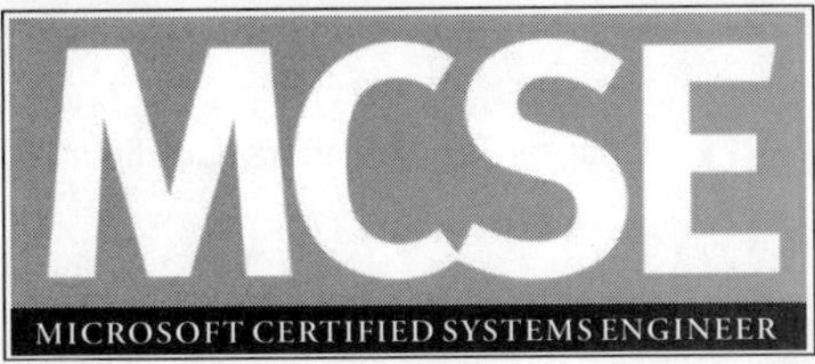

3

Installing, Configuring, and Troubleshooting DNS

CERTIFICATION OBJECTIVES

3.01	How Host Names Are Resolved
3.02	Windows 2000 DNS Server Roles
3.03	Integrating Windows 2000 Server with Active Directory
3.04	Integrating Windows 2000 Server with DHCP
3.05	Managing the Windows 2000 DNS Server
3.06	Monitoring and Troubleshooting DNS
✓	Two-Minute Drill
Q&A	Self Test

In the previous chapter, we covered some of the basic concepts underlying the Domain Name System. We compared the differences between NetBIOS and WinSock applications, and the different Session layer interfaces they use to access the TCP/IP protocol stack beneath the Application layer. We covered the DNS namespace and how to choose computer and domain names. You learned the difference between a zone and a domain, and how to put those differences into action. After you saw how zones worked, you learned about how information is transferred from one DNS server to another using the process of zone transfer. Finally, you learned how compatibility issues could affect the integrity of your zone transfers.

In this chapter, we'll look at more advanced concepts, such as DNS server roles and how the Windows 2000 DNS Server integrates with the Active Directory and the Windows 2000 DHCP Server. Then we'll look at the nuts and bolts of managing the actual zones and the Server itself via the DNS Management Console. Finally, you'll learn how to use some of the tools available that allow you to monitor and troubleshoot your Windows 2000 DNS installation.

CERTIFICATION OBJECTIVE 3.01

How Host Names Are Resolved

WinSock applications require the IP address of the destination host to establish a session. However, most people find numbers difficult to remember, so most users prefer to use host names to access resources. The process of matching up an IP address to a known host name is called *host name resolution.*

The DNS client must have some method of formulating a question that the DNS server can understand before it can send an answer. *Resolver* software on the DNS client formulates and issues query statements sent to the DNS server. Resolver software can be included in the WinSock application, or in the case of Windows 2000, be a component of the operating system. The Windows 2000 operating system has a system-wide caching resolver. Examples of WinSock programs that make use of resolver software include:

- Web browsers (such as Microsoft Internet Explorer)
- FTP clients (such as the command-line FTP program found in Windows 2000)
- Telnet clients
- DNS servers

exam Watch

Any program or service that issues DNS queries uses resolver software. The resolver can be included within the application itself, or it may take advantage of a system-wide resolver, such as that included with Windows 2000.

The Order of Host Name Resolution

No, this is not a secret religious order—it is the order of methods the DNS Client service uses in an attempt to resolve a host name to an IP address. You may remember learning this in your Windows NT 4.0 studies when you learned the Host Name Resolution Sequence: Large Hard Drives? Can We Buy Legally? (localhost, HOSTS, DNS, NetBIOS Remote Name Cache, WINS, Broadcast, LMHOSTS). Things have changed a little since Windows NT 4.0.

The Windows 2000 Resolver now caches the contents of the HOSTS file on system startup. You will remember the HOSTS file as a static text file that stores host name to IP address mappings. When an entry is entered into the HOSTS file and the file is saved, the entries will be immediately placed into the local computer's DNS cache. This saves some time since the HOSTS text file itself does not have to be loaded and searched each time access to those entries is required.

on the Job

You may find that you need to edit the HOSTS file from time to time on the job for troubleshooting purposes. You can find it at %systemroot%\system32\drivers\etc.

When the resolver receives a request for an entry that is longer than 15 bytes, or if it contains a period, it will be sent through the host name resolution sequence. If the request does not meet either of these specifications, it will be sent through the NetBIOS name resolution sequence.

Once the request begins the host name resolution sequence, the first step is to check whether the destination is the local host. If not, the local DNS client will check its own DNS cache. Note that at this point it does *not* check the HOSTS file, as was the case with Windows NT 4.0, because the contents of the HOSTS file have been loaded into cache. If the destination host's IP address is not in the local DNS cache, the query will be sent to the DNS client's Preferred DNS server. If the DNS server cannot resolve the query, the host name portion of the fully qualified domain name (FQDN) will be processed through the NetBIOS name resolution sequence.

So, when remembering the host name resolution sequence for Windows 2000, think of L C D C W B L (Liquid Crystal Displays? Can We Buy Legally?, or think of a better one yourself).

exam Watch

It is very important for you to understand and memorize the host name resolution sequence, not just for the exam, but also for your actual practice on the job. While it is unlikely that the exam will ask you to spit out the host name resolution sequence, you will need to know it in order to solve host name resolution troubleshooting problems.

The Windows 2000 Caching Resolver

We have touched on the local client's DNS cache in the preceding section. You should know that Windows 2000 includes a system-wide *caching resolver*. This caching resolver is responsible for formulating and issuing queries on behalf of the DNS client for host name resolution. The caching resolver is implemented as part of the *DNS Client Service.*

The caching resolver is able to cache both positive and negative responses. When a positive response is cached, the time-to-live (TTL) on the record returned to the client is respected by the DNS client receiving the DNS response. For example, if you resolve *www.shinder.net* to 209.217.17.13, the response from the DNS server resolving the request will include a TTL for that record.

The caching resolver not only caches queries that have been answered positively, but also caches negative results as well. When a DNS query fails, this failed result is placed in cache for five minutes, by default. If the machines issues a DNS query for the same object within five minutes, no query will be sent, and a failure message will be retrieved from cache. This can significantly reduce the overall DNS query traffic on a large network. Figure 3-1 shows an example of a negatively cached DNS query result.

Recursive Queries

When you type an FQDN in the address bar of a Web browser, the resolver formulates a DNS query and sends the query to the client's Preferred DNS server. The DNS client most often will send a *recursive query.* When a recursive query is sent to the client's Preferred DNS server, the server *must* respond to the query either positively or negatively. A positive response returns the IP address; a negative response returns a "host not found" or similar error. A recursive query is one that requires a definitive response, either affirmative or negative. A *Referral* response from the DNS server is not an option.

If you were asked "who was the 17th president of the United States?" how might you go about answering this question? You could give the correct answer (a positive response), or admit that you don't know (a negative response). This type of query

FIGURE 3-1 A negatively cached DNS query

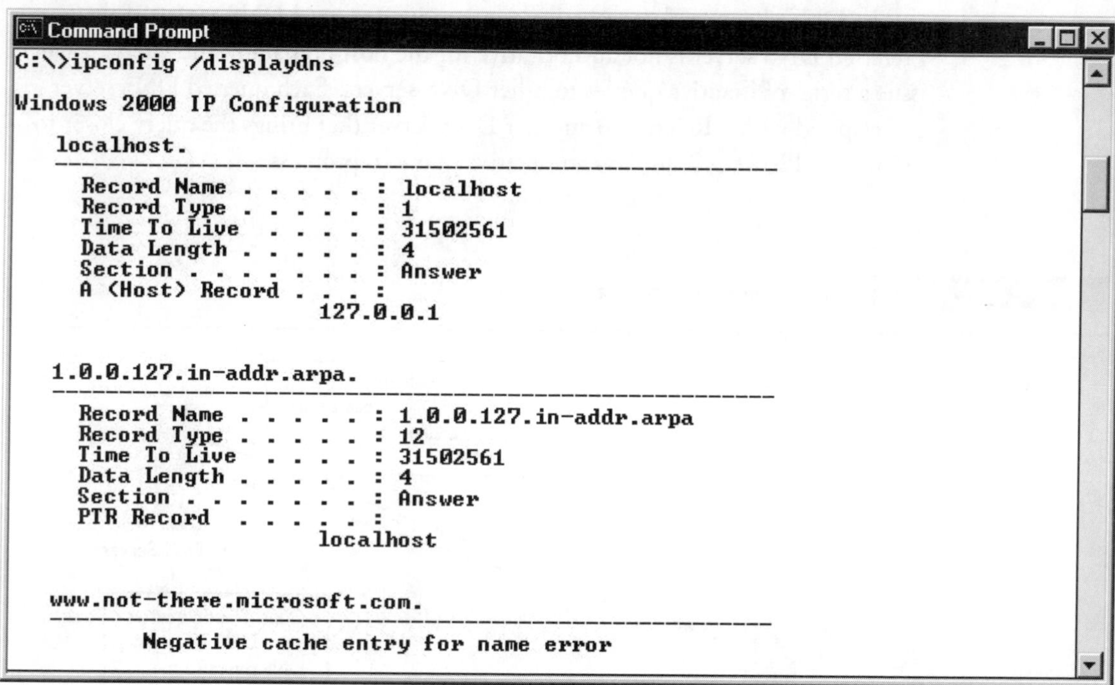
Command Prompt
C:\>ipconfig /displaydns
Windows 2000 IP Configuration
localhost.
Record Name . . . . . : localhost
Record Type . . . . . : 1
Time To Live . . . . : 31502561
Data Length . . . . . : 4
Section . . . . : Answer
A (Host) Record . . . :
127.0.0.1
1.0.0.127.in-addr.arpa.
Record Name . . . . . : 1.0.0.127.in-addr.arpa
Record Type . . . . . : 12
Time To Live . . . . : 31502561
Data Length . . . . . : 4
Section . . . . : Answer
PTR Record . . . . . :
localhost
www.not-there.microsoft.com.
Negative cache entry for name error

where you only have two options is an example of a recursive query. When you were in the process of figuring out the answer, you were performing recursion (i.e., coming up with a definitive answer).

Iterative Queries

Is there any other approach you can use to answer the question? Yes! You could say, "hold on, I'm going to find out and get some help with this recursion." Then you would ask other people, who might *refer* you to other people who *might* know the answer. You'd have this option if I were to issue to you an *iterative* query.

Iterative queries allow the DNS server responding to the request to make a best-effort attempt at resolving the DNS query. If the DNS server receiving an iterative query is not authoritative for the domain included in the query, it can return a *Referral* response. The Referral contains the IP address of another DNS server that may be able to service the query. The Referral is based on information contained in delegations (NS records) on the DNS server being queried.

The DNS client sends a recursive query to its Preferred DNS server. If the Preferred DNS server is not authoritative for the host domain in the query, it will issue a series of iterative queries to other DNS servers. Each queried DNS server can respond with a Referral to another DNS server that brings the query closer to resolution. Figure 3-2 displays an iterative query in progress.

FIGURE 3-2 Using iterative queries to resolve a host name

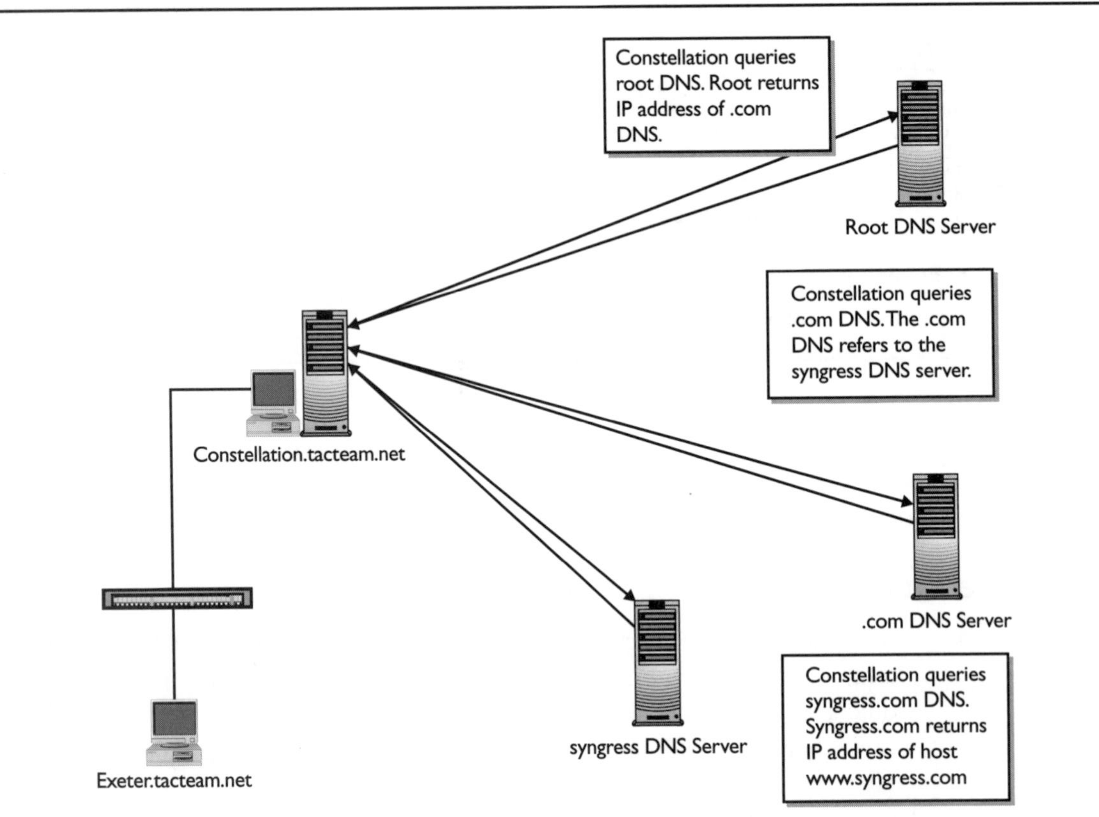

Passing the Buck

When the DNS client sends a recursive query to its Preferred DNS server, it asks for recursion. Think of this as a way for the DNS client to "pass the buck" and get someone else to do the actual work of resolving the DNS query. It becomes the DNS server's responsibility to find the answer. There are several advantages in having the DNS client issue recursive requests rather than having each DNS client perform its own recursion:

- There is much less network traffic when a DNS server performs recursion rather than having each client perform its own.
- The DNS server maintains a cache of host names and domains that it has recently resolved. All machines using a particular DNS server benefit from having access to this centralized cache.
- There are security risks to having machines access external DNS servers. You can strategically place your DNS servers so that no external DNS server ever requires access to a DNS server located on the internal network.

So, while "passing the buck" might sound like a bad thing at first, a lot of good comes out of having the DNS client issue recursive requests to its Preferred DNS servers.

There may be times when you need to connect to a resource on a server that uses Dynamic DNS to register its host name. If this server changes its IP address frequently, you may not be able to resolve the host name of the server to an IP address. To fix this problem, clear the DNS cache via the DNS console.

Looking Up an Address from a Name

The following represents the sequence of events during the host name resolution process using both recursive and iterative queries. In this example, we want to connect to a Web server named Exeter at tacteam.net (note that in this example, the query is for an FQDN and *not* an *unqualified* request).

1. Type **exeter.tacteam.net** in the address bar of the Web browser, and press Enter. After pressing Enter, the resolver formulates a recursive DNS query and sends it to the client's Preferred DNS server.

2. The Preferred DNS server will check to see if it is authoritative for the zone in the query. The server will also check its cache to see if it has recently resolved the same host name and to see if it has the IP address of a DNS server authoritative for the zone included in the query. If the required information is not in its cache, and if the DNS server is not authoritative for the queried domain, it will send an iterative query to an Internet Root Name server. At this point, the Preferred DNS server becomes a DNS client itself and uses its own caching resolver to formulate the iterative DNS queries. The Preferred DNS server starts the iterative query process in order to complete recursion. Once recursion is complete, a definitive answer can be returned to the client.
3. The Root Name server is not authoritative for tacteam.net. However, the Internet Root DNS server is authoritative for all top-level domains and contains delegations for all of them. This includes the .net domain. The Root server sends the IP address of a DNS server authoritative for the .net domain to the Preferred DNS server.
4. The Preferred DNS server connects to a DNS server authoritative for the .net domain. The .net domain DNS server is not authoritative for the tacteam.net domain. However, the .net DNS server does contain a delegation record that points to the DNS server authoritative for the tacteam.net domain. The .net domain DNS server returns to the Preferred DNS server the IP address for the DNS server authoritative for the tacteam.net domain.
5. At this point, the Preferred DNS server queries the DNS server authoritative for the tacteam.net domain. The tacteam.net DNS server checks its zone files for a Host (A) resource record for Exeter. Exeter is located in the tacteam.net domain, and there is an Address record for it in the zone database. The tacteam.net DNS server responds to the Preferred DNS server with the IP address of host computer Exeter.
6. The Preferred DNS server has completed recursion. It responds to the client with a recursive response and sends the IP address of exeter.tacteam.net. You can now establish a session to the destination host because the IP address is known. If the tacteam.net DNS server did not have a Host (A) resource record for Exeter, the Preferred server would have replied negatively to the query.

In this example, both the DNS client and the Preferred server acted as resolvers in the process. The example is depicted in Figure 3-3.

The DNS server caches the results of successful queries. This reduces Internet traffic to Internet Root servers. The longer the DNS server is online without rebooting, the longer it has to build its DNS cache. The contents of the cache are lost after a reboot. DNS requests speed up significantly after the DNS server has built up a large cache of successfully resolved queries.

FIGURE 3-3

Performing both recursive and iterative queries

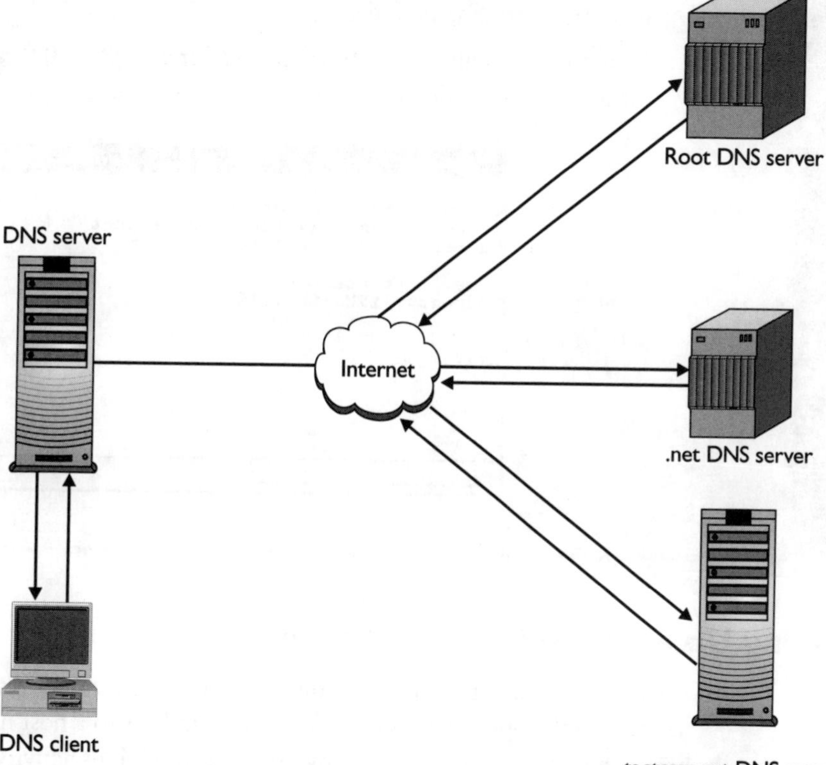

CertCam 3-1

EXERCISE 3-1

Performing a Forward Lookup

In this exercise, you will perform a forward lookup by querying a forward lookup zone. In order to complete this exercise, you will need to be connected to the Internet via a modem or a network connection that allows nslookup queries to pass through any existing firewalls.

1. Log on as Administrator.
2. Open the Command Prompt from the Accessories menu.
3. At the Command Prompt, type: **nslookup www.tacteam.net** (be sure to include the trailing period).
4. Note that you will see our Internet IP address 198.41.0.9 rather than the intranet address, which is shown in the screen shot.

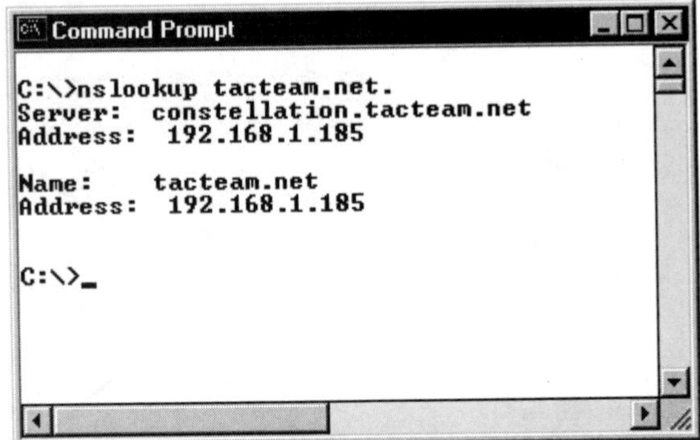
Command Prompt
C:\>nslookup tacteam.net.
Server: constellation.tacteam.net
Address: 192.168.1.185
Name: tacteam.net
Address: 192.168.1.185
C:\>_

Looking Up a Name from an Address

We have examined how a host name is resolved to an IP address. Occasionally, we need to do the opposite: resolve a known IP address to a host name. IP address to host name resolution can aid in investigating suspicious activity. Many security analysis programs use IP address to host name resolution. The process of resolving a known IP address to a host name is called a *reverse lookup*, in contrast to the forward lookup where a host name is resolved to an IP address. Reverse lookups query *reverse lookup zones.*

As you saw earlier, a HOSTS file can be used to map host names to IP addresses. It is simple to search the HOSTS file to find an IP address to host name mapping. However, this becomes much more complex when dealing with a worldwide distributed database.

Indexing the Domain Databases

The primary "index" for the Domain Name System is the domain name. The DNS is comparable to a phone book, which is indexed by last names. Forward lookups are based on a similar indexing scheme. Locating a domain name using the IP address as the value would require an exhaustive search of the entire DNS. This would be like trying to find the person associated with a particular phone number by using a conventional phone book. Reverse lookups could be accomplished this way, but performance would be so dismal, they would be of no use.

The in-addr.arpa Domain

The answer lies in creating *another* domain that uses Network IDs as the index value. Then we can search this domain in the same way we searched the forward lookup zones. This is the *in-addr.arpa* domain.

Each node in the in-addr.arpa domain is named after numbers found in the w, x, y, and z octets of the Network ID. Each level (or branch) in the in-addr.arpa domain can contain 256 (0–255) domains corresponding to the possible values for each octet. The leaf objects in the in-addr.arpa domain are the actual resource records (PTR records) that contain the IP address to host name mapping.

The in-addr.arpa zone file notation mimics the forward lookup zone construction. For example, if tacteam.net has a Network ID of 21.18.189.0, the in-addr.arpa subdomain is 189.18.21.in-addr.arpa. This maps to the domain name tacteam.net. Just as forward lookup zones go from specific to general when moving from left to right, so do the reverse lookup zones.

This arrangement allows Network ID based domains to be hierarchical in the same fashion as the forward lookup zones. The Network IDs themselves are assigned by central authorities in the same way that root, top-level, and second-level domain spaces are centrally managed. Like subdomains within the second-level domain, you can subdivide or subnet your Network ID any way you like.

We can delegate authority for a reverse lookup zone in the same way as is done for the forward lookup zones. For example, the 126.in-addr.arpa domain contains reverse mappings for all hosts and subdomains whose IP addresses start with 126. The administrator of network 126 can delegate authority for the 256 subdomains of the 126.in-addr.arpa domain. The American Registry for Internet Numbers is the central authority that manages the delegations for the in-addr.arpa domain. You can find more information about them at www.arin.net.

The iterative and recursive query process works the same when performing reverse lookups as it does when performing forward lookups.

EXERCISE 3-2

Looking Up a Host Name from an IP Address

In this exercise, you will perform a reverse lookup using the nslookup utility. To successfully complete this exercise, you must have a connection to the Internet that allows you to pass nslookup queries. If you are directly connected to the Internet via a modem, you will have no problem; if you are connected to the Internet via a network connection, a firewall may prevent you from successfully performing this exercise.

1. Log on as Administrator if you have not already done so.
2. Open the Command Prompt from the Accessories menu.
3. At the Command Prompt, type **nslookup 209.185.243.135**. You should see what appears next.

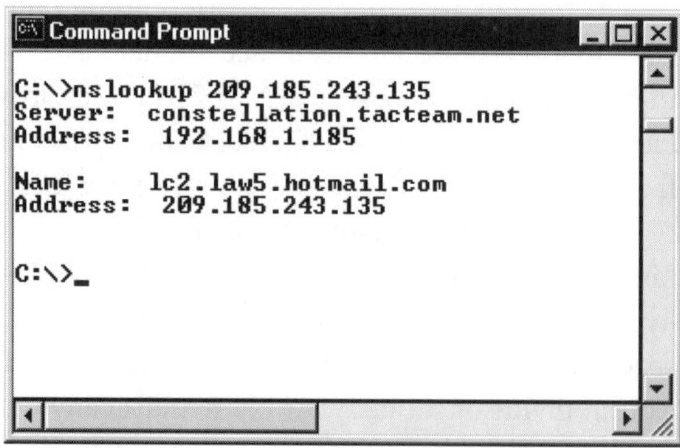
Command Prompt
C:\>nslookup 209.185.243.135
Server: constellation.tacteam.net
Address: 192.168.1.185
Name: lc2.law5.hotmail.com
Address: 209.185.243.135
C:\>_

exam Watch

As the administrator of your own subdomains, you are not required to create or maintain reverse lookup zones. Some network security analysis software will not work correctly if reverse lookup zones are not created. In addition, you will receive errors when doing nslookup queries directed to your DNS server, because a reverse lookup is performed first for the DNS server name during the nslookup process.

SCENARIO & SOLUTION	
How can I tell what entries are in the DNS client cache? How can I get rid of them?	You can use the ipconfig /displaydns command to see a list of cached entries. These entries respect the TTL listed on the records as they are received, so they don't stay in your cache forever. If you want to manually delete the entries in your local DNS cache, you can use the ipconfig /flushdns command. Note that there is no way to delete individual entries.
I have heard something about "negative caching." What is that all about?	When a query fails, it is reported to the DNS client service (the caching resolver). When an entry is negative cached, the fact that it was unsuccessful will stay in cache for five minutes. While the negatively cached entry remains in the DNS client cache, no queries will be sent for that entry, even when a request is made through a user agent (Web browser, ftp client, etc.).
Do I need to maintain a HOSTS file on my servers or workstations?	HOSTS files are not required. You can use a HOSTS file for fault tolerance; in case all DNS servers become unavailable, clients can refer to the cached entries in the local HOSTS file. The HOSTS file is also helpful for troubleshooting purposes. Remember that there are no "tags" that confer additional information in a HOSTS file, which is different from what you have available to you with LMHOSTS files. In addition, if there are erroneous entries in the HOSTS file, they will be used preferentially over entries in the DNS server, because of the nature of host name resolution. You should always check for bad entries in the HOSTS file when troubleshooting host name resolution problems.

CERTIFICATION OBJECTIVE 3.02

Windows 2000 DNS Server Roles

A Windows 2000 DNS Server can take on a variety of different roles. We will focus on Standard DNS zones in this section. Zone databases can be integrated with the Active Directory. When the zone database is integrated with the Active Directory, some of the concepts discussed in this section may not apply. We'll talk more about Active Directory integrated zones later in this chapter.

A Windows 2000 DNS Server may take the role of:

- Primary DNS server
- Secondary DNS server
- DNS Forwarder
- Caching-only server
- DNS slave server
- Dynamic update server

Each role determines how the zone database is handled on the server and/or how DNS client queries are evaluated. First, let's examine the different DNS server roles.

Primary DNS Server

A Primary DNS server contains the only copy of the zone database that can be changed. A Primary DNS server is *authoritative* for the domain or domains contained in its zone files. Primary DNS servers are authoritative because they can respond directly to DNS queries. Primary DNS servers share characteristics with all DNS servers, including:

- Zone database information is stored in the %systemroot%>\system32\dns directory.
- The ability to boot from either the registry or a boot file.
- The ability to cache resolved queries.

- A cache.dns file (or "*root hints*" file) that contains host name to IP address mappings for the Internet DNS Root servers.

All zone files are stored in the %systemroot%\system32\dns directory. Zone file names are based on the name of the zone and are appended with the ".dns" file extension. For example, the tacteam.net zone file is named tacteam.net.dns.

Configuring the DNS Server via the Boot File and DNS Management Console

A Windows 2000 DNS Server's configuration information is stored in the Registry. Server configuration is done via the DNS Management console. This is the default and preferred setting.

You may choose to administer the DNS server configuration via a file called BOOT. UNIX Administrators are accustomed to manipulating DNS server behavior by manipulating the BOOT file.

You can choose to boot from:

- The Registry
- The BOOT file
- Active Directory and the Registry

These configuration choices can be made in the Advanced tab for the DNS server you are administrating.

Microsoft recommends that you use either the BOOT file or the DNS Management Console exclusively, and not switch between the two. This is because errors may occur when editing the BOOT file directory that the DNS console may not be able to handle efficiently. Choose one or the other and stick with it.

DNS Server Caching

All DNS servers cache resolved queries. When a DNS server issues an iterative query to another DNS server, the results are placed in the requesting server's cache. Cached information is stored in system memory and is not written to disk. Because the cached DNS is stored solely in RAM, the information is lost after a server reboot. Therefore, DNS servers are most effective when reboots are avoided.

The cache.dns file (also known as the Root Hints file) will typically contain host name and IP address mappings for the Root Internet DNS servers. If a DNS server receives a recursive query for a domain for which it is not authoritative, it must complete recursion by issuing iterative queries. The iterative query process may begin with the Root DNS servers if the target domain in the DNS query is not contained in the DNS server's cache. The cache.dns file is located in the same directory as the zone files.

exam Watch

After you install the Windows 2000 DNS Server the cache.dns file will map the host names and IP addresses of the Internet Root servers. This allows the server to resolve Internet host names. However, if you are not interested in having the server resolve Internet host names, you should replace the entries in the cache.dns file with the Root servers in your organization. Those are your intranet servers that contain information about your company's root domain.

The Internet Root server mappings change periodically. You can download the current Internet Root server mappings from:

ftp://ftp.rs.internic.net/domain/root.zone.gz

DNS Servers Can Be Authoritative for Multiple Domains

A DNS server can be authoritative for multiple domains. For example, the tacteam.net.dns zone file can contain entries authoritative for tacteam.net and dev.tactem.net. Since it is authoritative for these domains, it does not need to issue iterative queries to other DNS servers in order to resolve the request.

As we learned earlier, a Primary DNS server can also be a Secondary DNS server. A Primary DNS server that receives zone transfers from another Primary server acts in the role of Secondary. Any DNS server can contain either or both Primary or Secondary zone files. The only difference between the two is that the Primary zone file is read/write, while the Secondary zone file is read-only.

This leads us to the next subject: How do we provide fault tolerance for zone database files? And how can we gain a measure of load balancing for our DNS servers? A corporation is highly dependent on reliable host name resolution in order to access both intranet and Internet servers. In order to provide for fault tolerance, we configure Secondary DNS servers.

You will find that various administrators, enterprise architects, and writers use the terms Primary and Secondary DNS servers. The server software is the same for both. What makes a machine a Primary or Secondary DNS server is the type of zone files it contains. This explains why a machine can be both a Primary and Secondary DNS server: because it contains both Primary and Secondary DNS zone files.

Secondary DNS Servers

The Domain Name System was designed to include at least two DNS servers authoritative for each zone. Secondary DNS servers are authoritative for the zones they contain. Secondary DNS servers provide the following functions:

- **Fault tolerance** If the Primary DNS server is somehow disabled, the Secondary can answer requests for the zone.
- **Load balancing** By distributing the query load, the Primary server is not as impacted by large volumes of query traffic.
- **Bandwidth conservation** Secondary servers can be placed in remote locations, which reduces the need to traverse a WAN for name resolution.

Zone Fault Tolerance

Like Primary servers, Secondary DNS servers contain zone database files. The copy is received via zone transfer. A Primary DNS server for the zone acts as a *Master server* and copies the zone file to the Secondary during a zone transfer. Secondary DNS servers can answer DNS client queries; therefore, they are also authoritative for the zones they contain. DNS clients are configured with the IP addresses of Preferred and Alternate DNS servers for fault tolerance. Name resolution services can continue without interruption by querying the Secondary server if the Primary should become disabled.

Zone Load Balancing and Bandwidth Preservation

Load balancing allows you to distribute the DNS query load among multiple DNS servers. A single DNS server could be overwhelmed by name query traffic if all client computers were to access a single Primary server simultaneously. Clients on different segments can be configured to query local Secondary servers. This disperses the query load among Primary and Secondary DNS servers for a zone.

Fault tolerance, load balancing, and bandwidth preservation provide cogent reasons to implement Secondary DNS servers. If you plan to maintain your own DNS servers on the Internet, the Domain Registrar will require you to have at least one Primary and one Secondary DNS server for your second-level domain.

Caching-Only Servers

All DNS servers cache results of queries they have resolved. The *caching-only* DNS server does not contain zone information or a zone file; it builds its database of host name and domain mappings over time from successful DNS queries it has resolved for DNS clients.

All DNS servers have a cache.dns file that contains the IP addresses of all Internet Root servers. The Windows 2000 cache.dns file is also referred to as the *root hints* file. You can view the contents of the Root Hints file via the DNS server properties dialog box, as seen in Figure 3-4. The caching-only server uses this list to begin building its cache. It adds to the cache as it issues iterative queries when responding to client requests.

Caching-only servers are valuable because:

- They do not generate zone transfer traffic.
- They can be placed on the far side of a slow WAN link and provide name resolution services for remote offices that do not require a high level of host name resolution support.
- They can be configured as secure DNS forwarders.

Satellite locations are often connected to the main office via slow WAN links. These locations benefit from caching-only servers for a couple of reasons:

- There is no zone transfer traffic. For large corporate intranets with small remote branches, eliminating zone transfer traffic can be very beneficial, since these offices often have a slow link to the corporate headquarters.
- DNS queries do not have to traverse the WAN after an adequate cache is built from successfully resolved queries.

FIGURE 3-4

The Root Hints tab in the DNS server Properties dialog box

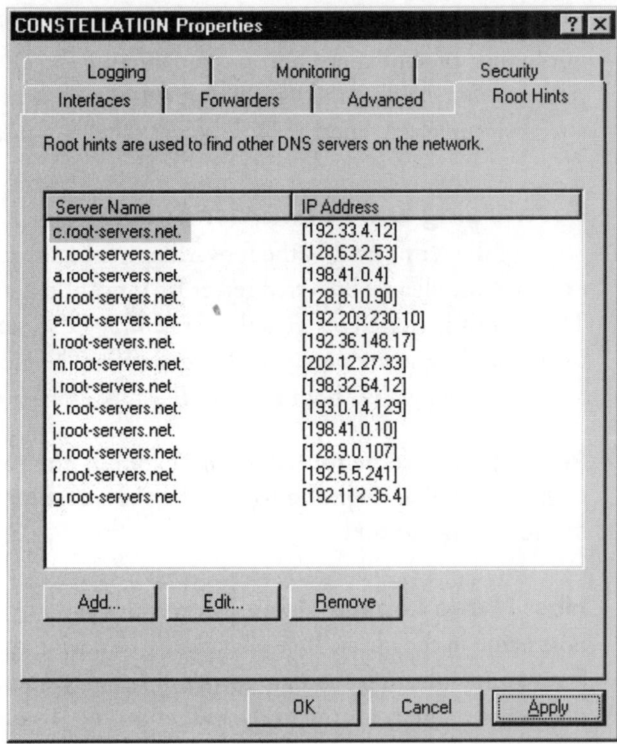

These caching-only servers do not require expert administration. A satellite office is unlikely to have trained DNS administrative staff onsite. This saves the cost of having an experienced DNS administrator visit the site.

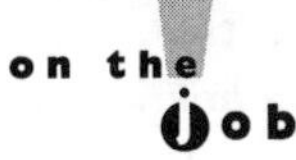

There is no risk of an intruder obtaining zone information from a caching-only server. Therefore, caching-only servers make excellent candidates for forwarders.

DNS Forwarders and Slave Servers

A DNS forwarder is a DNS server that accepts recursive queries from another DNS server. Caching-only servers make good forwarders. A forwarder can be used to protect internal zone files from Internet access.

For example, a DNS client sends a recursive query to its Preferred DNS server. The request is for a host in a domain for which the Preferred server is not authoritative.

The Preferred server must resolve the host name for the client or return a "host not found" or similar error. You can configure the DNS client's Preferred DNS server to *forward* all queries for which it is not authoritative. This DNS server issues a recursive query to another DNS server called a *forwarder*.

Forwarding and Forwarder Servers

Some of the terms used in the forwarding process require clarification. In our example, the client's Preferred server is "forwarding" the request to the "forwarder." The client's Preferred server is the *forwarding* DNS server. The DNS server receiving the forwarding server's query is the *forwarder*. Therefore, the process of forwarding a DNS query involves both a *forwarding* DNS server and a *forwarder* DNS server.

exam Watch

Be careful not to be fooled on the exam by the terms** forwarder **and** forwarding **DNS server. You might be tricked by the question using one or the other term in the wrong context.

Host Name Lookup Using Forwarders The forwarder begins to resolve the host name in the query. It can do this by retrieving the information from its cache, from a zone file, or by issuing a series of iterative queries. If successful, it will answer the recursive query affirmatively and return the IP address to the forwarding server. The forwarding server completes its recursion by returning this IP address to the DNS client that initiated the query (Figure 3-5).

If the forwarder cannot resolve the hostname to an IP address, it will return to the forwarding DNS server a "host not found" error. If this happens, the Preferred DNS server (the forwarding server) will attempt to resolve the host name itself. The forwarding server will check its cache, zone files, or perform iterative queries to resolve the host name. If unsuccessful, a "host not found" or similar error is finally returned to the client.

You may not want the forwarding DNS server to issue iterative queries to servers located on the Internet. This may be true when the forwarding server is an internal DNS server. Internal DNS servers that issue iterative queries for Internet host name resolution are easy targets for hackers.

You can configure the forwarding server to not resolve host names when the forwarder fails to return a valid IP address. When the forwarding computer is configured in this fashion, it is referred to as a *slave* server. The slave server accepts responses from the forwarder and relays them to the client without attempting host name resolution itself, which it would do if the forwarder were not able to answer the query.

FIGURE 3-5 Top: The forwarder completing recursion for the forwarding server
Bottom: The forwarding server completing recursion via its own iterative queries

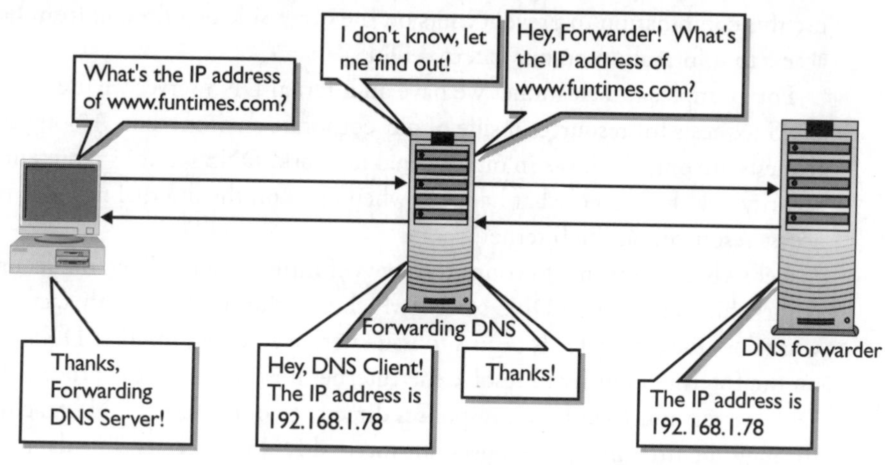

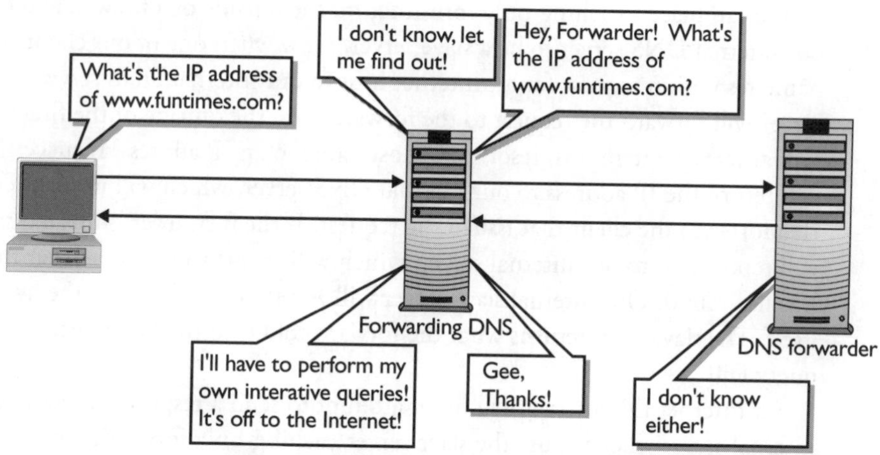

on the Job

In general, it's a good idea to disable recursion on machines that are using forwarders. Think about it: If the forwarder was unable to answer the query, what is the likelihood that the forwarding DNS server will be able to? By disabling recursion on the forwarding server, you reduce the amount of network traffic that would have been generated by the hapless attempts to resolve the host name by the forwarding computer.

Forwarders and Firewalls The *slave server/caching-only forwarder* combination is very helpful in protecting your intranet zone data from Internet intruders. We can use this combination to prevent users on the other side of a firewall from having access to information on our Internal DNS server.

For example, at tacteam.net we have an internal DNS server we use to resolve DNS requests for resources inside of our corporate environment. As long as the requests are only for hosts in our internal network, DNS requests represent no security risk. However, what happens when users on the internal network need to access resources on the Internet?

Let's say a user wants to connect to www.funtimes.com. When the recursive request hits our internal DNS server (which is authoritative for only tacteam.net), what does the server do? It begins to issue iterative queries to other DNS servers on the Internet in order to resolve the Internet host name. In the process, Internet DNS servers must send their responses directly to our internal DNS machine through the firewall. This exposes our internal DNS server, its zone data, and the nature of our requests to users on the Internet. How can we avoid this potentially dangerous situation?

We can place a caching-only forwarder on the outside of a firewall and configure our internal DNS server to be a slave server. Now when one of our clients issues a name resolution request for an Internet host to our internal DNS server, the internal server will forward the request to the forwarder on the outside of the firewall. The forwarder will attempt to resolve the host name to an IP address. If successful, it will return the IP address to our internal DNS server, which will in turn return the IP address to the client that issued the request. If the forwarder is unsuccessful, it will report that to our internal server, which will report to the client that the host was not found. Our internal slave server will *not* attempt to resolve the host name itself. The slave then returns what the forward told it to the DNS client, and the query fails.

An Internet DNS server will never attempt to send a response directly to our internal server when we use the slave server/caching-only forwarder combination. In this way, our internal zone records are safe. Figure 3-6 illustrates this setup.

Dynamic DNS Servers (DDNS)

If there is one characteristic that defines the difference between the Windows 2000 DNS Server and previous versions of Microsoft DNS servers, it is the Windows 2000 DNS Server's ability to dynamically update the information contained in its zone databases.

FIGURE 3-6 Forwarders and slaves

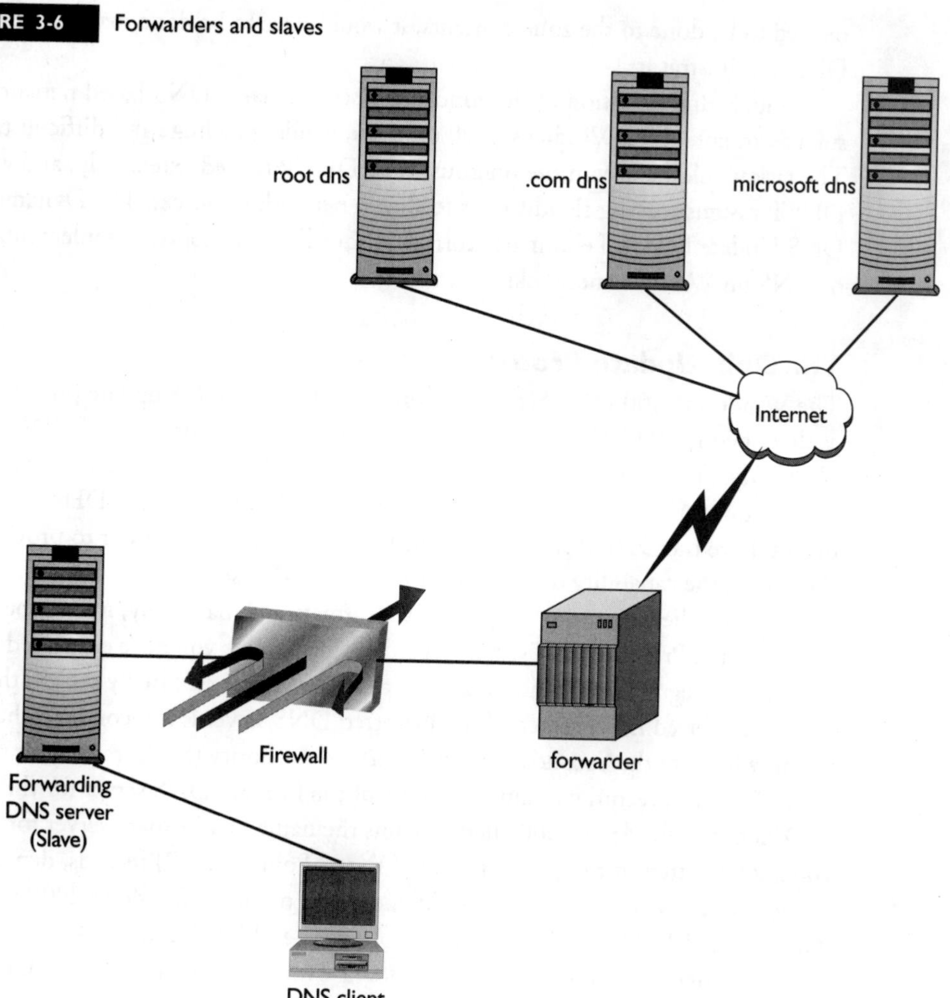

This behavior is very much like what you have seen with WINS servers. A WINS server allows NetBIOS nodes on the network to update their NetBIOS name and IP address mappings dynamically. This was a real advantage on earlier versions of Microsoft networks, since all of them had been NetBIOS based.

Windows 2000 is free of the shackles of NetBIOS (for the most part) and uses the DNS scheme for computer and domain naming. While there are many advantages to using the DNS rather than NetBIOS, there is a major problem: Zone database files were originally designed to be *static* databases. If any update needed to be done to the zone contents, it would have to be done manually by the DNS administrator.

Manual administration of the zone databases on a large DNS-based network, such as an enterprise Windows 2000 network, would be a huge and difficult task. The task would be even more onerous when DHCP is used extensively, and when DHCP assigns varying IP addresses to shared network resources. The Dynamic DNS Update Protocol eliminates this major hurdle to widespread implementation of DNS on Windows networks.

The DNS Update Protocol

The Windows 2000 DNS Server supports the Dynamic DNS update protocol as described in RFC 2136. Windows 2000 DNS clients actually use the *DHCP client service* to update a Dynamic DNS server with their host name and IP address information. All Windows 2000 computers, regardless if they are a DHCP client or not, have the DHCP client service installed and running in order to provide them with the capability of updating a Dynamic DNS server.

If a DNS client is going to update its information dynamically, it must be updated on a Primary DNS server, regardless of whether you have employed Active Directory integrated or Standard zone types. The update is initially sent to the DNS client's Preferred DNS server. If the Preferred DNS server is a Secondary, then the client will query the Secondary for the Start Of Authority (SOA) record for the zone. The SOA record contains the name of the Primary DNS server for the zone.

When the Windows 2000 client obtains the name of a Primary server for the zone, it will attempt to update its Host (A) and Pointer (PTR) records, depending on how you have configured dynamic updates to occur. A Windows 2000 machine with a static IP address always updates both its A and PTR records itself.

A Windows 2000 *DHCP client* updates its own A record, and the DHCP server updates the PTR record (by default, although you can alter this behavior). A downlevel client cannot directly update its information directly with a Dynamic DNS server, but can use a Windows 2000 DHCP server as a "proxy" to update its information.

When zone transfers are taking place, the zone file is locked and cannot be accessed. If DNS clients try to update the records during a zone transfer, the Windows 2000 Server will attempt to queue the update. This information is stored in memory, and if a server is heavily taxed and low in memory, errors may occur during the update.

RAS Clients and Dynamic Update RAS clients will always register their own information directly with the DNS server and never interact with a DHCP server. The RAS client registers both its A and PTR records itself. If an orderly disconnection of the RAS client occurs, it will remove its own records from the DNS before signing off. If a "disorderly" disconnection occurs, the RAS client's records will not be removed from the zone database. This can cause "stale" or outdated and inaccurate resource records to exist in the zone database.

Name Collisions

When a machine tries to update its name in the zone database, and finds that its name is already there with a different IP address, it has experienced a *name collision.* The default behavior of the DNS client is to overwrite the existing record with its own information.

This can be a bit of a problem, because it has the potential of being a security risk. There are two ways you can prevent the default update behavior from taking place:

- **Disable the client's ability to overwrite the existing record.** You can change the default setting so that instead of replacing the IP address, the client backs out of the registration process and logs the error in Event Viewer. To do so, add the **DisableReplaceAddressesInConflicts** entry with a value of 1 (DWORD) to the following registry subkey:

  ```
  HKEY_LOCAL_MACHINE\SYSTEM\CurrentControlSet\Services\
  Tcpip\Parameters
  ```

  The entry can be 1 or 0, which specify one of the following:

  - 1: If the name that the client is trying to create already exists, the client does not try to overwrite it.
  - 0: If the name that the client is trying to create already exists, the client tries to overwrite it. This is the default value.

- **Enable secure dynamic updates.** Secure updates can only be done with Active Directory integrated zones.

Name collisions can also take place in Active Directory integrated zones when two administrators enter differing information into the zone. When this situation occurs, the most recent record added will be considered the valid record, and will overwrite the older entry during replication. Prior to replication, there will be inaccurate data provided to some of the DNS clients. Microsoft has termed this temporary disparity "loose consistency." Therefore, the DNS database can be considered *loosely consistent.*

EXERCISE 3-3

Enabling Dynamic Updates on a Windows 2000 DNS Server

In this exercise, you will learn how to enable dynamic updates on a Windows 2000 DNS Server. The default setting is to not allow dynamic updates, so you must make this change manually. Note that dynamic updates are enabled on a *per zone* basis.

1. Log on as Administrator if you have not already done so.
2. Open the DNS Management Console from the Administrative Tools menu.
3. Expand all nodes in the left pane. Right-click on the tacteam.net zone and select Properties. You should see what appears in the following illustration.

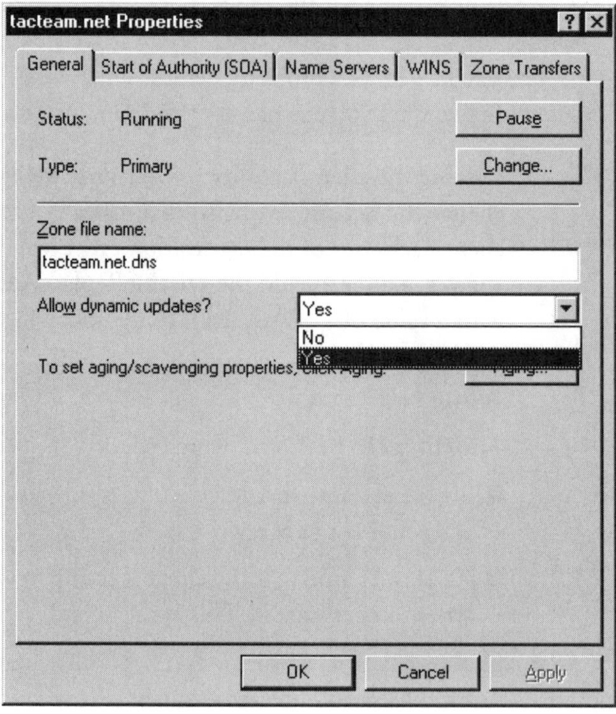

Note that you should not have to restart the DNS Server Service; however, you might want to be safe and restart the service. You can do this easily by right-clicking on the name of your server in the left pane, trace down to All Tasks, and then trace over and click Restart.

SCENARIO & SOLUTION	
Is there any way I can see the contents of the cache for caching-only DNS servers?	Yes, although this is not the default setting. In order to see the contents of the DNS cache in the DNS Management console, you must right-click the name of the server you want to view, trace down to the View command, then trace over and click Advanced. After activating the Advanced view, you will see the cached lookups node in the left pane. Expand all nodes under the cached lookups node. If there is an entry you wish to delete, right-click on that entry and click Delete.
What happens to dynamic updates on my Standard DNS zone if my Primary DNS server is not available?	When the Primary DNS server is offline or otherwise unavailable, no dynamic updates can take place. This is one of the major disadvantages of Standard zones, and one of the major reasons why you should consider implementing only Active Directory integrated zones. The Active Directory integrated zones are multimaster; therefore, if a single Primary DNS server becomes unavailable, there typically are others that can take its place.
What port numbers must I open in my firewall to allow DNS messages to pass between my forwarding and my forwarder DNS servers?	DNS uses TCP and UDP Port 53. Typically, DNS uses UDP to send and receive DNS messages. However, each message must fit in a single UDP segment, and if a single UDP segment is not large enough for the entire message, DNS servers will "fall-back" on TCP, which can accommodate larger message sizes.

CERTIFICATION OBJECTIVE 3.03

Integrating Windows 2000 DNS Server with Active Directory

Windows 2000 allows DNS integration with the Active Directory. There are significant advantages to integrating Windows 2000 zones with the Active Directory, including:

- Active Directory integrated zones use the Active Directory replication engine, thus obviating the need to create separate DNS and Active Directory replication topologies.
- Per property (rather than the entire record) zone transfers are available when the zone is Active Directory integrated.
- All Active Directory integrated DNS zones are Primary zones (multimaster). This offers a greater degree of fault tolerance when DNS clients need to dynamically update their records on a Dynamic DNS server.
- Secure dynamic updates of the DNS zone database prevents rogue machines from taking over a mapping that belongs to another machine.

DNS is required for Windows 2000 domains. Windows 2000 domain controllers are located via DNS queries. The Netlogon service searches for a logon server via DNS. Prior to Windows 2000, WINS servers provided a similar function. However, Windows 2000 is no longer dependent on NetBIOS. Core network functionality is mediated through the WinSock interface and not the NetBIOS interface.

When Active Directory is installed on a domain controller, it will seek out a DNS server authoritative for the domain. If it cannot find an authoritative DNS server, or if the authoritative DNS server does not support Dynamic updates and SRV records, the installer will require you create a DNS server on that machine. Active Directory domain names are DNS domain names.

FROM THE CLASSROOM

Domain Names

Active Directory domain names are also DNS domain names.This is in contrast to the NetBIOS name that is also assigned to a Windows 2000 domain controller, which allows it to act as a PDC Emulator for downlevel Microsoft clients (those running Windows NT and Windows 9*x* operating systems). In fact, if the leftmost label of your DNS name for the domain is longer than 15 characters, the NetBIOS name of the domain will be truncated. For this reason, it might be a good idea to keep the leftmost label of any domain name to less than 15 characters.

—*Thomas W. Shinder, M.D., MCSE, MCP+I, MCT*

Secure Dynamic Updates

Active Directory integrated zones can be protected from updates by invalid or rogue hosts. This can be accomplished by using *secure dynamic updates.* When secure updates are enabled on the Active Directory integrated zone, machines that register records in the zone become the owners of those records. Access controls are placed on the records to prevent other machines from overwriting them.

Mechanisms of Dynamic Updates

The mechanism by which this is accomplished is via the *Generic Security Service API (GSS-API)*, which is defined in RFC 2078. Other methods of secure update, such as *System Security Extensions* (RFC 2535) and *Secure Domain Name System Dynamic Update* (RFC 2137), are not supported in Windows 2000.

Security tokens are passed back and forth between the DNS client and secure DNS server. This token-passing process continues until the client and server settle on a security context in which information can be securely transferred between client and server.

The Windows 2000 implementation of the GSS-API uses Kerberos as the security method for establishing a secure connection. The GSS-API is defined in a way that allows other security providers to establish a secure context (such as smart cards and certificate-based authentication), but these haven't yet been implemented.

Two types of resource records are used to establish the secure context:

- **TKEY** The TKEY resource record is used to transfer security tokens between the DNS client and server. It allows for the establishment of the shared *secret key* that will be used with the TSIG resource record.
- **TSIG** The TSIG resource record is used to send and verify messages that have been signed with a hash algorithm.

exam Watch

Almost all secure negotiations in Windows 2000 employ aspects of a Public Key Infrastructure (PKI). In order to do well on any of your Windows 2000 exams, you must be comfortable with PKI concepts, including shared secret keys, public key, private key, and certificates. Check out the Syngress Study Guide for Exam 70-220, Designing Security for a Microsoft Windows 2000 Network.

Negotiating a Secure Context When a DNS client attempts to complete a secure update, it begins with a TKEY negotiation that will establish the shared secret. This will determine the security mechanism used during the actual data exchange. Keys are exchanged at this point.

The DNS client then sends its update request to the DNS server. This request is signed with the TSIG resource record, and the server acknowledges that it has received the signed request. The DNS server then attempts to update the Active Directory on behalf of the client.

Secure dynamic updates prevent machines from pirating the name of another legitimate machine on the network. You can configure security on resources records or entire domains via the Active Directory Users and Computers interface. Figure 3-7 shows the Secure dynamic update negotiation in progress.

DnsUpdateProxy

With secure DNS zone updates, only the "owner" of the record can update a resource record. This improves overall security, but it can cause some problems you might have to deal with. For example: You use a DHCP server to assign IP addresses to Windows 2000 clients. The default behavior for Windows 2000 DNS

FIGURE 3-7 Negotiating a secure context for dynamic updates

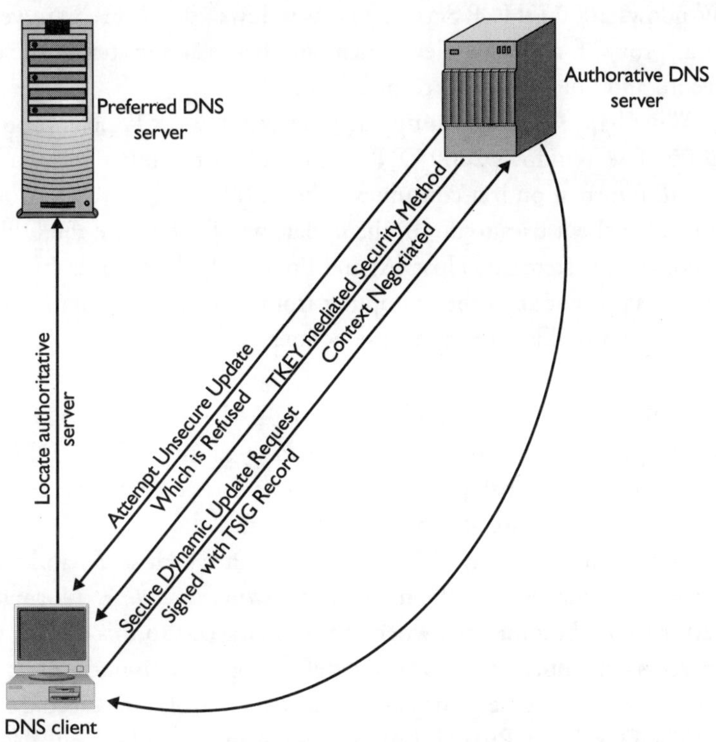

clients that are also DHCP clients is to update their own addresses record and to allow the DHCP server to update the Pointer PTR record. The DNS client therefore "owns" the Host (A) record, and the DHCP server "owns" the PTR record. Access controls are placed on these records so that no other machine can update or "touch" them.

The Problem Suppose your DHCP server crashes. You have a backup DHCP server, so you might not worry about it too much. However, when the backup DHCP server tries to update the PTR record for the DNS client, it won't be able to—it doesn't own that pointer record and therefore has no access to it.

Another problematic situation is when you are working with downlevel clients. Suppose you have a Windows NT 4.0 computer that is a DHCP client for a Windows 2000 DHCP Server. The Windows 2000 DHCP Server has been acting as a "proxy" for the downlevel client and has been registering the client's Host (A) record and Pointer (PTR) record for it.

What happens after you upgrade the Windows NT 4.0 computer to Windows 2000? The Windows 2000 DNS client will try to update its own DNS Host (A) record information if it continues to be a DHCP client. Unfortunately, when the upgraded client tries to do so, the update will fail because the DHCP server that originally registered its Host (A) and Pointer (PTR) records owns them, and access controls prevent any other computer from accessing and changing those records.

Figure 3-8 illustrates these interactions.

The Solution The solution to these problems is to place DHCP servers in a special group known as the *DnsUpdateProxy* group. When a DHCP server that is a member of the DnsUpdateProxy group creates an entry for a machine in DNS, no access controls are attached to the record.

For example, let's say a DHCP server creates a Host (A) and a Pointer (PTR) record for a machine by the name of *daedalus.tacteam.net*. Normally, the DHCP server would become the owner and restrict access to this record, but if the DHCP server is a member of the DnsUpdateProxy group, no one will be registered as the owner of the resource record and no access controls are placed on it.

The DnsUpdateProxy solution does create a complication: We've just eliminated the security in secure dynamic updates for DHCP clients (at least for the PTR records for Windows 2000 DHCP clients)! Any machine can be brought online and claim the name of a machine that has been legitimately registered by a DHCP server. Consider this the trade-off between convenience and security.

Domain Controllers in the DnsUpdateProxy Group The most significant issue relating to membership in the DnsUpdateProxy group is that of domain controllers that run the DHCP Server service. If the DHCP server is on a domain controller, it will register the domain controller's information in a nonsecure context. This allows any machine to register itself as the domain controller in question. This represents a significant security hole.

on the job

Microsoft recommends that you not implement DHCP servers on domain controllers because of the potentially adverse security consequences.

FIGURE 3-8 Problems when DHCP servers go offline and downlevel clients are upgraded

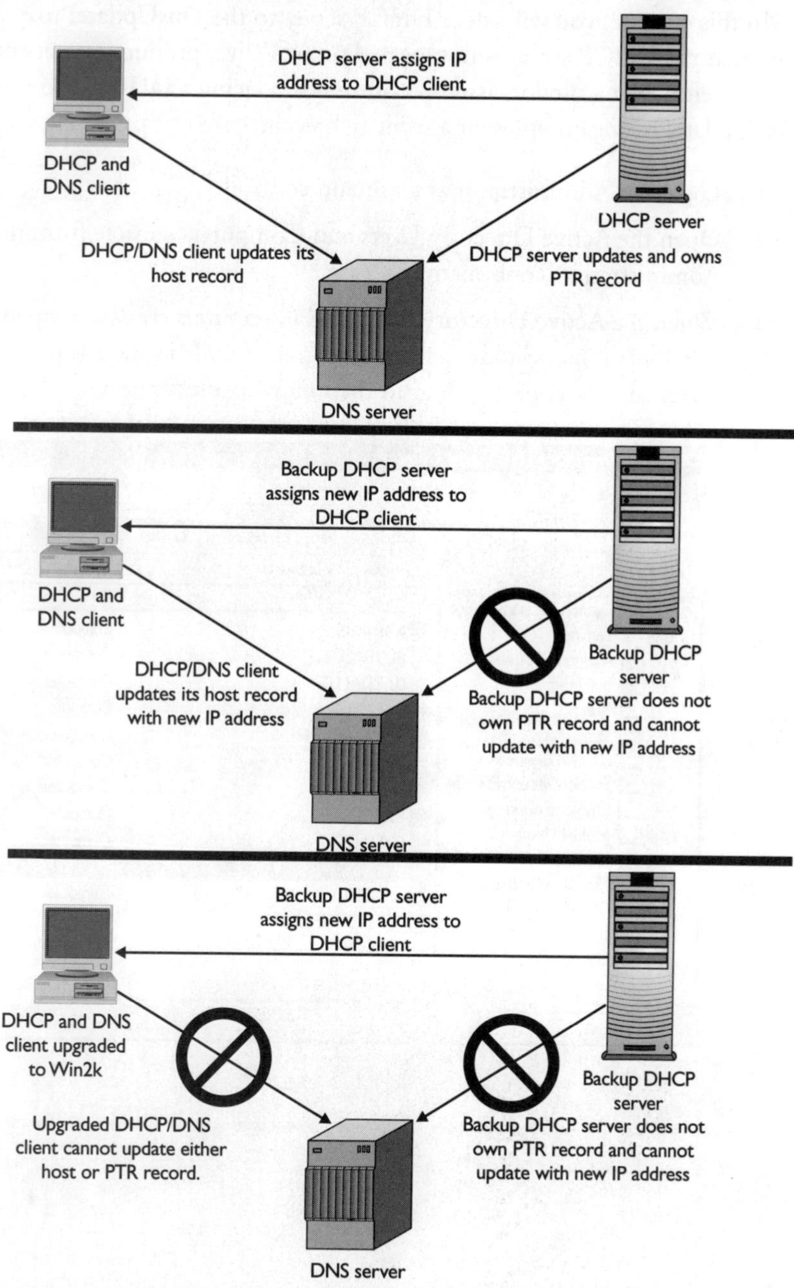

EXERCISE 3-4

Adding a DHCP Server to the DnsUpdateProxy Group

In this exercise, you will add a DHCP server to the DnsUpdateProxy group. Be sure that the DHCP server is not located on an active, production network, and is not presently being used to assign IP addresses. Placing a DHCP into the DnsUpdateProxy can represent a security breech.

1. Log on as Administrator at a domain controller.
2. Open the Active Directory Users and Computers console from the Administrative Tools menu.
3. When the Active Directory Users and Computers console is open, expand the domain name and open the Computers node in the left pane. Your screen should appear similar to the following illustration.

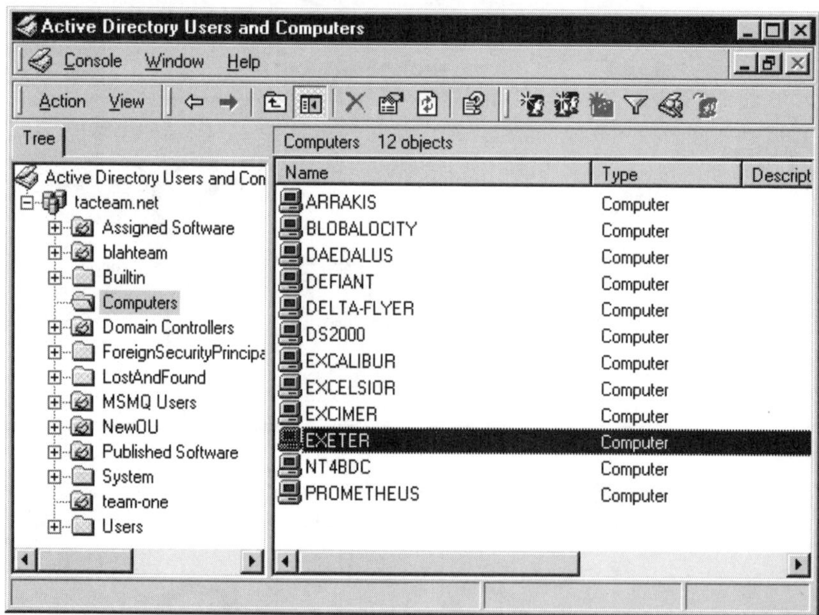

4. Examine the list in the right pane and select a computer that is a DHCP server. Right-click on the DHCP server, and click Properties. In the properties dialog box, click on the Member Of tab. You should see what appears next.

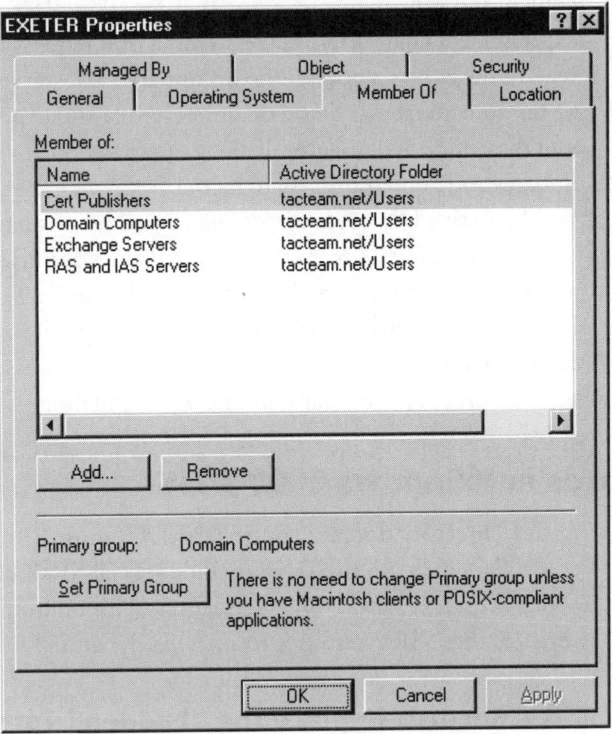

5. Click Add. you will see the Select Groups dialog box. Scroll down the list until you find DnsUpdatedProxy. Select it and then click Add. That will add the computer to the DnsUpdatedProxy group. Click OK.
6. You are returned to the <Computer> Properties box. Click Apply and then OK. The machine has been successfully added to the group.

Be aware at this point that no security will be applied to any records added by this DHCP server. However, no changes have been made to existing records.

Active Directory Integrated Zone Replication

In a Standard zone environment, the DNS Primary contains the only read/write copy of the zone database. Zone transfer takes place when the Refresh interval has expired. Secondary DNS servers send a pull request to a Master DNS server to receive the zone database. The Secondary DNS server contains a read-only copy of the zone database. Standard zones have a single point of failure for both manual and dynamic zone updates. If the Primary server for the zone is disabled, zone updates and zone transfers are halted.

The Active Directory integrated zone does not have a single point of failure because all Active Directory integrated zones are Primary. The Active Directory allows for *multimaster* replication using the Active Directory replication engine. DNS zone information is stored in the Active Directory and each authoritative server contains a read/write copy of the zone database. A single "downed" Primary will not prevent zone transfers and zone updates.

SRV Records in Windows 2000 DNS

Active Directory domain controllers (DC) must be registered in the DNS. Domain controller entries in the DNS include special SRV records that contain information about their DC status. The Netlogon service on domain controllers automatically registers these SRV resource records via dynamic DNS update.

SRV Records Replace the "Hidden" 16th Character (to some extent)

These *SRV* (Service Location) records provide a function similar to the service identifier used in the NetBIOS name. For WINS clients, the client could query the WINS database for the service desired by examining the 16th character service identifiers recorded in the WINS database. Windows 2000 domain controllers are able to dynamically update SRV records on a Dynamic DNS server and provide information about available services. Examples of such services include LDAP, FTP, and WWW (although all these service identifiers are not implemented at the present time). Domain clients must find a SRV record for a domain controller in the DNS database in order to authenticate logon. There is an SRV record for Kerberos information. This allows Kerberos clients to locate the Key Distribution server in their domain.

Manually Adding SRV Records

There may be times when you will have to manually add SRV records for domain controllers. An unfortunate example is the administrator who inadvertently deletes these records via the DNS console. It is important to restore these records on a timely basis, since domain clients are dependent on these records for domain activity.

To view the SRV resource records created by a domain controller, open and view the *netlogon.dns* file. The Active Directory Installation Wizard created this file during setup. It can be found in:

%systemroot%\System32\Config\Netlogon.dns

Each record contains the complete Active Directory path. Be sure when creating a new SRV record for a domain controller that the record is placed in the appropriate container object in the Active Directory as indicated by the path defined in the netlogon.dns file.

CertCam 3-5

EXERCISE 3-5

Adding a SRV Record Manually to the DNS

In this exercise, we'll look at a SRV record in the netlogon.dns file and add it manually to the DNS database. You may have to do this if a SRV record is deleted from the zone database file, or if you need to add SRV records to DNS servers that do not accept dynamic updates. Do not perform this exercise on a domain controller on your own network, as it will return invalid data to DNS clients searching for domain controllers on your network.

The record we will add is:

_ldap._tcp.dc._msdcs.tacteam.net. 600 IN SRV 0 100 389 CONSTELLATION.tacteam.net

1. Log on as Administrator if you haven't done so already.
2. Open the **DNS** Management Console from the Administrative Tools menu.
3. Find the forward lookup zone for your domain. Expand all nodes in the left pane for that forward lookup zone. You want to find that node that corresponds with the path: _msdcs\dc_tcp under your domain. Click on the _tcp node. Your screen should look something like what follows.

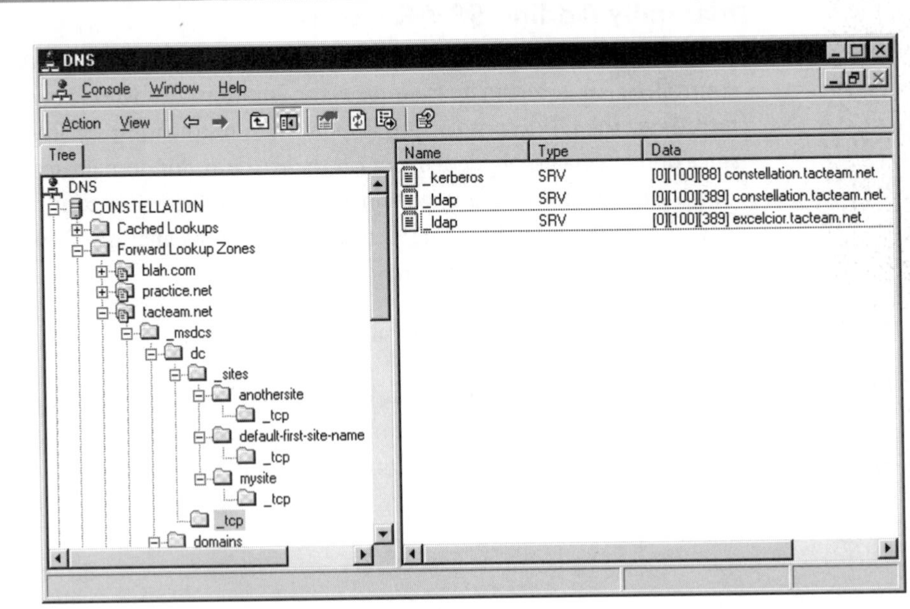

4. Right-click on the _msdcs node and click on Other New Records. Scroll down the list of resource record types until you find SRV, and select SRV. You should see what appears in the following illustration. Note the explanation of the SRV resource record type.

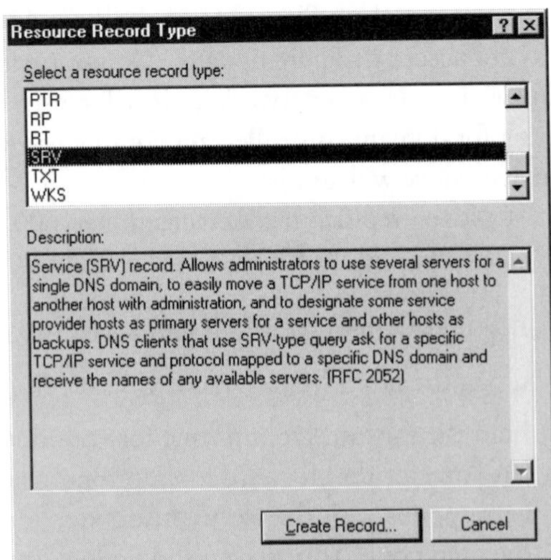

5. Click Create Record. You should see what appears next.

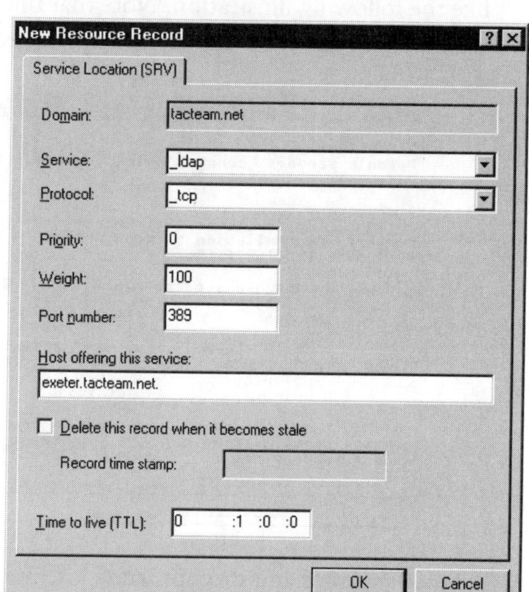

6. In the Service drop-down list, select _ldap, which indicates the service being offered. Other services offered in the list include ftp, nntp, telnet, Kerberos, and more. In the Protocol drop-down list, select _tcp to indicate the transport is TCP. You could also select _udp from the list for UDP transport dependent applications. Add 0 for Priority. Type **100** for weight. Confirm that the Port Number is 389. Then type the FQDN of the machine that will be a domain controller in the Windows 2000 domain. Click OK, and then click Done.
7. Return to the DNS console to confirm that the SRV record was added.
8. Open the Command Prompt. At the Command Prompt, type **nslookup**, and press Enter. Now that you are at the nslookup interactive command prompt, type **set q=srv**, which will set the query to search for SRV records. Press Enter. At the interactive nslookup command prompt, type: **_ldap._tcp.dc._msdcs.<your_domain_name>.**

I used tacteam.net for my domain name. The output should look something like the following illustration. Note that the names and the IP addresses of the domain controllers appear in this screen print.

```
Command Prompt - nslookup

F:\>nslookup
Default Server:  constellation.tacteam.net
Address:  192.168.1.185

> set q=srv
> _ldap._tcp.dc._msdcs.tacteam.net.
Server:  constellation.tacteam.net
Address:  192.168.1.185

_ldap._tcp.dc._msdcs.tacteam.net        SRV service location:
          priority       = 0
          weight         = 100
          port           = 389
          svr hostname   = constellation.tacteam.net
_ldap._tcp.dc._msdcs.tacteam.net        SRV service location:
          priority       = 0
          weight         = 100
          port           = 389
          svr hostname   = exeter.tacteam.net
constellation.tacteam.net       internet address = 192.168.1.185
exeter.tacteam.net      internet address = 192.168.1.186
> _
```

9. Close the Command Prompt, and close the DNS console.

As you can see from this exercise, manually adding the SRV records isn't a lot of fun. This is why Microsoft recommends that you have a Dynamic DNS server on line, or that you install one contemporaneously during the installation of the Active Directory domain services.

Another way to add SRV records that have been lost on domain controllers is to use the netdiag utility. If you open a command prompt and type netdiag /fix, it should reload the entries in the netlogon.dns file. You should confirm this by returning to the DNS console to see if the missing records reappear in the zone.

SCENARIO & SOLUTION

What are the meanings of the *priority* and *weight* values when we are setting up SRV records?	If there are multiple hosts offering the same service in a domain, you can give them different *priority* values. These values can range from 0–65535 with the *lower* value having the higher priority. If two hosts have the same priority value, the DNS client will pick one randomly. If you prefer to have some control over this random choice, you can manipulate the *weight*. This value can vary from 0 to 65535, and the *higher* value is chosen preferentially. One way to remember how this works is: "High priority and heavy weight."
What kind of control do I have over Active Directory integrated zone replication?	Active Directory integrated zones use both intrasite and intersite replication topologies and methodologies as defined for the Active Directory as a whole. Intrasite replication is "event" based, meaning that changes are replicated related to the time a change takes place to the Active Directory (which by default is five minutes). Intersite replication takes place every 15 minutes by default. Both of these values are configurable via the Active Directory.
I am running a mixed Windows 2000 and UNIX DNS environment. Can my Windows 2000 DNS Clients update my UNIX Dynamic DNS servers?	Maybe. There are a number of different Dynamic Update protocols, and your UNIX server may not support GSS (Generic Security Service), which is used by Windows 2000 DNS Servers. If your UNIX DNS servers are not using this protocol, the dynamic updates will fail.

CERTIFICATION OBJECTIVE 3.04

Integrating Windows 2000 DNS Server with DHCP

The Windows 2000 DHCP Server can deliver host name and IP addressing information to a Windows 2000 DNS Server. This added functionality allows even downlevel clients to take advantage of the services available via a Dynamic DNS server.

The Windows 2000 DHCP server interacts with a Windows 2000 DNS Server in one of three ways after assigning a DHCP client an IP address:

- It will update the DNS server by providing information to create a Host (A) resource record and PTR (Pointer) record depending on the DNS client request.
- The DHCP server will update both the Address and the Pointer Record regardless of the client request.
- The DHCP server will never register information about the DHCP client. However, the client itself may contact the Dynamic DNS server directly with this information.

The DCHP/DNS interaction varies with the client operating system receiving the IP addressing information from a DHCP server. The interplay between the Windows 2000 client and Windows 2000 DHCP Server encompasses the following:

- The Windows 2000 client broadcasts a DHCPREQUEST message and receives an IP address. The Windows 2000 client registers its own Address record with the Dynamic DNS server after obtaining a lease. The DHCP server registers the client's PTR record with the DNS server. This is the default behavior for a Windows 2000 client and Windows 2000 DHCP Server.
- Client and server parameters can be manipulated to allow the DHCP server to update both Address and PTR records. If desired, the DHCP server and DCHP client can be configured so that no dynamic updates are made to the DNS server via DHCP.

In a pure Windows 2000 environment, the Windows 2000 DNS client has several options in terms of how its information is registered in the DNS. Downlevel clients are not able to directly update their own records on the DNS server.

However, the DHCP server can act as "proxy" and will forward both Host (A) and PTR information to the DNS server for downlevel clients.

Figure 3-9 shows these interactions.

Windows 2000 computers configured with *static* IP addresses update their own Host (A) and Pointer (PTR) records with the DNS server. If you change the name or IP address of a Windows 2000 client with a static IP address, you can manually update the client's entry in the DDNS server by issuing the command:

```
ipconfig /registerdns
```

The /registerdns switch refreshes all DHCP leases and re-registers DNS names at the DNS server.

Downlevel clients with static IP addresses are not able to communicate directly with the DDNS server. You must manually add the Host (A) and Pointer (PTR) records for these clients.

exam Watch ***If you want the DHCP server to act as a "proxy" for downlevel clients that cannot update their own information with the Windows 2000 DNS Server, you must be sure to use only Windows 2000 DHCP Servers on your network.***

FIGURE 3-9 Windows 2000 DHCP client/server interaction with the DDNS server

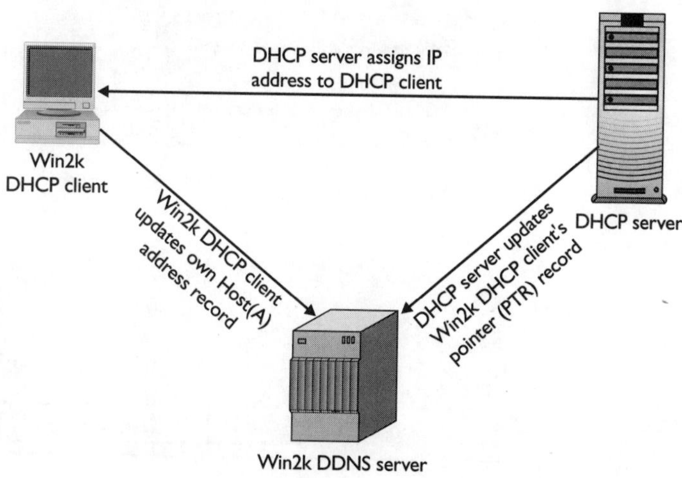

EXERCISE 3-6

Enabling Dynamic Updates for Downlevel DNS/DHCP Clients

In this exercise, you will learn how to enable the Windows 2000 DHCP Server to dynamically update the Host (A) and Pointer (PTR) records on a Dynamic DNS server. By doing so, the DHCP server becomes a Proxy between the downlevel DNS/DHCP client and the DDNS server.

Note: You will not be able to perform this exercise if the Windows 2000 DHCP Server service is not installed. If it is not yet installed, please refer to chapter 4 for information on how to install the Windows 2000 DHCP Server.

Do not perform this exercise on a live, production network without the permission of your network administrator.

1. Log on as Administrator if you have not already done so.
2. Open the DHCP console from the Administrative Tools menu.
3. Expand all nodes in the left pane. Right-click on the name of the server that you want to have dynamically update the DDNS server. Click on the Properties command and then click on the DNS tab in the DHCP server's Properties dialog box. You should see what appears next.

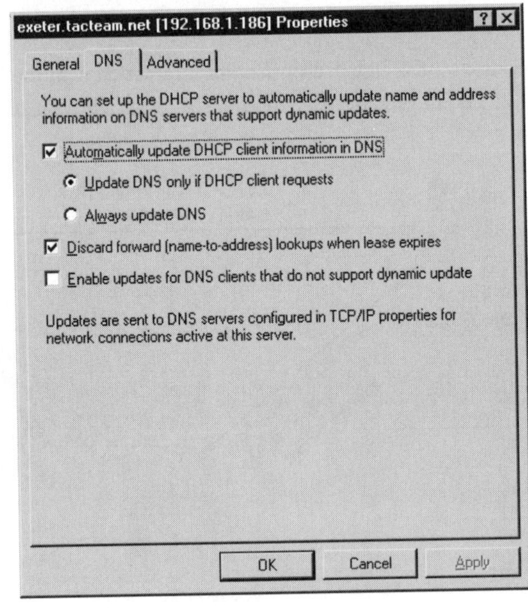

4. To enable dynamic updates for downlevel clients, place a check mark in the check box for "Enable updates for DNS clients that do not support dynamic update." Click OK.

Be aware that if you enable secure dynamic updates and then update the downlevel client to Windows 2000, the upgraded computer will not be able to update any of its records with the DDNS server.

CERTIFICATION OBJECTIVE 3.05

Managing the Windows 2000 DNS Server

Managing the Windows 2000 DNS Server involves a thorough understanding of the DNS console and the dialog boxes and options available to you, the DNS administrator. In this section, we will uncover some of the mysteries of the configuration parameters of the Windows 2000 DNS Server.

Configuring Server Properties

When configuring the Windows 2000 DNS Server properties, you are making decisions about how the entire system, including all zones, functions for that DNS installation. To access the DNS server properties, open the DNS console, and right-click on the name of the server you wish to configure. You should see what appears in Figure 3-10. The first tab you are presented is the Interfaces tabbed properties sheet (henceforth known as "tab").

The DNS Server Properties Interfaces Tab

If you are running a multihomed DNS server, you may wish to exclude an interface from answering DNS queries. Perhaps the server is used for other purposes, such as a file server. You may have added a second network interface card that you use exclusively for high-speed backups on a separate segment. You would not want other network traffic on the interface you use for the backups. In this case, you would select the "Only the following IP addresses" option and add the IP address of the interface that you want to answer the queries in the text box.

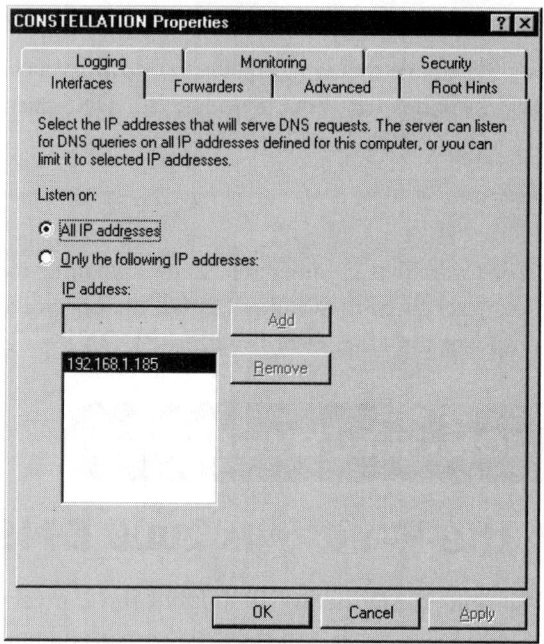

FIGURE 3-10 The Interfaces tab on the DNS server's Properties dialog box

The DNS Server Properties Forwarders Tab

Click on the Forwarders tab and you will see what appears in Figure 3-11.

If you choose to use a forwarder, you would place a check mark in the "Enable forwarders" check box. Then enter the IP address of the forwarder in the text box under "**IP address:**". If you wish to make the machine a slave server that does not perform recursion, place a check mark in the "Do not use recursion" check box.

The DNS Server Properties Advanced Tab

Click the Advanced tab and you will see what appears in Figure 3-12.

There are some pretty obscure entries on the Advanced tab, so pay close attention. Hey, didn't we see the "Disable recursion" option somewhere else? Yes, and if you place a check mark in the box located on the Advanced tab, it will have the same effect. Think of it as getting another chance in life.

The "BIND secondaries" option is selected if you have BIND secondaries that do not support the *fast transfer* we spoke about earlier. Versions of BIND prior to 4.9.4 do not support the fast transfer, so if you have any of these, you should put a check mark in the "BIND secondaries" check box.

FIGURE 3-11

The Forwarders tab

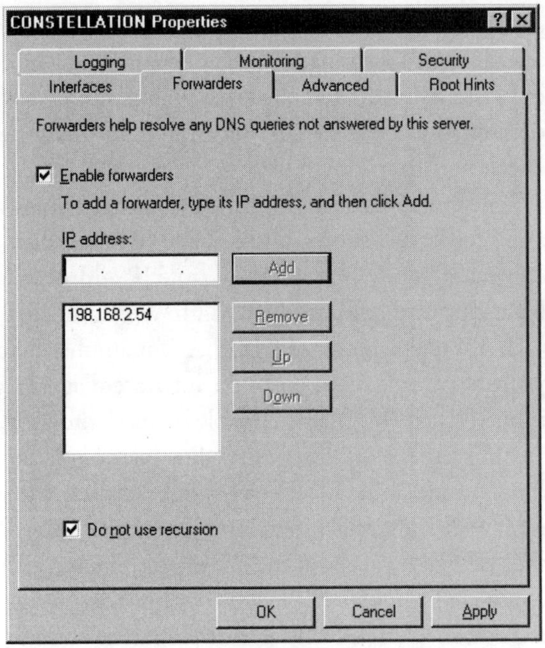

CONSTELLATION Properties
Logging
Monitoring
Security
Interfaces
Forwarders
Advanced
Root Hints
Forwarders help resolve any DNS queries not answered by this server.
Enable forwarders
To add a forwarder, type its IP address, and then click Add.
IP address:
Add
198.168.2.54
Remove
Up
Down
Do not use recursion
OK
Cancel
Apply

FIGURE 3-12

The Advanced tab

CONSTELLATION Properties
Logging
Monitoring
Security
Interfaces
Forwarders
Advanced
Root Hints
Server version number:
5.0 49664 (0xc200)
Server options:
Disable recursion
BIND secondaries
Fail on load if bad zone data
Enable round robin
Enable netmask ordering
Secure cache against pollution
Name checking:
Multibyte (UTF8)
Load zone data on startup:
From Active Directory and registry
Enable automatic scavenging of stale records
Scavenging period:
7
days
Reset to Default
OK
Cancel
Apply

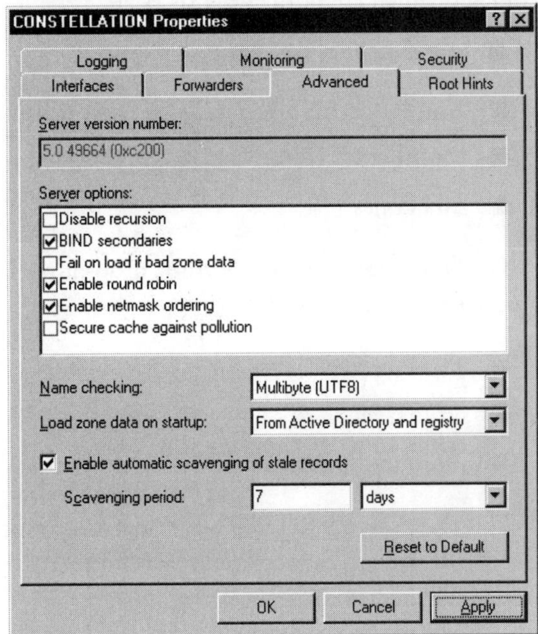

If you want the zone database file to load only if there are no faulty records in it, select the "Fail on load if bad zone data." If you don't select this option, the zone database will load and the error will be noted in the DNS log. Data will be determined as bad or not, depending on the options you selected in the "Name checking:" drop-down list box.

The "Enable round robin" option determines whether the DNS server rotates and reorders a list of multiple Host (A) records if a queried host name is for a computer configured with multiple IP addresses. *Round robin* is useful for load balancing and commonly used for Web and Proxy servers.

If a machine sends a DNS query for another machine that is multihomed, you probably want to connect to the interface that is located on your own subnet, if there is one. When you enable "Enable netmask ordering," this is exactly what you get.

Sometimes a DNS server sending back a referral will include "extra" information. For example, if the DNS server begins an iterative query process for stuff.microsoft.com, it may get additional referrals for msn.com. This is enabled by default because it allows the cache to learn about the namespace in a more timely fashion. However, this is considered *pollution* of the DNS cache. You can disable cache pollution by selecting the option "Secure cache against pollution."

The "Name Checking" drop-down list box is used to determine which names are valid and which are not. The choices are

- Strict RFC (ANSI)
- Non RFC (ANSI)
- Multibyte (UTF8)
- All Names

The "Load zone data on startup" drop-down list box allows you to choose to load the zone information from:

- The Registry
- From a file
- From the Active Directory and Registry

The Windows 2000 DNS Server defaults to booting from the Active Directory and the Registry. This accommodates both Active Directory integrated and Standard zones.

Scavenging is the process of removing stale entries from the zone. The default setting is not to allow scavenging from the DNS database. Scavenging can be set on a per-server or per-zone basis. The details of the scavenging process are beyond the scope of this book, and will be covered in detail in the *MCSE Designing a Windows 2000 Network Infrastructure Study Guide (Exam 70-221).*

The Root Hints Tab

Click on the Root Hints tab and you will see what appears in Figure 3-13.

The Root Hints tab displays servers that can be used to answer authoritatively for servers that are authoritative for *non-root* zones. For example, a non-root zone could be a subzone of the microsoft.com zone, such as sales.microsoft.com. The DNS servers authoritative for the sales.microsoft.com zone use the root hints in the process of performing iterative queries. It gives them a "leg up" in the process of learning about the DNS namespace.

For example, suppose a DNS server DAEDALUS has a zone called west.tacteam.net. In the process of answering a query for a higher-level domain, such as the tacteam.net domain, DAEDALUS needs some assistance to locate an authoritative server for this domain, which in this case is CONSTELLATION.

FIGURE 3-13

The DNS Server Properties Root Hints tab

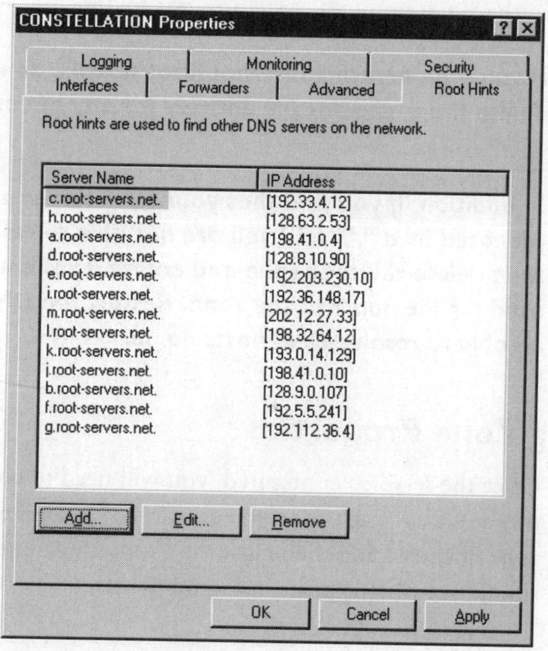

CONSTELLATION Properties

Logging | Monitoring | Security
Interfaces | Forwarders | Advanced | Root Hints

Root hints are used to find other DNS servers on the network.

Server Name	IP Address
c.root-servers.net.	[192.33.4.12]
h.root-servers.net.	[128.63.2.53]
a.root-servers.net.	[198.41.0.4]
d.root-servers.net.	[128.8.10.90]
e.root-servers.net.	[192.203.230.10]
i.root-servers.net.	[192.36.148.17]
m.root-servers.net.	[202.12.27.33]
l.root-servers.net.	[198.32.64.12]
k.root-servers.net.	[193.0.14.129]
j.root-servers.net.	[198.41.0.10]
b.root-servers.net.	[128.9.0.107]
f.root-servers.net.	[192.5.5.241]
g.root-servers.net.	[192.112.36.4]

Add... Edit... Remove

OK Cancel Apply

In order for DAEDALUS to find CONSTELLATION, or any other servers that are authoritative for the tacteam.net domain, it needs to be able to send a DNS query to the Root servers for the DNS namespace (with tacteam.net being the root in this example). The Root servers can then refer DAEDALUS to the authoritative servers for the .com domain. The servers for the .net domain can, in turn, offer referral to CONSTELLATION or other servers that are authoritative for the tacteam.net domain.

How to Use the Root Hints Tab In order to use the Root Hints properly, you need to make a few assessments:

- Will you be using DNS to resolve internal host names?
- Will you be using DNS to resolve external host names?
- Is the server used as a Root server?

Resolving Internet Host Names If the DNS server will be resolving names for Internet hosts, you must have the names and IP addresses of the Internet Root servers. The cache.dns file, which is included with your DNS server installation, provides the names and addresses of the Internet Root servers. This file is stored in the %systemroot%\system32\dns folder.

exam Watch

If you are operating internal Root servers, do not use root hints. Instead, delete the cache.dns file entirely for any of your Root servers.

In addition, if you find that your DNS server only has a "root" zone installed (denoted by a ".") and you are not able to resolve Internet DNS host names, then delete the root zone and create a zone with your internal namespace used for the name of the zone. Restart the DNS Server service and you should be able to resolve DNS hosts name.

Configuring Zone Properties

Once the server is configured, you will need to configure the zones you have created on the server. Each zone you create can be configured separately. Right-click on the zone of choice and then click the Properties command on the context menu. You should see what appears in Figure 3-14.

FIGURE 3-14

The Zone Properties dialog box General tab

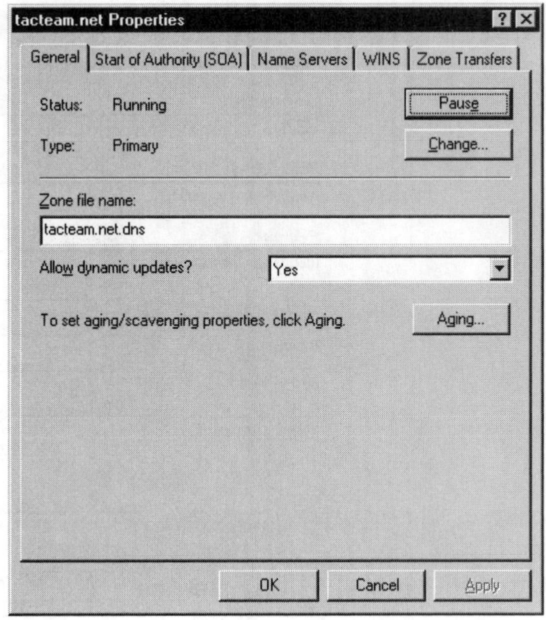

The first tab you are presented with is the General tab. If you are making changes to the server and you do not want any additional connections to it while you are working, click Pause. This will not disconnect any existing connections to the DNS server.

You can change the *type* of zone by clicking Change. Your choices are Primary, Secondary, and Active Directory integrated. Note that you cannot choose "Active Directory integrated" unless you are running the DNS server on a domain controller.

In the "Allow dynamic updates?" drop-down list box you can choose among Yes, No, or "Only secure updates." The latter is only available on DNS servers running on domain controllers and the zone is Active Directory integrated.

Aging is used to control the scavenging properties for the zone. We will go over scavenging in detail in the *Designing a Windows 2000 Network Infrastructure Study Guide.*

The Start of Authority (SOA) Tab

Click on the Start of Authority (SOA) tab and you will see what appears in Figure 3-15.

The "Serial number" text box tells you what the current serial number is for the zone. If for some reason you want to increment the serial number, you can click Increment.

FIGURE 3-15

The Start of Authority tab on the Zone Properties dialog box

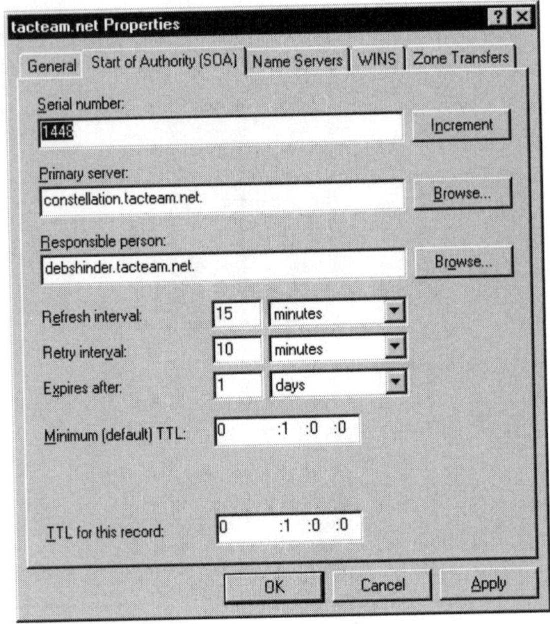

You might want to manually increment the serial number in order to force all Secondaries to download the zone database.

The "Primary server" text box contains the name of the DNS server that is Primary for the zone. If you want to change the name, you can type it in or click Browse and locate it via the GUI. The "Responsible person" is typically the DNS administrator who manages the zone. This is the e-mail address of that person, and the username and domain name are separated by a period rather than an @ sign.

"Refresh interval:" determines how often the Secondary will call a Primary to check for zone updates. "Retry interval:" is the amount of time a Secondary will wait after an unsuccessful refresh attempt. Be sure to make the refresh interval longer than the retry interval!

The "Expires after:" interval determines how long the Secondary can go without being about to update its zone data from a Primary before considering its zone data invalid. For example, if the Primary went down 25 hours ago and the expiration interval for the zone is 24 hours, the Secondary will no longer answer queries for the zone. This is because after the expiration interval has passed, the Secondary assumes that the zone data is no longer valid, and will not hand out potentially invalid DNS replies.

FIGURE 3-16

The Name Servers tab on the Zone Properties dialog box

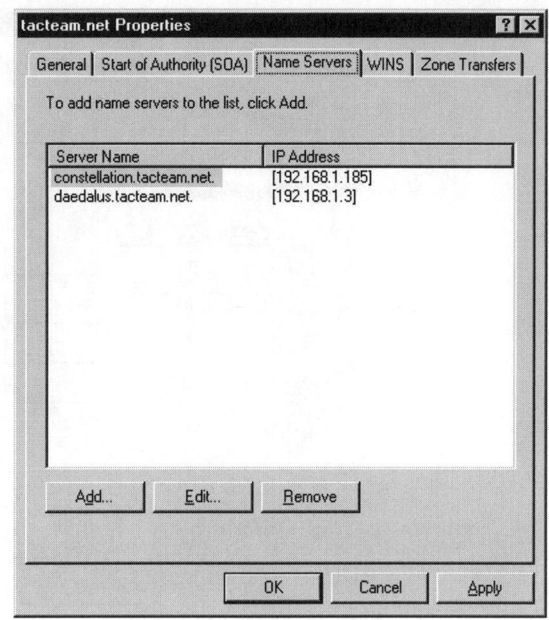

"Minimum (default) TTL:" determines the time-to-live for all records in the zone. Note that this is the *default* TTL for all records; you can assign TTLs more granularly by giving individual records their own TTL. "TTL for this record:" allows you just this sort of granular control over the TTL. However, since the SOA record is a resource record in its own right, you have the opportunity to change its TTL here.

The Name Servers Tab

Click on the Name Servers tab and you will see what appears in Figure 3-16.

The Name Servers tab allows you to manually add and remove the names of servers that are authoritative for the zone. This includes the Primary and all Secondaries in Standard DNS zones. These machines all require NS resource records. If you find that a server with an NS record does not enter itself onto this list, you must enter it manually. Also, if you manually enter a server onto this list, you will need an NS record for that server included in the zone.

The WINS Tab

Click on the WINS tab. You will see what appears in Figure 3-17.

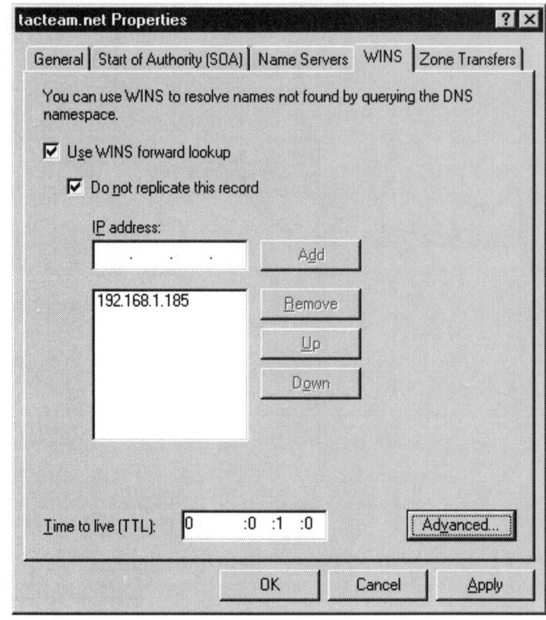

FIGURE 3-17 The WINS tab on the Zone Properties dialog box

The Windows 2000 DDNS Server can query a WINS server before finally giving up on a query. The WINS server is not queried until the DNS server confirms that it does not have a record for the host in any of its zones, and the results of iterative queries have failed.

You enabled WINS forward lookups by placing a check mark in the "Use WINS forward lookup" check box. Check the "Do not replicate this record" checkbox if you have downlevel DNS servers that are not Windows NT 4.0 or Windows 2000 DNS servers. Add the IP address of the WINS server you want the DNS server to query in the "IP address:" text box, and then click Add. You can also adjust the TTL on WINS lookups in the "Time to live (TTL):" text box.

The WINS tab looks a little different for reverse lookup zones. Right-click on one of your reverse lookup zones and click Properties, and then click on the WINS-R tab. You will see what appears in Figure 3-18.

A Windows 2000 DNS Server can also query a WINS server for reverse lookups if the standard DNS-centric approach is unsuccessful. To enable the server to perform reverse WINS lookups, place a check mark in the "Use WINS-R lookup:" checkbox. If you have Secondaries that are not Windows 2000 or Windows NT 4.0 DNS servers, place a check mark in the "Do not replicate this record" check box to prevent errors in zone transfer with those downlevel DNS servers.

FIGURE 3-18

The WINS-R tab in the Reverse Lookup Zone's Properties dialog box

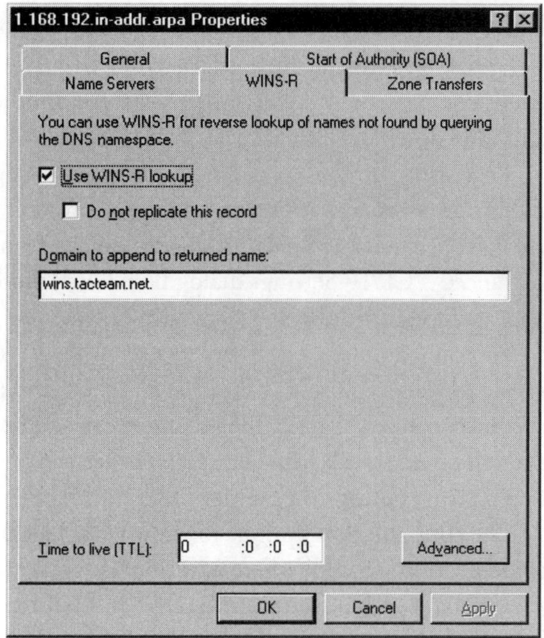

In the "Domain to append to returned name:" text box, place the domain name that you want appended to reverse WINS queries. This is important since security and network monitoring/inventory software will use this domain name when performing WINS reverse lookups.

Microsoft recommends that you enable only a single zone to answer forward WINS lookups and to designate that zone in the WINS-R record. This prevents confusion related to the domain location of clients that were located via WINS queries. See the *Designing a Windows 2000 Network Infrastructure Study Guide* ***for more details.***

Configuring Windows 2000 DNS Clients

You can configure your DNS clients in two ways:

- Manually
- Via Dynamic Host Configuration Protocol (DHCP)

The easier and less error-prone approach is to let the DHCP server hand out the relevant IP addressing information. We will take a look at both approaches in this section.

Manually Configuring DNS Client Settings

You must be sitting at the local machine to perform manual configuration. Right-click on the My Network Places icon on the desktop and select Properties, and then double-click on Local Area Connection and then click Properties.

This brings up the Local Area Connection Properties dialog box. Scroll down the list of network components, find the Internet Protocol (TCP/IP) option, and click Properties. Then click Advanced on the General tab. This brings you to the Advanced TCP/IP Settings dialog box. Click on the DNS tab and you will see what appears in Figure 3-19.

You can add more DNS servers to your DNS server search list in the "DNS server addresses, in order of use" area. Click Add to add more DNS servers. If the top entry is not available, the second entry will be contacted and will be moved to the top of the search list. The search order can be changed by using the up and down arrow buttons on the right side of the DNS servers list.

The configuration options for how to handle unqualified DNS queries are underneath the region where additional servers are added. The option "Append primary and connection specific DNS suffixes" refers to what DNS *suffixes* should be included in a request to a DNS server if an *unqualified* DNS query is issued to the DNS server.

FIGURE 3-19

The DNS tab in the Advanced TCP/IP Setting Properties dialog box

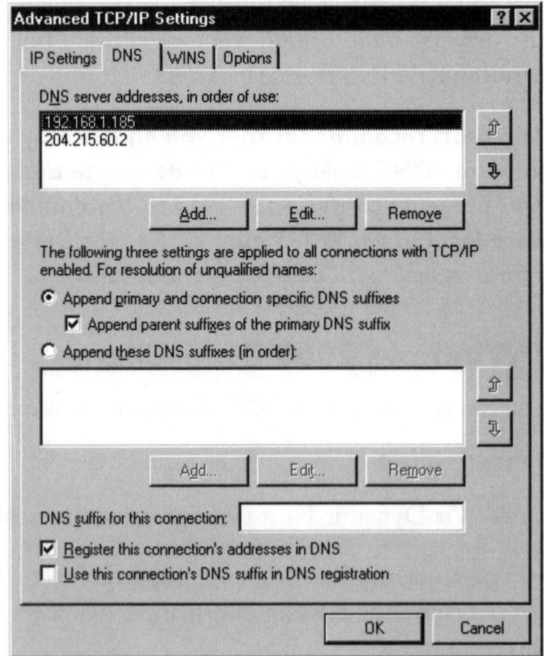

Issuing an Unqualified Request For example, if you were to type *http://constellation* in the address bar of your Web browser, you would be issuing an unqualified request. This is because no domain name is included in the request, just a host name. A DNS server must receive an FQDN in order to process a DNS query. The *Primary suffix* is the computer's domain membership included in the Network Identification tab of the System Properties dialog box, as seen in Figure 3-20.

The "Append parent suffixes of the primary DNS suffix" option specifies whether resolution for unqualified names issued by the computer includes the parent suffixes of the primary DNS suffix up to the second-level domain. This is sometimes referred to as *devolution* of the DNS query.

For example, your primary DNS suffix is dev.west.tacteam.net. You type **ping xyz** at a Windows 2000 command prompt. The first FQDN sent in the DNS query will be xyz.dev.west.tacteam.net. If this fails, Windows 2000 will query for xyz.west.tacteam.net, and if that fails, it will query for xyz.tacteam.net. Devolution will not extend past the second-level domain name.

If you choose "Append these DNS suffixes (in order)," you can configure a customized set of domain names to append to DNS queries. Click Add to add DNS suffixes to the list. One situation where you might wish to add your own DNS suffixes to the list is when you are deploying special *WINS referral* zones. When and how you configure these special zones is discussed in the *Designing a Windows 2000 Network Infrastructure Study Guide.*

FIGURE 3-20

The System Properties dialog box

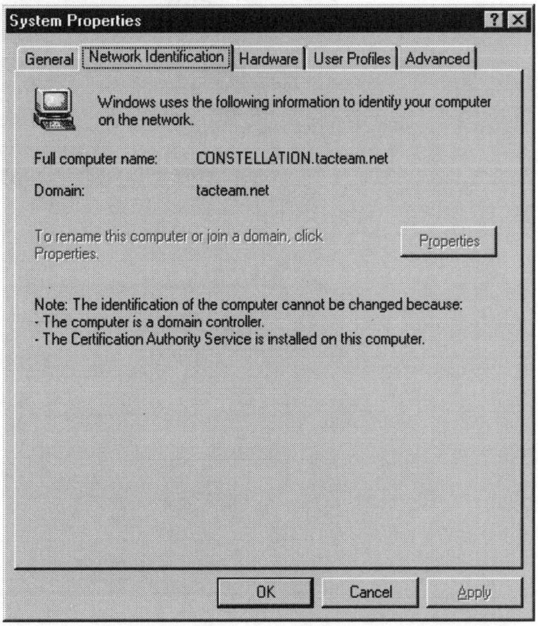

The Windows 2000 DNS client by default registers its own Host (A) address records with the Primary DDNS server for its zone. The "Register this connection's addresses in DNS" is selected by default. The domain name for this registration is defined in the System Properties dialog box. If you uncheck this box and the DNS client is also a DHCP client, the DHCP server will register both the Host (A) and Pointer (PTR) records for the host on the Dynamic DNS server.

Connection-specific domain name registrations can be made as well. By default, each connection-specific DNS suffix is also registered with the DNS server. You can prevent this by removing the check mark from that option.

Configuring DNS Clients Using DHCP

You can avoid a lot of administrative hassle by using a DHCP server to assign DNS configuration information to your Windows 2000 DHCP clients.

You must first create a scope on the DHCP server. After creating the scope, you need to define the 006 DNS server's option for the scope. When configuring your DNS server scope option, consider the placement of your DNS server. Ideally, you want the DHCP client to use a DNS server closest to it, and preferably on its own segment or subnet.

Figure 3-21 shows the Scope Options dialog box on a DHCP server. Note that you can include an entire DNS server search list in the 006 DNS server's option.

FIGURE 3-21 The Scope Options dialog box

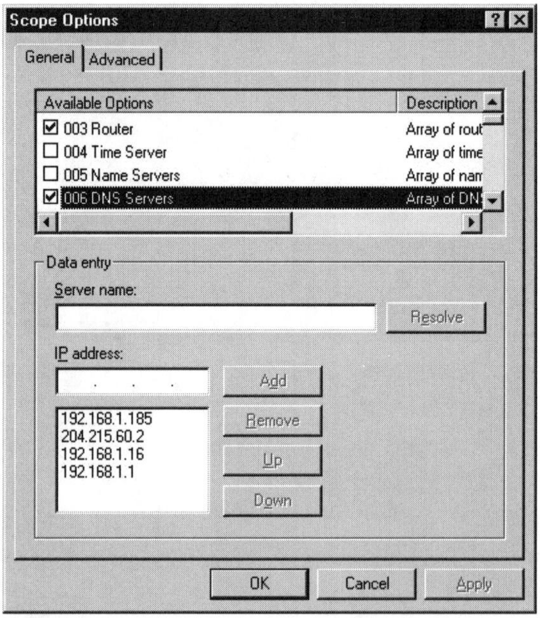

SCENARIO & SOLUTION

What is this "WINS Referral Zone" you mentioned? Is it something I need?	A WINS Referral Zone is usually a forward lookup zone that has no resource records in it. After creating the WINS Referral Zone, you disable WINS Referral for all other zones. After you have done this, any queries that are resolved via WINS are returned with the FQDN that contains the NetBIOS name returned from the WINS server with the WINS Referral Zone's domain name appended to it. In this way, it is easy to identify what queries have been resolved via WINS lookups.
What happens when I use Windows NT 4.0 DHCP servers for my Windows 2000 clients?	The Windows NT 4.0 DHCP Server cannot update the Dynamic DNS server. If you require the DHCP server to update the DDNS server, then you must use the Windows 2000 DHCP Server.
How often do I need to update the cache.dns file?	Not very often. The current implementation of the cache.dns file is circa 1997. Those Internet Root servers don't change much.

EXERCISE 3-7

Disabling Replication of WINS-Specific Resource Record Data

In this exercise, you will disable replication of WINS Resource record-related data in order to allow smooth integration with downlevel BIND servers.

1. Open the DNS console from the Administrative Tools menu.
2. Expand all nodes in the left pane. Right-click on one of the forward lookup zones and click Properties.
3. On the zone's Properties sheet, click on the WINS tab. Place a checkmark in the "Do not replicate this record" check box. Click OK.
4. Close the DNS console.

CERTIFICATION OBJECTIVE 3.06

Monitoring and Troubleshooting DNS

In this section, we will cover some important tools and techniques that you can use to monitor and troubleshoot your DNS configuration. The Windows 2000 DNS Server service works very well, once you have it configured correctly. However, there will be times when things go awry, and you must be ready for those circumstances.

IPCONFIG

If you are a seasoned Windows NT 4.0 professional, you know all about the ipconfig command. However, you should know that ipconfig has been improved in Windows 2000. Ipconfig includes new switches that increase its usefulness beyond a great tool for getting IP addressing information about your machines.

The Windows 2000 ipconfig utility includes three new switches that help in DNS management:

- **ipconfig /flushdns** The flushdns switch allows you to clear the local machine's DNS cache. When you make zone changes or machine IP address configuration changes and then do an nslookup, you may receive information that doesn't reflect the changes you thought you made. This is because the information is being retrieved from cache rather than from the DNS server itself. Use the flushdns switch to clear the cache, and then repeat the nslookup you were doing before.
- **ipconfig /displaydns** The displaydns switch prints out the local DNS cache. This is particularly helpful to use after you have completed the flushdns command, to confirm that the cache is indeed empty. The displaydns switch allows you to see the entries in the host file loaded into the cache.
- **ipconfig /registerdns** The registerdns switch will renew a DHCP client's lease and re-register the DNS client's address information with a DNS server. This is sometimes helpful in "reminding" the DNS server of the DNS clients' addressing information.

The ipconfig utility that was so helpful in Windows NT 4.0 has become even more so in Windows 2000. Use it early and often!

NSLOOKUP

Nslookup is a command-line utility that allows you to test and query your DNS server's zone databases. Nslookup works in two modes: *interactive mode* and *command mode.* Command mode is used when you only want to do a single query. For example, if you type the command:

```
nslookup exeter.tacteam.net.
```

you'll get the following output:

```
Server: constellation.tacteam.net
Address: 192.168.1.185

Name:    exeter.tacteam.net
Address: 192.168.1.186
```

Notice that we are returned to the command prompt when the lookup is completed. If you plan on doing a number of nslookup queries, you should use interactive mode. To enter interactive mode, just type **nslookup** at the command prompt. Your output should look like this:

```
C:\>nslookup
Default Server: constellation.tacteam.net
Address: 192.168.1.185
```

Observe that you are not returned to the command prompt, but to the nslookup command's *interactive prompt.* Once you enter interactive mode, you can use the "set" commands to determine the nature of your queries. Some of the "set" commands are listed in Table 3-1. When you're ready to leave interactive mode and return to the command prompt, just type **exit** at the interactive mode command prompt.

The d2 option gives you the most information about the query you're performing. If you want the benefits of debug mode while still in command mode, you can issue nslookup using –ds switch. For example, type the command:

```
nslookup -ds www.microsoft.com.
```

You get detailed information about the query with the –ds switch.

exam Watch

When you do an nslookup, be aware that the most likely reason that you might receive a "non-authoritative" answer to a query is because your DNS server is answering from cache.

TABLE 3-1

Selected "set" Commands that Are Used in Interactive Mode

Command	Description
all	Prints out a list of current options and server parameters
[no]debug	Prints out detailed information from the lookup
[no]d2	Prints out "exhaustive" debugging information
[no]defname	Appends a specific domain name to each query
[no]recurse	Asks for recursion for the query
[no]search	Uses the domain suffix search list
[no]vc	Always use a virtual circuit
domain=NAME	Allows you to set a default domain name for the lookup
root=NAME	Defines the name of the Root server to use for lookup
retry=X	Defines the number of retries for the lookup
timeout=X	Defines the timeout for the lookup
type=X	Defines the Query Type. For example: ANY,CNAME,MX,NS,PTR,SOA,SRV

You should become well versed in the use of the nslookup command. It is an extremely useful and powerful tool for troubleshooting your DNS server.

EXERCISE 3-8

Using the Nslookup Utility

In order to complete this exercise, you must be connected to the Internet via a dial-up connection or via your network. If a firewall is implemented on your network, it must support passing nslookup queries.

1. Log on as Administrator if you have not already done so.
2. Open a command prompt.

3. At the command prompt, type:

   nslookup

   Then press ENTER.
4. Note that the command prompt changes its appearance to that of the nslookup interactive prompt. At the interactive prompt, type:

   set debug

   Then press ENTER.
5. Note that the command prompt doesn't change its appearance. That's OK, since it doesn't give you any feedback after you set one of the nslookup options. At the interactive command prompt, type:

   www.syngress.com

   Then press ENTER.
6. Note the detailed information you receive. Here's a question: What is the "actual" name of the server for www.syngress.com? Check the Web site for the answer!

Using the System Monitor

When you install the Windows 2000 DNS Server, it will place a large number of DNS-related counters into the System Monitor application. Many new counters have been added to the Windows 2000 DNS Object counter list. Table 3-2 lists these counters and their functions.

The system monitor allows you to draw a fine bead on the activities of your DNS installation. There is a counter that will aid you in troubleshooting and baselining just about any situation you might run into.

TABLE 3-2 DNS Performance Counters

Counter	Description
AXFR Request Received	Total full zone transfer requests received by the Master DNS server
AXFR Request Sent	Total full zone transfer requests sent by the Secondary DNS server
AXFR Response Received	Total full zone transfer responses received by the Secondary DNS server
AXFR Success Received	Total successful full zone transfers received by the Secondary DNS server
AXFR Success Sent	Total successful full zone transfers of the Master DNS server
Caching Memory	Total amount of caching memory used by the DNS server
Database Node Memory	Total database node memory used by the DNS server
Dynamic Update NoOperation	Total number No-operation/empty dynamic update requests received by the DNS server
Dynamic Update NoOperation/sec	Rate at which No-operation/empty dynamic update requests are received by the DNS server
Dynamic Update Queued	Total dynamic updates that are queued by the DNS server
Dynamic Update Received	Total dynamic update requests that are received by the DNS server
Dynamic Update Received/sec	Rate at which dynamic update requests are received by the DNS server
Dynamic Update Rejected	Total dynamic updates rejected by the DNS server
Dynamic Update TimeOuts	Total dynamic update timeouts of the DNS server
Dynamic Update Written to Database	Total dynamic updates written to the database by the DNS server
Dynamic Update Written to Database/sec	Rate at which dynamic updates are written to the database by the DNS server

TABLE 3-2 DNS Performance Counters *(continued)*

Counter	Description
IXFR Request Received	Total incremental zone transfer requests received by the Master DNS server
IXFR Request Sent	Total incremental zone transfer requests sent by the Secondary DNS server
IXFR Response Received	Total incremental zone transfer responses received by the Secondary DNS server
IXFR Success Received	Total successful incremental zone transfers received by the Secondary DNS server
IXFR Success Sent	Total successful incremental zone transfers of the Master DNS server
IXFR TCP Success Received	Total successful TCP incremental zone transfers received by the Secondary DNS server
IXFR UDP Success Received	Total successful UDP incremental zone transfers received by the Secondary DNS server
Nbstat Memory	Total Nbstat memory used by the DNS server
Notify Received	Total notifies received by the Secondary DNS server
Notify Sent	Total notifies sent by the Master DNS server
Record Flow Memory	Total record flow memory used by the DNS server
Recursive Queries	Total recursive queries received by the DNS server
Recursive Queries/sec	Rate recursive queries are received by the DNS server
Recursive Query Failure	Total of recursive query failures
Recursive Query Failure/sec	Rate of recursive query failures
Recursive Send TimeOuts	Total of recursive query sending timeouts
Recursive TimeOut/sec	Rate recursive query sending timeouts
Secure Update Failure	Total secure update failures of the DNS server

TABLE 3-2 DNS Performance Counters *(continued)*

Counter	Description
Secure Update Received	Total secure update requests received by the DNS server
Secure Update Received/sec	Rate at which secure update requests are received by the DNS server
TCP Message Memory	Total TCP message memory used by the DNS server
TCP Query Received	Total TCP queries received by the DNS server
TCP Query Received/sec	Rate TCP queries are received by the DNS server
TCP Response Sent	Total TCP responses sent by the DNS server
TCP Response Sent/sec	Rate TCP responses are sent by the DNS server
Total Query Received	Total queries received by the DNS server
Total Query Received/sec	Rate queries are received by the DNS server
Total Response Sent	Total responses sent by the DNS server
Total Response Sent/sec	Rate responses are sent by the DNS server
UDP Message Memory	Total UDP message memory used by the DNS server
UDP Query Received	Total UDP queries received by the DNS server
UDP Query Received/sec	Rate UDP queries are received by the DNS server
UDP Response Sent	Total UDP responses sent by the DNS server
UDP Response Sent/sec	Rate UDP responses are sent by the DNS server
WINS Lookup Received	Total WINS lookup requests received by the DNS server
WINS Lookup Received/sec	Rate WINS lookup requests are received by the DNS server

TABLE 3-2 DNS Performance Counters *(continued)*

Counter	Description
WINS Response Sent	Total WINS lookup responses sent by the DNS server
WINS Response Sent/sec	Rate WINS lookup responses are sent by the server
WINS Reverse Lookup Received	Total WINS reverse lookup requests received by the DNS server
WINS Reverse Lookup Received/sec	Rate WINS reverse lookup requests are received by the DNS server
WINS Reverse Response Sent	Total WINS reverse lookup responses sent by the DNS server
WINS Reverse Response Sent/sec	Rate WINS reverse lookup responses are sent by the server
Zone Transfer Failure	Total failed zone transfers of the Master DNS server
Zone Transfer Request Received	Total zone transfer requests received by the Master DNS server
Zone Transfer SOA Request Sent	Total zone transfer start of authority (SOA) requests sent by the Secondary DNS server
Zone Transfer Success	Total successful zone transfers of the Master DNS server

Using Event Viewer

The Windows 2000 Event Viewer has a dedicated log for DNS-specific information. The Event Viewer can provide you information on when zone transfers have taken place, if there was a problem with a zone transfer, when changes have taken place within the zone, or even report that an excessive number of changes have occurred to the zone for a specific period of time.

Since the Event Viewer is easy to access and doesn't require configuration changes on your part, it is often wise to start there and see if it supplies any clues to any type of DNS-related problem you might have.

The Event View will often return cryptic error message numbers. The Windows 2000 Server Resource Kit has a help file that you can install on your computer that has very large and useful list of event codes and what they mean.

Using Trace Logs

The Windows 2000 DNS Server allows you to enable trace logging via the GUI interface if you require extremely detailed information about the DNS server's activities. The information gathered in the trace is saved to a text file on the local hard disk. A trace log can track all queries received and answered by the DNS server.

To enable trace logging, right-click on the server name in the DNS Management Console and click Properties. Click on the Logging tab, and you will see a dialog box similar to that in Figure 3-22.

exam Watch

Trace logging can be a very processor- and disk-intensive procedure, so be judicious in your use of this feature.

The logs are stored in a plain text file located at:

```
%system_root%\system32\dns\dns.log
```

Note that problems with trace logging observed in beta versions of the Windows 2000 DNS Server appear to continue with the final release version. You may find trace logging unreliable when attempting to perform traces on your own servers.

FIGURE 3-22

Configuring trace logging for the DNS server

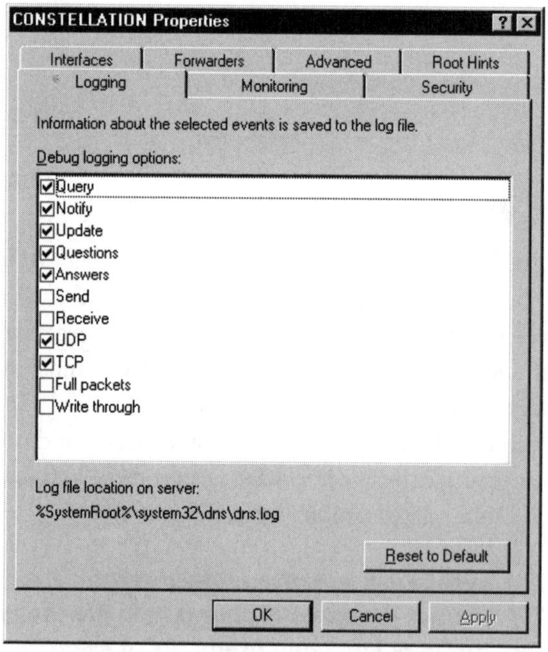

Network Monitor

The Network Monitor included "in the box" of the Windows 2000 Server products allows you to analyze packets coming to and leaving the server running the Network Monitor application.

exam **Watch**

If you want a "full-fledged" version of Network Monitor that allows you to listen to all traffic on the segment, you can purchase Microsoft Systems Management Server 2.0.

Network Monitor will allow you to identify problems with network communications, including the details of the DNS query frames. Figure 3-23 displays the Network Monitor screen after a capture of DNS frames has been done.

Something to focus on when analyzing a DNS message is the message identifier, which is the first value you see on the Description line. For example, look at frames 376 and 377. Each of those has at the beginning of the description line "0x174E," which is the query identifier. You can use this number to track related queries and responses.

FIGURE 3-23

Capture of DNS packets in Microsoft Network Monitor

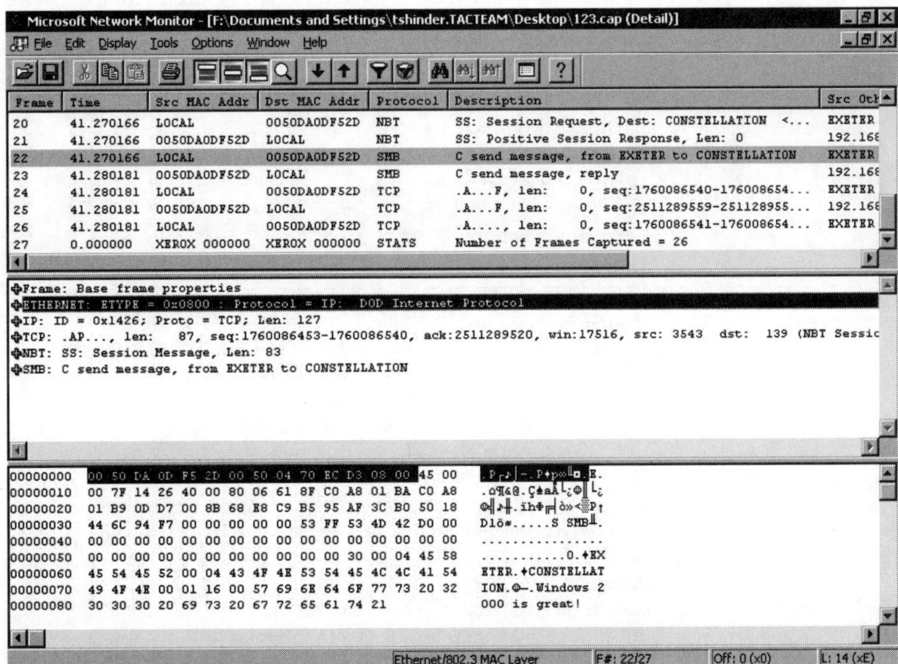

If there is a packet of particular interest—for example, a failure message is returned by the server—you can select the frame in the top pane and then click the Edit menu and then Copy. Open Notepad or another text editor and paste the contents of the frame into the application. For example, after copying packet 377 into Notepad, we see:

```
377 23.543854 LOCAL 0050DA62684E DNS 0x174E:Std Qry Resp.
www.dallasnews.com. of type Canonical name on class INET addr. CONSTELLATION
DAEDALUS IP
Frame: Base frame properties
    Frame: Time of capture = 1/1/2000 11:48:1
    Frame: Time delta from previous physical frame: 0 microseconds
    Frame: Frame number: 377
    Frame: Total frame length: 108 bytes
    Frame: Capture frame length: 108 bytes
    Frame: Frame data: Number of data bytes remaining = 108 (0x006C)
ETHERNET: ETYPE = 0x0800 : Protocol = IP: DOD Internet Protocol
    ETHERNET: Destination address : 0050DA62684E
        ETHERNET: .......0 = Individual address
        ETHERNET: ......0. = Universally administered address
    ETHERNET: Source address : 0050DA0DF52D
        ETHERNET: .......0 = No routing information present
        ETHERNET: ......0. = Universally administered address
    ETHERNET: Frame Length : 108 (0x006C)
    ETHERNET: Ethernet Type : 0x0800 (IP:  DOD Internet Protocol)
    ETHERNET: Ethernet Data: Number of data bytes remaining = 94 (0x005E)
IP: ID = 0x6A65; Proto = UDP; Len: 94
    IP: Version = 4 (0x4)
    IP: Header Length = 20
    IP: Precedence = Routine
    IP: Type of Service = Normal Service
    IP: Total Length = 94 (
    IP: Identification = 27237 (0x6A65)
    IP: Flags Summary = 0 (0x0)
        IP: .......0 = Last fragment in datagram
        IP: ......0. = May fragment datagram if necessary
    IP: Fragment Offset = 0 (0x0) bytes
    IP: Time to Live = 128 (0x80)
    IP: Protocol = UDP - User Datagram
    IP: Checksum = 0x4C1D
    IP: Source Address = 192.168.1.185
    IP: Destination Address = 192.168.1.3
    IP: Data: Number of data bytes remaining = 74 (0x004A)
UDP: Src Port: DNS, (53); Dst Port: Unknown (1068); Length = 74 (0x4A)
    UDP: Source Port = DNS
    UDP: Destination Port = 0x042C
    UDP: Total length = 74 (0x4A) bytes
    UDP: UDP Checksum = 0x2
    UDP: Data: Number of data bytes remaining = 66 (0x0042)
```

```
DNS: 0x174E:Std Qry Resp. for www.dallasnews.com. of type Canonical name on
class INET addr.
    DNS: Query Identifier = 5966 (0x174E)
    DNS: DNS Flags = Response, OpCode - Std Qry, RD RA Bits Set, RCode
error
        DNS: 1............... = Response
        DNS: .0000........... = Standard Query
        DNS: .....0.......... = Server not authority for
        DNS: ......0......... = Message complete
        DNS: .......1........ = Recursive query desired
        DNS: ........1....... = Recursive queries supported by server
        DNS: .........000.... = Reserved
        DNS: ............0000 = No error
    DNS: Question Entry Count = 1 (0x1)
    DNS: Answer Entry Count = 2 (0x2)
    DNS: Name Server Count = 0 (0x0)
    DNS: Additional Records Count = 0 (0x0)
    DNS: Question Section: www.dallasnews.com. of type Host Addr on class
INET addr.
        DNS: Question Name: www.dallasnews.com.
        DNS: Question Type = Host Address
        DNS: Question Class = Internet address class
    DNS: Answer section: www.dallasnews.com. of type Canonical name on class
INET addr.(2 records present)
        DNS: Resource Record: www.dallasnews.com. of type Canonical name on
class INET addr.
            DNS: Resource Name: www.dallasnews.com.
            DNS: Resource Type = Canonical name for alias
            DNS: Resource Class = Internet address class
            DNS: Time To Live = 10493 (0x28FD)
            DNS: Resource Data Length = 2 (0x2)
            DNS: Owner primary name: dallasnews.com.
        DNS: Resource Record: dallasnews.com. of type Host Addr on class
INET addr.
            DNS: Resource Name: dallasnews.com.
            DNS: Resource Type = Host Address
            DNS: Resource Class = Internet address class
            DNS: Time To Live = 10493 (0x28FD)
            DNS: Resource Data Length = 4 (0x4)
            DNS: IP address = 207.238.232.133
00000:  00 50 DA 62 68 4E 00 50 DA 0D F5 2D 08 00 45 00   .PÚbhN.PÚ.õ-..E.
00010:  00 5E 6A 65 00 00 80 11 4C 1D C0 A8 01 B9 C0 A8   .^je...L.À¨.¹À¨
00020:  01 03 00 35 04 2C 00 4A 23 D4 17 4E 81 80 00 01   ...5.,.J#Ô.N..
00030:  00 02 00 00 00 00 03 77 77 77 0A 64 61 6C 6C 61   .......www.dalla
00040:  73 6E 65 77 73 03 63 6F 6D 00 00 01 00 01 C0 0C   snews.com.....À.
00050:  00 05 00 01 00 00 28 FD 00 02 C0 10 C0 30 00 01   ......(ý..À.À0..
00060:  00 01 00 00 28 FD 00 04 CF EE E8 85               ....(ý..Ïîè…
```

You get all the details of Ethernet, IP, and DNS protocols, and it allows you to find any anomalies.

The Monitoring Tab

After you have completed your installation and configuration of the DNS server, you can perform a "quick check" to see if the server can successfully perform simple and iterative queries. A simple query would be one for which the server is authoritative, and an iterative query would be generated if a DNS request was received for which the server was not authoritative.

You can have the DNS server perform these queries for you automatically by right-clicking on the name of the server, selecting Properties, and clicking on the Monitoring tab. There you will be able to perform two different tests:

- **A simple query against the DNS server** A query will be sent to the local server for resolution of a name on a zone for which the server is authoritative. The server is not asked to perform recursion for this simple query.
- **A recursive query to other DNS servers** When you ask the server to perform a recursive query, it will act as a DNS client to other DNS servers in the process of performing recursion. This query will ask for the NS record information for the root of the Internet Domain Name Space. This requires that the cache.dns file is up to date and accurate.

You can also have the server perform these tests automatically, and the results of the automated testing will appear in the Test Results box. When configuring automated testing, you must choose an interval between tests. Each test will consume a small degree of network and processor resources.

If you have problems with your test failing using the tests in the Monitoring tab, try opening the Computer Management Console and using the DNS console from there. Often your queries will pass there when they have failed in the "official" DNS console. This is an "undocumented feature" included with Windows 2000 and should be repaired with the first service pack in July 2000.

CERTIFICATION SUMMARY

In this chapter, we covered more advanced concepts of how DNS and the Windows 2000 DNS Server function. We started with how host names are resolved and learned about the new Windows 2000 caching resolver. You saw how the host name resolution order has changed with Windows 2000, and that the entries in the HOSTS file are immediately copied into the DNS client's local DNS cache.

Different types of queries were covered next. DNS clients and DNS servers issue the two main types of queries, recursive and iterative, in the process of resolving a host name. A recursive query must be answered definitively, either with a positive or a negative response. An iterative query allows responses that include a referral to another DNS server that may aid in resolving the query.

There are two types of "lookups," the forward lookup and the reverse lookup. A forward lookup seeks to resolve a host name to an IP address, and a reverse lookup resolves an IP address to a host name.

We then covered the different DNS servers' roles, which include Primary DNS server, Secondary DNS server, caching-only server, forwarding and forwarder DNS servers, and dynamic update DNS servers.

A Primary DNS server contains a read/write copy of the zone database and is authoritative for the zones it contains. A Secondary DNS server contains a read-only copy of the zone database and receives its copy from a Primary DNS server. Caching-only DNS servers do not contain any zone data, and are able to answer queries based on iterative queries and an ever-growing cache that builds over time, as queries are successfully resolved.

A forwarding DNS server sends recursive requests to a DNS forwarder. This allows the forwarding DNS server to offload some of the responsibility for resolving queries. A slave DNS server is a forwarding server that has the ability to perform recursion by issuing its own iterative queries disabled.

A Dynamic DNS server is able to receive dynamic updates from either or both DNS clients and/or a DHCP server. Only Windows 2000 DNS clients and Windows 2000 DHCP servers are able to update the DDNS via the GSS Dynamic Update protocol.

The Windows 2000 DNS Server can integrate its zones with the Active Directory on a zone-by-zone basis. There are advantages to integrating zones with the Active Directory, including the advantage of not having to create a separate Active Directory and DNS replication topology, using the Active Directory replication scheme, and the multimaster nature of the Active Directory, which helps avoid problems with dynamic updates and zone transfers when a single DNS server becomes unavailable.

Managing the DNS server includes configuring both the server as a whole and the zones it contains. When configuring the server, you must make decisions about what "root hints" you will use, whether or not you will use forwarders, and what interfaces will participate in answering DNS queries. There are also several Advanced options that you can configure for the server.

Zone configuration involves reviewing and adjusting the Start of Authority (SOA) record, defining additional Secondary Name servers for the zone, and configuring zone update behavior.

There are several monitoring and troubleshooting tools available for the Windows 2000 DNS Server, including the nslookup utility, ipconfig and its new switches, the Event Viewer's DNS log, and trace logging. The Network Monitor allows you to view DNS traffic moving to and from the machine running the Network Monitor program.

TWO-MINUTE DRILL

How Host Names Are Resolved

- ❑ Host name resolution resolves DNS names to IP addresses. This is in contrast to NetBIOS name resolution, which resolves NetBIOS names to IP addresses.
- ❑ The contents of the HOSTS file are copied immediately to the DNS client local cache. This takes place at system startup, and whenever a change is saved to the HOSTS file.
- ❑ The order of host name resolution is localhost, DNS client cache, DNS, NetBIOS Remote Name cache, WINS, Broadcast, LMHOSTS.
- ❑ When a DNS server receives a recursive query, it must respond with a definitive answer.
- ❑ When a DNS server receives an iterative query, it has the option of returning a referral answer that will point the requestor to another DNS server that may be able to answer the question.
- ❑ A forward lookup is when a host name is resolved to an IP address.
- ❑ A reverse lookup is when an IP address is resolved to a host name.
- ❑ Reverse lookup zones all are members of the in-addr.arpa domain, which uses the Network ID as an index rather than a domain name.

Windows 2000 DNS Server Roles

- ❑ A Primary DNS server contains a read/write copy of the zone database file.
- ❑ In Standard zones, there is only a single Primary DNS server.
- ❑ A Windows 2000 DNS Server can be configured via a BOOT file or via the Registry and Active Directory.
- ❑ All Windows 2000 DNS Server types cache the results of successful and unsuccessful queries.
- ❑ A Single DNS server can be authoritative for multiple domains.
- ❑ Secondary DNS servers provide fault tolerance, load balancing, and bandwidth preservation.

- Caching-only DNS servers do not contain any zone database information. They build a cache over time from successfully resolved queries
- Caching-only servers are most effective if they are not rebooted. The cache is stored in RAM, and the contents are lost after a reboot.
- A DNS forwarder is a DNS server that performs recursion for another DNS server.
- A forwarding DNS server is a DNS server that forwards queries to a DNS forwarder.
- A slave DNS server is a forwarding DNS server that cannot perform iterative queries, and must accept the answer provided by the forwarder and return that to the requesting DNS client.
- A Dynamic DNS server can receive updates to the DNS zone database file from DNS clients and DHCP servers.
- When there is a name collision, the more recent record is considered the valid record.
- RAS clients release their Host (A) and Pointer (PTR) records after they gracefully sign off.

Integrating Windows 2000 with Active Directory

- Zones can be integrated with the Active Directory on a zone-by-zone basis.
- Active Directory integrated zones benefit from the Active Directory multimaster domain model, which prevents problems related to a single Primary domain controller, the Active Directory replication model and topology, and secure dynamic updates.
- Secure dynamic updates use GSS as their Secure Update protocol.
- When a record is securely updated, the machine that registers the name is the owner of the record, and no other machine is able to update that record.
- When you place a machine in the DnsUpdateProxy group, no security is placed on that record, and the next machine to "touch" the record becomes the owner of that record. DHCP servers can be placed in the DnsUpdateProxy group to avoid complications regarding access controls on secured DNS records.

- ☐ Active Directory integrated zones can replicate only the changed properties of records, rather than having to transfer the entire record during a zone transfer.
- ☐ Domain controllers register SRV records with DNS servers. A DNS server that supports SRV records must be available in order to create a new Windows 2000 domain.
- ☐ SRV records can be registered dynamically or manually. SRV records registered by domain controllers are stored in a text file named netlogon.dns.

Integrating Windows 2000 with DHCP

- ☐ A Windows 2000 DHCP Server can be configured to update records on a DDNS server.
- ☐ The default behavior for a Windows 2000 DHCP/DNS client is for the client to update its own Host (A) record, and for the DHCP server to update the Pointer (PTR) record.
- ☐ A Windows 2000 DHCP Server can act as a proxy for downlevel DNS clients that cannot interact with a DDNS server. The Windows 2000 DHCP Server will update both the Host (A) and Pointer (PTR) record on behalf of the downlevel client.

Managing Windows 2000 DNS Server

- ☐ The Windows 2000 DNS Server can be managed via the DNS console.
- ☐ The DNS server properties are managed separately from the zone properties.
- ☐ You configure the zones to perform WINS lookups via the WINS tab in forward lookup zones, and from the WINS-R tab in reverse lookup zones.
- ☐ The DNS client can be configured manually or via DHCP.
- ☐ You configure DNS clients to handle unqualified requests based on selections you make on the DNS tab in the Advanced TCP/IP Properties dialog box.
- ☐ DNS clients support multiple DNS servers. The one on the top of the list is referred to as the Preferred DNS server, and the others are called the Alternate DNS servers.

Monitoring and Troubleshooting DNS

- The ipconfig utility has added functionality, including the /flushdns and the /displaydns switches.
- The nslookup utility allows you to test and troubleshoot your DNS server and name resolution configuration.
- System Monitor provides a larger number of counters than the Windows NT 4.0 version of Performance Monitor.
- The Event Viewer contains a new log named the DNS Log, which is dedicated to logging DNS specific errors.
- Trace logs can be employed, which give very detailed accounts of the DNS server's activities. Trace logs are very disk and processor intensive
- The Network Monitor can be used to capture and view the details of DNS packets moving into and out of the machine that is running the Network Monitor application.

SELF TEST

The following questions will help you measure your understanding of the material presented in this chapter. Read all of the choices carefully, as there may be more than one correct answer. Choose all correct answers for each question.

How Host Names Are Resolved

1. What is the major difference between the Windows NT 4.0 host name resolution sequence and the Windows 2000 host name resolution sequence?

   A. The Windows 2000 host name resolution sequence begins with a DNS server query first.

   B. The Windows NT 4.0 host name resolution sequence did not include NetBIOS name resolution.

   C. The Windows NT 4.0 host name resolution sequence did not employ HOSTS files.

   D. The Windows 2000 host name resolution sequence uses the cached entries from the HOSTS file, rather than scanning the HOSTS file itself during the process of host name resolution.

2. You receive a call from one of your users, who tells you that he cannot connect to one of your intranet Web servers. He says that when he uses the FQDN name he is unable to connect, but when he uses the IP address that you gave him, he has no problem. You check the DNS servers configured for that client and find that the entry in DNS is correct for the Web server. What is a possible reason for this problem?

   A. There is a physical disconnection between the user's computer and the Web server.

   B. The caching resolver is not working properly, and the DHCP client service must be restarted.

   C. There is an incorrect HINFO record entered for the Web server.

   D. There is an incorrect entry in the users HOSTS file for the Web server.

3. A forward lookup is when:

   A. A query is sent to resolve a host name to an IP address.

   B. A query is sent to resolve an IP address to a host name.

   C. A query pre-fetches the IP addresses of the URLs contained on a Web page.

   D. A query downloads the contents of the zone database file to the DNS client so that all lookups can be resolved from cache.

Windows 2000 DNS Server Roles

4. Your company has 12,500 DNS clients who use intranet and Internet resources frequently. You have a single DNS server that contains Standard zone files that are used to answer queries for local resources. You have also configured the DNS server to answer Internet host name resolution requests. When you perform system monitoring, you see that the processor and disk counters are being taxed very heavily, and this seems to be correlated with jumps in the DNS server counters. What can you do to offload some of the burden on this DNS server?

A. Throttle the bandwidth to the DNS server so that it doesn't have to answer so many queries per second.

B. Install the DNS server service on other computers on the network, and create Secondary zones on these servers for the Primary zones located on the original DNS server.

C. Configure the DNS clients with different Preferred DNS servers.

D. Disable the DNS client service and have all name queries processed via WINS.

5. Some advantages of using caching-only DNS servers include:

A. They do not generate zone transfer traffic.

B. They can be configured as secure DNS forwarders.

C. You can store your external zone files on them for Internet user access.

D. They can be placed at remote office locations to reduce the amount of traffic over the slow WAN link.

6. A slave server is:

A. A DNS server that is dependent on the Active Directory for boot information.

B. A domain controller that must access domain resources via Windows NT 4.0 DNS servers.

C. A DNS server that uses forwarders and cannot perform its own iterative request requests.

D. A DHCP server that updates a Dynamic DNS server.

7. Your company has decided to enable secure dynamic updates for Host (A) and PTR (PTR) record information for the computers in the organization. After installing the DNS server and adding the appropriate zones, you start getting phone calls from users complaining that they are not able to access resources on each other's peer Web services Web servers. What is the problem, and how can you fix it?

A. The users must use the NetBIOS names of the destination computers when they are using peer Web services to share resources with each other.

B. You did not make the zone Active Directory integrated.

C. The users must put all WinSock accessible resources on a centralized IIS server in order to share resources with one another.

D. You did not enable dynamic updates for the zone.

8. You have a mix of Windows 2000 Dynamic DNS Servers and UNIX Dynamic DNS Servers on your network. All the client computers on the network are Windows 2000 Professional and Servers. The secure dynamic updates seem to work fine on the Windows 2000 DDNS Server, but they are not being registered on the UNIX DDNS Server. What is the explanation for this?

A. The Windows 2000 DDNS clients only support System Security Extensions as defined in RFC 2535.

B. The Windows 2000 DDNS clients only support Secure Domain Name System dynamic updates as defined in RFC 2137.

C. The UNIX DDNS Servers do not support Generic Security Service (GSS) dynamic update protocols.

D. UNIX servers do not support any type of secure dynamic updates.

Integrating Windows 2000 with Active Directory

9. Some of the advantages of Active Directory integrated zones include:

A. Active Directory integrated zones allows for per property transfer of zone updates.

B. Active Directory integrated zones are single master zones.

C. Active Directory integrated zones are multimaster zones.

D. Active Directory integrated zones use the same replication topology as the Active Directory; therefore, you do not need to create separate replication topologies for the Active Directory and DNS zones.

10. You have installed a Windows 2000 DNS Server and have enabled secure dynamic updates. A Windows 2000 DHCP Server assigns IP addresses to all computers on the network. The DHCP server updates all records for downlevel clients on the DDNS server. The DHCP server crashes, but you have a backup and bring that one online. Later, you start hearing complaints from users regarding not being able to access FTP, Web, and Mail servers on the network. What might the problem be, and how would you fix it?

A. The DHCP server that went offline was the owner of both the Host (A) record and the Pointer (PTR) record for all the machines, and now the backup DHCP server cannot update the records owned by the previous DHCP server.

B. Place the DHCP servers in the DnsUpdateProxy group.

C. The DNS/DHCP clients must be configured to use the new DHCP server.

D. The DHCP database is corrupt on the backup DHCP server.

Integrating Windows 2000 with DHCP

11. You are upgrading your Windows NT 4.0 Workstation computers to Windows 2000 Professional. These computers have been DHCP clients to a Windows 2000 DHCP Server that has been registering for the downlevel clients the Host (A) and Pointer (PTR) records for the Windows NT 4.0 Workstations. However, when you upgrade the Workstations to Windows 2000 Professional, the upgraded computers are not able to update their records with the DDNS server. Why?

    A. The Windows 2000 DHCP Server must be restarted before the upgraded clients can register their records.

    B. Windows 2000 Professional computers can only update the records on a DDNS server if they are part of a "fresh" installation. Dynamic update will not work after an upgrade installation.

    C. The Windows 2000 Professional clients must be authorized with in the Active Directory before they can upgrade their records.

    D. Windows NT 4.0 DNS clients cannot register with a DDNS server. When the DHCP server updated the Workstation's DNS Records it took ownership of them.

12. The default behavior of a Windows 2000 DHCP/DNS client is:

    A. The Windows 2000 DHCP/DNS client updates its own Host (A) address record, and the DHCP server updates the Pointer (PTR) record.

    B. The Windows 2000 DHCP/DNS client allows the DHCP server to update both records.

    C. The Windows 2000 DHCP/DNS client updates both records itself.

    D. The Windows 2000 DHCP/DNS client updates its Pointer (PTR) record, and the DHCP server updates the Host (A) record.

Managing Windows 2000 DNS Server

13. You have BIND Secondaries on your network that do not support the Fast Transfer method of zone transfer where multiple records can be included in a single message. What must you do at the DNS server to prevent zone transfer failures when copying the zone database from a Windows 2000 DNS Server to the BIND DNS server?

A. Select BIND Secondaries in the Advanced tab of the DNS server Properties dialog box.

B. Select Enable Netmask Ordering from the Advanced tab of the DNS server Properties dialog box.

C. Select "Do Not Replicate This Record" in the WINS tab of the Forward Lookup Zone's Properties dialog box.

D. Select "Do Not Replicate This Record" in the WINS-R tab of the Reverse Lookup Zone's Properties dialog box.

14. You are implementing a DNS server solution for your intranet. The DNS server will not be resolving queries for any Internet hosts. What changes would you make to the DNS server after you create a forward lookup domain for your organization's intranet domain name?

A. Replace the entries in the cache.dns file with entries for the Root servers for your intranet's domain.

B. Download the latest cache.dns file from its Internet location as internic.

C. Create a referral record to all external resources you will be accessing with this DNS server.

D. Block access to any external routes on the DNS server.

Monitoring and Troubleshooting DNS

15. Which utility would you use to clear the local client's DNS cache?

A. IPCONFIG

B. NSLOOKUP

C. NETDIAG

D. The Event Viewer

16. What does it mean when you do an nslookup and the answer is returned as "non-authoritative"?

A. A tertiary DNS server has answered the query.

B. A non-Windows 2000 DNS Server has answered the query.

C. The DNS client service is unsure if the answer is correct.

D. The answer was returned from the DNS server's cache and not from a direct query answer from another DNS server.

17. What utility would you use to examine the contents of DNS messages as they traverse the network?

A. Network Monitor

B. System Monitor

C. NETSTAT

D. NBTSTAT

LAB QUESTION

You are the new network administrator at ACME Incorporated. The company has both an intranet and an Internet presence. The ACME networking staff tells you that there have been some problems with the DNS servers on the intranet. Every few days, the Host Address records are altered on key intranet DNS servers. These changes seem to take place when external Internet connections are made to the affected DNS servers.

Diagram and then explain how you can configure DNS servers for this company to optimize intranet security, while maintaining full availability for Internet resources. In your solution, consider the types of DNS servers available to you, what network hardware or software you would use to secure the intranet resources, and what configuration changes you would need to make on the security principles to allow your solution to work. In addition, explain what a possible reason is for the mysterious changes taking place on the DNS servers zone databases.

SELF TEST ANSWERS

How Host Names Are Resolved

1. ☑ D. Windows NT 4.0 did not cache the contents of the HOSTS file, while Windows 2000 does cache the contents of the HOSTS file during system startup and whenever the contents of the file are changed and saved.
☒ A is incorrect because the Windows 2000 host name resolution sequence begins with localhost and then checks the DNS client cache. **B** is incorrect because both Windows 2000 and Windows NT 4.0 would go through the NetBIOS name resolution sequence in the quest of resolving a host name. **C** is incorrect because both Windows 2000 and Windows NT 4.0 are able to use the contents of the HOSTS file to help resolve a host name.

2. ☑ D. Erroneous entries in the HOSTS file will override correct entries at the DNS server because the contents of the HOSTS file are cached at system startup, and this cache is referenced between that queries are sent to a DNS server.
☒ A is incorrect because the physical connection must be intact, since the user is able to connect via the IP address. **B** is incorrect because the caching resolver is implemented as part of the DNS client service. The DHCP client service participates in the dynamic registration of DNS clients with a DDNS server. **C** is incorrect because the HINFO record only provides information about the DNS server itself, such as processor type and operating system, and has no effect on the validity or lack thereof of Host (A) records.

3. ☑ A. The definition of a forward lookup is resolving host names to IP addresses.
☒ B is incorrect because that is the definition of a reverse lookup. **C** is incorrect because the DNS client service does not initiate pre-fetching of any kind. Pre-fetching of Web pages is used frequently by Proxy servers to improve perceived performance by the user. **D** is incorrect because the forward lookup does not download the entire zone database file. However, you can use nslookup switches to download the contents of the zone file for troubleshooting purposes.

Windows 2000 DNS Server Roles

4. ☑ B, C. **B** is correct because you can implement Secondary DNS servers to help provide load balancing for the zones and reduce the overall processor usage dedicated to servicing DNS query requests. **C** is correct because after Secondary zones are created, you must distribute the assignment of Preferred DNS servers among the Primary and Secondary servers. If you assign the Primary DNS server as the Preferred server for all of the DNS clients, you will not have successfully enable load-balancing.

☒ A is incorrect because by throttling the overall bandwidth, you are just distributing the load over time, and you will not reduce the overall impact the query traffic has on the DNS server. In addition, query requests may be dropped, which will result in a user revolt against you. **D** is incorrect because WINS queries are not the same as DNS queries, and can provide disparate results depending on how the domain name and host name schemes match with the NetBIOS naming scheme.

5. ☑ **A, B, D. A** is correct because caching-only servers do not contain zone files; therefore, there is no need for zone transfer traffic. **B** is correct because caching-only servers are ideal as secure DNS forwarders because hackers will not be able to access any zone data on them, since there are no zone files to access. **D** is correct because you obviate the need for large zone transfer traffic with caching-only DNS servers; therefore, remote offices can benefit from having a cache of successfully resolved queries build up over time on the caching-only server.
☒ C is incorrect because caching-only forwarders do not contain zone files, and therefore would not be useful in providing name resolution for your external, Internet accessible resources.

6. ☑ **C.** This is one of the definitions of a slave server. Another definition for a slave server is a Secondary DNS server that receives zone database files from a Master DNS server.
☒ A is incorrect because this is not a definition of a slave server. **B** is incorrect because there is not a specific designation for a machine that uses only Windows NT 4.0 DNS Servers for host name resolution. **D** is incorrect because this is not a definition of a slave server.

7. ☑ **B, D. B** is correct because in order to have secure dynamic updates, the zone must be Active Directory integrated. **D** is correct because dynamic updates must be enabled in order for the DNS clients to register their names with the DNS server. The clients were not able to resolve the names for each other's Web servers because there were no entries in the zone database.
☒ A is incorrect because you do not need to use NetBIOS names to access resources contained on Web servers. The Windows 2000 Peer Web Services Web Server allows for workgroup Web access of up to 10 Web clients. **C** is incorrect because users can use the Peer Web Services Web Server to access resources on each other's computers. They are not required to use a central IIS server to share resources.

8. ☑ **C.** Many UNIX servers do not support the GSS-API.
☒ A is incorrect because Windows 2000 systems use the Generic Security Services API to establish secure dynamic updates. **B** is incorrect for the same reason. **D** is incorrect because UNIX DDNS servers are capable of receiving secure dynamic updates.

Integrating Windows 2000 with Active Directory

9. ☑ **A, C, D. A** is correct because Active Directory integrated zones are able to transfer only the changed properties of a record during a zone transfer, and do not need to transfer the entire changed record. **C** is correct because Active Directory integrated zones are multimaster, and all Active Directory integrated zones are Primary zones. **D** is correct because you do not need to create separate replication topologies when you integrate your DNS zones with the Active Directory.

☒ **B** is incorrect because the Active Directory integrated zone topology is multimaster, which confers an advantage of Standard DNS zones that are single master (single Primary DNS server).

10. ☑ **A, B. A** is correct because when secure dynamic updates are enabled, the computer that registers the record becomes the owner of the record, and no other computer can update the record. **B** is correct because you can avoid the problem of the backup DHCP server not being the owner of the record, and therefore not being able to update it by preventing the initial DHCP server from adding any security information regarding the record. You do this by adding the DHCP server to the DnsUpdateProxy group. DHCP servers that belong to the DnsUpdateProxy group do not register security information when updating the DNS zone database.

☒ **C** is incorrect because there is no way to "point" a DHCP client to a particular DHCP server because DHCP messages are broadcast messages. **D** is incorrect because although it is possible, it is not likely.

Integrating Windows 2000 with DHCP

11. ☑ **D.** Downlevel clients cannot update their information on the DDNS server; therefore, the DHCP server owns the records.

☒ **A** is incorrect because you do not need to restart a DHCP server to allow Windows 2000 clients to register their information on a DDNS server. **B** is incorrect because it doesn't matter whether you upgrade or install "fresh," a Windows 2000 Professional computer has the capability to upgrade its own records on a DNS server. **C** is incorrect because you must authorize the DHCP server in the Active Directory; you do not need to authorize DHCP clients.

12. ☑ A. The default behavior of Windows 2000 DHCP/DNS clients is to update their own Host (A) record, and allows the DHCP server to update the Pointer (PTR) record.
☒ B, C, and D are incorrect because the DHCP/DNS client does not, by default, allow the DHCP server to update both records, it does not update both records itself, and it does not update its Pointer record.

Managing Windows 2000 DNS Server

13. ☑ A. When you place a check mark in the BIND Secondaries check box in the Advanced tab of the DNS server's Properties dialog box, the fast transfer method will not be used.
☒ B is incorrect because netmask ordering is related to choosing the IP address of the destination host that is on the same subnet as the requesting host. C and D are incorrect because replication of WINS records is unrelated to the fast transfer method of zone transfers.

14. ☑ A. If you are using a DNS server to resolve only internal names, you should replace the entries in the cache.dns files with entries for your intranet Root servers.
☒ B is incorrect because the cache.dns file you would download from the Internet would contain entries for the Internet Root servers, and would not help in resolving host names for your intranet. C is incorrect because you do not need to create referral records for external resources, since you will not be resolving external host names from this computer. D is incorrect because you do not need to cut communication to a gateway just because you will not be resolving external host names. The machine may need access to the gateway for other reasons.

Monitoring and Troubleshooting DNS

15. ☑ A. You can clear the local DNS client cache by using the ipconfig /flushdns command.
☒ B is incorrect because you use the nslookup command to query DNS servers, but you cannot view the client cache with it. C is incorrect because the netdiag command can repair the DNS zone to some extent, but does not let you view the client cache. D is incorrect because the Event Viewer does not contain information regarding locally cached entries.

16. ☑ D. You will be notified that the answer was non-authoritative when answered from cache.
☒ A is incorrect because there are no tertiary DNS servers. B and C are also incorrect because a non-authoritative answer to a nslookup does not indicate that a non-Windows 2000 DNS Server has answered the query, nor does it mean that the DNS client service is unsure if the answer is correct.

17. ☑ A. Network Monitor allows you to view the contents of the packets on the network.
☒ B is incorrect because you cannot view the contents of packets with system monitor.
C is incorrect because you cannot view the contents of the packets with netstat.
D is incorrect because you cannot view the contents of packets using NBTSTAT.

LAB ANSWER

This scenario represents a common problem for companies that use DNS servers to access resources on both their intranet and the Internet. The DNS server located on the intranet contains zone databases containing IP addressing information for the company's internal resources.

Whenever an intranet host issues a recursive query to the internal DNS server, the DNS server first checks to see if it is authoritative for the queried zone. If the server is not authoritative, then it will issue a series of iterative queries to DNS servers on the Internet. Each Internet DNS server responds to the internal DNS server directly. This means that Internet hosts have direct access to the internal DNS server.

Intruders can intercept these queries made on UDP Port 53, and with the aid of a simple Network Analyzer, can obtain the IP address of the internal DNS server. Once the IP address of the internal DNS server is known, skilled hackers can access the server. Once they have access, they can change the contents of the DNS zone database file. This is a possible explanation for the mysterious changes in the host records on the internal DNS servers.

In order to solve this problem, we need to prevent direct communication between the internal DNS server and DNS servers on the Internet. This can be accomplished by making the internal DNS server a forwarding slave server to a DNS forwarder on the outside of a corporate firewall. The forwarder is configured as a caching-only DNS server, and therefore contains no zone database information.

With this arrangement, when an internal host issues a query to the internal DNS server for an Internet resource, the internal DNS server will forward the query to the DNS forwarder, which lies outside the firewall. The forwarder will issue iterative queries to Internet DNS servers in order to resolve the host name to an IP address. When the forwarder obtains the IP address, it returns the information to the internal forwarding DNS server, which, in turn, returns the answer to the request host.

If the forwarder is not able to resolve the host name to an IP address, it returns this information to the internal forwarding DNS server. Normally, if the forwarder is not able to resolve the host name to an IP address, the forwarding DNS server will then try to resolve the host name. However, because we have configured the forwarding server to be a slave server, it does not perform its own iterative queries, and returns the failure message directly to the requesting host. In Windows 2000, this is accomplished by selecting the "Do not use recursion" option on the DNS server, as seen in Figure 3-24.

FIGURE 3-24

Configuring a slave server

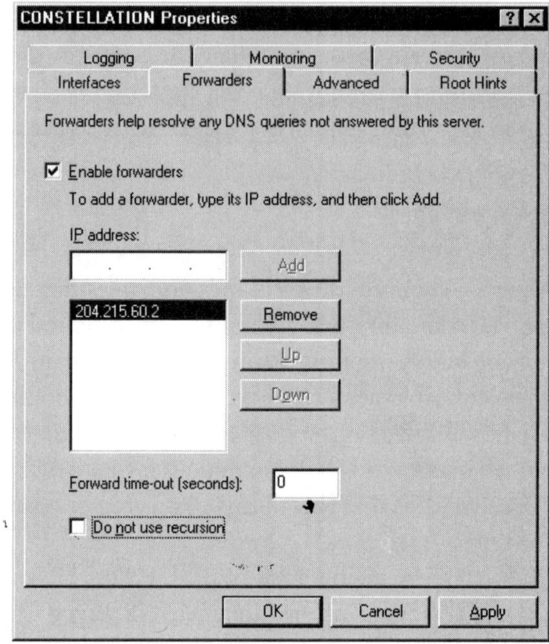

In this way, the internal DNS server is never in direct contact with Internet DNS servers. In order to secure the network further, the firewall should be configured to allow DNS traffic only between the intranet forwarding DNS server and the external forwarder DNS server. Traffic over UDP Port 53 and TCP Port 53 should be opened between the two servers. If a DNS response is longer than a single UDP packet, TCP will be used because of its larger packet size.

MCSE

MICROSOFT CERTIFIED SYSTEMS ENGINEER

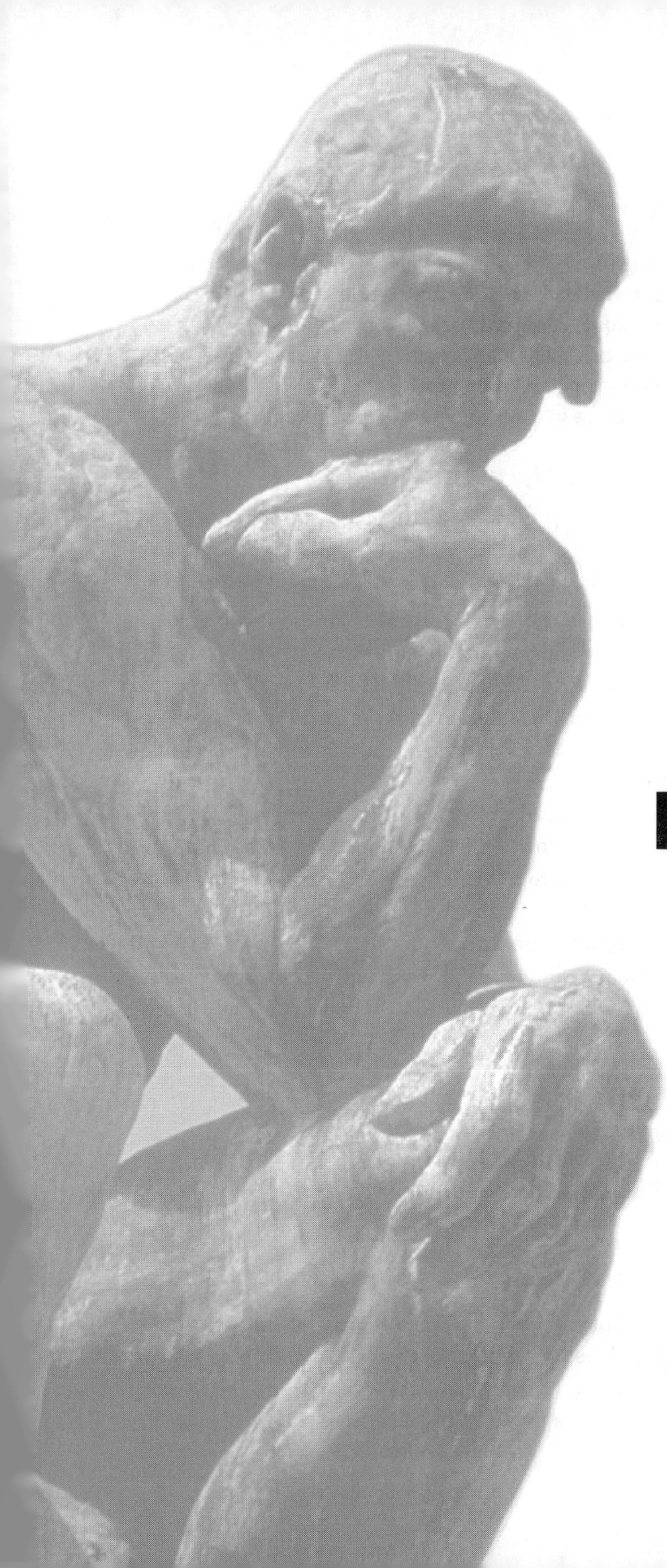

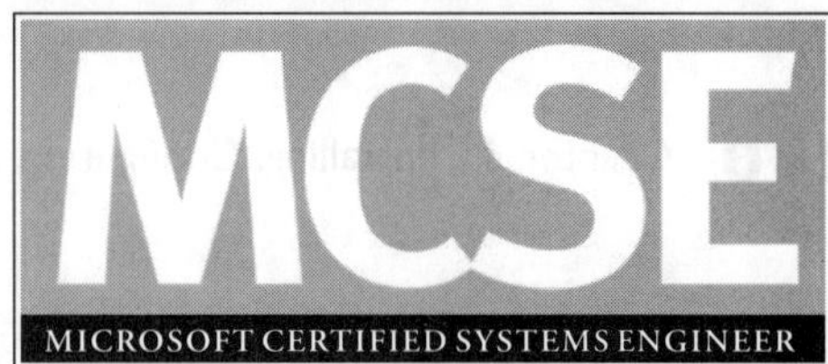

4

Installing, Configuring, and Troubleshooting DHCP

CERTIFICATION OBJECTIVES

4.01	Overview of DHCP
4.02	DHCP Server Configuration
4.03	DHCP Relay Agents in a Routed Environment
4.04	Integrating DHCP with DDNS
4.05	Integrating DHCP with RRAS
4.06	Integrating DHCP with Active Directory
4.07	DHCP and APIPA
4.08	Monitoring and Troubleshooting DHCP
✓	Two-Minute Drill
Q&A	Self Test

All common network protocols assign each computer a unique identifier. In the case of IPX, this number is assigned automatically by the workstation in a way that is guaranteed to make the number unique: NetBEUI uses a 16-byte NetBIOS name. The TCP/IP protocol uses an IP address. In its original implementation, TCP/IP was designed to connect a relatively small number of servers together. The designers of DHCP did not portend that hundreds or thousands of computers in a single network would require IP address assignment.

To solve the problem of managing the hundreds or thousands of IP addresses an organization might have, DCHP was developed to provide a way to dynamically assign IP addresses to computers when they connect to the LAN.

Having a DHCP server on your network makes it easier for users who use laptops to connect to various office and home networks. In addition to assigning basic IP addressing information such as an IP address and a subnet mask, the DHCP server gives out other TCP/IP configuration information to the client.
This additional information includes the IP address of the default gateway, DNS server, and the client's DNS domain name.

The Windows 2000 DHCP Server is integrated with the Windows 2000 DNS Server. This new feature allows a Windows 2000 DHCP Server to communicate IP addressing and host name information to a Windows 2000 Dynamic DNS (DDNS) Server. The Windows 2000 DHCP Server can now provide dynamically the host name and IP address mapping information directly to the DDNS server. As application standards move toward using the WinSock interface, and away from NetBIOS, it is critical in large corporate networks to locate clients by host name and IP address.

CERTIFICATION OBJECTIVE 4.01

Overview of DHCP

Dynamic Host Configuration Protocol provides IP addressing information for DHCP clients. To obtain IP addressing information, the client must obtain a *lease* from a DHCP server. In this section, we will examine the process of DHCP client lease assignment and the conversations that take place between a DHCP client and server.

DHCP Leases

When a DHCP server assigns IP addressing information to a DHCP client, the DHCP client does not own that IP address. The DHCP server continues to own the IP address, and the client has merely leased that information. Think of an IP address as a plot of land. When the DHCP server assigns the IP address to the DHCP client, it is renting out some land on the network. The DHCP client rents a parcel of land out on the network, but if its lease is not renewed, it won't be able to live on the network anymore.

In order to obtain a lease, a DHCP server and client participate in a conversation that includes four steps: Discover, Offer, Request, and Acknowledgement. Let's look at this process in more detail.

The DHCP Lease Process

The DHCP client and server participate in a dialog that consists of four primary interchanges:

- DHCPDISCOVER
- DHCPOFFER
- DHCPREQUEST
- DHCPACKNOWLEDGEMENT

The result of this dialog is the assignment of an IP address and additional TCP/IP parameters.

Discover

When the DHCP client initializes, it broadcasts a DHCPDISCOVER message to the local segment. The destination IP address is the limited broadcast address, 255.255.255.255. The destination hardware address is FFFFFFFFFFFF, which is the hardware broadcast address. All DHCP servers on the segment respond to the DHCPDISCOVER message. The DCHP client does not have an IP address yet, so it includes with the DHCPDISCOVER message its Media Access Control (MAC) address (identified as the *ciaddr* field in a packet analysis). Other information in the DHCPDISCOVER message includes:

- The client's host name.
- A "parameter request list" that includes DHCP option codes the client supports.

- A message ID that identifies this particular request, and will be included in each of the messages the DHCP client and server send to each other.
- The "hardware type" of the client's network interface card, such as 10-Mb Ethernet.

Offer

All DHCP servers that receive the DHCPDISCOVER message respond by offering an IP address from their *pool* of available IP addresses. This offer is made in the form of a DHCPOFFER message. The DHCP client will accept the IP address from the first server that it receives a DHCP offer from.

The DHCPOFFER message is a broadcast message like the DISCOVER message. In order for the correct client to receive the information, the destination MAC address is included in the *ciaddr* field. Other information in the DHCPOFFER message includes:

- DHCP server IP address
- The offered IP address
- The offered subnet mask
- DHCP option information: WINS and DNS servers, default gateway
- Lease interval
- First and second lease renewal intervals (Renewal Time Interval [T1] and Rebinding Time Value [T2])

The DHCPOFFER message contains the basic IP addressing information the client computer will use when the TCP/IP stack is initialized. This basic information includes the client's IP address and subnet mask.

Request

The client responds to the offer by issuing a DHCPREQUEST broadcast message. Some questions may come to mind at this point: "Why use a broadcast message? Doesn't the client now have an IP address?" Recall that all DHCP servers respond to the initial DCHPDISCOVER message. The purpose of the DHCPREQUEST broadcast is to inform other DHCP servers that their offers have been rejected. The rejected DHCP servers then return the IP addresses they offered back to their pools of available IP addresses.

The DCHPREQUEST message is a confirmation of the information sent to the client in the DHCPOFFER message. The DHCPREQUEST message includes

- The client's hardware address
- The DHCP server's IP address
- The client's requested IP address
- The client's host name

ACK/NACK

Finally, the DHCP server responds to the DHCPREQUEST message with a DHCPACK broadcast message. The reason this message is broadcast is that the client doesn't "officially" obtain its IP address until it is acknowledged. Again, the client's MAC address is included in order to identify the proper destination of this message.

The DHCPACK message contains similar information to that included with the DHCPOFFER message, and acts as a confirmation of the DHCPREQUEST message. At this point, the client has leased the IP address and can use it for network communication. The address is marked as "leased" by the DHCP server and will not be leased to any other client during the active lease period. It is also during the ACK phase that DHCP options are delivered to the client.

Lease Renewal

A lease is an agreement to let someone use something for a defined length of time. The DHCP client leases IP addressing information from the DHCP server. The DHCP client does not own this information, and does not get to keep it forever.

Because the DHCP server owns this information, it allows the DHCP server to maintain a dynamic pool of IP addresses. The lease process prevents computers no longer on the network from retaining IP addresses that other computers might use.

The length of the lease is defined at the DHCP server. The default lease period on a Windows 2000 DHCP Server is eight days. This can be changed depending on the needs of the network administrator and his or her specific network requirements.

A DHCP client must renew its lease. The DHCPOFFER and DHCPACK messages include the amount of time a client is allowed to keep its IP address, which is its lease period. Also included are the times when the client is required to *renew* its lease. The DHCPOFFER message includes not only the lease period, but also a *Renewal Time Interval (T1)* and the *Rebinding Time Value (T2).*

Renewal and Rebinding Intervals

The Renewal Time Value represents 50% of the lease period. If the lease period were eight days, then the Renewal Time Value (T1) would be four days. At T1, the DHCP client will attempt to renew its IP address by broadcasting a DHCPREQUEST message containing its current IP address. If the DHCP server that granted the IP address is available, it will renew the IP address for the period specified in the renewed lease. If the DHCP server is not available, the client will continue to use its lease, since it still has 50% of the lease period remaining.

The Rebinding Time Value represents 87.5% of the lease period. If the lease period is eight days, then the rebinding interval is 168 hours. The client will attempt to rebind its IP address at this time only if it was not able to renew its lease at the Renewal Time (T1). The client broadcasts a DHCPREQUEST message. If the server that granted the IP address does not respond, the client will enter the *Rebinding State* and begin the DHCPDISCOVER process, attempting to renew its IP address with any DHCP server. If it cannot renew its IP address, it will try to receive a new one from any responding DHCP server. If unsuccessful, TCP/IP services are shut down on that computer.

SCENARIO & SOLUTION	
Do I have to use DHCP on my network?	No, but it will make your life as an administrator a lot easier. You can centrally control the IP addressing assignments on your network from a single server in many instances.
Are there other DHCP messages than those we just talked about?	Yes. There is the DHCPINFORM message that is used by the DHCP client service to communicate with DHCP servers different types of information, such as querying for the name and location of a domain controller for purposes of rogue DHCP server detection. There is also the DHCPDECLINE message, which a DHCP client will send to a DHCP server if the DHCP client detects that the IP address it has been assigned is already in use.
When should I configure long lease periods?	If you network is stable, and you don't have a large number of computers joining and leaving the network. For example, if you rarely have users plug into the network with notebooks or other portable computers, you may not require short lease periods.

Leased DHCP information has other advantages over statically assigned IP addresses. If you want to make a change to the default gateway's IP address, or the WINS server's IP address, you only need to make this change once at the DHCP server. When the DHCP client renews its lease, it will reconfigure according to the new parameters you included at the DHCP server. If you have configured a short lease period initially, the clients will quickly receive this new information.

The four steps in the DHCP lease process are DISCOVER, OFFER, REQUEST, and ACKNOWLEDGEMENT. One way to remember this process is to think of "Aunt DORA."

The DHCP client first tries to renew its IP address at 50% of its lease interval, which is also known as T1. If the DHCP server that assigned its lease is online, and if the IP address is still available, then the DHCP client will keep its current IP address. If the server is not available, the client will continue to use its current IP address and attempt to renew the IP address lease later. At 87.5% of the lease period, the client attempts to renew its lease with any DHCP server (T2). If the DHCP server that assigned the original lease is online, and the IP address is still available, then it will renew the lease. If the IP address is not available, or the server is offline, then the DHCP client will start all over with the DHCPDISCOVER message.

Some advantages of using DHCP over manually assigned IP addresses include decreased risk of human error when entering IP addressing information on multiple clients, centralizing the management and tracking of IP addresses, and the eliminating the need to visit each client workstation or server to assign the manual IP address.

EXERCISE 4-1

The DHCP Lease Process

In this exercise, you are to answer some questions about how the DHCP lease process works.

1. What are the four steps in the DHCP lease process?
2. At what point does the DHCP client first attempt to renew its DHCP lease?
3. What are the advantages of using DHCP rather than manually assigning static IP addresses?

exam Watch

A DHCP client that has never owned an IP address will start with the DHCPDISCOVER message. When the DHCP client seeks to renew its IP address, it sends out a DHCPREQUEST message. When a DHCP client that already owns an IP address boots up, it will also send a DHCPREQUEST message. Even if the DHCP client's lease is not up, it will still do this during boot-up. This is a check to see if it is still on the same subnet. If the DHCP client has been moved, it will not receive a renewal, and will attempt to gain a new IP address.

EXERCISE 4-2

Installing the DHCP Server Service

In this exercise, you will install the DHCP Server Service on a Windows 2000 Advanced Server machine. This exercise will work fine on a Windows 2000 Server machine as well, but you cannot install the DHCP Server Service on a Windows 2000 Professional computer. Do not perform this exercise on a live, production network without the permission of your network administrator. Improper installation of a DHCP server can lead to network errors and communication disruptions.

1. Log on as Administrator.
2. Open Control Panel, and then double-click on Add/Remove Programs. You should see something similar to what appears next.

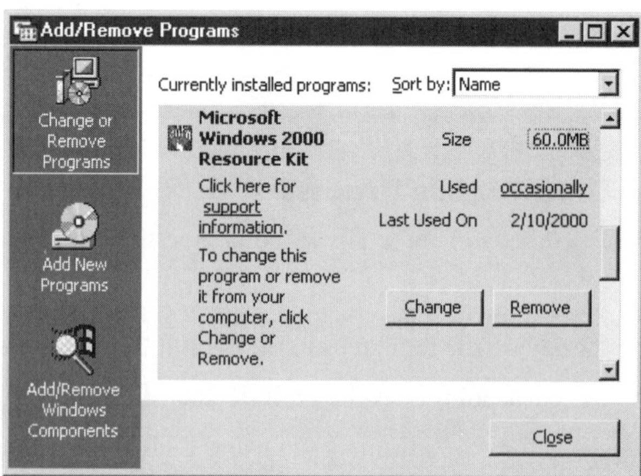

3. Click Add/Remove Windows Components in the left pane of the dialog box.
4. Scroll down the list of Components until you find Networking Services. If there is a check mark in the check box to the left of Networking Services, leave it there; if there is not, place a check in the box. Then click Details. You should see what appears next.

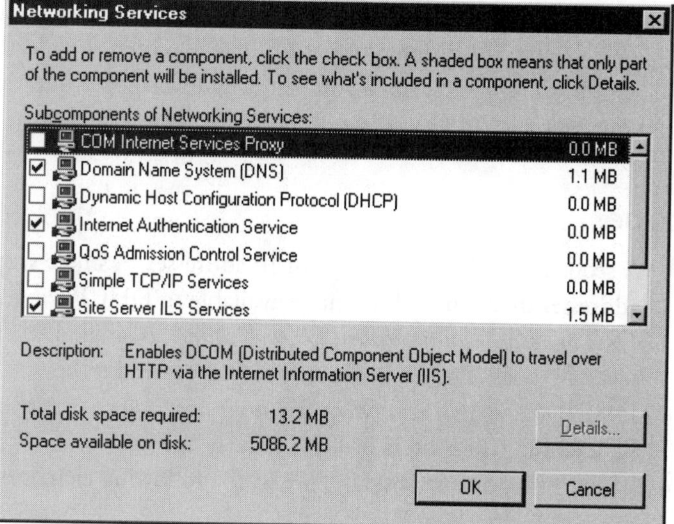

5. Place a check mark in the check box for Dynamic Host Configuration Protocol. Then Click OK.
6. You are returned to the Windows Components dialog box. Click Next.
7. The Configuring Components dialog box appears while the DHCP Server Service installs. You can monitor the progress of the installation by observing the progress bar.
8. When the installation finishes, you see the Completing the Windows Components Wizard dialog box. Click Finish.

You have successfully installed the DHCP Server Service. There is still some work to do, but before you continue, let's talk about one DHCP server configuration and, specifically, the creation and configuration of DHCP scopes.

CERTIFICATION OBJECTIVE 4.02

DHCP Server Configuration

Your major configuration task when implementing a DHCP solution for your organization is knowing how to set up and configure DHCP *scopes.* Scopes are the *containers* for the "sack" of IP addresses the server has to hand out. In this section, we'll explore the different types of DHCP scopes. In addition, we'll cover BOOTP and BOOTP tables, since you just might find some questions on those on your exam.

DHCP Scopes

A scope is a collection or pool of IP addresses. A single scope includes all the IP addresses that you wish to make available to DHCP clients on a single subnet. *Only one scope can be created for each subnet.* A single DHCP server can manage several scopes. The DHCP server does not need to be on the same subnet as the DHCP clients that it services. Remote hosts can access the DHCP server via RFC-compliant routers or DHCP relay agents.

Each scope must contain at least the following elements:

- Scope name
- Start and end IP address
- Lease duration
- Subnet mask

You should create the scope so that it includes all the IP addresses of your network or subnetwork ID. If you have clients with static IP addresses, such as WINS server, DNS server, or other DHCP servers, you can configure a range of excluded IP addresses. The excluded IP addresses are removed from the scope and are not available for distribution.

Creating a new scope in Windows 2000 is a much easier task because it is wizard driven. Most configuration options are included in the wizard, which helps you define and configure the scope.

DHCP Options

A DHCP server must be configured to supply a minimum amount of information, which includes the IP address and the subnet mask. Configuration details such as the IP address of the WINS server, DNS server, and default gateway can be included in a client lease. However, you don't have to include these values; they are *optional.* These optional configuration details are referred to as *DHCP options.*

There are several types of DHCP options, including

- Server options
- Scope options
- Client options
- Vendor class or user class options

There are a large number of options available in the Windows 2000 DHCP Server. However, Microsoft client operating systems support a small number of these options. Of the standard set of DHCP options, Microsoft clients support

- **003 Router** The IP address of the default gateway
- **006 DNS** The IP address of the DNS server
- **015 Domain Name** The DNS domain name the client should use
- **044 WINS/NBNS Servers** The IP address of the WINS server
- **046 WINS/NBT Node Type** The NetBIOS node type
- **047 NetBIOS Scope ID** The NetBIOS scope ID

Each of these options is configured at the DHCP server. Let's look at the different option types and see how to configure options at each level.

Remember, they are called DHCP options because their use is optional. You do not need to assign any options if you choose not to. However, you will find that using the appropriate DHCP options will make your life as an administrator a lot easier.

Server Options

Server options apply to all scopes configured on a single DHCP server. Server options were known as *global options* on the Windows NT 4.0 DHCP Server. For example, you have three scopes on your DHCP server that assign IP addresses for the following subnets:

192.168.1.0

192.168.2.0

192.168.3.0

Now you want all the DHCP clients from each of those subnets to receive the same WINS server address. You can do this by creating a WINS server option that includes the IP address of the WINS server. Clients receiving their lease from any of these scopes will be given the same WINS server address.

Figure 4-1 shows the WINS configuration option on the DHCP server.

FIGURE 4-1

The WINS Server Options dialog box

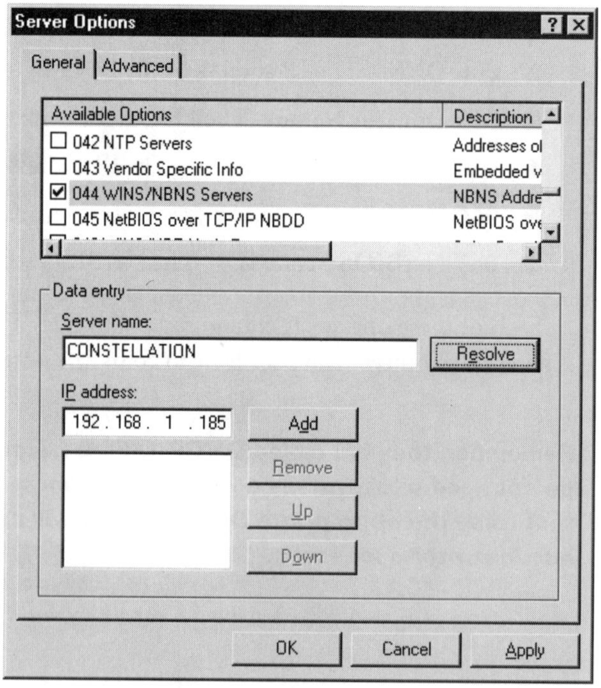

Scope Options

Scope options allow you to specify DHCP options that apply to a single scope. A good example of when you want to set scope options is when you want to automatically configure the IP address of the default gateway for the DHCP clients. Each subnet must have a different default gateway, since the default gateway must be local to each subnet. It wouldn't make much sense to assign the same default gateway to all the scopes. Therefore, you configure a scope option for the default gateway for each scope that has a different default gateway.

Figure 4-2 shows the Scope Options configuration dialog box, where you would configure the IP address of the DNS server for a particular scope.

Client Options

In order to assign client options, you must first create a *reserved client.* A reserved client is a DHCP client that you configure to always receive the same IP address. Creating reserved clients allows you to assign functionally *static* IP addresses to

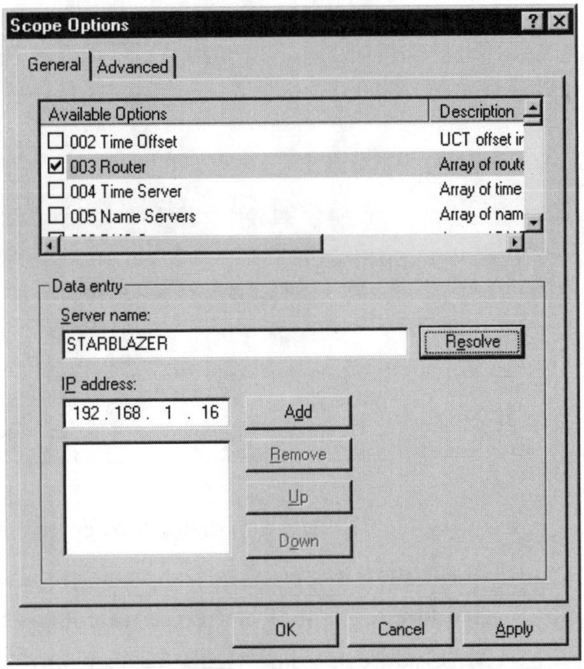

FIGURE 4-2

The DNS Scope Options dialog box

computers that require these, such as WINS and DNS servers. DHCP servers also require a static IP address. However, the DHCP server itself cannot be a DHCP client, so creating a client reservation for them would be a waste of IP addresses. Client reservations allow you to centrally manage virtually the entirety of your IP addresses space, with the exception being your DHCP servers.

To create a client reservation, perform the following steps:

1. Open the DHCP management console.
2. In the left pane, expand the server name, and then expand the scope object. You will need to already have a scope in place to do this. Click on the Reservations folder.
3. Right-click on the Reservations folder, and select New Reservation. You should see the New Reservation dialog box as it appears in Figure 4-3.

FIGURE 4-3

Creating a client reservation

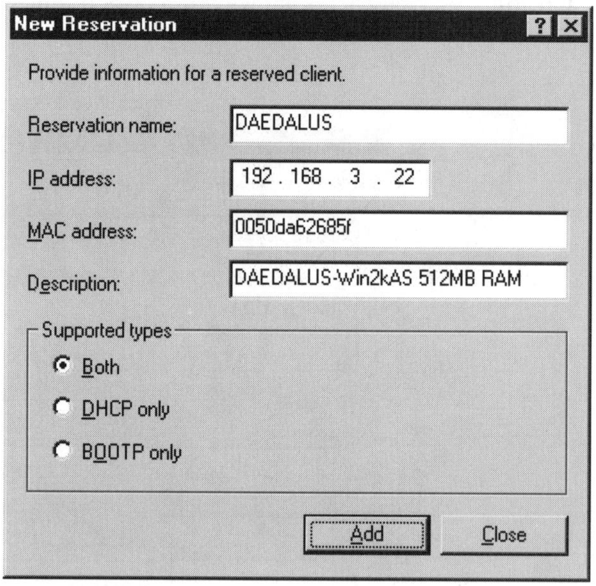

4. In the New Reservation dialog box, enter the following information:

   Reservation name: The host name of the computer

   IP address: The IP address of the computer

   MAC address: The Media Access Control address (do not include dashes)

   Description: An optional field to describe the reserved client

Supported types: Indicate whether this reservation is for a DHCP client, a BOOTP client, or either one

5. Click Add to complete the operation, then click Close

A reserved client's IP address must be one that is part of an existing scope. You do not need to create an exclusion for the IP address that has been given to the reserved client. Many administrators feel that they need to do this in order to prevent other computers from taking the reserved client's IP address. However, as you can see in Figure 4-4, once you create the client reservation, the IP address is automatically removed from the pool and assigned to the reserved client. In this example, the reserved client is offline and has not yet received its new IP address via the client reservation.

Client options can be now be configured. To create client options:

1. Open the DHCP management console.
2. In the left pane, expand the server name, expand the Scope folder, and then expand the Reservations folder. You need to have a scope in place to do this. Right-click on the name of the client reservation for which you want to configure options, and then click Configure Options.
3. Configure options in the Reservation Options dialog box as shown in Figure 4-5.

FIGURE 4-4

The reserved client's IP address is removed from the pool of available IP addresses

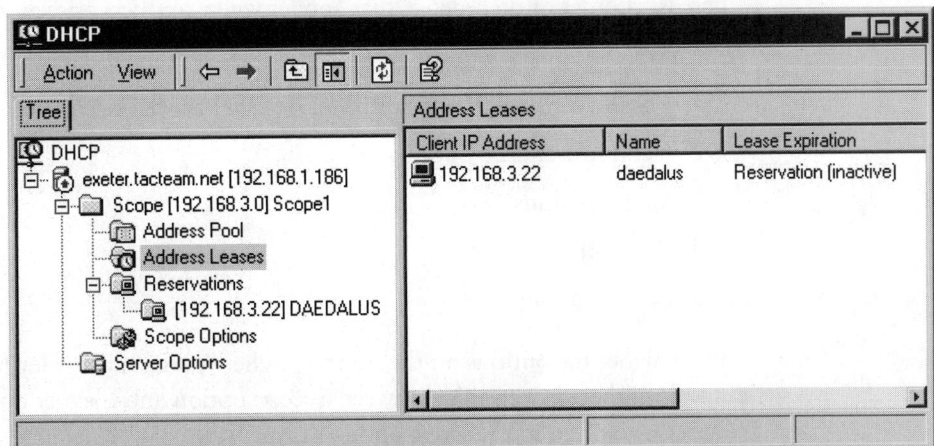

FIGURE 4-5

The Reservation Options dialog box

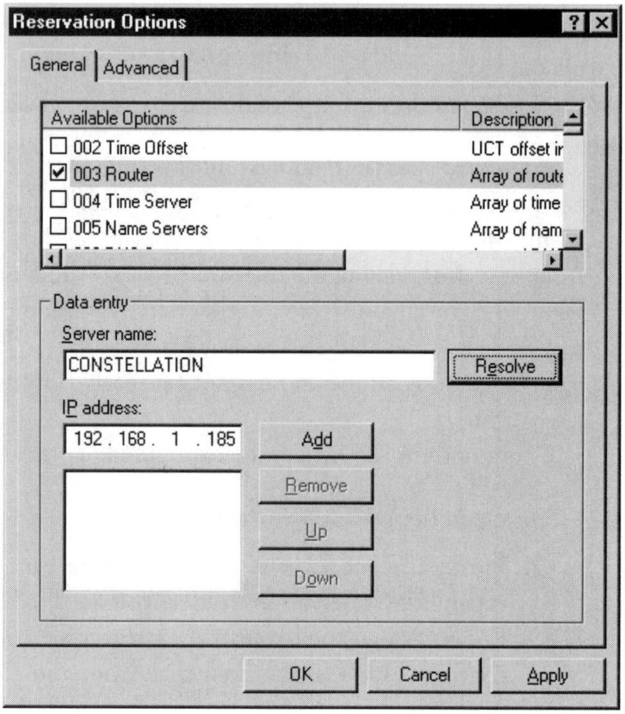

DHCP Options Order of Precedence

There is an order of precedence that applies when conflicts arise among DHCP options:

1. Locally configured options (the DHCP client has been manually configured)
2. Vendor/user class options
3. Client options
4. Scope options
5. Server options

The higher the options on the list, the higher "precedence" they have. For example, if there is a conflict between a scope option and a server option, the conflict is resolved in the scope option's favor.

exam Watch

When assessing DHCP option conflicts, be aware that all configured options, at whatever level they are assigned, will apply. For example, you configure server options that define the WINS server address as 192.168.1.2 and the DNS server address as 192.168.1.3. You also configure a reserved client to have the WINS server client option to be 192.168.1.10. The reserved client will have both options applied to it, with the WINS server being 192.168.1.10 and the DNS server for the reserved client being 192.168.1.3. The DHCP options are comparable to NTFS permissions, in that they are additive as you move through the various option types.

on the Job

There is another set of DHCP options that you can define at the DHCP server. These are the *predefined options.* ***You create predefined options when you want default option settings for the new scopes you create.***

Vendor-Specific Options

RFCs 2131 and 2132 define DHCP *vendor class options,* which allow hardware and software vendors to add their own options to the DHCP server. These options are additions to the list of standard DHCP options included with the Windows 2000 DHCP Server.

If a manufacturer wants custom DHCP options sent to the DHCP client, the DHCP client can be configured to request these options during the lease assignment process. The vendor's customized set of options is installed on the DHCP server itself, so that it can respond to the DHCP clients' request. The DHCP server will recognize the vendor's class identifiers sent by the DHCP client and forward the vendor-configured options to the client.

The vendor options must be installed and configured on the DHCP server. Microsoft has included vendor class options for Windows 2000 and Windows 98 clients, as well as a generic Microsoft operating system vendor class. The latter is used to deliver DHCP options to any Microsoft operating system that includes "MSFT" as a client identifier during the client initialization. You can see these options in Figure 4-6.

Microsoft vendor-specific options include:

- **Disable NetBIOS over TCP/IP (NetBT)** Allows an option to be sent to the client to disable NetBT.
- **Release DHCP lease on shutdown** Informs the client to release its lease at shut down. You might use this with laptop computers that move on and off the network frequently. This will free up IP addresses in the scope.

FIGURE 4-6

Vendor class options included with the Windows 2000 DHCP Server

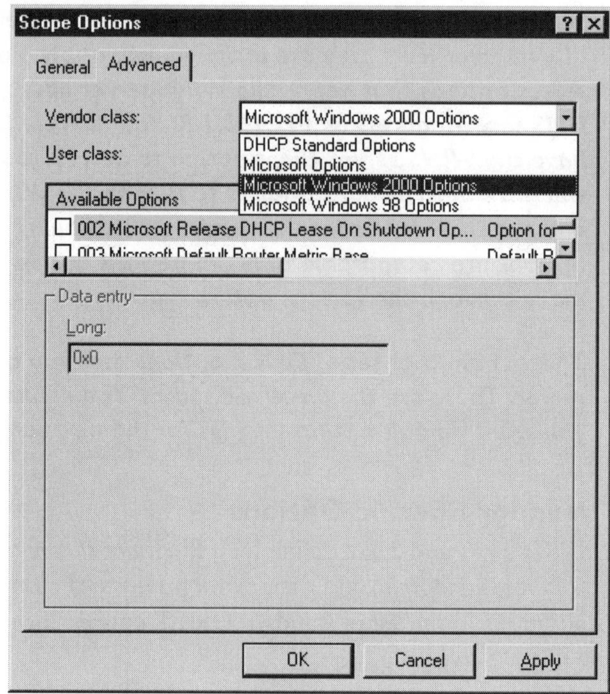

- **Default router metric base** Sets the default base metric for the DHCP client. This value is used to calculate the fastest and least-expensive routes.
- **Proxy Autodiscovery** Used only by clients that have Internet Explorer 5.0. This option informs the client of the location of the Internet Explorer 5.0 automatic configuration file.

The administrator cannot create vendor class options; the hardware or software vendor provides them. The administrator can implement these options when the software or hardware manufacturer makes them available.

User Class Options

User classes allow DHCP clients to identify their *class membership* to a DHCP server. The server can return to the client a specific set of options relevant to the *class*. The process is the same as how vendor class options are requested by the client and sent by the DHCP server.

You define the user classes at the DHCP server. User classes allow you as the administrator to customize a set of class options that fit your specific needs. For example, you could classify a group of computers that should use a specific WINS server and default gateway as "Portable." Then you create a Portable user class on the DHCP server and you configure the laptop computers to identify themselves as members of the Portable class.

Microsoft has included some built-in classes that are available "out of the box." These include user classes with special options for BOOTP and remote access clients, as depicted in Figure 4-7.

Scope options override server options, Client options override scope options, and user class options override all other options, except those manually configured on the DHCP client. For example, if we have a machine with a client reservation, this machine's reserved client options will override any other options that might be set for the server or for the scope. However, if the reserved client identifies itself as a member of a certain user class, the user class options will override any reserved client options that are in conflict.

FIGURE 4-7

User classes available "out of the box" on Windows 2000

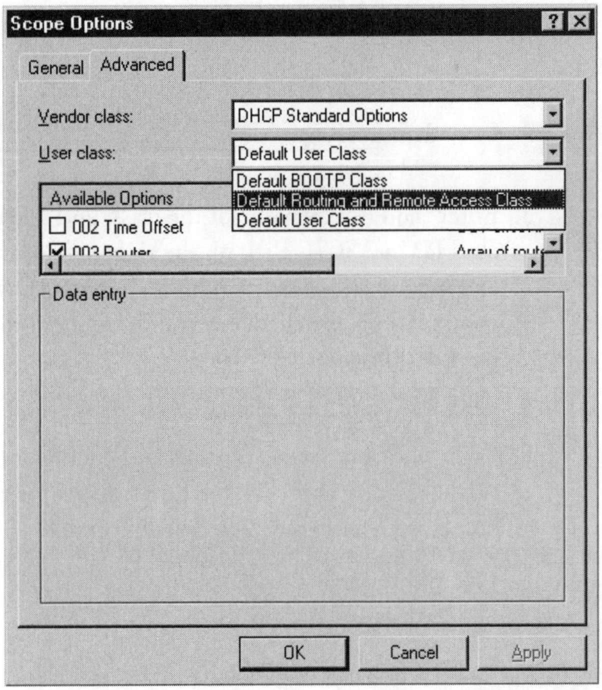

To create a new user class:

1. In the DHCP management console, right-click on the server name, and then click on Define User Classes.
2. The DHCP User Classes dialog box appears. Click Add. You should now see the New Class dialog box as shown in Figure 4-8.

FIGURE 4-8

Creating a new user class

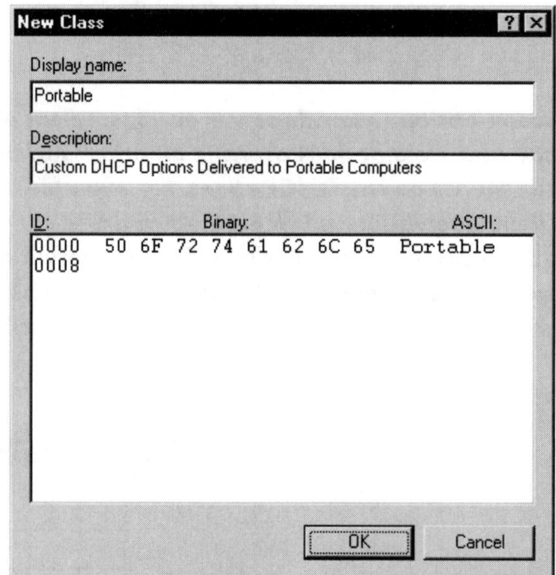

3. Enter the Display name of the class, and a Description. To enter the user class ID in ASCII, click on the right side of the lowest text box under ASCII and type in the class ID. This is the class ID you will use with the ipconfig command on the clients to configure them to send their class membership to the DHCP server.
4. Click OK, and then click Close to close the DHCP User Classes dialog box.
5. Right-click on Server Options and click Configure Options. Click on the Advanced tab, and click the down arrow for the "User class" drop-down list box, as seen in Figure 4-9. Select Portable.

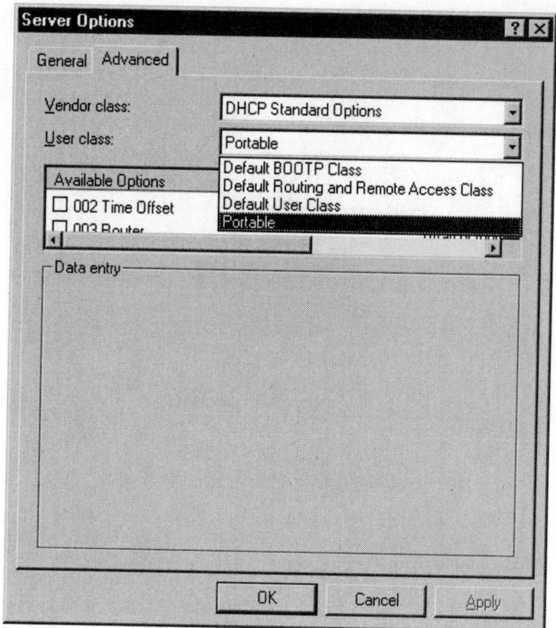

FIGURE 4-9 Selecting the Portable user class from the Advanced tab in the Server Options dialog box

6. After selecting the Portable user class, you will see a list of DHCP options you can set for the class. Note that this is just a list of the standard DHCP options. The difference is that members of the Portable class will have different values for the options that you select. Figure 4-10 shows an example of this.
7. Click Apply, then OK, and you're set.

At the client machine, type in the following command to have the client identify itself as a member of the class:

ipconfig /setclassid adapter [classidtoset]

In the preceding example, the new class ID was Portable. At the client we would open a command prompt and type

ipconfig /setclassid 3Com portable

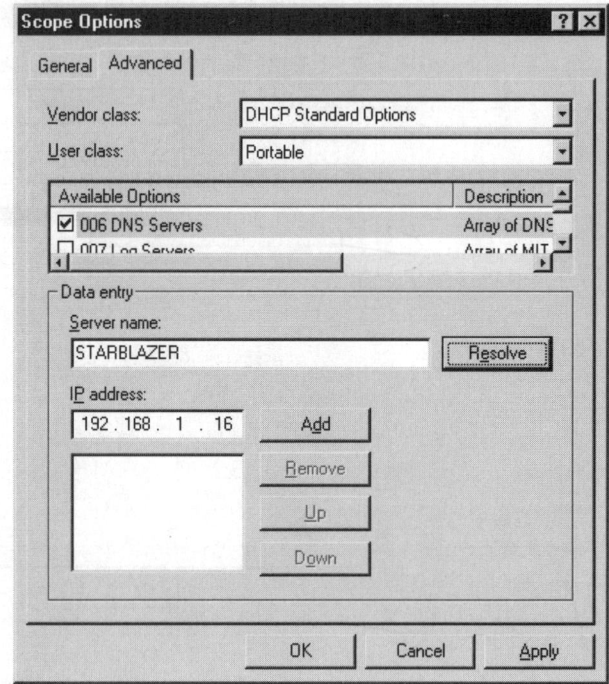

FIGURE 4-10

The Portable user class options

User options allow us a greater level of granularity in the assignment of DHCP options. This improved granularity gives the administrator greater control over the TCP/IP parameters configured on the DHCP clients in his network.

Something that might drive you nuts is the "adapter" argument of the setclassid switch. One would think this would be the name of the NIC itself, such as** 3Com EtherLink XL 10/100 PCI TX NIC (3C905B-TX)**, which can be found by looking at the properties of the network card. However, the name that you enter in the adapter argument is the name of the interface, which by default is** Local Area Connection. **To make your life easier when working with the adapter name in command-line arguments, change the name of the adapter from** Local Area Connection **to something simpler like** 3Com **or** LinkSys.. **You can do this by right-clicking on the Local Area Connection icon in the Network Properties window, selecting Rename, and typing in the new name.

BOOTP Tables

BOOTP (Bootstrap Protocol) is the predecessor to DHCP. It was originally designed to provide IP address configuration to diskless workstations, which not only received IP addressing information from a BOOTP server, but also received information regarding where to download its operating system image. DHCP was developed to improve on the host configuration services offered by BOOTP, and address some of the problems encountered in using it.

BOOTP specifications are defined in RFC 951.

Similarities between DHCP and BOOTP

Because DHCP is based on BOOTP, they are alike in many ways. For instance, the request and reply messages they use are basically the same, using one 576-byte UDP datagram for each message. The headers are almost the same as well, although there is a slight difference in the final message header field that carries optional data: It is called the *vendor-specific area* in BOOTP, whereas DHCP calls it the *options field*. The size of the field differs, too; the vendor-specific area is only 64 octets, while the DHCP options field can hold as much as 312 bytes of information. This allows DHCP to provide many more options than can be provided via the BOOTP protocol.

Another thing the two protocols have in common is the use of the same UDP ports for communication between server and client. UDP 67 is used for receiving client messages, and UDP 68 is used to accept replies from a server.

Because of these similarities, relay agents generally don't distinguish between BOOTP and DHCP packets, treating them both the same.

Differences between DHCP and BOOTP

Despite the similarities noted in the preceding section, there are some important differences between the two host configuration protocols. The IP address allocation methods are not alike—BOOTP normally allocates one IP address per client, which it permanently reserves in its database on the BOOTP server. DHCP, as its name implies, leases addresses dynamically, assigning an address to the client from a pool of available addresses and only temporarily reserving it in the server's database.

Many of the differences between BOOTP and DHCP stem from the difference in intended purpose. Unlike BOOTP, DHCP was originally designed to configure addressing information for computers with hard drives from which they could boot, especially laptops and other computers that are moved frequently.

Due to this, BOOTP uses a two-phase configuration process in which client computers first contact a BOOTP server for address assignment, and then contact a TFTP (Trivial File Transfer Protocol) server to transfer their boot image files to boot the operating system. DHCP clients, which are capable of booting from their own hard drives, use a one-phase configuration process: the client negotiates a leased IP address from the DHCP server, which contains any other needed TCP/IP configuration details (such as subnet mask, default gateway, DNS and WINS server addresses).

Another difference is that BOOTP clients must restart in order to renew the configuration with the server. DHCP clients, however, can automatically renew their leases with the DHCP servers at preset intervals. It is valuable for a Windows 2000 administrator to be aware of the characteristics of BOOTP, since it is the foundation upon which automatic host configuration was founded.

BOOTP clients can have the IP addressing information assigned statically, via client reservations, or dynamically via a scope configured to support BOOTP requests. However, if the client receives its information from a dynamic pool, it will not be able to download the boot image file.

Superscopes

Microsoft recommends the use of *superscopes* when you have more than one DHCP server on a subnet. A superscope is a Windows 2000 DHCP feature that lets you use more than one scope for a subnet. The superscope contains multiple "child" scopes, grouped together under one name and manageable as one entity. The situations in which superscopes should be used include:

- When many DHCP clients are added to a network, so that it has more than were originally planned for.
- When the IP addresses on a network must be renumbered.
- When two (or more) DHCP servers are on the same subnet for fault tolerance purposes.

Using superscopes gives the administrator the flexibility to support DHCP clients in *multinet* configurations. A multinet is a network configuration in which multiple logical networks reside on the same physical segment. The administrator is able to activate the individual scope ranges of IP addresses used on the network, and provide leases from multiple scopes to the DHCP clients on the same physical network.

Superscopes are valuable in situations where the available DHCP addresses have almost been used up, and additional computers need to join the same segment. Using a superscope will allow you to extend the address space for the network segment. In this situation, you can create a superscope with two child scopes: the original scope of addresses that is almost depleted, and a new scope for the additional computers that need to join the network.

To create a new superscope you must have at least two scopes already in place. After creating the two scopes, perform the following steps:

1. Right click on the DHCP server name in the left pane of the DHCP management console and click on New Superscope.
2. That starts the New Superscope Wizard; click Next to move past the welcome screen. Type in the name of the superscope in the Name text box and click Next.
3. In the Select Scopes dialog box, select two or more scopes from the list that will be members of the superscope. Figure 4-11 shows what this looks like. (Note that you have to hold down Ctrl while you click on multiple entries.)
4. Click Next to move to the last page of the wizard. The final page displays the name of the superscope and the member scopes you included in the superscope. If everything looks good, click Finish.
5. Now when you look at the DHCP management console, you see the individual scopes represented as objects within the Superscope container, as shown in Figure 4-12.

FIGURE 4-11

The Select Scopes dialog box

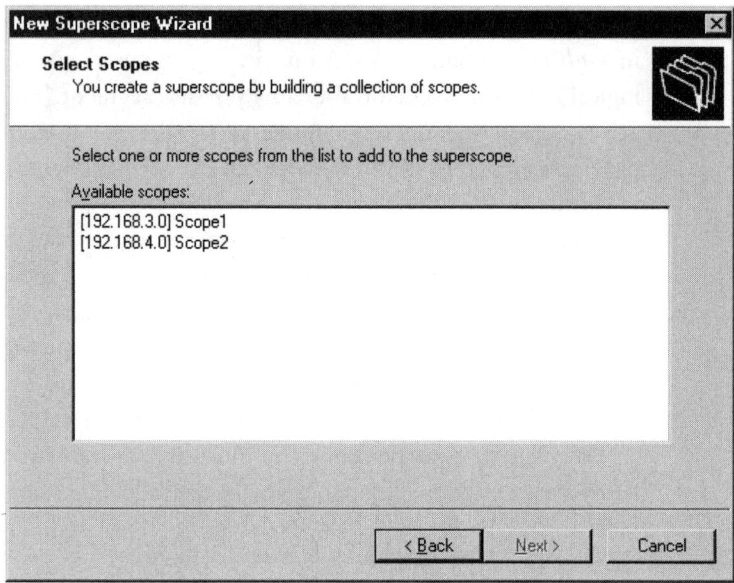

FIGURE 4-12

Member's scope objects inside a Superscope container object

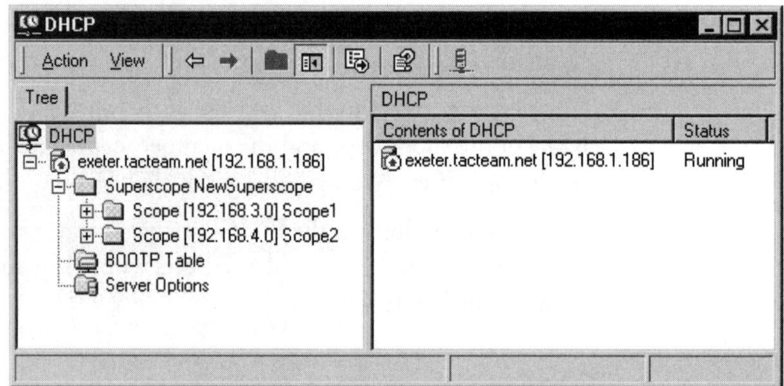

SCENARIO & SOLUTION

Do I have to create scope options?	No. You do not have to create or use any of the DHCP options if you don't want to; or, you can use just server options. However, you will probably want to create at least the default gateway option for each scope, since each subnet needs to use a different default gateway, and you don't want to have to manually configure the gateway address on all the DHCP client computers.
What computers should I create client reservations for?	You can create client reservations for all computers that need to have the same IP over time. Examples include WINS servers and DNS servers. The reason why these machines need the same IP address is that the client configuration for these services uses IP addresses rather than NetBIOS or host names. Client reservations are a good way for you to almost completely centralize the management of your IP address space. The only machines that typically can't be DHCP clients are the DHCP servers themselves.
I have tried to create a vendor class on my Windows 2000 DHCP Server, but I can't find where to do this. Is there something wrong with my DHCP server?	You cannot create your own vendor classes; you must obtain custom vendor class options from the product vendors that wish to create their own vendor class options on the Windows 2000 DHCP Server.

When you have two logical subnets on a single physical segment, how do machines communicate with each other? If a machine from the 192.168.3.0 subnet needs to communicate with a machine on the 192.168.4.0 subnet, it must send the message to its default gateway. The only difference from what you usually see is that the gateway interfaces for both of these network IDs will be on the same physical segment. The router(s) will need to be configured to recognize this situation correctly.

EXERCISE 4-3

Creating a New Scope

In this exercise, you will configure a scope on the DHCP server. Remember, a single DHCP server can host multiple scopes. We will configure a single scope using the Windows 2000 Scope Wizard.

1. Log on as Administrator.
2. Select Start | Programs | Administrative Tools. Click on DHCP to start the DHCP management console.
3. Expand all nodes in the left pane. Right now, the console doesn't look too exciting. All you should see is the name of your DHCP server and the Server Options node in the left pane, and some instructions on how to configure the DHCP 4-15.306 (shown as follows).

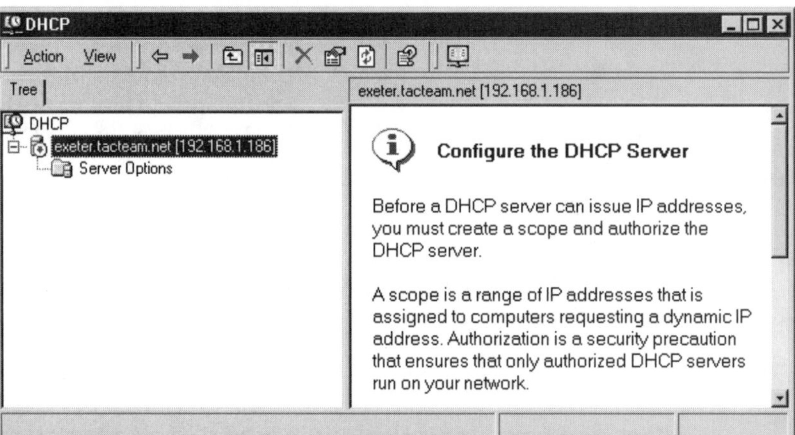

4. Right-click on your DHCP server's name, and click New Scope. This begins the New Scope Wizard. Click Next.
5. In the Name box, give the Scope the name NewScope1. In the description box, type **First Scope**. Click Next.
6. In the IP Address Range dialog box, type **192.168.3.1** for the Start IP address and **192.168.3.254** for the End IP address. Note that the Length and the Subnet mask text boxes are filled in for you automatically, as shown in the following illustration. Click Next.

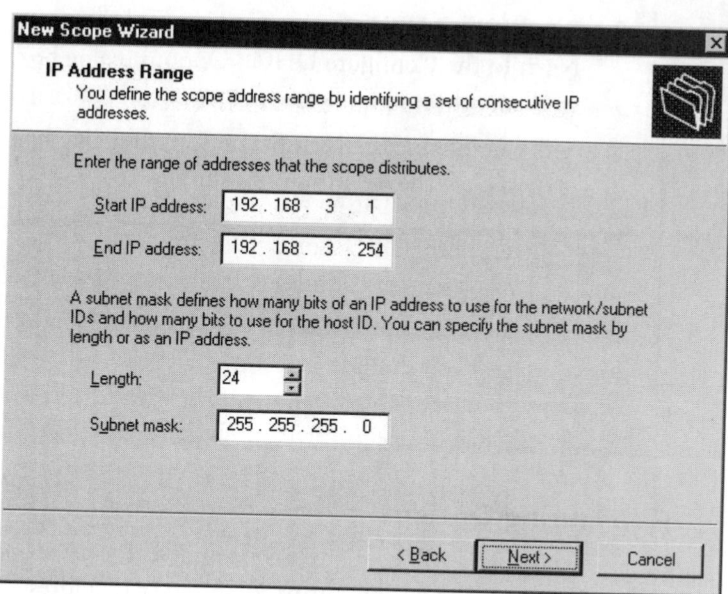

7. In the Add Exclusions dialog box, type **192.168.3.1** for the Start IP address and **192.168.1.10** for the End IP address. Then click Add. You screen should look like the following illustration. Click Next.

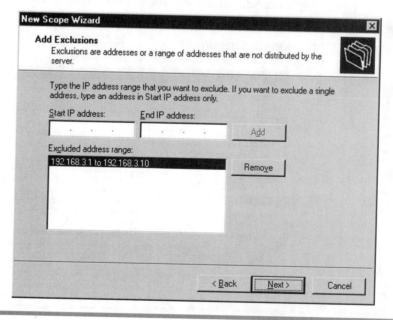

New Scope Wizard

Add Exclusions

Exclusions are addresses or a range of addresses that are not distributed by the server.

Type the IP address range that you want to exclude. If you want to exclude a single address, type an address in Start IP address only.

Start IP address: End IP address: Add

Excluded address range:

192.168.3.1 to 192.168.3.10

Remove

< Back Next > Cancel

8. For the Lease Duration, accept the default lease period of 8 Days and click Next. In the Configure DHCP Options dialog box, select "No, I will configure these options later," then click Next.
9. The Completing the New Scope Wizard dialog box appears. Click Finish to complete the definition of your new scope.

Now that you've defined your scope, let's configure some options.

EXERCISE 4-4

Configuring Options

In this exercise, you will configure scope options for the scope you just created. You will configure a scope option for the DNS server IP address. Do not perform this exercise on a live, production network without the permission of your network administrator.

1. Log on as Administrator if you have not done so already.
2. Expand all nodes in the left pane. You should see what appears in the following illustration.

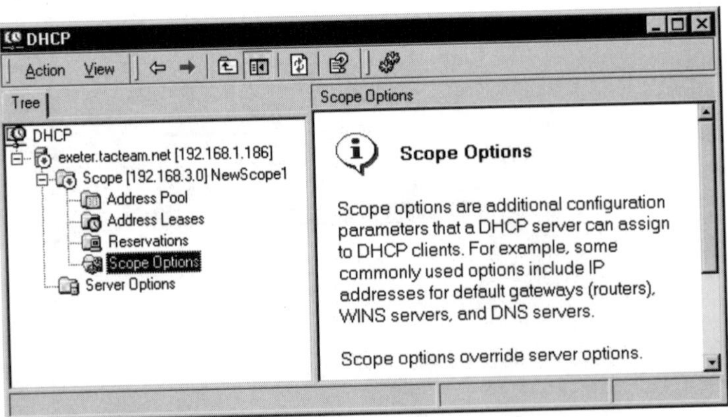

3. Right-click on Scope Options, and click on Configure Options.

4. On the General tab, scroll down the list of options until you find DNS Servers. Place a check mark in the check box next to DNS Servers. Type in the name of one of your DNS servers and then click Resolve. Your screen should look like the following illustration. Click Add, then click Apply, and then OK.

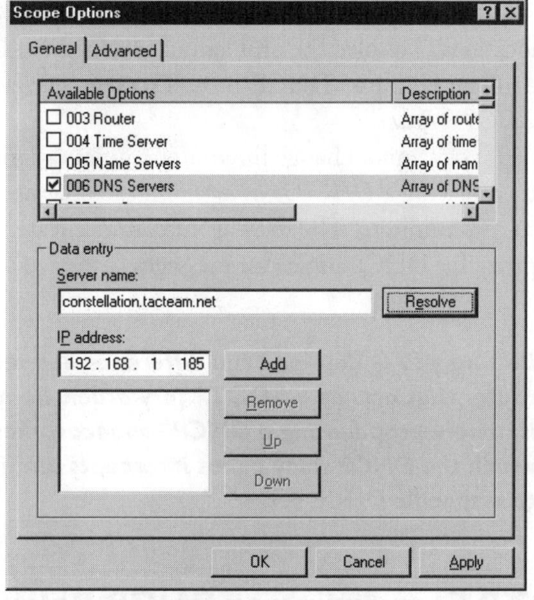

You have successfully configured a scope option that will deliver the DNS server IP address to the DHCP clients that receive IP addresses on the subnet represented by that scope.

CERTIFICATION OBJECTIVE 4.03

DHCP Relay Agents in a Routed Environment

Deploying DHCP in a single segment network is easy. Since all DHCP messages are broadcast messages, all the computers on the segment can listen and respond to these broadcasts. A single scope on a solitary DHCP server is all that is required.

The complexity of the DHCP server placement problem increases with the number of segments on the network. This is because the DHCP broadcast messages do not by default cross the routers. One solution is to put a DHCP server on each segment. This obviates the need for broadcast messages to traverse routers. This solution can be cost prohibitive and labor intensive if there are a large number of subnets. This also defeats your primary goal of centralizing management of IP addressing for your organization.

A better option is to use fewer DHCP servers and place these machines in central locations. To solve the problem of DHCP broadcast management, routers can be configured to pass DHCP/BOOTP messages selectively. This is referred to as *BOOTP Relay.*

If you cannot change the router configuration to accommodate BOOTP Relay, then placing a *DHCP relay agent* on each segment allows DHCP clients and servers to communicate. The relay agent communicates with a DHCP server and acts as a proxy for DHCP broadcast messages that need to be routed to remote segments.

exam Watch

Be sure you understand the difference between a DHCP relay agent and a router that acts as a BOOTP forwarder. Be aware that the BOOTP forwarder is merely propagating a DHCP broadcast message across multiple subnets, which the DHCP relay agent intercepts and forwards via a directed datagram to a specific DHCP server.

Using BOOTP Forwarding or DHCP Relay Agents

Routers that conform to RFC 2132 can be configured to pass DHCP/BOOTP broadcast messages. These broadcast packets pass through UDP Port 67, which is the DHCP server port number for receiving DHCP client messages. This is known as BOOTP Relay. Most modern routers support BOOTP Relay; if your router does not, contact the router manufacturer for a software or firmware upgrade.

If you cannot upgrade routers to support BOOTP Relay, you can configure a Windows NT 4.0 or Windows 2000 Server to become a DCHP relay agent. The DHCP relay agent will listen for DHCP broadcast messages and forward these to a DHCP server on a remote subnet. The relay agent itself does not depend on broadcasts when forwarding these messages because it is configured with the IP address of the DHCP server, and therefore can send directed datagrams to the

DHCP server. When the remote DHCP server receives the messages from the DHCP relay agent, it forwards replies to the DHCP relay agent, which broadcasts each reply on its local subnet.

The following are the details of this exchange when an RFC-compliant router acts as a relay agent via BOOTP Relay:

1. The DHCP client broadcasts a DHCPDISCOVER message.
2. The DHCP relay agent intercepts the message. In the message header there is a field for the gateway IP address. If the field is 0.0.0.0, the relay agent inserts its own IP address.
3. The DHCP relay agent forwards the DHCPDISCOVER message to the remote DHCP server.
4. When the DHCPDISCOVER message arrives at the DHCP server, the service examines the gateway IP address (*giaddr*). The server determines whether it has a scope for the network ID specified in the giaddr.
5. The DHCP server prepares a lease for the client, and issues a DHCPOFFER message directly to the address included in the giaddr.
6. Since the client does not yet have an IP address, the local router interface broadcasts the DHCPOFFER to the subnet.
7. The same processes take place for the DHCPREQUEST and DHCPACK messages.

A similar series of events takes place when a Windows computer is used as a DHCP relay agent.

Configuring the DHCP Relay Agent

The Routing and Remote Access Service (RRAS) must be installed prior to configuring the DHCP relay agent. After installing RRAS, open the Routing and Remote Access console, expand the server name, expand the IP routing node, then click on the DHCP Relay Agent node. In the right pane, you will see a list of Interfaces listening for DHCP broadcasts. Figure 4-13 shows how the Routing and Remote Access console should appear to you at this point.

Right-click on the DHCP Relay Agent node in the left pane and click on Properties. You should see what appears in Figure 4-14. This is where you enter the

FROM THE CLASSROOM

DHCP Relay Agents vs. BOOTP Forwarders

Remember that a DHCP relay agent and a BOOTP forwarder are two different entities. I have found in the classroom that students often confuse these two, and think they are just two terms for the same thing. they are not! A DHCP relay agent is typically, on a Windows 2000 network, a computer that is configured to intercept DHCP messages and forward them to a specific DHCP server. BOOTP forwarding is done at the router. The router can be a multihomed Windows 2000 machine configured as a router, or a dedicated hardware router. When BOOTP forwarding is enabled, DHCP broadcast messages are passed through the router interface to the next network. In order for BOOTP forwarding to work correctly, all router interfaces between the source of the DHCP broadcast and the destination must have BOOTP forwarding enabled.

—Thomas W. Shinder, M.D., MCSE, MCP+I, MCT

FIGURE 4-13

DHCP Relay Agent node in the Routing and Remote Access console

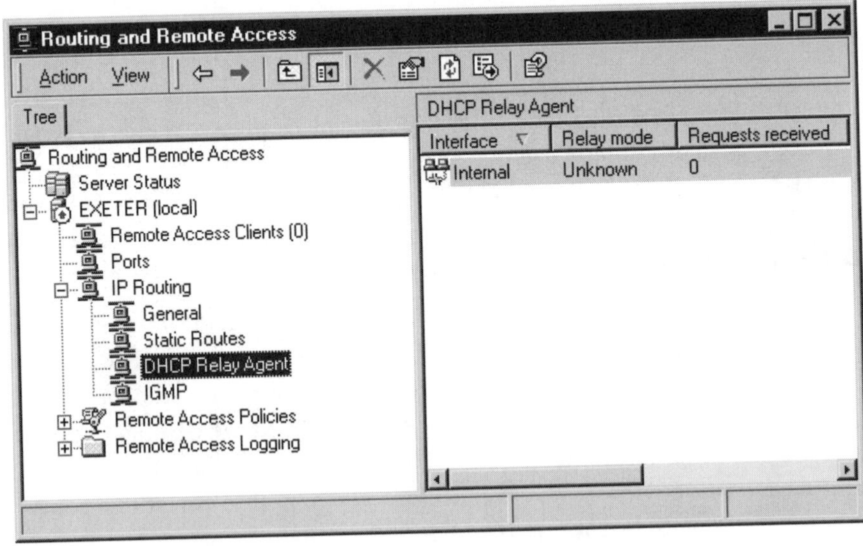

IP address of the DHCP server that the relay agent will forward the DHCP broadcast message to.

Double-click on the interface of choice. You will see the Internal Properties dialog box as shown in Figure 4-15.

Put a check mark in the "Relay DHCP packets" box to enable DHCP relay for the selected interface. The "Hop count threshold" allows you to configure the number of networks a DCHP broadcast message can pass through before being silently discarded. This prevents DHCP messages from looping endlessly throughout the network. The maximum setting is 16.

The "Boot threshold" defines the number of seconds the relay agent waits before forwarding DHCP messages. This option is useful if you are using a combination of local and remote DHCP servers, as in the case of fault tolerant setups. The relay agent should forward DHCP messages only if the local server fails to respond

FIGURE 4-14

The DHCP Relay Agent Properties box

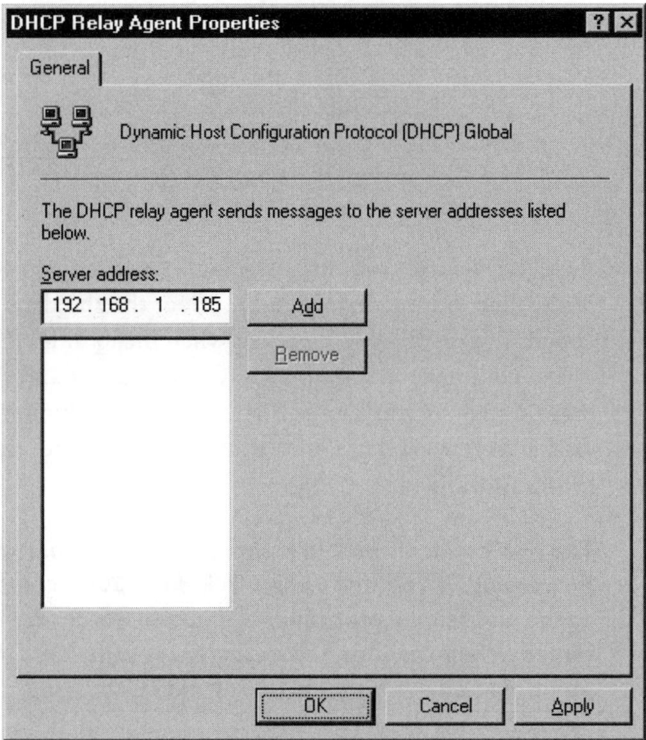

FIGURE 4-15

The DHCP Relay Agent Internal Interface Properties sheet

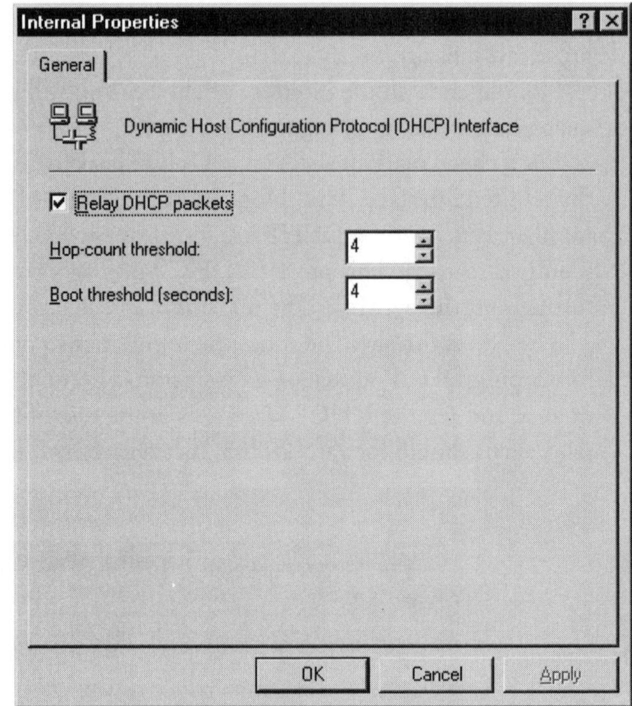

in the time interval defined in the "Boot threshold." This setting helps prevent a "flood" of routed DHCP packets when the local DHCP server is busy.

Do not implement both a DHCP relay agent and RFC-compliant router pass-through. If you choose the DHCP relay option, reconnoiter your network and disable BOOTP/DHCP forwarding on your routers to minimize pass-through broadcast traffic.

The hop count threshold is significant only when you are using BOOTP forwarding. If you are using a Windows 2000 computer as a DHCP relay agent, the relay agent sends a directed datagram to the configured DHCP server. When the directed datagram is sent, the DHCP message is not forwarded as a broadcast to any network.

All DHCP broadcast messages on the segment will now be forwarded to a remote DHCP server with a directed datagram.

SCENARIO & SOLUTION

Does the DHCP relay agent rebroadcast the messages sent by the DHCP clients?	No. When the DHCP relay agent intercepts the DHCP broadcast messages, it sends a directed datagram to a DHCP server whose IP address has been entered into the DHCP relay agent.
How does the DHCP server know what scope to use when it receives a request from a DHCP relay agent?	When the DHCP relay agent forwards the request to a DHCP server, it includes its IP address and subnet mask, from which the DHCP server can assess the network ID and select the appropriate scope.
Does Microsoft use DHCP relay agents or BOOTP forwarding at their campus in Redmond?	In an article entitled "Windows 2000 Infrastructure Services Design and Deployment: DNS and DHCP Deployment within Microsoft," it appears that they use primarily BOOTP Relay rather than DHCP. You can search for this article on your TechNet CD-ROM, or at: www.microsoft.com/technet.

EXERCISE 4-5

Configuring a DHCP Relay Agent

In this exercise, you will configure a DHCP relay agent to forward DHCP broadcast messages to a remote DHCP server. In order to complete this exercise, you must have already installed and configured the Routing and Remote Access Service on you computer. Do not perform this exercise on a live, production network without the permission of your network administrator.

1. Log on as Administrator.
2. From the Administrator Tools menu, open the Routing and Remote Access management console.
3. Expand all nodes in the left pane. Locate the DHCP Relay Agent node, which is a subobject of the IP Routing node. Right-click on the DHCP Relay Agent node and click Properties.
4. In the DHCP Relay Agent Properties dialog box, type in an IP address for a DHCP server that is located on a remote subnet in the "Server address" text box and click Add. Click Apply and then OK.

CERTIFICATION OBJECTIVE 4.04

Integrating DHCP with DDNS

The Windows 2000 DHCP Server has a number of improvements over the DHCP Server found in Windows NT 4.0. The most significant is the Windows 2000 DHCP Server's ability to deliver host name and IP addressing information to a Windows 2000 Dynamic DNS (DDNS) Server.

After the Windows 2000 DHCP Server assigns the DHCP client an IP address, the Windows 2000 DHCP Server can interact with a Windows 2000 Dynamic DNS Server in one of three ways:

- It will update the DNS server by providing information to create a Host (A) record and PTR (Pointer) record on the DNS at the client's request.
- The DHCP server will update both the Host (A) record and the Pointer (PTR) record regardless of the client request.
- The DHCP server will never register information about the DHCP client. However, the client itself may directly update its information with the DDNS server.

These configuration options are made at the DHCP server, as shown in Figure 4-16.

The Windows 2000 DHCP Server supports the Client FQDN Option (Option Code 81), which allows the DHCP client to send its FQDN to the DHCP server. Only Windows 2000 clients support Option Code 81. The Windows 2000 DHCP Client and Server interact in the following way:

1. The Windows 2000 DHCP Client and Server participate in the DORA process for lease assignment. After officially obtaining a lease, the Windows 2000 client registers its own Host (A) record with the Dynamic DNS server.
2. The DHCP server registers the client's Pointer (PTR) record with the DDNS server.
3. Client and server configuration can be manipulated to allow the DHCP server to update both Host (A) and Pointer (PTR) records. If desired, the DHCP server and DCHP client can be configured so that no dynamic update of client information reaches the DDNS server.

FIGURE 4-16

Configuring DNS updates from the DHCP server

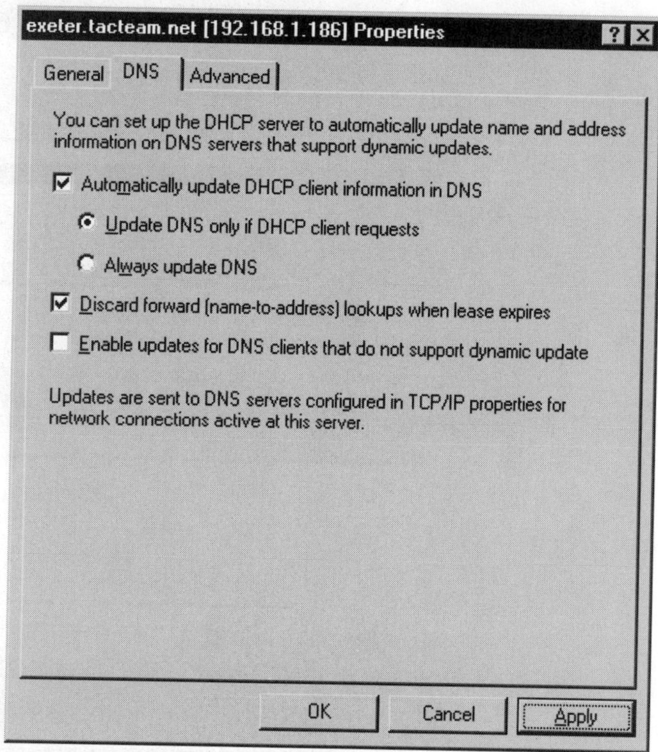

To prevent the client from registering directly with the DDNS server, you must alter the default settings. Figure 4-17 shows the Advanced TCP/IP settings dialog box on a DNS client. If you remove the check mark from the "Register this connection's addresses in DNS," it will not attempt to update the DNS directly.

The "Use this connection's DNS suffix in DNS registration" option refers to entries made in the textbox for the "DNS suffix for this connection." Each network connection can be customized to provide its own DNS domain suffix. If you remove the check mark from both of these, it will prevent the client from registering directly with the Dynamic DNS server.

Integrating Downlevel DHCP Clients and Dynamic DNS

Downlevel clients are not able to communicate directly with a DDNS server. In this case, the Windows 2000 DHCP Server can act as a "proxy" and forwards both Host (A) and Pointer (PTR) information on its behalf to the DDNS server. To enable

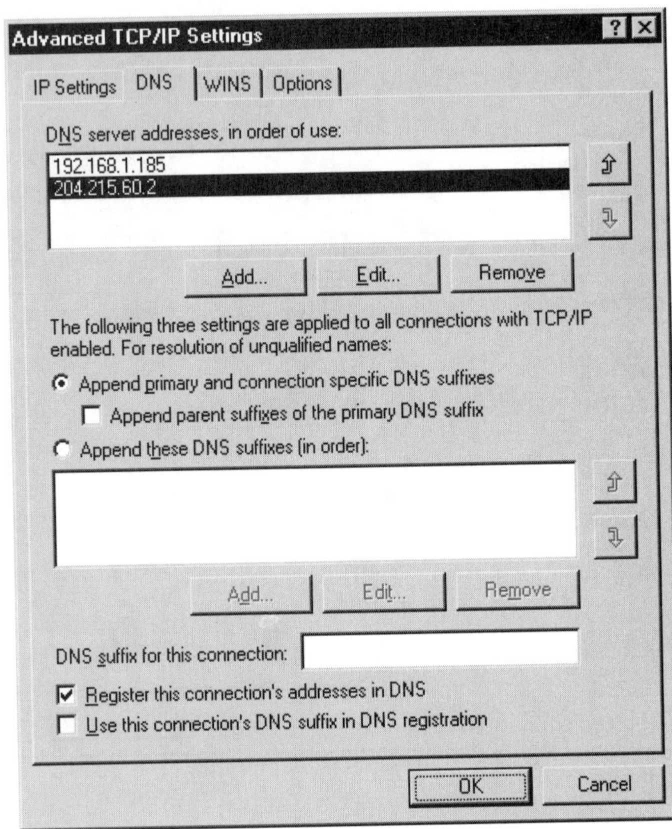

FIGURE 4-17 Advanced TCP/IP Settings dialog box and the DNS tab

support for these downlevel clients, place a check mark in the "Enable updates for DNS clients that do not support dynamic update" check box in the DHCP server's Properties dialog box.

Windows 2000 computers configured with static IP information will update their own Host (A) and Pointer (PTR) records with the DDNS server. If you change the name or IP address of a Windows 2000 client with manually configured IP addressing information, you can force an update to that client's entry in the DDNS server by issuing the command:

```
ipconfig /registerdns
```

Downlevel clients with static IP addresses are not able to communicate directly with the DDNS server. DDNS entries for these clients must be manually reconfigured at the DDNS server.

exam Watch

Downlevel Clients such as Windows NT 4.0 computers cannot communicate with a Windows 2000 DNS Server. To dynamically update downlevel client information on a DDNS server, you must use a Windows 2000 DHCP Server to assign the downlevel clients IP addressing information.

The DHCP server is now able to update Host (A) and Pointer (PTR) record information for the downlevel clients.

EXERCISE 4-6

Enabling a DHCP Server to Update Downlevel DHCP Client Information

In this exercise, you will enable the DHCP server to update both the Host (A) and Pointer (PTR) records on the DDNS server on the behalf of downlevel clients. Do not perform this exercise on a live, production network without the permission of your network administrator.

1. Log on as Administrator.
2. Open the DHCP management console from the Administrative Tools menu. Expand all nodes in the left pane. Right-click on the DHCP server name and click Properties.
3. In the DHCP server's Properties dialog box, place a check mark in the check box for "Enable updates for DNS clients that do not support dynamic update." Click Apply, and then OK.

CERTIFICATION OBJECTIVE 4.05

Integrating DHCP with RRAS

The Routing and Remote Access Service (RRAS) is able to obtain IP addresses to assign to RAS clients. The RRAS server acts as a *proxy* between the RRAS client and the DHCP server. The way the RRAS server uses the DHCP server to distribute IP addresses differs from how LAN clients receive DHCP IP address information.

If the RRAS server is configured to use DHCP to assign IP addresses, it will obtain a group of IP addresses from the DHCP server. This block is obtained when RRAS services initialize. RRAS *clients* do not directly interact with the DHCP server. However, they can obtain option information via DHCPINFORM packets that are forwarded by a DHCP relay agent installed on the RRAS server they have dialed in to. The number of IP addresses retrieved is equal to the number of RAS ports configured to receive calls on the RRAS server plus one. The RRAS server itself uses the additional IP address.

When the RRAS server obtains its group of IP addresses, any option information sent from the DHCP server to the RRAS server is ignored. Typical DHCP option parameters such as WINS and DNS IP addresses are obtained from the specific RRAS connection. Each RRAS connection can be independently configured. However, if a DHCP relay agent is installed on the RRAS server, the RAS clients will be able to obtain option information.

There is no effective lease period for the RRAS client; the lease immediately expires after the connection is terminated. You can perform an `ipconfig` on the client machine to see if the RRAS server has assigned DHCP configuration parameters.

Be aware that the RAS server may grab a *lot* ***of IP addresses from the DHCP server if you're not careful. The RRAS server will obtain IP addresses for all ports it has configured to take incoming calls. If you have 100 PPTP ports configured, the RRAS server will take that many IP addresses,*** *in advance.* ***If you notice that your scopes are becoming depleted faster than you had anticipated, check this out.***

EXERCISE 4-7

Configuring RRAS to Use DHCP to Assign IP Addresses

In this exercise, you will configure an RRAS server to use DHCP to assign IP addressing information to RAS clients. In order to do this exercise, you must have RRAS installed and configured. Do not perform this exercise on a live, production network without the permission of your network administrator.

1. Log on as Administrator.
2. From the Administrative Tools menu, click on Routing and Remote Access.
3. Expand all nodes in the left pane. Right-click on the RRAS server name in the left pane, and click on Properties. You should see what appears in the following illustration.

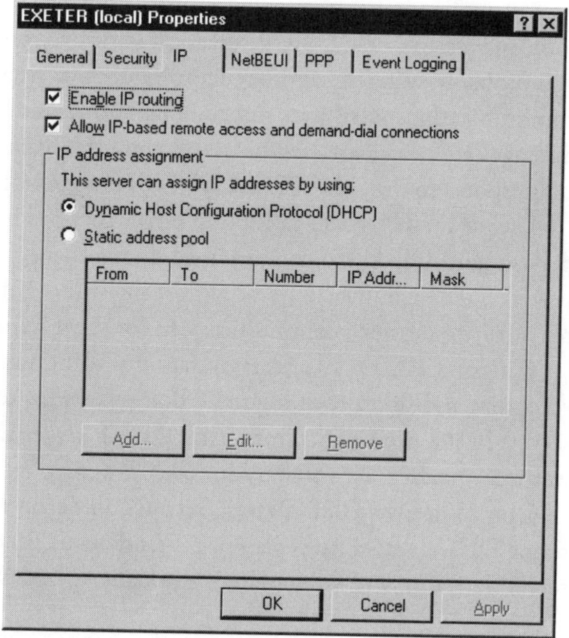

4. Select the option for Dynamic Host Configuration Protocol (DHCP) under "This server can assign IP addresses by using." Click Apply, and then OK.

CERTIFICATION OBJECTIVE 4.06

Integrating DHCP with Active Directory

The Windows 2000 DHCP Server is tightly integrated with the Windows 2000 Domain Security infrastructure. By integrating with the Active Directory, the Windows 2000 DCHP Server can prevent errors in network communication by shutting down DHCP servers that have not been approved by the network administrator. The process of approving these DHCP servers is called *authorizing*.

Authorizing DHCP Servers

As a network administrator, you probably have had the experience of having someone "test" a new DHCP server on your live, production network. And, you probably suffered from having to figure out what the problems with network communications were after someone had done this. The problem is that DHCP messages are broadcast messages, and any DHCP server that hears the broadcast can respond to the DHCPDISCOVER message from a DHCP client.

A *rogue* DHCP server (a DHCP server that has not been approved by the IT department) is likely to contain invalid scopes and DHCP options. Rogue DHCP servers can assign inaccurate IP addressing information to DHCP clients, which may disrupt network communications for these hapless clients.

Windows 2000 networks running only Windows 2000 DHCP Servers can recognize and shut down rogue DHCP servers by keeping a list of *authorized* DHCP servers in the Active Directory. Any DHCP server that starts up and is not included in the authorized list will have its DHCP Server Service shut down automatically.

Only Windows 2000 DHCP Servers can detect rogue DHCP servers, and the rogue DHCP server must also be a Windows 2000 computer. Rogue NT DHCP server detection will fail to detect an unauthorized Windows NT DHCP server.

Rogue DHCP Server Detection

When a Windows 2000 DHCP Server initializes, it broadcasts a DHCPINFORM message to the local segment. The DHCPINFORM message contains vendor-specific option codes that can be interpreted by Microsoft Windows 2000 DHCP Servers. These option types allow the Windows 2000 DHCP Server to obtain information about the network from other Windows 2000 DHCP Servers on the segment.

The DHCPINFORM message submits queries to other Windows 2000 DHCP Servers, and when a Windows 2000 DHCP Server on the segment receives this message, it responds to a DHCPINFORM query. This query asks for information about the Enterprise root name and location. The queried Windows 2000 DHCP Server responds by sending back a DHCPACK that includes Directory Services Enterprise Root information.

exam Watch

The new DHCP server will receive DHCPACK messages from all the DHCP servers on its segment. This allows the new DHCP server to collect domain membership information about all Windows 2000 DHCP Servers on its segment.

If the new DHCP server receives information about an existing Directory Services Enterprise Root, it will query the Active Directory, which maintains a list of authorized DHCP servers. If the machine's IP address is on the list, it will successfully initialize DHCP Server Services. If not, DHCP Server Services will not initialize.

The new DHCP server will start DHCP Server Services if:

- There are other DHCP servers on the segment that are authorized DHCP servers and the new DHCP server is listed in the Active Directory's list of authorized DHCP servers.
- The new DHCP server is the *only* DHCP server on the segment (If the new DHCP does not receive a response to the DHCPINFORM message query, the new DHCP server cannot be made aware of existing Directory Services Enterprise Roots).
- The new DHCP server is on a segment with other Windows 2000 DHCP Servers that are workgroup members, or all other DHCP servers on the segments are downlevel systems (such as Windows NT 4.0 DHCP servers).

In the second and third instances, the new DHCP server is unable to contact another DHCP server that has information about a Directory Services Enterprise Root. The "lone" DHCP server will continue to send a DHCPINFORM message every five minutes. If the new DHCP server later receives a DHCPACK from a DHCP server that contains information about the Enterprise Root, the new DHCP server will look to see if it is authorized in the Active Directory, and if not, will disable its DHCP Server Services.

EXERCISE 4-8

Authorizing a DHCP Server in the Active Directory

In this exercise, you will authorize a DHCP server in the Active Directory. Do not perform this exercise on a live, production network without the permission of your network administrator.

1. Log on as Administrator.
2. Open the DHCP management console from the Administrative Tools menu.
3. Right-click on the DHCP server's name in the left pane, and click Authorize, as seen in the following illustration.

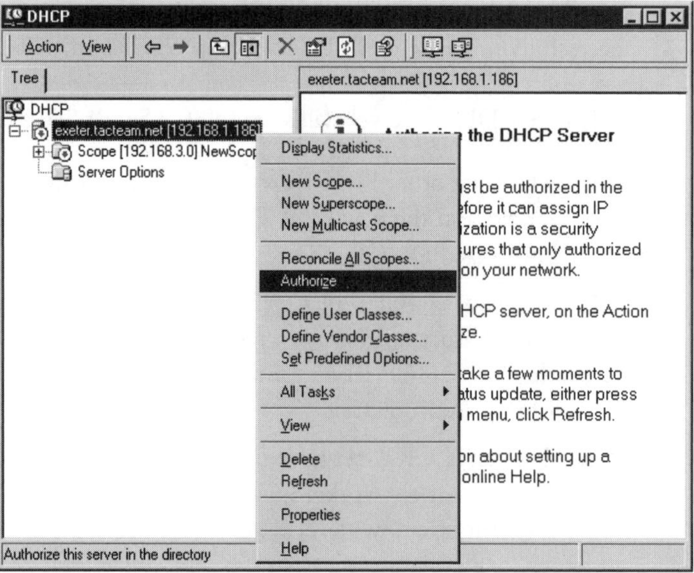

The DHCP server is now authorized. Because the DHCP Server is authorized, the DHCP Server Service will not be shut down as a rogue DHCP Server.

CERTIFICATION OBJECTIVE 4.07

DHCP and APIPA

Automatic Private IP Addressing, or *APIPA*, allows Windows 2000 computers configured as DHCP clients to assign their own IP addresses. This technology is available on Windows 98 clients and has been ported to Windows 2000. APIPA allows a Windows 2000 DHCP client unable to contact a DHCP server to assign itself an IP address.

There are two situations where APIPA is useful. The first scenario occurs when the machine has not previously bound an IP address. In this case:

1. The Windows 2000 computer configured as a DHCP Client starts up. A DHCPDISCOVER message is broadcast to the segment. If the machine does not receive a reply, it starts to autoconfigure its IP address.
2. The machine will select, at random, an IP address from the APIPA reserved Class B network ID 169.254.0.0 with the default Class B subnet mask of 255.255.0.0.
3. A *gratuitous ARP* message is broadcast for this randomly selected IP address. If no machine responds to the ARP request, the machine will bind the new IP address to the network adapter configured as a DHCP client.
4. If another machine on the segment responds to the ARP request, the self-configuring computer will choose another IP address and issue another ARP request. It will continue this process for up to 10 addresses. If the machine cannot configure an IP address after 10 attempts, it will stop and disable TCP/IP.

If a DHCP client who has an active lease starts up and cannot contact a DHCP server, the process is a little different.

1. When the DHCP client with a valid lease starts up, it issues a DHCPREQUEST broadcast to renew the lease.
2. If the client does not receive a DHCPACK from the DHCP server, it will start to PING the IP address of the default gateway configured in its lease.

3. If the default gateway responds, the machine "assumes" there must be a problem with the DHCP server itself. The DHCP client attempts to renew its lease at 50% and 87.5% of the lease period.
4. If the default gateway fails to respond to the PING, the machine assumes it has been moved. In this case, the DHCP client abandons its lease, and autoconfigures itself as described above.

In both cases, the DHCP client issues a DHCPDISCOVER message every five minutes, attempting to contact a DHCP server. If the client receives a DHCPOFFER message at any time, it will bind a valid IP address from the DHCP server sending the offer.

Windows 2000 DHCP computers communicate with NDIS 5.0 compliant network interface card drivers to obtain information about network connection status. This *media sense* capability allows the operating system to detect whether the computer has been disconnected from the network. If the operating system senses the computer has been removed from a network and plugged into another, it will begin the lease renewal and Autoconfiguration process.

EXERCISE 4-9

CertCam 4-9

Disabling Automatic Private IP Addressing

In this exercise, you will disable APIPA on your computer. Do not perform this exercise in a live, production networking environment without the permission of your network administrator.

1. Log on as Administrator.
2. Open the Registry editor. You can do this by clicking Start | Run. In the text box for the Run command, type **regedt32** and press Enter.
3. Maximize the Hkey Local Machine window. Expand CurrentControlSet, then expand Services, then expand TCP/IP, then expand Interfaces, and then click on the node that matches the name of your adapter.
4. Click the Edit menu and then click Add Value.
5. In the Value Name text box, type **IPAutoconfigurationEnabled** and make the Data Type REG_DWORD. Then Click OK.
6. In the DWORD Editor dialog box, set the value to 0 and Click OK.
7. The new value should show in the right pane. Close the Registry Editor.

Keep in mind that APIPA is only useful on single-segment networks where all machines are using APIPA. Otherwise, the self-configuring machines will assign themselves to a network ID that's unlikely to be in use on your network.

CERTIFICATION OBJECTIVE 4.08

Monitoring and Troubleshooting DHCP

The Windows 2000 DHCP Server is a self-tuning service for the most part. However, there are times when the Server will not function properly, and you will need to troubleshoot problems with your DHCP Server. In this section, we'll explore three tools provided with the Windows 2000 DHCP Server: the Event Viewer, System Monitor, and DCHP Logging.

Using Event Viewer

The DHCP Server will report significant errors to the Windows 2000 Event Viewer. Whenever you have problems related to the DHCP server, you should look at the Event Viewer first to assess what the problem might be. Typically, the DHCP Server Service will report an error code to the Event Viewer. The Windows 2000 Support Tools, which are on the Windows 2000 CD-ROM, include a help file that contains a large number of these error codes. Be sure to install these support tools and look up cryptic error codes when you encounter them.

Using System Monitor

The Windows 2000 System Monitor takes over for the Windows NT 4.0 Performance Monitor. The System Monitor allows you to monitor many different aspects of your Windows 2000 Server installation. The Windows 2000 System Monitor contains a large number of counters that allow you to track all types of messages a DHCP server sends and receives, how much processor time is devoted to the DHCP Server Service, and the volume of packets that are dropped by the DHCP server due to a heavily taxed server.

Table 4-1 includes a sample of the more important counters that you should be familiar with when monitoring and troubleshooting your DHCP server.

TABLE 4-1

System Monitor DHCP-Related Counters

Counter	Description
Packets Received/sec	The average number of DHCP messages received by the server. After performing a baseline, if you see an unusually large number, you should investigate the reasons for the excessive DHCP traffic.
Packets Expired/sec	If DHCP message packets are held in the DHCP server's queue for an excessive period of time, the server will expire these packets and drop them. After base lining, if you find a large number of packets are being expired, you should troubleshoot the problem with the server's slow response time to DHCP messages.
Nacks/sec	This is the average number of negative acknowledges received per second. If this value is high, it's likely that many machines are moving from segment to segment, or there is a configuration problem with the client or server. Common reasons for this sort of behavior include deactivated scopes and a large number of laptops moving on and off the network.
Declines/sec	A DHCP client issues a gratuitous ARP message when it receives an IP address from a DHCP server. If the DHCP client discovers that the IP address is already in use, it will send a DHCPDECLINE message to the DHCP server and reject the offered IP address. If this happens frequently, enable conflict detection on the DHCP server for troubleshooting purposes while you're investigating the problem. Do not leave conflict detection enabled for extended periods of time.

Using Logs

Windows 2000 has auditing to allow the administrator to monitor the DHCP server. However, auditing introduces another problem: logging. Since Windows 2000 now has disk quotas, it is much easier for the logs to fill the available disk space. Windows 2000 reduces the problems by introducing *registry keys* to change the logging settings for the DHCP's audit log. To edit the values, edit the key: HKEY_LOCAL_MACHINE\SYSTEM\CurrentControlSet\Services\DHCPServer\Parameters. The values for the registry key parameters are

```
DhcpLogFilePath
DhcpLogMinSpaceOnDisk
DhcpLogDiskSpaceCheckInterval
DhcpLogFileMaxSize
```

The DhcpLogFilePath key, which is of data type REG_SZ, lets the user specify the full path to the log file. The DhcpLogMinSpaceOnDisk, which is of data type REG_DWORD, allows the administrator to specify the amount of disk space left before the audit logging is stopped. The DhcpLogDiskSpaceCheckInterval, which is of data type REG_DWORD, is the number of times the log is written before the free space is checked. DhcpLogFileMaxSize, which is of data type REG_DWORD is the maximum size of the log file in megabytes. The default is 7 megabytes.

CertCam 4-10

EXERCISE 4-10

Enabling DHCP Server Logging

In this exercise, you will enable detailed logging on your DHCP server. Do not perform this exercise on a live, production DHCP server or network without the permission of your network administrator.

1. Log on as Administrator.
2. From the Start menu, go to the Administrative Tools and then click DHCP.
3. Right-click on the name of your DHCP server, and click Properties.
4. On the General tab in the Properties dialog box, place a check mark in the "Enable DHCP audit logging" check box.
5. Click OK and close the DHCP management console.

CERTIFICATION SUMMARY

The DHCP Server Service is designed to make the management and assignment of IP addresses easier for the network administrator. You can centrally manage all the IP addressing information for even the largest of organizations by employing just a handful of DHCP servers.

DHCP clients do not usually keep IP addresses indefinitely. Instead, IP addressing information is "leased" to DHCP clients. There are four steps to the lease process: DHCPDISCOVER, DHCPOFFER, DHCPREQUEST, and DHCPACK. All DHCP messages are broadcasts.

A client must have a valid lease to retain an IP address, and will not be able to continue network activity if is does not retain a valid lease.

Remember that broadcast messages do not traverse routers. DHCP messages can be communicated across routers if you configure a router to pass through BOOTP/DHCP messages via UDP Port 67 (BOOTP Relay), or if you implement a DHCP relay agent. A DHCP relay agent intercepts multicast DHCP messages and forwards them as unicast messages to a DHCP server.

The pool of available IP addresses is called a *scope*. Only one scope is allowed per logical subnet. Scopes typically include all the available IP addresses for a specific network ID. Clients that require static IP addresses can be excluded from the scope. Excluded addresses will not be allocated to DHCP clients.

The DHCP server can deliver additional IP addressing information in the form of *DHCP options*. A large number of DHCP options are available, but Microsoft network clients support only a small number of DHCP options.

DHCP options can be configured at several levels, including server options, scope options, client options, and vendor class/user class options. Server options apply to all scopes configured on a single server. Scope options apply only to a single scope. Scope options override server options.

A DHCP server can deliver the same IP address to a machine each time it renews a lease, if a client is designated as *reserved*. A reserved client is a computer whose MAC address and IP address have been configured at the DHCP server.

A reserved client can be configured with its own DHCP options, and reserved client options override scope options.

Vendor class options are introduced for the first time in the Windows 2000 DHCP Server.

The DHCP client can identify itself as a member of the Vendor's class, and the DHCP server will send class members a custom set of options.

The DHCP administrator configures user class options, which are delivered to machines identifying themselves as a member of a particular user class. For example, a user class named "laptops" could be created. All laptops would be configured to send their class ID to the DHCP server, and DHCP options configured for the "laptops" user class are then sent to these machines. Vendor and user class options override all other DHCP options.

DHCP clients unable to contact a DHCP server can autoconfigure their IP address. APIPA (Automatic Private IP Addressing) allows DHCP clients to self-assign an IP address from the 169.254.0.0 Class B network ID.

Autoconfiguration prevents TCP/IP from shutting down when a DHCP server cannot be contacted.

Routing and Remote Access Services (RRAS) can use DHCP to assign IP addresses to RRAS clients. The RRAS server obtains a block of IP addresses from a DHCP server during initialization. The RRAS server retains only the IP address itself and all options information is discarded. Then the RRAS server assigns WINS and DNS settings to the RRAS client based on connection-specific configuration on the RRAS server. This information does not come from the DHCP server. An RRAS client lease lasts for the duration of the connection.

The Windows 2000 DHCP Server also supports dynamic assignment of IP addresses to BOOTP clients, and client reservations can be configured for BOOTP clients as well. The name of a TFTP server and the location of the Boot Image are configured in the DHCP server Boot Table.

A single physical network containing multiple logical subnetworks is called a *multinet*. A *superscope* must be configured to support multinet configurations. To create a superscope, you need to first create individual scopes. Then you use the Superscope wizard to join the individual scopes into a single administrative unit.

TWO-MINUTE DRILL

Overview of DHCP

- The DHCP server centrally manages and assigns IP addresses for an organization, which simplifies the life of the network administrator
- A DHCP server leases addresses. DHCP clients do not keep their IP addressing information indefinitely.
- You can remember the lease process by thinking of DORA: DISCOVER, OFFER, REQUEST, ACKNOWLEDGEMENT.
- All DHCP messages are broadcast messages that are broadcast to the IP and MAC hardware addresses.
- DHCP clients first attempt to renew their lease at 50% of their lease period. They will try again at 87.5% of their lease period if they were not able to renew the lease at the 50% mark.
- DHCP broadcast messages can be forwarded to remote DHCP servers by enabling BOOTP Relay on RFC-compliant routers.
- DHCP broadcast messages can be conveyed without forwarding broadcasts to remote DHCP servers by using DHCP relay agents that intercept the broadcasts and forward the broadcast request as a unicast message to a remote DHCP server.

DHCP Server Configuration

- DHCP servers store groups of IP addresses to hand out to DHCP clients in *scopes*. Each scope represents a different subnet, and only a single subnet can be included in a scope.
- In addition to assigning an IP address and subnet mask, the DHCP can provide other information such as WINS server, DNS server, and default gateway addresses. These are configured as DHCP options.
- The Windows 2000 DHCP Server includes server options, scope options, client options, reserved client options, and vendor/user class options. Know what these options represent and their order of precedence.
- BOOTP is used to assign IP addressing information to diskless workstations such as Net PCs and other "dumb" client machines.

- ❑ A *superscope* is an administrative unit that allows you to manage multiple scopes as a single entity. Superscopes are useful when you wish to include multiple scopes on a single physical segment.

DHCP Relay Agents in a Routed Environment

- ❑ Use a DHCP relay agent on segments that do not have a DHCP server located on them. The DHCP relay agent will intercept DHCP messages from DHCP clients and forward those messages to a DHCP server on remote subnets.
- ❑ If you choose not to use a DHCP relay agent, you can configure your routers to provide *BOOTP forwarding*. When enabled, BOOTP forwarding allows DHCP messages to pass through the router. Be mindful of the hop count for DHCP messages when using BOOTP forwarding to allow DHCP clients to access remote DHCP servers.

Integrating DHCP with DDNS

- ❑ The Windows 2000 DHCP Server is able to convey information to a Windows 2000 Dynamic DNS Server. By default, Windows 2000 DHCP clients update their own Host (A) record, and the DHCP server updates its Pointer (PTR) record.
- ❑ The Windows 2000 DHCP Server can act as a proxy for downlevel DHCP clients that are unable to communicate directly with Dynamic DNS servers. In this case, the DHCP server will update both the Host (A) record and the Pointer (PTR) record on the behalf of the downlevel client.

Integrating DHCP and RRAS

- ❑ The Windows 2000 RRAS Server obtains blocks of IP address from a DHCP server when the RRAS server has been configured to assign IP addresses via DHCP. Any option information associated with the IP addresses it obtains is ignored.
- ❑ The RRAS client never communicates directly with the DHCP server. It receives its IP address and option-related information directly from the RRAS server. RRAS clients drop their lease when they shut down.

Integrating DHCP with Active Directory

- A Windows 2000 DHCP Server is able to detect rogue DHCP servers. Rogue DCHP servers are those that are not authorized for use in the Active Directory. Rogue DHCP server detection is performed with the help of DHCPINFORM messages.
- Rogue server detection only works when all operating systems are Active Directory aware. Therefore, if you introduce a Windows NT 4.0 DCHP server into the network, it will not be detected as a rogue DHCP server, because the Windows NT 4.0 DHCP server does not register itself with the Active Directory.

DHCP and APIPA

- DHCP clients can self-configure their IP addressing information using Automatic Private IP Addressing (APIPA). If the DHCP client is not able to contact a DHCP server, it will self assign an IP address in the Class B network ID of 168.254.0.0.
- You can disable APIPA by editing the Registry. It is often a good idea to disable APIPA on certain machines, such as servers, on your network.

SELF TEST

The following questions will help you measure your understanding of the material presented in this chapter. Read all of the choices carefully, as there may be more than one correct answer. Choose all correct answers for each question.

Overview of DHCP

1. Which of the following messages are passed between a DHCP server and client?
   A. DHCPDISCOVER
   B. DHCPOFFER
   C. DHCPREQUEST
   D. HCPACKNOWLEDGEMENT
2. The Windows 2000 DHCP Server default lease period is:
   A. Two days
   B. Four days
   C. Six days
   D. Eight days
3. You have recently implemented a new network that has 3500 client machines. You are still in the "shakedown" period for several segments, and the IP addresses of the WINS server, DHCP servers, and default gateways are likely to change frequently during this period. You will be using DHCP to assign IP addressing information during this shakedown period. What should you do with your DHCP leases during this period to make change management easier?
   A. Keep the lease period relatively short.
   B. Increase the lease period as long as possible so as to introduce a level of stability to this unstable network.
   C. Manually configure all of your client's IP addressing information until everything is stable; you have no alternatives.
   D. Use WINS server to assign IP addressing information until your DHCP lease information can be permanently defined.

DHCP Server Configuration

4. What must you create in order for your DHCP server to assign IP addresses to DHCP clients?

   A. Exclusion

   B. Scope

   C. Users class option

   D. DHCP relay agent

5. Which option type allows you to have the DHCP server deliver an option that disables NetBIOS over TCP/IP (NetBT)?

   A. Server options

   B. Scope options

   C. Reserved client options

   D. Vendor Class options

6. You have both desktop PCs and dumb terminals at your facility. You wish to use DHCP to assign IP addressing information to all the computers on your network. You want to dynamically assign IP addresses to your dumb terminal clients, so you enable your scopes to support BOOTP requests and DHCP requests. When you make changes to the options information at the DHCP server, you find that all the DHCP clients obtain the new DHCP parameters within five days, but the BOOTP clients do not appear to receive them. What might be one cause of this problem?

   A. BOOTP clients do not receive DHCP option information.

   B. You must create a dedicated BOOTP scope that assigns IP addresses only to BOOTP clients.

   C. BOOTP clients must have client reservations in order to receive IP addressing information from the DHCP server.

   D. BOOTP clients only renew their IP addressing information when they boot up and do not issue REQUEST messages at 50% of the lease period.

7. A single physical segment that contains multiple logical subnets is called a:

   A. Parapet

   B. Internet

   C. Intranet

   D. Multinet

DHCP Relay Agents in a Routed Environment

8. Richard is having problems with DHCP clients obtaining IP addressing information from DHCP servers on remote subnets. He has decided to enable BOOTP Relay. A Proxy server separates one of his segments from the rest of the network and is placed between the segment's clients and the router interface. None of the DHCP clients are able to obtain IP addresses from the DHCP server on the remote subnet, in spite of his confirming that DHCP relay is configured correctly. He has opened UDP Port 68 on the Proxy server. What might be causing the problem?

   A. Richard must remove the Proxy server in order for BOOTP Relay to work correctly.

   B. Richard must open UDP Ports 67 and 68 on the Proxy server.

   C. DHCP servers and clients use TCP Ports, not UDP Ports.

   D. You must place a DHCP relay agent on the subnet to forward the DHCP messages to the BOOTP Relay enabled routers.

9. The setting that determines how many networks a DHCP message can pass through before being silently dropped is:

   A. The boot threshold setting

   B. The hop count threshold setting

   C. The giaddr base metric setting

   D. The destination DHCP server IP address limit threshold

Integrating DHCP with DDNS

10. You are running a mixed network of Windows 2000 and Windows NT 4.0 DHCP clients. You have installed a Windows 2000 DNS Server and a Windows NT 4.0 DHCP Server. Dynamic updates have been enabled on the DDNS server. You begin to receive calls from some of your users who are unable to connect to your intranet FTP and Web servers. What might be the cause of the problem for these users?

    A. The downlevel clients must have the Windows 2000 DHCP client service add-on installed in order to have the Windows NT 4.0 DHCP Server forward information to the DDNS server.

    B. The Windows NT 4.0 DHCP Server needs to have DDNS forwarding enabled before updating information on the Windows 2000 DDNS Server.

    C. The Windows NT 4.0 DHCP Server cannot communicate with a Win2 DDNS Server because it does not support the Dynamic Update protocol.

    D. You must restart the Windows NT 4.0 DHCP Server Service in order to enable dynamic updates.

11. You oversee a mixed-mode network that contains both Windows 2000 and Windows NT 4.0 computers. The domain controllers exist in a mixed-mode environment with both Windows 2000 and Windows NT 4.0 domain controllers. The network clients are also a mix, including Windows 95, Windows 98, and Windows NT 4.0 Workstation computers. You use DHCP to assign IP addressing information to the machines on the network, and you have integrated DHCP with DDNS. However, your downlevel clients are not having their information registered into the DDNS. What is a possible cause for this problem?

    A. Downlevel clients cannot register with the DDNS.

    B. The DDNS server and the DHCP server are not members of the same Windows 2000 domain.

    C. Dynamic update only works in native mode domains.

    D. The "Enable updates for DNS clients that do not support dynamic update" switch has not been set.

Integrating DHCP with RRAS

12. The number of IP addresses that the RRAS server obtains from the DHCP server to use for dynamic IP address assignment to RRAS clients is:

    A. Equal to the number of network interface cards installed on the RRAS server.

    B. Equal to the number of modem connections on the RRAS server.

    C. Equal to the number of RAS client licenses installed on the RRAS server.

    D. Equal to the total number of RAS ports configured to answer calls on the RRAS server.

13. All computers in your company use DHCP to obtain IP addressing information so that they can participate in network activity. This includes RAS clients that call in to your modem pool connected to your RRAS server. You decide to take advantage of the special RRAS user class and assign special WINS and DNS server option values to be used by the RAS clients only. When RAS client connections are established, the RAS clients are unable to browse the network or access resources using a fully qualified domain name (FQDN). What is a possible cause(s) of this problem?

    A. RAS clients obtain option information from the RAS server or RAS connection settings, which is independent of DHCP server settings.

    B. You must install and configure the DHCP relay agent on the RRAS server in order to obtain option information from a DHCP server via an RAS connection.

    C. Poor link quality on the RRAS server prevents them from obtaining IP addressing information from the DHCP server.

    D. APIPA has been disabled on the RAS clients.

Integrating DHCP with Active Directory

14. A rogue DHCP server is:

A. A Windows 2000 DHCP Server that has not been authorized in the Active Directory.

B. A Windows NT 4.0 DHCP Server introduced on a Windows 2000 network segment.

C. A Windows 2000 DHCP Server that has no configured scopes.

D. A Windows 2000 DHCP Server that has a runaway service that is pegging its processor activity.

15. Your junior administrator asks your permission to install a Windows NT 4.0 DHCP Server on one of your production network segments so that he can get some practice. You tell him it's all right because you want to have a little fun with him. You know that his DHCP server is not authorized in the Active Directory and will be shut down when he restarts the computer after installing the Windows NT 4.0 DHCP Server Service on the machine. The next day, you get a number of calls from people who can no longer connect to other computers on the network. What caused the problem?

A. The Windows NT 4.0 DHCP Server issues locator broadcasts, which are flooding the network segment and preventing other computers from communicating.

B. Windows NT 4.0 DHCP Servers are able to self-register with the Active Directory; therefore, the new DHCP server was able to hand out invalid IP addresses.

C. Windows NT 4.0 DHCP Servers are unaware of the Active Directory and are not shut down by the rogue DHCP Server detection process.

D. The Windows 2000 computers on the network intercepted the Windows NT 4.0 DHCP Server's DHCPINFORM message and forwarded it for authorization to a domain controller on the domain.

DHCP and APIPA

16. How does a DHCP client that has a valid lease assess whether it has been moved to another network when it boots up and cannot contact a DHCP server?

A. The DHCP client pings the DNS server in its lease.

B. The DHCP client pings the WINS server in its lease.

C. The DHCP client pings the default gateway in its lease.

D. The DHCP client cannot tell whether it has been moved to another network.

Monitoring and Troubleshooting DHCP

17. You have been having trouble with the IP addressing scheme on your new network. Several of the users have been manually configuring IP addressing information locally on their machines, which has been causing conflicts with the IP addresses delivered via the DHCP server. You would like to get a measure of the overall impact of these manually configured workstations that are causing conflicts with the DHCP server. What counter should you use to assess this situation?

A. ACKs/sec.

B. NACKs/sec

C. DECLINEs/sec

LAB QUESTION

In this exercise, you will build a DHCP Deployment plan.

You are the network administrator for a new firm. You plan on using DHCP to dynamically assign IP addressing information to all of your network clients, except those that require static IP addresses such as WINS and DNS servers. You would also like to use DHCP to assign their information too. Because DHCP is so important to the proper functioning of your network, you want to create a fault tolerance plan for your DHCP servers.

Your network consists of two physical segments that have been assigned the logical network IDs 192.168.1.0 and 192.168.2.0. You want to be sure that if the DHCP server on one segment becomes disabled, the DHCP clients on that segment will still be able to obtain IP addresses.

When answering the question, consider the following:

- Where will you place your DHCP servers?
- How many DHCP servers will you place?
- Will you use BOOTP forwarding?
- Will you use a DHCP relay agent?
- What scopes will you create on your DHCP server or servers?

SELF TEST ANSWERS

Overview of DHCP

1. ☑ **A, B, C, D.** The DHCP lease process includes the DISCOVER message which the DHCP client sends when it attempts to obtain a new lease. The OFFER message which is returned by all DHCP servers that received the DISCOVER message. The REQUEST message that the DHCP client sends to the DHCP server to request that it keep the lease in the OFFER message, and the ACKNOWLEDGEMENT message sent from the DHCP server confirming the lease and providing DHCP options information.

2. ☑ **D.** The default lease period for the Windows 2000 DHCP Server is eight days. This is in contrast to the default lease period for the Windows NT 4.0 DHCP Server, which was six days.
   ☒ **A, B,** and **C** are incorrect because the Windows 2000 DHCP Server default lease period is eight days.

3. ☑ **A.** If you keep your leases short, the DHCP clients will issue DHCPREQUEST messages more frequently. When the DHCP client's lease is renewed, it also receives new option parameters such as WINS, DNS, and gateway addresses.
   ☒ **C** is incorrect because manually reconfiguring client IP addresses will end up causing more work for the administrator. **B** is incorrect because if you make the lease periods longer, the clients will not receive updated option information on a timely basis. **D** is incorrect because WINS servers do not assign IP addressing information.

DHCP Server Configuration

4. ☑ **B.** A DHCP scope must be in place before a DHCP server can respond to DHCPDISCOVER messages.
   ☒ **A** is incorrect because an Exclusion or Exclusion Range is a group of IP addresses that are excluded from the range of IP addresses contained within a single scope. **C** is incorrect because user class options are optional, and DHCP servers work fine without any options defined for the scopes they contain. **D** is incorrect because the DHCP relay agent forwards DHCP messages to and from a DHCP server on remote subnets, but is not required in order for a DHCP server to respond to DHCPDISCOVER messages.

5. ☑ **D.** The Microsoft Windows 2000 Vendor Class Options allow you to send information to the DHCP client that will disable NetBIOS over TCP/IP.
   ☒ **A, B,** and **C** are incorrect because these option types do not provide this functionality.

6. ☑ **D.** BOOTP clients only obtain option information during bootup, and do not renew their IP addressing information. If the administrator wants the BOOTP clients to obtain the new default gateway information, he will have to reboot the BOOTP client computers.
☒ **A** is incorrect because BOOTP clients can and do receive DHCP option information from DHCP servers. **B** is incorrect because you can create a scope using the Windows 2000 DHCP Server that will assign IP addressing information to both DHCP and BOOTP clients. **C** is incorrect because the Windows 2000 DHCP Server allows you to dynamically assign IP addressing information to BOOTP clients.

7. ☑ **D.** A single physical network that contains multiple logical IP networks is called a multinet. You can use superscopes to assign IP addresses via a DHCP server to machines on a multinet.
☒ **A** is incorrect because a parapet is a low protective wall or railing along the edge of a raised structure such as a roof or balcony. **B** is incorrect because an internet is a collection of interconnected networks. **C** is incorrect because an intranet is an internal network that uses Internet technologies to accomplish business goals.

DHCP Relay Agents in a Routed Environment

8. ☑ **B.** You must open outbound UDP Port 67 and inbound UDP Port 68 on the Proxy server in order for DHCP clients to send and receive messages via BOOTP Relay.
☒ **A** is incorrect because you do not need to remove the Proxy server in order for BOOTP Relay to work correctly. **C** is incorrect because DHCP messages are limited to 576 bytes, and therefore always can fit within a UDP packet; DHCP messages are sent via UDP. **D** is incorrect because DHCP relay agents do not forward DHCP messages to BOOTP forwarders; they relay messages directly to DHCP servers.

9. ☑ **B.** The hop count is a measure of how many BOOTP Relays the DHCP message traverses before being silently dropped.
☒ **A** is incorrect because the boot threshold setting determines how long the DHCP relay agent will wait before forwarding the DHCP message to a remote DHCP server. If a local DHCP server answers the DHCPDISCOVER message before the boot threshold period, the relay agent will drop the message. **C** is incorrect because there is no giaddr base metric setting. **D** is incorrect because there is no destination DHCP server IP address limit threshold.

Integrating DHCP with DDNS

10. ☑ **C.** A Windows NT 4.0 DHCP Server cannot update records in the zone database on the behalf of DHCP clients. In order to allow the DHCP server to update records in the zone database, you will need to upgrade the DHCP server to Windows 2000.

☒ A is incorrect because there is no DHCP client add-in utility. **B** is incorrect because there is no DDNS forwarding capability for Windows NT 4.0 DHCP Servers. **D** is incorrect because restarting the Windows NT 4.0 DHCP Server will not have any effect.

11. ☑ **D.** You must enable support for downlevel clients in the DHCP server's Properties sheet.
☒ **A** is incorrect because downlevel clients can register with the DDNS if they use a Windows 2000 DHCP Server as a proxy between them. **B** is incorrect because the DDNS server and the DHCP server do not need to be in the same Windows 2000 domain. **C** is incorrect because dynamic update works in both native and mixed-mode environments.

Integrating DHCP with RRAS

12. ☑ **D.** The RRAS server will obtain a block of IP addresses when the RRAS server starts up that is equal to the number of RAS ports that are configured to accept calls. These ports can be serial ports, parallel ports, network interface card connections, or virtual private network connections via PPTP or L2TP/IPSec.
☒ **A, B,** and **C** are incorrect because they represent only a portion of the number of ports for which IP addresses are obtained.

13. ☑ **A, B. A** is correct because RAS clients, by default, obtain their IP addressing information directly from the DHCP server. The RAS clients never communicate with a DHCP server, and receive typical DHCP options such as WINS and DNS server addresses from the configuration of the DHCP server or from connection-specific options on the RRAS port. **B** is correct because an RAS client can obtain DHCP server options indirectly from a DHCP server by issuing DHCPINFORM messages that are relayed through a DHCP relay agent to the DHCP server.
☒ **C** is incorrect because poor link quality should not have a selective effect on option assignment to the RAS client. **D** is incorrect because APIPA, or Automatic Private IP Addressing, is used by DHCP clients that cannot "find" a DHCP server. This has no effect on RAS client IP addressing assignments.

Integrating DHCP with Active Directory

14. ☑ **A, B. A** is correct because a Windows 2000 DHCP Server that is not authorized in the Active Directory is considered a rogue DHCP server and therefore will have its DHCP Server Service shut down. **B** is correct because a Windows NT 4.0 DHCP Server cannot be authorized in the Active Directory and therefore is considered a rogue.
☒ **C** is incorrect because a DHCP server without scopes is not considered a rogue DHCP server. **D** is incorrect because a runaway service might cause other problems, but does not make the DHCP server a rogue.

15. ☑ **C.** Windows NT 4.0 DHCP Servers are unaware of the Active Directory and, therefore, are not subject to the rogue DHCP server detection process. Only Windows 2000 computers can be shut down as rogue DHCP servers.

☒ A is incorrect because Windows NT 4.0 DHCP Servers do not issue locator broadcasts. **B** is incorrect because Windows NT 4.0 DHCP Servers do not self-register with the Active Directory. **D** is incorrect because Windows NT 4.0 DHCP Servers do not issue DHCPINFORM messages.

DHCP and APIPA

16. ☑ C. The DHCP client will ping the default gateway in its lease if it does not receive a reply from its DHCPREQUEST message during bootup. If the default gateway responds, and there is still time left on the lease, the DHCP client will keep the IP addressing information in the lease. If the default gateway does not respond to the ping, the DHCP client assumes that it has been moved, and since there is no DHCP server on the network that can respond with a valid IP address, it configures itself via APIPA.
☒ A is incorrect because the DHCP client does not ping the DNS server. **B** is incorrect because the DHCP client does not ping the WINS server. **D** is incorrect because the DHCP client can assess whether it has been moved.

Monitoring and Troubleshooting DHCP

17. ☑ **B.** If a computer is assigned an IP address that is already in use, it will receive a Negative Acknowledgement from the DHCP server. The NACKs/sec counter will let you know how profound the problem is for a particular server.
☒ Answer **A** is incorrect because the ACKs/sec counter will only tell you about machines that have successfully received IP addressing information from the DHCP server. Answer **C** is incorrect because DECLINE messages are received from a DHCP client that declines an offered IP address.

LAB ANSWER

This is a common scenario. In order to provide for fault tolerance, you need backups for each of your scopes. One solution is to place a DHCP server on each segment. You would also place a DHCP relay agent on each segment, so that if the local DHCP server should become disabled, DHCP broadcast messages can be intercepted by the DHCP relay agent and forwarded to the DHCP server on the remote segment.

When allocating your IP addresses, Microsoft recommends that you assign 80% of the IP addresses to the local DHCP server, and 20% of the IP addresses to the remote DHCP server. For example, if we have IP addresses 192.168.1.1–192.168.1.100 available, we would assign 192.168.1.1–192.168.1.80 to a scope on the 192.168.1.0 network, and then we would create a scope on the DHCP server on the 192.168.2.0 network with the IP address range 192.168.1.80–192.168.1.100. If the DHCP server on the 192.168.1.0 network becomes disabled, a DHCP relay agent on that segment would forward requests to the DHCP server on 192.168.2.0, and IP addresses can be obtained for the 192.168.1.0 scope configured on that DHCP server.

You would do the same thing for the 192.168.2.0 scope, just in reverse.

For a small network like the one in this example, you could forego using a DHCP relay agent, and enable BOOTP forwarding on your router instead. The propagation of DHCP broadcast traffic is unlikely to have a significant impact on network performance unless you use very short lease periods.

MCSE

MICROSOFT CERTIFIED SYSTEMS ENGINEER

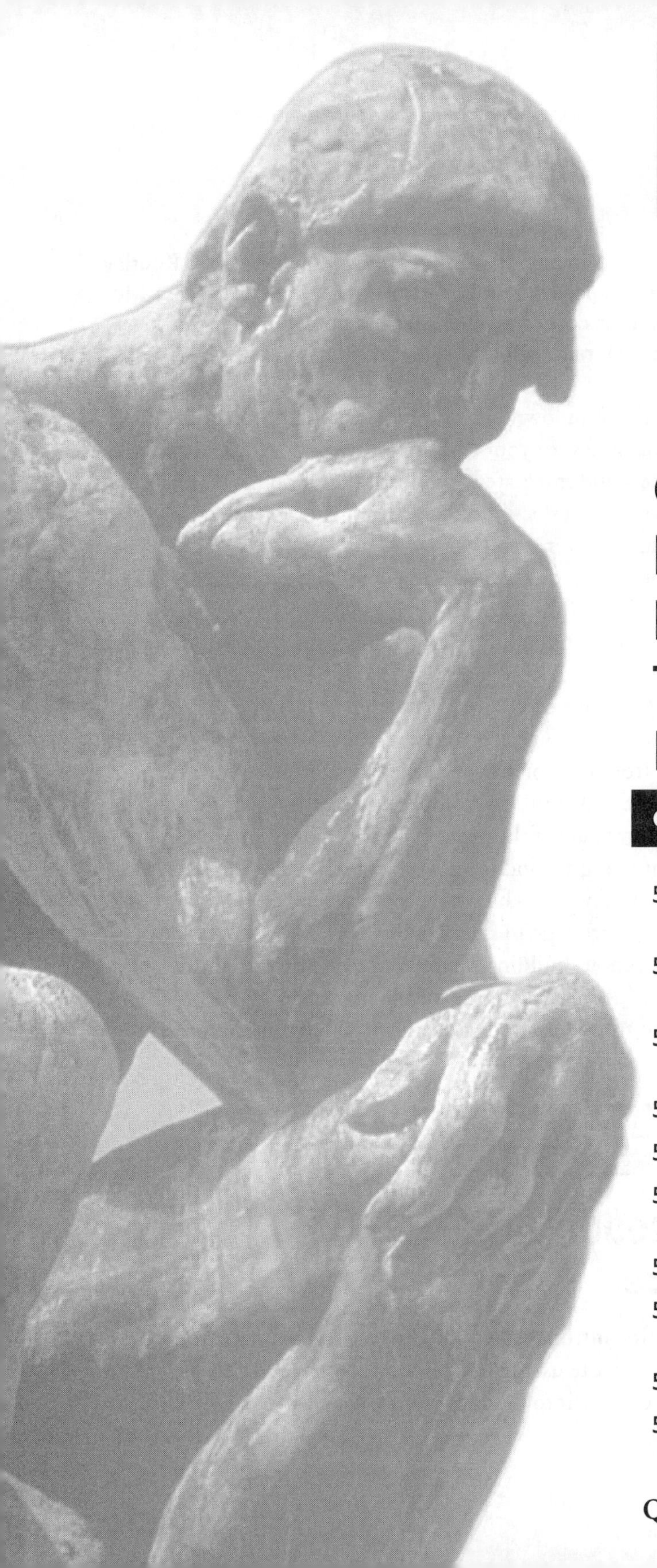

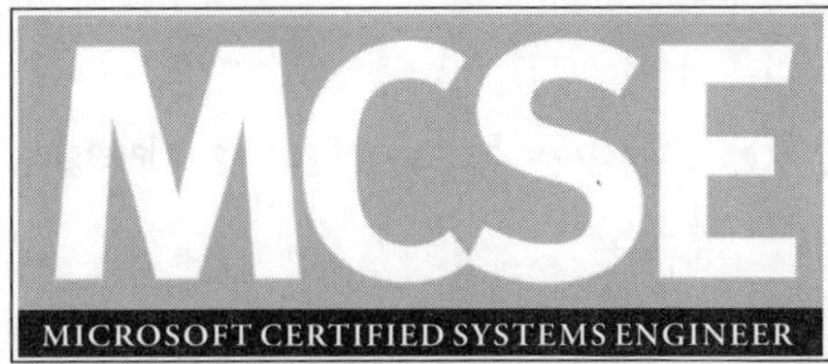

5

Configuring, Managing, Monitoring, and Troubleshooting Remote Access

CERTIFICATION OBJECTIVES

5.01	Overview: Windows 2000 Routing and Remote Access Service
5.02	Installing and Configuring the Remote Access Service
5.03	Configuring the Remote Access Server
5.04	Assigning Remote Access Permissions
5.05	Virtual Private Networking
5.06	Connections using PPP Multilink and BAP
5.07	Integrating Remote Access and DHCP
5.08	Managing and Monitoring Remote Access
5.09	Remote Access Security
5.10	Remote Access Best Practices and Tips
✓	Two-Minute Drill
Q&A	Self Test

This chapter discusses some of the elements that make up the Windows 2000 Routing and Remote Access Service, but in particular it concentrates on Remote Access with dial-up or dedicated connections. It covers essential information you will need to know in the exam, as well as practical considerations for a live environment.

It is not difficult to set up the Windows 2000 Routing and Remote Access Service to provide users with remote access to your corporate network. In fact, it is very easy with the Windows 2000 new and integrated administration tool, the Routing and Remote Access snap-in. However, it does not follow that it is easy to set it up correctly and securely for a particular environment.

Being connected over public networks means that a remote access server is a high security risk and potentially one of the most vulnerable gateways into your company's resources and confidential information. If it is your responsibility to set up and configure remote access, a thorough understanding of the underlying concepts will help you make informed choices of how best to configure it to meet the needs of your company without unnecessarily compromising security. You will also be better equipped to troubleshoot any problems if you can break down and analyze each component that makes up this complex service.

Finally, a thorough understanding of this service will be required for the exam "Implementing and Administering a Windows 2000 Network Infrastructure"—either directly with questions specifically on such favorite topics as VPNs and dial-up, or indirectly with questions on security, permissions, and routing.

This chapter details the various building blocks that make up the Routing and Remote Access Service to help you make some informed choices for configuring, managing, monitoring, and troubleshooting a Windows 2000 remote access server.

CERTIFICATION OBJECTIVE 5.01

Overview: Windows 2000 Routing and Remote Access Service

Remote access (RAS) was first introduced with NT3.51 Service Pack 2 to offer an inexpensive solution for remote users to access local resources via a dial-up connection. This was carried over into Windows NT 4.0 and then significantly changed when Microsoft released the Routing and Remote Access Server (RRAS) with considerable improvements to replace the previous version with a single integrated service that provided both remote access and multiprotocol routing.

The Routing and Remote Access Service for Windows 2000 Server continues its line of evolution with the following new features:

- Internet Group Management Protocol (IGMP) support, and support for multicast boundaries
- Network Address Translation with addressing/name resolution components that simplify Internet connections for a Small Office/Home Office (SOHO)
- Integrated AppleTalk routing
- Layer Two Tunneling Protocol (L2TP) over IP Security (IPSec) support for router-to-router VPN connections
- Improved administration and management tools with a Routing and Remote Access MMC snap-in and a command-line utility called *Netsh* (the latter also allows scripting for automated configuration)
- Improved support for RADIUS

FROM THE CLASSROOM

What is RADIUS?

Support for RADIUS has been available for a long time in Windows NT 4.0; however, many people are unaware of what it is or how it works. This is partly because it was introduced after NT 4.0 was released in one of the NT 4 Option Pack components called Internet Connection Services For MS RAS, which offered a RADIUS Server, and RADIUS proxying services in the form of Internet Authentication Services. Typically, it was not used on medium-sized corporate networks and therefore rarely mentioned in textbooks or documentation. However, because Windows 2000 is more suited to large enterprise environments and is more integrated with the Internet, RADIUS now plays a more important role in Windows 2000 Routing and Remote Access Service. Options for RADIUS abound in RRAS, because it can now act as a RADIUS client either with or without the Microsoft

FROM THE CLASSROOM

Internet Authentication Service, so it's important to know what RADIUS is and how it works.

The Remote Authentication Dial-In User Service is an industry-standard protocol providing what's often referred to as the three "A"s—Authentication, Authorization, and Accounting services for distributed dial-up networking. RADIUS is actually a client/server protocol— in the context of Windows 2000 Routing and Remote Access, the RAS server is actually the RADIUS client, because although it physically accepts the incoming connections, it passes all connection requests and information about the connections to the RADIUS server. That RADIUS server is usually devoted to running a large user account database against which it can identify remote users. This setup allows for wide-scale central management—for example, you can see how several Windows 2000 Servers providing dial-in services can all authenticate and log to one centrally managed server dedicated to such a job.

RADIUS can authenticate users from a variety of user accounts, including NT domains, Novell Directory Services, Lightweight Directory Access Protocol directories (such as Windows 2000 Active Directory), Microsoft SQL Server databases, ODBC databases, and UNIX password files. This provides much greater interoperability within multivendor environments, because such a wide range of user accounts can be pooled together to provide a common service.

RADIUS authorization can restrict authenticated user access to certain network services, and can log information on what services they accessed and how long they were connected. This "accounting" aspect allows ISPs, for example, to use this information for billing purposes and network traffic analysis. Similarly, corporate network managers can use the accounting information to verify ISP charges and allocate expenses to individual departments.

Typically, RADIUS servers run on powerful UNIX servers, but you can also run them on the Intel platform. Examples of RADIUS servers available that will run on Windows NT 4.0 servers include RADIUS from Lucent Technologies, NTRadius from Advanced Instruments, BillNet from PrimeData, NTX Access from Internet Transaction Services, and Steel-Belted RADIUS from Funk Software.

Windows 2000 offers its own RADIUS server when Windows 2000 Server is configured with Internet Authentication Service (IAS). Therefore, if your company

FROM THE CLASSROOM

wanted to benefit from a centralized management for remote access services that complimented Windows 2000 Routing and Remote Access, and you wanted a Microsoft solution that neatly fits in with your existing Windows 2000 network infrastructure, you could configure the server(s) running the Routing and Remote Access as RADIUS client(s) for another Windows 2000 server running IAS. However, traditionally the more common setup for medium-sized companies has been to not use a RADIUS server, and all the authentication, authorization, and accounting are handled by the remote access server itself.

—*Carol Bailey, MCSE+I*

The following are components of the Routing and Remote Access Service:

- Multiprotocol router—routing IP, IPX, AppleTalk
- Demand-dial router
- Routing IP and IPX over on-demand or persistent WAN links (e.g., telephone lines, ISDN, or over VPN connections with PPTP or L2TP/IPSec)
- Remote Access Server—providing remote access connectivity to remote dial-up or VPN clients using a range of LAN protocols including IP, IPX, AppleTalk, and NetBEUI

Note that some of the components such as NAT, IPSec, routing, IGMP, and multicasting are covered in other chapters in this book.

What Is Remote Access?

A Windows 2000 Server running the Routing and Remote Access Service enables a computer to be a remote access server that accepts connections from users who are physically separated from the corporate network but connect to it when needed over a WAN. This connection has traditionally used standard dial-up technologies such as analog telephone lines with modems.

Depending on your remote access requirements and corporate security policies, successfully connected and authenticated remote users can then either:

- Access resources on that server but not beyond the server.
- Access resources on both that server and on other machines that have a connection with the server, so that remote users can access all resources on the corporate network as if they were locally connected.

exam Watch

If remote access is restricted to the remote access server only, this is called Point-to-Point remote access and no routing is involved. If remote access is allowed beyond the Remote Access Server, the server acts as a router, a multiprotocol router, or a NetBIOS gateway (depending on which protocol the remote user specifies)— this is called point-to-LAN remote access.

Remote Access vs. Remote Control

Many people get confused with the difference between remote access (such as RRAS supports) and remote control (such as Terminal Service supports or third-party applications such as PCAnywhere).

Although both involve connecting two computers usually over a WAN, the two are fundamentally different.

Remote access is when a workstation connects to a remote network so that remote resources can be transparently accessed. All applications are still run on the workstation—the only processing done on the remote access server involves the connection process (e.g., routing, authentication, encryption) rather than running any applications for the remote client.

Remote control is when a workstation shares (controls) a remote machine's resources (screen, keyboard, mouse, processor) over a remote link. This means that the remote machine can run applications for the client workstation because the CPU is shared. In this case, the workstation effectively becomes a dumb terminal, because it is not running applications itself but using the CPU on the remote machine.

Remote Access Connections

Similar to the new RRAS service in Windows NT 4.0, the Windows 2000 Routing and Remote Access Service provides two remote access connection methods for remote users:

- Dial-up networking
- Virtual private networking

Dial-Up Networking

Remote users make a nonpermanent dial-up connection using telecommunications services (e.g., analog telephone line with modem, ISDN, or X25) that connect similarly to a physical port on the remote access server. This is a direct physical connection between the client and the server. For added security, you can encrypt the data sent over this connection, but because the connection is point-to-point, this is not usually deemed necessary.

Typically, a mobile user will dial up with a modem and connect to a remote access server with a bank of dedicated modems listening for incoming calls.

Virtual Private Networking

Remote users make use of an IP internetwork to tunnel their remote access connection, making a virtual private network between them and the Remote Access Server (acting as a VPN Server). In contrast to dial-up networking, virtual private networking is a logical and indirect connection between remote user and connecting server. It is not necessary to encrypt the data sent over this connection, but it is usually considered advisable if connecting over a public internetwork. Typically, a remote user will connect to the Internet via an ISP, and from there initiate a virtual private network call to the VPN server that is also connected to the Internet.

Remote Access Clients

The following clients can connect to a Windows 2000 Server running Routing and Remote Access Service:

- Windows 2000
- Windows NT 3.5
- Windows NT 4.0
- Windows 9*x*
- Windows for Workgroups
- MS-DOS
- Microsoft LAN Manager remote access clients

Additionally, almost any third-party client using the Point-to-Point Protocol (PPP) can connect, which includes UNIX and Apple Macintosh clients

exam Watch

As in Windows NT 4.0, although the Microsoft remote access client can use the older Serial Line Interface Protocol (SLIP) to dial out, the Windows 2000 RRAS Server does not support inbound SLIP connections. In practice, SLIP is normally only required when connecting to older UNIX servers that cannot support the later PPP protocol.

Remote Access Administration

There are two main utilities you use for Remote Access administration:

- The GUI Routing And Remote Access snap-in
- The Net Shell command line

The Routing and Remote Access Snap-In

The Routing And Remote Access snap-in allows you to perform a variety of administration tasks, including:

- Enabling/disabling routing and remote access
- Managing routing interfaces
- Configuring ports
- Controlling security
- Controlling remote access permissions
- Assigning network addresses
- Configuring remote access policies

This utility is available from the Administrative Tools folder, and is the primary management utility for configuring your company computers running Windows 2000 Server with Routing and Remote Access Service.

Additionally, you will need to configure the Dial-In tab on a user's account properties. If you are unsure how to do this, refer to Table 5-1.

TABLE 5-1 How to Configure the Dial-in tab

Server Type	Where to Specify Dial-In Permissions
Stand-alone server	Specify the dial-in permissions and other related properties on the Dial-in tab of the user account properties in the Local Users and Groups snap-in.
Active Directory based server	Specify the dial-in permissions and other related properties on the Dial-in tab of the user account properties in the Active Directory Users and Computers snap-in.

The Dial-in options are shown in Figure 5-1. Refer to Table 5-2 for an explanation of these user properties.

FIGURE 5-1 Dial-in tab on the User Properties sheet

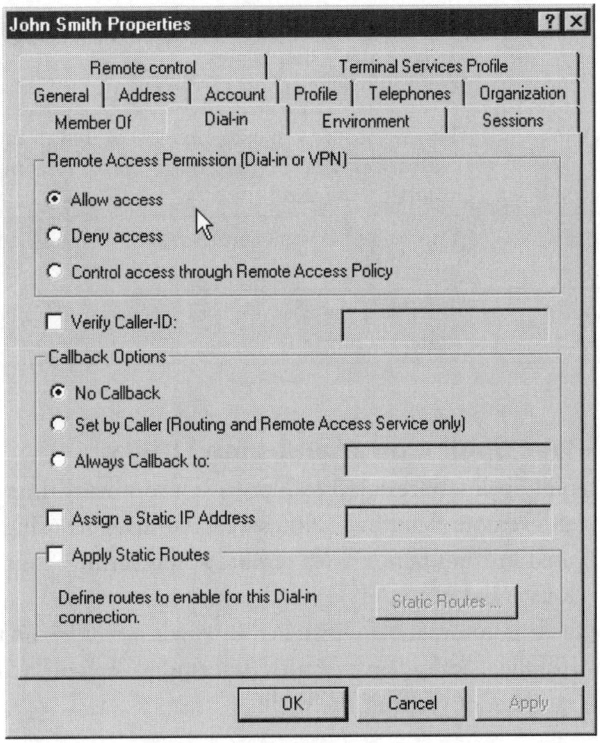

TABLE 5-2 Dial-in Properties on User Account

User Account Properties - Dial-in Options	Explanation
Remote Access Permission (Dial-in or VPN)	This is used to verify whether remote access is allowed. An explanation of these three options is in "Assigning Remote Access Permissions" later in this chapter.
Verify Caller ID	This is used to verify the caller by the hardware being used rather than username/password; if used, you must specify the Caller ID here. See the section " Caller ID" under "Remote Access Security."
Callback Options	Callback is when the remote user dials in and requests the server to call back, so the connection cost of the remote access session is charged to the server's line and not the user.
No Callback	This option doesn't allow the user to request being called back.
Set by Caller	This option doesn't automatically call back the user; however, if the user requests to be called back, it will do so.
Always Callback to	This is "Secure Callback" and is covered in more detail in the section "Secure Callback under "Remote Access Security." If used, you must specify the number to be used here.
Assign a Static IP Address	This is used if you want to assign a static IP address to this user rather than using DHCP or allowing them to choose their own IP address.
Apply Static Routes	Use this if the user needs to access resources beyond the server, and automatic routes do not exist.

Net Shell Command-Line Utility

Net Shell (abbreviated to **Netsh**) is a command-line and scripting tool for both local and remote Windows 2000 servers running Routing and Remote Access. It can be used in conjunction with remote access settings, but is also for routing, DHCP Relay, and NAT.

It is automatically installed in *%systemroot%\system32* when Windows 2000 is installed, and when executed will run taking commands in either Online or Offline mode until you exit the shell:

- **Online mode** Commands are executed immediately.
- **Offline mode** Commands are accumulated and executed as a batch only when the special command "commit" is issued (you can discard accumulated commands with the "flush" command).

One example of using this utility is for doing a quick backup of your Routing and Remote Access server. To do so, type:

Netsh dump >*filename*.txt

This dumps your current RRAS configuration to the named text file (which you can view with any text editor). To restore this configuration, ensure you have a default RRAS server enabled, and then type:

Netsh exec <*filename*.txt>

exam Watch

When you issue this command, Netsh will report what it restored and whether it was successful. There may be some components that couldn't be restored because of the current RRAS configuration (for example, it cannot restore remote access ports if remote access is not currently enabled, but it will restore remote access policies). It is a wise precaution to pipe the Netsh display to a file to review later so you can reconfigure manually (as suggested by Netsh) any components that failed to restore. In practice, however, if you can manually reconfigure the basics, try the restore again. And always check that the restored settings look correct!

on the Job

Do not be tempted to directly edit the Registry to change RRAS settings if an alternative exists in the Routing and Remote Access snap-in or with the Netsh command. For performance reasons, most of the RRAS configuration is stored in binary across large configuration blocks, rather than separate Registry entries that can be easily viewed/changed/exported.

Other useful Netsh commands for remote access include **ras show client** to display currently connected remote access clients, **ras show activeservers** to display all Windows 2000 Servers running RRAS on your network, and **ras show authtype**, which displays the permitted authentication types. Refer to the Windows Help for more information on Netsh and other available commands.

CERTIFICATION OBJECTIVE 5.02

Installing and Configuring the Remote Access Service

This section will cover typical hardware environments, and how to enable and configure remote access service on a Windows 2000 Server.

Hardware Requirements

First of all, ensure your Windows 2000 uses hardware that complies with the Windows 2000 Hardware Compatibility List (HCL), and bear in mind that additional processing power will be required—particularly if you intend to use data encryption.

Dial-Up Hardware and WAN Infrastructure

The physical or logical connection between the Routing and Remote Access server and the remote access client uses dial-up equipment (e.g., modem or ISDN) and the telecommunications infrastructure that may be one of the following:

- Public Switched Telephone Network (PSTN)
- Digital Links and V90
- Integrated Services Digital Network (ISDN)
- X25
- Asynchronous Transfer Mode (ATM) over Asymmetric Digital Subscriber Line (ADSL)

Public Switched Telephone Network (PSTN) Also known as POTS (Plain Old Telephone Service), this is the analog telephone system originally designed to transfer human voice. The dial-up equipment consists of an analog modem at the client and at the server. The maximum bit rate is low.

Digital Links and V.90 Instead of the Routing and Remote Access server having to convert analog signals to digital and vice versa (which is what a standard modem does), a connection through a digital switch based on a T-Carrier or ISDN will greatly improve the bit rate throughput because of the reduction in quantization noise. This presupposes that no other conversion is carried out before reaching the remote modem. Although this setup can only eliminate noise on one side of the connection, it does greatly improve the throughput from server to client.

The remote access client must be using a V90 modem, and the RRAS server must be using a V90 digital switch and using a digital link to connect to the PSTN (e.g., T-Carrier or ISDN).

Integrated Services Digital Network This offers a fully digital connection more suited for data transmissions by using an ISDN adapter on both sides of the connection (remote access client and Routing and Remote Access server).

ISDN offers multiple channels, which means that two or more data channels can be combined for greater throughput—this is called *multilink.*

Typically, remote access users will use Basic Rate ISDN (BRI) with two 64-Kbps channels, and large organizations that require a high throughput will use Primary Rate ISDN (PRI) with 23 64-Kbps channels.

X25 X25 uses an international standard for sending data across public packet-switching networks.

The Windows 2000 Routing and Remote Access server will only support direct connections to X25 networks by using an X25 smart card.

ATM over ADSL ADSL offers a new technology aimed at small businesses and residential customers. It offers a higher throughput than PSTN and ISDN connections, but the bit rate is higher downstream than upstream—typically 384 Kbps when going out and 384 Kbps–1.544 Mbps when coming in (this usually suits Internet traffic usage where users download a much higher percentage of data than they upload).

ADSL equipment can appear to a Windows 2000 Server as one of two interfaces: Ethernet or dial-up. When seen as an Ethernet interface, the ASDL behaves in the same way as a standard network adapter connected to the Internet. When seen as a dial-up interface, ADSL provides the physical connection for ATM traffic.

Other, Slower Connections Slower connections are also possible via direct connection over:

- RS-232C null modem cable
- Parallel port
- Infrared port

Enabling the Routing and Remote Access Service

This is one service that you don't install as you would normally with Add/Remove Programs in Control Panel. Instead, it is automatically installed in Windows 2000, but in a disabled state. However, before you enable it, ensure that all interfaces and protocols you want to use for the Routing and Remote Access Service are installed, configured, and working correctly. This may include dial-up equipment and Internet interfaces.

EXERCISE 5-1

CertCam 5-1

Enabling the Routing and Remote Access Service

1. Ensure you are logged on with Administrator privileges, and choose Routing and Remote Access from Start | Programs | Administrative Tools.

If Routing and Remote Access hasn't been previously enabled on this server, it will show your local server status as disabled with a red cross as shown in the following illustration.

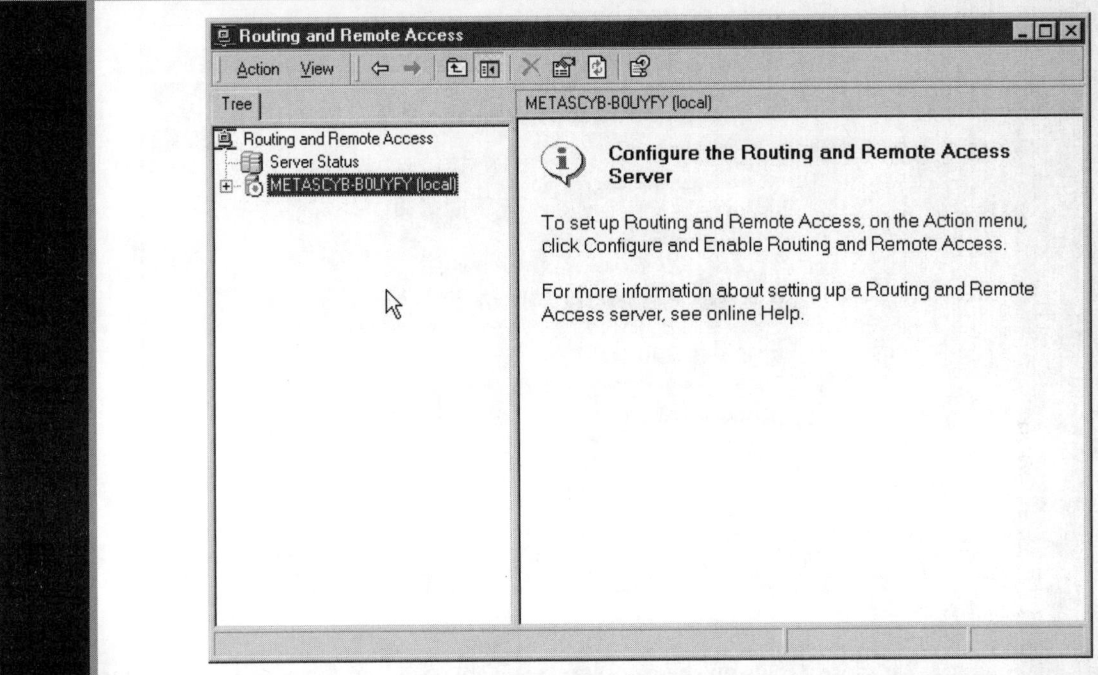

2. Right-click on your server and from the shortcut menu, select Configure and Enable Routing and Remote Access. This starts the Routing and Remote Access Server Setup Wizard. Click Next.
3. You will have a choice of common configurations to choose from as shown in the following illustration.

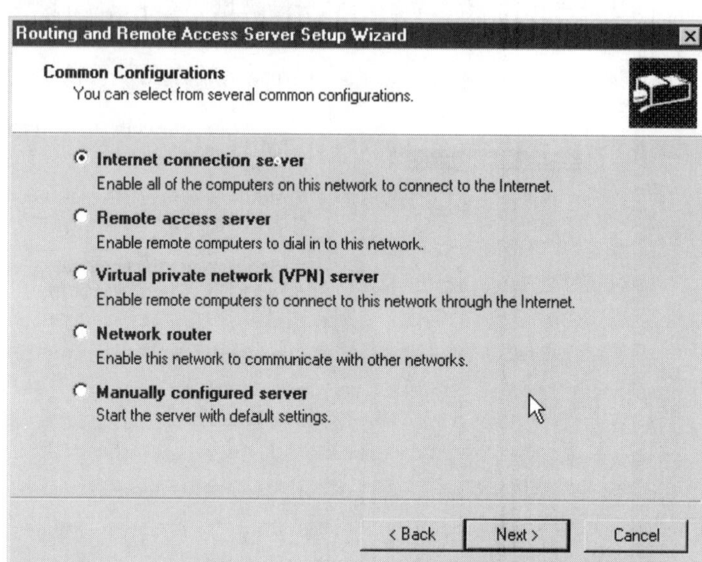

For more details on these choices, see Table 5-3, but for now, select "Remote access server" and click Next.

4. You will be asked to verify that the protocols you want to use are already installed with a list of installed protocols displayed. If you select the option to install other protocols and click Next, the wizard will inform you that it cannot continue until the protocols you need are installed. You will be given a choice to Finish (so you can install the protocols you need and then call up the Routing and Remote Access Server Setup Wizard again), or Back.
5. When you select "Yes, all of the required protocols are on this list" and click Next, you will be prompted for the Network Selection you want to use. If your server is multihomed, this is particularly important. You will see a list of all network adapters with their description and assigned IP address—select the one you want to use on your internal network. Click Next.
6. You will then be asked about IP Address Assignment, whether to use DHCP or define a static pool of addresses. The recommended setting is "Automatically" if you have a DHCP server on the same subnet as your remote access server. Even if you don't have a DHCP server on the same

subnet, you can still use this setting—see the section "Integrating Remote Access and DHCP" for more information on this.

After selecting your IP address assignment, click Next.

7. If you chose to use a static pool of addresses, you will be asked to specify a range (pool) of addresses to use. If you do not have enough free contiguous addresses, you can specify multiple pools, each with different start and end addresses. The following illustration shows two pools of IP addresses. Click Next.

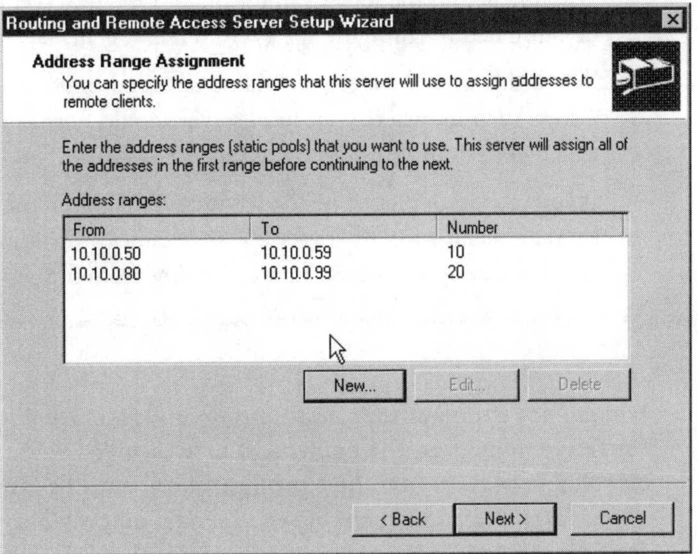

8. The next dialog asks whether you want to use Windows authentication or RADIUS. Choosing RADIUS configures RRAS to be a RADIUS client, which means it doesn't authenticate remote access clients itself, but passes authentication requests to another server that holds such authentication information.

   If you do select the RADIUS option, you will then be prompted to specify details of the RADIUS server(s) and the password (shared secret) to connect to it. When you Click OK, your RRAS server will attempt to connect to the RADIUS server with the credentials provided to verify that it can communicate with it. If the RADIUS server cannot be located, setup cannot continue.

The default setting is "No, I don't want to set up this server to use RADIUS now." Select this and click Next.

9. The final screen tells you that you have successfully completed the setup configuration, and prompts you to click Finish if you want to automatically load Help.

   Note at this time if you have selected to use automatic TCP/IP address assignment and the server cannot find a DHCP server on its subnet, you will be reminded to configure the DHCP relay agent.

10. When this wizard closes you will be returned to the Routing and Remote Access snap-in, where your local server should now show a green up arrow assigned to it, indicating that the service is enabled and started.

11. If you wish to stop or pause the service, right-click on the server, and from the shortcut menu select All Tasks, and then either Stop or Pause. To revert to an enabled state again, choose Start or Resume from the same shortcut menu.

on the Job

You cannot install or uninstall Routing and Remote Access with Add/Remove Programs. However, the equivalent is to disable the service. Usually most disabled services retain their configuration, but this is not the case with RRAS! If you later decide to reenable the service, all previously configured options for Remote Access (including protocol, routing information and port settings, etc.) will be lost and these must be reconfigured from scratch.

To disable the service, select the Disable Routing and Remote Access option from the relevant server when you right-click on it in the Routing and Remote Access snap-in.

exam Watch

If the person enabling the RRAS service is not an administrator, the remote access server must be manually added to the RAS and IAS servers security group. If it is added manually, reboot the RRAS server afterward to ensure the new group membership is in effect.

Table 5-3 lists the installation options in the Routing and Remote Access Server Setup Wizard.

TABLE 5-3 The Installation Options in the Routing and Remote Access Server Setup Wizard

Internet connection server	This offers two ways of sharing a single Internet connection with other computers on your network: Internet Connection Sharing (ICS) is the simplest setup, and selecting this will to prompt you to use the Network and Dial-up Connections folder to configure an Internet connection, which is then shared. Network Address Translation (NAT) is another way to provide Internet access to other computers on your network. NAT requires more configuration, but has greater flexibility. It is installed as a routing protocol within RRAS.
Remote access server	This is what we will be configuring, and the typical scenario is a dial-up modem or bank of modems attached to the server that allow remote clients to dial in and then access local resources.
Virtual private network (VPN) server	We will also be configuring a VPN server, and the typical scenario is a multihomed server with one adapter connected to the Internet and the other connected to your company network. Remote clients dial up to the Internet and then tunnel a second connection over the first to connect securely to the server.
Network router	This allows the server to route packets to other routers when required, which could be over a persistent link or on demand. Multicasting and unicast boundaries are also supported.
Manually configured server	This simply loads the Routing and Remote Access snap-in so you can manually configure the options you need without being prompted by the Setup wizard.

CERTIFICATION OBJECTIVE 5.03

Configuring the Remote Access Server

There are several configuration options you should check and change if necessary before allowing remote access clients to connect to this server, including:

- Allowing remote access
- Settings for authentication and auditing
- IP address assignment

EXERCISE 5-2

Configuring the Remote Access Server

1. If not already open, load the Routing and Remote Access Service snap-in from the Administrative Tools folder.
2. Right-click your remote access server in the left pane and select Properties. This will display the dialog box shown next.

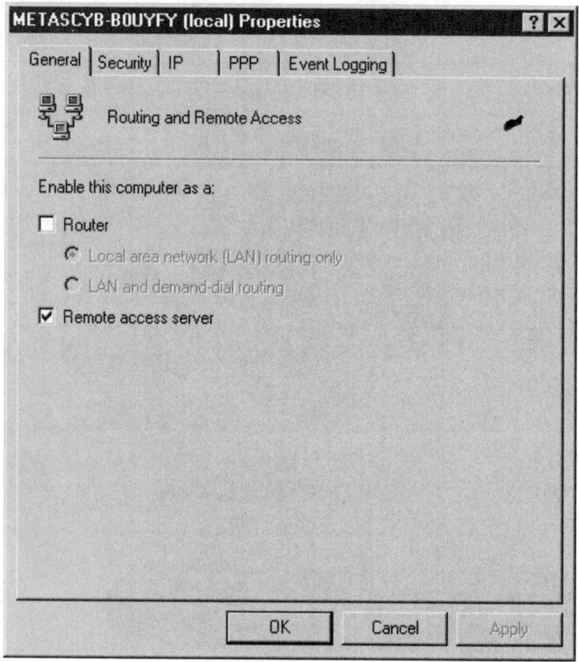

3. Under the General tab, you will find the most important setting that enables Routing and Remote Access to accept remote connections. Ensure the check box "Remote access server" is selected.
4. Under the Security tab, you will find properties for authentication and accounting. Unless you are using a RADIUS server, select Windows Authentication and Windows Accounting.

   Authentication Methods allow you to choose the authentication protocols you want the server to use. If a remote access client cannot match one of your chosen authentication protocols, they will not successfully connect.

For more details on each of these authentication protocols, see "Secure Authentication" under the "Remote Access Security" section later in this chapter. The default setting is MS-CHAP and MS-CHAP v2.

5. The IP tab shows the current settings for the internal connection to your company network. Here you can stop remote access clients from connecting to resources beyond your remote access server with the **"Enable IP routing"** option, change your IP address assignment, and specify an alternative network adapter to use if your server is multihomed.

   Note that you can switch between using DHCP and a static IP address pool without losing the address pool details, as shown next.

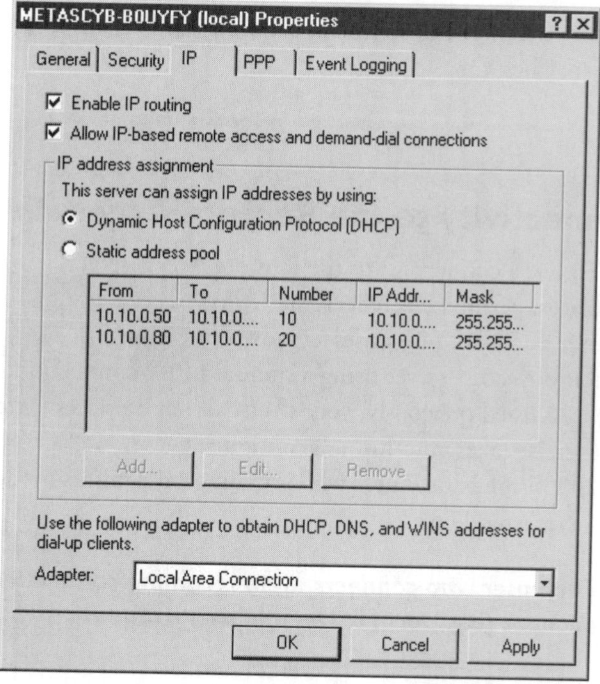

6. The PPP tab allows you to set options for enabling Multilink, BAP, LCP extensions, and software compression. See the section "Connections using PPP Multilink and BAP" later in this chapter for more details on these options.
7. The Event Logging tab allows you specify the level of information that the remote access server automatically sends to the Event Log. The default is errors and warnings. For more information about logging, see the section "Event Logging" under "Managing and Monitoring Remote Access" later in the chapter.

   You can also set PPP logging in this dialog box. For more information, see the section "PPP Tracing" under "Managing and Monitoring Remote Access" later in the chapter.
8. When you have finished looking at or changing the server's properties, Click OK.

Testing Connectivity to the Remote Access Server

To test a connection to the Remote Access server, ensure that your test user has dial-in permissions (check the "Allow access" option under the Dial-in tab of the user's account properties as shown in Figure 5-1), and attempt to connect to your remote access server using a standard PPP connection.

As listed previously, your choice of remote access clients is varied but the following exercise takes you through configuring a remote access connection for a Windows 2000 Professional user who is dialing in from his modem to the remote access server's modem.

exam Watch

Each user who connects to an incoming connection must have a valid user account (e.g., local or domain user account).

EXERCISE 5-3

Configuring a Remote Access Connection with Windows 2000 Professional

In Windows 2000, you configure your dial-up remote access with the Network Connection Wizard.

1. Under Network and Dial-up Connection, select Make New Connection.

This loads the Network Connection Wizard, which steps you through your configuration choices, as shown in the following illustration.

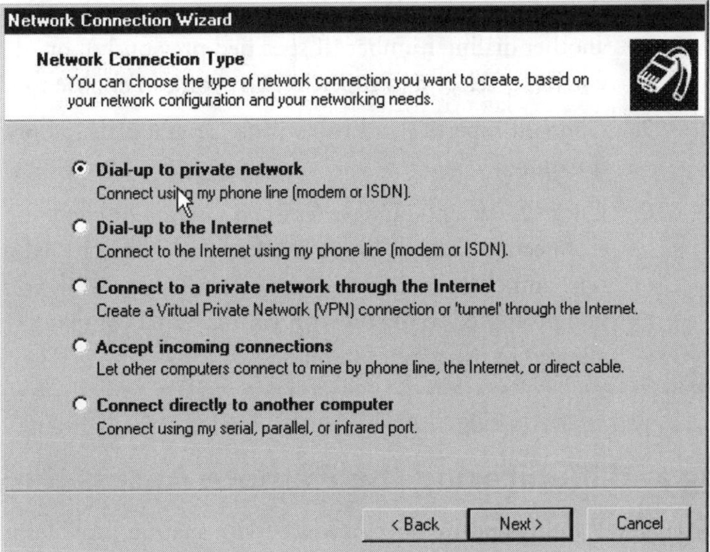

2. Select the "Dial-up to private network" option, and click Next.
3. In the next dialog box, specify the telephone number (and other information if necessary) of the remote access server, and select Next.
4. The next dialog box asks whether you want to share this connection with others (the default), or ensure only one person can use it. Note that even if sharing, it will only be shared when you are logged on. Select "Only for myself," and select Next.

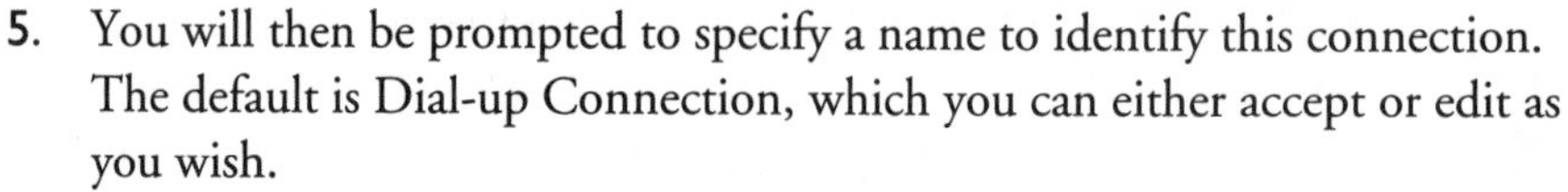

5. You will then be prompted to specify a name to identify this connection. The default is Dial-up Connection, which you can either accept or edit as you wish.
6. If you want to automatically create a shortcut for this connection on your desktop, click the "Add a shortcut to my desktop."
7. Click Finish and the final dialog box will prompt you for your username and password that should be used when dialing this connection, with a check box to save the password.
8. From here, you either dial the number you have just specified, choose another dialing number (if specified previously), or edit your connection entries by selecting Properties. Or, you can choose to Cancel.
9. Choose Properties and you will see several dial-up options you can change if required.
10. Click OK when you have finished viewing or changing any Dial-up Connection Properties to return to the Connect Dial-up Connection dialog box, and click Dial. If the connection is successful, you will be connected and prompted to log on with your internal company credentials before being allowed to use remote resources.

Managing and Monitoring the Remote Access Server

The Routing and Remote Access Service snap-in provides most of the dynamic information you will need to manage and monitor remote access connections.

If you expand Ports, you should see all the external ports available to the remote access server. For example if you have a bank of modems, these should be displayed with their name, device (modem), and status. When a connection comes in, the status will change from Inactive to Active, and if you right-click on it to obtain Status information, you will be able to see information such as the line speed, bytes in and out, errors such as CRC failures, and network registration (e.g., assigned IP address). You can reset a port from this status dialog box.

If your remote access server is connected to the Internet, you will also see VPN ports listed as WAN Miniports—the default being 5 using PPTP and 5 using L2TP. See the section "Virtual Private Networking" for more information on configuring VPNs.

Remote Access Clients will indicate a number in brackets, which is the number of currently connected users. Expand Remote Access Clients to view details of who is connected, with details of their username, the duration of the call, and the number of ports allocated (the latter is applicable only when using multilink—see the section "Connections using PPP Multilink and BAP" later in this chapter for more information). When a user is connected, you can send him or her a message by right-clicking on the session, and selecting Send Message. Similarly, you can choose to send a message to all currently connected remote clients.

The Event Log will record certain events to help provide a history of what happened on your remote access server; for example, who connected and when, and what IP address they were assigned. You can change the level of information written to the Event Log, but this not advisable unless you are experiencing technical difficulties and require detailed information for analysis. See the section "Managing and Monitoring Remote Access" for more information on logging and recording events.

CERTIFICATION OBJECTIVE 5.04

Assigning Remote Access Permissions

In Windows NT 3.51 and Windows NT 4.0, remote access was granted to domain users based solely on whether the user's account had dial-in permission—configured in User Manager or the Remote Access Administration utility.

In Windows 2000, remote access authorization can still be determined by the dial-in properties for the user account. For a stand-alone server, you specify the dial-in permission and other related properties on the Dial-In tab of the user account properties in the Local Users and Groups snap-in. For an Active Directory based server, you specify these dial-in options on the Dial-In tab of the user account properties in the Active Directory Users and Computers snap-in as we saw previously in Figure 5-1.

For those of you familiar with configuring dial-in properties in Windows NT 4.0, you will probably notice an option for dial-in permission that's new with Windows 2000. It's rather an unusual one, because it's only available when running in a native mode domain: Control access through Remote Access Policy. Irrespective of whether your Windows 2000 Server running Routing and Remote Access Service is in a mixed or native domain, the Remote Access Permission setting here is very important when it comes to assigning remote access permissions.

Remote Policies

New to Windows 2000, Routing and Remote Access uses remote access policies to allow greater flexibility in configuring and managing remote access.

A remote access policy not only allows you to manage who has remote access permission and under what circumstances (e.g., only on certain days and times), but also allows you to impose conditions and connection settings for your remote users. For example, you can set the maximum session time allowed, require certain authentication, require encryption and so forth. If the remote user does not meet these conditions and constraints, the connection is refused or disconnected.

If you use multiple remote access policies, you can have different sets of conditions for different remote access clients, and/or you could have different requirements for the same remote user based on certain factors (for example, if connecting over the Internet rather than your modem pool, impose higher security restrictions such as a strong authentication protocol and encryption).

The Default Remote Access Policy

When you first enable Routing and Remote Access Service, you will see a single built-in policy: "Allow access if dial-in permission is enabled." This is referred to as "The Default Policy." You would have seen this when you finished enabling the Routing And Remote Access service. If it is not displayed in the right pane, expand the Remote Access Policies in the console tree. The details pane lists this policy, and if you right-click it and choose Properties, you will see as in Figure 5-2 that this policy consists of a single condition that must be met before a remote access client can connect.

If you click Edit, you will see it allows you to specify the times of day as shown in Figure 5-3.

Because the only condition is Any Day, Any Time, this effectively makes this policy transparent (not effective), but you could restrict your condition to certain days and times (for example, designated office working hours).

However, on the Settings dialog box there is another section labeled "If a user matches the conditions" with two choices:

- Grant remote access permission
- Deny remote access permission (the default)

FIGURE 5-2

Settings in the Default Policy

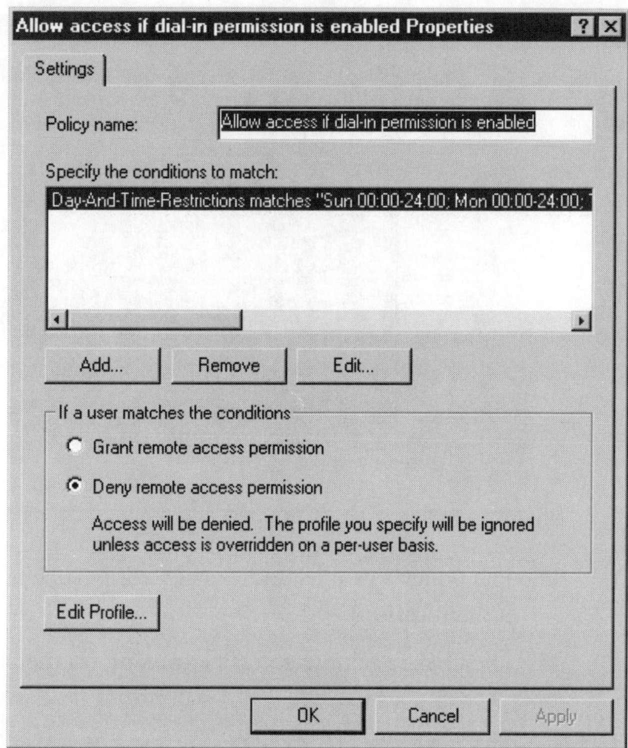

Therefore, the default condition of this policy is Any Day, Any Time, but Deny remote access permission. You might deduce that this Default Policy would deny anybody connecting to the remote access server; however, the deny permission can be overwritten by the Dial-in properties on a user's account. If a user's account explicitly grants dial-in permission (rather than "Deny access" or "Control access through Remote Access Policy" as shown in Figure 5-1), with the Default Policy in place a user can (when authorized and authenticated) connect to this server any day or any time.

Therefore, the final remote access permission consists of four elements:

- The conditions of the remote access policy or policies
- The remote access permission for the policy ("If a user matches the conditions")

FIGURE 5-3

Time of day constraints within the Default Policy

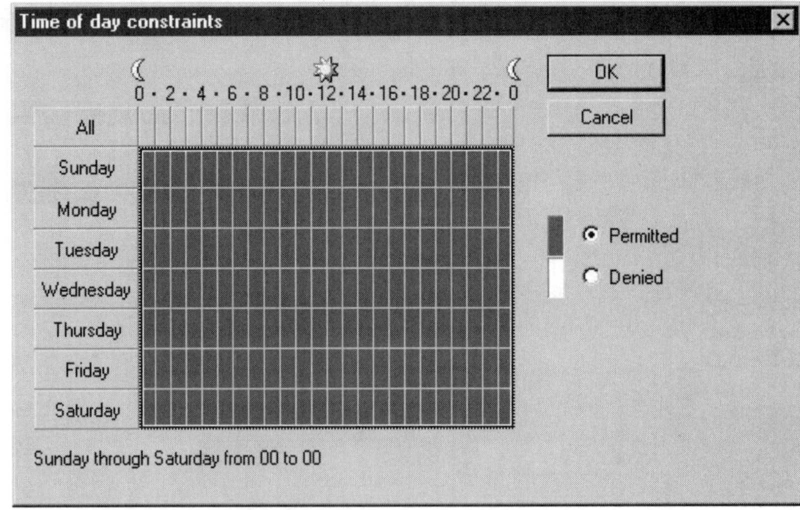

- The policy's profile (additional settings such as permitted media and required authentication)
- The Dial-in remote access permission on the user's account

The Administrative Models for Remote Access Policy

The four elements that control who has remote access permissions work together, and how you choose to configure them will depend on factors such as whether your network is a mixed– or native–mode domain, the numbers of users you have, and the degree of control you require when configuring remote access. Microsoft recommends that you choose one of the following three administrative models when designing and implementing your Remote Access Policies:

- Access by User
- Access by Policy in a Windows 2000 mixed-mode domain
- Access by Policy in a Windows 2000 native-mode domain

Remember that a mixed-mode domain is when you have Windows NT 4.0 domains and Windows 2000 Servers, and a native-mode domain consists of only Windows 2000 Servers with Active Directory.

Remote Access Permission by User

This is simplest to administer for a small number of users.

As in Windows NT 4.0, remote access permission is granted on individual user accounts. As we have seen in Windows 2000, this is from the remote access permission on the Dial-in tab of the Properties window for the user account.

Even with the Remote Access Default Policy in place (of "Deny remote access permission"), the individual users with dial-in permission will have permission to connect to remote access servers, because their account setting will override the Remote Access Policy.

Remote Access Permission by Policy for a Native-Mode Domain

When running in native mode, user accounts have a new option available under the remote access permission in the Dial-in tab: Control Access Through Remote Access Policy. When this is selected, remote access permission is solely determined by the Remote Access Policy or policies.

This model is easier to administer for a large number of users.

Because you have no individual user account settings overriding any remote access policies, you must change or create a new Remote Access Policy that gives remote access permission to users–or no user will be able to connect to your remote access server. The simplest way to do this would be to edit the Default Profile such that the "Deny remote access permission" is changed to "Grant remote access permission." However, this would mean that all users would have remote access permission at all times; usually, for security reasons, you would want to restrict this to either certain users/groups or to other conditions.

on the Job

If you want to grant permission to all users with the "Grant remote access permission," remember that this will apply to all accounts, including the Guest account. For security, verify that the Guest account is disabled and/or that its remote access permission is set to "Deny access" to override your remote access policy.

If you prefer a more secure policy design and do not want to grant remote access permission to everybody, it is better to grant or deny access by group membership. Group membership is granted with the Windows-Group attribute, which will be explained in more detail later.

Decide whether you want to explicitly grant permission only if users belong to a selected group (and implicitly reject access if users don't belong to your selected groups), or whether you want to explicitly deny permission if users belong to a selected group (and implicitly accept users if they don't belong to your selected groups). You will then need to delete or edit the Default Policy and have a new policy (or policies) to reflect your choice.

If you want to grant access by group membership:

1. Create a new policy called something similar to "Allow Access If Member of Selected Groups."
2. Add the Windows-Groups attribute to the policy, and then select the group or groups to be granted access. On the policy itself, select the "Grant remote access permission" option.

If you want to deny access by group membership:

1. Create a new policy called something similar to "Deny Access If Member of Selected Groups."
2. Add the Windows-Group attribute to the policy, and then select the group or groups to be denied access.
3. On the policy itself, select the "Deny remote access permission" option.

Remote Access Permission by Policy for a Mixed-Mode Domain

In this model, you cannot enable the "Control access through Remote Access Policy" option in the user account properties under the Dial-in tab. Instead, the remote access permission can be set to either "Allow access" or "Deny access."

Set this option to "Allow access" for all users, and then delete or modify the Default Policy to control who has remote access permission. If you don't delete or change the Default Policy, all users will be granted permission (because the profile overrides the "Deny remote access permission" in the policy).

As described in the native mode model, you can create policies that explicitly or implicitly grant or deny access by group membership.

However, if you decide to explicitly deny access by membership, you cannot as before use the "Deny remote access permission" in the policy, because each user profile has "Allow access," which will override the policy.

One alternative is to add a condition to your profile that is impossible to match; for example, specify that the user has to be calling in to the server with an invalid telephone number. To do this, edit the profile, and on the Dial-In Constraints tab, select Restrict Dial-In To This Number Only and specify a number that isn't valid for your remote access server.

Now that you have an understanding of the three remote access administration models, you should be able to identify which model to use in different circumstances.

SCENARIO & SOLUTION

Which remote access administrative model should I use if…	Administrative Model
I only have a small number of users who need access to one RRAS server?	Access by user. It's probably easier to assign permission on each account if additional conditions are not required that you only find in the remote access policies.
Many users require access to one or more RRAS servers?	Access by policy (in either a mixed- or native-mode domain, depending on whether you're running a mixed- or native-mode domain). You can more easily manage a large number of users through remote access policies (for example, define specific groups) and have different remote access policies on different RRAS servers.
A large number of users have accounts on a Windows NT4.0 domain?	Access by Policy in a mixed-mode domain. The Control Access through Remote Access Policy option is only available when running in native-mode, so you cannot use just this setting. However, the large number of users to manage will be easier if using remote access policies, and control can be more granular.
I want to specify which groups should be allowed remote access rather than defining this on each individual account?	Access by Policy (in either a mixed- or native-mode domain, depending on whether you're running a mixed- or native-mode domain). You can only define groups in remote access policies.
I have a small number of users that should only be able to connect at specified times?	Access by Policy (in either a mixed- or native-mode domain, depending on whether you're running a mixed- or native-mode domain). You cannot set this restriction within the user account Dial-in properties.

Remote Access Policy Conditions

The Default Policy has only the one condition: the Day-And-Time-Restriction. We mentioned earlier that you could add another condition by adding an attribute called Windows-Group, which allowed you to explicitly grant or deny access permission based on group membership. Remember that with Windows 2000, you can have both nested groups and universal groups.

Table 5-4 lists the Remote Access Policy conditions.

NAS is an abbreviation for "Network Access Server," and is a generic term for a server offering remote access services. ISPs will use this generic term, while Microsoft's two specific products that deliver these services are the "Routing and

TABLE 5-4 Remote Access Policy Conditions

Condition Attribute	Explanation
Called-Station-ID	The telephone number of the remote access server. Note that the telephone line, hardware, and hardware drivers must all support passing the station-ID.
Calling-Station-ID	The telephone number used by the remote user. Note that the telephone line, remote server, and all connecting hardware must support passing the caller ID; if not, the connection will be denied.
Client-Friendly Name	Only applicable if the RRAS server is acting as a RADIUS client.
Client-IP-Address	Only applicable if the RRAS server is acting as a RADIUS client.
Client-Vendor	Only applicable if the RRAS server is acting as a RADIUS client.
Day-And-Time-Restriction	Days and times that are valid for connections; note the time taken from the RRAS server.
Framed-Protocol	Only applicable if the RRAS server is acting as a RADIUS client.
NAS-Identifier	Only applicable if the RRAS server is acting as a RADIUS client.
NAS-IP-Address	Only applicable if the RRAS server is acting as a RADIUS client.
NAS-Port-Type	The type of media used by the caller; for example, analog telephone lines (asynch), ISDN, virtual private networks (virtual).
Service-Type	Only applicable if the RRAS server is acting as a RADIUS client.
Tunnel-Type	Tunneling protocols to be used (PPTP and L2TP).
Windows-Groups	Domain groups (can be nested or universal) of which the remote user is a member. Note local groups not supported.

Remote Access Service" (often abbreviated as RRAS) and the "Internet Authentication Service" (abbreviated as IAS).

Remote Access Policy Profiles

The policy's profile is a further set of conditions that apply after a connection is authorized. The profile applies irrespective of whether access permission has been granted by user or policy.

Click Edit Profile on the policy's Properties sheet to view/edit the Profile. You will see the six tabbed options as shown in Figure 5-4.

Policy Profile Options Under Dial-In Constraints

This tab has the following options where you can define with a high degree of control these dial-in conditions:

- **Restrict access to the following days and times** By default, this is not set, but allows you to specify when a connection will be allowed. Connection attempts outside permitted times will be denied, although currently connected sessions will not be disconnected.

FROM THE CLASSROOM

What's the Difference Between Authentication and Authorization?

Authentication is when a user is identified (usually by means of a username and password). If this is done in an encrypted form, an authentication protocol is used. A successful authentication proves that users are who they say they are, but has nothing to do with what resources they can access.

Authorization is when it is determined whether users can have access to requested resources based on their identity. By definition, this can only happen after a successful authentication. In the context of RRAS, remote users' connection attempts can be authenticated (because they have proved who they are), but their connection can still be denied because their authorization failed if they did not have permission to dial in, for example.

—*Carol Bailey, MCSE+I*

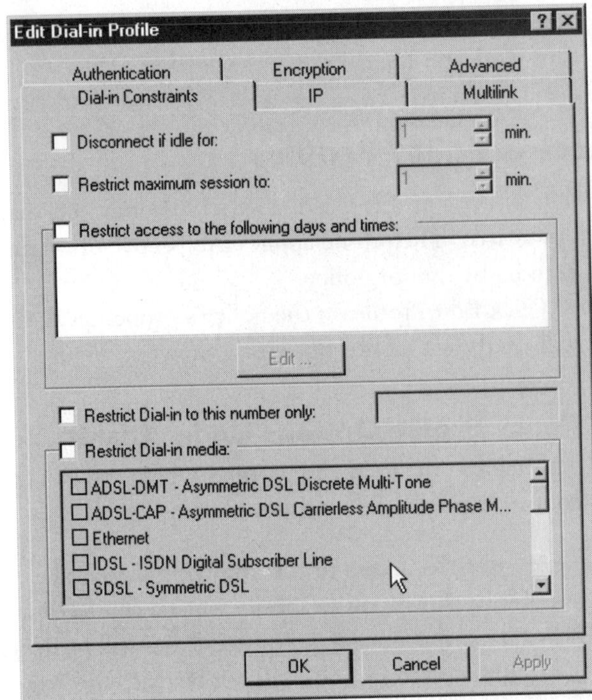

FIGURE 5-4

Remote Access Policy's Profile options

- **Restrict Dial-In to this number only** By default, this is not specified, but allows you to set a specific number that the remote user must call for a connection to be allowed.
- **Restrict Dial-In media** By default, this is not specified, but allows you to restrict exactly which medium the remote access user should use (e.g., ISDN, T1). If the medium being used is not the one specified when this option is set, the connection will be rejected.

Policy Profile Options Under IP Address Policies

This tab has the following options where you can define a high degree of control over the IP options for a connecting remote user:

- **IP address assignment policy** By default, the remote access server supplies an IP address for the remote access clients when they connect. However, this option allows you to explicitly specify whether the server must specify an address, or whether the remote access user can request to use its own choice of IP address.

- **IP packet filters** By default, no packet filtering is enabled, but for security purposes, you could specify parameters such as inbound and outbound protocols, IP addresses, ports, etc. You can set these on an exception basis—either all traffic except the packets specified in the filters, or no traffic except the packets specified in the filters.
- **Disconnect if idle for** By default, this is not set, but allows you to set a period of time after which you can disconnect the remote user if the link has been idle.
- **Restrict maximum session to** By default, this is not set, but allows you to specify the maximum time a remote user can be connected at any one time.

Policy Profile Options Under Multilink

This allows you to enable multilink and the Bandwidth Allocation Protocol (BAP) if the remote access server has these enabled. Multilink allows you to combine multiple physical connections into a single logical connection to increase the available bandwidth for a single connection.

Because multilink cannot automatically adapt to changing bandwidth requirements, you should also enable BAP so that the multilinks can be automatically added, dropped, and managed as needed:

- **Multilink Settings** This takes the default setting from the server itself, but here it allows you to disable multilink, or to set the maximum number of ports that a connection can use.
- **Bandwidth Allocation Protocol Settings** This allows a multilink connection to be reduced automatically if the throughput on the link falls below a specified capacity for a specific time.

For more information on multilink and BAP, see the section "Connections using PPP Multilink and BAP" later in this chapter.

Policy Profile Options Under Authentication

You can specify the authentication methods allowed for the connection. The authentication protocols specified here must also be enabled on the server. For more information on authentication protocols, see "Authentication Protocols" in the "Remote Access Security" section.

Policy Profile Options Under Encryption

This tab has the following options, where you can specify a high degree of control over the encryption required for remote access users:

- **No Encryption** This allows nonencrypted data over the connection, which may be preferable if the need for performance is higher than security.
- **Basic** This is for dial-up and PPTP connections and uses Microsoft Point-to-Point Encryption (MPPE) with a 40-bit key, and for L2TP over IPSec connections, uses 56-bit Data Encryption Standard (DES) encryption.
- **Strong** This is for dial-up and PPTP connections, and uses MPPE with a 56-bit key, and for L2TP over IPSec connections, uses 56-bit DES encryption.

Policy Profile Options Under Advanced

These are not relevant to routing and remote access, but are for RADIUS attributes that are sent to the RADIUS client by the IAS server.

CertCam 5-4

EXERCISE 5-4

Modifying the Default Remote Access Policy

Remember that we looked at the Default Policy, which was effectively any day, any time. This exercise takes you through modifying this by adding a further condition that is to only accept Domain Users to make the condition more restrictive.

1. Expand the Remote Access Policies to display the Default Policy in the details pane. Right-click on it and select Properties.

2. Click Add and you will see that you can add conditions mentioned in Table 5-4 as shown in the following illustration.

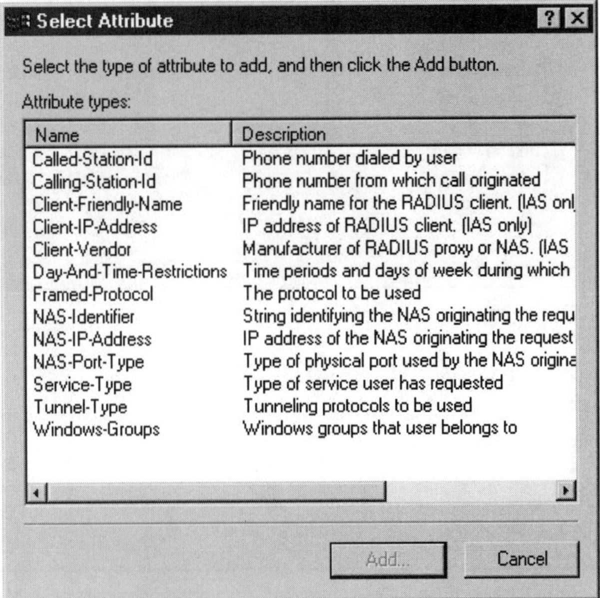

3. Each attribute when selected has a further prompt to ask for more information relevant to the attribute you have selected. For example, we need to select the Windows-Groups, so select it, and click Add. You will now see a list of all groups already in the condition, and you can add or remove them.
4. Since we have no existing groups defined, click Add to see a list of available groups. Select Domain Users, and then Click OK.

   After adding the group to the policy, it should look similar to the following illustration.

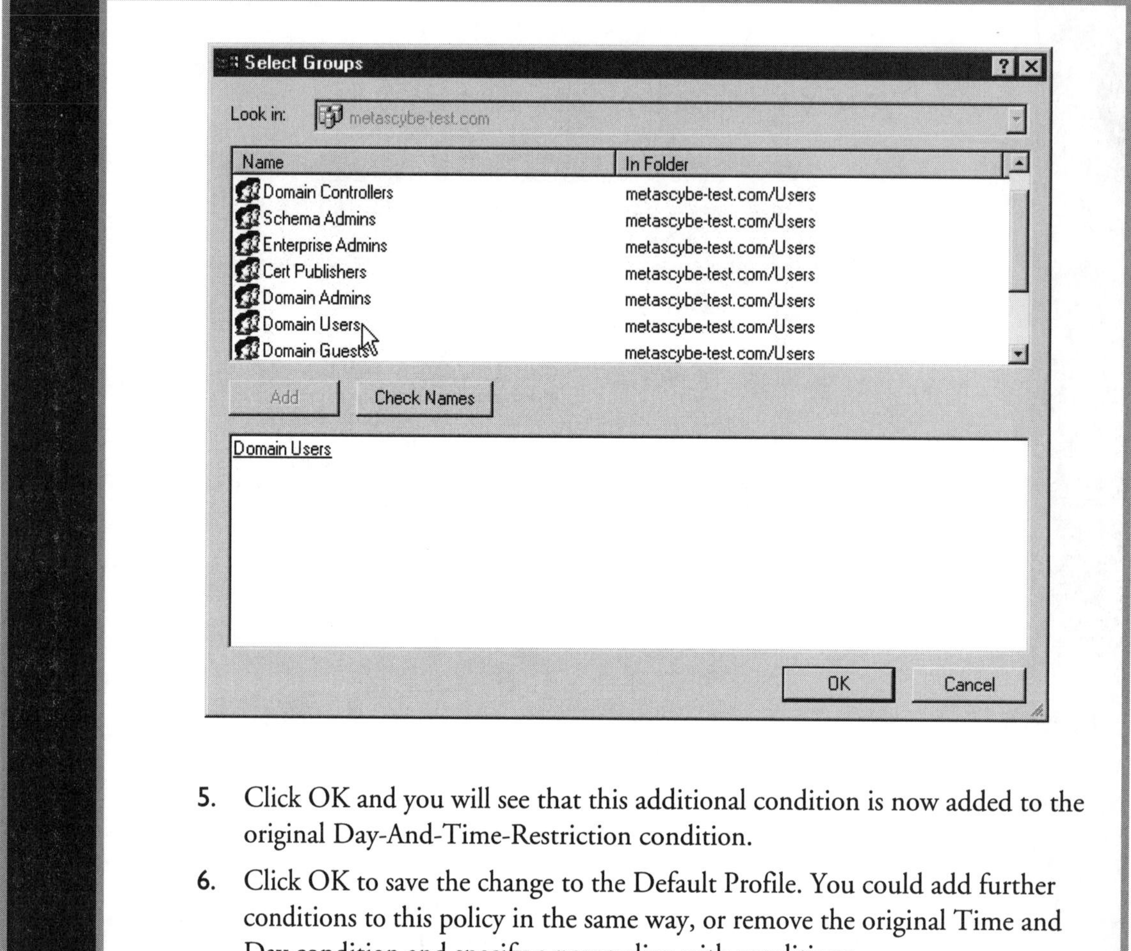

5. Click OK and you will see that this additional condition is now added to the original Day-And-Time-Restriction condition.
6. Click OK to save the change to the Default Profile. You could add further conditions to this policy in the same way, or remove the original Time and Day condition and specify a new policy with conditions.

EXERCISE 5-5

Creating a New Remote Access Policy

1. Right-click on Remote Access Policies and select New Remote Access Policy.
2. You will be prompted to supply a name for your new policy. The new policy in our exercise will only allow users to connect over PPTP on a VPN, so this new policy could be called "Only PPTP Users." Click Next.
3. You will then be prompted to specify the conditions by clicking Add, Remove, or Edit. Because we only want to accept users who connect with a VPN connection using PPTP, click Add and select Tunnel-Type and then Point-to-Point Tunneling Protocol (PPTP).
4. Click OK and you will see your new condition displayed. If you wanted to add more conditions to the same policy, repeat the Add and select your next condition in the same way. When you have multiple conditions in the same policy, you see that all but the last have AND statements to indicate that the policy is a combination of all these conditions.
5. When you have finished specifying all your conditions, click Next. You will be prompted about permissions. Your choice is what action to take if all the conditions match—should it result in remote access permission being granted or denied? Select "Allow permissions" and click Next.
6. The final screen prompts you to edit the policy's profile, which can further filter permissions and settings. Click Finish.
7. Under the Remote Access Policies, you should now see two policies as in the following illustration and a number allocated to them to indicate the sequential order in which they should be assessed. If you want to reorder these, right-click on the policy you want to move up or down, and then select Move Up or Move Down as appropriate.

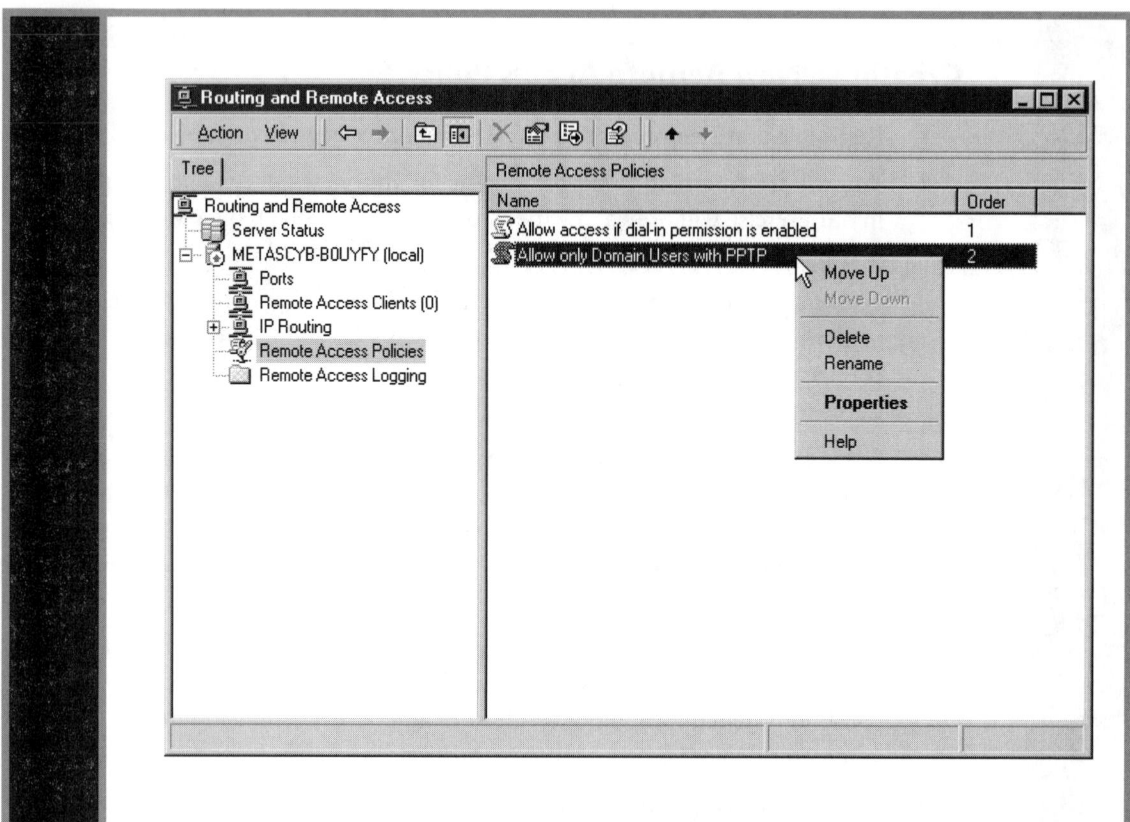

Determining Access Permissions—Putting It All Together

We have looked at the various elements that determine whether a remote access connection is allowed or denied, but how do you put them all together? For a quick check list, refer to the following:

Windows 2000 allows remote access when:

- It matches the conditions of a Remote Access Policy.
- It is allowed by the combination of the remote access permission on the user account and the remote access permission of the matching Remote Access Policy.

- It meets the connection constraints of the matching Remote Access Policy profile and the dial-up properties of the user account.

Windows 2000 denies remote access when:

- It matches the conditions of a Remote Access Policy, but is not allowed by the combination of the remote access permission of the user account and the remote access permission of the policy.
- It matches the conditions of a Remote Access Policy, but does not meet the connection constraints of the matching Remote Access Policy profile or the dial-up properties of the user account.
- It does not match the conditions of any Remote Access Policy.

exam Watch

If a remote access connection attempt does not match any of the remote access policies, the connection is rejected regardless of the remote access permission setting on the user account.

Troubleshooting Remote Access Connections

The following lists some basic checks and common problems/resolutions you should bear in mind if you are having problems connecting your remote access clients through the Windows 2000 Routing and Remote Access Server:

- Verify that the Routing and Remote Access Service is running on the remote access server.
- Verify that remote access is enabled on the remote server.
- Verify that the dial-up ports on the remote access server are configured to allow inbound remote access connections.
- Verify that dial-in properties of the user account, together with remote access policies and profiles, permit dial-in access.
- Verify that settings in the Remote Access Policy profile do not conflict with properties of the remote access server; for example, check settings for multilink, BAP, authentication.
- Verify that any dial-up equipment being used is working correctly.

- Verify that you have free dial-up ports to accept new connections on the remote access server.
- Verify the user's specified credentials are correct (username, password).
- Verify connectivity from the remote access server to other resources on your network.
- Verify that the LAN protocols used by remote clients are either enabled for routing or remote access.
- For a remote access server that is a member of a Windows 2000 native-mode domain, verify that the remote access server has joined the domain.
- If the Routing and Remote Access server was manually added to the RAS and IAS servers security group, bear in mind this addition will not take effect immediately because of the way Active Directory caches directory service information. Your safest bet in this scenario is to reboot the remote access server.
- Verify that the remote client and server have at least one LAN protocol in common.
- If the remote client's protocol is TCP/IP and the access server is configured with a static address pool, verify that there are free addresses available.
- If the remote client's protocol is TCP/IP and the remote access server is configured for DHCP, ensure that a DHCP server is reachable from the server.
- If the remote client's protocol is IPX and tries to use its own IPX node number, verify the server's configuration allows this.
- If the remote client's protocol is IPX and the remote access server allocates an IPX node number, ensure this number is not being used elsewhere on your network.
- If the remote client's protocol is IPX and they cannot create file or printer shares, NetBIOS over IPX broadcast forwarding must be enabled on the LAN adapter connected to your company network.
- If the remote access server shares a modem with the Windows 2000 Fax service, ensure the modem supports adaptive answer. If not, you must disable fax on the modem when you need to accept remote client connections.
- Make use of the tools (tracing and logging facilities) mentioned later in this chapter to help diagnose the problem.

CERTIFICATION OBJECTIVE 5.05

Virtual Private Networking

This section provides an overview of virtual private networks (VPNs), describing the various components and how they work together, and outlines some of the key technologies that permit private networking over public internetworks.

VPN Overview

A virtual private network (VPN) is an extension of a corporate network that uses encapsulated, encrypted, and authenticated links across shared or public networks.

In practice, this means that remote users can connect to a corporate server over a standard Internet connection. Instead of directly connecting to the remote access server, they first connect to the Internet (or other public or shared network); for example, via their local ISP. Then using the first connection, they make another connection to the remote access server. This second connection is "tunneling" over the first, and the actual data packets sent are said to be "encapsulated."

The second connection from client to server creates a virtual network that is private to the client and server, despite the first connection being over a public network. VPNs actually use the in-place routing infrastructure of the Internet, but to remote users, it will seem as if they have a dedicated (private) link.

Why connect in this way, rather than simply connecting directly? Cost. A long distance call from client to server will cost much more than if the client connects via the Internet, because they only pay the cost of a local call to their local ISP.

Note that both sides (client and server) must be connected to the Internet, and the server's connection must be dedicated.

The Internet, by definition being an open and public network, is not a secure medium on which to securely transfer data. However, when that data is encrypted, it then becomes secure.

In addition to remote users connecting to the corporate network, the same technology can be used to connect branch offices, with either dedicated lines or dial-up.

It is even possible to use the same technology within the corporate network itself where privacy is the main benefit of having a virtual network within the main network. The use of IPSec would normally be more appropriate here, but IPSec is not available to down-level clients such as Win9*x* and Windows NT4.0. In a mixed environment, a VPN within the corporate network may be a viable solution to securely transferring data.

Encapsulation and Encryption

To emulate a point-to-point link, data is encapsulated with a header that provides routing information that allows it to travel across the shared or public internetwork, and reach its final destination. This provides the virtual network. To achieve this securely, the data within the packets must also be encrypted. This provides the virtual private network.

Although it is possible to create a virtual network with a tunnel and not encrypt the data, this is not by definition a virtual private network. With VPNs, encapsulation and encryption always go together.

Components of Windows 2000 VPN

These consist of:

- A VPN server
- A VPN client
- A VPN connection using a tunneling protocols

VPN Server

This is the Windows 2000 Server running Routing and Remote Access, with one connection to the Internet and a separate connection to your corporate network. Typically, the connection to the Internet will be over a dedicated line (e.g., T1, Fractional T1, or Frame Relay).

The server must be configured to support VPN connections as either remote access, or as a router-to-router connection.

Because the WAN adapter appears as a network adapter, you must configure this external interface with the IP address and subnet mask supplied by your ISP (or assigned for your domain), and configure the default gateway as being the IP address of the router that connects to the Internet.

When you enable Routing and Remote Access with Internet connectivity, it automatically creates VPN ports (10 in all).

VPN Client

This computer initiates the VPN connection to the VPN Server. For remote access, this will be a user calling up remote access software. However, this connection could also be an automatic router-to-router call.

Many clients can initiate a VPN call, including

- Windows NT 4.0
- Windows 2000
- Windows 9*x*
- Any third-party dial-up clients that support the tunneling protocols in Windows 2000

Additionally, both Windows 2000 Servers and Windows NT 4.0 Servers can create router-to-router VPN connections.

LAN Protocols

Although the initial connection to the Internet has to be TCP/IP (because this is the common protocol of the Internet), the client can use either TCP/IP or other network protocols within the tunnel. Remember that for a client to access a resource, there must be at least one protocol in common; therefore, if your internal network runs IPX rather than TCP/IP, the client should use IPX as the protocol to be tunneled over the VPN.

The choice of which LAN protocol should be used is no different from the same choice when configuring a direct point-to-point connection to a remote access server. And similarly to remote access, you must correctly configure onward routes if remote clients need to access resources on the network rather than just on the Routing and Remote Access server.

Tunneling Protocols

Windows 2000 supports two tunneling protocols: Point to Point Tunneling Protocol (PPTP) and Layer 2 Tunneling Protocol (L2TP).

Both sides of the connection must agree to the creation of a tunnel and be aware that it exists so it can be monitored and maintained (e.g., keep-alive messages if no data is being transferred). However, it does not guarantee reliable data delivery.

PPTP uses TCP with a modified Generic Routing Encapsulation (GRE) protocol, and L2TP uses UDP.

PPTP The Point-to-Point Tunneling Protocol is an extension of PPP that allows the encapsulation of PPP frames into IP datagrams for transmission over an IP internetwork.

PPTP uses a TCP connection for tunnel maintenance, and uses modified GRE encapsulated PPP frames for tunneled data. The data can be encrypted and compressed.

PPTP tunnels must be authenticated by using the same authentication methods as PPP. However, to compress and encrypt (with MPPE) the tunneled data, you must use either MSCHAP or EAP-TLS. Remember that the encryption is only from remote client to VPN server, which may not be the final resource destination if the remote access server allows remote routing. This is another way of saying PPTP does not support end-to-end security.

If you need end-to-end security, your choices include either using L2TP with IPSec as an alternative tunneling protocol, or using PPTP to the VPN server and then employing IPSec from the VPN server to the remote resource machine.

Sometimes GRE is used by ISPs to forward routing information within their own network, which may mean they filter out GRE packets to prevent their routing information being forwarded to Internet backbone routers. If your ISP blocks GRE packets, this will stop your VPN connection from working properly (the tunnel will be created but no data will transfer). If you experience this problem when trying to establish a VPN connection using PPTP, ask the ISP whether they filter GRE packets. If they do and cannot accommodate your VPN connection using PPTP, your alternatives will include using L2TP/IPSec (if your remote clients can support this). Ask if your ISP provides a tunneling service (see the section "WAN and Internet Support," or change your ISP to one that does not filter out GRE packets.

L2TP Layer 2 Tunneling Protocol is a combination of PPTP and Layer 2 Forwarding.

In theory, L2TP encapsulates PPP frames to be sent over any one of the following networks:

- IP
- X25
- Frame Relay
- ATM

In practice, however, Windows 2000 only supports L2TP over IP, and in this scenario it is suitable to be used as a tunneling protocol over the Internet.

L2TP uses UDP and a series of L2TP messages for maintaining the tunnel. L2TP also uses UDP to send L2TP-encapsulated PPP frames as the tunneled data. The data can be encrypted and compressed.

Windows 2000 supports IPSec instead of PPP encryption for L2TP; however, it is possible for third-party implementations to use PPP encryption with L2TP.

L2TP is very similar to PPTP in that an L2TP must be supported on both sides of the connection, and standard PPP authentication is still required. However, where L2TP differs from PPTP is that although it supports (inherits) PPP data compression, PPP encryption is not supported due to lack of security. This is why you must encrypt the data with IPSec.

WAN Options and Internet Support

There may be reasons why you want all your remote connections to be over a VPN but don't want your remote users to initiate it; for example, you don't want the support overhead of the additional dial-up configuration at the client end, and/or the client computer does not have the required tunneling protocol installed.

Access Concentrators and Network Access Servers In this scenario, it is possible to still obtain your VPN connection by using another computer or network device to create the tunnel on the client's behalf. This intermediary device is referred to as an "access concentrator." The access concentrator must have the appropriate tunneling protocol installed (matches the tunneling protocol on your VPN server) and be capable of establishing the tunnel for remote clients when they initiate a connection to connect to your VPN server.

An ISP, for example, may offer a company the service of running a tunneling-enabled Network Access Server (NAS), so that specifically identified remote users can connect to this ISP with a standard PPP connection. The access concentrator on the NAS automatically creates the tunnel for them into the company network VPN server. Because the connecting user does not choose to connect over a tunnel, this configuration is called *compulsory tunneling*.

An extension of this is *realm-based tunneling*, where the access concentrator makes decisions on the tunnel's final destination (VPN server) based on additional group information about the user (referred to as the *realm*). For example, one user called JohnB@domain1.com is always directed to one VPN server that serves the realm domain1.com, and another user called JackD@domain2.com is always directed to a different VPN server that serves the realm domain2.com. Realm compulsory tunnels that work in this way are "static," because a set of rules predetermines the route for each realm and cannot accommodate any flexibility at connection time.

on the Job

A realm name can be either a prefix (such as /domain1) or suffix (such as @domain1). Users can include their realm name as part of their username at logon. However, with some dialling programs, you could add the realm automatically. For example, Microsoft's Connection Manager Administration Kit (CMAK) can be used with Connection Manager to do this automatically for your remote users.

An elaboration on this is when you have *dynamic compulsory tunnels* where a connection is dynamically assessed and the tunnel directed accordingly. For example, based on certain criteria, the same user may be directed to different VPN servers depending on what time of day the connection is made. Or, realms can be further divided into usernames, departments, the telephone number being used, and so forth. In this way, dynamic compulsory tunnels offer the highest degree of flexibility and granularity. An additional advantage for the owner of the Network Access Server is that it can simultaneously support both tunneling and nontunneling connections.

Each concentrator can store its own database for this filtering process; however, for large-scale solutions it would be better to host this information on a centrally maintained server and reference it when needed. RADIUS provides this type of solution.

exam Watch

A* transit internetwork *refers to the shared or public internetwork used by the encapsulated data. Although the transit internetwork can be either the public Internet or a private IP-based network, in Windows 2000 scenarios it invariably refers to the Internet.

Security

Security is an important aspect of a VPN, because you are potentially offering your corporate resources to the open Internet.

In addition to deciding upon which authentication and encryption methods you will employ, you should also filter for only PPTP and/or L2TP packets (as appropriate) on the VPN server and/or your company firewall or router that connects to the Internet.

For more information on configuring packet filters, see the section "Configuring Firewalls with VPNs."

Security When Using PPTP PPTP offers user authentication and encryption in the same way that a PPP connection can—inheriting Microsoft Point-to-Point Encryption (MPPE) when used with MSCHAP (both versions) or EAP-TLS. MPPE can use 40-bit, 56-bit, or 128-bit encryption keys, and by default, the highest key strength supported by both client and server is negotiated during the connection establishment. If the server is configured to require a higher key strength than the client can support, the connection attempt fails. Note that 40-bit encryption provides backward compatibility for clients that aren't running Windows 2000.

One other added security change to PPTP over a standard PPP connection is that the encryption key is changed for every packet sent.

Security When Using L2TP over IPSec L2TP over IPSec offers user authentication, mutual computer authentication, encryption, data authentication, and data integrity:

- Authentication of the VPN client occurs at both the computer and then the user.
- Mutual computer authentication is performed when an IPSec Encapsulating Security Payload security association is established through the exchange of computer certificates. IPSec security association is established with an agreed encryption algorithm, hash algorithm, and encryption keys.

You must have computer certificates on both the VPN server and client before being able to use L2TP over IPSec connections. Computer certificates can be automatically obtained by configuring an auto-enrollment Windows 2000 Group Policy, or manually using the Certificates snap-in. For more information, refer to the chapter 7, "Configuring and Troubleshooting IPSec."

User authentication is performed with the usual PPP user authentication protocols such as EAP, MSCHAP, CHAP, SAP, and PAP (see "Authentication Protocols" in the "Remote Access Security" section later in this chapter for more information on these authentication protocols). Any authentication protocol can be used, but for stronger security with mutual authentication, use MS-CHAPv2 or EAP-TLS.

You can also authenticate the endpoints of an L2TP tunnel (L2TP tunnel authentication), although this isn't configured on Windows 2000 by default.

Encryption is determined by the IPSec Security Authority, and available encryption algorithms include:

- DES with a 56-bit key
- Triple DES (3DES)—three 56-bit keys designed for high-security environments

Data authentication and integrity is provided with one of the following:

- The hash message authentication code (HMAC) Message Digest 5 (MD5)—128-bit hash
- The hash message authentication code Secure Hash Algorithm (HMAC SHA-1)—160-bit hash

Now that you have an understanding about the two tunneling protocols, you should be able to decide which is better to use in different circumstances.

SCENARIO & SOLUTION

Which Tunneling Protocol Should Be Used?	Tunneling Protocol to Use
If security is important, and remote access clients are running Windows 2000 Professional?	L2TP/IPSec. This offers a higher degree of security than PPTP, and data is encrypted from client to final resource. When using encryption with PPTP, the data is only encrypted from client to server, and not beyond the server.
If security is important, and remote access clients are Windows NT 4.0 workstations?	PPTP. Down-level clients such as Windows NT 4.0 and Windows 9*x* cannot support L2TP/IPSec.
If performance is more important than security?	PPTP. This requires less processing than L2TP/IPSec.
If I require mutual authentication of both client and server for better security?	Either PPTP or L2TP/IPSec, providing you disable the MS-CHAP authentication. The authentication protocol is independent of the tunneling protocol used, because it inherits these settings from the tunneled PPP connection.

SCENARIO & SOLUTION

If I have been instructed to use 3DES encryption for a high security environment?	L2TP/IPSec. PPTP does not support this high encryption standard.
If I want to quickly set up and use just one standard tunneling protocol for everybody?	PPTP, because this is the easiest to set up (no IPSec policies required) and is supported by the widest range of client platforms.

Installing and Configuring the VPN Server

You must have a permanent and dedicated link to the Internet to support a VPN. This dedicated connection is typically a second network adapter that connects to an Internet router. In this configuration, the Routing and Remote Access Service will automatically assign VPN ports that appear as WAN Miniports under Ports in the main console tree.

The default configuration is five ports that support PPTP and five ports that support L2TP. To enable or disable these for inbound traffic, right-click Ports and then select Properties from the shortcut menu. This will display the Devices dialog box similar to the one shown in Figure 5-5.

FIGURE 5-5

Device Ports Properties dialog box

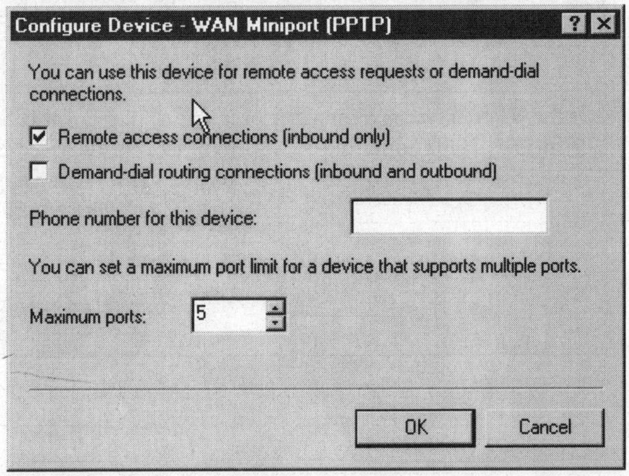

For each tunneling protocol (e.g., PPTP) you can configure whether to allow remote access, specify the telephone number being used (if any), and change the number of simultaneously supported ports for that particular device.

Note that as with any security setting in Windows 2000, the strongest setting will be tried first, and only if that fails will it try to negotiate down to the next strongest level. For VPN connections, this means that if a Windows 2000 Professional attempts to connect to the VPN server, the client's default Server Type of "Automatic" will try a L2TP/IPSec connection first, and then a PPTP connection if the first fails. This behavior may explain unexpected connection patterns for the VPN ports you have configured.

exam Watch

By default, both PPTP and L2TP ports are enabled on a VPN server. If you want the VPN server to accept one of these tunneling protocols only, set the number of ports on the unwanted protocol to zero. You cannot as you might expect, simply delete either of these ports. Alternatively, you could disable the remote access permission on the port.

If you are using L2TP over IPSec, you must ensure the IPSec policies are in place for the remote access server. Table 5-5 shows where to configure these IPSec settings.

TABLE 5-5 Where to Set IPSec Settings for Your VPN Server

Role of VPN Server	How to Create IPSec Policies
If the VPN server is a stand-alone server or a member of a Windows NT 4.0 domain	Configure local machine IPSec policy.
If the VPN server is a member of a Windows 2000 domain	Local IPSec policies are overwritten by assigned domain IPSec policies. To create an IPSec policy that only applies to the VPN server, create an organizational unit in the Active Directory, put the VPN server computer account in this OU, and then use the Group Policy to create and assign IPSec policies for the VPN server's OU.

How to configure the IP options for the two adapters: On your internal adapter (local network connection) you will need to specify the standard company TCP/IP options you would for any internal computer: IP address, subnet mask, default gateway, and so forth. You can do this either statically (recommended) or via DHCP. However, on the external adapter (the one connected to the Internet), you must assign to it the static IP address details provided by your ISP or equivalent. Your default gateway on this external adapter should be the IP address of the router that connects directly to the Internet (e.g., ISP). You should not have assigned to the external adapter details for DNS or WINS.

Configuring Firewalls with VPNs

How to correctly configure a firewall when using a VPN is a very commonly asked question, and this is information you need to know irrespective of whether you pass on this information to somebody else who manages the firewall, or you manage it yourself. There's no point in having a perfectly configured VPN if the firewall won't let connections through!

Although you can have the scenario where the VPN server is attached to the Internet and the firewall is between the VPN server and the intranet, the more typical firewall setup is such that the firewall is attached to the Internet, and the VPN server is between the firewall and the intranet. In this way, the VPN server is another Internet resource on the *demilitarized zone* (DMZ), perhaps sharing it with Web servers, proxy servers, ftp servers, and so forth.

In addition to any standard filters designed for protecting your other DMZ resources, for your VPN server you must configure the firewall with input and output filters on its Internet interface to allow the relevant tunneling protocols and data to pass from the Internet to the VPN server.

The information in this section can also be applied if you decide to use packet filtering on the Routing and Remote Access server itself.

Packet Filters for PPTP

Configure the following input filters to drop all packets except those that meet the criteria listed:

Input Filter	Explanation
Destination IP address of the VPN server's Internet interface and TCP destination port 1723	This allows PPTP tunnel maintenance traffic from PPTP client to PPTP server.
Destination IP address of the VPN server's Internet interface and TCP destination port 1723	This allows PPTP tunnel maintenance traffic from PPTP client to PPTP server.
Destination IP address of the VPN server's Internet interface and IP Protocol ID 47	This allows PPTP tunneled data from the PPTP client to PPTP server.
Destination IP address of the VPN server's Internet interface and TCP (established) source port 1723	This is required only if VPN server is acting as a VPN client (i.e., calling router) in a router-to-router VPN connection.

Configure the following output filters to drop all packets *except* those that meet the criteria listed:

Output Filter	Explanation
Source IP address of the VPN server's Internet interface and TCP source port 1723	This allows PPTP tunnel maintenance traffic from VPN server to VPN client.
Source IP address of the VPN server's Internet interface and IP Protocol ID 47	This allows PPTP tunneled data from VPN server to VPN client.
Source IP address of the VPN server's Internet interface and TCP (established) destination port 1723	This filter is only required if the VPN server is acting as a VPN client (i.e., calling router) in a router-to-router VPN connection.

Packet Filters for L2PT over IPSec

Configure the following input filters to drop all packets *except* those that meet the criteria listed:

Input Filter	Explanation
Destination IP address of VPN server's Internet interface and UDP destination port 500	This allows Internet Key Exchange (IKE) traffic through to the VPN server.
Destination IP address of VPN server's Internet interface and IP Protocol ID 50	This allows IPSec Encapsulating Security Payload traffic from VPN client to VPN server.

Configure the following output filters to drop all packets *except* those that meet the criteria listed:

Output Filter	Explanation
Source address of the VPN server's Internet interface and UDP source port 500.	This allows Internet Key Exchange traffic from the VPN server.
Source IP address of the VPN server's Internet interface and IP Protocol ID 50.	This allows IPSec Encapsulating Security Payload traffic from VPN server to VPN client.

There are no filters required for L2TP traffic at UDP port 1701; at the firewall, all L2TP traffic (including tunnel maintenance and tunneled data) is encrypted as part of the IPSec Encapsulating Security Payload.

Testing Connectivity to the VPN Server

You will need to configure a VPN client to connect to your VPN server, and although many remote access clients support this (e.g., Windows NT 4.0, Windows 98), we will look at how to configure a VPN client on Windows 2000 Professional.

The underlying concept remains the same for other clients. You must first have a valid Internet connection that is dialed first and connected, and then dial a second connection that specifies the VPN server's address (e.g., IP address or DNS name) as the destination rather than specifying a telephone number.

When you dial the VPN server, you will be asked to log on, and once authenticated, your remote access permissions will be assessed. If all goes well and you pass the security checks, you will be connected to your internal network and should be able to access resources just as if you were locally connected (albeit more slowly).

Note that if you want to use L2TP with IPSec (rather than PPTP), you must use Windows 2000 Professional as your VPN client—this tunneling protocol is not supported on other Microsoft platforms.

EXERCISE 5-6

Configuring a VPN Remote Access Client on Windows 2000 Professional

If you haven't already configured a dial-up connection to the Internet, you will need to do this first. Select Dial-up to the Internet to load the Internet Connection Wizard, which will walk you through setting up your Internet connection. When you have completed this step, test the connection to ensure you can connect to the Internet without problems. You are then ready to configure your VPN connection.

1. Under Network and Dial-up Connection, select Make New Connection.
2. This loads the Network Connection Wizard. Select the option "Connect to a private network through the Internet," and click Next.
3. You will then be prompted whether you want the required Internet connection to be automatically dialed before trying the VPN connection (recommended). If you choose to automatically dial up to the Internet first, select the Internet connection you need from the drop-down list box. Click Next.
4. You will then be prompted for the destination address of the VPN server as shown in the following illustration. You can enter this in any valid Internet format, which may be IP address, DNS name, or host name.

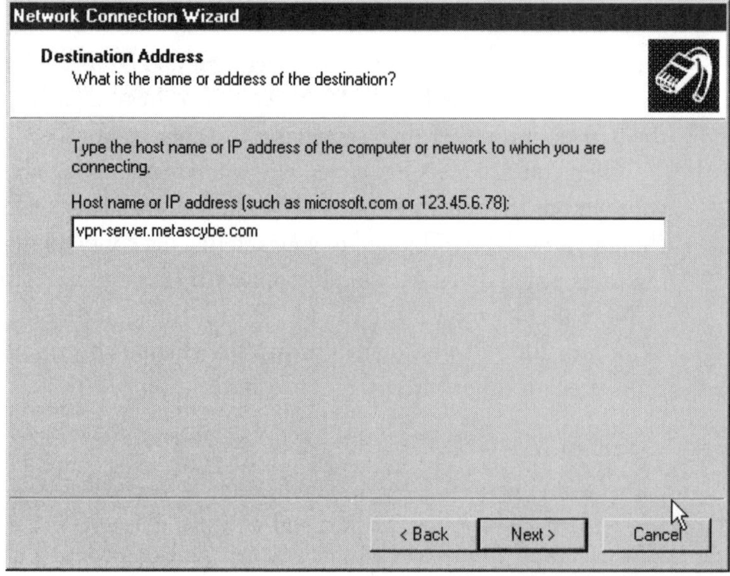

If in doubt, specify the IP address to eliminate any name resolution problems. Click Next.

5. You will next be prompted whether you want exclusive access to this connection, or share it with others. Note that even if sharing, it will only be shared when you are logged on. Select "Only for myself," and click Next.
6. You will then be prompted to specify a name to identify this connection. The default is Virtual Private Connection, which you can either accept or edit as you wish.
7. If you want to automatically create a shortcut for this connection on your desktop, click the "Add a shortcut to my desktop" check box at the bottom of the dialog box.
8. Click Finish and you will be prompted whether to connect your chosen Internet connection now, with a check box to say whether you want this reminder displayed again. Click Yes, which will prompt you to dial your Internet connection, and once connected, prompt to dial your VPN connection.

Troubleshooting VPNs

The VPN problems you encounter will probably fall into one of these categories:

- Connection attempt fails when it should be accepted
- Connection attempt is accepted when it should fail
- Unable to access resources beyond the VPN server
- Unable to establish a tunnel

Check through the previous Routing and Remote Access server troubleshooting list to eliminate any standard remote access problems. The following are specific to VPN problems:

- If you are not using packet filtering on the VPN server and/or your firewall allows through a ping command from the Internet, try pinging the VPN server from the client to test basic connectivity. If this works, ping by the same host name specified in the client's VPN connection destination if an IP address isn't being used (this ensures correct name to IP resolution).

- Verify that PPTP and/or L2TP ports are enabled for inbound remote access.
- Verify that free PPTP and/or L2TP ports are available; increase if necessary.
- Verify that the VPN client's tunneling protocol is supported by the VPN server, and vice versa.
- If using L2TP over IPSec, verify that computer certificates are installed on both the VPN server and the VPN client.
- If using PPTP, verify that GRE isn't being filtered out by your ISP.
- Verify there are no TCP/IP filters on the profile properties of the Remote Access Policy being used by the VPN connection that block required packets.
- Verify there are no IP packet filters that block required packets from the server, the Internet connected adapter, or within remote access policies.
- Verify firewall configuration is not blocking required packets.
- Verify the VPN connection configuration on the remote access client. If identifying the VPN server by DNS name, change this to the actual IP address.
- Check to see whether the remote access client has a policy that excludes tunneling.
- Verify that the WinSock Proxy client is not currently running on the VPN client (which will forward all IP traffic to the proxy server rather than the VPN server).
- To improve the performance of VPN connections, look to improve the processor and memory on *both* sides of the connection (i.e., server and client) that is required to support the additional encapsulation and encryption.

on the Job

If the remote user has problems accessing local resources once connected, check the default gateway setting on the client computer once it has successfully connected to the VPN server (e.g., route print command or winipcfg/ipconfig). A VPN connection should replace the previous (ISP's) default gateway with a new default gateway for the VPN connection; however, some clients (e.g., Windows 95) have been known to have problems relinquishing the initial default gateway. If this happens, all traffic sent over the Internet connection by the remote client continues to be directed to the ISP rather than the company's router. If necessary, use the route add command to manually assign the default gateway for the VPN connection.

CERTIFICATION OBJECTIVE 5.06

Connections Using PPP Multilink and BAP

Windows 2000 remote access supports the following when aggregating multiple physical links into a single logical link:

- PPP Multilink Protocol (MP)
- Bandwidth Allocation Protocol (BAP)
- Bandwidth Allocation Control Protocol (BACP)

These protocols are explained in Table 5-6.

PPP Multilink and BAP are enabled on the remote access server through the PPP tab on the Properties sheet of the remote access server in the Routing and Remote Access snap-in. Settings for multilink and BAP can also be configured from the Multilink tab on the Properties sheet of a Remote Access Policy profile. However, you must have multilink and BAP enabled on the server before you can fine-tune these settings in the remote policy profile.

Multilink supports multiple devices but not multiple servers—you cannot span multilinked devices over more than one Routing and Remote Access server.

TABLE 5-6 MP, BAP, and BACP

Protocol	Explanation
MP	MP allows multiple physical links to appear as a single local link over which data can be sent and received at a higher throughput than if going over a single physical link.
BAP	BAP is a PPP control protocol that is used to dynamically add or remove additional links to an MP connection.
BACP	BACP polices multiple peers using MP; for example, electing a favored peer when more than one PPP peer requests to add or remove a connection at the same time.

PPP Multilink Protocol

This protocol is used to combine multiple physical links into a single logical link to increase throughput. The most common use of multilink is the aggregation of the two B-channels of an ISDN Basic Rate Interface connection.

MP fragments, sequences, and reorders alternating packets are sent across multiple physical connections, the resulting bandwidth becoming the sum of the combined links. Although MP can be done for any ISDN adapter, MP must be supported on both sides of the connection.

On the Windows 2000 Routing and Remote Access Service, you can enable multilink as one of the server's properties, and you can also enable it in a policy's profile.

BAP

Although MP allows multiple physical links to be combined, there is no automatic way of adapting to changing conditions; for example, adding additional links when greater throughput is required, or closing links that are no longer required.

This extra facility is provided by the Bandwidth Allocation Protocol (BAP) and the Bandwidth Allocation Control Protocol (BACP).

An example of this working is when an MP- and BAP-enabled remote client and remote access server create an MP connection that is only a single physical link because they are not sending much data. However, should the throughput increase, at a configured level, the remote client could issue a *BAP Call Request* to add an additional link (e.g., additional ISDN channel, or modem). The remote access server responds with a *BAP Call Response* that contains the information needed to access one of its available ports (e.g., telephone number).

When the throughput then drops again, either side could send a BAP Link Drop Query Request so that the additional link that is no longer needed is dropped and becomes available again (e.g., for another connecting client).

on the job

Adding or dropping telephone lines may not work successfully with generic modem drivers that don't correctly provide send/receive status information—causing BAP to use false throughput values. The result of this can be unexpected and expensive dial-up costs! Monitor line activity, and if you suspect this to be a problem, try to obtain the latest modem drivers, or disable BAP.

To set the telephone number of a port that is sent in the BAP Call Response message:

1. Use the Routing and Remote Access snap-in to obtain properties on the Ports object.
2. Select the port you want to configure and click Configure.
3. Type in the telephone number in the "Phone number of this device" text box.

Bandwidth Allocation Control Protocol (BACP)

The sole job of this protocol is to elect a favored peer when necessary. If both peers of an MP- and BAP-enabled connection send a BAP Call Request or BAP Link Drop Query Request message at the same time, only one request can succeed, and it is the responsibility of this protocol to elect which peer wins.

on the job

Configure multilink and BAP on Windows 2000 Professional by editing the remote access connection's Properties, and then in the Options tab you can select how to configure multilink in the "Multiple devices" section. If you want to use all devices, select the "Dial all devices" option. Enabling BAP and configuring it is available when you select the "Dial devices only as needed" and then Configure to specify conditions and thresholds.

EXERCISE 5-7

CertCam 5-7

Configuring Multilink Support on Your Remote Access Server

Your Routing and Remote Access server has a multiport serial adapter that supports 16 modems for a small group of homeworkers. Some of these users have requested to use multilink to improve the speed of their connection, but you are keen to restrict this to just two modems per user to ensure that enough free ports are available for other users.

You therefore configure your Routing and Remote Access server to enable multilink, but you also set up a Remote Access Policy for these homeworkers that restricts them to only two links.

1. If you haven't already done so, load up the Routing and Remote Access snap-in, select your server, right-click and select Properties.
2. On the PPP tab, ensure that all options are selected. Click OK.

3. Click on Remote Access Policies and right-click to select New Remote Access Policy.
4. Enter as the Policy Friendly Name: "Restrict Homeworkers to 2 modems only" and Click OK.
5. On the Conditions dialog box, click Add, select Windows-Group, and click Add.
6. Select the user group that contains your homeworkers (for this exercise, if you don't have any additional groups set up, you could select the Domain Users group). Click Add and Click OK.
7. Click OK again and you will see your one condition displayed. Click Next to continue.
8. On the Permissions dialog box, select to "Grant remote access permission" and click Next.
9. Before you click Finish, click Edit Profile. It is in the profile where you can fine-tune your settings that include multilink settings.
10. Select the Multilink tab and under the Multilink Settings instead of the default "Default to server settings," select "Allow Multilink," and underneath the Limit Maximum Ports will automatically default to 2, which is the setting we require.
11. Click OK to close the Profile dialog box, and then click Finish to complete this Remote Access Policy.

You have now successfully enabled multilink on your remote access server, but are restricting all users in this group to just two ports.

CERTIFICATION OBJECTIVE 5.07

Integrating Remote Access and DHCP

Although you have a choice of whether to use a static address pool defined on the Routing and Remote Access server or use DHCP, Microsoft recommends using

DHCP where possible. This means that IP address assignment is centrally configured and maintained, and therefore less prone to errors such as duplicate addresses. However, there are some considerations to be taken into account when using DHCP with remote access, which are discussed in the following sections.

Obtaining DHCP Addresses via RRAS

When the Routing and Remote Access Service first starts and it is configured to automatically assign IP addresses, it looks to obtain from a DHCP server a pool of 10 addresses. These addresses are stored in the remote access server's Registry to allocate as needed to remote access clients when they connect. The remote access server manages these IP leases, noting from which DHCP server they were assigned and their lease time, so it can renew them appropriately. Note that the lease is actually between the DHCP server and the RAS server, rather than the DHCP server and the remote access client.

When remote access clients disconnect from the RAS server, their IP address is returned to the RAS server rather than to the DHCP server. This means that other connecting remote clients can reuse their IP addresses. However, if there are no more free addresses, a further block of 10 addresses are obtained from a DHCP server. When the Routing and Remote Access Service is stopped, all addresses obtained by the remote access server are released. You cannot release them manually on the server—for example, issuing an **ipconfig /release all** command.

If you know the number of simultaneous addresses your RAS server will need (for example, you know on average you will have 20 simultaneous RAS connections), you can change the number of "pre-booked" addresses so that an adequate number is initially cached on startup of the RRAS service. To change this number of addresses, modify the following Registry key and change the default value of 10 to the number you require:

```
HKEY_LOCAL_MACHINE\SYSTEM\CurrentControlSet\Services\
RemoteAccess\Parameters\IP\ InitialAddressPoolSize
```

Obtaining DHCP Options via RRAS

The IP address is not the only DHCP setting that can be passed to DHCP clients. Once the IP address has been offered and accepted, DHCP clients send a DHCPInform message to the DHCP server to obtain any DHCP configured options, such as WINS servers, DNS servers, Class options, and the domain name. However, when a remote access client has been allocated an address by the RAS server through DHCP, and sends its DHCPInform message to the RAS server, the RAS server discards this message and does not pass it on to the originating DHCP server.

This means that remote access clients by default will not obtain any DHCP scope options. Instead, the RAS server allocates to the remote access workstation its own default gateway address, and its own WINS and DNS server addresses (if configured). In most cases, this will ensure successful network connectivity for the remote access clients beyond the RAS server. It also allows workstations to automatically receive appropriate configurations depending on whether they are connecting directly on the local area network or remotely by the RAS server.

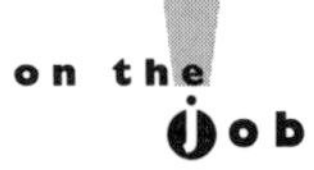

The Windows 2000 RRAS Server caches an IP address pool (10 by default) from a DHCP server. These IP addresses are allocated to remote access clients as they connect, but other DHCP configured options are by default discarded. If the RAS server is configured with a DNS and/or WINS address, these details will be automatically inherited by connecting remote access clients.

on the Job

Windows 95 clients do not inherit WINS information from the remote access server, and therefore by default will resolve NetBIOS names by broadcast.

However, if the RAS server is configured to use the DHCP relay agent on the internal interface, DHCPInform messages will be passed to the DHCP server, and in this way remote workstations can receive DHCP scope options (such as a WINS and DNS address) from the DHCP server. This applies even if you are using static addresses.

The settings from the DHCP server override (replace) settings inherited from the RAS server (such as WINS server, DNS server). This is particularly useful for configuring the domain name, which cannot be inherited from the RAS server, and if you specifically want remote access clients to obtain other configured DHCP options.

If you want your remote access clients to receive DHCP scope options, use the DHCP relay agent on the RAS server.

Location of the DHCP Server

The DHCP server may be the same server that's hosting the Routing and Remote Access Service; however, in all but a very small network environment, this is unlikely.

If there is a DHCP server on the same subnet as the Routing and Remote Access server, the RAS server will be able to obtain IP addresses directly for remote clients because both servers are on the same subnetwork. If there is no DHCP server on the same subnet as the Routing and Remote Access server, the DHCP relay agent must be running on the Routing and Remote Access server so that it can forward requests to the DHCP server in order to obtain the IP addresses it needs for remote access clients.

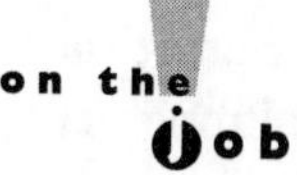

To install the DHCP relay agent, double-click on IP Routing in the Routing and Remote Access snap-in. Right-click on General, and then select New Routing Protocol. Select DHCP relay agent, and then Click OK. Right-click on the installed DHCP Relay Agent and choose Properties. In the General tab, add at least one address of a DHCP server. Note that you cannot install the DHCP relay agent if the server is also running the DHCP service, or NAT. For more information about DHCP, see Chapter 4, "Installing, Configuring, and Troubleshooting DHCP."

Automatic Private IP Addresses—APIPA

If the Routing and Remote Access server is configured to automatically assign IP addresses for remote access clients, but no DHCP server can be found when the Routing and Remote Access Service starts, the server will still be able to assign IP addresses through the Windows 2000 support of Automatic Private IP Addresses, or APIPA.

The private address range is 169.254.0.1–169.254.255.254.

The remote access server will randomly choose an address from this range for connecting remote access clients, so the lack of a DHCP server will not prevent remote connections. However, this use of APIPA is only practical with remote access when all your internal computers are also using APIPA (including the remote access server itself) and there are no routers on the internal network. This setup is very unusual and not recommended except for the smallest of networks.

Multihomed Servers

If remote access clients are being connected but cannot access resources on the internal network, check the allocated IP address of the connecting remote access client (under Remote Access Clients in the Routing and Remote Access snap-in) to see if they are using a 169.254.xxx.xxx address instead of the one you were expecting had a DHCP server been available.

If a DHCP server is available and your remote access server is multihomed, check the adapter selected for DHCP requests. When multiple network adapters exist on a server running Routing and Remote Access, it will by default randomly choose an adapter for sending out DHCP requests. Obviously, it may select an adapter that has no link to a DHCP server, in which case you will have to manually change the selected adapter (Routing and Remote Access snap-in | <server-name> | Properties | IP tab | Adapter dropdown box).

If DHCP has been enabled to assign IP addresses to remote clients, but no DHCP server could be located, by default this will be recorded in the Event Log displaying which private address was used in the absence of a DHCP server (see Exercise 5-8).

Typically, in this scenario users will not be aware that they do not have their expected IP address because they will be successfully connected. However, they will not be able to access resources beyond the server and will receive a "The network path was not found" error message.

Off-Subnet Addressing and On-Subnet Addressing

Another consideration is when the DHCP server allocates an IP address that is on a different subnet to the remote access server itself; this is called *off-subnet addressing*. When the allocated addresses are on the same subnet as the remote access server, this is called *on-subnet addressing* and is by far the more common setup.

Why might you want to use off-sub addressing? Well, you might decide that all your remote users, although transparently connected to your network as if they were locally connected, should be differentiated logically with a different subnet address. In this case, the remote access server is acting as a router between the remote access workstations and your company resources.

When a remote access user obtains a different subnet address to the RAS server, the RAS server automatically adds a new route for the remote access client to its routing table so it can forward packets to and from the remote access users and the company network.

Additionally, if the RAS server has installed an IP routing protocol, this new route will be automatically advertised to neighboring routers on the company network so they too will add the network path of the remote access users to their routing tables. This ensures that traffic can flow between the remote access workstations and resources on the company network.

However, if the RAS server does not have an IP routing protocol installed, other routers and other computers will not know about the new network route, and packets destined for the remote access users from any computer other than the RAS server will have no automatic path back to them. If this is the case, static routes should be added that define a path back to the remote access clients via the RAS server. If you do not add static routes in this situation, the connection between the remote access client and company resource (beyond the RAS server) will fail. You may decide to turn this into a security advantage by only adding static routes on certain computers to ensure that only these resources can be accessed remotely.

EXERCISE 5-8

Demonstrating APIPA

This exercise steps through showing APIPA in action so that remote access clients can still connect. However, it does require you to stop the DHCP server to simulate a network or DHCP problem.

1. Ensure that your remote access server is set to allocate IP addresses automatically to remote access clients (within the Routing and Remote Access snap-in, this is specified under your server, Properties, and then the IP tab), and your server has a static address. Ensure that a DHCP server is not available. How you make the DHCP server unavailable depends on your setup. See the following table for various solutions.

DHCP Setup	How to Stop the Routing and Remote Access Server from Obtaining IP Addresses from a DHCP Server
If the DHCP service is running on the same server as the remote access server	Stop the service (Start | Programs | Administrative Tools | DHCP Manager), then select your server in the left pane, right-click, select All Tasks, then either Stop or Pause.
If the DHCP server is on another subnet and you are using the DHCP relay agent to locate it	Stop this service under IP Routing, DHCP relay agent. Right-click and select All Tasks | Stop.

DHCP Setup	How to Stop the Routing and Remote Access Server from Obtaining IP Addresses from a DHCP Server
If the DHCP server is on the same subnet and you are able to temporarily pause or stop the DHCP service	Pause or stop the DHCP service.
If you cannot stop the DHCP service (because it's servicing live clients) but your RRAS server is a standalone server	Change your internal IP address to be a different network address, which will mean that the DHCP broadcast will now fail.

2. Before you connect a remote access client, stop and restart the Windows 2000 Routing and Remote Access Service. Then connect the workstation to the Remote Access server (refer to Exercise 5-3 if necessary). Expand Remote Access Clients in the Routing and Remote Access snap-in, and double-click on the connected user to view the connected IP address. As in the following illustration, the IP address should now be in the APIPA address range.

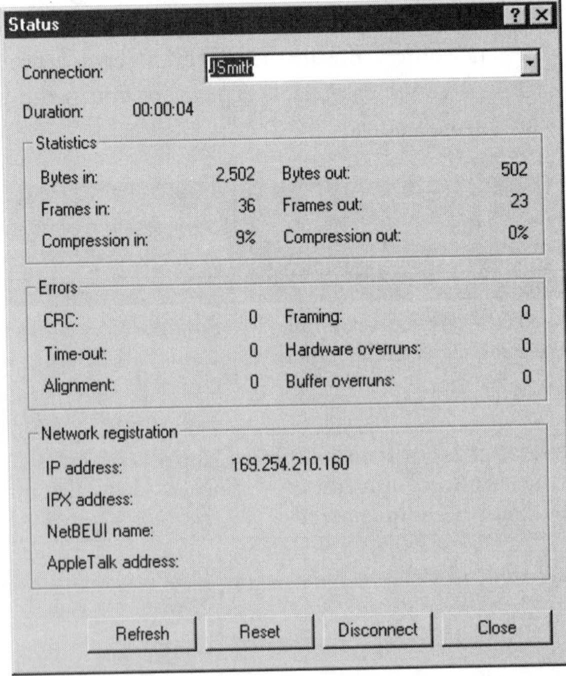

3. The user has connected successfully, but are remote resources available beyond the server? Try connecting a mapped drive on your internal network to a share that would normally be accessible. You should see the "The network path was not found" error message similar to the one shown as follows.

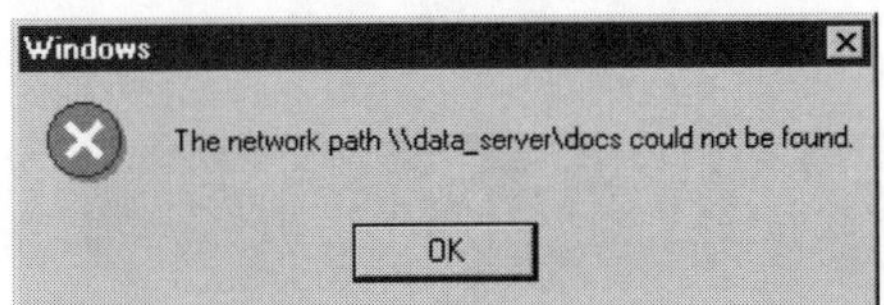

4. Look in the System Event Log; providing you haven't disabled all logging on the RRAS server, you should see something similar to the following illustration, the evidence as to why remote access paths beyond the server are failing.

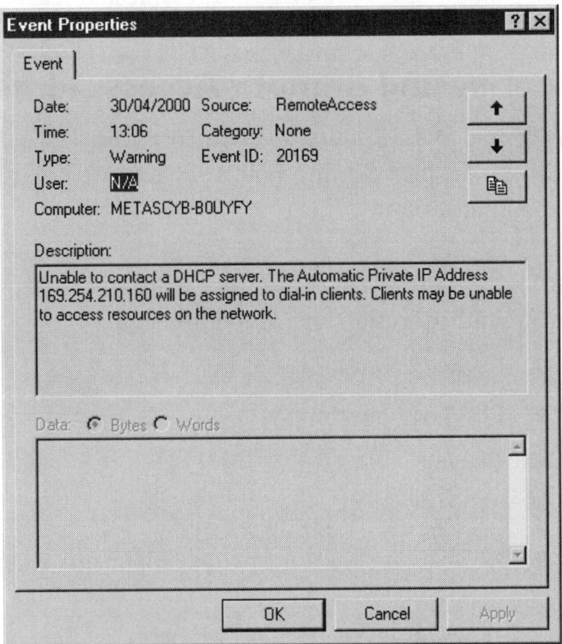

You will see in the System log multiple errors—the RAS server tries to obtain its initial pool of addresses. As the network administrator, you would now know you had to resolve a DHCP problem rather than have to check other possible causes (e.g., modem problems, remote access permission, authentication issues, etc).

Once you have completed this exercise, don't forget to restart your DHCP service and stop/restart the Windows 2000 Routing and Remote Access Service!

CERTIFICATION OBJECTIVE 5.08

Managing and Monitoring Remote Access

Once you decide on your remote access strategies and configure your remote connections accordingly, you will still need to manage and monitor this service to ensure that it offers and delivers a reliable and secure service.

Additional Routing and Remote Access Administration Tools

In addition to the Routing and Remote Access Service snap-in, and the command-line utility Netsh, the following tools are available to help support various RRAS administrative tasks:

- Event Logging
- Authentication and Account Logging
- Network Monitor
- PPP Logging
- Tracing
- SNMP MIB Support
- API Support for third-party components and utilities

Event Logging

Four levels of logging can be set for recording RRAS information to the Event Log. These can be seen on the Properties sheet of the remote access server's Event Logging tab:

- Log errors only
- Log errors and warnings
- Log the maximum amount of information
- Disable event logging

The DHCP error we saw earlier was one of the "Log errors and warnings" entries that will be recorded. Other events relate to the general functionality of the remote access server (for example, which user connected at what line speed, what IP addresses were allocated, and any security or authentication messages).

Obviously, the more detailed the logging, the more resources your computer must devote to this job, which may be at the expense of the Routing and Remote Access service itself.

Authentication and Accounting Logging

The remote access server can log authentication and accounting information in local logging files that are separate from events written to the Event Log.

This sort of logging is very helpful for troubleshooting Remote Access Policy problems, because for each authentication attempt, it logs the name of the Remote Access Policy that either accepts or rejects the connection.

If the remote access server is configured for Windows 2000 authentication and accounting, the authentication and accounting information is stored locally by default in:

%SystemRoot%\System32\LogFiles

If the remote access server is configured for RADIUS authentication and accounting, and this RADIUS server is a Windows 2000 Server running IAS, the same log path and file will be used, but on the IAS computer instead.

The default format of this file is IAS 1.0, which is a comma-delimited file displaying various attributes about each connection. However, the alternative *Database compatible file format* is often the more useful setting since it not only supports the use of ODBC-compliant tools so that the raw data when imported into a database can be easily interpreted and analyzed, but unlike the IAS-format log it saves the data in a standard structure that is compatible with other Network Access Servers. In a multivendor environment, this setting would be more appropriate.

Set authentication and accounting logging (and an alternative path for the log file if preferred) from the server's Remote Access Logging properties from the Routing and Remote Access snap-in. To do this, expand Remote Access Logging in the left pane, right-click Local File in the details pane, and select Properties. This reveals two tabs, one for Settings (where you specify what you want to log) and another for Local File (where you specify the log format and path, and how often you want to save log information).

Network Monitor

This allows you to capture the PPP traffic (connection establishment and PPP-encapsulated user data) sent between the remote client and the remote access server. Note that Network Monitor does not interpret the compressed or encrypted portions of remote access traffic, but it can be useful in determining the following:

- What is happening during the PPP connection establishment process
- Whether data is being encrypted
- Whether data is being compressed

Although you cannot read the contents of encrypted/compressed packets, you can identify them by their protocol ID, which is 0x3D.

Network Monitor captures can be saved and sent to Microsoft support for analysis.

PPP Tracing

PPP tracing was available in Windows NT 4.0 and is useful to help track down connecting problems, because it specifically logs detailed information on the PPP connection establishment process. It does not log any user data once the connection is established.

It is set by selecting Enable Point-to-Point Protocol (PPP) Logging from the Event Logging tab on the properties of the remote access server in the Routing and Remote Access snap-in.

Information is saved to a file called *Ppp.log* in the *%Systemroot%*\tracing folder and includes the programming calls and actual packet contents of PPP packets for PPP control protocols.

Tracing

Tracing can be used to help diagnose complex network problems, such as recording internal component variables, function calls, and interactions. Additionally, separate routing and remote access components can be independently enabled to log tracing information to files, and you can even enable/disable these without disruption to a live router.

Bear in mind not only will tracing put additional load on your computer's resources, but this level of information is aimed at network specialists rather than general network administrators.

Tracing can only be enabled by setting to 1 each component (e.g., RIP2) under the following Registry key:

```
HKEY_LOCAL_MACHINE\SOFTWARE\Microsoft\Tracing\<component>
```

By default all tracing files are saved to *%systemroot%*\Tracing and are named after the component they are tracing. However, you can specify an alternative path under the same key as above.

The default level of tracing is set to maximum, but this can also be changed for each component by setting the value of the FileTracingMask under the same key as above—range from 0 to FFFF0000.

The default maximum trace file size is 64 K, but this can be changed for each component by setting the value of the MaxFileSize under the same key as above (64 K is represented as 10000).

SNMP MIB Support

Windows 2000 with Routing and Remote Access supports Simple Network Management Protocol (SNMP) agent functionality with support for Internet MIB II.

Network Management Stations such as the popular HP OpenView can compile the MIB to manage IP Network layer events relating to Windows 2000 remote access router functions—providing the remote access server itself has the SNMP agent installed and running.

API Support for Third-Party Components and Utilities

Routing and Remote Access has fully published API sets for unicast, multicast routing protocol, and administration support, which means that third-party developers can write their own routing protocols, interfaces, and management tools that directly interface with the Routing and Remote Access architecture.

EXERCISE 5-9

Setting Up a Log File for Database Analysis

You have been asked to set up and provide monthly log files of remote connections from your Windows 2000 Routing and Remote Access Server so that the Accounting Department can import them into Microsoft Access. The logged data can then be easily sorted and presented to indicate which users and departments are using the remote access services—and charge by department accordingly.

Your one Routing and Remote Access server is configured to use Windows as both the Authentication and Accounting Provider.

1. Load up the Routing and Remote Access snap-in and expand the Remote Access Logging.
2. Right-click on the Local File in the right pane and select Properties.
3. On the Settings tab, ensure the first option, "Account logging requests" is selected, but no others.
4. Click on the Local File and select "Database compatible file format" rather than the default of IAS Format.
5. Because you have been asked for monthly logs, select the "New log time period" of Monthly—you will see the log file name displayed below change to Inyymm.log to indicate which year and month the log will refer to.
6. Finally, because you don't want the logging to be in competition with the server's system files, you know that specifying the log path to go to an alternative partition would be preferable to keeping to the default of *%systemroot%*\System32\LogFiles. If you can use a different partition (or even machine) to store the log files, enter it in the Log file directory field.
7. Click OK. If you changed the file path, this will be reflected in the Description field against the Local File in the right pane.

Your monthly accounting log files are now set up.

CERTIFICATION OBJECTIVE 5.09

Remote Access Security

In addition to the dial-in permission and remote access policies, Windows 2000 Routing and Remote Access offers a wide range of security features, including

- Secure authentication (of both user and server)
- Data encryption
- Packet filtering
- Secure callback
- Caller ID
- Remote access account lockout

Which security options you choose to implement will depend on the level of security required, which must be decided within the considerations of administration overheads (e.g., setting, monitoring, maintaining, and troubleshooting failed valid connections).

Secure Authentication

Part of the PPP connection establishment is the authentication of the remote access client. Both sides must agree on a single, specific authentication protocol.

A secure authentication provides protection from

- Replay attacks
- Client impersonation
- Server impersonation

Table 5-7 lists the authentication risks.

TABLE 5-7

Authentication Risks

Authentication Risk	Explanation
Replay attack	This is when somebody captures the packets of a successful connection attempt and then later replays the same packets in an attempt to obtain an authenticated connection.
Client impersonation	This is when somebody takes over an existing authenticated connection by obtaining connection parameters from a successfully authenticated client, disconnecting the client, and then taking control of the original connection.
Server impersonation	This is when a bogus server appears to be a valid server so that it can capture credentials of a remote user trying to connect so it can use these to connect to the valid server.

Secure user authentication occurs through the encrypted exchange of user credentials using PPP with an authentication protocol. Windows 2000 Routing and Remote Access offers two different security Authentication Providers:

- Windows authentication
- RADIUS authentication

This is configured under the Routing and Remote Access server Properties, Security tab; the default setting is for Windows authentication.

Windows Authentication

User credentials sent by users attempting remote access connections are authenticated using normal Windows authentication mechanisms.

RADIUS Authentication

User credentials and connection request parameters are sent as a series of RADIUS request messages to a RADIUS server, which might be another Windows 2000 server running the Internet Authentication Service (IAS). In this mode, the Windows 2000 RRAS Server is acting as a RADIUS client.

The RADIUS server authenticates the remote access client against its authentication database, and it can also inform the RRAS server of other connection parameters for the particular user, such as the maximum time it can be connected, and how it assigns IP addresses.

RADIUS can use its own database for authenticating users, or it can use a database on another server running an ODBC interface, or even on a Windows 2000 DC.

exam Watch

If the RRAS server is a member server in mixed- or native-Windows 2000 domains, the computer account of the RRAS server when using Windows Authentication must be a member of the RAS and IAS Servers security group. If a domain administrator installed RRAS, the computer account would have automatically been added to this security group. However, if a nondomain administrator were to install RRAS, a domain administrator should add the computer account to the group with the Active Directory user and Groups MMC snap-in, or use the following Netsh command: ras add <registeredserver>

Authentication Protocols

Both authentication providers allow you to specify which authentication protocols you require the remote access clients to use. Click Authentication Methods on the same Security tab to view and edit the authentication protocols.

If the connecting remote access client cannot perform a secure authentication with your selected authentication protocol/s, the connection will be denied.

To the other extreme, you can have an open Routing and Remote Access server without any authentication by selecting the last option to allow unauthenticated access. Although this is obviously not a secure configuration, there may be appropriate reasons for selecting unauthenticated PPP connections:

- When using Automatic Number Identification/Calling Line Identification (ANI/CLI) authentication, where the authentication is based on the telephone number of the remote user rather than on a username/password basis.
- When using guest authentication, and the Guest account is being used as the identity of the remote user.

PAP (Password Authentication Protocol)

The Password Authentication Protocol is the least secure of the authentication protocols provided using a simple, plain-text authentication. It offers no protection against replay attacks, client impersonation, or server impersonation. However, it is offered in Windows 2000 Routing and Remote Access for downward compatibility for older clients and non-Microsoft clients that cannot support a stronger authentication protocol.

on the Job

Allow PAP authentication only with caution and good reason!

SPAP

The Shiva Password Authentication Protocol is a reversible encryption mechanism used by Shiva remote access servers. Although a remote access client might use SPAP to authenticate on a Windows 2000 Routing and Remote Access Server, this protocol is more likely to be used by clients who need to connect to a Shiva remote access client.

This protocol is more secure than PAP, but less secure than the other protocols, and offers no protection against server impersonation. It is unlikely you would need it on a server running Windows 2000 Routing and Remote Access Service.

CHAP

The Challenge Handshake Authentication Protocol is a challenge-response authentication protocol that uses the industry-standard Message Digest 5 (MD5) one-way encryption scheme to hash the response to a challenge issued by the remote access server.

This protocol is more secure than PAP and SPAP because the password is never actually transferred, so it cannot be captured. It protects against replay attacks by using an arbitrary challenge string for each authentication, but offers no protection against server impersonation. It is useful for non-Microsoft clients but should not be needed if your remote access clients are running any version of Windows.

MS-CHAP

This is Microsoft's version of the Challenge Handshake Authentication Protocol, and offers the same features as CHAP with some additional advantages. It is supported on all versions of Windows, and as such, makes a suitable default authentication protocol. However, where you have the choice, you should instead use the later version, MS-CHAPv2, which is a more secure protocol that protects against server impersonation.

If mutual authentication (where both sides can verify they are who they say they are) is important to your security policies, then you should ensure that Microsoft clients have the latest MS-CHAPv2 and disable MS-CHAP on the server.

MS-CHAPv2

This later version of the Challenge Handshake Authentication Protocol provides stronger security for remote access connections because of the following additions:

- LAN Manager encoding of responses/password changes is no longer supported.
- Mutual authentication occurs, which eliminates both client and server impersonation.
- Separate cryptographic keys are generated for transmitted and received data.
- Cryptographic keys are based on user's password and the arbitrary challenge string, so even when the user reconnects with same password, a different cryptographic key will be used.

MS-CHAPv2 is supported on Windows 2000 without modification. It is supported on Service Pack 4 or later for NT 4.0, on Service Pack 1 or later for Windows 98,and in Windows Dial-up Networking 1.3 Performance & Security Upgrade for Windows 95 for PPTP connections. However, it is not supported for PPP connections.

EAP

The Extensible Authentication Protocol is an extension to PPP that allows for arbitrary authentication mechanisms to be used to validate a PPP connection. Its design is such that it allows authentication plug-in modules at both the client and server. One example is using security token cards ("smart cards"), where the remote access server queries the client for a name, PIN, and card token value. Another example is using biometrics; for example, a retina scan or finger print match to uniquely identify an individual.

Once the connection authentication phase is reached, the client negotiates which EAP authentication it wants to use, which is known as the EAP type. Once the EAP type is agreed upon, the server can issue multiple authentication requests to the client (as in the client name, then PIN, then card token value).

EAP offers the highest flexibility in authentication uniqueness and variations, even offering the ability for third-party vendors to supply their own EAP type library (which would need to be installed on both the server and client).

Of all Microsoft platforms, Windows 2000 is the only one to support EAP, and it is required for smart cards.

EAP-MD5 This is the CHAP authentication used with EAP.

EAP-TLS This is the Transport Layer Security protocol, based on Secure Sockets Layer (SSL), that allows applications to communicate securely. It offers the following:

- Client and two-way authentication using encryption
- Negotiation of the specific encryption algorithm
- Secured exchange of encryption keys used for encrypting messages
- Message integrity and user authentication using a message authentication code

The mutual authentication is done by the exchange and verification of certificates—the connecting client sends a user certificate, and the server sends a machine certificate.

exam Watch

Although EAP-TLS offers the highest level of EAP security, it is only supported on Windows 2000 Server remote access servers that are members of a Windows 2000 mixed- or native-domain; stand-alone Windows 2000 Remote Access Servers cannot support EAP-TLS.

EAP-RADIUS

EAP-RADIUS passes EAP messages from the remote access server to the RADIUS server for authentication. In this way, the remote access server simply passes through the EAP messages from the client to the destination RADIUS server and does not process them. Because the remote access server is not processing the EAP messages, it does not need to have the EAP type installed, which is certainly an advantage if using multiple remote access servers.

In a typical use of EAP-RADIUS, the remote access server is configured to use EAP, and to use RADIUS as the authentication provider rather than Windows 2000. Then when a remote client attempts to connect and sends its EAP message, the remote access server will pass on to the RADIUS server any EAP messages until the connection is successfully authenticated or denied.

Data Encryption

Just as you can configure the Routing and Remote Access server to require that a certain authentication occurs, so the server can require that remote access clients encrypt data sent between them and the server. If the connecting remote access client cannot encrypt as required, the connection will be denied.

Note that data encryption over PPP does not ensure end-to-end encryption if the remote access client is connecting *beyond* the RRAS server. If this is required, IPSec should be used and configured to encrypt data that can be used with or without L2TP.

If you don't use IPSec, data encryption can still be used between the remote client and remote access server. However, data encryption can only be supported when one of the following authentication protocols is also being used:

- EAP-TLS
- MS-CHAP
- MS-CHAP v2

All Microsoft's 32-bit remote access clients support the Microsoft Point-to-Point Encryption Protocol (MPPE) for encrypting data. This uses the Rivest-Shamir-Adleman (RSA) RC4 stream cipher, and 40-bit, 56-bit, or 128-bit secret keys (the higher the key number, the stronger the security). These MPPE keys are generated during the authentication process.

Although encryption can be set by the client (and is set by default on a Windows 2000 Professional VPN connection), you can only set encryption for all data on a Routing and Remote Access server within a remote access policy. Select Edit Profile, and then under the Encryption tab are options for No Encryption, Basic, or Strong.

Packet Filtering

Usually, packet filtering for a device that communicates with the outside world would be configured at a firewall. However, you can configure these on the server itself, and there may be good reasons why you may want to do this in addition to the firewall's settings (for example, use packet filtering on certain users with no fixed source address).

There are actually three places where you can employ packet filtering on a Windows 2000 Server running Routing and Remote Access Service, and each allows you to specify the filtering with a higher degree of control. These levels are at the server (all adapters), at a particular adapter (e.g., adapter connected to the Internet), and for individual policies.

If you decide to use packet filtering, don't forget to check all three places and ensure that you haven't blocked valid packets at a higher level that are needed at a lower level. For example, there's no point in configuring a Remote Access Policy to allow only packets through for PPTP if packet filtering at the Internet adapter has been set to block PPTP packets!

Packet Filtering at the Server

This is rather well-hidden under the properties of the TCP/IP protocol, General | Advanced Options | TCP/IP filtering with the option Enable TCP/IP Filtering (All adapters) where you can specify TCP and UDP ports and Protocol IDs. You cannot specify source and destination addresses here. This dialog box is very similar to the one in Windows NT 4.0, but the important difference is that these settings apply to *all adapters* in the computer.

Packet Filtering on Individual Adapters

This is specified within the Routing and Remote Access snap-in. Select IP Routing | General, and then right-click on the interface you want to use (e.g., your Internet connected adapter) and select Properties. From there, select the buttons for Input Filters and Output Filters, supplying in each the source/destination address, protocol and ports to filter. This setting applies to all packets on that interface.

Packet Filtering on Individual Remote Access Policies

Finally, you can specify packet filtering in the Profile of a remote access policy, under the IP tab. You will see under IP packet filters two buttons: From client and To client. These are the equivalent to the Input and Output filters. Select one button and then click Add to define source and destination addresses, protocols, and ports. Figure 5-6 shows an example of an Input filter that blocks any packets coming in to the server (from any client) except those suitable for the VPN. You can then add the Windows-Group condition to this profile so that these filters would only apply to a specific group of users.

Refer to the section "Configuring Firewalls with VPNs" for more information on the settings you should know for secure connections. For other connections, decide what services you need to allow or block, and with reference to a list of well-known ports and protocol IDs, build these into your packet filtering. Don't forget to reboot and test after any changes to ensure you are not blocking valid connections.

Secure Callback

This is when the remote access server calls back the remote client after a successful authentication, and is used particularly when the connection charge should be the responsibility of the server rather than the client. Either the client can specify the number that should be called back (greatest flexibility so they can dial in from

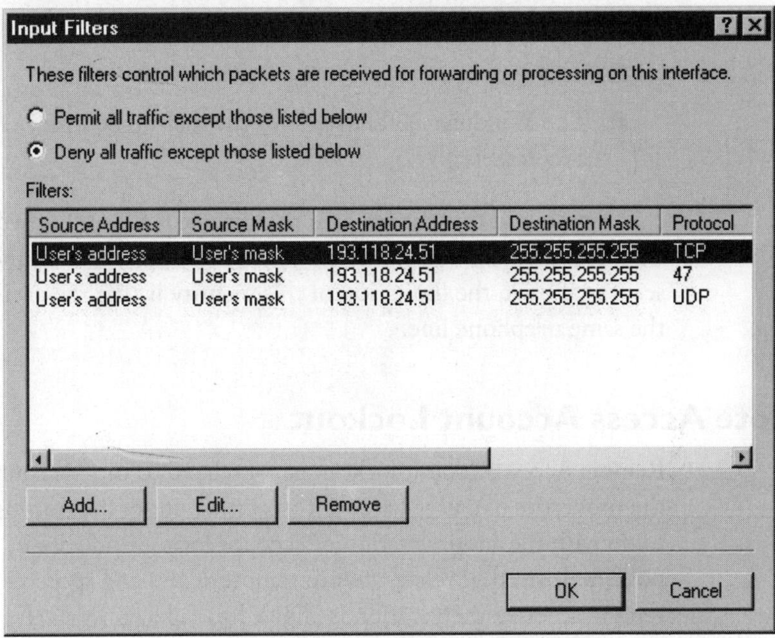

FIGURE 5-6 Example Input filters within a Remote Access Policy

anywhere), or this feature can be restricted for security to only call back on a specific number (secure callback).

Callback uses the *Callback Control Protocol (CBCP)* immediately after authentication. Before remote clients can be called back, the dial-in properties of their accounts must be enabled for callback, and the number to be called back must be specified by either the client (if allowed) or the server.

You cannot use this facility with VPN solutions.

Caller ID

Caller ID can also be used to verify that the incoming connection is from a specified telephone number; again, it is configured in the dial-in properties of the user account.

If the Caller ID number of the incoming connection for the user does not match the specified Caller ID, the connection is denied.

Caller ID requires that the following all support Caller ID:

- The remote user's telephone line

- The telephone system being used
- The remote access server's telephone line
- The Windows 2000 driver for the dial-up equipment (modem, ATM adapter, etc.)

If any link in this path fails to pass on the Caller ID, it will not get through and an account configured for Caller ID will not be able to connect. Note that as with secure callback, the limitation of this security is that the user is restricted to using the same telephone line.

Remote Access Account Lockout

Remote Access Account lockout is *not* related to the "Account locked out" setting in the properties of a user's account (specified under the Account tab) and has nothing to do with the administration of account lockout policies in Windows 2000 group policies. Instead, it relates *only* to remote access and specifies how many times a remote access authentication is allowed to fail against a valid user account before denying the user remote access (not allow them to try another password).

The RAS specific account lockout is particularly relevant for VPN servers that are connected to the Internet and will help combat a *dictionary attack*, which is when a malicious user attempts to gain access by "cracking" a password by automatically trying a list of words or commonly used phrases. By enabling the remote access account lockout feature, such an attack will be thwarted after a specified number of failed attempts.

However, remember that this setting has no compassion for genuine users who have forgotten their password and in desperation retry every password they have ever used, so set the threshold number of attempts with care or you might be spending your time constantly resetting lockouts!

on the job

It is also possible that a malicious user who knows or guesses usernames but not passwords can deliberately lock out accounts, which results in remote users being unable to gain the lawful remote resources they need in order to work productively. There is usually a flip side to security settings, and there is no right or wrong policy you should decide upon. Instead, make an informed choice after considering all the options and consequences.

Setting RAS Account Lockout

You cannot set the remote access lockout setting with the usual Routing and Remote Access administrative tools; it must be set directly in the Registry of the computer that provides the authentication. In most cases, this will be on the Routing and Remote Access server itself, but if you are using RADIUS authentication to a Windows 2000 Server running the Internet Authentication Service (IAS), you will need to edit the Registry on the IAS computer.

There are two settings:

- **MaxDenials**, which is the number of failed attempts permitted before the account is locked out.
- **ResetTime (Mins)**, which is for an automatic release after a specified period of time.

Set the MaxDenials to enable remote account lockout:

```
HKEY_LOCAL_MACHINE\SYSTEM\CurrentControlSet\Services\
RemoteAccess\Parameters\AccountLockout
```

This should be set to 1 or greater (the default is 0, which disables this setting). Change the automatic reset (if required), by setting the ResetTime (Mins) under:

```
HKEY_LOCAL_MACHINE\SYSTEM\CurrentControlSet\Services\
RemoteAccess\Parameters\ AccountLockout
```

This should be set in hours (but in hex values; for example, the default of b40 is 48 hours).

If you cannot wait for the automatic reset, you can *manually unlock* a locked account by deleting the Registry subkey that corresponds to the user's account name under:

```
HKEY_LOCAL_MACHINE\SYSTEM\CurrentControlSet\Services\
RemoteAccess\Parameters\ AccountLockout\<domain_name:user_name>
```

EXERCISE 5-10

Enabling and Configuring Suitable Authentication Protocols for Different Types of Users

You have two different types of users who need remote access:

1. Traveling salespeople who have been issued Windows 2000 laptops with smart cards who need to dial in over the Internet.
2. Occasional homeworkers running Windows 98 (with SP1) and dialing in with V90 modems.

You have been asked to configure security to accommodate remote access for both types of users at the same time, so you decide to configure the following:

- VPN connections with L2TP/IPSec for the salespeople, accepting only EAP-TLS authentication
- Modem connections with PPP for the homeworkers, accepting only MS-CHAP v2 authentication

This exercise involves creating two new remote access policies, and because this has been covered in previous exercises, it assumes you know what they are and how to create them. If you are unsure of how to complete these steps with the following instructions, refer to Exercises 5-4 and 5-5.

1. Ensure these users have dial-in permission, either directly from their user account (with Allow access) or by using Control access through Remote Access Policy.
2. If you haven't already done so, load the Routing and Remote Access snap-in, select your server, and right-click on it to select Properties.
3. Ensure that Remote Access Server is selected under the General tab, and then select the Security tab.
4. Ensure that the Authentication Provider is set to Windows Authentication, and then click Authentication Methods.
5. Click the Extensible Authentication Protocol box, and then click EAP Methods.
6. Under the EAP Methods listed, select Smart Card or other Certificate, and Click OK to return to the Authentication Methods dialog box.

7. Ensure the Microsoft encrypted authentication version 2 (MS-CHAP v2) is selected. Deselect the option called Microsoft encrypted authentication (MS-CHAP).
8. Ensure no other option on this dialog box is selected, and Click OK.
9. Click OK again to finish configuring your server properties.

The server is now configured to support these authentication protocols, but by default, either will be accepted—and you do not want the salespeople to be able to authenticate with the less-secure protocol. Therefore, you need to set up two remote access policies, one for salespeople that only allows EAP authentication, and another for homeworkers that allows MS-CHAP-v2 (strictly speaking, the second policy isn't needed, because if the stronger authentication protocol fails, a weaker one will then be tried, and if supported on the server, the connection will succeed).

1. Right click on Remote Access Policies and then Add New Policy—call it "Restrict to Salespeople with smart cards over VPN."
2. Add the following conditions:

   Windows-Group The group that contains the Salespeople
   Tunnel-Type Layer Two Tunneling Protocol (L2TP)
3. Edit the profile, and on the Authentication tab, select the Extensible Authentication Protocol, and underneath ensure that Smart Card or other Certificate is selected and configured. Deselect any other authentication protocol on this dialog box. Finish the policy with a Grant permission.
4. Repeat the Add New Policy, and this time call it "Homeworkers with MS-CHAP v2."
5. Add the following condition:

   Windows-Group The group that contains the Homeworkers
6. Edit the profile and on the Authentication tab, deselect Microsoft Encrypted Authentication (MS-CHAP), and make sure the only protocol selected is Microsoft Encrypted Authentication version 2 (MS-CHAP-2). Finish the policy with a Grant permission.

That's it; your server now allows both authentication protocols, but you have implemented different security restrictions appropriate to different groups of users without the risk of negotiating down to a less-secure connection.

Troubleshooting Remote Access Security

The following provides some common problems/resolutions when experiencing authentication problems with remote access connections:

- If connections using callback and/or Caller ID fail, verify that these are enabled and configured correctly on the dial-in properties of the user account. In addition, verify the Link Control Protocol (LCP) Extensions are enabled on the PPP tab on the properties of the remote access server.
- If Caller ID is failing, verify that all communication hardware supports this feature.
- There are actually three places where you can specify packet filters on the remote access computer; make sure none of these are blocking valid packets.
- Unless you allow unauthenticated access, ensure both the remote access client and the remote access server are enabled to use at least one common authentication protocol.
- If either the client or server requires encryption, ensure that both have a common encryption method.
- For connections using MS-CHAP, verify that the user's password is not longer than 14 characters (this restriction does not apply to MS-CHAP v2). If it is, either change the password so it is less than 14 characters, or use a different authentication protocol.
- Verify that the user's account has not been disabled or locked out on the properties of the user account; for example, if the password has expired. If the password has expired, the remote client must use MSCHAP or MSCHAPv2 to be able to change an expired password during a remote access connection attempt.
- Check the Registry to see if the remote account lockout is enabled, and if so, reset the user account in the Registry.
- Verify that the correct authentication provider is configured on the remote access server, and if using RADIUS authentication, verify communication between the two computers (network and password authentication).

- If using L2TP over IPSec, temporarily disable the encryption to eliminate the IPSec authentication and negotiation process—don't forget to reset this after your tests!

In a native-mode domain, the callback number can be up to 128 characters. However, if the user account is on a remote access server running Windows 2000 as a stand-alone server, or in a mixed-mode domain, the callback number is restricted to 24–48 characters. If your RRAS server is not in a native-mode domain and callback connections are failing, check the length of the callback number being used by the RRAS server, because it may become truncated in this setup.

CERTIFICATION OBJECTIVE 5.10

Remote Access Best Practices and Tips

The following lists our recommended best practices and tips for running a successful and secure remote access server:

- Disable any protocols and services not being used on the Routing and Remote Access server, for security reasons and to ensure the best performance from your server. For this reason, a dedicated member server is preferable to running Routing and Remote Access on a domain controller, and it is a more secure solution.
- There is no reason why you can't run a Routing and Remote Access Service on a Windows 2000 Server in an otherwise completely Windows NT 4.0 domain—you can immediately benefit from the added granular control of remote access permission with remote policies. However, bear in mind that Windows 2000 itself does require a higher specification of computer than if you were running the equivalent service on a Windows NT 4.0 member server.
- Particularly when being used as a VPN server, baseline your server with the Performance Monitor utility and ensure the processor is not unduly stressed. If necessary, upgrade or rethink your remote access strategies (e.g., use multiple remote access servers). The overhead of encryption comes at a price! Bear in mind that the new tunneling protocol L2TP over IPSec requires greater processing than PPTP.

- Use DHCP when DHCP servers are installed on your network—centrally configured and maintained IP addresses are less prone to configuration errors than statically configured addresses.
- To help avoid routing problems when the LAN protocol being used is TCP/IP, ensure that remote access clients and the remote access server are on the same subnet.
- Similarly, use automatic IPX network IDs for remote access clients wishing to use IPX as their LAN protocol, and use the same network ID as the one your remote access server is using.
- Use strong authentication with long passwords that are a mixture of letters and numbers, and not a common name or word that can be found in dictionaries.
- If you are using EAP-TLS as your authentication protocol, Microsoft recommends using smart cards rather than Registry-based certificates.
- If all your remote access clients will be running Windows 2000 Professional, disable MS-CHAP on your remote access server to ensure a stronger and mutual authentication. Consider also using IPSec for all remote connections. For Microsoft remote access clients that are Windows NT 4.0 or Windows 9*x*, obtain the latest MS-CHAP v2 from Microsoft.
- Avoid unnecessarily complicated remote access policies—plan in advance how to construct the simplest set of conditions and settings with the minimal number of policies. In particular, avoid configuring remote policies such that more than one policy applies to the same user.
- Remote access policies are tried in order, so typically you would want to place more specific policies before more general policies.
- If remote access is important to your company, consider putting in place contingencies so that you can ensure minimal downtime. For example, if using a VPN, install and preconfigure a point-to-point connection as well (e.g., a modem), which by default is not enabled for incoming remote access.

Then if there are problems with the VPN (e.g., ISP problems), you can enable the modem connection so that remote users can still connect (albeit at a slower throughput).

- If throughput performance is a high priority, and especially if you want to transfer voice and video over your remote connections, a dedicated high-speed private line is a better choice than a VPN.
- If you have a large number of remote access clients, consider using Connection Manager and the Connection Manager Administration Kit to provide a custom dialer with preconfigured connections to your remote access server(s). This ensures a consistent client configuration and will reap rewards from fewer support calls!
- If you have multiple remote access servers, consider configuring them as RADIUS clients connecting to a Windows 2000 Server running the Internet Authentication Service. This will provide and support central configuration for remote access policies, accounting, and logging, rather than having to specify these individually for each server. An additional benefit of this solution is that the Windows 2000 with IAS will allow a Windows NT 4.0 Server running Routing and Remote Access Server to take advantage of remote access policies.
- Remember, Routing and Remote Access Services should not only provide remote access to users who require this facility, but also provide protection from outside attack. If in doubt, use stronger security configuration rather than weaker—users will always tell you when something isn't working, but you won't be aware of security holes or potential breaches until it's too late!
- The Routing and Remote Access Service is more complex in Windows 2000 than in previous versions. When you have decided upon the configuration you want and have thoroughly tested it, document the settings (particularly the policies)—not just what the settings are, but why they are configured as they are. If you ever need to troubleshoot problems, or review/configure settings in the future, this document could be a lifesaver!

EXERCISE 5-11

Streamlining your RRAS Server and Disabling a Backup Modem

This exercise demonstrates how to achieve two of the suggestions listed previously: streamlining the services on your RRAS server, and having a disabled modem port for backup emergencies ready to be enabled if your VPN access fails.

1. To streamline the RRAS server, go through the list of services it is running and stop any that aren't required. For safety reasons, do not immediately change their startup type, and do not remove them until you are sure your RRAS server is still functioning correctly without them. To view the services click on Start | Programs | Administrative Tools | Services.
2. You should now see a list of services and see the Status of each (e.g., "Started" or blank) and another column for their StartupType (e.g., "Automatic").
3. For those services that are started, double-click on them to view their Properties. The Properties will display a description of what the service is to help you decide whether it is required on this server. Check also the Dependencies tab, which lists any other services that are linked to the one you are viewing.
4. For those services you think you do not need, click Stop under the General tab. You can either stop and then test the results of each service on the RRAS server one at a time, or if you are confident that the service is not needed, you can stop more than one and then test.
5. When you have finished with the Services, stop and restart the RRAS server and test that connections are still functioning and that the RRAS snap-in is still functioning.
6. If something is no longer functioning, restart the service you stopped, and then restart the RRAS service again. If you previously stopped more than one service, identifying the service you need will be a process of elimination.
7. When you are happy that your stopped services do not prevent the RRAS server from functioning, change the service Startup Type from *Automatic* to *Manual.* You do this in the Service properties in the General tab where a drop-down list called Startup Type allows you to select Manual for those services you stopped.

8. Reboot the RRAS server and test again that your RRAS connections and the RRAS snap-in are still functioning. At this point, you can either remove the stopped services if you are sure you will not need them (this is the more secure choice), or you can leave them installed but stopped (this is the safest option).
9. To have your modem on standby but not actually active for RAS until needed, first verify that connections over the modem work as required. Then load the RRAS snap-in and right-click on Ports and then Properties. Highlight your modem port(s) and click Configure. Deselect the "Remote access connections (inbound only)" so it looks like the following illustration.

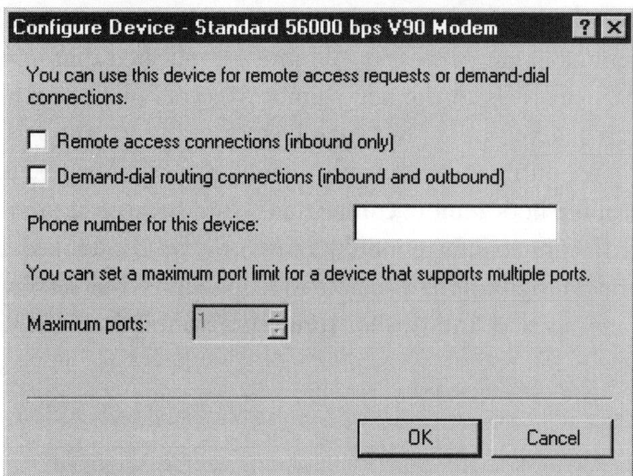

10. Click on Ok and the modem port should now be removed from the list of ports in the RRAS snap-in. When you need to enable it, repeat this procedure and reselect the "Remote access connections (inbound only)" option.

CERTIFICATION SUMMARY

This chapter introduced you to some of the new services, components, and interfaces that make up the Windows 2000 Routing and Remote Access services. Remote access is a vital resource for many companies, but it goes hand-in-hand with the need for security and managing such connections.

Windows 2000 is able to take advantage of new technologies and hardware, while the Routing and Remote Access Service allows you to take advantage of secure connections that can be configured with a high degree of flexibility.

We examined some of the basic components that make up the Windows 2000 Routing and Remote Access Service, looked at both dial-up and virtual private networking, and detailed the main configurations required on the server. Assigning remote access permission is more complicated that it was in Windows NT 4.0, and particularly with the new Remote Access Policies, each connection and permission can be fined-tuned to a high degree.

We outlined various utilities and tools that can be used to help monitor and troubleshoot remote connections. And because security is very important for a server with connections to a public network, we also looked at the various security options and configurations available to help secure your server. Finally we offered a list of best practices and tips for running a trouble-free and secure remote access server.

✓ TWO-MINUTE DRILL

Overview: Windows 2000 Routing and Remote Access Service

- ❑ Routing and Remote Access Service (RRAS) in Windows 2000 builds on previous versions, with new features offering IGMP and support for multicasting, Network Address Translation (NAT), integrated AppleTalk routing, L2TP over IPSec, improved administration tools, and better support for RADIUS.
- ❑ Remote access allows users who are physically separated from the company network to access company resources on either just the RRAS server itself, or on the whole network.
- ❑ Remote access connections are either dial-up or use a virtual private network (VPN).
- ❑ Two main utilities are the Routing and Remote Access MMC and the command-line shell Netsh.

Installing and Configuring the Remote Access Service

- ❑ A variety of new hardware is supported, including ATM over ADSL, digital links with V90 modems and X25 smart cards, in addition to the traditional modem. Check your choice of communication hardware against the Hardware Compatibility List before installing it.
- ❑ RRAS is automatically installed; you must enable it rather than use the normal Add/Remove Programs procedure.
- ❑ The RRAS Setup Wizard guides you through choices of connection services, including Remote Access Server, Virtual Private Network, Routing, Network Address Translation, and Internet Connection Sharing.

Configuring the Remote Access Server

- ❑ Dynamic information about currently connected remote access clients can be obtained by expanding Remote Access Clients in the MMC—you will see information such as their assigned network address, username, etc.

- VPN ports are referred to as WAN Miniports; the default is five PPTP ports and five L2TP ports.
- The Event Log by default records information about RRAS, which includes information on connecting clients; this level of information can be changed under the server properties.

Assigning Remote Access Permissions

- Remote Access Policies are new to Windows 2000 and allow you to centrally control remote access and also more finely control connection restrictions and settings.
- The three Administrative models for Remote Access Policy are "Access by User," "Access by policy in mixed-mode," and "Access by policy in native-mode." Choose the one most appropriate for your environment and requirements.
- A remote access policy consists of Conditions, Permission, and a Profile. You can have multiple profiles and define the order in which they should be applied.
- Remote access permission is a combination of the dial-in options in the user's account and any applicable remote access policies.

Virtual Private Networking

- A VPN connection uses encapsulated, encrypted, and authenticated links across a shared or public network.
- A VPN offers a low-cost solution, because it only incurs local charges to the user's ISP, rather than long distance charges from user to server.
- VPNs require a tunneling protocol, either PPTP or L2TP with IPSec. Which one you use may depend on factors such as which protocol the client supports, your priorities for security or performance, or a lower administrative overhead.

Connections using PPP Multilink and BAP

- Multilink is when you combine multiple physical links into a single logical link for greater throughput. It needs to be supported at both ends of the connection—enable multilink for the server and you can fine-tune settings with remote access policies.

- ❑ Multilink now supports the Bandwidth Allocation Protocol (BAP), which dynamically adds or removes links in a multilink connection.

Integrating Remote Access and DHCP

- ❑ DHCP is recommended over static address pools for assigning IP addresses to remote clients.
- ❑ When configured for DHCP, the RRAS server precaches a pool of addresses from a DHCP when the service first starts, and the RRAS server then manages these leases—assigning IP addresses to remote access clients when they connect.
- ❑ When using DHCP with RRAS, only the IP address is passed from the DHCP server to the remote access clients; other configured options on the DHCP are discarded by the RRAS server. Remote access clients inherit other IP configuration options such as those for DNS and/or WINS from the RRAS server.
- ❑ If you want remote access clients to obtain DHCP scope options, configure the DHCP relay agent on the internal interface on the RRAS server.
- ❑ If you subnet your network, there may be considerations that have to be taken into account when using DHCP for remote access clients, such as assigning static routes or enabling routing protocols, a relay agent, and the consequences of APIPA.

Managing and Monitoring Remote Access

- ❑ Additional tools that help you manage, monitor, and troubleshoot remote access include the Event Log, authentication and account logging, Network Monitor, PPP logging, tracing, SNMP, and third-party utilities that use the RRAS APIs.

Remote Access Security

- ❑ Security features in RRAS include authentication, data encryption, packet filtering, secure callback, caller ID, and remote access account lockout.
- ❑ The two security providers supported for remote access are Windows and RADIUS. With Windows authentication, Windows 2000 security verifies

the authentication, the dial-up properties of the user account, and any locally stored remote access policies. With RADIUS authentication, the credentials of the connection attempt will be passed to a specified RADIUS server for authentication and authorization, and if accepted, it will pass this confirmation back to the RRAS server.

- The default authentication protocols are MS-CHAP and MS-CHAP-v2. MSCHAP does not support mutual authentication, but is included for older clients.
- EAP-TLS is the highest security authentication protocol RRAS offers, and is used with smart cards.

Remote Access Best Practices and Tips

- Disable any unused services and protocols on the RRAS server—it's better to have a dedicated member server running RRAS rather than a domain controller.
- Use strong security rather than weak.
- Document how your RRAS server is configured.

SELF TEST

The following questions will help you measure your understanding of the material presented in this chapter. Read all of the choices carefully, as there may be more than one correct answer. Choose all correct answers for each question.

Overview: Windows 2000 Routing and Remote Access Service

1. If a remote access client connects using data encryption to a modem on your remote access server, and then accesses other resources on the company network, what is this called?

   A. Point to Point remote access

   B. Point-to-LAN remote access

   C. Point-to-network remote access

   D. VPN connection

2. You are about to make some major configuration changes to your Routing and Remote Access server. What's the easiest way of ensuring you can easily revert to your previously configured and working RRAS server if it all goes horribly wrong?

   A. Export the relevant RRAS entries in the Registry so you can re-import them if necessary.

   B. Use the Backup utility to back up your server, taking care to include the Registry.

   C. Use the RRAS MMC, select your server, All Tasks, Backup before making changes.

   D. Use the RRAS command-line utility.

Installing and Configuring the Remote Access Service

3. Which of the following are valid choices when you are choosing communication hardware for your RRAS server? (Select all that apply.)

   A. X25 smart card

   B. ISDN adapter

   C. Infrared port

   D. Parallel cable

Configuring the Remote Access Server

4. You have a mixture of remote access clients that need to connect to your remote access server. These include Windows for Workgroups, Windows 98, Windows NT 4.0, and Windows 2000 Professional. With the default authentication setting on the remote access server, which of them would be able to authenticate?

A. All but Windows for Workgroups

B. Only Windows 2000 Professional

C. Windows NT 4.0 and Windows 2000 Professional

D. All of them

5. Where do you specify whether remote access clients should be restricted to the remote access server, or can use resources beyond the server?

A. When enabling the RRAS service, this is one of the questions asked by the Routing and Remote Access Setup Wizard after selecting the Remote Access Server option.

B. In the RRAS MMC under <server>, Properties | General, next to the setting for the Remote access server.

C. In the RRAS MMC under <server>, Properties, IP tab.

D. As part of the Default Remote Access Policy.

Assigning Remote Access Permissions

6. If you decide to use the Remote Access Permission by User model and delete the single Default Remote Access Policy, which of the following would be true?

A. Users would only be able to connect if their account had the Remote Access Permission set to "Allow access."

B. Users would be able to connect even if their account had the Remote Access Permission set to "Deny access."

C. Users would only be able to connect if their account had the Remote Access Permission set to "Control access through Remote Access Policy" and they were a member of Domain Users.

D. Users would not be able to connect.

7. You are tasked with deciding how best to implement remote access permissions. You have a large number of users who require remote access, and your network is running a mixture of Windows 2000 domains and Windows NT 4.0 domains. All the users who need remote access are in the Accounting group, and you also need to restrict them to dialing in during office hours only. Which is the best way to implement this?

A. Enable dial-in access in each user account in the Accounting group, and change the Default Policy to only allow access during office hours.

B. Disable dial-in access in each account, create a new policy for the Accounting group with the days/times restricted in the profile, and grant remote access permission to this profile.

C. Use the Control Access by Policy in the user account, change the Default Policy for office hours only, and add the Accounting group with the additional Windows-Group condition.

D. Use the Control Access through Remote Access Policy in the user account, leave the Default Policy as it is, and create a new policy with the Day-and-Time restriction of office hours, the Windows-Group condition specifying the Accounting group, and use the Grant access permission.

Virtual Private Networking

8. Which of the following conditions must be met before a remote access client can connect to your Windows 2000 Server that is running the Routing and Remote Access Service as a VPN server? (Select all that apply.)

A. The remote access client must be running TCP/IP.

B. The remote access client must have a valid company user account.

C. The remote access client must be running Windows 2000.

D. The remote access client must support a high-level authentication protocol.

9. Which of the following ports and protocols is incorrect when configuring either a firewall or packet filtering for VPN support if using both PPTP and L2TP/IPSec?

A. TCP port 1723

B. Protocol 47

C. TCP port 500

D. Protocol ID 50

Connections Using PPP Multilink and BAP

10. A remote access client has complained about slow throughput when she connects to your RRAS server. She discovered that when she connects, one of her ISDN links is immediately disconnected, which explains why the line speed is halved and consequently throughput is slow. Where do you check whether multilink is enabled for this user? (Choose all that apply.)

A. In the server properties

B. As one of the Remote Access Policy Conditions

C. As one of the settings in the Remote Access Policy Profile

D. On the Internet connected adapter under IP Routing

Integrating Remote Access and DHCP

11. What are some of the possible causes if clients can connect to the RRAS server but cannot access resources beyond the server? (Choose all that apply.)

A. The remote access server is using the wrong adapter to send out DHCP discover messages.

B. The DHCP server is down.

C. The DHCP relay agent on the Routing and Remote Access server has been stopped.

D. There are network problems.

12. If a remote client dials in to your remote access server that is configured for automatic IP address assignment but no DHCP server is available, how does the remote client know she has been assigned an IP address through APIPA, which would explain why she is unable to access resources beyond the RRAS server?

A. On connection, the remote access client will receive a message from the remote access server warning it that a DHCP server was not available.

B. No warning message will be displayed to the remote client until the remote access client tries to connect to a remote network resource.

C. No warning message is displayed to the remote client and the user will not know that a DHCP server was unavailable.

D. No warning message is displayed to the remote client, but an error is logged on the remote client's computer.

Managing and Monitoring Remote Access

13. By default, where are authentication and accounting log files saved?

A. %systemroot% System32\RRAS

B. %systemroot%System32\LogFiles

C. %systemroot%System32\RRASLogs

D. %systemroot%System\RRAS

14. Even though a different department has been asked to add the necessary filters on the company firewall, you have been asked to apply appropriate packet filters for the VPN server yourself, as a "belt and braces" approach. Your server only offers PPTP connections. Where's the best place to configure these packet filters?

A. As one of the TCP/IP protocol properties

B. Under IP Routing in the RRAS MMC

C. By modifying the Default Policy and adding the Condition Tunnel-Type and setting this to PPTP

D. By modifying a policy profile under the IP tab (From client and To client)

Remote Access Security

15. If you wanted to use Caller ID as your authentication method rather than asking a remote access client for a username/password, which of the following conditions must be met? (Select all that apply.)

A. Caller ID is supported on the remote user's telephone line.

B. Caller ID is supported on the server's ATM adapter they will connect to.

C. Caller ID must be specified in the user account.

D. Caller ID must be specified in a remote access policy that applies to the user.

16. Your boss has asked you to only allow secure authentication protocols on the server that supports mutual authentication and encrypted data. Which authentication protocols meet these conditions?

A. MS-CHAP and MS-CHAP v2

B. MS-CHAP and MS-CHAP v2 and EAP-TLS

C. MS-CHAP v2 and EAP-TLS

D. EAP-TLS only

17. When would it be acceptable to allow unauthenticated access? (Choose all that apply.)

A. When older clients such as DOS and Windows for Workgroups need to connect

B. When a UNIX workstation needs to connect

C. When you are using Caller ID for all connections

D. When valid connections are being rejected

Remote Access Best Practices and Tips

18. You have a large number of users who require remote access. What's the best method for configuring the client side?

A. Document and e-mail to users.

B. Use Connection Manager to provide preconfigured connections.

C. Export the relevant Registry keys from a working client on the same operating system.

D. Visit each PC and configure it for them.

LAB QUESTION

You are asked to set up and configure a Windows 2000 member server on your company extranet to offer remote access. The priority is to enable remote access at all times to all employees. However, your company also hires part-time contractors who should not be allowed remote access. Your network is in Windows 2000 native mode, but some workstations have yet to be upgraded and are still running Windows NT 4.0 with SP6a. IPSec is not implemented on your network. Outline your plan of how best to meet these requirements, including the hardware required, the configuration of the server, and how to manage remote access permission.

SELF TEST ANSWERS

Overview: Windows 2000 Routing and Remote Access Service

1. ☑ **B.** Point-to-LAN remote access is the correct term here, since it describes a modem connection to a resource on the remote network.
   ☒ **A** is incorrect because the user is connecting beyond the RRAS server; if they were only connecting to resources on the remote access server itself, this would be the correct term. **C** is incorrect because there's no such term. **D** is incorrect because although the data is encrypted, this is not the definition of a VPN, because the connection is a direct physical connection to the server's modem rather than connecting over the Internet first.

2. ☑ **D.** Use the RRAS command-line utility is correct because the command-line utility Netsh allows you to issue a "dump" command, which is the quickest way to make a backup of your RRAS server.
   ☒ **A** is incorrect because RRAS configuration options are not neatly stored in separate Registry keys. **B** would work, but would take much longer than using Netsh. **C** is incorrect because there is no such option within the RRAS MMC—backing up a known good configuration is a sensible precaution before making configuration changes, but there's no option within the MMC to help you do that.

Installing and Configuring the Remote Access Service

3. ☑ **A, B, C, D** are all valid choices. **A**, X25 smart cards, is a valid hardware choice for RRAS. Note that an X25 smart card has nothing to do with smart cards used for security. **B**, ISDN adapter, is a valid and popular choice for a dial-up connection, particularly when aggregating channels together for higher throughput. **C**, infrared port, is a valid choice now that Windows 2000 supports infrared. However, the throughput would be low and therefore not a good choice. **D**, parallel cable, is also valid, but as with infrared only offers low throughput, which might be suitable if you just wanted to test inhouse remote authentication, for example.

Configuring the Remote Access Server

4. ☑ **D** is correct because the default authentication protocols are MS-CHAP and MS-CHAP v2. Windows 2000 supports MS-CHAP v2 out of the box, and Windows NT 4.0 and Windows 98 support MS-CHAP v2 with later service packs. All Microsoft Windows clients support MS-CHAP. Because stronger protocols are tried first, the clients that support MS-CHAP v2 would use that protocol, and any others (e.g., Windows for Workgroups) would negotiate down to use MS-CHAP.

5. ☑ **C.** The Enable IP routing option allows remote access clients to connect to other remote resources, and under the same tab you can specify whether you want to use static or automatic IP address assignment.
☒ **A** is incorrect. The wizard does not ask you this question and it's up to you to manually configure it. **B** is incorrect. It is true that you can enable or disable the remote access server from here, but there is no other option for remote access clients. **D** is also incorrect. There is no such policy setting, and this setting is server-wide. You cannot restrict this option to a subset of users.

Assigning Remote Access Permissions

6. ☑ **D.** You must have at least one policy match before the remote access permission is evaluated. If no match is found (and you can't match a nonexistent policy!), then the connection will be denied irrespective of the remote access permission in the user account.
☒ **A**, **B**, and **C** are all incorrect because these settings have no relevance when there are no remote access policies. Additionally, the setting in **C** with the Control access through Remote Access Policy would not be used with the Remote Access Permission by User model.

7. ☑ **A.** Normally, if you have a large number of users and you want to give access to a whole group rather than individual users, the Control access through Remote Access Policy is the one to go for—but it's only available if running in native mode, which isn't the case here. The Default Policy has a Deny access, which is overridden by the Allow access in the user account, and if you change the day/time restriction in the Default Policy, all requirements are met.
☒ **C** and **D** are incorrect because you cannot select an option that isn't available. The other important factor here is that the Allow Access or Deny Access in the user account will override the Grant or Deny in any policies. Therefore, if you disable access in the user account as **B** suggests, the user will not be able to connect irrespective of any policy conditions that match.

Virtual Private Networking

8. ☑ **A, B.** The remote access client must be running TCP/IP is correct because a VPN connection uses an Internet connection first, and TCP/IP is the only protocol supported on the Internet. However, once the remote access client had connected to an ISP, the subsequent connection to the VPN server could be over any LAN protocol such as IPX or NetBEUI as long as the server also had this protocol installed. **B,** the remote access client must have a valid company user account, is also correct because remote users must be authenticated (prove they are who they say they are) against an account that stores their username and password details.

☒ C is incorrect. Although only Windows 2000 currently supports the newer L2TP/IPSec tunneling protocol, other clients can use PPTP. **D** is also incorrect because although it is advisable to use a high-level authentication protocol, it is not a requirement of a VPN.

9. ☑ C. It should be UDP (and not TCP) port 500 that allows through Internet Key Exchange traffic.
☒ A is incorrect. TCP port 1723 is needed for PPTP tunnel maintenance. **B** is incorrect. Protocol 47 is the GRE protocol that supports sending the data through the tunnel. **D** is also incorrect. Protocol ID 50 is needed for L2TP security encapsulation.

Connections Using PPP Multilink and BAP

10. ☑ A, C. You can specify settings for multilink in these two places, but settings in the profile will not work unless the setting for multilink is first enabled under the server.
☒ B is incorrect because it is not one of the policy conditions. Windows-Group, Time-and-Day-Restriction, and Tunneling-Type are the more commonly used policy conditions. **D** is also incorrect because multilink support is not a general setting for the adapter; it is specifically for remote access and as such, appears under the remote access server or one of its policies.

Integrating Remote Access and DHCP

11. ☑ A, B, C and D are all possible causes if clients can connect to the server but not access resources beyond the server. **A**, the remote access server is using the wrong adapter to send out DHCP discover messages, could be correct particularly if your remote access server is multihomed, because in this case, an adapter is randomly chosen to send out DHCP discover messages. Make sure you have the correct one specified under the IP tab in the server properties. **B**, the DHCP server is down, could be very possible and consequently the remote access server defaults to APIPA. Check the Event Log to see if there were reports of being unable to access a DHCP server. **C**, the DHCP Relay Agent on the Routing and Remote Access server has been stopped, is a possibility if there were no DHCP servers on the same subnet as the remote access server. In this scenario, you need a DHCP Relay Agent installed and configured within Routing and Remote Access so it can locate a DHCP server. **D**, there are network problems, may also be a valid reason why resources are unavailable. If the server cannot make a valid connection to other computers on the network, your remote user will also have problems irrespective of whether it was able to allocate a DHCP assigned address for the remote client.

12. ☑ C. Your remote user will not know that a DHCP server failed to assign a correct IP address, and therefore the server used APIPA to assign the address.

☒ **A** and **B** are incorrect. The only time the user will know something is wrong is when she tries to connect to a resource beyond the RRAS server and receives a standard Windows error that the network path could not be found, rather than a specific remote access error as suggested. **D** is also incorrect because the client computer cannot log an error it doesn't know about—only the remote access server will know that it failed to contact a DHCP server and it will log the error in the Event Log.

Managing and Monitoring Remote Access

13. ☑ **B.** %systemroot%System32\LogFiles is the correct answer, although it is usually a good idea to place the log files on a different partition from the one that holds the system files. When you change the path of the log files, the new location will be displayed in the RRAS MMC when you expand Remote Access Logging.
☒ **A**, **C**, and **D** are incorrect. These directories are not created by the remote access service.

14. ☑ **B.** This allows you to choose the interface on which you want to restrict packets, and you should select your Internet connected interface. If your remote access server is only offering PPTP connections, you might as well restrict the Internet adapter to only accept these kinds of connections, and reject any others at the lowest level you can.
☒ **A** is incorrect. Although you could do this in Windows NT 4.0, the equivalent option in Windows 2000 will set the filtering for all adapters and not just the one connected to the Internet. **C** could potentially work with many "ifs" (e.g., if there were no other policies, and if each user had dial-in permission on their account, or the Default Policy was changed to grant remote access, and if they never needed dial-up access). Not only are the proviso "ifs" making this unnecessarily and dangerously complicated, but if you want a general setting that applies to all Internet connections, you are better defining this at the adapter level rather than at the policy level. Similarly, defining it within a policy profile as **D** suggests could work with the same sort of "ifs." However, it would be far easier and safer to simply set this as an interface setting—at least until you are asked to configure additional connection types!

Remote Access Security

15. ☑ **A, B, C.** Caller ID must be supported on all hardware aspects of the call from the user's telephone line, the telephone system being used, the server's telephone line, and the server's dial-up equipment being used. Additionally, the option for Caller ID is set in the user account.
☒ **D** is incorrect because there is no such option in the remote access policy—as either a condition or a setting in the profile.

16. ☑ C. This is the only combination that supports mutual authentication and data encryption.
☒ A is incorrect because although MS-CHAP supports data encryption, it doesn't support mutual authentication. **B** is incorrect because although MS-CHAP v2 and EAP-TLS support both data encryption and mutual authentication, MS-CHAP does not support mutual authentication. **D** is incorrect because although it supports both of the requirements, so does MS-CHAP v2, and because EAP-TLS is a lesser-used authentication protocol (e.g., used with smart cards), many clients will not be able to use it.

17. ☑ C. The authentication is done on the known calling telephone number rather than supplying a username/password.
☒ A is incorrect because although older clients cannot use some of the higher security protocols like EAP and MSCHAP-v2, they can still use some of the other protocols such as MSCHAP or even SPAP or PAP. A low-grade authentication protocols is always better than none! **B** is incorrect because this also should be able to use either SPAP or PAP. **D** is not a good choice unless you are purely in a testing environment without any connection to the outside world. If you leave your server wide open because one valid user cannot connect, you also leave it wide open for anybody to connect to it. Instead, try to find out why the authentication is failing, and use some of the logging facilities mentioned in this chapter.

Remote Access Best Practices and Tips

18. ☑ B. This option is your best bet here to save yourself a lot of support time.
☒ A is incorrect because most users don't read detailed instructions, even if they are clearly and unambiguously written. C is not a good bet—one man's working Registry keys could be another man's disaster when imported! **D** would probably get the job done, but at considerable cost in terms of your time and patience!

LAB ANSWER

Because you are running in a purely Windows 2000 environment, you can use the "Control access by Remote Policy," which makes this an easier model to configure, maintain, and extend later. All user accounts should have the "Control access by Remote Policy" option set in their dial-in tab.

The first thing to think about is the communications equipment for your connections, and because you need to ensure users can access this server, you decide to offer both VPN connections and dial-up connections as backup. You therefore purchase and install (after checking against the HCL) a bank of fast modems, and install a fast Ethernet adapter for your intranet and a WAN adapter for your Internet connection. On the Internet adapter, you configure this with a static IP address/subnet mask that is registered on the Internet, set the default gateway on this adapter to be the IP address of the router that connects to the Internet, and do not specify a WINS or DNS server address. On the other adapter, you assign a static private IP address/subnet mask, and you specify your DNS and WINS server details.

To streamline your server, you then carefully examine all the services it is running automatically, and either remove or set to manual any that are not needed (e.g., Web server, ftp server). You enable packet filtering on the adapter connected to the Internet, and supply packet filters for PPTP.

You then enable Routing and Remote Access, which immediately configures ports for your modem and 10 ports for your VPN. Because your company is not using IPSec, you change the number of L2TP ports to zero and increase the number of PPTP ports you think you need to accommodate your remote users. Some users may have ISDN adapters, so you ensure multilink is enabled on the server. For added security, you deselect MSCHAP and leave just MSCHAP-v2 as the server's authentication protocol. Additionally, you configure RRAS to automatically assign IP addresses, and you know your DHCP server is on the same subnet as your RRAS server.

You then configure the following policies:

- Rename the default profile called "Allow access if dial-in permission is enabled" and call it "Allow access to employees." and select the Grant remote access permission.
- Create a new policy called "Deny contractors remote access all the time" and add the Windows-Group: Contractors, and select "Deny remote access permission."
- Move the "Deny contractors remote access all the time" to the top of the list.

You ensure your company firewall will allow through your PPTP packets and your ISP doesn't filter on GRE packets. Then you power down the server, connect the adapter to the Internet, and reboot the server. Check that the RRAS server started successfully with no errors in the Event Log, and test two connections: the first one as a member of the Contractors group (connection should be rejected), and the second one as a standard user (connection should be accepted). If it doesn't work, fix it. If it does work, back it up and then document the configuration.

MCSE

MICROSOFT CERTIFIED SYSTEMS ENGINEER

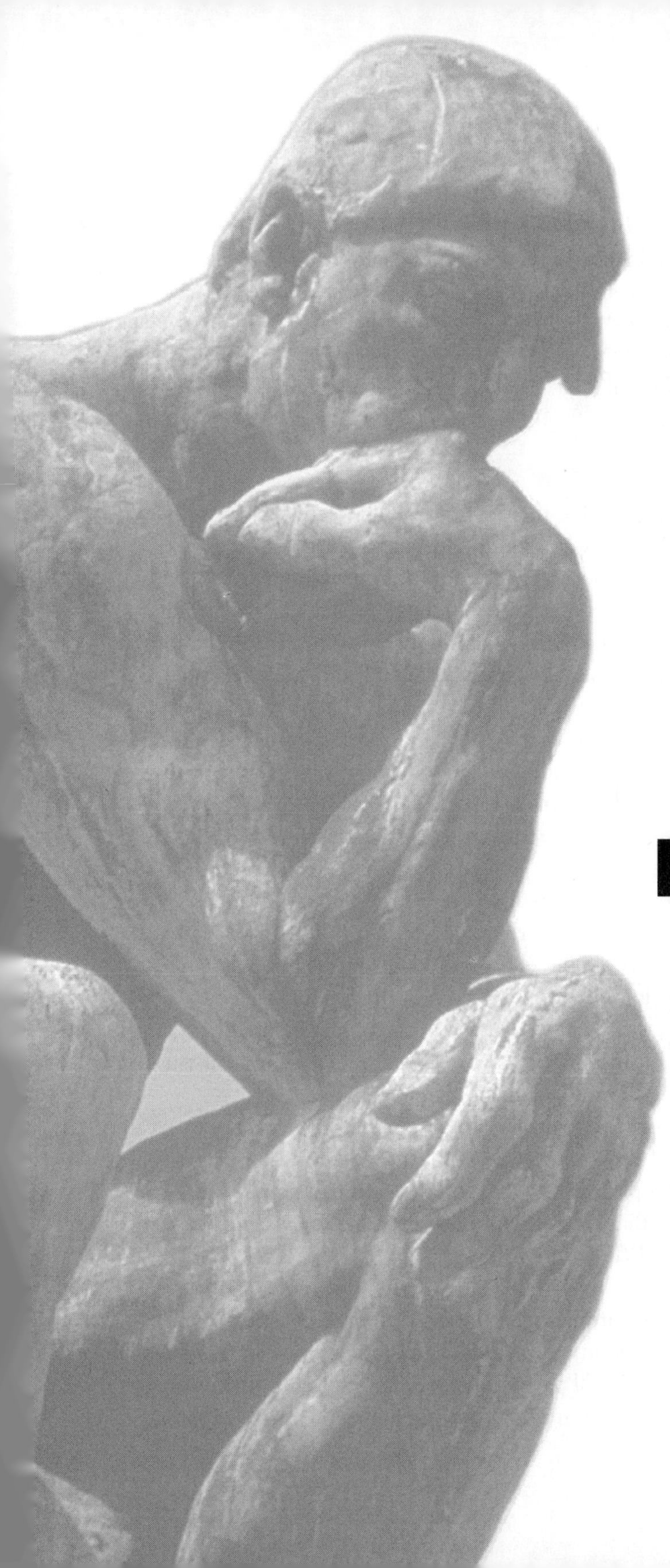

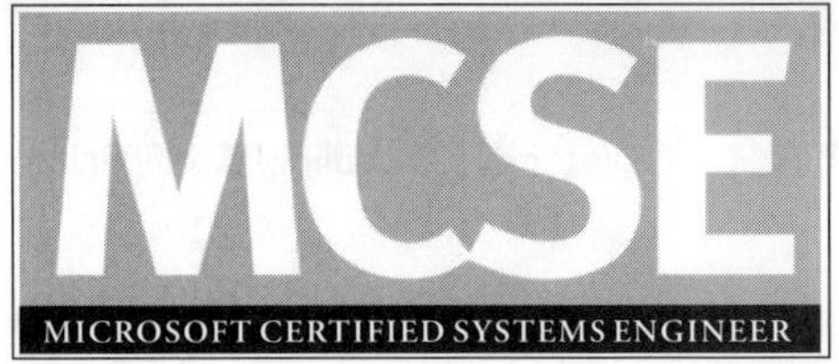

6

Installing, Configuring, Managing, Monitoring, and Troubleshooting Network Protocols

CERTIFICATION OBJECTIVES

6.01	Windows 2000 TCP/IP
6.02	IP Addressing
6.03	Installing, Configuring, Managing, and Monitoring TCP/IP
6.04	Installing and Configuring NWLink
✓	Two-Minute Drill
Q&A	Self Test

The Windows NT 4.0 certification track included an elective exam (taken by the vast majority of MCSE candidates) on the intricacies of the TCP/IP protocol suite and its implementation in various network environments. The new Windows 2000 track does not include an exam on this topic, which may lead some candidates to mistakenly believe that it is no longer necessary to study and understand TCP/IP. Nothing could be farther from the truth

Introduction

There is a good reason for the fact that there is no TCP/IP elective in the Windows 2000 MCSE track: a thorough knowledge and understanding of this set of protocols is no longer optional. TCP/IP is the foundation upon which Windows 2000 networking is built, and it is the default protocol stack installed with the operating system. The components of the suite and how to use them will be integral topics in the Windows 2000 core exams, especially Exam 70-216, "Implementing and Administering a Windows 2000 Network Infrastructure."

TCP/IP is not peculiar to Microsoft networks. In fact, not so long ago, TCP/IP was regarded as a somewhat sluggish, difficult-to-configure protocol used primarily by university or government networks participating in an exotic wide area networking project called ARPAnet. Few private organizations used it for their LANS because it was considered too slow and complex.

There were other protocols available that seemed to offer many advantages over the TCP/IP suite. Microsoft and IBM workgroups could use NetBEUI, a fast and simple transport protocol that could be set up easily and quickly by someone without a great deal of expertise. Novell NetWare networks, prior to NetWare 5.0, required the IPX/SPX stack, which was routable and thus could be used with larger server-based networks. Few business networks had any need for a powerful but high-overhead set of protocols like TCP/IP.

That was before the explosive popularity of the global wide area network we call the Internet. Inexpensive and easy to implement instant worldwide connectivity changed the lives of many people—and it changed the nature of networking. The growth of the Internet, more than any other single phenomenon, was responsible for the popularity enjoyed by TCP/IP in networking today. TCP/IP is *the* protocol stack on which the Internet runs.

In this chapter, we will focus primarily on the TCP/IP protocol suite. We'll briefly discuss the history and evolution of TCP/IP, and the purposes of the various protocols included in the suite. We'll pay particular attention to how to configure and use TCP/IP in a Windows 2000 network, and we'll examine some common troubleshooting scenarios.

An important part of implementing and administering a TCP/IP-based network is working with IP addressing issues, and we will delve into this topic in some depth. We will include information on IP subnetting and supernetting, and talk about new developments on the TCP/IP front, such as Classless InterDomain Routing (CIDR) and IPv6, the future incarnation of the Internet Protocol.

Although TCP/IP is Microsoft's obvious protocol of choice for Windows 2000 local area networks, there are still many hybrid networks in existence, in which Windows 2000 machines must coexist with current and older versions of Novell NetWare. Microsoft provides support for NWLink, its own implementation of the IPX/SPX protocol stack that is necessary for connection to NetWare networks prior to version 5. We will look briefly at how to install and configure the NWLink protocol, and discuss the importance of binding orders when running multiple protocols on a Windows 2000 computer.

CERTIFICATION OBJECTIVE 6.01

Windows 2000 TCP/IP

The Transmission Control Protocol/Internet Protocol (TCP/IP) stack is often called the protocol of the Internet. It is also the protocol of choice for Windows 2000. The Windows 2000 implementation of TCP/IP is based on industry standards and designed to support networks of all sizes, up to the largest enterprise environments, as well as providing connectivity to the Internet.

Windows 2000 TCP/IP also includes a variety of built-in utilities used to configure, maintain, and troubleshoot the protocols, and to provide connectivity to many different types of systems, such as:

- Internet host computers
- Apple Macintosh systems
- IBM mainframe systems
- UNIX systems
- Open VMS systems
- Microsoft Windows NT and Windows 2000 computers
- Microsoft Windows 95 and 98 computers

- Microsoft Windows for Workgroups computers
- Microsoft LAN Manager networks
- Network-ready printers, such as HP JetDirect-equipped printers

Windows 2000 TCP/IP also includes utilities such as File Transfer Protocol (FTP) and Telnet. FTP is a character-based application protocol that allows you to connect to FTP servers and transfer files. Telnet is an application that allows you to log in to remote computers and issue commands as if you were sitting at the keyboard of the remote computer. There are many variations of FTP, Telnet, and other programs based on earlier Internet standards available on the Internet as freeware/shareware or for purchase from third-party vendors.

We will take a more detailed look at these utilities and how they are used, later in this chapter.

Introduction to TCP/IP

Before we can understand the function of the TCP/IP protocols, we must first understand the role of protocols in computing and computer networking. A *protocol* is sometimes likened to a language that computers "speak" to communicate with one another, but a better analogy would be to think of the protocol as the syntax of a language. Protocols are sets of rules that specify the order and manner in which processes occur (in this case, the elements of the network communications process). A common protocol is necessary for two computers to "understand" one another.

Although TCP/IP is often referred to as "a" LAN protocol, in reality it is a set of protocols, also called a *protocol stack* or *protocol suite.* A *stack* consists of two or more protocols working together to accomplish a purpose (communication with another computer across a network). A *suite* is a more elaborate collection of communication protocols, utilities, tools, and applications. TCP and IP make up the stack, which handles the most important tasks of communication such as handling addressing and routing issues, error checking, and flow control. The suite includes a large number of additional protocols, used in various situations and for different purposes. Different vendors may include different tools and utilities in their implementations of the TCP/IP suite.

exam Watch

Some protocols that were developed specifically for the TCP/IP suite include Simple Mail Transfer Protocol (SMTP), Simple Network Management Protocol (SNMP), and File Transfer Protocol (FTP).

TCP/IP is known as an *open standard protocol.* In other words, it does not "belong" to any specific vendor, but is open to implementation by different companies. Thus we have not only Windows 2000 TCP/IP, but Novell's TCP/IP stack, UNIX stacks, TCP/IP stacks that are designed to run on Macintosh systems or mainframe computers, and so on. In order to maintain compatibility across these different operating systems and environments, all these vendors must adhere to certain standards.

TCP/IP Standards

Standards and specifications relating to various aspects of the TCP/IP suite are published as RFCs (Requests for Comments) on the Internet and serve as guidelines to promote standardization. The Windows 2000 implementation of Microsoft TCP/IP supports a large number of RFCs that define how the protocols work. These documents are used to describe Internet standards, and go through a formal approval process before being adopted.

FROM THE CLASSROOM

RFCs

RFCs are submitted by any interested party and assigned an RFC number. Not all RFCs describe standards, but if a document is to become a standard, it goes through three stages: Proposed Standard, Draft Standard, and Internet Standard (RFC 2226, "Instructions to Authors," contains information on how to write and format a draft). The Internet Engineering Steering Group (IESG) then reviews the document. The IESG is a part of the Internet Engineering Task Force (IETF). The IETF's working groups (WGs) create a large number of the Internet Drafts. (For more detailed information, see *www.ietf.org/home.html).* After review and approval, it is edited and published. The RFC editor, employed by the Internet Society, maintains and publishes a master list of RFCs, and is also responsible for final editing of the documents. The RFC Editor's homepage is located at *www.rfc-editor.org/.* For more information about the RFC submission and approval process, see RFC 2026, at *ftp://ftp.isi.edu/in-notes/rfc2026.txt* . Request For Comments (RFC) 1180, available on the Web, provides an authoritative tutorial on the TCP/IP protocol suite.

—Debra Littlejohn Shinder, MCSE, MCP+I, MCT

Standards are also supported through the use of common networking models, such as the Open Systems Interconnection (OSI) model, developed by the International Organization for Standardization, and the DoD (Department of Defense) model, developed by the U.S. government in conjunction with the design of the TCP/IP protocols themselves during the creation of the ARPAnet. ARPAnet was a wide area network of U.S. military installations and major educational institutions that was the predecessor to today's Internet.

Brief History of TCP/IP

In the 1960s, at the height of the cold war, the U.S. Department of Defense recognized that it would be valuable to establish electronic communications links between its major military installations, to ensure continued communication capabilities in the event of the mass destruction that would prevail if a nuclear war occurred. Major universities were already involved in their own networking projects. The DoD established the Advanced Research Projects Agency (ARPA), which funded research sites throughout the United States. In 1968, ARPA contracted with a company called BNN to build a network based on *packet-switching* technology.

exam Watch

A packet-switching network is one in which there is no dedicated pathway or circuit established. It is also known as a "connectionless" technology. If you send data from your computer to your company's national headquarters in New York over a packet-switched network, each individual packet, or chunk of data, can take a different physical route to get there. Most traffic sent across the Internet uses packet switching.

The ARPAnet grew, as nodes (computers attached to the network) were added each year. Eventually the military network split off, calling itself MILNET. The remaining membership of the ARPAnet consisted primarily of an elite group of academics at major universities. However, in the late 1980s and early 1990s, the international network caught the eye of the business world. As commercial enterprises moved onto the network (which changed its name again during this period), access became less expensive and widely available to companies and individuals. The original ARPAnet thus evolved into today's global Internet. According to most estimates, by 1999 there were over 50 million host computers connected to the Internet. Figure 6-1 illustrates the growth of the Internet.

From its ARPAnet beginnings, the Internet has grown into a huge, world-wide network. The protocol suite upon which the ARPAnet was built was the TCP/IP suite. The DoD designed it for that purpose, and the focus was reliability, rather

FIGURE 6-1

The growth of the Internet over the years

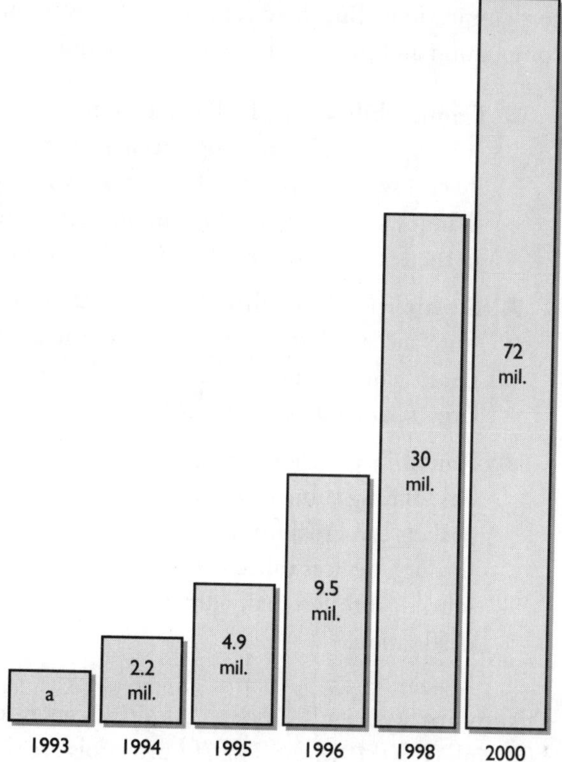

than speed. Despite later efforts to replace it with "better" protocols, such as the OSI suite, TCP/IP has endured. In addition to the Internet, the majority of medium to large networks today run on some implementation of the TCP/IP protocols.

Advantages and Disadvantages of TCP/IP vs. Other LAN Protocols

As noted, TCP/IP is relatively slow, it requires more overhead than most other LAN protocols, and it is also more difficult to configure and more complex to troubleshoot. Why, then, has it become so popular? Despite its shortcomings, the TCP/IP suite offers several advantages over other common LAN protocols such as IPX/SPX and NetBEUI.

The TCP/IP Advantages Reliability is TCP/IP's strong suit—the Department of Defense designed it that way. It is highly appropriate for mission-critical communications. But there are many other ways in which TCP/IP outdoes the competition and justifies the extra effort required to implement it:

- **Compatibility** TCP/IP could almost be considered the universal protocol. It is supported by most operating systems and platforms, and allows highly diverse systems—such as Macintosh workstations, UNIX servers, and Windows computers—to communicate with one another. Connection to the Internet *requires* the TCP/IP protocols.
- **Scalability** More than any other set of protocols in use, TCP/IP can scale from the smallest home network to the largest network of all: the Internet. Because of its unique addressing scheme, TCP/IP is especially suitable for large *internetworks* (networks that are interconnected with other networks).
- **Routability** Closely related to scalability is the protocol stack's capability of spanning subnets. Unlike unroutable protocols such as NetBEUI, its data packets can cross from one network, or *subnet,* to another by traveling through devices called *routers.* Internet communication often involves a journey through many different networks before the data reaches its destination.

Disadvantages of TCP/IP As already mentioned, compared to NetBEUI and NWLink (IPX/SPX), the TCP/IP protocols are slow. More resource overhead is required, and configuring the protocols correctly (IP address, subnet mask, default gateway) requires more knowledge and expertise. Most networking professionals feel that these are small prices to pay for TCP/IP's flexibility and power.

The TCP/IP Protocol Suite

TCP and IP make up the protocol "stack" that gets the messages to their destination, and ensures that they get there reliably. However, an entire suite of protocols has come to be associated with the name and included with most vendors' implementations.

Some of these are used to provide additional services, while others are useful primarily as information-gathering or troubleshooting tools. The different members of the suite work at different "layers" of the networking process. In order to understand this, let's take a look at the concept of layered networking models.

TCP/IP and the DOD/OSI Networking Models

In the early days of computer networking, protocols were *proprietary*; that is, each vendor of networking products developed its own set of rules. This meant that computers using the same vendor's products would be able to communicate with each other, but not with computers that were using the networking product of a different vendor.

The solution to this problem was to develop protocols that are based on *open standards*. Organizations such as the International Organization for Standardization (also called the ISO, which derives from the Greek word for "equal") took on the responsibility of overseeing the definition and control of these standards, and publishing them so that they would be available to any vendor who wanted to create products that adhered to them. This is an advantage to consumers, because they are no longer forced to use the products of only one vendor. It can also benefit the vendors, in that its products are more widely compatible and can be used in networks that started out using a different vendor's products.

Graphical models were developed to represent these open standards. Models provide an easy-to-understand description of the networking architecture and serve as the framework for the standards. The ISO's OSI model has become a common reference point for discussion of network protocols and connection devices. Another widely used model is the DoD (Department of Defense) networking model, on which TCP/IP is based. Both of these are *layered* models that represent the communication process as a series of steps or levels. This layered approach provides a logical division of responsibility, where each layer handles prescribed functions.

The Open Systems Interconnection Model The OSI model consists of seven layers. The data is passed from one layer down to the next lower layer at the sending computer, until the Physical layer finally puts it out onto the network cable. At the receiving end, it travels back up in reverse order. Although the data travels down the layers on one side and up the layers on the other, the logical communication link is between each layer and its matching counterpart, as shown in Figure 6-2.

As the data is passed down through the layers, it is enclosed within a larger unit as each layer adds its own header information. When it reaches the receiving computer, the process occurs in reverse; the information is passed upward through each layer, and as it does so, the encapsulation information is stripped off one layer at a time. After processing, each layer removes the header information that was added by its corresponding layer on the sending side.

FIGURE 6-2

Each of the seven layers of the OSI model communicates with its corresponding layer on the receiving side

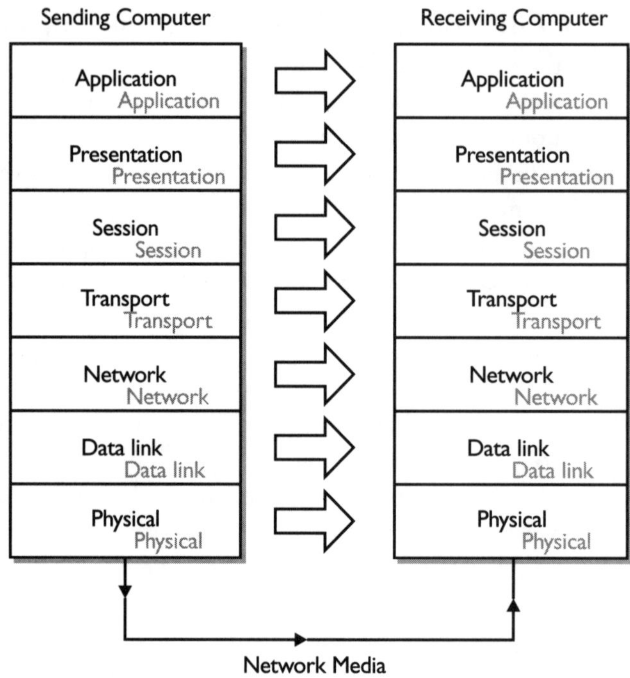

exam Watch

The process of enclosing data within a larger unit, with header information added by the protocol that is doing the enclosing, is called encapsulation.

By the time the data is finally presented to the Application layer, which then passes it up to the user application at the receiving computer, the data is once again in the form it was in when it was sent by the user application at the sending machine. Figure 6-3 shows how the header information is added to the data as it moves down through the layers.

The layers of the OSI model (from the top down), and a brief summary of the functions of each, are as follows:

- **Application** This is the part of the networking component that interfaces with the user application.
- **Presentation** This layer handles issues such as compression and encryption.
- **Session** This layer is responsible for establishing a one-to-one connection, or session, between computers.
- **Transport** The protocols at this layer handle error checking, flow control, and acknowledgments.

FIGURE 6-3

The protocols at each networking layer add header information that will be processed by the corresponding layer at the receiving computer

	Data	Link hdr	Application					
	Data	Link hdr	Pres hdr	Presentation				
	Data	Link hdr	Pres hdr	Ses hdr	Session			
	Data	Link hd	Pres hdr	Ses hdr	Transp hdr	Transport		
	Data	Link hdr	Pres hdr	Ses hdr	Transp hdr	Net hdr	Network	
Link trailer	Data	Link hdr	Pres hdr	Ses hdr	Transp hdr	Net hdr	Link hdr	Data link

- **Network** This layer is responsible for routing and logical addressing issues.
- **Data Link** This layer deals with the physical addressing and link establishment.
- **Physical** This layer interfaces with the hardware, and does not add headers to the data.

The Department of Defense Networking Model TCP/IP is often discussed in reference to the OSI networking model. However, the protocol suite was developed prior to development of the OSI model, and in conjunction with the DoD model. Therefore, the TCP/IP protocols do not map exactly to the seven OSI layers, but do map directly to the four layers of the DoD model.

Figure 6-4 shows how the OSI and DoD layers correlate.

Again beginning at the top and working our way down, the four DoD layers are as follows:

- **Application/Process** The Application layer of the DoD model corresponds to the top three layers of the OSI model, and handles the functions performed by the Application, Presentation, and Session layers. A number of the protocols included in the TCP/IP suite operate here, including File Transfer Protocol (FTP), Telnet, HyperText Transfer Protocol (HTTP), Simple Mail Transfer Protocol (SMTP), and others. Two Application Programming Interfaces (APIs) also reside here: NetBIOS and WinSock

FIGURE 6-4

The four layers of the DoD (TCP/IP) model can be roughly mapped to the seven layers of the OSI model

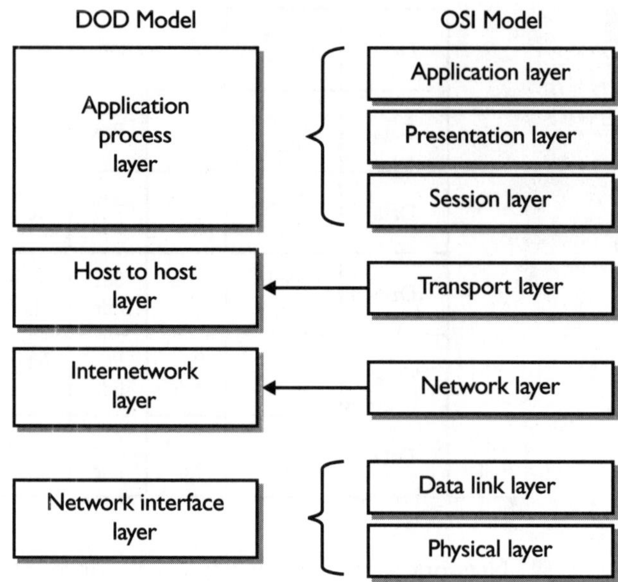

(Windows Sockets), which provide access to the transport protocols. Many *gateways* also operate in this layer. A gateway is software or a device that provides an interface to allow network communications between two disparate systems.

Since the Presentation layer handles the very important task of protocol translation, this layer is where many gateways operate. The gateway acts as a translator, and allows computers using different protocols to communicate with one another. There are many types of gateway programs available that you may encounter in the field, such as:

E-mail gateway *This software translates the messages from diverse, noncompatible e-mail systems into a common Internet format such as the Simple Mail Transfer Protocol (SMTP).*

SNA gateway *Systems Network Architecture is a proprietary IBM architecture used in mainframe computer systems such as the AS/400. An SNA gateway allows personal computers on a local area network to access files and applications on the mainframe computer.*

Gateway Services for Netware (GSNW) *This software is included with Windows 2000 (and Windows NT) Server operating systems to allow the Windows server's clients to access files on a Novell NetWare server. It translates between the SMB (Server Message Block) used by Microsoft to NCP (Netware Core Protocol) used by NetWare.*

- **Host to Host (Transport)** This layer is basically the same as the Transport layer in the OSI model. It is responsible for flow control, acknowledgments, sequencing (ordering) of packets, and establishment of end-to-end communications. TCP and the User Datagram Protocol (UDP) operate at this level.
- **Internetwork** This layer matches the Network layer in the OSI model. The Internet Protocol (IP) works here to route and deliver packets to the correct destination address. Other protocols that operate at this layer include the Address Resolution Protocol (ARP), Reverse Address Resolution Protocol (RARP), and the Internet Control Message Protocol (ICMP).
- **Network Interface** This bottom layer of the DoD model corresponds to both the Data Link and Physical layers of OSI. It provides the interface between the network architecture (Ethernet, Token Ring, AppleTalk, etc.) and the upper layers, as well as the physical (hardware) issues.

The most critical members of the TCP/IP suite are the Network and Transport layer protocols (or Internetwork and Host-to-Host): TCP/UDP and IP.

The Internetwork Layer Protocols

The protocols that operate at the Internet layer of the DoD model (Network layer of the OSI model) handle logical (IP) addressing issues and routing.

Routers work at the Internetwork layer. A router can be a dedicated device, or you can configure a Windows NT or Windows 2000 computer to route IP packets by installing multiple network interface cards and enabling IP forwarding. Routers are necessary for communication to take place between computers that are not on the same network (subnet).

IP routing involves discovering a pathway from the sending computer (or forwarding router) to the destination computer whose address is designated in the IP header.

The protocol most commonly associated with this layer is IP, the Internet Protocol (IPX, as part of the IPX/SPX stack, also operates at this layer, and Windows 2000 also supports IPX routing).

IP IP is a *connectionless* protocol; this means it must depend on TCP at the Transport layer above it to provide a connection if necessary.

exam Watch

A connection-oriented protocol is one that establishes a direct connection before sending data. A connection-oriented protocol works something like a phone call: If you wish to have a conversion with Mr. Smith, you would dial his number, ask for him, and verify that he is the party to whom you're speaking before plunging into the discussion. Connectionless protocols work more like sending a postcard: You write your message, address it to Mr. Smith, and drop it in the mailbox, hoping it will reach its destination. Mr. Smith was not aware that the message was coming until it arrived, and you have no way of knowing whether or not Mr. Smith received your communication.

Although IP does not establish a connection or acknowledgment receipt of messages, it is able to use number sequencing to break down and reassemble messages, and uses a checksum to perform error checking on the IP header.

ICMP and IGMP The Internet Control Message Protocol (ICMP) is a TCP/IP standard that allows hosts and routers that use IP communication to report errors and exchange limited control and status information. The PING utility (discussed later in this chapter) works by sending an ICMP echo request message and recording the response of echo replies.

The Internet Group Management Protocol is used for *multicasting,* which is a method of sending a message to multiple hosts but only addressing it to a single address. Members of a multicast group can be defined, and then when a message is sent to the group address, only those computers that belong to the group will receive it. IGMP is used to exchange membership status information between IP routers that support multicasting and members of multicast groups.

ARP and RARP The Address Resolution Protocol (ARP) is used to resolve IP (logical) addresses to Media Access Control (MAC) physical hardware addresses. ARP uses broadcasts to discover the hardware addresses, and stores the information in its *arp cache.*

RARP is the Reverse Address Resolution Protocol, which does the same thing in reverse; that is, it takes a physical address and resolves it to an IP address. The **arp –a** command can be used to view the current entries in the ARP cache. See Figure 6-5 for an illustration of this IP address to MAC address list.

The Transport Layer Protocols

Remember that the Transport layer's primary responsibility is reliability; it must verify that the data arrives complete and in good condition,. It also must have a way

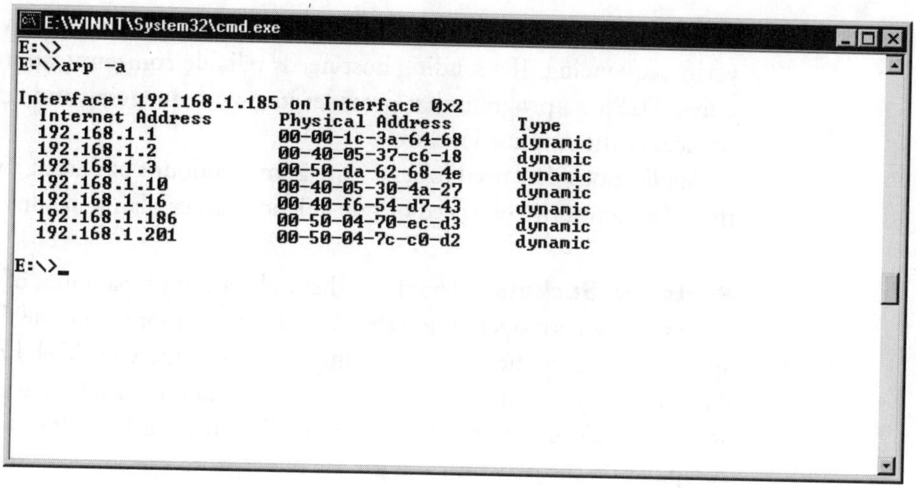

FIGURE 6-5 The current entries in the ARP cache, which matches IP addresses to MAC (hardware) addresses

```
E:\WINNT\System32\cmd.exe
E:\>
E:\>arp -a

Interface: 192.168.1.185 on Interface 0x2
  Internet Address      Physical Address      Type
  192.168.1.1           00-00-1c-3a-64-68     dynamic
  192.168.1.2           00-40-05-37-c6-18     dynamic
  192.168.1.3           00-50-da-62-68-4e     dynamic
  192.168.1.10          00-40-05-30-4a-27     dynamic
  192.168.1.16          00-40-f6-54-d7-43     dynamic
  192.168.1.186         00-50-04-70-ec-d3     dynamic
  192.168.1.201         00-50-04-7c-c0-d2     dynamic

E:\>_
```

to differentiate between the communications that may be coming to the same network address (the IP address) from—or to—different applications.

There are two protocols in the TCP/IP suite that operate at the Transport layer: the Transmission Control Protocol (TCP) and the User Datagram Protocol (UDP). TCP is called a *connection-oriented* protocol, and UDP is a *connectionless* protocol. A connection-oriented protocol such as TCP offers better error control, but its higher overhead means a loss of performance. A connectionless protocol like UDP, on the other hand, suffers in the reliability department but, because it doesn't have to bother with error-checking duties, is faster.

TCP TCP is based on *point-to-point communication* between two network hosts. This means a session is established before data transmission begins. This is done using a process called a *three-way handshake.* This is a way of synchronizing communications and establishing a virtual connection.

TCP processes data as a stream of bytes, which are divided into groups called *segments.* TCP bytes are grouped into segments that TCP then numbers and sequences for delivery. TCP sends *acknowledgments* when segments are received, to let the sending computer know that the data arrived. If data segments arrive out of sequence, TCP/IP can reassemble them in the correct order. If a segment fails to arrive, TCP lets the sending computer know so that segment can be sent again.

UDP UDP provides a service similar to that of TCP, but it does so in a different way. UDP is a connectionless protocol, which offers what is called *best-effort delivery.* This means that UDP does not guarantee delivery, nor does it verify sequencing. If a sending host needs reliable communication, it should use either TCP or a program that provides its own sequencing and acknowledgment services at the Application level.

Applications that need to send only a small amount of data at a time, or those that place a priority on speed of transmission rather than reliability, use UDP.

Ports and Sockets Thanks to the multitasking capabilities of Windows 2000 and other modern operating systems, you can use more than one network application simultaneously. For example, you can use your Web browser to access your company's homepage at the same time your e-mail software is downloading your e-mail. You probably know that TCP/IP uses an IP address to identify your computer on the network, and get the messages to the correct system, but how does it separate the response to your browser's request from your incoming mail when both arrive at the same IP address?

That's where ports come in. Remember we said that the two parts of an IP address that represent the network identification and the host (individual computer) identification are somewhat like a street name and an individual street number. In this analogy, the port number designates the specific apartment or suite within the building.

TCP and UDP, the Transport layer protocols, both use port numbers to ensure that the data intended for Apartment A doesn't get sent to Apartment B instead.

A *socket* is the combination of an IP address and a port number.

TCP Sliding Windows TCP is a reliable protocol, and as a result, in a TCP communication, every segment sent must be acknowledged. That way, if one segment doesn't arrive at its destination (and thus the receiving computer does not send back an acknowledgment for it), it will be sent again.

TCP has to have a way to control the "flow" of data transmission when multiple TCP connections have to share a busy link. Flow control is necessary so that the receiving computer doesn't get "overwhelmed" by a sending computer that deluges it with data faster than it can be processed, or alternately so that the receiver doesn't sit around waiting for the data to "trickle" in.

Flow control is the process of matching the outflow of data from the sending computer to the receiving computer's inflow. This is done by setting a limit on the number of packets that can be sent before acknowledgment is required, which signals the sender to slow down (or stop and wait) if data is "piling up" in the receiver's buffer. If the buffer overflows, data will be lost and must be retransmitted. Think of flow control as the effective management of the data flow between devices in a network so that the data can be handled at an efficient pace.

In the TCP communication process, those bytes of data that can be considered active are called the "window." These are the bytes that are ready to be sent, or they have been sent and are awaiting acknowledgment. As acknowledgments are received, the window "slides" past those bytes, to send additional bytes. The *sliding window protocol* determines how much data is being transmitted based on actual bytes, rather than segments. See Figure 6-6 for an illustration of how the sliding window concept works.

Other Members of the Suite

There are several other protocols that belong to the TCP/IP suite. Many of these operate at the Application layer, and are used for such tasks as transferring files, remote terminal emulation, messaging, and network management. Some of these protocols include:

- **File Transfer Protocol (FTP)** Used to download files from another computer, or to upload files to another computer.
- **Telnet** Used to connect to a remote computer and run programs or view files.

FIGURE 6-6

TCP uses "sliding windows" for flow control

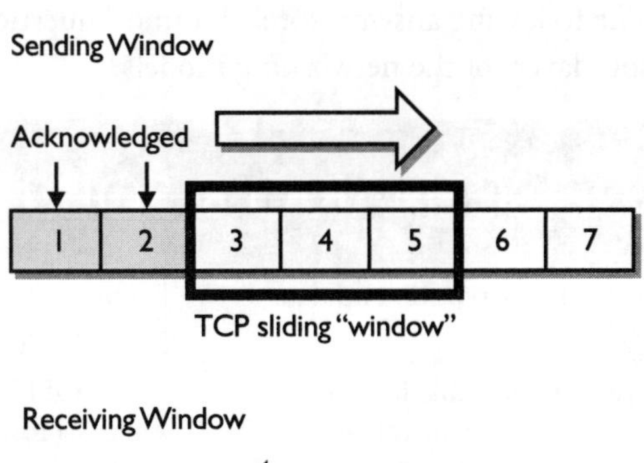

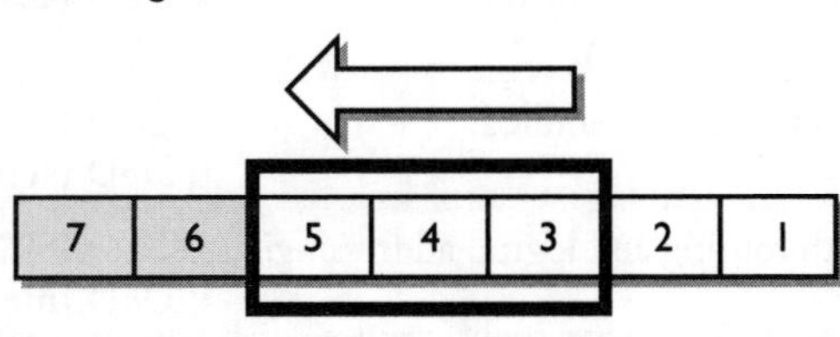

- **Simple Mail Transfer Protocol** Used for sending Internet mail (usually used in conjunction with the Post Office Protocol (POP), which is used to retrieve incoming mail from the mail server.
- **Simple Network Management Protocol (SNMP)** Used to monitor and manage TCP/IP networks. SNMP has two components, the SNMP Agent and the SNMP Management System, which use SNMP messages sent using UDP to communicate host information, which is stored in a Management Information Base (MIB).

exam Watch

The Application Programming Interfaces, APIs, are called boundary layers in Microsoft's own Windows networking model. The two supported APIs in Windows 2000 networking are NetBIOS and WinSock. NetBIOS communications use a destination name (called a NetBIOS name) and a message location to get the data to the correct destination. NetBIOS supports a session mode, for establishing a connection and transfer of large messages, and a datagram mode, for connectionless transmissions such as broadcast messages. A WinSock program handles input/output requests for Internet applications in a Windows operating system, using the sockets convention for connecting with and exchanging data between two processes. WinSock runs as a .dll file (dynamic link library). A .dll file is a collection of small programs, any of which can be loaded when an application needs to use it, but it isn't required to be included as part of the application.

The following answers some common questions about the responsibilities of various layers of the networking models.

SCENARIO & SOLUTION	
At what networking layer do encryption and data compression take place?	The OSI Presentation layer DoD Application layer
Which networking layer is responsible for acknowledgment of receipts, flow control, and sequencing of packets?	The OSI Transport layer DoD Host-to-Host (Transport) layer
At what layer are hardware issues handled?	The OSI Physical layer DoD Network Interface layer
Which layer deals with routing and logical addressing?	The OSI Network layer DoD Internetwork layer

CertCam 6-1

EXERCISE 6-1

Using the Windows 2000 FTP Client

To use the built-in FTP client in Windows 2000, perform the following steps:

1. Click the Run selection on the Start menu.
2. Type **cmd** in the Run box to invoke a command prompt.
3. At the command line, type **ftp**.
4. You should see a prompt displayed as **ftp>**.
5. At the prompt, type **open ftp.microsoft.com**.
6. You will be prompted for a username. Type **anonymous**.
7. You will receive a message that anonymous connections are allowed, and asked to give your e-mail address. Type in your e-mail address.
8. You will be welcomed to the Microsoft FTP site.
9. To get a list of files available for download, type **dir**. You will see a list such as that shown in the following illustration.

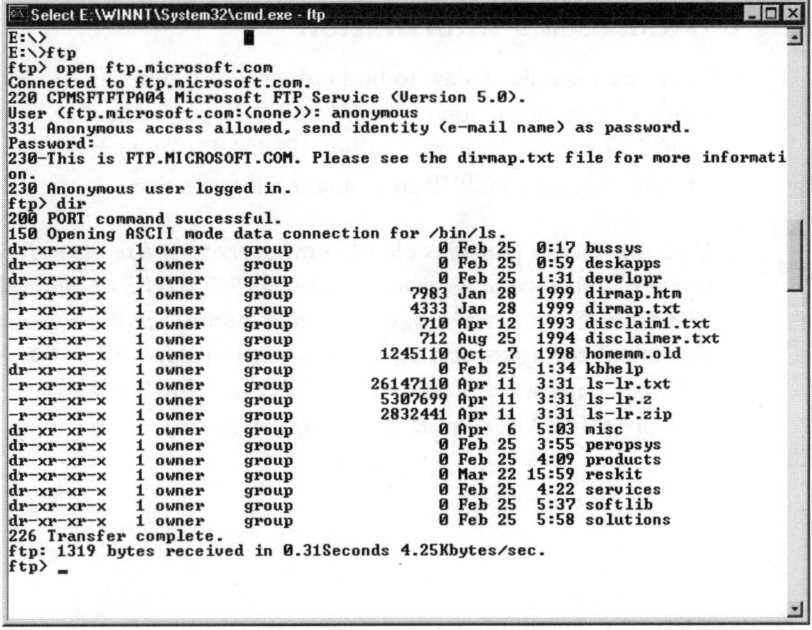

You can use the **GET** command to specify a file to be downloaded, or the **PUT** command to specify a file to be uploaded. For a complete listing of FTP commands, type **help** at the ftp prompt.

CERTIFICATION OBJECTIVE 6.02

IP Addressing

The IP address is a *logical* address, assigned by the network administrator. It bears no *direct* relation to the network interface card's *physical* address (called the MAC address because it is used at the Media Access Control sublayer of the OSI's Data Link layer). The MAC address is hard-coded into a chip on the network card in 1the typical Ethernet network. The *Address Resolution Protocol* (ARP), which was discussed earlier in this chapter, has the task of translating IP addresses to MAC addresses.

Locating IP Addressing Information

There are a couple of ways to find out what a computer's IP address is. TCP/IP configuration information is found in the Properties box for the protocol. Windows 2000 TCP/IP also includes a utility, IPCONFIG, which displays the computer's IP address and other TCP/IP configuration information.

If your network contains client computers that use older Microsoft operating systems, you should be aware that the IPCONFIG command also works with Windows NT (all versions) and with Windows for Workgroups 3.11. However, to view IP configuration information in Windows 95 or 98, you must use a different command: WINIPCFG. This will display the same information, but in a Graphical User Interface (GUI) dialog box.

EXERCISE 6-2

Finding Your Computer's IP Addressing Information

To determine your computer's IP address and related information (subnet mask and default gateway), follow these steps:

Locating IP information via the TCP/IP Properties box.

1. Select Start | Settings | Network and Dial-up Connections.
2. In the Network and Dial-up Connections Folder, right-click on your local area connection and select Properties, shown as follows.

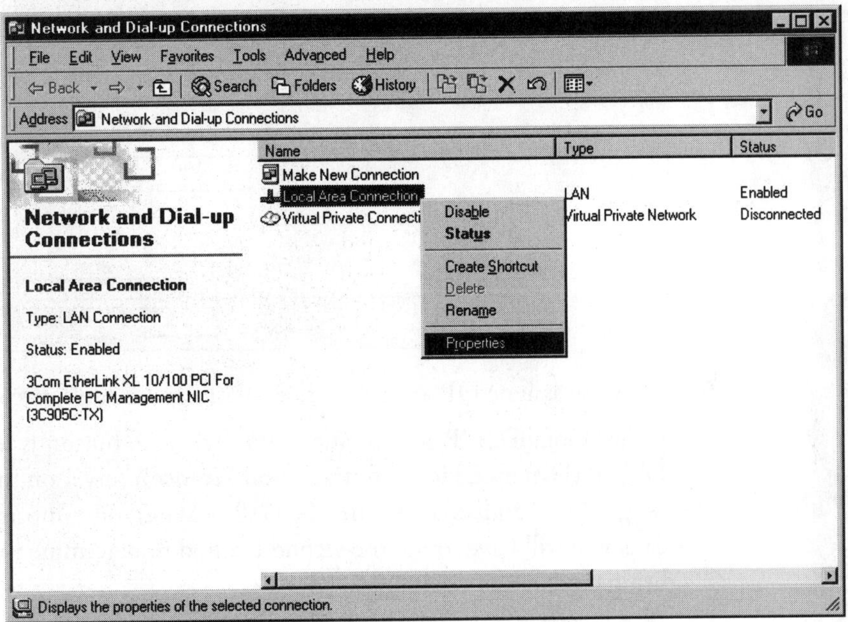

3. In the Properties dialog box, double-click on Internet Protocol (TCP/IP), or highlight it and click Properties.

4. You will see a dialog box displayed similar to the one shown next.

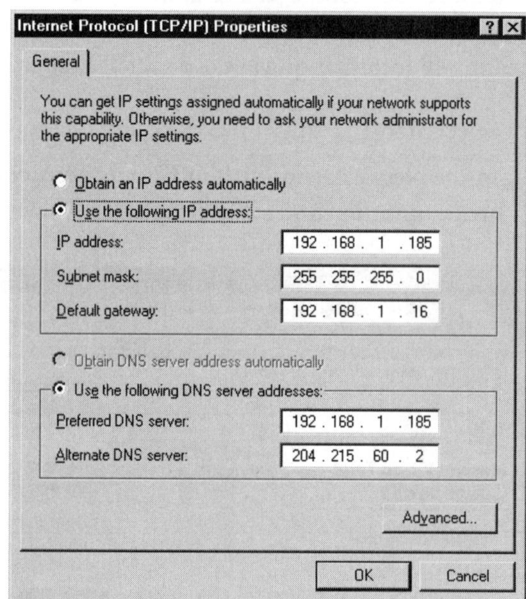

5. Note the assigned IP address, subnet mask, and default gateway information.

   If the "Obtain an IP address automatically" radio button is selected, a DHCP (Dynamic Host Configuration Protocol) server on the network will assign the IP address and other TCP/IP configuration information. In that case, you will have to use the second method to determine the IP address being used by the computer.

   Locating IP information via the IPCONFIG command.

   The best way to determine IP addressing information is by using the TCP/IP command-line utility IPCONFIG. To do so, follow these steps:

6. Bring up a command window (select Start | Run and type **cmd**).
7. Type **ipconfig** at the prompt.

8. You will see information displayed similar to that shown in the following illustration.

```
E:\WINNT\System32\cmd.exe
Microsoft Windows 2000 [Version 5.00.2195]
(C) Copyright 1985-1999 Microsoft Corp.

E:\Documents and Settings\debshinder.TACTEAM>cd\

E:\>ipconfig

Windows 2000 IP Configuration

Ethernet adapter Local Area Connection:

        Connection-specific DNS Suffix  . :
        IP Address. . . . . . . . . . . . : 192.168.1.185
        Subnet Mask . . . . . . . . . . . : 255.255.255.0
        Default Gateway . . . . . . . . . : 192.168.1.16

PPP adapter RAS Server (Dial In) Interface:

        Connection-specific DNS Suffix  . :
        IP Address. . . . . . . . . . . . : 192.168.1.214
        Subnet Mask . . . . . . . . . . . : 255.0.0.0
        Default Gateway . . . . . . . . . :

E:\>_
```

The IP address and subnet mask are always required for TCP/IP communication. The default gateway value is required to communicate on a routed network.

How IP Addressing Works

In order to communicate over the network using the TCP/IP protocols, a computer must have an IP address that is unique on that network. A network administrator can manually assign the IP address, or it can be automatically assigned by an addressing service such as DHCP, APIPA (Automatic Private IP Addressing),or ICS (Internet Connection Sharing).

The IP address is usually represented as shown in the screenshots, in "dotted decimal" (also called "dotted quad") notation with four sections, called *octets,* separated by dots. This decimal notation is merely a "user friendly" way to express the binary number used by the computers to communicate. The *octets* are called that because each represents eight binary digits.

FROM THE CLASSROOM

The IP address

IP addressing, used by the network protocols to deliver packets to the proper destination, is analogous to street addressing used by the postal service to deliver mail to the proper home or office. If you wish to send a letter to a specific location, you must indicate the street address on the envelope. Similarly, the computer's IP address is placed on the data packet's "envelope," in the form of header information. You also place a return address on the envelope so the post office will know where it originated in case it can't be delivered. The sending computer's address, called the source address, is likewise included in the header (there may be other information in addition to the source and destination address in some headers, just as you might have additional information or instructions, such as "Do not forward" or "Fragile—Do not bend" on the envelope you send through the postal system).

—Debra Littlejohn Shinder, MCSE, MCP+I, MCT

To identify which octet we're talking about, they are often referred to as the "W," "X," "Y," and "Z" as follows:

w.x.y.z

Ones and Zeros: Binary Addressing

Let's take a look at how IP addresses look in binary. This will help you to understand what the numbers really represent and how the computer uses them for communication.

For example: The IP address 192.168.1.185 *really* represents the following binary number: 11000000.10101000.00000001.10111001.

This number is made up of four groups of eight binary digits, the *octets* mentioned earlier. Binary uses only two digits—0 and 1—to represent all numerical values. Binary is a *base two* system, as opposed to decimal, which is a *base ten* system because it uses ten digits—0 through 9—to represent all numerical values.

How do you convert decimal to its binary equivalent? Well, you *could* just use the Windows calculator in scientific mode (choose "Scientific" from the View menu). Check the dec radio button and enter the number in decimal, then click on the bin radio button and Tada! As if by magic, you have the binary equivalent.

But you also need to know how to perform the calculation without the assistance of a calculator. It's really not as difficult as you may think.

Converting Decimal to Binary

Let's take a look at an octet:

11111111

We have eight binary digits, and each of them represents a decimal value, beginning with the rightmost digit and working our way back to the leftmost. The rightmost digits are sometimes referred to as the low order bits, and the leftmost as the high order bits.

Each bit that is "turned on" (that is, shows a 1 instead of a 0) represents the value of that bit as shown in Table 6-1.

You'll notice that the value increases by a power of 2 as you move from right to left. A bit that is turned "off" (represented by a 0) counts as 0. All we have to do then is add up the values of the bits that are "on."

If the octet we wish to convert is 10011011, we would add 1 + 2 + 8 + 16 +128 (the values of all the bits that are turned "on"), for a total of 155. So, 10011011 equals 155 in decimal notation.

TABLE 6-1 Values of Binary Digits in an Octet

1	1	1	1	1	1	1	1
128	64	32	16	8	4	2	1

The Components of an IP Address

What does this mean, then, in terms of the IP addresses we work with every day? Generally, when we configure TCP/IP properties, we enter IP addresses in *dotted decimal notation.* An IP address in its "pure" binary form consists of four octets (each octet being made up of eight binary digits), or 32 bits. The dotted decimal form shows the octets converted to their decimal equivalent with each octet separated by a dot. Thus, the address that the computer sees as 10011110 11101000 00011001 11111001 will be expressed as 158.232.25.249 (do the calculations as shown earlier or use the scientific calculator to make the conversion).

Network and Host ID This address is really made up of two parts, just as your street address contains both the *house number* and the *street name*; for example, 123 Main Street. Many houses share the "street name" portion of the address (everyone else on your street). There may also be other houses in your neighborhood that have the house number "123," but they will be on different streets. It's the combination of the house number and street name that makes up the unique identifier that describes to others which house is yours.

IP addresses work in a similar fashion. Part of the address is the *network ID,* which identifies the network (or subnet) on which the computer is located. All computers on the subnet share this part of the address. The second part of an IP address is called the *host ID,* and identifies the individual computer on that network or subnet. Combined, they create a unique address that differentiates this computer from all others on the internetwork.

The Role of the Subnet Mask How do we know *which* of the octets, or parts of the IP address, indicate the network ID, and which ones indicate the host ID? It would be easier if, for instance, the first octet always indicated the network, and the last three always indicated the host. Unfortunately, it's not that simple. However, we can determine what part of the IP address pertains to which by taking a look at our *subnet mask.*

The subnet mask is another 32-bit binary number, expressed in the same form as an IP address, but its purpose is to tell us (and more importantly, to tell the computers) which part of the IP address is *masked* (and thus represents the network ID). In the binary form of the subnet mask, the *masked bits* are those that are "on," or set to 1.

If the first eight bits from the left in the subnet mask (the first octet) are all ones, and the rest of the bits are zeros, that means the first octet represents the network ID and the remaining three octets represent the host ID. Let's convert that to decimal, since we usually see the subnet mask expressed in dotted decimal in the TCP/IP configuration.

11111111.00000000.00000000.00000000 =
255.0.0.0.

This generally means the first portion of the IP address identifies the network on which the computer "lives," and the last three parts identify the specific computer (host) on that network. In other words, if our IP address is 103.24.125.6 with a subnet mask of 255.0.0.0, the first octet (103) identifies the network, and the remaining three (24.125.6) identify the host computer on that network.

exam Watch

Certain addresses are used for special purposes. A host number of all 0s is used to identify the network, and a host number of all 255s is used as the broadcast address, to send messages to all computers on that network.

There is one more thing we must factor in: the *address class* to which the IP address belongs.

Address Classes

In order for computers to communicate on a worldwide global internetwork like the Internet, which requires that each computer have a unique IP address, there must be some centralized authority in charge of assigning addresses and ensuring that none are duplicated. This has been handled by the Internet Assigned Numbers Authority (IANA) and the InterNIC, a company tasked with that responsibility. Traditionally, blocks of IP addresses have been assigned in "lumps" to organizations and Internet Service Providers (ISPs), depending on how many host addresses were needed for their networks.

These blocks of addresses came in three basic sizes: large, medium, and small. The networks for which these blocks of addresses were assigned were called Class A, B, and C networks.

Class A Addresses

Class A addresses are for the "large size" networks, those that have a tremendous number of computers, and thus a need for many host addresses. Class A addresses always begin with a 0 in the first octet (also called the W octet). This will be the first bit on the left. This leaves seven bits for the individual network ID, and 24 bits to identify the host computers. When we convert to decimal, we see that this means a Class A address will have a decimal value in the first octet of 127 or less.

exam Watch

Class A networks can be assigned addresses with a first octet of 1–126. The 127.0.0.0 network, although technically a Class A, is reserved for use as the "loopback Network ID." This is a test Network ID used to troubleshoot TCP/IP connectivity. The address 127.0.0.1 is generally known as the "loopback" address, but a message sent to any valid IP address with the loopback network will "loop back" to the sender (regardless of the sender's IP address). Unfortunately, this means the more than 24 million additional addresses in the 127.0.0.0 network cannot be assigned and are wasted.

Class A addresses, because they use only the first octet to identify the network, are limited in number. However, each Class A network can have a huge number of host computers, over 16 million. The Class A network numbers were all used up some time ago; they have been assigned to very large organizations such as IBM, MIT, and General Electric.

Class B Addresses

Class B networks are the "medium size" networks. Class B networks use the first two octets (the 16 leftmost bits) to identify the network, and the last two octets (or the 16 rightmost bits) to identify the host computers. This means there can be far more Class B networks than Class As (over 16,000), but each can have fewer hosts ("only" 65,535 each). Class B addresses always begin with a 10 for the two leftmost bits in the W octet, and the network is defined by the first two octets, which translates to decimal values of 128 through 191 for the first octet. 16 bits identify the Network ID, and the remaining 16 bits identify the Host ID. Microsoft's network is an example of a Class B network.

Class C Addresses

The smallest sized block of addresses designated by a class is the Class C network, each of which can have only 254 hosts. However, there can be over 2 million Class C networks. A Class C network always has 110 as its first three bits. This leaves 24 bits to identify the network, with only 8 bits to use for host IDs. A Class C network, in decimal notation, will have a first octet decimal value of 192 through 223.

on the job

Don't be confused if you read in some texts that the network ID in a Class B network is identified by 14 bits rather than 16, or in a Class C by 21 instead of 24. Technically this is correct—the first 2 bits define the address class, and the next 14 define the individual network. To simplify our understanding of addressing, these two are usually referred to together as the "network ID."

There are many, many class C networks. Most Internet Service Providers (ISPs) have been assigned Class C network numbers.

The address ranges 10.x.x.x, 172.16.x.x, and 192.168.x.x are reserved for use as private addresses. That is, these address ranges cannot be assigned by the Internet authorities to any network connected to the public Internet, but can be used as internal addresses that are not connected to the public network, without being required to be registered. Private addresses cannot send to or receive traffic from the Internet—at least, not directly. If a LAN is using private addresses, and the computers on the LAN need to communicate with Internet locations, the private addresses must be translated to a public address. NAT (Network Address Translation) software is used for this purpose, and Windows 2000 includes built-in NAT support.

Class D and E Addresses

We said there are *three* network sizes, so where do the Class D and E addresses fit in? These two classes are *not* assigned to networks, but are reserved and used for special purposes.

Class D addresses, whose four high order (leftmost) bits in the W octet are 1110, are used for *multicasting.* This is a method of sending a message to multiple computers simultaneously.

Class E addresses, with four high order bits of 1111, are reserved to be used for experimental and testing purposes.

The following provides a quick reference for defining the ranges of IP address classes.

SCENARIO & SOLUTION	
What is the first octet range for Class A networks?	1–126
What is the first octet 127 used for?	The loopback address, for verifying that the TCP/IP stack is installed and configured properly.
What is the first octet range for Class B networks?	128–191
What is the first octet range for Class C networks?	192–223
What does a first octet value that exceeds 223 indicate?	Addresses used for special purposes, such as multicasting and experimental use, which are not assigned to networks (these are called Class D and E addresses).

Default Subnet Masks

When an entire block of addresses from a specified class is assigned and used as one network (either a Class A, B, or C), the subnet mask is easy to determine and understand. Either the first, first two, or first three octets are "masked"; that is, all bits in those octets are 1s (turned "on"), indicating that those bits represent the network ID. The subnet masks used in these cases are called the *default subnet masks* for each address class. The default masks are as follows:

- **Class A** 255.0.0.0 (11111111.00000000.00000000.00000000)
- **Class B** 255.255.0.0. (11111111.11111111.00000000.00000000)
- **Class C** 255.255.255.0 (11111111.11111111.11111111.00000000)

Often, however, a block of addresses (such as the 254 addresses available in an assigned Class C network) needs to be split into two or more smaller networks. This is called *subnetting.* There are many reasons for subnetting a network, one of which is to cut down on broadcast traffic (broadcast messages go only to the computers on the same subnet) and make better use of network bandwidth.

It is also possible to do the opposite: combine two or more Class C networks together to create a larger network. This is referred to as *supernetting.*

Remember that the default subnet masks indicate unsubnetted networks only when applied to the network class listed. This means the subnet mask of 255.255.0.0 *when applied to a Class B* ***network indicates an unsubnetted network. However, the same mask of 255.255.0.0, if applied to a Class A network, would be a subnetted network. The network class is always determined by the high order (leftmost) bits, as discussed earlier. A common mistake for new administrators is to assume that if the subnet mask is 255.255.255.0, for example, the network is a Class C network.***

Subnetting and Supernetting

Both subnetting and supernetting are ways of modifying the IP address by "stealing" bits from one portion (network ID or host ID) to "give" to the other. To do this, you must use a *variable length (or custom) subnet mask* to indicate which bits in the IP address pertain to the network ID and which to the host. Routers use the subnet mask to determine to which subnetwork a data packet should be sent.

Subnetting a network turns it into a routed network, as an IP router (either a dedicated device or a computer configured to function as a router) will be required for computers on one subnet to communicate with the computers on other subnets.

Subnetting Basics

If you are allocated an entire Class C network, remember that the default subnet mask is 255.255.255.0, or in binary, 11111111.11111111.11111111.00000000.

The eight bits on the right, represented as zeroes, are "yours." You can use all of them for host addresses, *or* you can "loan" some of them to the network ID, to divide your Class C network into two or more smaller networks.

To understand variable-length subnet masks, which indicate that the network is divided into subnets, you must work with the binary or you will probably end up hopelessly confused. Variable-length subnet masks are created by taking bits from the portion of the IP address normally used for the host ID and using it for the network (or subnet) ID. For instance, if you borrow four bits from the host portion of a class C network address, your subnet mask will look like this:

11111111 11111111 11111111 11110000

or, in decimal:

255 255 255 240

This technique allows us to divide our Class C network into 14 usable subnets with 14 hosts on each subnet, using the following formula:

Number of subnets = 2^x *-2*, where x = the number of bits borrowed from the host ID.

Number of hosts = $2^x - 2$, where x = the number of unmasked host ID bits remaining.

Note that we subtract two from the number of subnets, because conventional IP subnetting rules say we can't have a subnet ID that is all 1s or all 0s. Thus we must "throw out" the first and last subnet IDs. We also subtract two from the number of hosts, because two host addresses are always reserved for use as the network ID and the broadcast address.

Determining the Number of Subnets The first step in creating a subnetted network is to decide how many subnets you want to define. Remember that the more bits you "steal" from the host ID portion of the address, the more subnets you can create—*but* this reduces the number of hosts you can have per subnet. See Table 6-2.

TABLE 6-2 Determining How Many Bits Are Needed for a Given Number of Subnets

Subnets	Bits Needed	Mask
2	2	192
6	3	224
14	4	240
30	5	248
62	6	252
126	7	254
254	8	255

Table 6-2 illustrates how many new subnets can be created for each bit that you "steal" from the host ID. Use the formula 2^n–2 (where n is the number of bits that are available to be used for the host ID) to figure out the number of host addresses you will have. Remember that Class A addresses have 24 bits minus the number of bits used for the mask, Class B addresses have 16 bits minus the number used in the mask, and Class C addresses have 8 bits minus the number used in the mask.

Determining the Mask There are three basic steps involved in determining the appropriate subnet mask:

1. Determine the number of subnets you want.
2. Convert the number to binary. Notice how many bits were required.
3. Covert the number of bits required to decimal.

About Supernetting

Supernetting is a way of combining several small networks into a larger one. For example, a company may need a Class B network, but because those have all been assigned, it can't get one. However, Class C networks *are* available, so the company can be assigned multiple Class C networks with contiguous addresses. By "stealing" bits again, but in the opposite direction (sort of like taking from the poor and giving to the rich instead of vice versa), you can use some of the bits that originally represented the network ID to represent host IDs, reducing the number of networks but increasing the number of hosts available per network.

For instance, you can combine two Class C networks using a subnet mask of 255.255.254.0, to provide for 512 hosts on the network instead of the 254 to which a Class C network is traditionally limited. Or, we could combine 1024 Class C networks with a subnet mask of 255.252.0.0 and obtain 262,144 host addresses (although we probably wouldn't want to).

The addresses of the two Class C networks must be contiguous for this to work.

Supernetting often is used in conjunction with an IP addressing scheme called CIDR.

Classless Addressing: CIDR

The use of address classes is the traditional way of working with IP addressing and subnetting. A more recent development is called *Classless InterDomain Routing,* abbreviated as CIDR (and pronounced "cider").

One Internet resource describes CIDR as "subnetting on steroids." CIDR networks are referred to as "slash x" networks, with the "x" representing the number of bits assigned originally as the network ID (before subnetting). Think of this as the number of bits that don't "belong" to you.

With CIDR, the subnet mask actually becomes part of the routing tables. CIDR allows us to break networks into subnets and combine networks into supernets.

A traditional Class C network, you'll recall, contained 8 bits in the IP address that you could use as you wished for host IDs or subnetting, leaving 24 bits that were not under your control. Using CIDR, this would be designated as a "slash 24" network. Thus, a CIDR IP address would look like this: 192.168.1.27/24. Using the same formula, a traditional unsubnetted Class A network would be a /8, and a traditional unsubnetted Class B would be designated as /16. Of course, subnetted networks that would use variable length subnet masks are also designated in the same way. See Table 6-3 for the correlation of the subnet masks to the "slash x" designations.

TABLE 6-3

CIDR Network Designations as They Correlate to Subnet Masks

"Slash x" Designation	Subnet Mask
/8	255.0.0.0
/12	255.240.0.0
/16	255.255.0.0
/20	255.255.240.0
/21	255.255.248.0
/22	255.255.252.0
/23	255.255.254.0
/24	255.255.255.0
/25	255.255.255.128
/26	255.255.255.192
/27	255.255.255.224
/28	255.255.255.248
/29	255.255.255.252
/30	255.255.255.254

CERTIFICATION OBJECTIVE 6.03

Installing, Configuring, Managing, and Monitoring TCP/IP

In order to put all this theory into practice, you must first install (if you haven't already) and configure the TCP/IP protocol on your Windows 2000 computer. Network protocols are installed via the Network and Dial-up Connections window (this is different from NT 4.0, where you could right-click on Network Neighborhood and bring up the Properties sheet to install new protocols). In this case, you will select your local area connection, right-click, and choose Properties.

Installing TCP/IP in Windows 2000

The Properties sheet will list the networking protocols and components that are already installed, and will allow you to install, uninstall, and configure the properties of your networking components (Figure 6-7).

In the following exercise, we will walk through the steps of installing and configuring TCP/IP on a Windows 2000 computer. Note that you must be logged on with administrative privileges to install TCP/IP or other network protocols.

FIGURE 6-7

The Properties sheet for the Local Area Connection

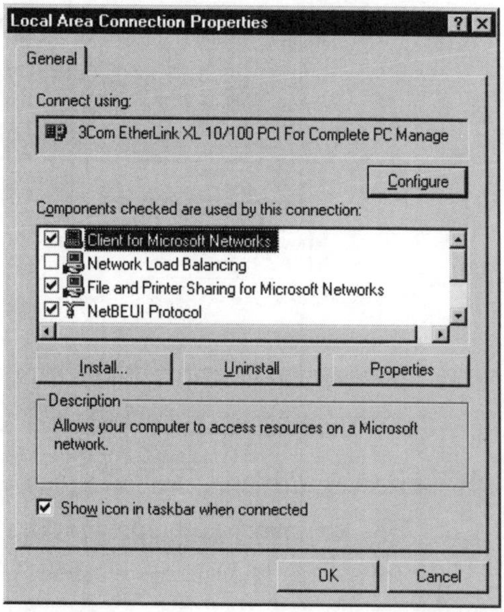

EXERCISE 6-3

Installing TCP/IP in Windows 2000

1. Select Start | Settings | Network and Dial-up Connections.
2. In the windows displaying the contents of the Network and Dial-up Connections folder, right-click on your local area connection and choose Properties.
3. Click Install, and you will see a dialog box as shown in the following illustration.

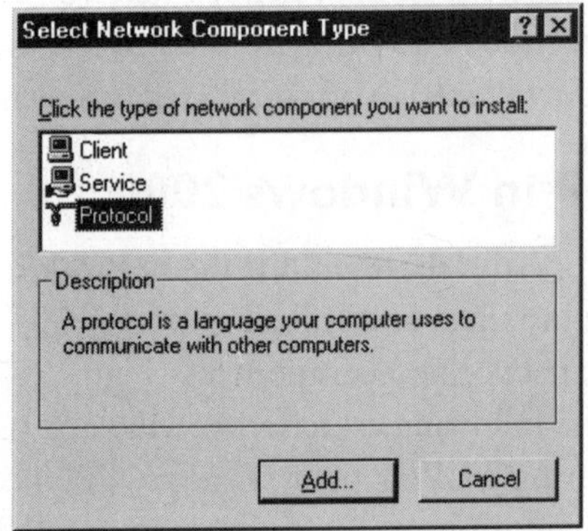

4. A list of available protocols will be shown, as shown next.

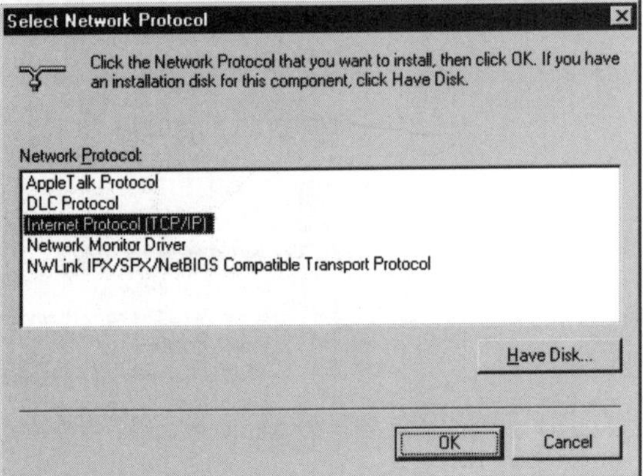

5. Select Internet Protocol (TCP/IP).
6. Click OK. You may be prompted for the Windows 2000 installation CD. The protocol will be installed, and can now be configured.

Configuring TCP/IP in Windows 2000

Once TCP/IP has been installed, you must enter the proper configuration information before the computer can communicate on the network using the TCP/IP protocols. The following exercise will walk you through the process.

EXERCISE 6-4

Configuring TCP/IP

Return to the Properties sheet for the local area connection, and select Internet Protocol (TCP/IP), then double-click or click Properties.

You will then see the TCP/IP Properties dialog box, as shown in the following illustration.

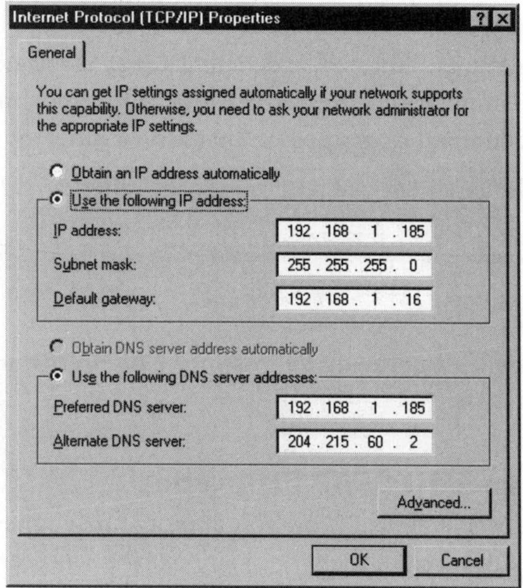

1. If your network has a DHCP server that will be used to obtain an IP address for this computer, select the "Obtain an IP address automatically" radio button. The DHCP server will provide both the IP address and other configuration information, such as the subnet mask and default gateway. If the network does not have a DHCP server, or you will not use the DHCP server to obtain an address automatically, skip to Step 4.

2. Select "Obtain DNS server address automatically" if the DHCP server will provide this information. Otherwise, select "Use the following DNS server address" and enter a preferred DNS server and, if available, an alternate DNS server to perform host-name-to-IP-address resolution.
3. Click OK and skip the remaining steps.
4. If you will not use DHCP to assign an address, select the "Use the following IP address" radio button, then complete the remaining steps.
5. In the IP address field, enter a valid IP address for the subnet on which this computer is located. Remember that the network ID must be the same as other computers on the subnet, and the host ID must be unique to the subnet.
6. Enter the correct subnet mask, based on the address class and whether and how the network is subnetted.
7. If the network is routed (contains more than one subnet), enter a *default gateway* address. The default gateway is the address of the router (or computer functioning as a router) to which messages are sent when they are addressed to destination that is on a different subnet.
8. Enter a preferred and (optionally) alternate DNS server. Click OK.

exam Watch

The default gateway address must be on the same subnet as the computer's IP address.

Advanced TCP/IP Properties

Windows 2000 will allow you to more finely tune your TCP/IP settings. When you click Advanced in the Properties box, you will see the tabbed Advanced TCP/IP Settings Properties sheet shown in Figure 6-8.

The Advanced Settings allow you to further configure the IP settings, DNS, WINS, and other options.

IP Settings Under Advanced IP Settings, you can configure the computer to use more than one IP address or default gateway. Note that you can add, remove, or edit the properties of both in this dialog box.

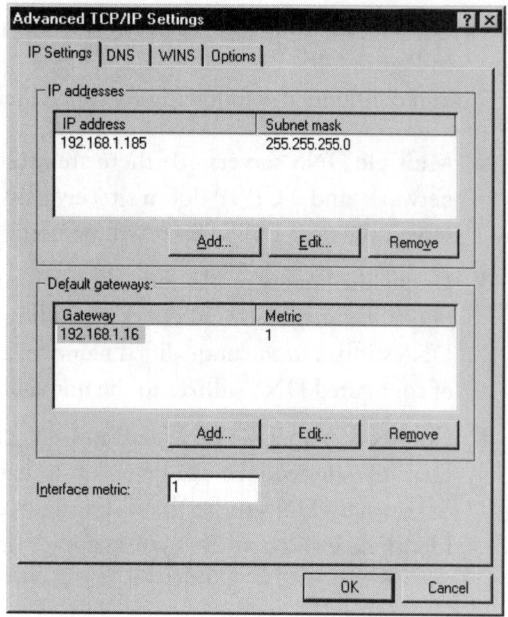

FIGURE 6-8

The Advanced TCP/IP Settings Property sheet

Assigning Multiple IP Addresses You can use multiple IP addresses in various situations, such as public addresses used for the Internet and private addresses used for an internal network, or for multiple logical IP networks on the same physical network segment.

Assigning Multiple Default Gateways Windows 2000 supports a feature called *dead gateway detection,* which is used to detect routers that have gone down. If multiple default gateways are configured, a failing TCP connection will update the IP routing table with the next default gateway in the list. Although you can assign multiple gateways, the second (or subsequent) gateway(s) will be used *only* if the first fails. In other words, more than one default gateway cannot be active simultaneously.

The Interface Metric You can specify a custom metric for the connection by typing a value in this field (the default value is 1). A *metric* is the cost of using a particular route from one destination to another. Generally this will be the number of *hops* to the IP destination. Anything on the local subnet is one hop, and every time a router is crossed, this adds 1 to the *hop count.* The value of this is that it lets Windows 2000 select the route with the lowest metric if there are multiple routes to the same destination.

Advanced DNS Settings The DNS tab on the Advanced Settings sheet is shown in Figure 6-9.

You can configure the following Advanced settings for DNS:

- **Multiple DNS servers** If there are multiple DNS servers configured on the network, and TCP/IP doesn't receive any response from the current DNS server, the next DNS server will be used.
- **Unqualified name resolution** You can configure TCP/IP to resolve unqualified names by either (1) appending the primary and connection- specific DNS suffixes to the unqualified name for DNS queries, or (2) appending a series of configured DNS suffixes to the unqualified name for DNS queries.
- **Connection-specific DNS suffixes** Each connection in the Network and Dial-up Connections can be set up to have its own DNS suffix, along with the primary DNS suffix that is configured for the computer on the Network Identification tab in the System applet (in Control Panel).

FIGURE 6-9

You can fine-tune DNS settings with the Advanced Settings Property sheet

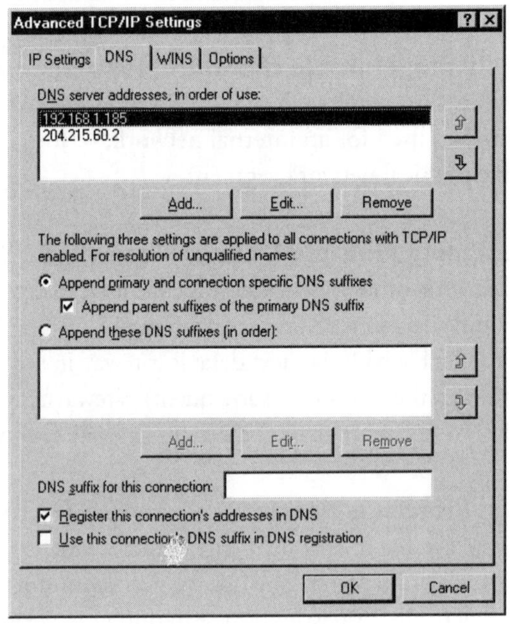

- **DNS dynamic update behavior** If you have DNS servers that support DNS dynamic update (DDNS), you can enable the DNS dynamic update of the domain name and IP addresses for the computer. Windows 2000 DNS Servers support dynamic update.

Advanced WINS Settings You can also make advanced settings to WINS, using the WINS tab shown in Figure 6-10.

Some settings that can be configured include:

- **Multiple WINS servers** If you have multiple WINS on the network, and TCP/IP fails to receive any response from the current WINS server, the next WINS server in the list will be tried.
- **Enabling and disabling the use of the Lmhosts file** You can use this selection to enable or disable the LMHOSTS file. If it is enabled, TCP/IP will use the LMHOSTS file found in the *systemroot*\System32\Drivers\Etc folder during the process of NetBIOS name resolution. The LMHOSTS file is enabled by default.
- **Enabling and disabling the use of NetBIOS over TCP/IP** You can enable or disable the use of NetBIOS over TCP/IP here. When it is disabled, NetBIOS programs cannot run over TCP/IP, which means you may not be able to connect to computers that are running downlevel operating systems such as Windows 95 or NT. NetBIOS over TCP/IP should be disabled only if all computers on your network have been upgraded to Windows 2000 and your network is not using NetBIOS-based applications.

Other Advanced Options The last tab in the Advanced TCP/IP Settings sheet is the Options tab, shown in Figure 6-11.

The two available options allow you to do the following:

- **Enable Internet Protocol security (IPSec)** You can provide for secure end-to-end communication of IP-based traffic on a private network or the Internet by enabling IPSec (it is disabled by default). When IPSec is enabled, you can also specify an IPSec security policy.

FIGURE 6-10

The WINS Advanced Properties tab allows you to fine-tune your WINS settings

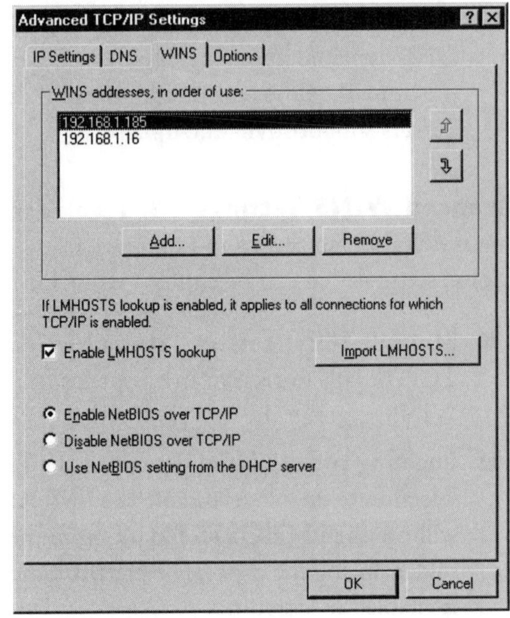

- **Enable TCP/IP filtering** This option allows you to enable filtering of TCP/IP packets. If TCP/IP filtering is enabled, you can specify what types of TCP/IP traffic are processed.

Although the help file indicates that the settings apply to all adapters, the filtering is specific for the adapter for which you are adjusting the filters. TCP/IP filtering specifies the types of incoming traffic destined for this adapter and passed up to the TCP/IP protocol for processing.

To configure TCP/IP filtering, select this check box and specify the types of allowed TCP/IP traffic for all adapters on this computer in terms of IP protocols, TCP ports, and UDP ports. The protocols are determined by the protocol number. You can determine protocol numbers by looking at the contents of the RFC 1700.

Configuring TCP/IP filtering can get a little tricky, because when you first enable it, all traffic is filtered out. You add filters for protocols and ports that will want to

FIGURE 6-11

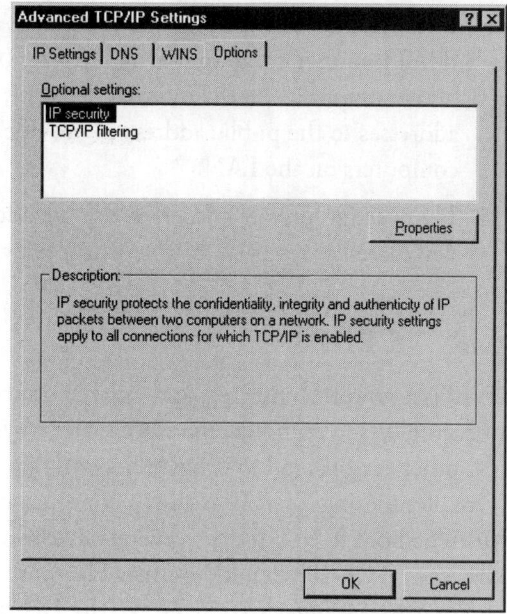

The Options tab allows you to configure IPSec and TCP/IP filtering

allow traffic to pass through. If you run into problems with network communications after enabling the filters, you should first disable TCP/IP filtering and see if that fixes the problem. If so, there is a protocol or port that you must add in order to resume normal network functioning.

TCP/IP Best Practices

Microsoft recommends the following best practices when setting up a TCP/IP-based Windows 2000 network:

- If your local network will be connected to the Internet, either obtain registered public IP addresses for all computers that will access the Internet and use an IP router to send traffic to the public network, or establish the

Internet connection using one computer, install *Network Address Translation* (NAT) on that computer, assign private (nonregistered) IP addresses to the other computers on the internal network, and let NAT translate the private addresses to the public address to provide access to the Internet for all the computers on the LAN.

- If you assign private addresses, use the address ranges in each class that are designated as reserved for that purpose by IANA.

Troubleshooting TCP/IP

TCP/IP is a powerful, flexible, and reliable protocol suite. Generally it works well, but because it is so complex, there are many ways in which it can be misconfigured or, for other reasons, fail to provide network communications.

Troubleshooting TCP/IP is thus a complicated topic, and an entire book could be written about it (and in fact, several have been). This chapter can only touch on the basics of TCP/IP troubleshooting. For more detailed information, see our book *Troubleshooting Windows 2000 TCP/IP* by Debra Littlejohn Shinder and Thomas W. Shinder, published by Syngress Media.

Windows 2000 TCP/IP comes with several useful utilities that can provide you with valuable troubleshooting information and help you to diagnose the problem when your TCP/IP network experiences connectivity problems. These include the command-line utilities IPCONFIG, PING/PATHPING, TRACERT, and NETSTAT/NBTSTAT, as well as Windows 2000's protocol analysis tool, Network Monitor.

Using TCP/IP Utilities

The command-line utilities included with Windows 2000 are useful in identifying and resolving TCP/IP problems.

IPCONFIG This utility displays current TCP/IP configuration values, and can be used to manually release and renew (with the /release and /renew switches, respectively) a TCP/IP configuration lease assigned by a DHCP server. It can also be used to reset DNS name registrations with the /registerdns switch. Typing **IPCONFIG** provides basic configuration information: IP address, subnet mask, and default gateway. Typing **IPCONFIG /ALL** provides more detailed information, as shown in Figure 6-12.

FIGURE 6-12

Using the /all switch with the IPCONFIG command provides more detailed information

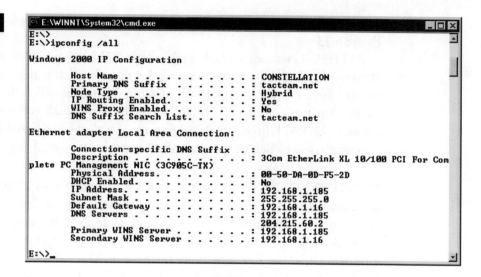

```
E:\WINNT\System32\cmd.exe
E:\>
E:\>ipconfig /all

Windows 2000 IP Configuration

        Host Name . . . . . . . . . . . . : CONSTELLATION
        Primary DNS Suffix  . . . . . . . : tacteam.net
        Node Type . . . . . . . . . . . . : Hybrid
        IP Routing Enabled. . . . . . . . : Yes
        WINS Proxy Enabled. . . . . . . . : No
        DNS Suffix Search List. . . . . . : tacteam.net

Ethernet adapter Local Area Connection:

        Connection-specific DNS Suffix  . :
        Description . . . . . . . . . . . : 3Com EtherLink XL 10/100 PCI For Com
plete PC Management NIC (3C905C-TX)
        Physical Address. . . . . . . . . : 00-50-DA-0D-F5-2D
        DHCP Enabled. . . . . . . . . . . : No
        IP Address. . . . . . . . . . . . : 192.168.1.185
        Subnet Mask . . . . . . . . . . . : 255.255.255.0
        Default Gateway . . . . . . . . . : 192.168.1.16
        DNS Servers . . . . . . . . . . . : 192.168.1.185
                                            204.215.60.2
        Primary WINS Server . . . . . . . : 192.168.1.185
        Secondary WINS Server . . . . . . : 192.168.1.16

E:\>_
```

As you can see, the /all switch provides much more information, including the host name, DNS suffix, node type being used, whether IP routing and WINS proxy are enabled, as well as the MAC (physical) address of the network card and the addresses of assigned DNS and WINS servers.

PING and PATHPING The PING command is used to verify whether TCP/IP is configured correctly and to test connectivity to other host systems. It is often used as the first step in diagnosing network problems. Microsoft recommends that PING be used, in the following order, to isolate a connectivity problem on the TCP/IP network:

1. First, ping the loopback address (127.0.0.1) to verify that TCP/IP is installed and configured correctly on the local computer.
2. Next, try pinging the IP address of the local computer itself, to verify that it was added to the network correctly.
3. Then ping the IP address of the default gateway (sometimes called the "near side of the router") to verify that the default gateway is functioning and that you can communicate with a local host on the local network.
4. Finally, ping the IP address of a remote host (called the "far side of the router") to verify that packets are being forwarded and you can communicate through the router.

If the TCP/IP connection is working, PING will return a response as shown in Figure 6-13.

PATHPING was not available in Windows NT, but is provided in Windows 2000 to allow you to trace the route a packet takes to a destination and display information on packet losses for each router in the path as well as the links between routers. You can also use PATHPING to troubleshoot *Quality of Service* (QoS) connectivity. PATHPING combines features of both the PING and the TRACERT commands, and includes additional information that neither of those tools provides.

TRACERT TRACER traces the network route taken by an IP datagram to its destination. It does this by sending Internet Control Message Protocol (ICMP) echo packets with varying Time-To-Live (TTL) values to the destination address. Each router along the path must decrease the TTL on a packet by at least 1 before forwarding it, so the TTL is basically a hop count. When the TTL on a packet reaches 0, the router is supposed to send back an *ICMP Time Exceeded* message to the source system. TRACERT determines the route by sending the first echo packet with a TTL of 1 and then incrementing the TTL by 1 on each additional transmission until a response is received or the maximum TTL count occurs. Examining the ICMP Time Exceeded messages sent back by intermediate routers allows the route to be determined.

The results of a TRACERT command are shown in Figure 6-14.

FIGURE 6-13

PING returns a response indicating TCP/IP connectivity is good

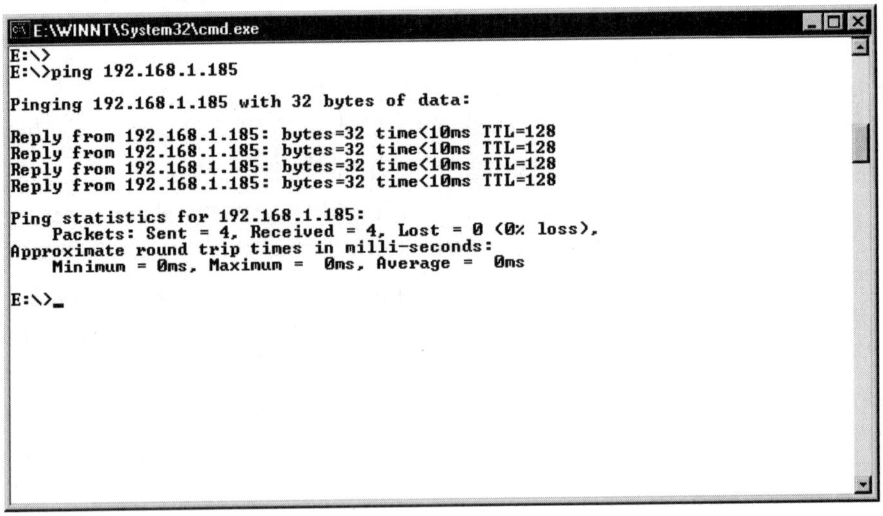

```
E:\WINNT\System32\cmd.exe
E:\>
E:\>ping 192.168.1.185

Pinging 192.168.1.185 with 32 bytes of data:

Reply from 192.168.1.185: bytes=32 time<10ms TTL=128
Reply from 192.168.1.185: bytes=32 time<10ms TTL=128
Reply from 192.168.1.185: bytes=32 time<10ms TTL=128
Reply from 192.168.1.185: bytes=32 time<10ms TTL=128

Ping statistics for 192.168.1.185:
    Packets: Sent = 4, Received = 4, Lost = 0 (0% loss),
Approximate round trip times in milli-seconds:
    Minimum = 0ms, Maximum =  0ms, Average =  0ms

E:\>_
```

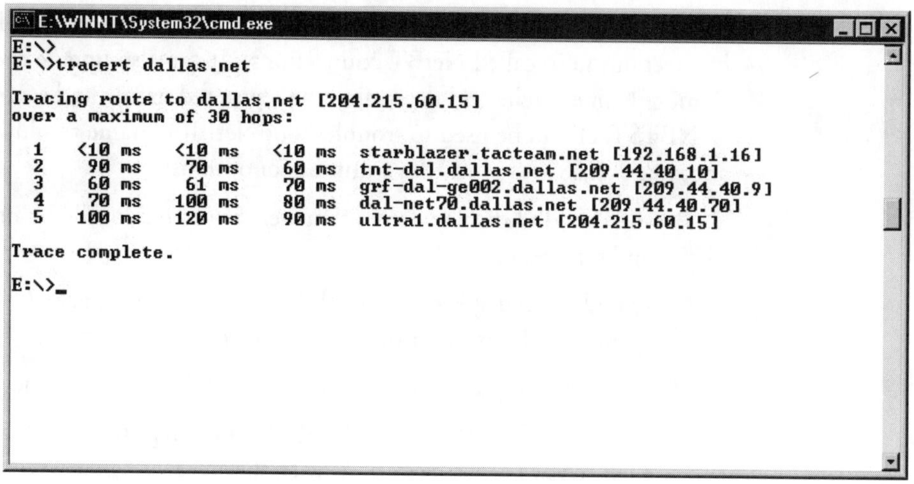

FIGURE 6-14

TRACERT returns information about each router passed through to reach the destination address

```
E:\WINNT\System32\cmd.exe
E:\>
E:\>tracert dallas.net

Tracing route to dallas.net [204.215.60.15]
over a maximum of 30 hops:

  1    <10 ms   <10 ms   <10 ms  starblazer.tacteam.net [192.168.1.16]
  2     90 ms    70 ms    60 ms  tnt-dal.dallas.net [209.44.40.10]
  3     60 ms    61 ms    70 ms  grf-dal-ge002.dallas.net [209.44.40.9]
  4     70 ms   100 ms    80 ms  dal-net70.dallas.net [209.44.40.70]
  5    100 ms   120 ms    90 ms  ultra1.dallas.net [204.215.60.15]

Trace complete.

E:\>_
```

You can ping or trace by either the IP address or by the fully qualified domain name. If you are able to get a response using the IP address but not by using the host name, you should suspect a problem with the name resolution server or the computer's DNS configuration.

NETSTAT and NBTSTAT NETSTAT displays protocol statistics and information on current TCP/IP connections. There are several options available for the NETSTAT command, listed as follows.

SCENARIO & SOLUTION

What does the –a option in NETSTAT do?	Causes all connections and listening ports to be displayed (server connections are not normally shown).
What is the –e option used for?	To display Ethernet statistics.
What is the purpose of the –n option?	Used to display addresses and port numbers in numerical form instead of by name.
How is the –s option used?	To display statistics on a per-protocol basis (type **netstat –p <protocol type>**).
Why would you use the –r option?	To display the routing table.

NBTSTAT is used to check the state of current NetBIOS over TCP/IP connections (also called NetBT connections). It can also update the NetBIOS Remote Name Cache and determine the registered names and scope IDs.

NBTSTAT can be used to troubleshoot NetBIOS name resolution problems and, like NETSTAT, includes a number of options:

- **-n** Used to display names that were registered locally by programs and services
- **-c** Used to display the NetBIOS Remote Name Cache (a mapping of names to addresses for other computers)
- **-R** Used to purge the name cache and reload it (from the LMHOSTS file)
- **-RR** Used to release the NetBIOS names registered with the WINS server, then renew their registrations with the server
- **-a** Used in conjunction with a computer name (in the format *nbtstat –a <computername>)* to return the NetBIOS name table for the computer named, as well as the MAC address of the network adapter
- **-s** Used to list current NetBIOS sessions and the status of each, with statistical information as shown in Figure 6-15

NETDIAG The Resource Kit for Windows 2000 Professional includes the NETDIAG utility. This is a command-line diagnostic tool that helps isolate networking and connectivity problems. It does this by performing a series of tests designed to determine the state of the network client software, and ascertain whether it is functional. This tool does not require that parameters or switches be specified,

FIGURE 6-15

The **NBTSTAT –S** command lists current NetBIOS sessions, status, and statistics

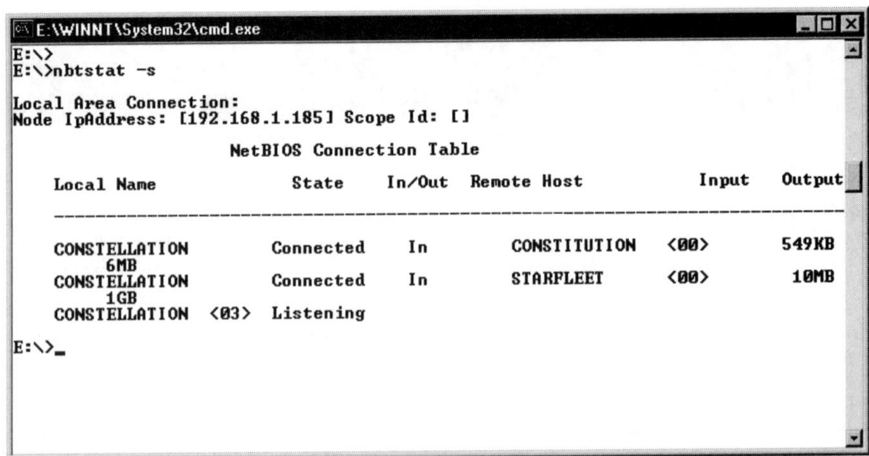

which means support personnel and network administrators can focus on analyzing the output, rather than training users on how to use the tool.

The resource kits for both Windows 2000 Professional and Server contain many useful tools for isolating, diagnosing, and sometimes even fixing problems. It is an excellent idea to familiarize yourself with the tools included in the resource kits, as well as those that ship with the product. Third parties also provide a variety of troubleshooting utilities for Windows 2000.

Managing and Monitoring Network Traffic

Because TCP/IP is such a widely used set of protocols, there are numerous hardware and software tools available for monitoring and managing traffic on a TCP/IP network. You can practice preventative maintenance, establish baselines, or troubleshoot existing problems. One of the most popular types of tools is called a *protocol analyzer*. This is usually a software program that allows you to copy the individual packets and analyze their structure. The process of copying frames for review and analysis is called *capturing*.

Windows 2000 Server includes a "lite" version of the protocol monitor that comes with Systems Management Server (SMS), Network Monitor. This tool can be used to capture and display the frames or packets that a Windows 2000 Server receives from a LAN. You can use Network Monitor to detect and troubleshoot many networking problems.

Installing the Windows 2000 Network Monitor

The Network Monitor tool can be installed on Windows 2000 Server from the Add/Remove Programs applet in Control Panel. Open the applet and click on Add/Remove Windows Components, select Management and Monitoring Tools, and then click Details. Select the Network Monitor check box. You may be prompted to insert your Windows 2000 installation CD.

After installation is complete, the Network Monitor will appear in the Administrative Tools submenu of the Programs menu.

Using the Windows 2000 Network Monitor

The version of Network Monitor included in Windows 2000 has some limitations. It cannot run in what is referred to as *promiscuous mode*. This is a state in which the network card can listen to all the traffic on the network, not just that which is sent from or received by the computer running the Network Monitor software. The more sophisticated version of Network Monitor that comes with SMS is capable of

promiscuous mode. Even so, there is a great deal of information that can be collected with Windows 2000's Network Monitor utility. Figure 6-16 shows the Network Monitor interface, with information from a capture.

As you can see, there is a great deal of statistical information available, including such useful values as the percentage of network utilization during the capture, the number of frames and bytes transferred, as well as how many frames were dropped.

After you have captured the data, you can view it by selecting Display Captured Data from the Capture menu. You will then see detailed information for each frame (packet) as shown in Figure 6-17.

Network Monitor Best Practices

Microsoft recommends that you run Network Monitor at off-peak (low-usage) times or only for short periods of time, in order to decrease the detrimental impact on system performance that can be caused by Network Monitor.

You can filter the data captured, as well as the data displayed. A *capture filter* works somewhat like a database query; you can use it to specify the types of network information you want to monitor. For example, you can capture packets based on the protocol or based on the addresses of two computers whose interactions you wish to monitor. When a capture filter is applied, all packets are examined and compared to the filter's parameters; those that do not fulfill the filter requirements

FIGURE 6-16

The Windows 2000 Network Monitor interface

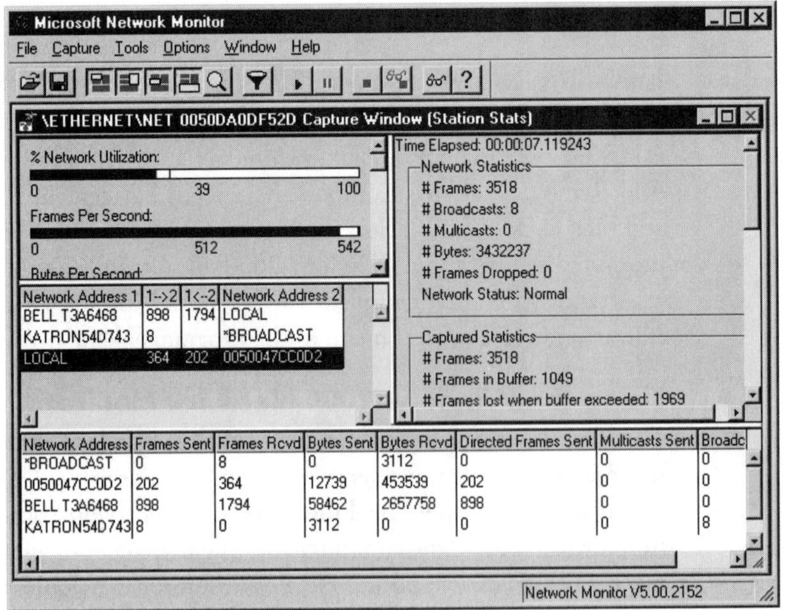

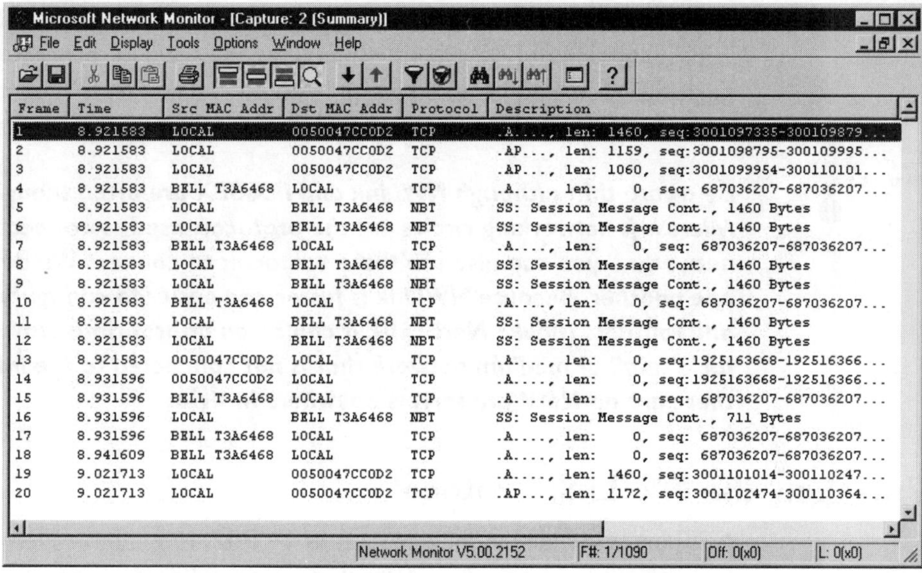

FIGURE 6-17 Capture detail summary displays information about each data frame

are dropped. This can be a processor-intensive activity during periods of moderate or high network utilization when the network card is placed in promiscuous mode.

Display filters work on data that has already been captured. They do not affect the contents of the Network Monitor capture buffer. You can use a display filter to determine which frames you want to display. The frames can be filtered by source or destination address, protocols used to send it, or the properties and values it contains.

You can also use *capture triggers* to specify a set of conditions that will cause ("trigger") an event to occur in a Network Monitor capture filter. Triggers allow Network Monitor to respond to events on your network. For example, you can set triggers so that if Network Monitor detects a particular set of circumstances on the network, it will start an executable file.

CERTIFICATION OBJECTIVE 6.04

Installing and Configuring NWLink

Despite Microsoft's emphasis on TCP/IP for Windows 2000 networks, there are situations in which other LAN protocols are required or desirable. For instance, connectivity to NetWare servers (prior to version 5) requires that the connecting computer(s) be running an IPX/SPX protocol stack. NWLink is Microsoft's implementation of IPX/SPX (the Internetwork Packet Exchange/Sequenced Packet Exchange protocols). You can install NWLink on Windows 2000 machines to allow them to access NetWare servers.

Be aware that although NWLink and IPX/SPX are often thought of in Microsoft networking circles as "the protocols used to connect to NetWare networks," you can also use these protocols to connect Windows machines to one another. Because NWLink is faster and easier to configure than TCP/IP and routable (unlike NetBEUI), it can be an appropriate LAN protocol choice for a small or medium network that is not connected to the Internet, even if there are no NetWare servers anywhere in sight.

Installing the NWLink Protocol

NWLink is installed in the same way as TCP/IP, through the Network and Dial-up Connections properties box. Note that you must be logged on with administrative privileges to install NWLink or other network protocols.

When you install the NWLink protocols, they will be installed on all your network connections. However, you can change this. After the installation is completed, if you do not want to use NWLink on a particular connection, you can right-click that connection, click Properties and uncheck the NWLink IPX/SPX/NetBIOS Compatible Transport Protocol check box on either the General or Networking tab.

Configuring NWLink

There is less configuration information required to set up NWLink than is necessary for TCP/IP, but there are still a few pieces of information you will need to have on hand. The configuration box asks you for a network number; if you are uncertain of this number, the default value of 00000000 will usually work.

Another setting that can be configured is the *frame type.* You can use automatic frame type detection, however. In most cases, this is preferred.

You can use the **IPXROUTE CONFIG** command to get information about the internal network number being used by the routers on the network, as well as the frame type being used by the servers.

EXERCISE 6-5

Installing and Configuring NWLink in Windows 2000

To install NWLink on your Windows 2000 computer, follow these steps:

1. Select Start | Settings | Network and Dial-up Connections.
2. Right-click on the icon for the local area connection, and click Properties.
3. On the General tab, click Install.
4. In the Select Network Component Type dialog box, click Protocol, and then click Add.
5. In the Select Network Protocol dialog box, click NWLink IPX/SPX/NetBIOS Compatible Transport Protocol, and then click OK.

To configure NWLink, follow these steps:

1. In the Local Area Connection properties box, select NWLink IPX/SPX NetBIOS Compatible Transport Protocol, and click Properties. You will see the General Properties sheet displayed, as shown in the following illustration.

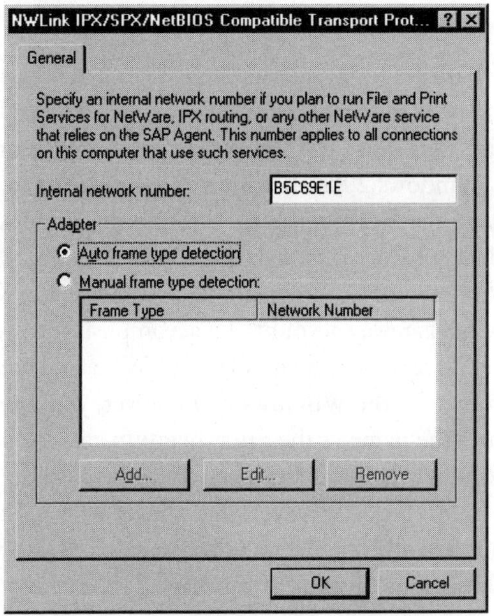

2. Enter the internal network number used on your network, or use the default of 00000000.
3. Select "Auto frame type detection" unless there is a compelling reason for manual frame type specification (this may be necessary if you have servers using different frame types on the same network).
4. If you choose "Manual frame type detection," you will need to specify a network number and select from the supported frame types shown in the following illustration.

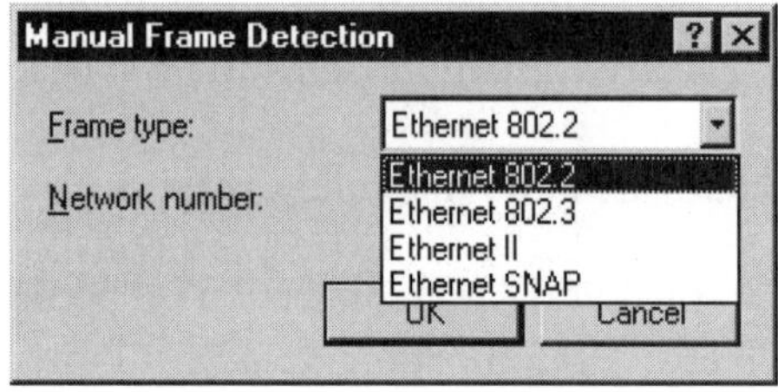

In order for Windows 2000 clients to access a NetWare server directly, you will also need to install *Client Services for NetWare* (CSNW) on the client computer(s). The users must also have valid user accounts on the NetWare server to log on.

Windows 2000 machines that are clients to a Windows 2000 Server can also access the NetWare server through the Windows 2000 Server, without having extra client software installed, if you install *Gateway Services for NetWare* (GSNW) on the Windows 2000 Server and configure the NetWare server to allow access through a special gateway account. To accomplish this, you must create a group on the NetWare server called NTGATEWAY and create a NetWare user account in that group. On the Windows 2000 Server, you must then enable the gateway service and enter the name of the gateway group and the password for the gateway account. All Windows 2000 clients can now connect to the NetWare server through this same account. Note, however, that all will be using the same user account for access, and thus will all have the same permissions. If you wish for a user to have different permissions, that user must have a valid individual user account on the NetWare server through which he or she can access the server's resources and client software installed on the client machine.

Protocol Binding Order

Network protocols are bound to network services installed on a particular client or server. Multiple protocols can be bound to multiple network services. For example, you can bind NetBEUI, TCP/IP, and NWLink to the Microsoft network client.

When a client attempts to establish a session with a server, it will request to use the protocol on the top of its binding order for the particular service. If the service is the Microsoft Network Client, then the protocol binding order for that list is processed. Just as was the case with Windows NT 4.0, the client determines the preferred protocol.

For example, the Microsoft network client service on the client has NetBEUI and TCP/IP installed, with NetBEUI on the top of the binding order. The destination server also has NetBEUI and TCP/IP installed, but has TCP/IP on top of the binding order. Since the caller determines the binding order, they will negotiate using TCP/IP first, because that is on top of the client's binding order.

exam Watch

To change the binding order you must open the Network and Dial-up Connections folder first. After opening the folder, click on the Advanced menu and click Advanced Settings. On the Adapters and Bindings tab, you will be able to use the* UP *and* DOWN *arrows to change the binding order.

CERTIFICATION SUMMARY

This chapter has covered a wide scope of topics pertaining to the networking protocols used for communication by the Windows 2000 operating systems, particularly the members of the TCP/IP protocol suite. In fact, we started the chapter with an introduction to the Windows 2000 implementation of TCP/IP and a brief history of the protocols, discussed the advantages and disadvantages of TCP/IP and where it fits into the popular networking models, the Open Systems Interconnection (OSI) model and the Department of Defense (DoD) model.

TCP/IP is the protocol stack of the global Internet, so we discussed the growth of the Internet and how TCP/IP played a part in that growth. We talked about IP addressing, including subnetting and supernetting, and we walked through an exercise on how to install and configure the TCP/IP protocols in Windows 2000.

Then we briefly discussed troubleshooting TCP/IP connectivity problems, and some of the tools and utilities included in Windows 2000 or available elsewhere that make troubleshooting easier. We examined the Network Monitor protocol analysis tool that Windows 2000 includes, and learned how to install it and how to use it to capture packets on the network.

Finally, we turned our attention to another popular protocol stack, IPX/SPX, which is used in many NetWare networks and is implemented in Windows 2000 as NWLink. We completed an exercise in installing and configuring NWLink, and we discussed the services—Client Services for NetWare and Gateway Services for NetWare—that are used, along with the NWLink protocols, to allow Windows 2000 machines to connect to and access the resources of NetWare servers.

TWO-MINUTE DRILL

Windows 2000 TCP/IP

- ❑ TCP/IP is the default network transport protocol in Windows 2000, and is required for connectivity to the Internet.
- ❑ The TCP/IP protocol suite is relatively slow and difficult to configure, but has the advantages over NWLink and NetBEUI of a flexible, scalable addressing scheme, compatibility with many platforms and operating systems, and routability.
- ❑ The TCP/IP suite consists of many different protocols that operate at different layers of the networking model, including IP, ICMP and IGMP, ARP/RARP, TCP, UDP, FTP, Telnet, SMTP, SNMP, and others.

IP Addressing

- ❑ IP addresses are 32-bit binary numbers (often expressed as their dotted decimal equivalent), in which one portion represents the network ID and the other portion represents the host ID.
- ❑ The subnet mask is a 32-bit binary number used to indicate which bits in the IP address represent the network and which represent the host.
- ❑ IP networks were traditionally divided into three classes: Class A for large networks, Class B for medium-sized networks, and Class C for small networks.
- ❑ Classless InterDomain Routing (CIDR) is a newer method of allocating addresses to networks that does not use the class system, but instead appends a "slash x" number to the end of the IP address that indicates how many bits are used for the network ID.
- ❑ Subnetting is a method of "stealing" bits from the designated host ID and adding them to the network ID in order to create more networks, but with fewer hosts each.
- ❑ Supernetting is a method of combining two or more smaller networks into one larger network, by "stealing" bits from the network ID portion of the IP address and adding them to the host portion, to create a network that allows for more hosts.

Installing, Configuring, and Monitoring TCP/IP

- ❑ Utilities included with TCP/IP that are useful for troubleshooting include IPCONFIG, PING and PATHPING, TRACERT, NETSTAT and NBTSTAT, and a resource kit utility called NETDIAG.
- ❑ Network Monitor is a software protocol analyzer included with Windows 2000 Server that allows you to capture and analyze packets sent to or from the Windows 2000 machine on which the software is installed.
- ❑ Windows 2000 supports assigning multiple IP addresses, multiple gateways, and setting the interface metric under Advanced TCP/IP settings.
- ❑ Disabling of NetBIOS over TCP/IP (NetBT) is done via the Advanced WINS configuration options, and should only be done if your network does not have any non-Windows 2000 machines and does not use NetBIOS applications.
- ❑ TCP/IP filtering allows you to specify what types of TCP/IP traffic are processed.

Installing and Configuring NWLink

- ❑ NWLink is Microsoft's implementation of the IPX/SPX protocol stack used by Novell for its NetWare networks. It can be installed, along with NetWare client or gateway software, to provide access by Windows 2000 machines to a NetWare server, or it can be used as the LAN protocol for Microsoft networks that don't need to connect to the Internet.
- ❑ Connectivity to NetWare servers (prior to version 5) requires that the connecting computer(s) be running an IPX/SPX protocol stack.
- ❑ Configuration settings for NWLink include the internal and external network numbers and the frame type.
- ❑ The protocol binding order on the client machine determines which LAN protocol will be used for the connection if multiple protocols are installed and configured.

SELF TEST

The following questions will help you measure your understanding of the material presented in this chapter. Read all of the choices carefully, as there may be more than one correct answer. Choose all correct answers for each question.

Windows 2000 TCP/IP

1. Which of the following is an advantage of the TCP/IP protocol stack over other common LAN protocols such as NetBEUI and IPX/SPX (NWLink)?

A. TCP/IP is faster than other LAN protocols.

B. TCP/IP is more scalable than other LAN protocols.

C. TCP/IP is easier to configure than other LAN protocols.

D. TCP/IP has lower overhead than other LAN protocols.

2. Your network is experiencing problems that seem to be related to IP addressing and routing. At which layer of the OSI networking model should you start the diagnostic procedure?

A. The Physical Layer

B. The Transport Layer

C. The Application Layer

D. The Network Layer

3. You have an application that needs to send messages quickly, in real time. Speed of transfer is more important in this case than reliability. Which Transport layer protocol will this application most likely use to communicate?

A. UDP

B. TCP

C. IP

D. SNMP

4. You do not know the IP address of your computer. You look at the TCP/IP properties settings for your local area connection, but discover that your computer is obtaining an IP address from a DHCP server. How can you find out what IP address has been assigned by the DHCP server?

A. Click Advanced on the TCP/IP properties sheet.

B. Use the IPCONFIG command-line utility.

C. Right-click on Network Neighborhood and select "IP address" from the right context menu.

D. Reboot the computer and enter Setup to locate your IP address in the CMOS settings.

IP Addressing

5. You have a Class C network, which you wish to divide into six usable subnets with an equal number of hosts on each. Which of the following default subnet masks would you use to identify the network and host portions of the IP address?

A. 255.255.255.252

B. 255.255.255.248

C. 255.255.255.224

D. 255.255.255.128

6. Which of the following "slash x" designations would represent a network with a subnet mask of 255.255.252.0 in CIDR terminology?

A. /12

B. /16

C. /18

D. /22

7. Using traditional classful addressing, which of the following would be an IP address of a computer on a Class B network?

A. 192.168.2.34

B. 14.244.22.9

C. 185.21.1.1

D. 224.32.128.4

8. Which of the following defines the cost of using a particular route from a source to a destination?

A. The default route

B. The metric

C. The address class

D. The TTL

9. You wish to configure your TCP/IP computer so there will be fault tolerance if the assigned default gateway (router) should fail. How can you accomplish this?

A. Configure a secondary gateway in the TCP/IP properties sheet.

B. Configure a static route in the routing table.

C. Configure multiple default gateways in the Advanced TCP/IP properties.

D. There is no way to provide fault tolerance in case of failure of a default gateway.

Installing, Configuring, and Monitoring TCP/IP

10. You need to provide end-to-end security for your TCP/IP communications. How can you accomplish this in Windows 2000, using no third-party utilities?

A. Enable IP forwarding.

B. Enable IP filtering.

C. Enable RIP.

D. Enable IPSec.

11. You have a small private unsubnetted, unrouted Class C network. One of your users is unable to connect to the other computers on the network. You run IPCONFIG and it shows the following: IP address 192.168.1.2, subnet mask 255.0.0.0, default gateway (none). Which, if any, of these settings is your first suspect as to the source of the trouble?

A. Invalid IP address.

B. Incorrect subnet mask.

C. Missing default gateway.

D. None of these is the source of the problem.

12. You have a medium size Class B network that is connected to the Internet via a routed connection. One of the computers on the network is unable to communicate with computers on its subnet or with the Internet. You run IPCONFIG and it displays the following: IP address – 192.168.255.255, subnet mask 255.255.0.0, default gateway – 161.23.2.1. Which, if any, of these settings do you first suspect as the source of the problem?

A. Invalid IP address.

B. Incorrect subnet mask.

C. Incorrect default gateway.

D. None of these is the source of the problem.

13. You need to know what node type is being used by your computer. Which of the following commands could you use to display that information?

A. IPCONFIG

B. NETSTAT -R

C. NBTSTAT

D. IPCONFIG /ALL

Installing and Configuring NWLink

14. You have a small private network running Windows 2000 and Windows 9*x* computers. You wish to have routing capability, but you do not need to connect to the Internet. You need a protocol stack that is fast and easy to configure. Which of the following would best fit that requirement?

A. NWLink

B. NetBEUI

C. TCP/IP

D. DLC

15. At which layer of the OSI networking model does IPX operate?

A. Physical

B. Data Link

C. Network

D. Presentation

16. Which of the following information do you supply when configuring the NWLink protocol? (Select all that apply.)

A. DNS server

B. External network number

C. Internal network number

D. Frame type

17. You have a Windows 2000 client computer that has NWLink, TCP/IP, and NetBEUI installed, with the binding order set in that order. This machine is connecting to a Windows 2000 Server that has TCP/IP and NWLink installed, bound in that order. Which protocol will be used to communicate between the machines?

A. TCP/IP

B. NWLink

C. NetBEUI

D. None of the above

LAB QUESTION

You have two laptop computers belonging to two employees in the Accounting department, Fred and Joe. Both are configured with both TCP/IP and NWLink. Fred complains that when he connects to the network, he is able to communicate with Joe using NWLink, but not TCP/IP. He is also unable to communicate with other computers using TCP/IP on the network. Joe tells you the same thing happened to him earlier in the week, although today he is able to communicate with other computers on the network using TCP/IP. Which of the following do you first suspect as the source of the problem?

A. Fred's and Joe's computers have the same NetBIOS name.

B. Fred's and Joe's computers have the same subnet mask.

C. Fred's and Joe's computers have the same default gateway.

D. Fred's and Joe's computers have the same IP address.

SELF TEST ANSWERS

Windows 2000 TCP/IP

1. ☑ **B.** TCP/IP is more scalable than other LAN protocols.
   ☒ **A, C,** and **D** are incorrect, because although TCP/IP is more flexible, routable, and scalable and thus appropriate for large networks, and although it is the protocol required to connect to the global Internet, it is slower than the other two common LAN protocols, is more difficult to configure, and has higher overhead.

2. ☑ **D.** The Network Layer of the OSI model (which corresponds to the Internetwork layer of the DoD model) is responsible for logical addressing and routing tasks.
   ☒ **A, B,** and **C** are incorrect because the Physical layer handles hardware, media and signaling issues; the Transport layer is responsible for reliability and acknowledgments; and the Application layer interfaces between the networking components and the user applications.

3. ☑ **A.** The User Datagram Protocol, UDP, is the Transport layer protocol used for sending data when speed is more important than reliability.
   ☒ **B** is incorrect because TCP is a slower, but more reliable Transport layer protocol. **C** is incorrect because IP is a Network layer protocol, responsible for routing and logical addressing. **D** is incorrect because SNMP is an Application layer protocol, used for monitoring and managing TCP/IP networks.

4. ☑ **B.** Type IPCONFIG at the command line and your IP address, subnet mask and default gateway will be displayed.
   ☒ **A** is incorrect because the IP address will not be indicated in the Advanced properties. **C** is incorrect because there is no Network Neighborhood in Windows 2000, and if you right-click on its replacement (My Network Places), there is no "IP address" selection in the right context menu. **D** is incorrect because the IP address is assigned in the operating system software and is not displayed in the CMOS settings for the computer.

IP Addressing

5. ☑ **C.** In order to create six subnets, you will need to "borrow" three bits from the host ID to create the subnet ID. This makes your last octet 11100000. If you convert the binary number to decimal by adding the values of the bits that are "on," 128+64+32, you end up with 224.
   ☒ **A, B,** and **D** are all incorrect.

6. ☑ **D.** The subnet mask 255.255.252.0 signifies that 22 bits are used for the network ID, and the remaining 10 are used for the host ID. In CIDR terms, this is indicated as a "slash 22" network, and would be expressed with "/22" following the IP address.
☒ **A**, **B**, and **C** are incorrect.

7. ☑ **C.** Network class is indicated by the high order, or leftmost bits. Class A networks always start with 0 as the high order bit, Class B with 10, and Class C with 110. This means when we convert to binary, Class A addresses have 1–126 as their first octet, Class B addresses have 128–191 as the first octet, and Class C addresses have 192–223 as the first octet. Only C, which begins with 185, falls into the Class B range.
☒ **A**, **B**, and **D** are incorrect. **A** would be a member of a Class C network, **B** would be a member of a Class A network, and **D** would be a multicast address.

8. ☑ **B.** The metric is the term used to indicate the cost of a route.
☒ **A** is incorrect; the default route is the route to be used when there is no route to a particular network specified in the routing table. **C** is incorrect because the address class indicates the size of the network, not the cost of a route. **D** is incorrect because the TTL is the Time to Live, used to indicate how long a receiving computer or router should hold or use the packet before it expires.

9. ☑ **C.** If you configure multiple default gateways, the first will always be used *unless* it fails, in which case the next on the list will be tried.
☒ **A** is incorrect because there is no option to configure a "secondary" gateway. **B** is incorrect because configuring a static route will not provide fault tolerance for a gateway failure. **D** is incorrect because there is a way to provide fault tolerance in case of a gateway failure.

Installing, Configuring, and Monitoring TCP/IP

10. ☑ **D.** IPSecurity (IPSec) can be used to provide for secure end-to-end communications.
☒ **A** is incorrect because IP forwarding is used to route messages from one subnet to another but does not provide security. **B** is incorrect because IP filtering will allow you to block certain messages but does not provide end-to-end security for your communications. **C** is incorrect because RIP (Routing Information Protocols) allows for dynamic routing, but does not address end-to-end security.

11. ☑ **B.** 255.0.0.0 is the default subnet mask for a Class A network. Because the network is not subnetted, the default Class C mask 255.255.255.0 should be used.
☒ **A** is incorrect because this IP address is a valid private class C address. **C** is incorrect because no default gateway is needed for an unsubnetted, unrouted network. **D** is incorrect because **B** is most likely the problem. You should check the other computers on the network to verify that they are using the standard Class C default mask.

12. ☑ **A.** The IP address has several problems: First, the 192.168.x.x address range is reserved for private addresses and cannot be used on the Internet. Second, the 255 host address is reserved for broadcast messages.
☒ **B** is incorrect because 255.255.0.0 is the correct default subnet mask for a Class B network. **C** is incorrect because this is a valid default gateway address for a Class B network (although if the IP address were valid, you would want to check the router and ensure this is the correct gateway address). **D** is incorrect because **A** is a likely cause of the problem.

13. ☑ **D.** IPCONFIG with the /all switch will display information that includes host name, DNS suffix, node type, MAC address, and DNS and WINS server addresses.
☒ **A** is incorrect because IPCONFIG alone only displays IP address, subnet mask, and default gateway information. **B** and **C** are incorrect because the NETSTAT and NBTSTAT commands do not display node type information.

Installing and Configuring NWLink

14. ☑ **A.** Although usually used for connecting to NetWare networks, NWLink can be used as the LAN protocol for a Windows 2000 network if Internet connection is not required (you must have TCP/IP for Internet connection).
☒ **B**, **C**, and **D** are incorrect. NWLink is faster and easier to configure than TCP/IP, and unlike NetBEUI, can be routed. DLC is used to communicate with mainframes and some network printers and is not routable.

15. ☑ **C.** The IPX protocol, like IP, operates at the Network layer to provide routing and addressing.
☒ **A**, **B**, and **D** are incorrect because IPX does not operate at these layers.

16. ☑ **B, C, D.** Configuration for the NWLink protocol requires an internal and external network number, and a frame type designation. However, in most cases the defaults will work. Frame type must be configured if there is more than one frame type being used on the network.
☒ **A** is incorrect because the NWLink protocol does not include configuration of a DNS server.

17. ☑ **B.** Because NWLink is at the top of the binding order on the client machine, it will first try to connect using NWLink if that protocol is installed on the server. Because NWLink is installed, the connection will be made with that protocol stack. To ensure that the two connect using TCP/IP, you should move TCP/IP to the top of the binding order on the client machine.
☒ **A** is incorrect because although TCP/IP is installed on both machines, it is the binding order on the client machine that determines the connection. **C** is incorrect because NetBEUI is not installed on the server, so the two machines cannot connect using that protocol. **D** is incorrect because **B** is correct.

LAB ANSWER

☑ **D.** The most likely cause of the problem is an IP address conflict. When Joe connects to the network first, he is able to use the IP address for TCP/IP communications, but when Fred then attempts to connect, he is unable to use TCP/IP because the IP address configured in his TCP/IP properties is still in use. If both had the same NetBIOS name, the second user to attempt to connect would receive an error message that the name already exists. Fred's and Joe's computers *should* have the same subnet mask and default gateway if they are on the same subnet; this would not hinder communications. To solve the problem, you should change the IP address on one of the machines to one not in use. A better solution might be to configure all the machines to use DHCP if there is a DHCP server on the network. This reduces the likelihood of duplicate addresses.

7

Configuring and Troubleshooting IPSec

CERTIFICATION OBJECTIVES

7.01 Overview of IP Security

7.02 Enabling and Configuring IPSec

7.03 Managing, Monitoring, and Troubleshooting IPSec

✓ Two-Minute Drill

Q&A Self Test

"Security is the chief enemy of mortals." —William Shakespeare

"Shun security." —Thales of Miletos

"One has to abandon altogether the search for security."—Morris L. West

As you read the preceding quotations, you realized that Morris, Thales, and old Bill had one thing in common: none of them were network administrators. For those who are responsible for the integrity of millions of bytes of data that travel over our networks, much of it sensitive information, security is a real and growing concern. We would be inclined to agree with E. R. Stettinius who said, *"happiness has many roots, but none more important than security."*

Computer and network security is the hot topic of the new decade, and the topic of objectives for several of the Windows 2000 certification exams, including 70-216, "Implementing and Administering a Windows 2000 Network Infrastructure." Despite the fact that there is an entire elective exam devoted to designing a security plan for your network (70-220), security issues are incorporated into *all* of the Windows 2000 exams to one degree or another. This should be an indication of how much importance Microsoft—and the industry—places on the subject.

Computer security is a term that encompasses many different issues, and in designing their new operating system, Microsoft has attempted to cover as many of the bases as possible. Improved authentication technologies, using Kerberos, certificates, Secure Sockets Layer (SSL), and—for compatibility with previous Microsoft operating systems—NTLM, provide for positive confirmation of the user's identity at logon. The new Encrypting File System (EFS) provides the means to encode data stored on disk so that it is not readable to unauthorized users.

But what about the safety of that data as it travels over the network? That's where IP Security (IPSec) comes in. Most network traffic today uses the TCP/IP protocol stack, including that which is sent over the Internet. IPSec allows you to encrypt data at the Network layer of the popular OSI network communications model to protect it from malicious or accidental access by persons for whom it was not destined.

In this chapter, we will look at what IPSec is, how it works, how it is enabled and configured in Windows 2000, and methods for managing, monitoring, and troubleshooting IP Security on your network.

CERTIFICATION OBJECTIVE 7.01

Overview of IP Security

IP Security, as its name implies, operates at the same layer as the Internet Protocol (IP), and this allows for a high level of protection with little overhead, and with no requirement to change your existing applications.

This is important because, unlike other security methods that operate at higher layers (for example, SSL), IPSec can provide security to applications that do not have to be aware of its existence (SSL works only with application programs that were designed to use SSL). And, unlike security methods that operate at lower layers of the OSI model, such as link layer encryption, IPSec is able to protect data from host to host, even when routed across the Internet or another internetwork. IPSec protects not only the IP protocol, but also those protocols that operate at higher levels in the TCP/IP protocol suite, such as TCP, UDP, and ICMP.

IPSec is a set of protocols that were developed to provide for highly reliable, standardized, cryptographic-based security for data communications over IPv4 and IPv6 (sometimes referred to as IPng).

Elements of IP Security include:

- The Authentication Header (AH) and Encapsulating Security Payload (ESP) protocols, sometimes referred to as "traffic security" protocols
- Cryptographic key management protocols
- Security Policy Database (SPD), which defines the security services
- Security Associations (SA), which are relationships between two or more systems that define how the systems will use the security services

IPSec supports two security association modes: tunnel mode and transport mode. A primary use of the IP Security protocol is to provide more protection for virtual private network (VPN) connections. IPSec works in conjunction with the Layer 2 Tunneling Protocol (L2TP)—which is included with Windows 2000 along with the more traditional Point-to-Point Tunneling Protocol (PPTP)—to accomplish this.

FROM THE CLASSROOM

Understanding IPSec

You are probably familiar with the way the TCP/IP protocols, as members of a protocol suite, work together to provide network communications. It may help you to understand IPSec if you realize that it, too, is made up of a suite of protocols that work together to provide security for IP communications. Components of IP Security include AH (Authentication Header), ESP (Encapsulating Security Payload), IKE (Internet Key Exchange), ISAKMP (Internet Security Association and Key Management Protocol), Oakley, and transforms (which define the algorithm, key sizes and how they are derived, and the transformation process used to secure the data). A true understanding of IPSec requires that you understand how all these protocols interact with one another and with the other protocols in the TCP/IP suite.

—Debra Littlejohn Shinder, MCSE, MCP+I, MCT

IPSec can be used to provide security to workgroups, client/server LANs, and remote access connections.

IPSec Terminology

One of the biggest barriers to understanding IPSec and some of the other security features built into Windows 2000 is the avalanche of new terms and unfamiliar acronyms with which you will be bombarded when you start to study in this area.

Before we discuss encryption, IPSec standards, and how they are implemented in Windows 2000, we will attempt to untangle some of this bewildering jungle of words and abbreviations you may not have previously encountered, even as an experienced NT administrator.

Glance through the following list of quick definitions and familiarize yourself with the terminology before you tackle the rest of the chapter:

- **Algorithm** A procedure or formula used to solve a problem.

- **Asymmetric algorithm** A cryptographic algorithm that utilizes a different key for encrypting data from the one used to decrypt the data. Also see *symmetric algorithm.*
- **Authentication** The validation of the identity claimed by an end user or a device.
- **Certificate** A message that contains the digital signature of a trusted third party, called a *certificate authority*, which ensures that a specific public key belongs to a specific user or device.
- **Certificate Authority** A third-party entity that is trusted to sign digital certificates verifying the identity of others.
- **Cipher** The process that turns readable text data into *ciphertext,* which is encrypted data that must be *deciphered* before it is readable.
- **Cryptography** The science of encrypting and decrypting data. The science (and art) of breaking cryptographic code is called *cryptanalysis.*
- **Diffie-Hellman key exchange** Provides a method for two parties to construct a *shared secret* (key) that is known only to the two of them, even though they are communicating via an insecure channel.
- **Digital signature** A string of bits that is added to a message (an encrypted hash), which provides for data integrity and authentication.
- **ESP (Encapsulating Security Payload)** A header used by IPSec when encrypting the contents of a packet.
- **Hash function** A mathematical calculation that produces a fixed-length string of bits, which cannot be reverse-engineered to produce the original.
- **ISAKMP (Internet Security Association and Key Management Protocol)** An IPSec protocol required as part of the IPSec implementation, which provides a framework for Internet key management.
- **MAC (Message Authentication Code)** A cryptographically generated fixed-length code associated with a message in order to ensure the authenticity of the message (a digital signature is a *public key MAC).*
- **Private key** A digital code used to decrypt data, which is kept secret and works in conjunction with a published *public key.*

- **Public key** A digital code used to encrypt or decrypt data, which is published and made available to the public, used in conjunction with a secret *private key.*
- **Public Key Infrastructure (PKI)** A key and certificate management system that is trusted.
- **Secret key** Also called a *shared secret,* a digital code shared between two parties and used for both encrypting and decrypting data.
- **Symmetric algorithm** A cryptographic algorithm that uses the same key to both encrypt and decrypt, also called a *secret key* algorithm. See *asymmetric algorithm.*

on the Job

IPSec should be implemented as one part of an overall security policy. Never rely on just one line of defense to protect your network, and remember that IP Security offers protection of data only in very specific circumstances—when it is transmitted over the network using the Internet Protocol. Other considerations in designing a strong network security plan include password security, encryption of data on the hard disk—which can be done using EFS in Windows 2000—and physical security of servers, workstations, cable/media, and connectivity devices.

Basics of Encryption

IPSec uses *encryption algorithms* to protect data. What is encryption, and how did modern encryption technologies develop? It might be useful to take a brief look at the history of cryptography and various encryption methods of the past and present.

A (Very) Brief History of Cryptography

The science of cryptography is an old one; some sources estimate that it goes back at least 4000 years, to the cryptic hieroglyphics used to decorate the tombs of ancient Egyptian rulers and ancient Chinese ideographs. It is perhaps human nature to want to keep secrets—what child hasn't yearned for some form of the infamous secret decoder ring, or an "invisible ink" that can only be seen by the intended recipient, or experimented with speaking "pig latin" so the uninitiated could not (at least in theory) understand him? And for better or worse, the innate desire to uncover the secrets of others also seems to be inborn.

The Origins of Encryption In early cultures, most information was imparted through the spoken word, in a face-to-face transaction. You had to be on the lookout for eavesdroppers, but you could be fairly sure to whom you were speaking. However, as societies developed sophisticated means of communication, more and more information was transferred by nonverbal methods. Written communications were more vulnerable to interception by unauthorized third parties, so ways had to be devised to disguise the meaning of confidential messages.

The first encryption methods were crude and, although often effective at protecting written communications from the prying eyes of casual observers, could be "cracked" relatively easily by knowledgeable—or merely persistent—persons.

Simple Encoding Methods One of the simplest "codes," usually discovered and delighted in by elementary school children, involves transposing letters of the alphabet and/or replacing letters with numbers. Under the former method, for instance, each letter of the alphabet would be "moved forward" by five letters, so that an "f" in the encoded message, for instance, represented an "a" in the real message. It's easy to construct a "key" to decipher this simple form of encryption, as seen in Table 7-1.

This simple key makes it easy to create a message that says:

gzd utyfytjs

that makes no sense to someone who doesn't have the "key." To another who is working from the same table, however, it's obvious that I'm saying:

buy potatoes

The latter method is just as simple—a number is assigned to each letter of the alphabet; for example, we could start numbering with "a" as "8." In this case, our "buy potatoes" message would be encoded as 9-28-32 23-22-27-8-27-22-12-26. Again, without the key, it's meaningless, and with the key, it's a simple matter of substitution.

TABLE 7-1 A Simple Form of Encryption

a	b	c	d	e	f	g	h	i	j	k	l	m	n	o	p	q	r	s	t	u	v	w	x	y	z
f	g	h	i	j	k	l	m	n	o	p	q	r	s	t	u	v	w	x	y	z	a	b	c	d	e

Added Complexity Increases Security The problem with these "secret codes" is obvious: Someone who has enough patience can eventually hit on the correct substitution process (or *algorithm*), and if our low-tech hacker ever got his or her hot little hands on a decrypted message, the entire key would be readily reconstructed, and all future communications that used it could be deciphered.

This led to the creation of more complex encryption methods. For instance, in order to decode a numerical message, you might follow this procedure:

1. Subtract 7 from the encoded number.
2. Go to the page of the Bible represented by the result.
3. Add 3 to the original number.
4. Count the words on the page and go to the one represented by the result in step 3.
5. The last letter in that word represents the character in the actual message that corresponds to the original number.

The key is knowing the precise steps of the formula. So long as this is kept secret and known only to the sender and the recipient, there would be a certain amount of security provided by this encoding method. Of course, it is important that both parties' versions of the Bible match exactly; even if both use the King James version, the method falls apart if the pages are not printed precisely alike.

Modern Encryption Methods

All of the early encryption methods described so far can be referred to as *secret key* technologies. The same key (substitution formula or set of steps) is used to encrypt and then decrypt the information. When the same key is used to both encrypt and decrypt the data, it is referred to as a *symmetric key* encryption method.

Secret Key Encryption Secret key encryption methods are still used today. The widely used Data Encryption Standard (DES) uses secret key algorthms. Standard DES operates on 64-bit "blocks" of data, and uses a series of complex steps (even more complex than our Bible-assisted method) to transform the original input bits to encoded output bits.

In secret key encryption, the key is called a *shared secret* because two (or more) people know the key. The problem with *this* comes if you want to send encoded messages to more than one person. If you used one of the keys discussed earlier to send secret messages to Jim, and then you wish to encode a message to send to Jack, you'll probably need to come up with a different key. If you use the same one you know and are used to, Jim will be able to read the messages that pass between you and Jack, *and* Jack will be able to read all the past and future messages sent to Jim. Having to remember and use all these different keys could become a real pain.

Enter a new type of encryption technology: *asymmetric encryption.* This is popularly used in *public key encryption.*

Public Key Encryption Doesn't *sound* very secure, does it? If the key is public, won't any and everyone be able to decrypt your data? Certainly "secret key technology" sounds much more secure than "public key technology." However, this is one of those instances where names can be deceiving. Actually public key, or *asymmetric* encryption methods, are more secure than secret key methods. This is because public key technologies actually involve the use of not one, but *two* keys. The "public" key is only half of the equation. A better term for public key encryption would be "public/private key encryption."

Three methods of Public Key Encryption are as follows:

- **Confidential Data Exchange** Think of the method used to secure safety deposit boxes at banks. When you rent a box, you have a key to it—but your key alone won't unlock it. The bank officer also has a key, but again, that key by itself isn't of much value. When *both* keys are used, however, the authorized person can access the box. Likewise, with public key encryption technologies, it takes two keys to tango. One is the public key, which is made available to all those who want to send you an encrypted message. They can all use that public key to encrypt their messages, but they *can't* use it to decrypt them—only your private key, which you keep secret, can do that. This is called a *confidential data exchange.*
- **Authenticated Data Exchange** The only problem with the preceding scenario is that there is no assurance that the person who used your public key to encrypt and send you a message is really whomever he or she claims to be. How can we ensure that?

  Well, let's look at using the public and private keys in a slightly different way: What if the sender encrypted the message using his or her *private* key, and then you decrypted it using his or her public key? What would this accomplish? We get the same confidentiality of the data as with the first method, but since presumably only the sender has the private key, we can be confident of his identity. Now we have an *authenticated data exchange.*

exam watch

A property of a security system that ensures the identity of the sender and prevents that sender from later being able to deny having sent the message is called nonrepudiation.

- **Double the Protection** If we want the benefits of both methods, we can combine them and double the protection. That is, the sender would encrypt the message with the recipient's public key, then sign it again with the sender's private key.

Key Generation Of course, the mechanisms that are used to generate these keys is much more complex than our five-step process discussed earlier.

One method that is used to create secret session keys that allow the communicating parties to share a secret key known only to them is called the *Diffie-Hellman algorithm.*

Public/private *key pairs* are generated by complicated algorithms such as the RSA algorithm (named after its creators, Ron Rivest, Adi Shamir, and Leonard Adelman).

on the job

Best practice is for the private key to be generated by the person identified by the key, and for it to never leave the possession of that person. Public keys should be distributed by trusted third parties (certificate authorities) to ensure that they belong to the claimed user if authentication— rather than just confidentiality—is required.

Data Encryption Standard (DES) The most commonly used encryption algorithm used with IPSec is the Data Encryption Standard (DES) algorithm. DES is the current U.S. government standard for encryption. The DES algorithm is an example of a symmetric encryption algorithm. A symmetric encryption algorithm has each side of the communication employ the same "secret key" for encryption and decryption. This is in contrast to a public key infrastructure, where two different keys are used. The public key approach is referred to as "asymmetric" encryption.

DES works on 64-bit "blocks" of data. The DES algorithm converts 64 input bits from the original data into 64 encrypted output bits. While DES starts with 64-bit keys, only 56 bits are actually used in the encryption process. The remaining 8 bits are used for parity.

A stronger version of DES is also available for use in Windows 2000 IPSec. This is called 3DES, or *Triple DES*. Triple DES processes each block three times, which increases the degree of complexity over that found in DES.

Cipher Block Chaining (CBC) Because the blocks of data are encrypted in 64-bit chunks, there must be a way to "chain" these blocks together. The chaining algorithm will define how the combination of the unencrypted text, the secret key, and the encrypted text (also known as *ciphertext*) will be combined to send to the destination host.

DES can be combined with Cipher Block Chaining (CBC) to prevent identical messages from looking the same. This DES-CBC algorithm will make each ciphertext message appear different by using a different "initialization vector" (IV). The IV is a random block of encrypted data that begins each chain. In this fashion, we are able to make each message's ciphertext appear different, even if we were to send the exact same message a hundred times.

IPSec Standards

In the past decade, communications over the Internet and other large networks that use the TCP/IP protocols has increased exponentially. As more data flows across these public and corporate networks, it has become more important to devise methods of providing security for information that is intended to remain private.

IPSec is actually a collection of open standards, developed by the Internet Engineering Task Force (IETF), for providing secure communications over IP networks. The IETF is a huge international community of network designers, operators, vendors, and researchers, which was established by the Internet Architecture Board (IAB) and is organized into *working groups* devoted to various Internet-related topics.

The IPSec working group issues RFCs (Requests for Comments), which are documents that propose and establish standards for protocol implementation. A collection of their working papers on IPSec can be found at

www.ietf.org/ids.by.wg/ipsec.html

RFCs

Numerous RFCs have been published addressing various aspects of IP Security. All published RFCs can be accessed via the Web site of the RFC Editor, who is funded by the Internet Society (ISOC) and is responsible for their official publication. The following Scenario & Solutions defines some of the more important IPSec-related RFCs.

IPSec Resources

The IETF produces the IPSec Working Group news on the Web, accessible at

www.cs.arizona.edu/xkernel/www/ipsec/ipsec.html.

For general discussions about IP Security, you can also join the IPSec mailing list. To subscribe, send e-mail to ipsec-request@lists.tislabs.com. Or check the IPSec archives at ftp://ftp.tis.com/pub/lists/ipsec or ftp.ans.net/pub/archive/ipsec.

IPSec Architecture

IPSec defines a network security architecture that allows secure networking for the enterprise, allowing you to secure packets at the network layer. By performing its services at the network layer, IPSec secures information in a manner that is transparent to the user and to the protocols that lie above the transport layer. IPSec provides "layer 3" protection.

The IPSec security architecture provides an "end to end" security model. This means that only the "endpoints" of a communication need to be IPSec aware. In other words, computers and devices that serve as intermediaries of message transfer do not need to be IPSec enabled. This allows the administrator of a Windows 2000 network to implement IPSec for end-to-end security over diverse network infrastructures, including the

SCENARIO & SOLUTION	
Where can I find the IP Security Document Roadmap?	RFC 2411
Where can I find standards relating to the IP Authentication Header (AH)?	RFC 2402
Where can I find information about the Encapsulating Security Payload (ESP)?	RFC 2496
Where can I find an RFC relating to the Internet Security Association and Key Management Protocol (ISAKMP)?	RFC 2407
Which RFC addresses the Internet Key Exchange (IKE)?	RFC 2409

Internet. Network devices that are in between the sending and receiving computers, such as bridges, switches, and routers, can be oblivious to IPSec.

This end-to-end capability can be extended to different communication scenarios, including:

- Client to client
- Gateway to gateway (also called "tunneling")

Transport vs. Tunnel Mode

IPSec can operate in two different modes, depending upon the scope of the secure communication. These are known as *transport mode* and *tunnel mode.*

Transport Mode When IPSec is used to protect communications between two clients (for example, two computers on the same LAN), the machines can utilize IPSec in what is known as *transport mode.* In this example, the endpoints of the secure communication are the source machine and the destination host.

exam Watch

In transport mode, both clients must use TCP/IP as their network protocol.

Tunnel Mode The second communication mode is a gateway-to-gateway solution. IPSec protects information that travels through a transit network (such as the Internet). Packets are protected as they leave the exit gateway, and then decrypted or authenticated at the destination network's gateway.

When gateways represent the endpoints of the secure communication, IPSec is operating in *tunnel mode.* A tunnel is created between the gateways, and client-to-client communications are encapsulated in the tunnel protocol headers.

Tunnels can be created using IPSec as the tunneling protocol, or you can combine IPSec with L2TP (Layer Two Tunneling Protocol) to establish a virtual private networking (VPN) connection. In this case, it is L2TP rather than IPSec that creates the tunnel.

exam Watch

In tunnel mode, the host and destination computers do not employ IPSec, and can use any LAN protocol supported by IPSec (IPX/SPX, AppleTalk, NetBEUI, TCP/IP).

IPSec Protocols

The IPSec protocols used by Windows 2000 to provide security for IP packets consist of the following:

- Authentication Header (AH)
- Encapsulating Security Payload (ESP)

We will examine each of these protocols and how they work.

AH

The Authentication Header ensures data integrity and authentication. The AH does not encrypt data, and therefore provides no confidentiality, but does protect the data from modification. When the AH protocol is applied in transport mode, the Authentication Header is inserted between the original IP header and the TCP or UDP header, as depicted in Figure 7-1.

Note that the entire datagram is authenticated using AH.

The Authentication Header signs the entire packet, using HMAC (Hash-based Message Authentication Code) algorithms. This ensures that the source and destination addresses in the IP header, as well as the data, cannot be changed without invalidating the packet.

Microsoft refers to AH as a "medium security method," and recommends it when your network requires standard—but not high—levels of security.

FIGURE 7-1

Datagram after the application of AH in transport mode

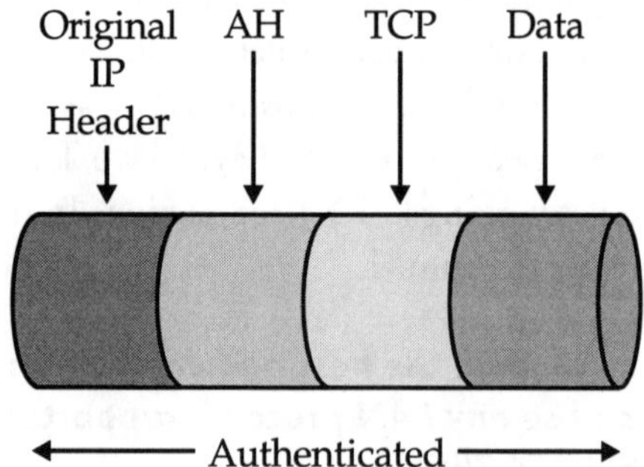

ESP

The Encapsulating Security Payload (ESP) protocol, like AH, provides authentication, integrity, and anti-replay to an IP datagram—but it does more; it also provides *confidentiality.* Note that, although authentication services are available with ESP, the original IP header (prior to application of the ESP header) is not authenticated by ESP.

The ESP header, in transport mode, is placed between the original header and the TCP header, as seen in Figure 7-2.

As you can see, only the TCP header, data, and ESP trailer are encrypted. Unlike AH, ESP normally does not sign the entire packet (the exception is in tunneling mode). This means there is no protection provided for the IP header.

If authentication of the original IP header is required, you can combine and use AH and ESP together as shown in Figure 7-2.

Microsoft recommends that ESP be used in high security environments, where encryption of the data is required. To use ESP and AH together, to provide security for both the data and the IP header (and the addressing information it contains),

FIGURE 7-2

The ESP header in transport mode, used in conjunction with AH

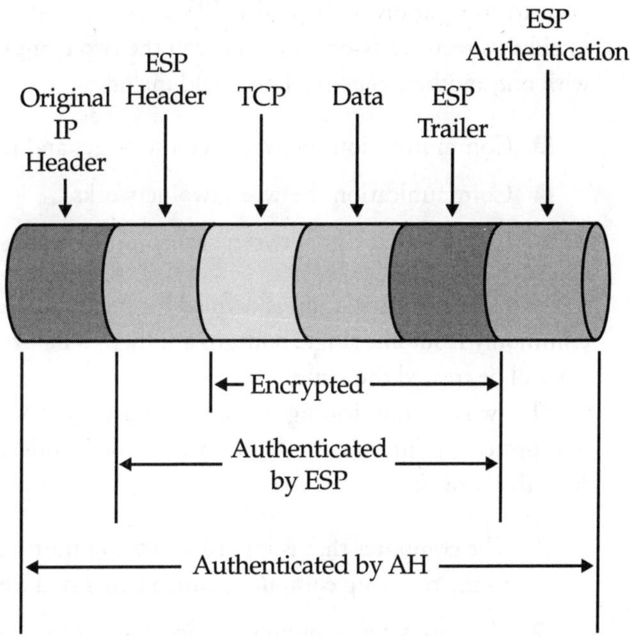

you must create a *custom security method* in Windows 2000's security method configuration.

See the section on enabling and configuring IPSec later in this chapter for information on how to select AH, ESP, or a combination (customized) as your security method.

Security Negotiation

Security negotiation ensures that the authentication and encryption methods used by the sending and receiving computers are the same. If they are not, reliable communication cannot take place. To provide for compatibility between the security systems being used, there must be protocols in place to negotiate the security methods. IPSec uses ISAKMP and IKE (discussed later in this chapter) to define the way in which *security associations* are negotiated. Let's look at what security associations are, and how they work.

Security Associations

Security associations (SAs) define IPSec secured links. One of the tasks of IPSec is to establish a security association between the two computers desiring to communicate with one another securely. This could include:

- Communications between remote nodes and the network
- Communications between two networks
- Communications between two computers on a local area network (LAN)

Each security association is defined for one unidirectional flow of data, most commonly from one single point to another. Whatever traffic flows over a specific SA will be treated the same.

The two communicating computers must agree on the method for exchanging and protecting information before secure communications can take place. Here is how that works:

1. The computer that is initiating the communication will transmit an *offer list* to the receiving computer, which contains a list of potential levels of security.
2. The receiving computer can accept the offer, or reject it. If the latter, it transmits a message back to the sender that notifies the sender that no offer was accepted.

Security Association Types One of two types of Security Associations can be established:

- A *soft SA* is established if the active security policies are set to permit unsecured communications with computers that are not IPSec-capable.
- A *hard SA* is established if the active policies are compatible. A hard SA is a secured security association.

Number of Security Associations A separate SA is established for outgoing and incoming messages, necessitating at least two security associations for each IPSec connection. In addition, a single SA can be applied to either AH or ESP, but not both. If both are used, then two more security associations are created.

Security Parameters Index A Security Parameters Index (SPI) tracks each SA. The SPI uniquely identifies each SA as separate and distinct from any other IPSec connections current on a particular machine. The index itself is derived from the destination host's IP address and a randomly assigned number. When a computer communicates with another computer via IPSec, it checks its database for an applicable SA. It then applies the appropriate algorithms, protocols, and keys, and inserts the SPI into the IPSec header.

Key Exchange

The first phase of security negotiation is *key exchange.* IPSec standards support either manual or automated key exchange, but large-scale implementations necessitate automated key exchange.

Automated Key Management uses a combination of the Internet Security Association Key Management Protocol and the Oakley Protocol (ISAKMP/Oakley). This combination of protocols is often referred to collectively as the Internet Key Exchange (IKE). The IKE is responsible for exchange of "key material" (groups of numbers that will form the basis of new key), session keys, SA negotiation, and authentication of peers participating in an IPSec interaction. During this exchange, the Oakley protocol protects the identities of the negotiating parties.

There are two phases involved in the key exchange:

- Establishment of the ISAKMP SA
- Establishment of the IPSec SA

Establishing the ISAKMP Security Association The steps involved in establishing the ISAKMP SA are:

1. The computers establish a common encryption algorithm (either DES or 3DES).
2. A common hash algorithm is agreed upon (either MD5 or SHA1).
3. An authentication method is established. (Depending on policy, this can be Kerberos, public-key encryption, or prearranged shared secret).
4. A Diffie-Hellman group is agreed upon in order to allow the Oakley protocol to manage the key exchange process.

FROM THE CLASSROOM

Diffie-Hellman Groups

Diffie-Hellman provides a mechanism for two parties to agree on a shared "master" key, which can be used immediately or can provide keying material for subsequent session key generation. Oakley determines key refresh and regeneration parameters. Diffie-Hellman groups are used to determine the length of the base prime numbers that are used during the key exchange. Group 1 (low strength) is not as strong as Group 2 (medium). Group 1 provides 768 bits of key material, and Group 2 provides 1024 bits. A larger group results in a key that is more difficult to break. The group cannot be switched during the negotiation, and if the groups specified on the two communicating computers don't match, the negotiation will fail. The drawback of larger key lengths is that more processor time is required to generate the keys, which increases the overhead of the encryption process.

—Debra Littlejohn Shinder, MCSE, MCP+I, MCT

Establishing the IPSec Security Association In the second phase of key exchange, security associations are negotiated for security protocols (AH, ESP, or both).

After a secure channel has been established by the creation of the ISAKMP SA, the IPSec SA(s) will be established. The process is similar, except that a separate IPSec SA is created for each protocol (AH or ESP) and for each direction of traffic (inbound and outbound). Each IPSec SA must establish the following:

- Encryption algorithm
- Hash algorithm
- Authentication method.

Each IPSec SA uses a different shared key than that negotiated during the ISAKMP SA. Depending on how policy is configured, the IPSec SA works by repeating the Diffie-Hellman exchange, or by reusing "key material" derived from the original ISAKMP SA. All data transferred between the two computers will take place in the context of the IPSec SA.

The following scenario and solution answers some common questions about key exchange in Windows 2000.

SCENARIO & SOLUTION	
What happens when a key's lifetime reaches the lifetime setting?	The associated security association is renegotiated and a new key is generated.
Why might you consider specifying a key session limit?	Rekeying (generating keys) off the same master key repeatedly could compromise the key.
What is the effect of enabling Perfect Forward Secrecy for the master key?	Any session limit that has been set will be ignored, and key generation will be forced each time so that a key cannot be used to generate more keys. This has the same effect as setting a session key limit of one.

Using Perfect Forward Secrecy (PFS) for the master key can slow performance of the domain controllers, as it requires re-authentication and thus results in additional overhead.

Data Protection

IPSec uses authentication to ensure that data is not changed, and encryption to protect the confidentiality of the data. The Windows 2000 implementation of IPSec can use DES (Data Encryption Standard), or it can use a strong encryption algorithm such as 3DES, which provides a higher level of security than DES because it uses a longer key.

The High Encryption Pack needs to be installed to use 3DES, and if the computer does not have the High Encryption Pack installed and receives a policy with 3DES settings, it will revert to DES.

DES Standard DES is 64-bit encryption. The key used by the algorithm is 64 bits long, and 56 bits are selected randomly, while 8 bits are for parity. (There is also a 40-bit version of DES, but it basically exists only to comply with U.S. export regulations).

3DES This stronger version of DES can be supported by IPSec policies, but the Windows 2000 High Encryption Pack (HEP) must be installed. The HEP provides for 128-bit encryption, and affects not only IPSec, but file encryption on the disk, NDIS connections, SSL, and Terminal services. The High Encryption Pack can be downloaded from the Microsoft Web site (before installing, note that there is no provision for uninstalling the HEP).

Use, and especially export, of strong encryption is subject to federal regulations. For more information, see the Department of Commerce Commercial Encryption Export Controls Web site at:

www.bxa.doc.gov/encryption

How IPSec Works

Let's look now at some of the important components of IP Security and how it actually works. In this section, we'll discuss IPSec authentication, the IPSec driver, the IPSec filter list, and the ISAKMP service in Windows 2000.

IPSec Authentication

Authentication methods are the means used by IPSec to define the way in which identities are verified. In order for two computers to communicate securely using IPSec, they must have at least one authentication method in common. A computer can have multiple authentication methods, and configuring multiple methods will increase the chances that, in attempting communication with another computer, there will be a common method. We will explore how IPSec rules affect authentication methods a little later in this chapter.

The authentication methods that can be used by IPSec include:

- Kerberos v5
- Public Key certificates
- Preshared keys

We will briefly discuss the characteristics of each.

Kerberos v5 Version 5 of the Kerberos security protocol is the default authentication method in Windows 2000. Client computers that belong to a trusted domain can use the Kerberos authentication method, which is based on a *shared secret,* as long as they are running the Kerberos v5 protocol. They do not have to be Windows 2000 machines to use this method.

Public Key Certificates A second authentication method involves the use of public key certificates in conjunction with a trusted certificate authority (CA). An advantage of this method is that it can be used with computers that are not running the Kerberos v5 protocol. Public key certificates are appropriately used for remote access communications or those that go across the public Internet.

A viable public key infrastructure includes the following three elements:

- Secret private keys
- Freely available public keys
- A trusted third party to confirm the authenticity of the public key

The trusted third party is required to digitally sign each party's public key. This is to prevent people from providing a public key that they "claim" is theirs, but is in fact not; it is the public key of the person they are impersonating.

Preshared Keys The third option is to use a *preshared key,* which is a secret key that was agreed upon previously by the two users conducting the transaction. This method, like the public key certificate, has the advantage of working with computers that are not running Kerberos v5. The disadvantage is that IPSec must be configured, on both sides, to use the specified preshared key. However, this simple method is also appropriate for non-Windows 2000 computers, and works well in cases where only authentication protection is required.

The process for authenticating using a preshared key is as follows:

1. The sending computer can hash a piece of data (a challenge) using the shared key and forward this to the destination computer.
2. The destination computer will receive the challenge, perform a hash using the same secret key, and send this back.
3. If the hashed results are identical, both computers share the same secret and are thus authenticated.

The ISAKMP Service

ISAKMP is used in conjunction with session key establishment protocols like Oakley, which is a leading *key management* method. The ISAKMP service is responsible for managing the exchange of the cryptographic keys used in IPSec communications, and Oakley generates and manages the authenticated keys used to secure the information.

ISAKMP centralizes the management of security associations, which in turn reduces connection time.

IPSec Driver

The IPSec driver, along with the other IPSec components, is incorporated into the Windows 2000 TCP/IP protocol. If the driver becomes corrupted, it can be reinstalled by removing and reinstalling TCP/IP. The IPSec driver is the component that first checks the *IP filter list* in the policy that is active, and notifies the ISAKMP service to begin security negotiations.

To force the restart of the IPSec driver, you can restart the** IPSec Policy Agent, **using the Services console in the Administrative Tools menu.

IPSec Packet Handling

Let's look now at how IPSec handles data at the packet level. A typical IPSec transaction involves the following steps:

1. The IPSec driver receives the filter list.
2. The driver inspects each packet (both inbound and outbound traffic) and compares it to the filter list.
3. The driver applies the filter to any matching packets.
4. The packet is allowed through (received or sent) if the filter action allows transmission. The packet is discarded if the filter action blocks transmission.

The security association (SA) that has been negotiated is used to process the incoming and outgoing packets. If there are multiple SAs configured, the SPI (Security Parameters Index) is used to determine which SA goes with the packet.

IPSec Filter Lists

IPSec uses *IP filter lists,* each of which contains one or more filters. An IP filter defines IP addresses and types of IP traffic. The administrator can specify the source or destination address, and/or the traffic type to be filtered. Each IP packet will be checked against the filter list.

IP Filters *Inbound filters* are, as the name suggests, applied to incoming IP packets, while *outbound filters* are applied to IP packets being sent out onto the network. The filter list triggers a security negotiation when a match is made to the source or destination address or the type of IP traffic.

Filter Settings Filter settings include the following:

- **Source/destination address** This is the IP address of the sending and receiving computer. It can be one IP address or a group of addresses, a subnet, a network, or multiple networks.

- **Protocol** This is the protocol being used to transfer the packet. The default is TCP/IP and all related protocols in the TCP/IP suite.
- **Source/destination port for TCP or UDP** The default setting is all ports, but the administrator can configure this setting to specify only a particular port(s).

In the section "Enabling and Configuring IPSec" later in this chapter, you will learn how to configure IP filter settings in Windows 2000.

IPSec and SNMP

The Simple Network Management Protocol (SNMP) is a protocol included in most implementations of the TCP/IP suite, which is used to monitor and manage networks and network devices. When the SNMP service is running and IPSec is used, SNMP messages will be blocked unless you configure a rule in your current active IPSec policy to prevent this.

In order to do this, the IP filter list needs to specify the source and destination addresses of the SNMP management systems and agents for the UDP protocol on ports 161 and 162 (inbound and outbound). Two filters will have to be configured to accomplish this, one for each port. *Filter action* should be configured to permit the traffic that matches the filter list. In this way, the SNMP packets will be allowed through.

IPSec and L2TP

One of the new features in Windows 2000 is the ability to establish a secure virtual private network (VPN) connection using L2TP (the Layer Two Tunneling Protocol) in combination with IPSec for improved security. Windows NT 4.0 supported only the Point-to-Point Tunneling Protocol (PPTP) for virtual private networking.

Windows 2000 supports both L2TP and PPTP for VPN connections, but IPSec can be used only with L2TP.

A secure VPN is created by using L2TP to establish the tunnel through which the data is transferred, and IPSec to provide security to that data.

When to Use L2TP

Instances in which you might use the L2TP/IPSec combination (referred to as *L2TP over IPSec)* include:

- Providing a secure link between remote clients and a corporate network (End to End security).
- Providing a secure connection for a company's offices located at multiple sites (Secure tunneling).

The configuration properties sheet for L2TP is used, instead of IPSec policies, to configure IP security over the VPN connection. This creates a *virtual private network* within the public network. L2TP determines authentication, and the IP filters and filter lists are set, dynamically, during the time the connection is active.

You can provide *end-to-end encryption* for the data in this way. That is, the data is encrypted from the remote client to the destination host. This differs from the *link encryption* provided by Microsoft Point-to-Point Encryption (MPPE), used by PPTP in establishing VPNs.

exam watch

In order to use L2TP over IPSec, both the Layer Two Tunneling Protocol and IPSec must be supported by both the VPN client and the VPN server.

How L2TP Security Works

L2TP over IPSec provides data security by using both encryption and *encapsulation.* Encapsulation refers to the enclosing of one thing inside another. In this context, we're talking about putting one data structure within another structure so that the first data structure is hidden temporarily. An encapsulated packet or frame of data is recognized according to the outer headers.

This concept is the basis for the term *tunneling,* which refers to the process of hiding the original packet inside a new packet. The *tunnel* is the path through which the encapsulated packets travel across the network.

Two-Tiered Encapsulation Packets are encapsulated twice first by L2TP and then by IPSec, so that we end up with "encapsulation inside encapsulation."

- **L2TP encapsulation** First the PPP frame (the IP datagram, or an IPX datagram or NetBEUI frame) is encapsulated, or wrapped, inside an L2TP header. A UDP header is also added.
- **IPSec encapsulation** The L2TP packet created by the preceding process is then wrapped by an IPSec ESP header and trailer, an IPSec authentication trailer, and finally an IP header.

Encryption IPSec encrypts the L2TP message. This is done using keys that have been created during the IPSec authentication process. Although you can establish an L2TP connection that is not encrypted (and therefore does not use IPSec), this is not recommended if you are transmitting over the public Internet. The PPP frame would then be sent in plain text and the data would not be secure.

The following scenario and solution answers some questions about the encryption levels that can be configured when using IPSec with L2TP for VPN connections.

The L2TP settings are configured through Network and Dial-up Connections on the VPN client. For the VPN server, and for gateway-to-gateway connections, the configuration is done via the RRAS console.

SCENARIO & SOLUTION	
If I configure L2TP for "no encryption," does this mean IPSec will not be used?	No. The "no encryption" security level still uses IPSec to negotiate AH, which authenticates the IP header. AH can ensure authentication and integrity.
What happens if I set L2TP for "optional encryption?" What determines whether encryption is used for a particular communication?	When L2TP is configured for "optional encryption," the security level used by IPSec will depend on the request or requirements of the other computer with which you are communicating.
What is the effect of configuring L2TP's security level as "required encryption?"	Secured communication will be required; the computer will not allow unsecured communication.

EXERCISE 7-1

Setting the Encryption Level on a VPN Client

To set the security level for a VPN client, perform the following steps:

1. From the Start | Settings | Network and Dial-up Connections folder, select the VPN connection that you wish to configure, as shown in the following illustration.

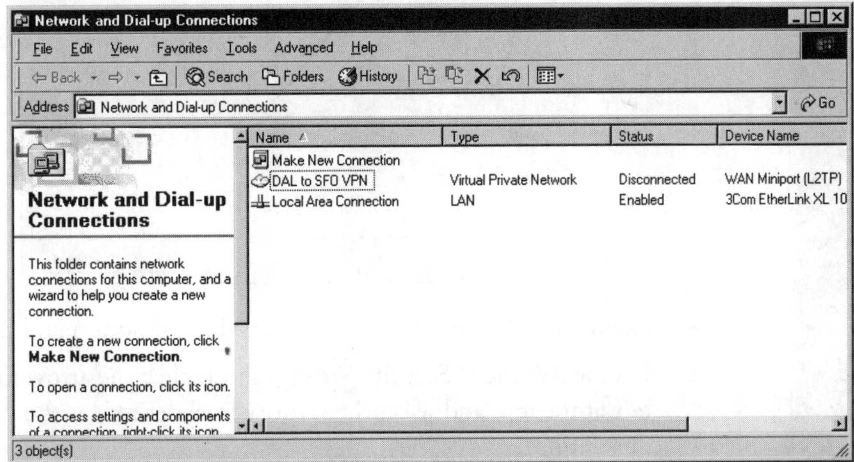

2. Right-click on the selected VPN connection name, and choose Properties from the context menu.
3. On the Properties sheet, select the Security tab, as shown in the following illustration.

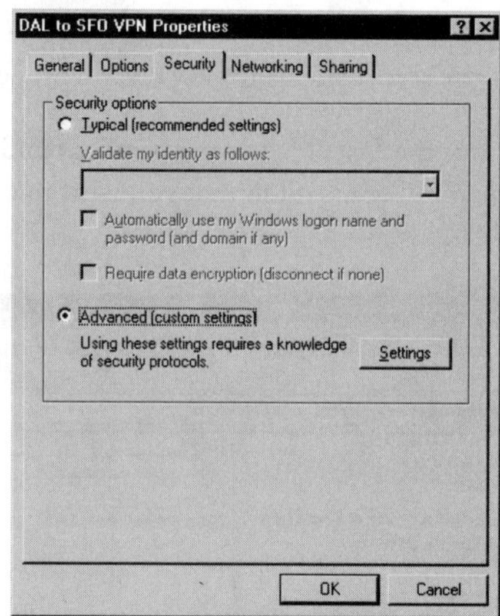

4. Choose the Advanced (custom settings) radio button and click Settings.
5. On the Advanced Security Settings sheet, click the arrow for the drop-down box at the top, and select the security level desired, as shown in the following illustration.

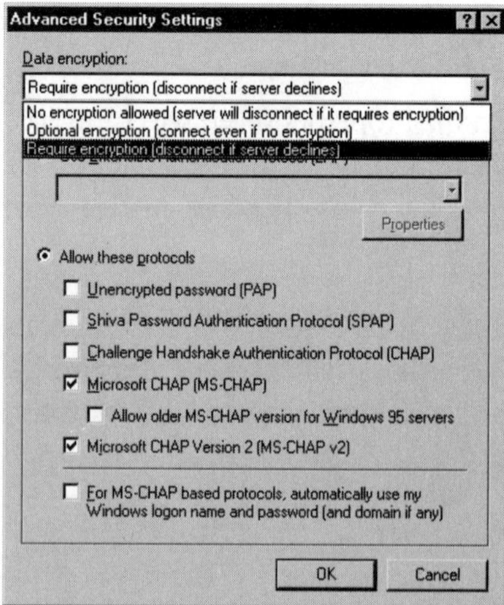

6. Click OK, then Click OK again to close the VPN Properties sheet.

CERTIFICATION OBJECTIVE 7.02

Enabling and Configuring IPSec

Now that you know something about the concepts behind IP Security, let's turn to some issues that are more practical: how to enable and configure IPSec for your network. We will discuss the configuration of IPSec for both transport and tunnel modes, but first, you need an understanding of IPSec policies, how they are created, and how they are applied.

IPSec Policies

Microsoft, in an attempt to make management of IP Security easier, has implemented *policy-based* administration for IPSec in Windows 2000. In other words, you, as a network administrator, create policies to configure IPSec. Windows 2000 provides the IP Security Policy Management snap-in, which is used to define and manage IPSec policies.

See Exercise 7-2 in this section for instructions on how to use the snap-in. Before you can create policies to govern IP Security, you must consider an overall security strategy for your network.

Factors to Consider

Developing a security plan begins with the awareness that security represents a balance. Complete security means no one has access to anything. All assets would be protected at the cost of no one being able to use them; this is not a very practical solution. On the other end of the continuum is total "openness," where no security controls are placed on any of the network's assets or resources. No one will have any problem accessing the information or resources needed, but the downside is that your information has essentially become public domain.

To implement an effective security policy, you will have to balance accessibility with security. The more secure the resource, the more difficult it will be to access, even for those who are allowed access. The easier the access, the more chance that an unauthorized person will be able to view, use, change, or delete the data.

Prior to implementing them on the network, you should design, create, and test the IPSec policies to determine which policies are truly necessary. Microsoft recommends that during the testing of your deployment scenarios, you should run normal workloads on applications to gain realistic feedback. Also note that during the initial tests, if you want to view the packet contents with Network Monitor or a sniffer, you should use the Medium security method level (or a custom security method set to AH), because using High or ESP will prevent you from being able to view the packets.

Evaluating Security Needs

Some of the things you will want to assess in developing the plan upon which your policies will be based include:

- The type of information typically sent over the network. How sensitive is it? Does it include trade secrets, confidential financial data, sensitive client records, and the like?
- Where is the sensitive information stored, and how will it be routed through the network?
- What is your vulnerability to network attacks? Do you have an always-on Internet connection? Do you have a remote access server to which outside users can dial in? Do you have a Web server or FTP server open to the public?

Your security plan should focus on the basic issues illustrated by the following scenario and solution.

SCENARIO & SOLUTION	
What network traffic should be secured?	Determine whether you need to secure the traffic between all computers or only some of them. Also, decide if security is needed for only some protocols and ports, or all of them.
What levels of security are needed?	Determine whether you need only data authentication and integrity, or whether you want to ensure confidentiality of the data.
Which connections should be secured?	Decide whether you need security only on remote access connections, or also on the internal network.
What about interoperability issues?	Determine whether the encryption settings selected will work with all computers that need access.

Evaluating Potential Security Threats

Part of developing your security plan involves evaluating the potential threats to which your network may be exposed. Many administrators envision the black-hat "hacker" as the most dangerous enemy of the network's information store, but this may not be entirely true. Depending on the nature of the data and the physical infrastructure of your network, more likely dangers may include:

- The "power user" who is interested in what he can "do" over the network
- The casual user who stumbles upon information that was not secured properly
- The authorized user who accesses a document or file that has poorly designed access control, leading to a misinformation situation that can create havoc in the corporation
- The disgruntled employee seeking revenge from a former employer
- The greed driven individual who sells his legitimate access controls to others for a profit
- Competing companies that hire agents to carry out corporate espionage in order to access your proprietary secrets

Although many companies go to great lengths to "harden" the network against outside intrusion, it is a fact of life that most risk emanates from within the company. While it is important to shore up portals to the Internet and other external networks, the security analyst's major concerns should usually be directed toward security breeches from* within*—both malicious and accidental.

Designing and Implementing IP Security Policies

In Windows 2000, IPSec configuration and deployment is intimately intertwined with the Active Directory and Group Policy. You must create a policy in order to deploy IPSec in your organization.

exam Watch

A policy can be applied to a forest, a tree, a domain, an organizational unit, or to a single computer.

Within the Group Policy, we can choose from built-in policies or create custom policies to meet our specialized needs. We configure these policies by creating an MMC and then using the appropriate MMC plug in.

EXERCISE 7-2

Creating a Custom IPSec MMC

1. Create a new console by starting the Run command and typing **mmc**.
2. Click OK to open up an empty console.
3. Click the Console menu, and then click Add/Remove Snap-in, as shown in the following illustration

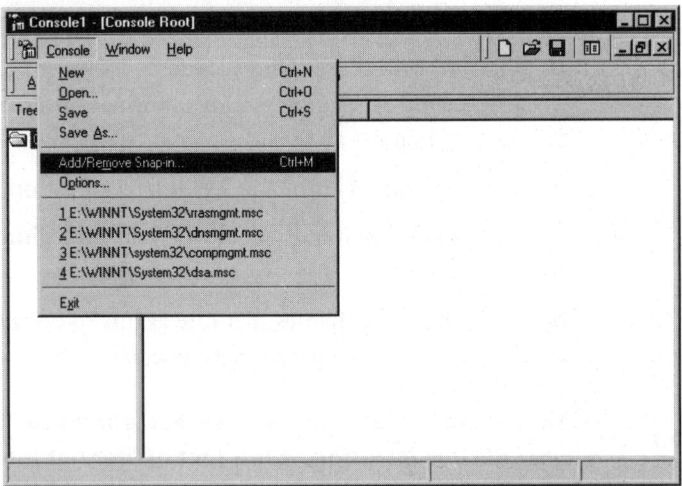

4. Click Add, select Computer Management, as shown in the following illustration, and click Add.

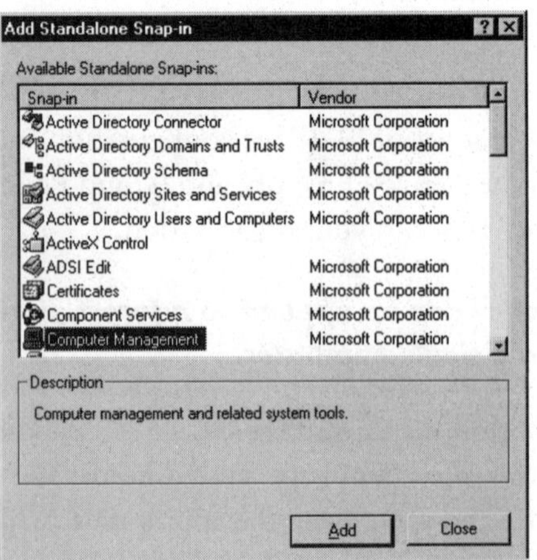

5. A dialog box will appear, asking which computer the snap-in will manage. Select Local Computer (the computer this console is running on). Then click Finish.
6. Scroll through the list of available snap-ins, and select Group Policy, and click Add.
7. At this point, a wizard will appear, shown in the following illustration.

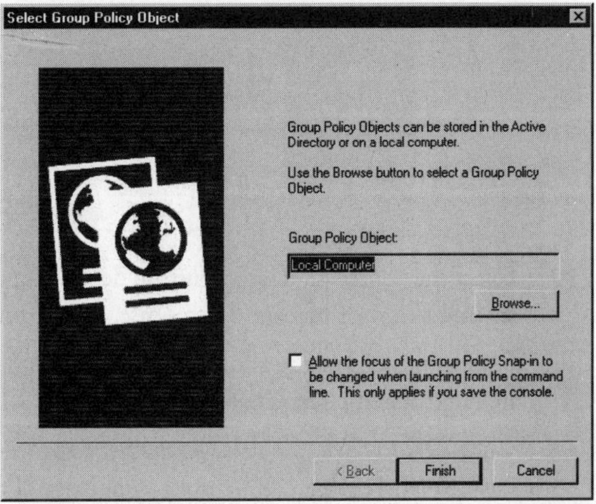

8. The wizard will query you on what group policy object you want to manage. In this case, confirm that it says Local Computer in the text box, and click Finish. If you want to define a policy for another group policy object, you would click Browse and select from the list.
9. Scroll through the list of snap-ins one more time, this time looking for Certificates. Select Certificates and click Add. A dialog box will appear, as shown in the following illustration.

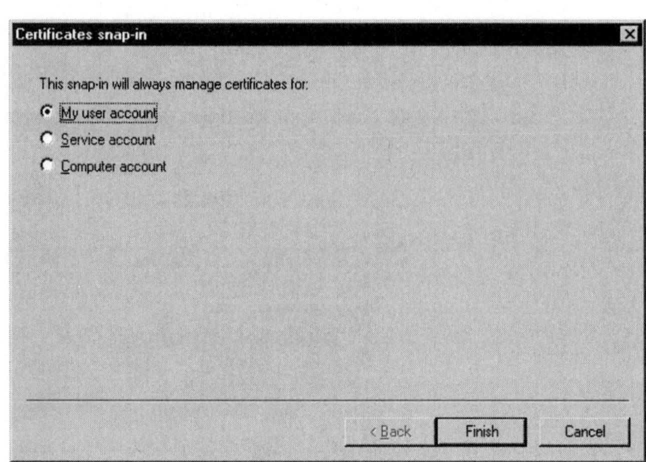

10. Select the appropriate radio button, depending upon what account you want the snap-in to always manage. In this case, select Computer Account, and click Next.
11. Select Local Computer for the computer that you want the snap-in to manage. Then click Finish.
12. Click OK to close the Add/Remove Snap-ins dialog box. You now have a custom MMC that can be used to manage IPSec policies, which should look something like the one shown as follows.

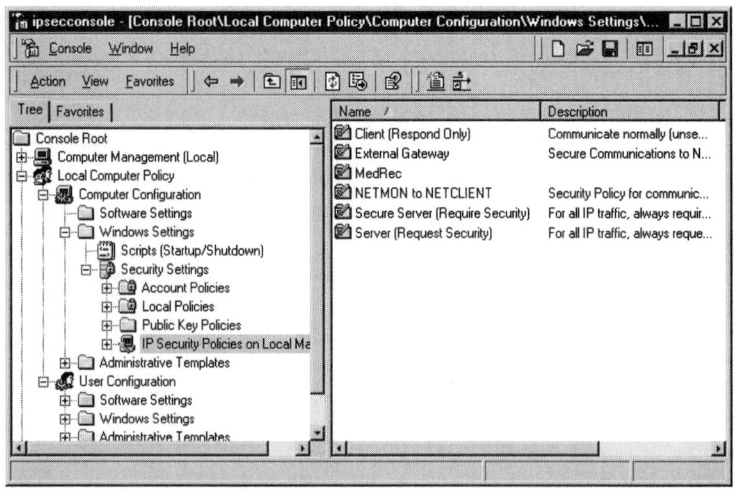

IPSec policies for the local machine will be located in the Local Computer Policy container, under Computer Configuration | Windows Settings | Security Settings, as shown in the previous illustration.

For this exercise, we have chosen to manage IPSec policy for this single machine. This might be appropriate if you were configuring IPSec policy for a file or application server. To manage policy for an entire domain or organizational unit, you would select the appropriate policy when selecting the Group Policy snap-in configuration.

IPSec Policy Properties

Because IPSec policies are implemented via Group Policy, we have a great deal of flexibility in how they are implemented. We can choose from three built-in IPSec Policies, or create our own custom policies. Let's first examine the built-in policies.

The Built-In IPSec Policies

The three built-in IPSec policies are as follows:

- **The Client (Respond Only) policy** Used when you require secure IPSec connections when another computer requests them. For example, you are using a machine as a workstation that wants to connect to a file server that requires IPSec security. The workstation with the built-in Client policy enabled will negotiate an IPSec security association. However, this client will never *require* IPSec security; it will only use IPSec to secure communications when requested to do so by another computer.
- **The Server (Request Security) policy** Used when you want to request IPSec security for all connections. This might be used for a file server that must serve both IPSec-aware (Windows 2000) clients and non-IPSec aware clients (such as Windows 9*x* and NT). If a connection is established with an IPSec-aware computer, the session will be secure. Unsecured sessions will be established with non-IPSec aware computers, and soft security associations will be established. This allows greater flexibility during the transition from mixed Windows networks to Native Windows 2000 networks.
- **The Secure Server (Require Security) policy** Used when all communications with a particular server *must* be secured. Examples include file servers with high impact information, and security gateways at either end of an L2TP/IPSec tunnel. The server with the Secure Server policy will

always request a secure channel. Connections will be denied to computers that are not able to respond to the request.

exam Watch

You must have appropriate administrator rights to Group Policy, or be a member of the local system Administrators group in order to define IPSec policies.

Creating Custom Policies

You will often need to define your own custom policies. To add or edit IPSec policies, follow these steps:

1. In IP Security Policy Management, choose whether to define a new policy or edit a current one. If you wish to create a new policy, click on the IP Security Policies folder in the console tree, then click Create IP Security Policy in the Action menu, as shown in Figure 7-3. This will invoke the IP Security Policy wizard. Complete the instructions in the wizard until the Properties dialog box for your new policy appears.

FIGURE 7-3

Creating a new IP security policy

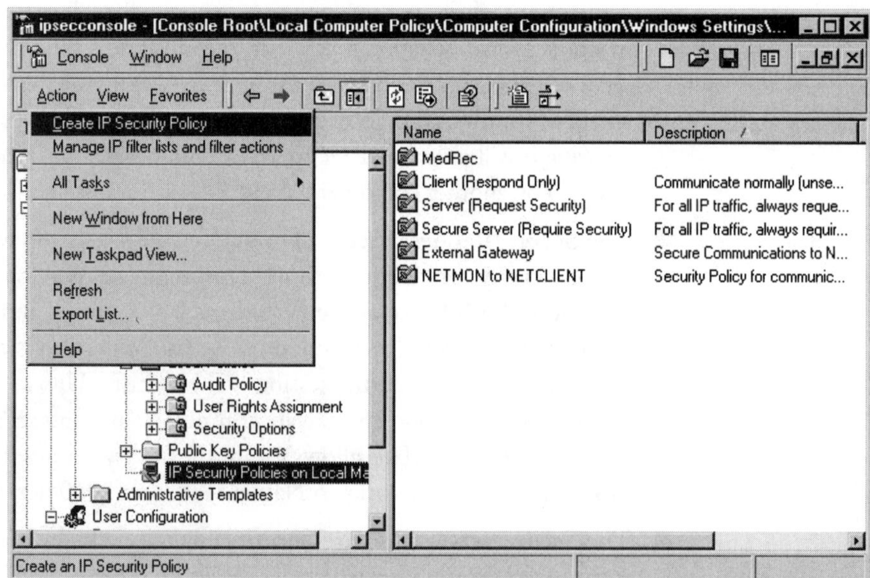

2. If you wish to edit an existing policy, just right-click the policy, and then click Properties. You will see the dialog box displayed in Figure 7-4.
3. Click the General tab, then in the Name field, enter a unique name.
4. In the Description field, type a description of the security policy, such as which groups or domains it affects.
5. If this computer is part of a domain, type a value in "Check for policy changes every" *number* minute(s) to specify how often the policy agent will check Group Policy for updates,
6. Click Advanced if you have special requirements for the security on the key exchange.
7. Click the Rules tab and create any necessary rules for the policy.

New policies may not be displayed immediately in the console tree. If you do not see the new policy, right-click on IP Security Policies in the Description folder, then select Refresh from the context menu.

FIGURE 7-4

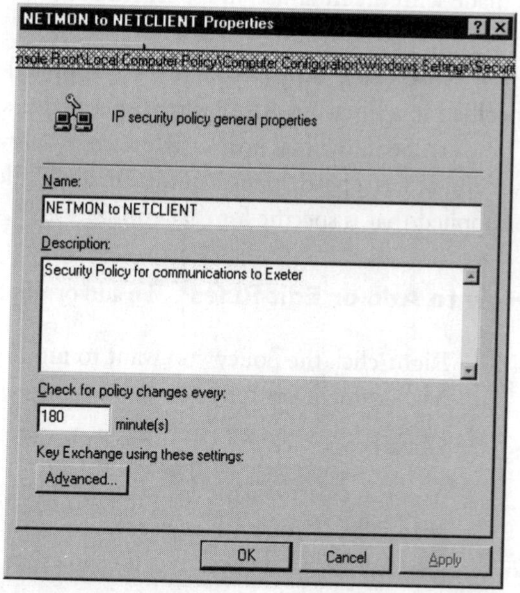

The Properties dialog box for an existing security policy

on the job

You cannot delete the built-in policies, but you can edit them. However, it is recommended that you leave the built-in policies as they are, and create new policies for custom requirements.

Configuring IPSec Policy Components

An IPSec policy has three main components:

- IP Filter rules
- IP Filter lists
- IP Filter actions

Let's look at each of those in more detail.

Configuring Filter Rules

Filter rules are created to specify how and when communication is to be secured. Each rule contains a list of filters, and a collection of security actions. When a match is made with the filter list, the specified actions will occur.

How Rules Are Applied Rules are applied to computers that match criteria specified in a filter list. An IP filter list contains source and destination IP Addresses. These can be individual host IP addresses or network IDs. When a communication is identified as a participant included in an IP filter list, a particular filter action will be applied that is specific for that connection.

How to Add or Edit Rules To add or edit filter rules, perform the following steps:

1. Right-click the policy you want to modify in the IP Security Policy Management console.
2. Click Properties and select the Rules tab.
3. You can either use the Security Rule wizard, or you can add or edit the rule manually. If you wish to use the Security Rule wizard to add a rule, check the Use Add Wizard check box, as shown in Figure 7-5.

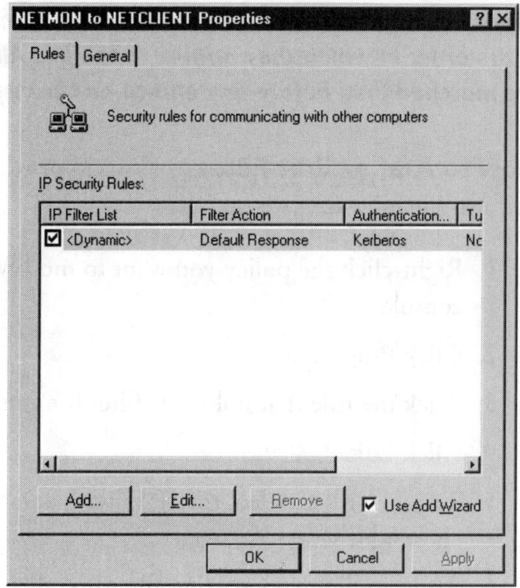

FIGURE 7-5 The Rules tab on the IP Security Policy Properties sheet

4. Click Next, and then follow the instructions in the wizard.
5. If you wish to add or edit a rule manually, clear the Use Add Wizard check box. Click Add or Edit. Continue to the next step.
6. Define the IP Filter List, Filter Action, Connection Type, Authentication Methods, and Tunnel Setting properties.

New rules are automatically applied to the policy being edited or created. The Default Response rule is automatically added in each new IPSec policy that you create. If you do not want this rule to be part of your policy, you will need to deactivate it, as predefined rules are not removable.

Configuring Filters and Filter Lists

Filters are the most important part of IPSec policy, because if you fail to specify the proper filters (in either the client or the server policies), the connection may not be secured. This is also true if the IP addresses change before the policy's filters are updated.

Filter Lists The IP filter list is a collection of filters.

Filters are applied in the order of most-specific filters first. Filters are not applied in the order in which they appear in the list. All of the filters used in tunnel rules are matched first, before any end-to-end transport filters are matched.

How to Add or Edit Filters To add or edit filters in Windows 2000 IPSec, perform the following steps:

1. Right-click the policy you want to modify in the IPSec Security Management console.
2. Click Properties.
3. Click the rule that holds the filter list you want to modify.
4. Click Edit.
5. To add a filter, select the IP Filter List tab, as shown in Figure 7-6, and click Add.
6. To reconfigure an existing filter list, click the IP filter, and then click Edit.

FIGURE 7-6

Selecting the IP Filter List tab

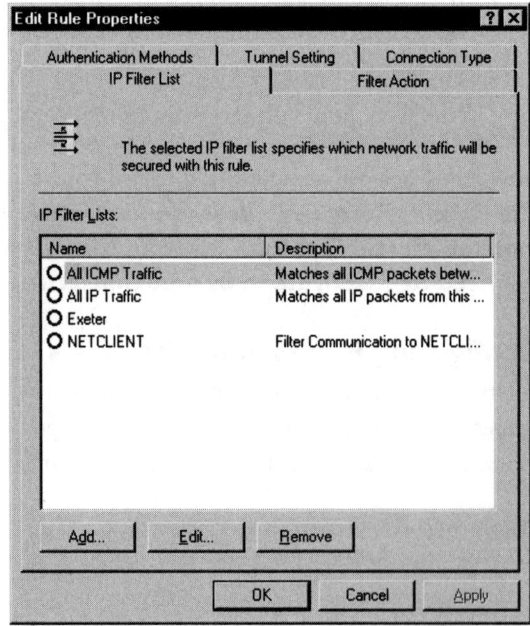

7. In the IP filter list, you can use the IP Filter wizard to create a filter. Just check the Use Add Wizard check box and follow the instructions of the wizard. (You can also create a filter manually, by clearing the Use Add Wizard check box and clicking Add, or reconfigure an existing filter by clearing the check box and clicking Edit).
8. Select the Addressing tab, as shown in Figure 7-7.
9. Select the Source address. Choose from the following options:
   - **My IP Address** Secures packets from all IP addresses on the computer for which the filter is configured.
   - **Any IP Address** Secures packets from all computers.
   - **A Specific IP Address** Secures packets from the IP address you type into the IP Address field.
   - **A Specific IP subnet** Secures packets from the subnet you designate in the Subnet Mask field.
10. Click the Destination address and repeat step 5 for the destination address.

FIGURE 7-7

Specifying the source address from which packets are to be secured

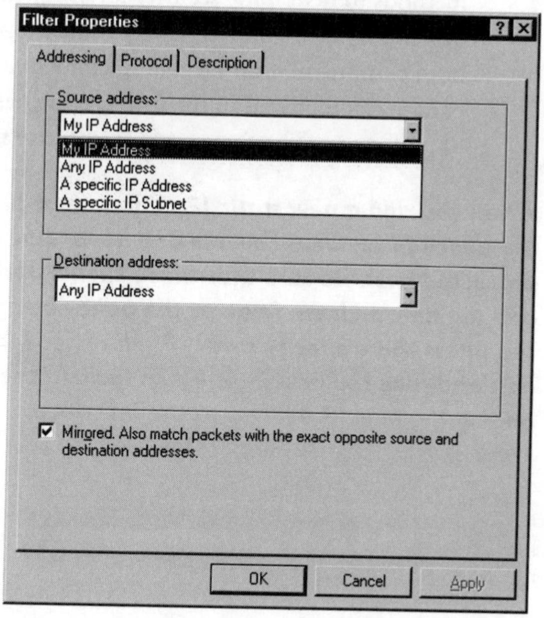

Filter Properties

Addressing | Protocol | Description

Source address:
My IP Address
My IP Address
Any IP Address
A specific IP Address
A specific IP Subnet

Destination address:
Any IP Address

Mirrored. Also match packets with the exact opposite source and destination addresses.

OK | Cancel | Apply

11. Select the desired setting under Mirrored, from the following options:
    - Check the Mirrored check box to create a filter for end-to-end security (to secure packets from the source to the destination computer).
    - Clear the Mirrored check box to create a filter for an IPSec tunnel (you must also create two rules, one inbound and one outbound, with different filter lists).
12. In the Description field, type a description for this filter (such as what hosts and traffic types are applicable).

Filter Actions

Filter actions define the type of security and the methods in which security is established. The primary methods are: Permit, Block, and Negotiate security.

- The Permit option blocks negotiation for IP security. This is appropriate if you never want to secure traffic to which this rule applies.
- The Block action blocks all traffic from computers specified in the IP filter list.
- The Negotiate security action allows the computer to use a list of security methods to determine security levels for the communication. The list is in descending order of preference. If the Negotiate security action is selected, both computers must be able to come to an agreement regarding the security parameters included in the list. The entries are processed sequentially in order of preference. The first common security method is enacted.

on the job

When you add a new static IP address to a protected host, you should modify the policy filters on all clients and hosts that make security requests to the protected host. Be sure that those clients updated their policies before you add the new address. Look at the policy being used on the protected host. If the filters there specify static IP addresses for local connections, you should edit and save the new filter list to include the new static IP address after adding the new IP address to the interface.

Configuring IPSec Authentication Methods

You can define the authentication method(s) to be used by IPSec, and set the order of preference, by following these steps:

1. Right-click on the policy in the IPSec Policy Management console and select Properties, as shown in Figure 7-8.
2. On the Properties sheet, select the rule you wish to edit, as shown in Figure 7-9, and click Edit.
3. Now select the Authentication Methods tab, as shown in Figure 7-10.
4. You can add or remove authentication methods, edit the properties of the existing methods, and move a method up or down in the preference order using this dialog box.

FIGURE 7-8

Selecting the IPSec policy to be modified

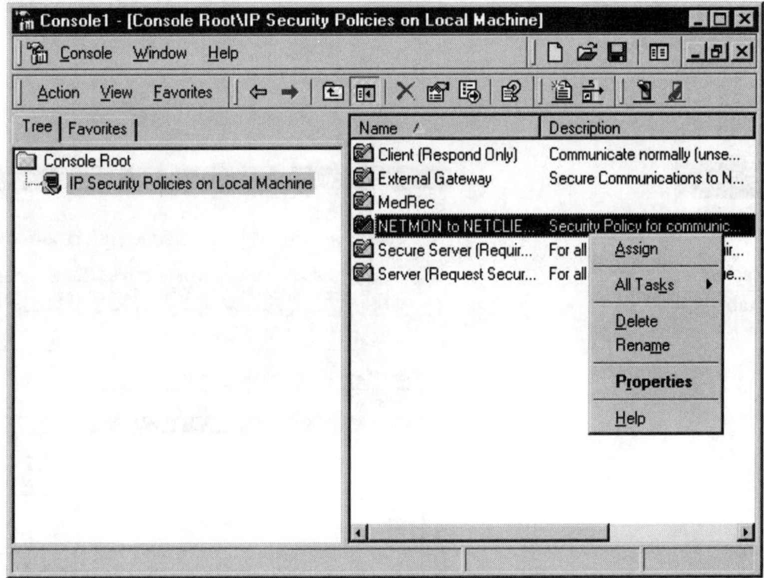

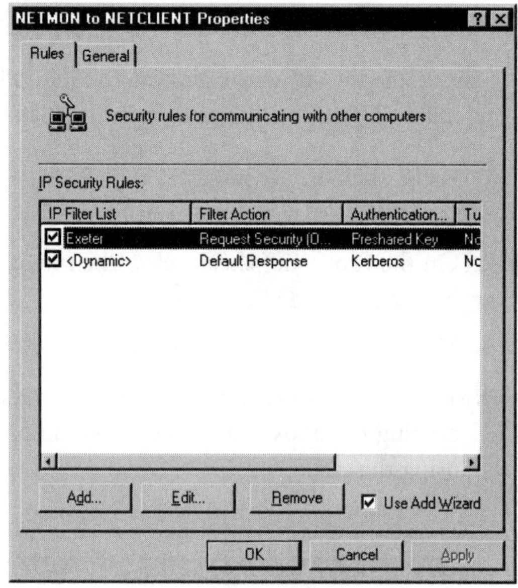

FIGURE 7-9 Selecting the IPSec rule to be edited

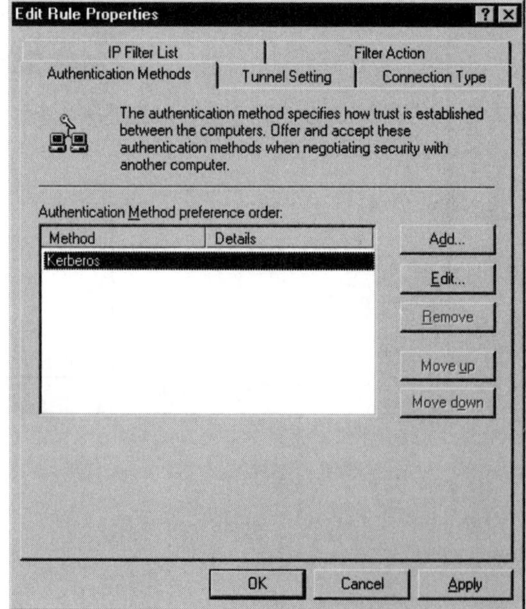

FIGURE 7-10 The Authentication Methods tab

Configuring Connection Types

For each IPSec rule, you must define which connection types on your computer will be affected by the rule. These connection types apply to all network and dial-up connections on the computer for which you are configuring the IPSec policy. There are three connection type settings:

- **All Network Connections** If you select this option, the rule will apply to communications sent over any of the network connections that are configured on the computer.
- **Local Area Network (LAN)** If you select this option, the rule will only apply to communications sent over the LAN connection(s) that are configured on the computer.
- **Remote Access** If you select this option, the rule will only apply to communications sent over remote access or dial-up connections that are configured on the computer.

To specify IPSec connection types for an IPSec rule, perform the following steps:

1. In the IP Security Policy Management console, right-click on the policy you want to edit.
2. Click Properties.
3. Click the rule to which you want to make changes.
4. Click Edit.
5. On the Connection Type tab, select the type of network connections to which this rule will apply, according to the three options discussed earlier (Figure 7-11).

Each rule can have one connection type specified. The rule will be applied only to connections of the type specified.

Configuring IPSec Tunneling

As mentioned earlier, an IPSec tunnel requires two separate IPSec rules to define the endpoints. This is done via the Tunneling Setting tab on the Edit Rules Properties sheet, as shown in Figure 7-12.

FIGURE 7-11

Selecting the network connection type

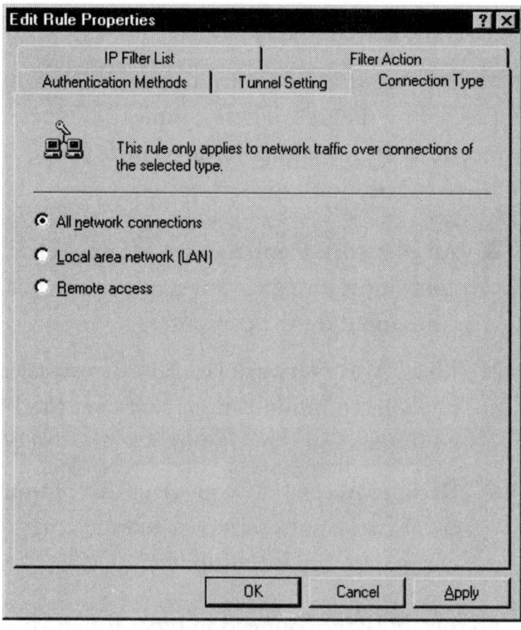

FIGURE 7-12

Configuring IPSec tunneling

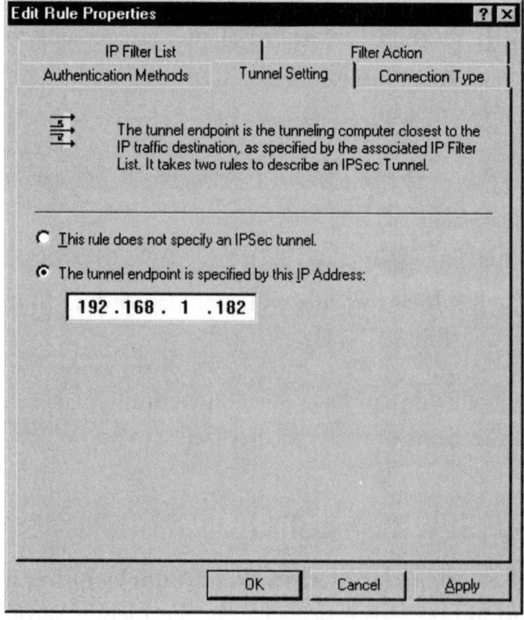

A second rule must be created to specify the other endpoint of the tunnel.

Configuring Advanced Settings

Key Exchange settings are specified by clicking Advanced on the General tab of the IPSec policy Properties sheet, as shown in Figure 7-13.

When you click Advanced, you will see the Key Exchange Settings dialog box shown in Figure 7-14.

This is where you control the security of the Internet Key Exchange (IKE) process and configure the security methods that are used to protect identities during the Key Exchange process. Methods that may be selected include 3DES and DES for encryption, and SHA1 and MD5 for integrity, as shown in Figure 7-15.

FIGURE 7-13

To specify Key Exchange settings, click Advanced

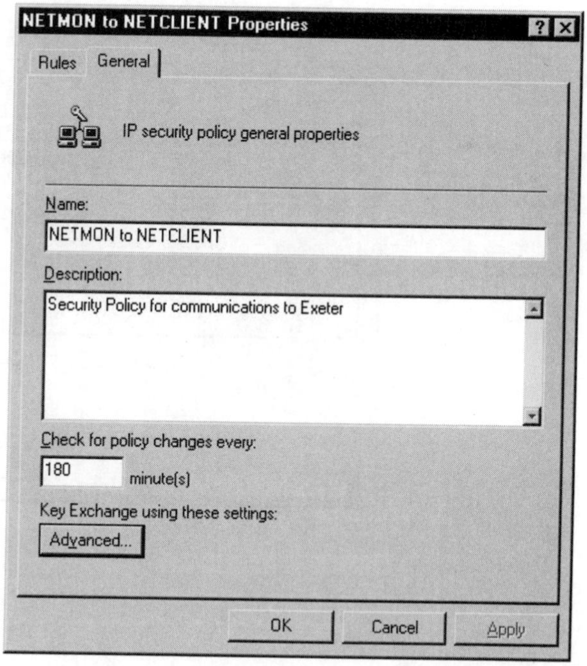

FIGURE 7-14

The Key Exchange Settings dialog box

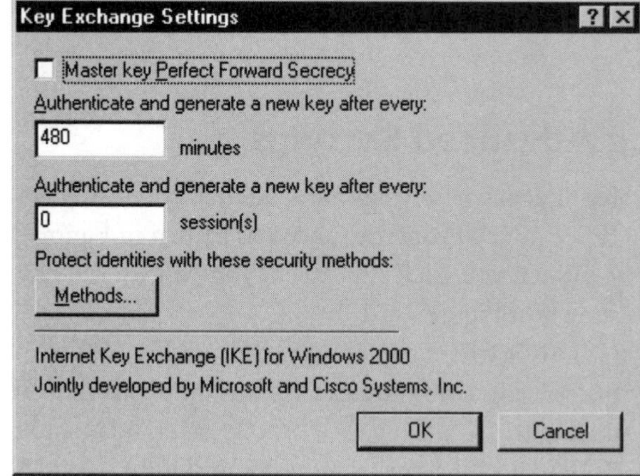

FIGURE 7-15

The available Key Exchange Security Methods

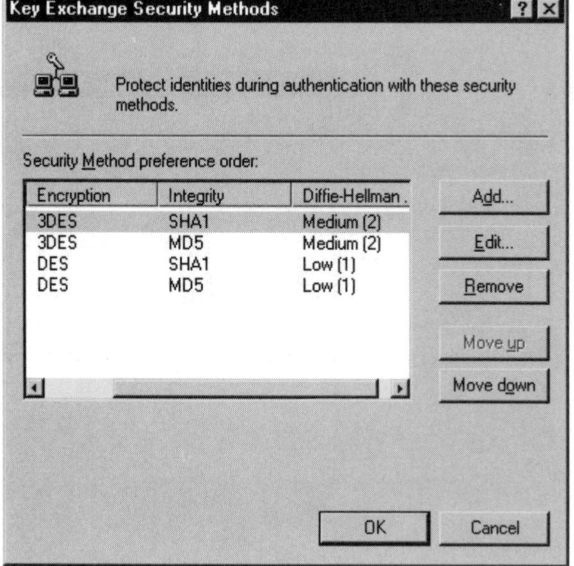

CERTIFICATION OBJECTIVE 7.03

Managing, Monitoring, and Troubleshooting IPSec

As you no doubt have discerned, IP Security is a complex feature, and working with IPSec in Windows 2000, despite the wizards and management tools provided, is no simple matter. In this last section, we will look at how to manage, monitor, and troubleshoot IPSec.

Managing IPSec

Managing IPSec policies involves the following activities:

- Testing IPSec policy integrity
- Restoring predefined IPSec policies
- Exporting IPSec policies
- Importing IPSec policies
- Refreshing the list of IPSec policies
- Deleting IPSec policies
- Renaming IPSec policies

Let's look at each of these a little more closely.

Testing Policy Integrity

Microsoft has made it easy to check the integrity of IPSec policies in Windows 2000. Just follow these steps:

1. In the IP Security Policy Management console, click on the folder labeled IP Security Policies on Local Machine.

2. Click Action, or right-click on the folder.
3. Select All Tasks, as shown in Figure 7-16.
4. Click Check Policy Integrity.

The Policy Integrity Check provides verification that the changes that have been made to policy settings have been properly propagated by Group Policy to the computer accounts in the GPO.

This same context menu will be used for most of the common policy management tasks.

Restoring Predefined IPSec Policies

There may be times when you wish to restore the predefined default policies (Client, Server, and Secure Server, as noted earlier) to replace custom policies you may have created. To return to the defaults, following these steps:

1. In the IP Security Policy Management console, click on the folder labeled IP Security Policies on Local Machine.
2. Click Action, or right-click on the folder.

FIGURE 7-16

Many policy management tasks are accomplished from the All Tasks menu

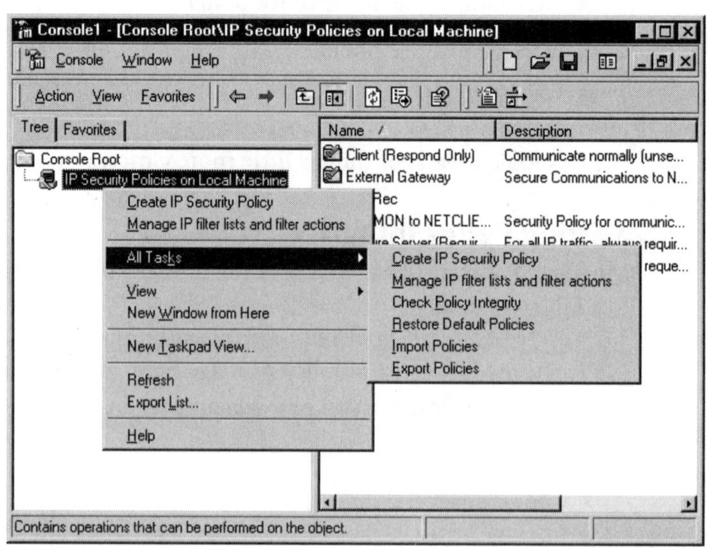

3. Select All Tasks.
4. Click Restore Default Policies.
5. Click Yes in response to the "Are you sure?" dialog box, and the predefined policies will be restored.

Exporting and Importing IPSec Policies

To export or import IPSec policies, follow the first three steps in the preceding section, then from the All Tasks context menu, select Export Policies or Import Policies, as the case may be. Type in the path and name of the file.

Refreshing the IPSec Policy List

Because a new policy may not show up immediately after you create it, Microsoft has made it easy to refresh the policy list—all it takes is a couple of clicks of the mouse. In the IPSec Policy Management console, right-click on the folder labeled IP Security Policies on Local Machine. Select Refresh from the context menu. The list will be updated, and any additions or deletions you have made will be reflected.

Deleting IPSec Policies

To delete an IPSec policy, select the policy you wish to remove in the IPSec Policy Management console, right-click on it, and choose Delete. Remember that you may have to refresh the policy list, as discussed previously, to see the effect of the change.

Renaming IPSec Policies

Renaming an IPSec policy is similar to renaming a file in the Windows Explorer. Just right-click the policy name in the IPSec Policy Management console, select Rename in the context menu, and type in the new name. Press Enter to apply the change, and refresh the list, if necessary, to display the new name.

Using IPSec Monitor

Windows 2000 includes a monitoring tool, the IPSec Monitor, which allows you to view the active security associations both on local and remote computers.

EXERCISE 7-3

Accessing the IPSec Monitor

To use the Monitor, perform the following steps:

1. Click Start.
2. Select the Run command.
3. Type **ipsecmon <computername>** in the Run box. You will see the IPSec Monitor, as shown in the following illustration.

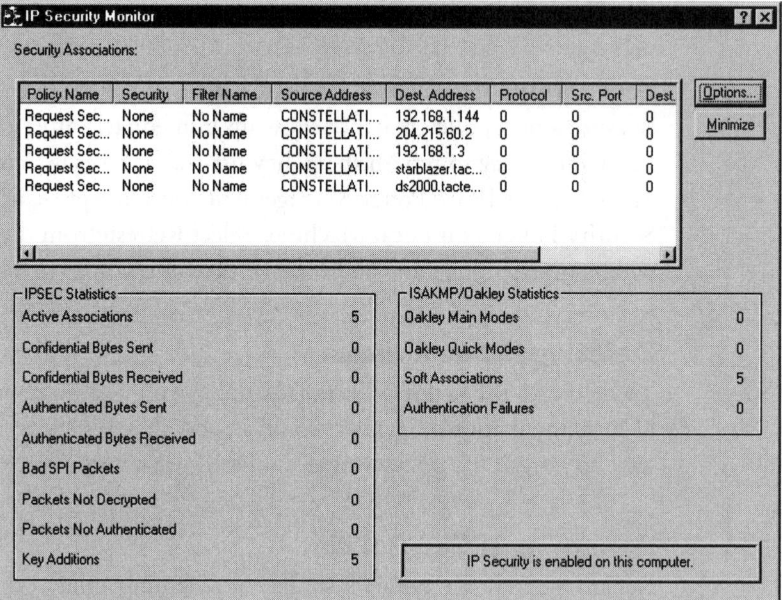

If you type the command without designating a computer name, the Monitor will default to the local machine.

The Components of the IPSec Monitor

When you run the Monitor, you should see an entry for each security association that is currently active. The policy name, security level, filter name, and the source and destination address will be shown. If tunneling mode is used, the endpoint of the tunnel will be shown. The Monitor also displays statistical information such as:

- The number of active security associations
- The types of security associations that are active
- The number of keys generated
- The number of confidential (ESP) and authenticated (ESP and AH) bytes sent and received

Using the IPSec Monitor

You can use the IPSec Monitor to perform the following:

- Verify that your communications have been secured successfully
- Track patterns of authentication failures or security association failures
- Aid in performance tuning

You can confirm IPSec policy assignments with the monitor. The message in the lower-right corner of the display tells you whether IPSec is enabled on the computer being monitored. If no policies have been assigned, IPSec is not enabled. If policies have been assigned, but no security associations are active with another computer, there will be nothing listed in the SA list.

The monitor's display will be updated every 15 seconds by default. You can change the refresh interval, by clicking Options and typing in a new setting, in number of seconds. This is the only option that can be configured.

IPSec Policy Agent Entries in the System and Security Logs

Windows 2000 starts event logging automatically whenever the operating system is booted. The System and Security logs in Event Viewer can be used in troubleshooting IPSec.

The System Log

The System log is used in troubleshooting the Policy Agent. IPSec-related messages you might encounter in the System log include:

- **Event (Informational) 279** This event is logged for informational purposes and does not indicate a problem. It tells you if an IPSec policy is in effect, and if so, whether it is a local or domain policy. If a change has been made to the policy, the message "updating IPSec policy" will be displayed.
- **Event (Error) 284** This is an error message, which indicates a problem. In this case, it means the policy agent was not able to access the Active Directory.

The Security Log

Messages pertaining to ISAKMP/Oakley appear in the Security log. An example would be the establishment of a security association in conjunction with a successful logon.

Common Troubleshooting Scenarios

Following are a few common troubleshooting scenarios related to IPSec, and suggestions for resolving them.

IPSec Communications Are Not Working as Expected

If communications that should be secured with IPSec do not appear to be secured, you should first verify that IPSec is enabled. You can do this with the IPSec Monitor as described earlier. Ensure that a policy is assigned.

You should also check to be sure that the network connection between the two computers is working properly. Network problems could appear to be IPSec communication failures. Determine whether you can PING. If you are using the Server or Secure Server policies, the ICMP packet sent when you PING will match the IP Filter List in these policies, and IPSec will attempt to apply security to the PING. Note that this may take longer than it usually takes to respond to the PING command.

on the Job

If the computer with which you are trying to communicate is not capable of using IPSec, you may get a "timed out" response. You can exempt ICMP packets in all of your IPSec policies to avoid this. To do this, you must create a rule (you can use the Security Rule wizard), select the All ICMP traffic filter list, and choose Permit as the filter action.

You can use PING in combination with the IPSec Monitor. When a PING command is successful, the Monitor should display a security association.

No Security Associations Indicated in IPSec Monitor

Soft security associations may be preventing hard SAs from occurring. You may need to restart the IPSec Policy Agent. To do so, right-click the IPSec Policy Agent in the Services console (accessed from the Administrative Tools menu), and click Restart, as shown in Figure 7-17.

An alternate method of restarting the service is to double-click on the service name, click Stop and then Start.

Security Negotiations Fail

Negotiations may fail if the IPSec policy settings on the two communicating computers are not compatible. If the Security log in Event Viewer shows failed attempts at Oakley negotiation, perform the following steps to find the source of the policy incompatibility:

1. Check the *authentication* methods on both computers and ensure they are compatible.

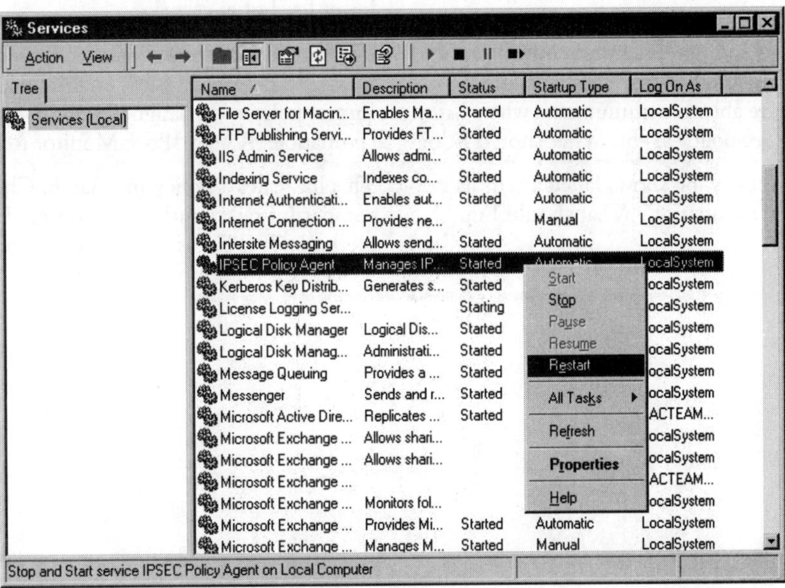

FIGURE 7-17 Restarting the IPSec Policy Agent

2. Check the *security* method(s) specified on both. There must be at least one common security method.
3. If *tunneling* mode is being used, make certain that the tunnel endpoint settings are correct.

Accidental Deletion of the IPSec Files

IPSec requires the IPSec driver and policy agent files, as well as the files for ISAKMP/Oakley. If any of the components of IPSec are deleted, or the files become corrupted, you can reinstall the IPSec files by removing and reinstalling the TCP/IP protocols.

The following scenario and solution answers some common questions in regard to troubleshooting IPSec.

SCENARIO & SOLUTION	
After I enabled IPSec, things seemed to slow down. Is this normal, and what can I do about it?	When you enable IPSec, you will find that IP traffic and packet size increase. Additionally, the computer's processor will be taxed more. This can cause a slowdown in performance. You should evaluate whether you need the level of security provided by IPSec and if not, disable it or choose a lower level of encryption.
My two computers cannot communicate with one another with IPSec enabled. They are able to communicate when I stop the IPSec policy agent. What should I do?	You should first consult the Security log and address any error messages. Be sure an SA is established, using IPSec Monitor. Ensure policies are assigned to both computers, and they are compatible. Restart IPSec Monitor to apply any changes.
The Security log shows failed attempts at Oakley negotiation. What should I do?	This indicates a policy mismatch. Check the following for compatibility: 1) authentication methods, and 2) security methods. If IPSec is used in tunneling mode, check the settings on the tunnel endpoints.

CERTIFICATION SUMMARY

In this chapter, we discussed both the concepts and practical implementation of the IP Security protocol, IPSec, in Windows 2000. We began with an overview of IP Security—what it is, why it's needed, and how it works. We discussed the components of security: authentication, integrity, and confidentiality, and you learned how IPSec provides each. We provided some background information about the history and development of cryptography and encryption methods of the past and present.

You became acquainted with the two IPSec protocols: Authentication Header (AH) and the Encapsulating Security Payload protocol (ESP). You learned that AH provides authentication for the entire packet, but does not encrypt data for confidentiality, while ESP does encrypt the data, but ordinarily does not protect the IP header.

We discussed the two modes in which IPSec can operate: transport mode and tunnel mode. We also examined how IPSec works in conjunction with L2TP to provide end-to-end security over a virtual private networking connection that is transmitted through the public Internet.

You learned how to configure IPSec, and how to use the IPSec Monitor and the System and Security event logs to aid in the troubleshooting process. Finally, we looked at some common troubleshooting scenarios, and suggestions for how to resolve them.

IP Security is an important topic—both on the Microsoft Implementing and Administering a Windows 2000 Network Infrastructure exam, and (more and more so every day) in the day-to-day world of a professional network administrator.

✓ TWO-MINUTE DRILL

Overview of IP Security

- ❑ IPSec operates at the Network layer of the OSI model, and provides protection to data that travels across the network, without a requirement to make changes to your applications.
- ❑ The elements of IPSec include the Authentication Header (AH) and Encapsulating Security Payload (ESP) protocols, cryptographic key management protocols, the Security Policy Database (SPD), and Security Associations (SAs).
- ❑ AH provides authentication and signs the entire packet, while ESP provides encryption but does not, in transport mode, protect the IP header. The two can be used in combination.
- ❑ IPSec supports two security association modes: transport and tunneling.
- ❑ IPSec uses encryption algorithms to protect data; the most common is the Data Encryption Standard (DES). 3DES is a stronger version. DES can be combined with Cipher Block Chaining (CBC) to prevent identical messages from looking the same in encrypted form.
- ❑ The IPSec security architecture provides an "end to end" security model. This means that only the "endpoints" of a communication need to be IPSec aware.
- ❑ Key Exchange is the first phase of security negotiation. This involves the use of the Internet Security Association Key Management Protocol (ISAKMP) and the Oakley protocol, collectively referred to as the Internet Key Exchange (IKE).
- ❑ IPSec will block SNMP messages unless you configure a rule to prevent it.
- ❑ IPSec is used in conjunction with the Layer Two Tunneling Protocol (L2TP) to provide a secure link over a virtual private network connection.

Enabling and Configuring IPSec

- ❑ Windows 2000 provides policy-based administration of IP Security, accomplished via the IP Security Management console.

- Before you can create and implement security policies, you must develop an overall security plan by assessing the organization's security needs and evaluating potential security threats.
- There are three built-in (predefined) IPSec policies: Client (Respond Only), Server (Request Security), and Secure Server (Require Security). You can also create custom policies.
- An IPSec policy has three main components: IP Security rules, IP filter lists, and IP filter actions.
- Each IPSec rule must be configured with one of three possible connection types: Local Area Network (LAN), Remote Access, or All Network Connections.
- Key Exchange settings, including intervals for authentication and generation of new keys, can be set using the Advanced settings dialog box.

Managing, Monitoring, and Troubleshooting IPSec

- Managing IPSec policies involves testing policy integrity, restoring predefined policies, exporting and importing policies, refreshing the list of IPSec policies, and deleting and renaming policies. These tasks can be accomplished via the IP Security Policy Management console.
- The IPSec Monitor allows you to view the active security associations on both local and remote computers.
- The Monitor is accessed via the command line **ipsecmon <computername>.** If you type the command without the computer name, the Monitor will default to the local machine.
- Information displayed by the IPSec Monitor includes the number and types of active security associations, number of keys generated, and number of confidential (ESP) and authenticated (AH and ESP) bytes sent and received.
- The IPSec Monitor can be used to verify that communications have been secured successfully, to track patterns of authentication failures of security association failures, and aid in performance tuning.
- The Windows 2000 Event Viewer can be used to view IPSec-related messages via the System log and (Oakley authentication messages) the Security log.

SELF TEST

The following questions will help you measure your understanding of the material presented in this chapter. Read all of the choices carefully, as there may be more than one correct answer. Choose all correct answers for each question.

Overview of IP Security

1. At what layer of the OSI networking model does IPSec operate?

   A. Application layer

   B. Transport layer

   C. Network layer

   D. Physical layer

2. You are the network administrator for a small law firm that has two branch offices in different cities, in addition to the headquarters office at your location. You would like for the users in the branch offices to be able to connect to the file server at the headquarters location via a virtual private network over the Internet, but the communications require end-to-end security to protect confidential client data. Which of the following solutions would you choose?

   A. Use PPTP with MPPE.

   B. Use PPTP with IPSec.

   C. Use L2TP.

   D. Use L2TP with IPSec.

3. Which of the following is defined as "a message that contains the digital signature of a trusted third party?"

   A. Cipher

   B. Certificate

   C. Certificate authority

   D. Algorithm

4. Which of the following is a method used to generate secret keys?

   A. Diffie-Hellman

   B. RSA

C. Both of the above

D. None of the above

5. You are a network administrator, and you wish to provide protection for IP packets that travel across your network. You need to ensure the authentication, integrity, and confidentiality of the data in transport mode, and you also wish to protect the integrity of the IP header. Which of the following IPSec protocols can be used to accomplish this?

A. You can accomplish this using the AH protocol only.

B. You can accomplish this using the ESP protocol only.

C. The only way to accomplish this is to use both AH and ESP together.

D. There is no way to accomplish this.

6. Which of the following describes a hard security association? (Select all that apply.)

A. It is established if active policies are set to allow unsecured communications with computers that are not IPSec capable.

B. It is established if the active policies on two communicating computers are compatible.

C. It is a secured security association.

D. It is an unsecured security association.

Enabling and Configuring IPSec

7. Which of the following are components of an IPSec policy? (Select all that apply.)

A. IP Security filter lists

B. IP Security rules

C. IP Security descriptions

D. IP Security filter actions

8. You have configured a new custom IPSec policy. You note that the Default Response rule has been automatically added to the new policy. You do not want this rule to be a part of this policy. What can you do?

A. Remove the rule.

B. Deactivate the rule.

C. Edit the rule.

D. There is no way to prevent the Default Response rule from being part of the policy.

9. You are the administrator of a large network. You have added a new static IP address to a host that is protected by IP Security, and now IPSec does not seem to be working. You have already modified and updated the policies on the clients that make security requests to the host. You view the policy that is being used on the host in question, and find that the filters specify static IP addresses for local connections. What action should you take after adding the new static IP address to the network interface?

   A. Remove all filter lists on the host and create new ones.

   B. Remove and reinstall the TCP/IP protocol, as it is obvious that the IPSec driver must have become corrupt or deleted.

   C. Edit the new filter list to include the new static IP address, and save the filter list.

   D. Reboot the computer, and IPSec will work with the new static address.

10. Which of following are true of the IPSec authentication methods? (Select all that apply.)

   A. You can add only one authentication method per rule.

   B. If you have multiple authentication methods enabled, Kerberos will always be the preferred method.

   C. You can designate a preshared key, which you type in manually, as the authentication method.

   D. Authentication methods are specified by editing the Filter rule Properties sheet.

11. You have created a new IPSec rule. You wish to have the communications sent over the local area network, as well as remote access communications, affected by this rule. How will you configure the connection types to accomplish this?

   A. Select the LAN connection type setting. If LAN connections are secured, remote access connections are automatically affected as well.

   B. Select the Remote Access connection type setting. The LAN setting affects only local connections, but if you select the Remote Access type, both remote and LAN connections will be affected.

   C. Select both the LAN and Remote Access connections.

   D. Select All Network Connections.

12. Which of the following is true of IPSec tunneling mode? (Select all that apply.)

   A. Two rules are required to describe an IP tunnel.

   B. Tunnel endpoints are specified by DNS names.

   C. Tunneling mode is used only when IPSec is used with L2TP.

D. IPSec tunneling encapsulates the original packet inside a new packet.

Managing, Monitoring, and Troubleshooting IPSec

13. You have created custom IPSec policies, but they are not working properly, and now you wish to restore the predefined policies (Client, Server, and Secure Server). What actions would you take to return to the default policies?

    A. In the IP Security Policy Management console, right-click on the IP Security Policies folder, select All Tasks, and click Restore Default Policies.

    B. In the IP Security Policy Management console, click on the Local Policies folder, click Action, and select Restore Predefined Policies.

    C. Start the IPSec Monitor by typing **ipsecmon** at the command line, select the security association that is active, and click Restore.

    D. On the Start menu, select Programs | Administrative Tools | IPSec | Restore Default Policies.

14. You have created a new IPSec policy, but it does not show up in the policy list. What must you do to make it display in the list?

    A. Double-click on the policy name in the IPSec Policy Management console and click Display on the Properties sheet.

    B. Right-click on the IP Security Policies folder and select Refresh from the context menu.

    C. Restart the computer.

    D. Type **ipsecupdate** at the command line.

15. You type **ipsecmon** at the command line. What happens?

    A. The IPSec Security Policy Management console will open, in monitoring mode.

    B. You will receive an error message because you did not specify a computer name.

    C. The IPSec Monitor will display current security associations for the local machine if IPSec is enabled on the computer.

    D. The IPSec Monitor will display current security associations for all machines on the network.

16. What type of IPSec-related messages would you be able to view through the Security log in Windows 2000's Event Viewer?

    A. Messages indicating that an IPSec policy is in effect, and whether it is a local or domain policy.

    B. Messages pertaining to the IPSec policy agent.

C. Messages pertaining to ISAKMP/Oakley authentication.

D. No IPSec-related messages appear in the Security log; all such messages are displayed in the IPSec Monitor.

17. Which of the following statistics are displayed by the IPSec Monitor? (Select all that apply.)

A. Number of active security associations.

B. Number of inactive security associations.

C. Number of authentication failures.

D. Number of ESP bytes sent and received.

LAB QUESTION

You are the network administrator for a company with 300 users at the local office, and 125 users at a branch office in another state. You are attempting to establish a secure communication between two computers on your local network; however, the computers are failing to establish a security association.

When you look in the Event Viewer, you see a message that indicates the ISAKMP/Oakley negotiation failed.

You examine the Rule properties in effect for each machine. On Computer 1, you see the following the Properties tabs as displayed in Figures 7-18, 7-19, and 7-20.

The Properties tabs for Computer 2 are shown in Figures 7-21, 7-22, and 7-23.

What is the problem that is preventing secured communications, and how can it be rectified?

FIGURE 7-18

The Tunnel Setting tab for Computer 1

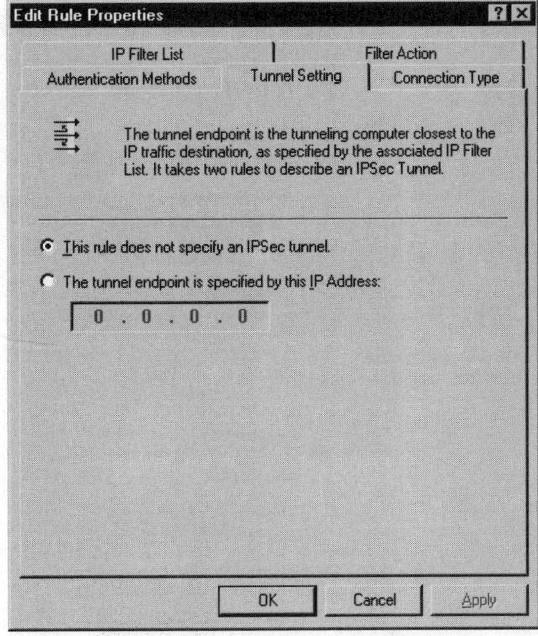

FIGURE 7-19

The Authentication Methods tab for Computer 1

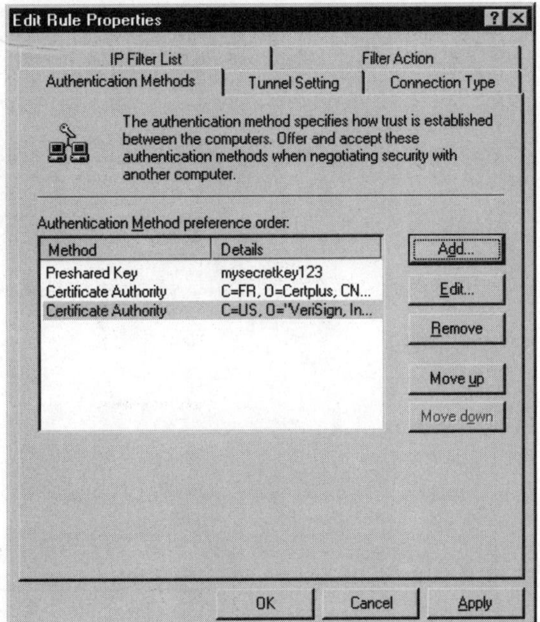

FIGURE 7-20

The Connection Type tab for Computer 1

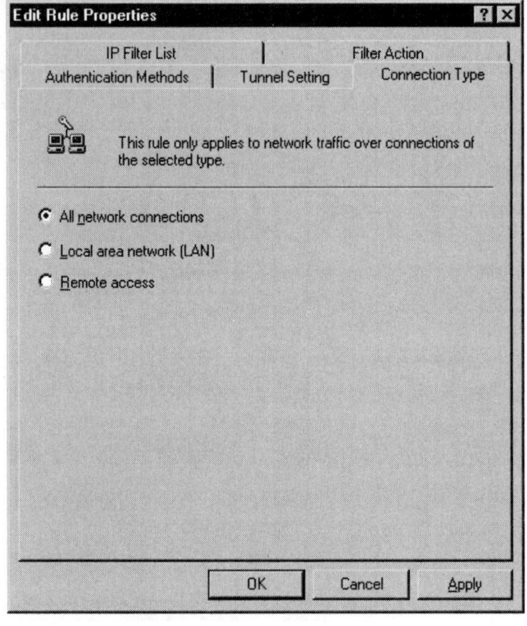

FIGURE 7-21

The Tunnel Setting tab for Computer 2

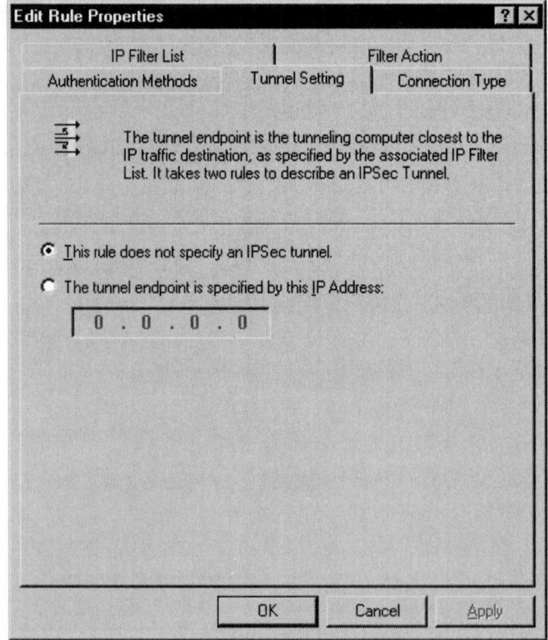

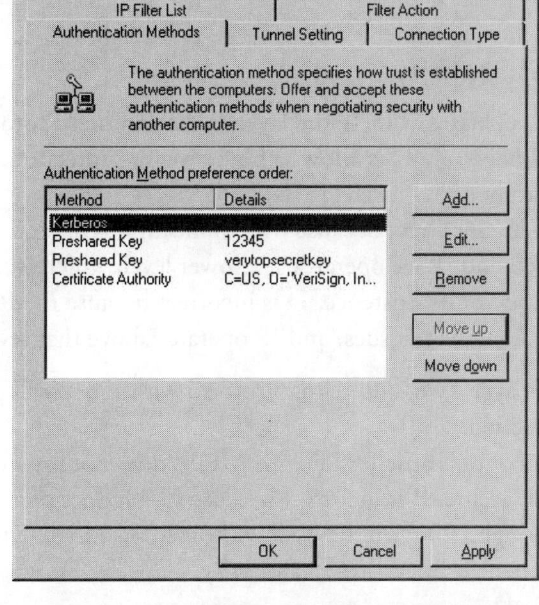

FIGURE 7-22 The Authentication Methods tab for Computer 2

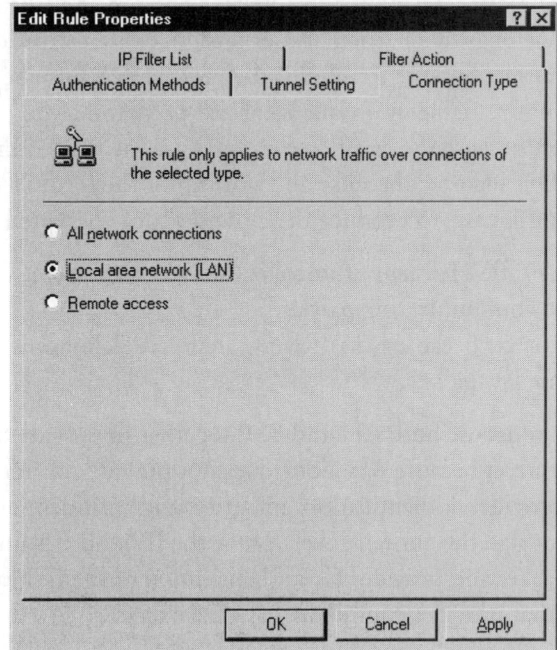

FIGURE 7-23 The Connection Type tab for Computer 2

SELF TEST ANSWERS

Overview of IP Security

1. ☑ C. IPSec operates at the same layer as the Internet Protocol (IP), the Network layer (also referred to as Layer 2). This allows a high level of protection, and no requirement for the applications to be IPSec aware.
   ☒ A and **B** are incorrect because the Application layer and the Transport layer are above the Network layer, and IPSec operates at a lower level, which is the reason the applications do not have to be aware of its existence. **D** is incorrect because the Physical layer deals with signaling, topology, and hardware issues, and IP operates above that level.

2. ☑ **D.** The Layer Two Tunneling Protocol with IPSec will provide for end-to-end security on a VPN connection.
   ☒ A is incorrect because PPTP with MPPE does not provide end-to-end security; only the tunnel itself is secure. **B** is incorrect because PPTP does not work with IPSec. **C** is incorrect because, although L2TP can be used without IPSec, there will be no encryption, and you will not have the benefit of end-to-end security.

3. ☑ **B.** A message that contains the digital signature of a trusted third party, ensuring that a specific key belongs to a particular user or device, is a certificate.
   ☒ A is incorrect because a cipher is the process that turns readable text data into encrypted data that is not readable by an unauthorized party (one who does not have the correct key). C is incorrect because the certificate authority is the trusted third party that signs the certificate. **D** is incorrect because an algorithm is the formula or procedure used to solve a problem (in this case, to produce the ciphertext, or encrypted data).

4. ☑ **A.** The Diffie-Hellman protocol is used to create secret session keys that are shared between two communicating parties.
   ☒ **B** is incorrect because RSA (Rivest, Shamir, Adelman) is an algorithm used to generate public/private key pairs.

5. ☑ C. You must use both AH and ESP together to provide this level of protection.
   ☒ A is incorrect because AH alone does not provide confidentiality. **B** is incorrect because, while ESP provides authentication, integrity, and confidentiality of data, in transport mode ESP does not sign the entire packet. Thus, the IP header is unprotected. AH, however, signs the entire packet and provides for authentication of the IP header in conjunction with ESP's encryption that provides confidentiality of the data.

6. ☑ **B, C.** A hard SA is established if the active security policies on two communicating computers are compatible, and a hard SA is a secured SA.
☒ **A** is incorrect because a soft SA is established if active policies are set to allow unsecured communications with computers that are not IPSec capable. Soft associations may prevent hard associations from being established, and you may have to restart the policy agent to rectify the situation. **D** is incorrect because the hard SA is a secured SA.

Enabling and Configuring IPSec

7. ☑ **A, B, D.** The three main components of an IPSec policy are filter lists, filter actions, and rules.
☒ **C** is incorrect because Description is a column header in the right details pane of the management console, not a component of an IPSec policy.

8. ☑ **B.** You must deactivate the rule if you do not wish for it to be part of your new custom policy.
☒ **A** is incorrect because you cannot remove a predefined rule. **C** is incorrect because editing the rule would not keep it from being part of the policy. **D** is incorrect because there *is* a way to prevent the rule from being part of this policy, by deactivating it.

9. ☑ **C.** You should edit and save the new filter list to include the new static IP address after adding the IP address to the network interface.
☒ **A** is incorrect because it is not necessary to remove all filter lists. **B** is incorrect because, although this is the correct procedure to repair damaged, corrupt, or deleted IPSec files, there is no indication that this is the problem. **D** is incorrect because rebooting the computer will not fix the problem unless you edit the filter list to add the new IP address.

10. ☑ **C, D.** You can designate a preshared key for authentication, which you type in manually, or you can use Kerberos (the default), or a designated certificate authority.
☒ **A** is incorrect because you can add multiple authentication methods to a rule. **B** is incorrect because when you have multiple methods enabled, you can move them up and down in the order of preference to indicate which one will be preferred.

11. ☑ **D.** To apply the rule to both LAN and remote connections, you must select the All Network Connections type.
☒ **A** is incorrect because the LAN setting will affect only local connections, not remote connections. **B** is incorrect because the Remote Access setting will affect only remote connections, not LAN connections. **C** is incorrect because you cannot choose two of the selections at the same time.

12. ☑ A, D. You must create two separate rules to define the two endpoints of the tunnel, and tunneling, by definition, involves encapsulating one packet inside another.
☒ B is incorrect because the tunnel endpoints are specified by IP addresses, not DNS names. C is incorrect because tunneling mode can be used in conjunction with L2TP to create a virtual private networking connection, but IPSec tunnel mode can be used alone, in which case IPSec itself encapsulates IP traffic.

Managing, Monitoring, and Troubleshooting IPSec

13. ☑ A. The default policies are restored from the IPSec Policy Management console, by right-clicking on the IP Security Policies folder, selecting All Tasks, and clicking Restore Default Policies.
☒ B is incorrect because IPSec is not administered from the Local Policies folder, which sets audit policies, user rights, and local security policies, and there is no Restore Predefined Policies option on the Action menu. C is incorrect because the IPSec Monitor is used to monitor and troubleshoot IPSec, not to restore the default policies. D is incorrect because there is no IPSec | Restore Default Policies selection in the Administrative Tools menu.

14. ☑ B. You can force an update of the IPSec Policy list by selecting Refresh from the context menu after right-clicking on the IP Security Policies folder.
☒ A is incorrect because there is no Display button. C is incorrect because it is not necessary to restart the computer to refresh the policy list. D is incorrect because there is no such thing as the ipsecupdate command.

15. ☑ C. If you do not type a computer name with the **ipsecmon** command, the Monitor will default to display of IPSec information for the local computer.
☒ A is incorrect because the **ipsecmon** command does not open the IPSec Security Policy Management console. B is incorrect because the command can be used without a computer name specified, which causes it to default to the local machine. D is incorrect because the Monitor will display the information only for the local machine (if IPSec is enabled on that machine), not for all machines on the network.

16. ☑ C. Messages related to ISAKMP/Oakley, such as the establishment of a security association in conjunction with a successful logon, appear in the Windows 2000 Security log.
☒ A and B are incorrect because messages indicating that an IPSec policy is in effect or pertaining to the IPSec policy agent appear in the System log, not the Security log. D is incorrect because IPSec-related messages are displayed in the Security log.

17. ☑ **A, C, D.** IPSec Monitor displays a great deal of pertinent information, including the number of active security associations, authentication failures, and confidential (ESP) bytes sent and received.

☒ **B** is incorrect because the number of inactive security associations is not displayed.

LAB ANSWER

There is a policy mismatch—the computers must have a common security method, authentication method, and, if IPSec is used in tunneling mode, the endpoint settings must be correct. We know from the Properties sheets that IPSec is not being used in tunnel mode; however, Computer 1 is set to use Certificate Authorities and a preshared key for authentication, whereas Computer 2 has only Kerberos designated as an authentication method. Thus, there is no common authentication method by which the two computers can negotiate authentication. Although the connection type settings are not the same on both machines, this will not prevent their establishing a secure communication, because they are on the local network and Computer 1 is configured to use this rule for all network connections, while Computer 2 is configured to use its rule for the local area connection only.

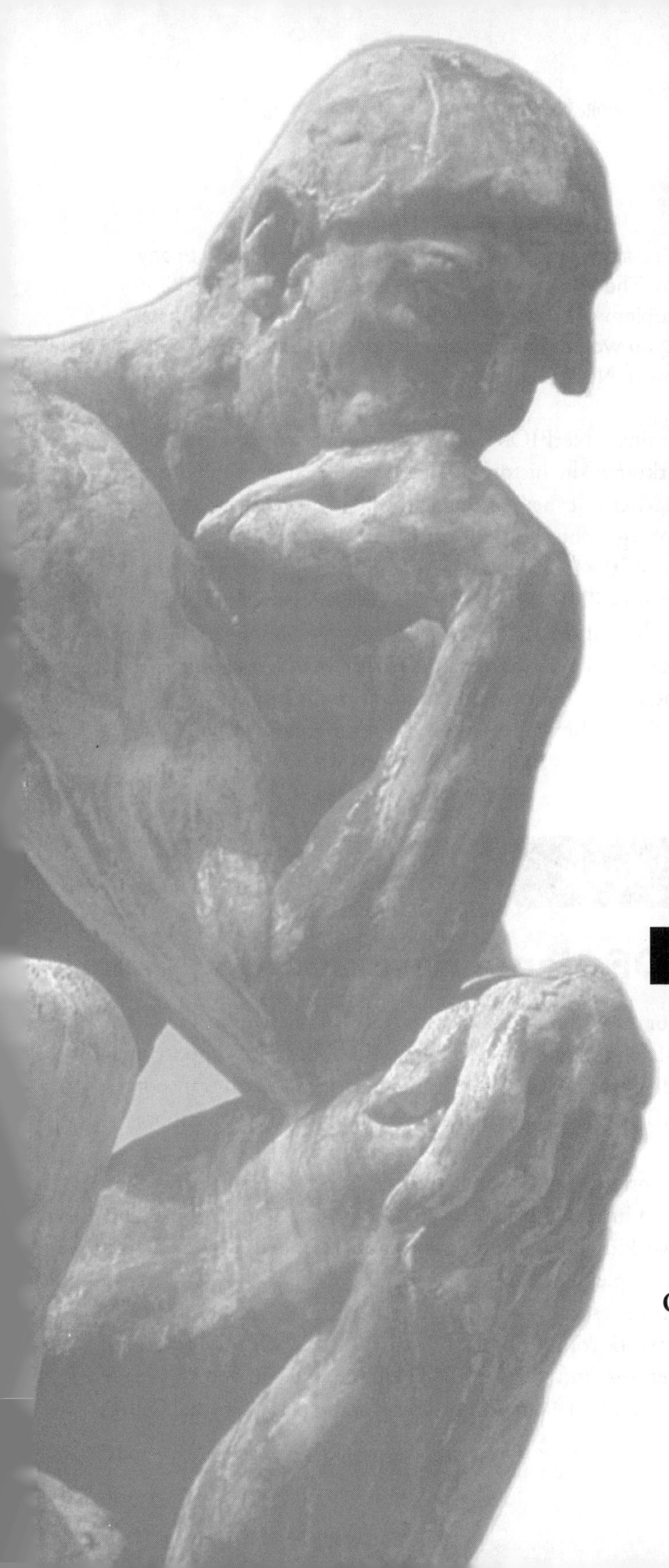

8

Installing, Configuring, Managing, Monitoring, and Troubleshooting WINS

CERTIFICATION OBJECTIVES

8.01	Introduction to NetBIOS Name Resolution
8.02	Planning and Implementing a WINS Solution
8.03	Interoperability Issues
8.04	Monitoring and Troubleshooting WINS
 ✓	Two-Minute Drill
Q&A	Self Test

In this chapter, we'll focus on a service familiar to those who have been working with any Microsoft network operating system: The Windows Internet Name Service, or WINS. WINS solves the very important problem of resolving NetBIOS names for remote hosts on Microsoft networks. Without WINS, you would need to use methods such as LMHOSTS files in order to resolve the names of remote NetBIOS hosts.

Microsoft's goal is to eliminate NetBIOS from Microsoft networks. However, the history of Microsoft networking is the history of NetBIOS. Because of the intimate ties between NetBIOS and Microsoft networking and Microsoft networked applications, a large cadre of legacy applications exists that depend on the NetBIOS interface. Therefore, in spite of the long-term goal of eliminating WINS, it's likely that NetBIOS name resolution will be an important problem for the network administrator in the foreseeable future.

In the chapter, we will look at the mechanics of NetBIOS name resolution, how to plan and implement a WINS networking solution, some important interoperability issues, and finally, how to monitor and troubleshoot your WINS implementation.

CERTIFICATION OBJECTIVE 8.01

Introduction to NetBIOS Name Resolution

All Microsoft networks prior to Windows 2000 were NetBIOS networks. NetBIOS was developed for IBM by a company name Sytek in 1983 in order to support small local area networks (LANs). It was initially a broadcast-based, monolith transport protocol for workgroups. Microsoft's implementation of the NetBIOS transport protocol is the NetBIOS Extend User Interface, or NetBEUI. NetBEUI was the workhorse of Microsoft networks during the early growth of the Microsoft networking model. In fact, Microsoft had intended NetBEUI to become even more robust, and even routable. They were working on a networking protocol dubbed "JetBEUI" that would have been a routable implementation of NetBEUI.

Everything changed with the ascendance of the Internet. In 1995, Microsoft recognized the future of network computing as intimately tied in with the Internet. The protocol of the Internet was, and is, TCP/IP. Therefore, the decision was made to abandon NetBEUI as the standard Microsoft protocol, and replace it with TCP/IP.

However, the changeover from NetBIOS networking to TCP/IP-based networking would not be easy or seamless. NetBIOS protocols use the NetBIOS name of the destination host as the endpoint of communication. TCP/IP is unaware of NetBIOS names. TCP/IP uses IP addresses and port numbers as the endpoints of communication. The vast majority of programs written for Microsoft networks were written to the NetBIOS programming interface. A mechanism had to be put into place that would solve this problem.

NetBIOS over TCP/IP

To understand the solution to the problem, you need to understand a little more about what the problem is with programs written specifically for NetBIOS-based networks.

When programs are designed, they are written with a particular protocol in mind. NetBIOS programs were written for NetBIOS based networks; in other words, all Microsoft networks prior to Windows 2000. These programs are able to access the network protocols via the NetBIOS Session layer interface. NetBIOS programs establish sessions with other computers via their NetBIOS names by broadcasting the destination computer's name over the segment, and waiting for the destination computer to respond with its MAC address.

The challenge was to get NetBIOS-based programs to work over TCP/IP-based networks. Since TCP/IP uses destination IP addresses and port numbers as the endpoint of communication, a NetBIOS *Session layer interface* was added. This NetBIOS Session layer interface is known as NetBIOS over TCP/IP, or NetBT.

NetBT is one of two session layer interfaces programs can use to access the networking protocols. The other is the *Windows Sockets interface*, or *WinSock.* Programs written expressly for TCP/IP-based networks access the TCP/IP protocol stack via the WinSock interface.

The main job for NetBT is to resolve NetBIOS names to IP addresses. In this way, we can get programs that are unaware of IP addresses to work with a protocol that is unaware of NetBIOS names. Once the destination computer's NetBIOS name is matched up, or *resolved* to an IP address, the request can be passed from the Application layer to the lower layers of the protocol stack.

exam Watch

The Microsoft courses and documentation state that NetBIOS is both a transport protocol and a session layer interface. You will see articles in Microsoft TechNet that state that NetBIOS is not a transport protocol. Remember for the exams that when we talk about NetBT, we are referring to a session layer interface.

Names and Naming Conventions

NetBIOS names are 16-byte names. You can configure the first 15 bytes with legal NetBIOS name characters, and the 16th byte is reserved for a service identifier. The NetBIOS convention is that all characters are treated as uppercase regardless of how you type them in various dialog boxes. Legal characters in NetBIOS names include A–Z, 0–9, #, $, !, -, _, @, %, (,), [,]. However, some of these *exotic* (non-alphanumeric) characters have other meanings in the Microsoft NetBIOS implementation, so you need to be careful in your use of these characters.

No two computers on a NetBIOS-based network can have the same NetBIOS name. This has caused many administrators to pull their hair out because in large networks of 40,000 computers or more, the challenge of coming up with a meaningful, yet different name for each computer required a certain level of creativity.

The NetBIOS namespace is a *flat* namespace. It is flat because the single NetBIOS name represents the only *partition* of the namespace. It's as if everyone in the world was required to have a different first name. What a challenge it would be to find a meaningful name for every person in the world if that were the case!

Although you can use any number of unusual characters in your NetBIOS names, you should limit yourself to the DNS-compatible characters. Otherwise, you can create a schism between your DNS host name and NetBIOS naming conventions, which can make troubleshooting name resolution problems on the network difficult. Be particularly careful to avoid the use of the underscore (_) character. Although this character was popular in the past, you should divorce yourself from this habit immediately in your Windows 2000 NetBIOS implementations.

Service Identifiers A computer running the TCP/IP NetBIOS interface actually has several NetBIOS names. Each name is used by a service to "advertise" that the service is running on that particular computer. It's like putting a sign on the door saying "these people live here." For example, if a Windows 2000 machine is running both the Server service and the Workstation (Microsoft *Redirector*) service, it will register two NetBIOS names, one for each of the services running. This is a way for the NetBIOS applications to let other machines know that they are running and available.

You can see a list of the registered NetBIOS names for your computer by using the nbtstat utility from the command line. Open a command prompt and type:

nbtstat –n

You'll see something similar to what appears in Figure 8-1.

FIGURE 8-1

Registered NetBIOS names for a computer named Constellation

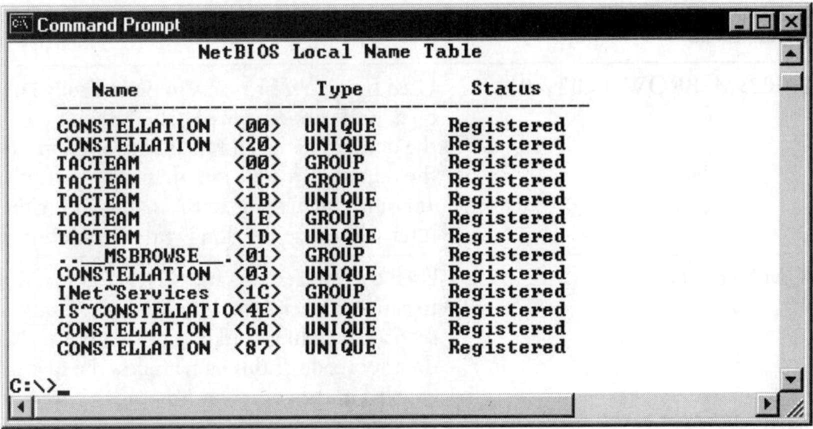

The key concept to appreciate is that computers running NetBIOS services don't typically have a NetBIOS name; they have *NetBIOS Names.*

Table 8-1 lists some of the common NetBIOS name service identifiers.

TABLE 8-1 Common NetBIOS Name Suffixes

<USERNAME><03>	Used to register the name of the user currently logged on in the WINS database so that the messenger service can locate users via their NetBIOS names.
<COMPUTER><00>	Used by the Microsoft Redirector to indicate that the computer is running the Microsoft Networking Client Service. This is the computer name registered by the Workstation Service.
<COMPUTER><03>	Used as the computer name that is registered for the Messenger Service on a computer that is a WINS client.
<COMPUTER><20>	Used as the name that is registered for a computer running the Server service on a Windows 2000 computer that is a WINS client.
<COMPUTER><Be>	Used as the *unique name* that is registered when the Network Monitor agent is started on the computer. Unique means that the name used is not a *group* name.
<COMPUTER><Bf>	Used as the *group* name that is registered when the Network Monitor agent is started on the computer. If this name is not 15 characters in length, it is padded with plus (+) symbols.
<COMPUTER><1f>	Used as the unique name that is registered for network dynamic data exchange (NetDDE) when the NetDDE service is started on the computer.

TABLE 8-1 Common NetBIOS Name Suffixes *(continued)*

<01><02>MSBROWSE<02><01>	Used by master browsers to periodically announce their domain on a local subnet. This master browser announcement contains the domain name and the name of the master browser server for the domain. In addition, master browsers receive the domain announcements sent to this name and maintain them in their internal browse list along with the announcer's computer name.
<DOMAIN><00>	Used by workstations and servers to process server announcements to support Microsoft LAN Manager. Computers running the Server service, including Windows 95, Windows NT, and Windows 2000, do not broadcast this name unless the LMAnnounce option is enabled in the computer running the Server service.
<DOMAIN><1b>	Used to identify the *domain master browser* name, which is a unique name that only the primary domain controller (PDC) or PDC Emulator can add. WINS assumes that the computer that registers a domain name with the <1b>character is the PDC.
<DOMAIN><1c>	Used for the internet group name, which all the domain controllers register. The internet group name is a dynamic list of up to 25 computers that have registered the name. This is the name used to find a Windows NT domain controller for pass-through authentication.
<DOMAIN><1d>	Used to identify a segment master browser (*not a domain master browser*). The master browser adds this name as a unique NetBIOS name when it starts. Computers running the Server service announce their presence to this name so that master browsers can build their browse list.
<DOMAIN><1e>	Used for all domain-wide announcements by browser servers in a Windows 2000 based server domain. This name is added by all browsers and potential browsers in the workgroup or domain. All browser election packets are sent to this name.

exam Watch

Be aware that Windows 2000 domains have both a DNS name and a NetBIOS equivalent. Windows 2000 domain operations are not dependent on NetBIOS, as was the case with Windows NT 4.0. Typically, the NetBIOS domain name is equivalent to the leftmost label in the DNS name. However, these names do not have to be the same.

SCENARIO & SOLUTION	
Why shouldn't I use the underscore character in my NetBIOS names? I've been doing that on my Windows Networking for the last five years.	The underscore character is not a legal character in most DNS server installations. When you name a Windows 2000 computer, it will recommend that you do not use the underscore because it will lead you to have different NetBIOS and host names for the machine. This can cause queries for either the NetBIOS name or the DNS name to fail if one of the name resolution services becomes unavailable.
I thought TCP/IP only had four layers—the Application, Transport, Internet, and Network Interface. How can there be a Session layer interface?	Although the DoD model on which the TCP/IP protocol stack was built only named four layers, the functions associated with the OSI Session layer are incorporated into the DoD Application layer.
Why is it that when I enter computer names or domain names into the GUI interfaces, they are always converted to all capital letters, regardless of how I type them?	The NetBIOS standard is that all NetBIOS names are capitalized. Although some operating systems will represent NetBIOS names in mixed case, their "true" names are all caps. Remember, the Windows NT 4.0 domain names are NetBIOS names too!

Resolving NetBIOS Names to IP Addresses

In order for NetBIOS applications to communicate with each other on TCP/IP-based networks, the destination NetBIOS name must be matched up, or *resolved*, to an IP address. This is known as *NetBIOS name resolution.*

There are multiple ways to resolve a NetBIOS name to an IP address. This is because resolving a NetBIOS name to an IP address is critical to communications on most Microsoft networks. The NetBIOS-specific methods of resolving a NetBIOS name to an IP address are

- NetBIOS Name Servers (WINS)
- Broadcasts
- LMHOSTS file

Let's look at each of these methods and see how they work, and how they *don't* work, on your TCP/IP network.

Broadcasts

NetBT can use broadcasts to resolve a NetBIOS name to an IP address. Broadcasts are of limited utility, because the destination host must be on the same segment in order for NetBIOS name resolution to be successful via broadcast. Routers do not, and should not, forward NetBIOS broadcast messages. If routers were configured to pass NetBIOS messages via UDP Ports 137 (NetBIOS Name Service) and 138 (NetBIOS Data Service), the network could become flooded with NetBIOS name registration and query traffic.

When the broadcast is issued, a request is sent for the IP address of a given NetBIOS name. When the IP address is returned, another broadcast takes place in the form of an ARP (Address Resolution Protocol) request. The ARP request broadcasts a query onto the segment requesting resolution of the IP address to a hardware (Media Access Control, or MAC) address. After the MAC address is obtained, a session can be established.

exam watch

NetBIOS is not the only protocol that issues broadcasts for resolution purposes. Network architectures such as Ethernet are broadcast dependent, because logical addresses must be resolved to hardware addresses. This is in contrast to ATM networks, where a MARS (Media Access Resolution Service) server is used to resolve logical addresses to hardware addresses.

LMHOSTS

An LMHOSTS file is a plain-text file that contains NetBIOS names to IP address mappings. LMHOSTS can be useful as a backup method of resolving names of especially important computers when other methods fail.

An example LMHOSTS file for our small office network appears in Figure 8-2.

FIGURE 8-2

A sample LMHOSTS file

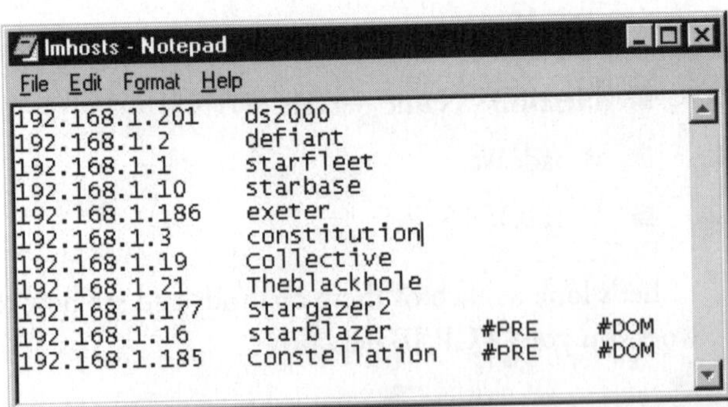

The LMHOSTS file looks somewhat like the HOSTS file, the major difference being that the LMHOSTS file resolves NetBIOS names, and the HOSTS file resolves host names. Another significant difference between LMHOSTS and HOSTS is that the LMHOSTS file supports a number of *tags* that enhance its utility.

A list of the supported LMHOSTS tags appears in Table 8-2.

TABLE 8-2 Commonly Used LMHOSTS File Tags

#BEGIN_ALTERNATE	Used to group multiple #INCLUDE statements. Any single successful #INCLUDE statement in a group causes the group to succeed. The included groups will not be searched until a successful name resolution is accomplished. Rather, the success of an included group is determined by whether or not access to the file is successful.
#END_ALTERNATE	Used to mark the end of a group of #INCLUDE statements.
#DOM:*<domain>*	Determines that the NetBIOS name mapping is for a domain controller. This keyword affects how the Browser and Logon services behave in routed TCP/IP environments. Since domain controllers are important for many domain-related functions, it is often preferred to preload a #DOM entry; the #PRE keyword must appear first in the entry.
#INCLUDE *<file name>*	An *included* LMHOSTS file is located on a remote server that has a shared directory with a file that can provide NetBIOS name to IP address mappings. Specifying a Universal Naming Convention (UNC) <file name> allows you to use a centralized LMHOSTS file on a server. If the server on which <file name> exists is outside of the local broadcast subnet, you must add a mapping in the LMHOSTS file for that server above the #BEGIN_ALTERNATE statement.
#MH	Multihomed machines have multiple IP addresses. Typically, a search for a NetBIOS name to IP address mapping will stop with the first successful match. However, if you append the #MH tag to the entry, the search will continue to find subsequent entries for the same NetBIOS name in the LMHOSTS file. The maximum number of addresses that can be assigned to a unique name is 25.
#PRE	Part of the NetBIOS name to IP address mapping entry that causes that entry to be preloaded into the NetBIOS remote name cache. By default, entries are not preloaded into the name cache, but are parsed only after WINS and name query broadcasts fail to resolve a name. *The #PRE keyword must be appended to entries that also appear in #INCLUDE statements; otherwise, the entry in the #INCLUDE statement is ignored.* Therefore, be sure when you create the mapping for the server that has the included LMHOSTS file that you put the #PRE tag on it.

Some things to note about the LMHOSTS file:

- The file is parsed (read and processed) from top to bottom.
- Parsing stops after the first successful match (unless the #MH tag is used).
- The *NetBIOS Names* are not case sensitive.
- The *tags* are case sensitive.
- The LMHOSTS file does not have a file extension.

Because the file is parsed from top to bottom, you should put the entries with the #PRE tags on the bottom of the list. This is because those entries have already been evaluated when the NetBIOS remote name cache has been evaluated at the beginning of the NetBIOS name resolution sequence.

The tags in the LMHOSTS file are case sensitive and should be entered in uppercase.

EXERCISE 8-1

Creating an LMHOSTS File

In this exercise, you will create an LMHOSTS file for your network. Do not perform this exercise on a live, production environment without your network administrator's permission.

1. Identify three computers on your network by NetBIOS name and IP address. If possible, find one that is a domain controller.
2. Open Notepad from the Start menu.
3. Type in the names of the three computers and their IP addresses in Notepad. Separate the computer name from the IP address with a Tab. Make the domain controller the last entry in the list, and use both the #DOM: and the #PRE tags for the domain controller. Be sure to press Enter after completing the last line. Your LMHOSTS file should look something like the following illustration.

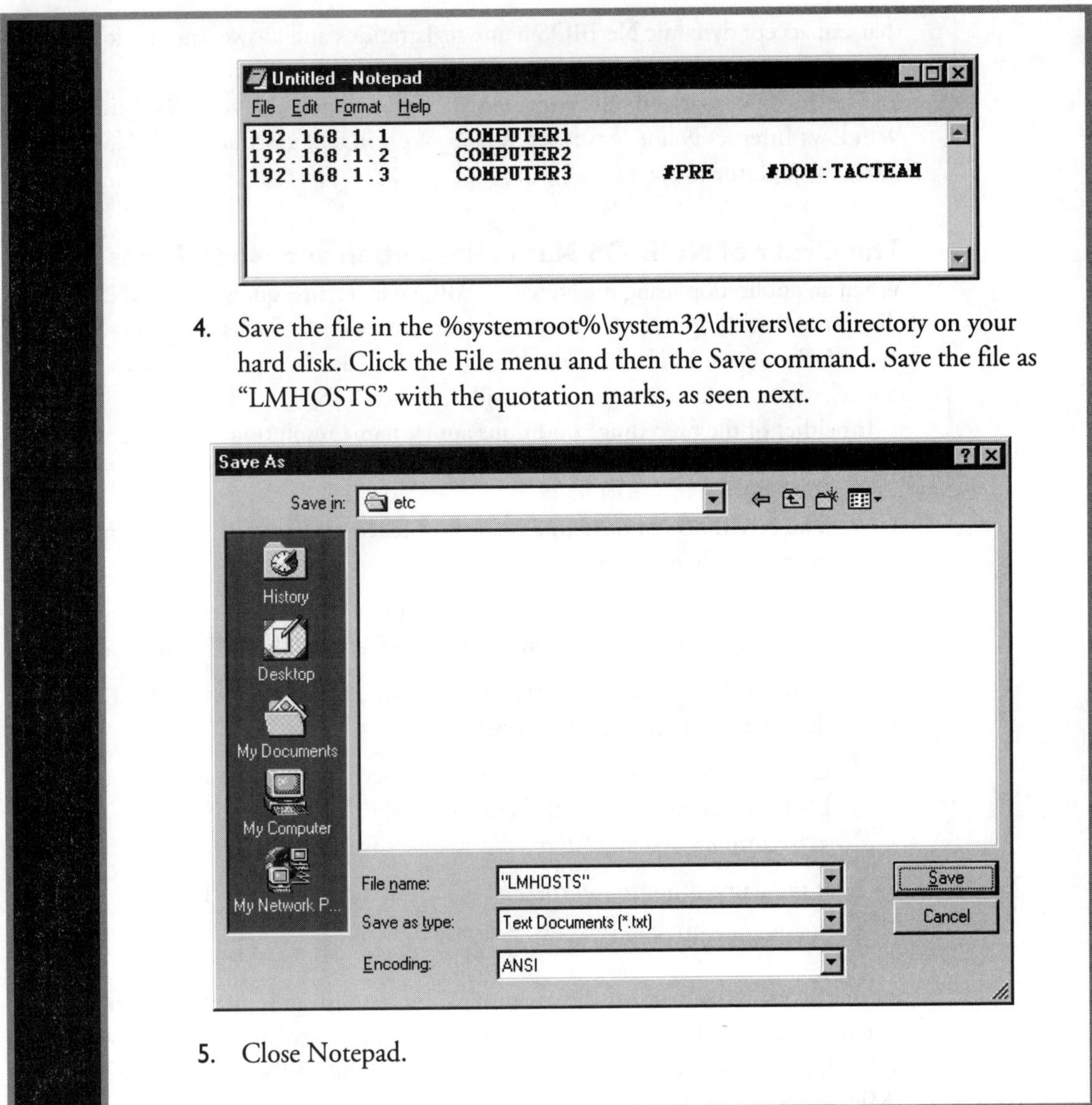

4. Save the file in the %systemroot%\system32\drivers\etc directory on your hard disk. Click the File menu and then the Save command. Save the file as "LMHOSTS" with the quotation marks, as seen next.

5. Close Notepad.

NetBIOS Name Server

A NetBIOS Name Server (NBNS) is a machine that runs server software dedicated to resolving NetBIOS names to IP addresses. The NBNS contains a database file that can accept dynamic NetBIOS name registrations and answer queries for NetBIOS name resolution.

The most popular and only widely used NetBIOS name server is the Microsoft Windows Internet Name Server, or WINS. We will talk more about WINS as we move through the chapter.

The Order of NetBIOS Name Resolution and Node Types

When an application using the NetBIOS API issues a name query on a WINS-enabled client, the first thing the operating system does is evaluate the name. If it is longer than 15 characters, or if it is hierarchical (contains "dots" or periods, such as constellation.tacteam.net), the query will be sent to DNS.

If neither of the preceding conditions apply, name resolution will proceed in the follow sequence:

1. The NetBIOS remote name cache is checked to determine if the name has been recently resolved.
2. If the name is not found there, it will contact the WINS server(s) whose address(es) have been entered in the WINS clients' TCP/IP properties.
3. If the WINS server cannot resolve the name, it will issue a broadcast to the other computers on its subnet.
4. If this doesn't work, and the TCP/IP properties are configured to use LMHOSTS lookup, it will check the LMHOSTS file in the <systemroot>\system32\Drivers\Etc directory.
5. If the name is not found there, it will next check the HOSTS file.
6. Finally, it will attempt to query a DNS server.

An easy way to remember the order of WINS resolution is by memorizing the sentence "Can We Buy Large Hard Drives." The first letter of each word—C, W, B, L, H, D—stands for the resolution methods: Cache, WINS, Broadcast, LMHOSTS, Hosts, DNS.

This NetBIOS name resolution sequence does not exactly tell the whole story, but should be adequate when taking your Windows 2000 exams. For example, while the HOSTS file is parsed, it's done a little differently from how it was in Windows NT 4.0. Entries in the HOSTS file are immediately put into the DNS client's caching resolver, and it's the resolver cache that is inspected during name resolution, and not the HOSTS file itself.

This is the sequence when the Windows 2000 machine is configured as an H-node client. When NetBIOS machines are configured as other node types, the name resolution sequence is slightly altered.

NetBIOS clients must be configured with a *node type* that defines how they process NetBIOS queries. The NetBIOS node type will determine which services are invoked, and in what order. The NetBIOS node types include

- b-node
- p-node
- m-node
- h-node

Let's look at each node type in a little more detail, and examine the circumstances in which each node might find its best use.

B-Node A *b-node* (broadcast node) client uses broadcasts instead of a WINS server. A Windows NetBIOS client computer without a configured WINS server is a b-node client. The NetBIOS name resolution order for the b-node client is

1. NetBIOS remote name cache
2. Broadcast
3. LMHOSTS
4. HOSTS
5. DNS server

There is another node type that is a subset of the b-node referred to as the Microsoft enhanced b-node. The enhanced b-node client uses entries that have the #PRE tag in the LMHOSTS file, and parses those cached entries before issuing the NetBIOS Name Query Request on the local segment.

P-Node A *p-node* (peer node) WINS client uses a WINS server and does not issue broadcasts. When a WINS client is configured as a p-node WINS client, it will *not* broadcast to resolve a NetBIOS name to an IP address. The advantage of configuring WINS clients as p-nodes is that there is no possibility of NetBIOS broadcast traffic using up valuable network bandwidth. On the other hand, if the p-node client is not able to access a WINS server, it will have to use alternate methods to resolve the NetBIOS name to an IP address, even if the destination host is local. This can lead to strange things, like the p-node client accessing a remote DNS server to resolve the IP address of a host on the local segment.

The NetBIOS name resolution order for the p-node client is

1. NetBIOS remote name cache
2. WINS server
3. LMHOSTS
4. HOSTS
5. DNS server

M-Node *M-node* (mixed node) WINS clients use both broadcasts *and* WINS servers to resolve NetBIOS names to IP addresses. The mixed-node client preferentially uses broadcasts before querying a WINS server.

Consider this example. You have a company with three sites. The main site is located in Dallas, and has 1200 computers. The company also maintains two satellite offices, one in Houston and another in Amarillo, which have 20 computers each. The satellite offices require very little network services support from the main office, and most sessions take place among the machines located within the remote sites. The only WINS server is in Dallas.

In this situation, you would be better off to configure the computers in the satellite offices as m-node clients, since these computers are all located on the same segment, and broadcasts will easily resolve the NetBIOS names to IP addresses. This will prevent the machines from having to query a remote WINS server for local addresses. If the client needs to resolve names for machines on remote segments, they can still query the remote WINS server.

The NetBIOS name resolution order for the m-node client is

1. NetBIOS remote name cache
2. Broadcast

3. WINS server
4. LMHOSTS
5. HOSTS
6. DNS server

H-Node H-node (hybrid node) WINS clients are similar to M-node, but use WINS NetBIOS name resolution first, before initiating a NetBIOS broadcast message.

The NetBIOS name resolution order for the h-node client is

1. NetBIOS remote name cache
2. WINS server
3. Broadcast
4. LMHOSTS
5. HOSTS
6. DNS server

exam Watch

The node type can be changed manually by editing the Registry, or can be automatically assigned when using a DHCP server. The NetBIOS node type setting is stored in the registry at:

HKLM\System\CurrentControlSet\Services\NetBT\Parameters

The Entry is named NodeType and is of type REG_DWORD. The possible values are
B-node = 0x1
P-node = 0x2
M-node = 0x4
H-node = 0x8
Hybrid node clients are best suited for a multiple segment LAN/WAN environment, where destination NetBIOS clients and resources are located on remote segments.

WINS Network Components

In order to resolve NetBIOS names using WINS, you need to architect the components of your WINS network. A *WINS network* is the collection of WINS servers on your network that will service the NetBIOS name query requests they receive from network clients.

WINS Servers

At the heart of your WINS network are the WINS servers. The WINS server maintains a database of NetBIOS name to IP address mappings. A single WINS server and a backup WINS server can easily accommodate up to 10,000 computers. One issue many Windows NT 4.0 networks faced was that of deploying too many WINS servers. This is because when you increase the number of WINS servers, you also increase the probability that you will have lags in the WINS database consistency. No matter how large the organization, you should limit yourself to less than 20 WINS servers total. If you believe your require more, Microsoft strongly recommends that you consult the Microsoft Consulting Services division.

While the WINS servers are the heart of your WINS network, there are other components that you need to set up: WINS clients, and possibly WINS Proxies.

WINS Clients

A WINS client is any computer that can register with and query a WINS server. The Microsoft operating systems that can act as WINS clients include

- Windows 2000
- Windows NT Server
- Windows NT Workstation
- Windows 98
- Windows 95
- Windows for Workgroups
- LAN Manager 2.*x*

In addition to these Microsoft operating systems, non-Microsoft client operating systems can be WINS enabled, although this is rarely seen in actual practice.

WINS clients are configured with at least one IP address for a WINS server. Figure 8-3 shows the Windows 2000 Advanced TCP/IP Settings Properties dialog box where WINS client configuration is accomplished.

The Windows NT 4.0 WINS client configuration allowed you to enter a Primary and Secondary WINS server. The WINS client would initially try to register its NetBIOS names with the Primary WINS server, and if that machine were not available, it would attempt to register with the Secondary WINS server. The same applied to the NetBIOS name query process. The Windows 2000 WINS Client allows you to enter up to 12 Secondary WINS servers. This allows an extra measure of fault tolerance for your WINS client NetBIOS name resolution requirements.

WINS Proxy Agents

WINS Proxies are similar to DHCP relay agents. A WINS Proxy intercepts NetBIOS name resolution requests for b-node clients that cannot be configured

FIGURE 8-3

WINS Client Configuration dialog box

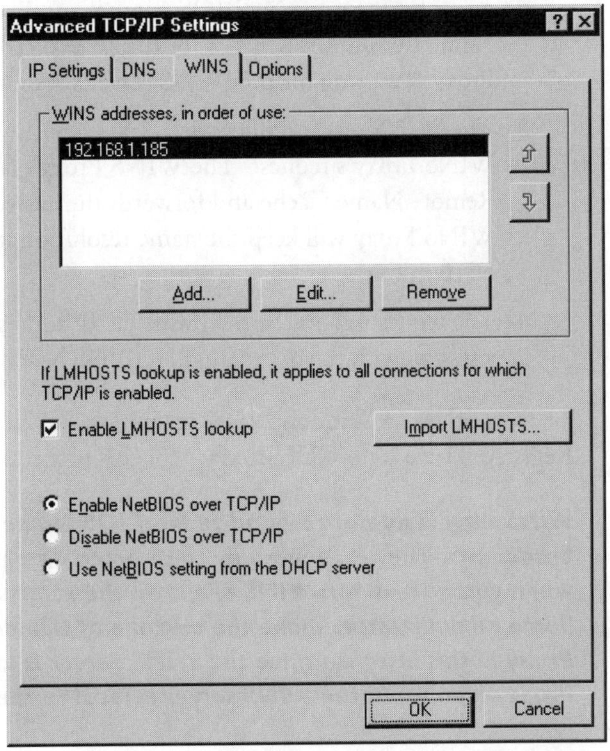

as WINS clients. The most common example of the non-WINS client you might encounter is the UNIX computer that is running a NetBIOS service and requires NetBIOS name resolution for remote NetBIOS hosts.

When a non-WINS client needs to resolve a NetBIOS name of a remote host, it issues a *NetBIOS Name Query Request.* If there is a WINS Proxy on the local subnet, it intercepts the request. After intercepting the request, the WINS Proxy does the following:

1. Checks its own NetBIOS Remote Name Cache for an entry for the destination NetBIOS host. If the name and IP address mapping are contained in the cache, this information is returned to the requesting machine.
2. If the name of the destination computer is not in the WINS Proxy's NetBIOS Remote Name Cache, it will query a WINS server via a directed datagram. The original query is placed in a *resolving state* until the WINS server responds. This is done so that the WINS Proxy does not send another query for the same NetBIOS name if another machine issues a NetBIOS Name Resolution Request for the same NetBIOS name while the WINS Proxy is waiting for the WINS server's response.
3. The WINS server replies with either a positive or negative response to the WINS Proxy's request. The WINS Proxy places the result in its NetBIOS Remote Name Cache and forwards the answer to the requesting host. The WINS Proxy will keep the name resolution in its cache for a default period of 10 minutes.
4. The requesting host, armed with the IP address of the remote host, establishes a session with the destination NetBIOS host.

To configure a Windows 2000 machine as a WINS Proxy, you must edit the Registry. There is no GUI interface for this procedure.

on the Job

WINS servers do not respond to NetBIOS Name Resolution Query Request broadcasts. They respond only to directed datagrams. This becomes an issue when you have a non-WINS client on the same segment as a WINS server. Some administrators make the mistake of thinking they do not need a WINS Proxy in this instance since the WINS Server is local. You do need a WINS Proxy, even when the WINS server is local to the non-WINS client.

EXERCISE 8-2

Configuring a Windows 2000 Member Server as a WINS Proxy Agent

In this exercise, you will edit the Registry to create a WINS Proxy Agent on a Windows 2000 computer. Do not perform this exercise on a live, production network without the permission of your network administrator.

1. From the Run command, open the Registry editor by typing **regedt32** in the command line. Navigate to the following location:

   ```
   HKEY_LOCAL_MACHINE\SYSTEM\CurrentControlSet\
   Services\Netbt\Parameters
   ```

2. Click the Edit menu, and then click the **Add Value** command. In the Value Name text box, type **Enable Proxy**. Set the Data Type to REG_DWORD. You should see what appears in the following illustration. Click OK.

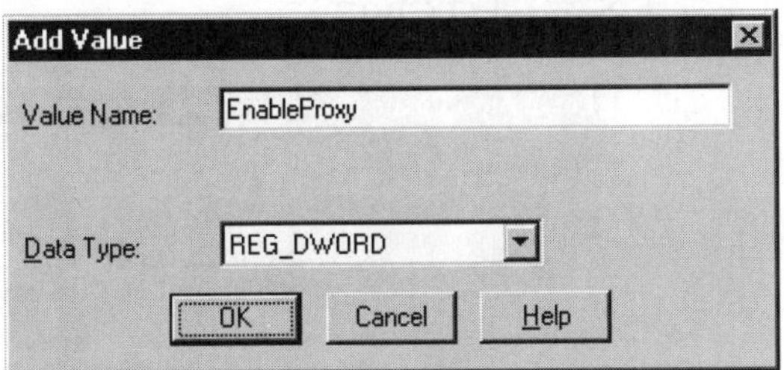

3. In the DWORD Editor dialog box, type **1** in the Data text box. Your screen should look like the following illustration.

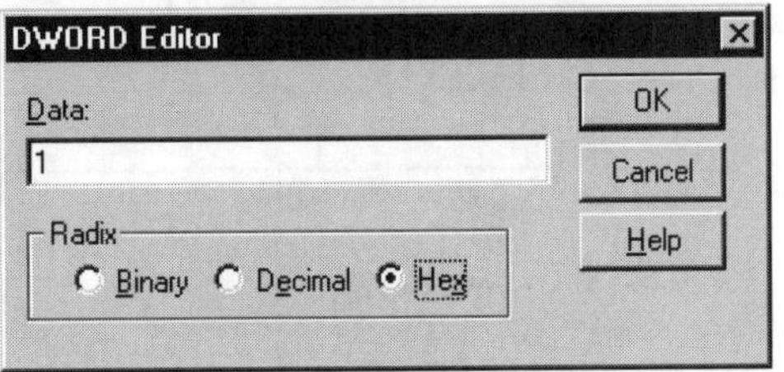

4. Click OK in the DWORD Editor dialog box. The new entry should show up in the right pane of the registry editor, and the WINS Proxy Agent is enabled immediately. You should not need to restart the computer.

EXERCISE 8-3

Configuring a Windows 2000 WINS Client

In this exercise, you will configure the WINS client. Do not perform this exercise on a live, production network without the permission of your network administrator.

1. Log on as Administrator.
2. Right click on the My Network Places icon on the desktop, and click the Properties command.
3. Right-click on Local Area Connection or any other active interface that appears in the Network and Dial-up Connections window, and click Properties.
4. You will see the Local Area Connection Properties dialog box as shown in the following illustration. Scroll down the list of components until you find Internet Protocol (TCP/IP).

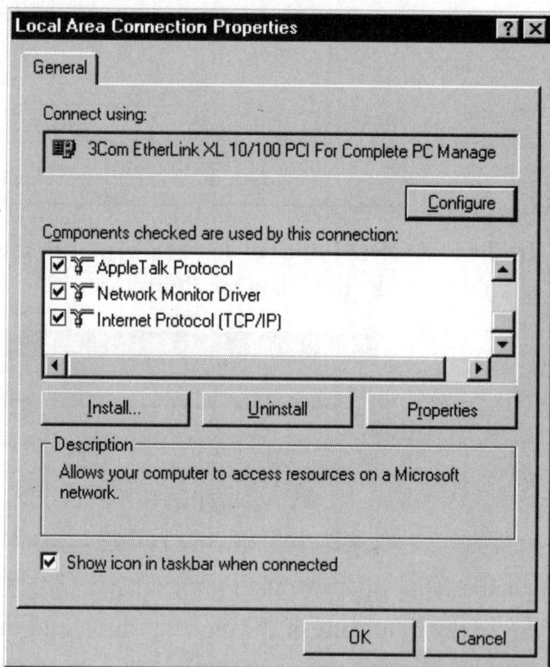

5. Double-click on Internet Protocol (TCP/IP). This takes you to the Internet Protocol (TCP/IP) Properties dialog box. Click Advanced.
6. In the Advanced TCP/IP Settings dialog box, click on the WINS tab. You should see what appears in next.

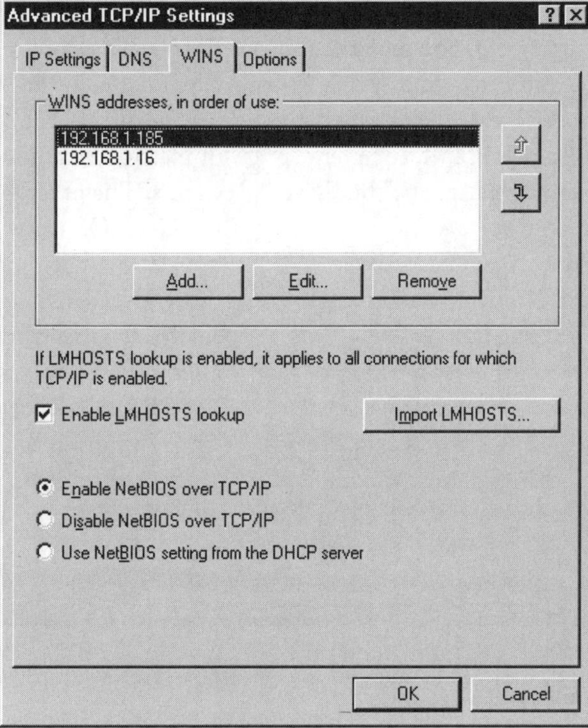

7. Click Add to add the IP address of a WINS server on your network.
8. Note the "Enable LMHOSTS lookup" check box. There must be a check in this check box if you wish to enable using the LMHOSTS file for NetBIOS name resolution. By default, this box is checked. If you have an LMHOSTS file located on the hard disk, or another computer on the network, you can import those entries into the local LMHOSTS file by clicking Import LMHOSTS and then indicating the location of the file.
9. Click OK. Click OK again, and click OK one more time. Close the Network and Dial-up Connections window.

FROM THE CLASSROOM

The WINS Proxy Agent

I don't think a class goes by without having a number of students confused over the purpose of the WINS Proxy Agent, and whether they should call it a WINS Proxy or a WINS Proxy Agent—both are correct. Don't get the WINS Proxy Agent and the DHCP Relay Agent confused! They are both "Agents," but have very different functions.

The WINS Proxy Agent has a single purpose: to resolve NetBIOS names for non-WINS clients. The non-WINS clients can be UNIX servers, or even Windows computers that are configured as b-node clients. Keep in mind that the WINS Proxy Agent resolves NetBIOS names, it does *not* register them. When a non-WINS client starts up, it may broadcast its name to the local segment, but the WINS Proxy Agent on that segment does not register the non-WINS client name in the WINS database.

The WINS Proxy Agent solves the problem of NetBIOS name resolution for non-WINS clients. The other side of the coin is resolving the NetBIOS name of a non-WINS client. A non-WINS client does not register its name in the WINS database. If a WINS client tries to resolve the name of a non-WINS client, the attempt fails, because there is no entry in the WINS database for the non-WINS client. The solution to this problem is to add a *static entry* into the WINS database for the non-WINS client.

—Thomas W. Shinder, M.D., MCSE, MCP+I, MCT

How WINS Works

The WINS server is a client/server application. Think of the WINS server as a database server, since it contains a database of NetBIOS names to IP address mappings. The WINS client and server participate in four basic activities: *name registration*, *name renewal*, *name release*, and *name resolution*.

Name Registration

When a WINS client starts up, it tries to register its NetBIOS names with its Primary WINS server. If the Primary WINS server does not respond after the first attempt, it will try two more times, 500ms apart. If the first WINS server fails to respond after a total of three connection attempts, the WINS client proceeds down its list and attempts to register with its Secondary WINS servers until it is successful.

If none of the Secondary WINS servers respond, it begins again at the top of the list with the Primary WINS server.

on the job

In Windows NT 4.0, there was a specific text box that said "Primary WINS Server." The Windows 2000 WINS Client does not contain a dedicated text box for the Primary WINS server. The Primary is the WINS server located at the top of the list.

The WINS server checks to see if the name already exists in the WINS database. If it does not, then the WINS client receives a *Positive Name Registration Response.* If it does exist in the WINS database, the WINS server sends the WINS client a *Wait for Acknowledgement (WACK)* message. Then it sends up to three challenges 500ms apart to the computer with the IP address of the requesting WINS client. If it receives no response, the WINS client receives a *Positive Name Registration Response.* If the WINS server does receive a response from the owner of the WINS database record, the WINS client attempting to register the same name receives a *Negative Name Registration Response.*

Note that if the WINS client tries to register a name and IP address that are the same as one already contained in the WINS database (i.e., its own name and IP address), the registration request become a *NetBIOS Name Renewal.*

Renewal

When the WINS server sends the WINS client a Positive NetBIOS Name Registration Response, it also sends with that a *Renewal Interval* or *TTL (Time-to-Live)* for the name it just registered. The WINS client must renew its name periodically to keep its name *Active* in the WINS database.

When a WINS client renews its name, its sends a *Name Refresh Request* to its Primary WINS server. This request is sent at one-half of the renewal interval. If the Primary WINS server does not respond, it will try at 10-minute intervals for up to an hour, then move on to its Secondary WINS servers. If the Secondaries do not respond, it goes back to the Primary WINS server and starts the whole process over again. Once the name is refreshed, it may receive a *new* renewal interval.

exam watch

WINS clients typically receive the same renewal interval after name refreshes. However, under certain circumstances the renewal interval may change, such as when the WINS administrator makes changes to the renewal interval or when Burst Handling Mode ***is in effect.***

Release

When a WINS client shuts down "gracefully" (the operating system didn't crash and wasn't powered off before shutting down), it will send a *NetBIOS Name Release* message to its Primary WINS server. If the name and IP address of the WINS client sending the release message is the same as that contained in the WINS database, then the entry is marked as released in the WINS database, and becomes *inactive.*

If the IP address is different from the WINS client that is seeking a release, the release request is ignored.

After the record is marked as inactive, it stays that way for the period known as the *extinction interval.* During this period, if another computer wants to register the name, no challenge will be issued. After the extinction interval has passed, the record is marked *extinct* and is *tombstoned.* The record remains tombstoned for a period called the *extinction timeout.* After the expiration of the extinction timeout period, the record is deleted, or *scavenged,* from the WINS database.

We'll talk more about tombstoning later in this chapter.

Resolution

A WINS client will go through the following process to resolve a NetBIOS name to an IP address:

1. After a request is sent to the TCP/IP protocol stack from the NetBIOS application, it will first check its *NetBIOS Remote Name Cache.*
2. If the mapping is not in the NetBIOS Remote Name Cache, the WINS client will send a *Name Query Request* directly to its Primary WINS server. If the WINS server does not respond, it will query two more times, for a total of three attempts. If the Primary WINS server fails to respond, then the Secondary WINS servers will be contacted.
3. When a WINS server is contacted, it will respond with either a *Positive Name Query Response* or a *Negative Name Query Response,* depending on whether the server did or did not have a mapping for the requested NetBIOS name.
4. If a Negative Name Query Response is received, the WINS client will issue up to three NetBIOS Name Query Request broadcasts to the local segment, 750ms apart. If this fails, the client may use other methods of NetBIOS name resolution.

EXERCISE 8-4

Installing the WINS Server Service

In this exercise, you will install the WINS Server service onto either a Windows 2000 Server or Windows 2000 Advanced Server computer, whichever you have available. Do not perform this exercise on a live, production network without the permission of your network administrator.

1. Log on as Administrator.
2. Open the Control Panel and double-click on Add/Remove Programs.
3. In the Add/Remove Program dialog box, click Add/Remove Windows Components in the left side of the dialog box.
4. In the Windows Components Wizard dialog box, scroll through the list and double-click on Networking Services. Place a check mark in the checkbox next to Windows Internet Name Service (WINS) as it appears in the following illustration. Then click OK.

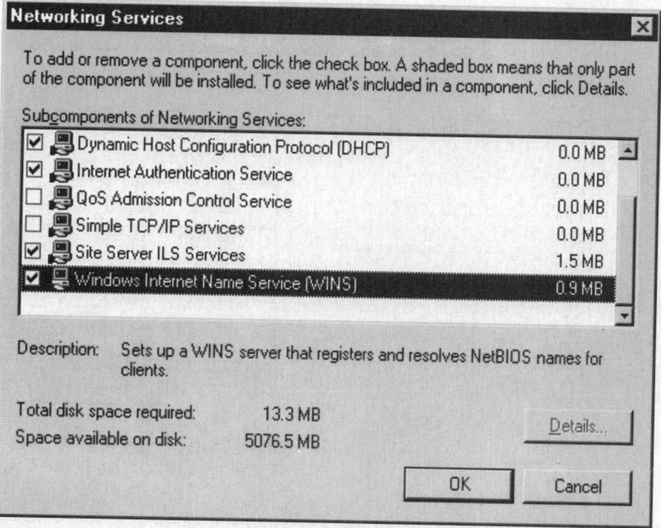

5. Click Next. The wizard will display a progress bar indicating how far the installation has completed. If asked for the CD-ROM, point the wizard to the correct location of the Windows 2000 installation files.
6. When the files have completed copying, the Completing the Windows Components Wizard dialog box appears. Click Finish to complete the installation.

exam Watch

Note that you do not need to restart the computer after installing the WINS Server service.

EXERCISE 8-5

Configuring Intervals on the WINS Server

In this exercise, you will configure the various intervals related to WINS database record aging. Do not perform this exercise on a live, production network without the permission of your network administrator.

1. Open the WINS console from the Administrative Tools menu.
2. Right-click on the name of your WINS server in the left pane. (If your server does not appear in the left pane, right-click on where it says WINS in the left pane, click Add Server and type in the name or IP address of your WINS server.) After right-clicking on the name of your WINS server, click Properties.
3. Select the Intervals tab, and you will see what appears next.

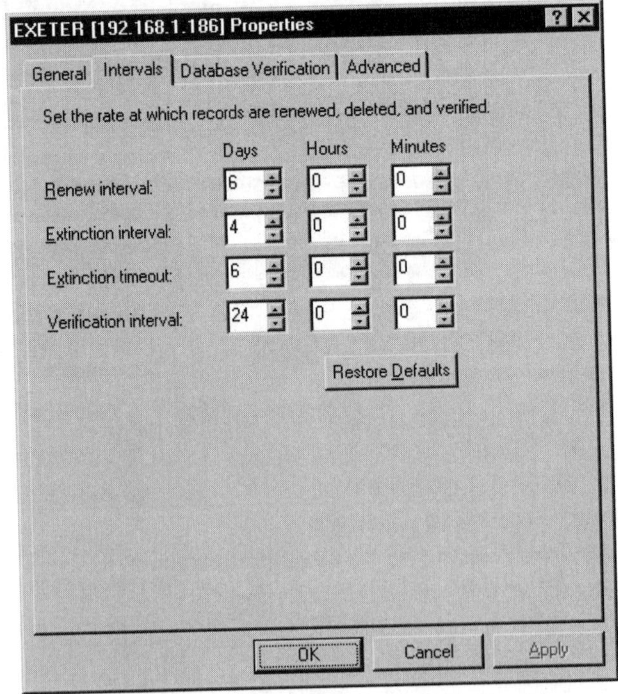

4. Increase the renewal interval to 8 days, and the extinction timeout to 10 days, then click OK.

SCENARIO & SOLUTION	
Do I have to have a WINS server on my network? Can't I just use DNS?	You do not have to have a WINS server on your network. However, if you run distributed NetBIOS applications, WINS is the most effective method of name resolution. DNS can be used to resolve NetBIOS names, but because of how NetBIOS name resolution is processed, it isn't the fastest or most efficient way to proceed.
Should I place more than one WINS Proxy Agent on a segment for fault tolerance?	It is generally not a good idea to place more than one WINS Proxy Agent on a single segment. This is because each WINS Proxy Agent will intercept all NetBIOS Name Query Request Broadcasts and forward them to the WINS server. This increases the amount of traffic sent to the WINS server for identical name resolution requests. However, if you have only a single WINS Proxy Agent, you have no fault tolerance. Since a limited number of segments will require a WINS Proxy Agent, your own baselining is the best indicator of the most prudent action.
What entries should I put into my LMHOSTS file?	The answer for Windows NT 4.0 machines was to put the mapping for domain controllers into your LMHOSTS file, since the domain locator for NT was NetBIOS dependent. This is no longer the case in Windows 2000. However, if you are dependent on NetBIOS network application servers, you should place entries for those machines in the LMHOSTS file. If you are dependent on the Browser service, you should put entries for the master browsers on each segment in the LMHOSTS files of each master browser, including a mapping for the PDC emulator for the domain.

New and Improved Windows 2000 WINS Server Features

Although Microsoft's long-term goal is to phase out NetBIOS from Microsoft networks, the WINS server will continue to hold an important place on Windows 2000 networks. The history of Microsoft networking is imbued with NetBIOS, and it will be many years before all important network applications move completely over to the WinSock interface.

Three new or improved features you will find of particular utility are *persistent connections*, *burst handling*, and *manual tombstoning*.

Persistent Connections

You can configure a Windows 2000 WINS Server to maintain a *persistent connection* with its replication partners. By maintaining an open channel, the session setup process between partners only needs to be done once. This reduces the amount of overhead incurred with creating and tearing down sessions between WINS replication partners.

Microsoft states that this should have a positive effect on server performance with a minimum of network overhead, since no data is being transferred over the open connection the majority of the time.

on the Job

While persistent connections sound good in theory, the overall impact of establishing and tearing down sessions between WINS Replication Partners is nominal on K7 (Athlon) or P-III class machines.

Burst Handling

In a large organization, there are times when WINS servers can be overwhelmed with NetBIOS name registration requests. The typical example is when a systemwide power outage takes place, and all machines come online simultaneously and attempt to register their NetBIOS names. Normally, the WINS server can cache a certain number of requests, after which it begins to drop NetBIOS Name Registration Requests.

Windows NT 4.0 WINS Server with Service Pack 3 and above supports high-volume WINS registration requests through a process called *burst handling.* Windows 2000 WINS Servers also support WINS server *burst mode* responses.

The number of simultaneous requests may be so great that the efficiency and accuracy of name registration may suffer. In this scenario, the WINS server will switch into *burst mode.* When the WINS server is in burst mode, any name registration requests received over a predefined number receive immediate acknowledgement. However, the WINS server does not check the NetBIOS against the WINS database; it does not issue a challenge against duplicate names, and it does not write an entry to the WINS database.

exam Watch

Remember that once burst mode takes effect, no entries are recorded into the WINS database for those machines that are offered the short TTLs.

The default queue size is 500. When the number of pending registration requests exceeds 500, the WINS server switches into burst mode, immediately acknowledges the WINS client's request for NetBIOS name registration, and sends with the acknowledgement a shortened renewal interval or Time-to-Live (TTL). For the first 100 registrations over 500, the clients are given a name renewal period of 5 minutes. For the next 100 pending name registrations, the WINS clients receive a name renewal interval of 10 minutes. This pattern of incrementing the name renewal period by 5 minutes per 100 pending requests continues until the TTL reaches 50 minutes (1000 pending registrations). Then the process starts all over with the WINS server sending the next 100 pending registration requests a TTL of 5 minutes. The maximum number of queued responses is 25,000. After that point, the WINS server starts dropping the requests without providing an acknowledgement or TTL.

Burst handling allows the WINS server to accommodate WINS clients' attempts at name registration at times when the WINS server is too busy to write to the database.

on the job

Remember that burst handling is not new to Windows 2000, and is available on your Windows NT 4.0 WINS Servers after they have been upgraded to Service Pack 3 or above.

Tombstoning Records

To understand tombstoning, you need to understand the WINS record life cycle. When a WINS client registers its NetBIOS names with a WINS server, a WINS database record is created for that WINS client. This record stays *active* in the WINS database for a period of time determined by the *renewal interval.* While the record is active, the WINS server will defend it by issuing challenges when another machine attempts to register the same NetBIOS name to a different IP address. The WINS client must update its record with the WINS server before the renewal interval expires. The expired record is then marked as *inactive.* The main difference between an active and an inactive WINS database record is that no challenge is issued when another computer tries to register the name.

An inactive record remains in the WINS database for a period known as the *extinction interval.* After remaining in the inactive state for the period defined by the extinction interval, the record is marked as *extinct.* Another term for an extinct record is *tombstoned.* The record remains in the tombstoned state for a period defined by the *extinction timeout,* after which it is removed, or *scavenged,* by the WINS server that owns it.

If a WINS server has a copy of a replicated tombstoned record owned by another WINS server, it checks with the owner WINS server after the expiration of the *verification interval* to see if the record still exists. If the record is no longer at the owner WINS server, it is scavenged from the non-owner WINS servers.

The Value of Tombstoning Imagine that we have three WINS servers in our WINS network: WINS-A, WINS-B, and WINS-C. WINS-B is the hub of the WINS network, and WINS-A and WINS-C are spokes (Figure 8-4). WINS-A receives a

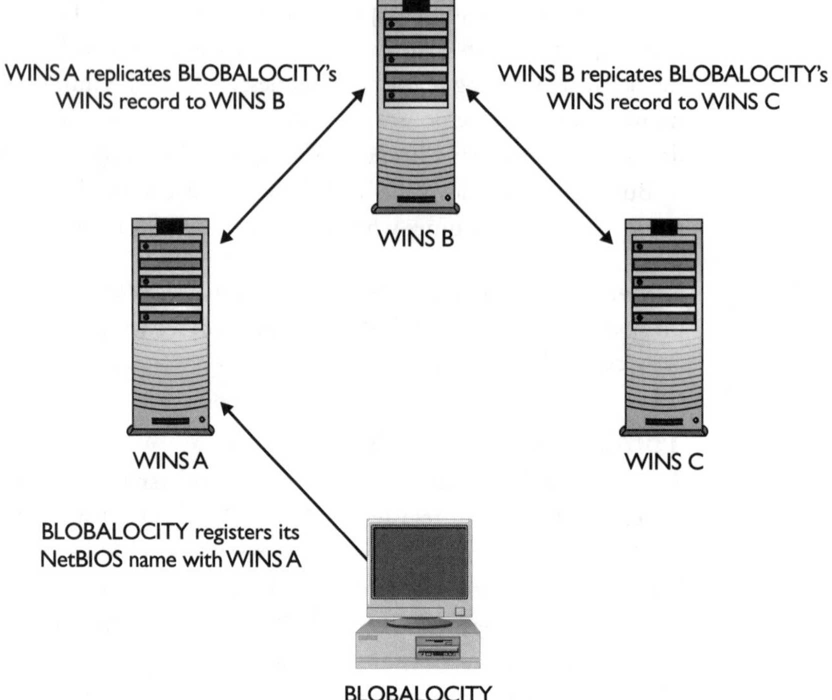
WINS A replicates BLOBALOCITY's
WINS record to WINS B
WINS B repicates BLOBALOCITY's
WINS record to WINS C
WINS B
WINS A
WINS C
BLOBALOCITY registers its
NetBIOS name with WINS A
BLOBALOCITY

FIGURE 8-4 The example WINS network

NetBIOS name registration for a computer named BLOBALOCITY. After registering its NetBIOS name, we decide that we're going to take BLOBALOCITY off the network. Meanwhile, BLOBALOCITY's record is replicated to WINS-B, and WINS-B replicates the record to WINS-C.

To increase the speed and responsiveness of WINS registrations and queries, you want to keep the WINS database lean and mean. You open your WINS management console and delete the record for BLOBALOCITY. You figure the fact that the record was deleted will be replicated over to the other WINS servers, and you can bid adieu to BLOBALOCITY from your WINS network.

When WINS-A next replicates with WINS-B, it doesn't replicate BLOBALOCITY's WINS record—it can't, since the record was deleted. What happens when WINS-B replicates with WINS-A? Since WINS-B still has BLOBALOCITY's record in its database, it replicates it back to WINS-A. Now BLOBALOCITY has risen from the dead and its record reappears, marked active, in the WINS-A database.

Eventually, BLOBALOCITY's record will exceed its renewal interval, then its extinction interval, then its extinction timeout, and finally will be deleted. But, if you just delete records, the entire process will take longer than it should, and the stale WINS database records will have a negative impact on WINS server performance.

Manual Tombstoning The Windows 2000 WINS console allows you to manually tombstone WINS database records, rather than delete them outright. When a record is tombstoned, its tombstoned status is replicated with it. When you tombstone a record, it doesn't "magically" reappear as an active record. The tombstoned record is removed from the owner WINS database after completion of the extinction timeout, and will be removed from replication partners WINS databases after expiration of the verification interval.

To tombstone a WINS record, open the WINS management console and click on Active Registrations. Right-click on Active Registrations and select Find by Owner. On the Owners tab, select the option button for "All owners," and click Find Now. Right-click on one of the records in the right pane and select Delete. You will see a dialog box as shown in Figure 8-5.

Manual tombstoning of WINS database records is not entirely new with Windows 2000. In Windows NT 4.0, you could use the command-line utility *winscl.exe* ***to manually tombstone records, but it was a kludgy solution for a simple problem. The Windows 2000 GUI interface makes a simple task simple to execute.***

FIGURE 8-5

The Delete Record dialog box

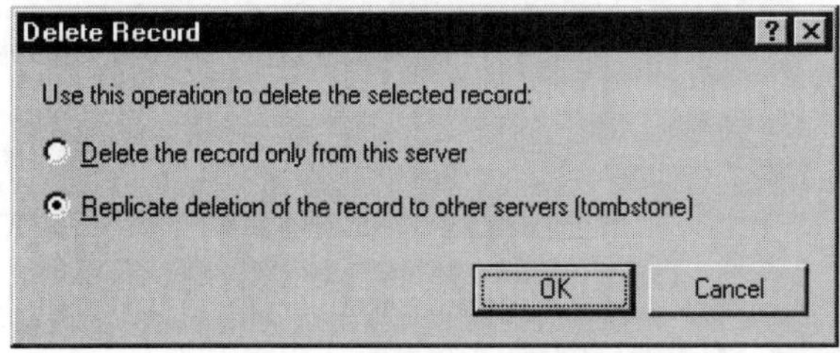

EXERCISE 8-6

Configuring Burst Handling

In this exercise, you will see how to configure WINS server burst handle parameters. Do not perform this exercise on a live, production network without the permission of your network administrator.

1. Log on as Administrator.
2. Open the WINS management console from the Administrative Tools menu.
3. Right-click on your WINS server's name in the left pane and click Properties.
4. Click on the Advanced tab. You will see what appears next.

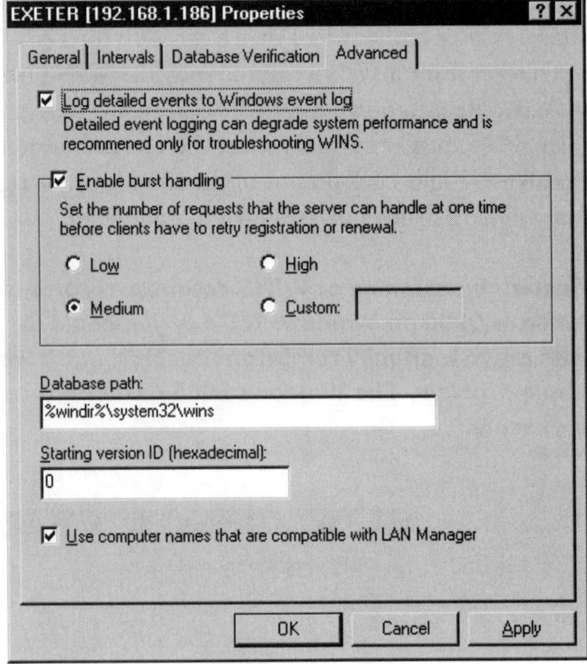

5. Place a check mark in the "Enable burst handling" check box, and select Medium. Click Apply and then OK.

WINS Replication

You should deploy multiple WINS servers for fault tolerance and efficient NetBIOS name resolution. To maintain consistency among all WINS servers on a network, there must be a way for all the WINS servers to share what they "know" with each other. This method of sharing information is known as *WINS replication.*

WINS clients normally register their NetBIOS names with their Primary WINS server, and if the Primary WINS server is not reachable, the WINS client registers with one of its Secondary WINS server. In large internetworks, multiple WINS servers handle the name registration requests of WINS clients near them. Those same WINS servers also answer NetBIOS name queries for these same WINS clients.

A problem arises as WINS clients register their names with different WINS servers. Imagine we have the following setup:

WINS server IP address:

192.168.1.2

WINS clients from subnets:

192.168.1.0

192.168.2.0

Register with and query this WINS server

WINS server IP address:

192.168.3.2

WINS clients from subnets:

192.168.3.0

192.168.4.0

Register with and query this WINS server

When clients on the 192.168.1.0 subnet need to resolve a NetBIOS name for a client on subnet 192.168.2.0 they can query the WINS server at 192.168.1.2, and a mapping for that client is located in the WINS database. If a client on the 192.168.3.0 subnet needs to resolve a NetBIOS name for a client on the 192.168.4.0 subnet, it can do so successfully because a mapping for clients on both the 192.168.3.0 and 192.168.4.0 subnets are at the WINS server 192.168.3.2. However, what happens when a client on the 192.168.1.0 subnet needs to resolve a NetBIOS name of a client on the 192.168.4.0 subnet?

The client on the 192.168.1.0 subnet issues a NetBIOS Name Query Request to its Preferred WINS server at 192.168.1.2. However, no clients on the 192.168.4.0 registered their NetBIOS names with this WINS server; therefore, no mapping exists for computers on that segment. To solve this problem, we configure the WINS servers to be replication partners.

WINS Replication Partners

Replication partners share their information. This makes it possible for any WINS client to query any WINS server and successfully resolve a NetBIOS name, regardless of what WINS server originally received the NetBIOS name registration.

WINS servers are configured as replication partners in two ways: *pull* and *push.* The pull partner receives WINS database information based on a configured replication interval. A push partner sends database information based on how many changes have taken place in the WINS database.

Pull Partners A WINS server is notified by its pull partner when it's *time* to request the changes to the WINS database since the last time it received replicated information. This determination is made based on WINS database version IDs. If the PULL partner's WINS database has a version ID higher than the one last *pulled* by the pull partner, it will request the changes. If the pull partner's database version is the same or smaller (an unlikely event, but possible), then records are not replicated from the pull partner.

Push Partners Push replication causes the push partner to send changes based on *the number of* changes made in the WINS database. After the minimum number of changes have been made, the push partner sends a pull notification to the WINS server to request the changes. Windows 2000 WINS Servers are able to maintain persistent connections, which allow push partners to push changes as soon as they take place.

Automatic Partner Discovery You can configure your WINS servers to find other WINS servers on the network and create a replication partnership with them automatically. When you enable *Automatic Partner Discovery*, WINS servers use the multicast address 224.0.1.24 to discover or find other WINS servers.

How many of your WINS servers can be found through Autodiscovery depends on how the routers on your network have been configured. If routers do not support IGMP (multicasting), WINS servers only find other WINS servers on the same segment. WINS servers that set up partner arrangements via Autodiscovery will become push/pull partners with a replication pull interval of 2 hours. Microsoft documentation does not state what push trigger number is, however. Automatic partner discovery can be configured on the Advanced tab of the WINS server's Properties dialog box.

Push and Pull Partner Recommendations Microsoft recommends that replication partners be configured as both push and pull partners. This reduces the chance of inconsistencies or lags in the WINS database. A notable exception to this policy is when WINS servers are separated by slow WAN connections. In this circumstance, it may be more efficient to configure the WINS servers on both sides to be PULL partners. These pull partners are configured to exchange WINS database information during times of reduced network utilization, and therefore not impact normal network communications to such a large extent.

exam Watch

The definition of a slow versus fast link is a moving target in the fast-paced world of network hardware. However, many authorities consider a connection supporting 512 kbps or higher as being fast. However, in the Microsoft documentation, fast seems to be a relative term based on how fast the site links are. You'll have to use good judgment when you encounter these questions.

Disabling NetBT

Windows 2000 allows you to disable NetBIOS (NetBT) on any network interface installed on the computer. You should be very careful about disabling NetBIOS on the computers on your network. The great majority of network applications designed to work on Microsoft networks were written for, and dependent on, the NetBIOS interface. There are some specialized situations when you definitely would want to disable NetBIOS. These include computers in specialized or secured roles for your network, such as an edge Proxy server or bastion host in a firewall environment. In these environments, you improve security by disabling NetBT.

The following are considerations for disabling NetBT on computers running Windows 2000:

- The Browser service was no longer functioning on the computer with NetBIOS disabled. The computer will not act as a browser, nor will it issue announcements of its server status to the Master Browser on its segment.
- You will no longer be able to use certain core Windows 2000 networking utilities, such as net send and the Alerter service.
- If the computer must be a WINS client, it will need to have NetBIOS enabled. The only reason why you would want the machine to be a WINS client is that it runs either NetBIOS server or client services.
- If you want to install the WINS server on a Windows 2000 Server family computer, you must have NetBIOS enabled, even if the server will not be used for any other NetBIOS functions.

The classic example of when it's a good time to disable NetBIOS is on the external public interface on a Proxy server. By disabling NetBT on only the Internet connection, the multihomed computer continues to function as either a WINS server or client for the internal network, and WINS clients are still serviced for connections made by using other physical network adapters installed on the computer.

There are a couple of ways you can disable NetBIOS on your Windows 2000 machine: You can go to the WINS tab in the Advanced TCP/IP Settings, or you can use the Microsoft vendor-specific options at a DHCP server. Figure 8-6 shows the WINS tab.

on the job

It is imperative to confirm that NetBIOS is not required on the machine on which you disable the NetBIOS interface. Carefully inventory the client and server applications in use on the computer, and research whether or not they are NetBIOS dependent. After you have completed the research, test the machine with NetBIOS disabled in a nonproduction environment before putting it back into production.

FIGURE 8-6

Disabling NetBIOS via the WINS tab on the Advanced TCP/IP Settings Properties dialog box

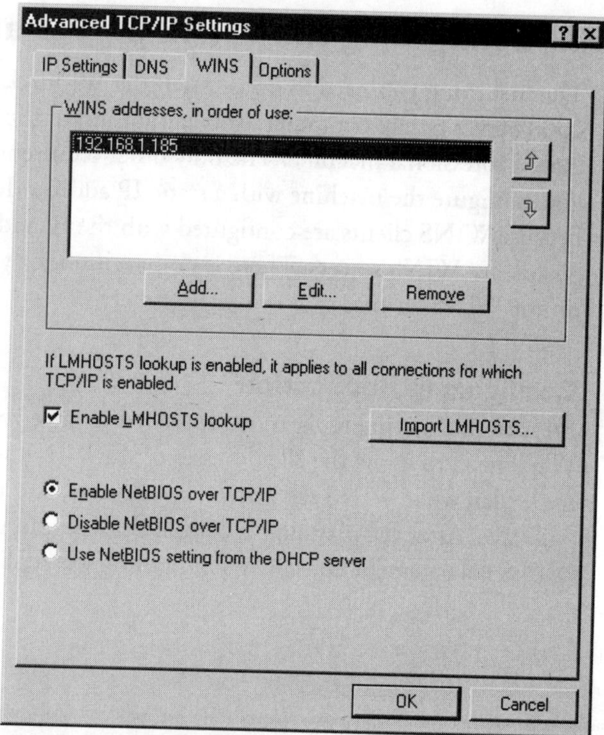

CERTIFICATION OBJECTIVE 8.02

Planning and Implementing a WINS Solution

When you are ready to implement a WINS solution for the NetBIOS environment, make sure that you have planned where you want to place the WINS servers, and how the WINS servers will be configured to support your WINS networking plan. In this section, we will focus on the installation and configuration of the WINS server. In the *Designing a Windows 2000 Networking Infrastructure Study Guide*, we'll go over the more complex issues regarding how to design a reliable, fault-tolerant WINS network.

Installing and Configuring the WINS Server and Client

The first thing you need to do is install the WINS Server service on a Windows 2000 Server family computer. You cannot install the WINS service on a Windows 2000 Professional machine. The only other requirement for the WINS server is that you configure the machine with a static IP address. It requires a static IP address because WINS clients are configured with the IP addresses for their Primary and Secondary WINS servers. There is no provision for you to enter a NetBIOS name on the WINS clients.

Configuring Replication

Prior to configuring replication, you need to have your WINS network planned. You'll need to know the IP addresses of the WINS servers on the network, and you must plan what WINS servers will be partners, and the types of partnerships they will have. After the planning is completed, you can get to the task of using the WINS management console to configuring the replication parameters.

EXERCISE 8-7

Configuring WINS Replication

In this exercise, you will configure WINS Replication parameters. You will need at least two WINS servers available in order to complete this lesson. Do not perform this exercise on a live, production network without the permission of your network administrator.

1. Log on as Administrator.
2. Open the WINS console from the Administrative Tools menu.
3. Expand all nodes in the left pane. Right-click on Replication Partners, and click Properties.
4. Click on the Push Replication tab. You should see what appears in the following illustration. Type 5 in the "Number of changes in version ID before replication" text box. Place a check mark in the "Use persistent connection for push replication partners" check box to enable persistent connections.

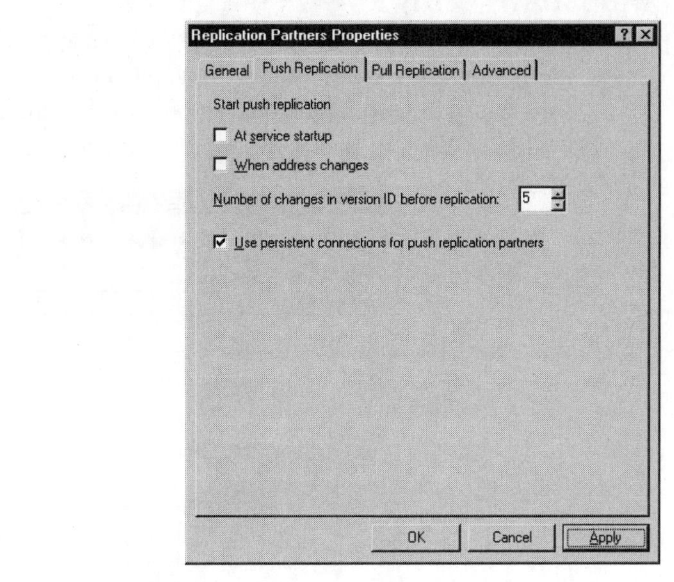

5. Click on the Pull Replication tab. You will see what appears in the following illustration. Change the Start time to 2:00 A.M. by typing **2** in the Hours text box. Change the replication interval to every 24 hours by typing **1** into the Days text box on the replication interval line.

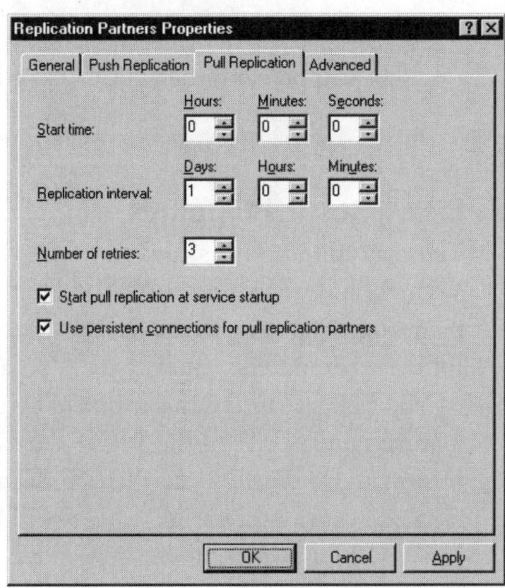

6. Click on the Advanced tab. You will see what appears in the following illustration. To enable Autodiscovery, put a check in the check box for "Enable automatic partner configuration." Note that the multicast interval is 40 minutes by default. You can change this value to meet your particular needs.

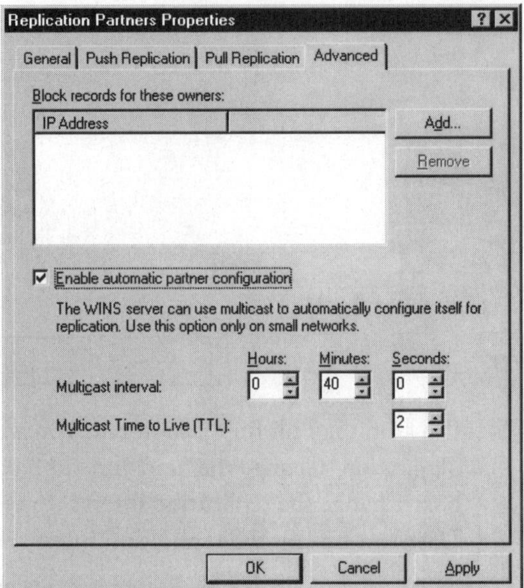

7. Click Apply, and then click OK. Close the WINS management console.

Using Static Mappings

You may run into the situation where you need to resolve the NetBIOS name of a remote host that is *not* a WINS client. Non-WINS clients do not register their names automatically in the WINS database. If you try to query the WINS server for these computers, you will get a Negative NetBIOS Name Query Response.

You can get around this problem by using *static* mappings. A static mapping is a nondynamic entry in the WINS database. You must enter the static mapping information *manually* into the WINS database. This is similar to traditional DNS databases, such as those in Windows NT 4.0, where you had to manually add the host record information yourself. Static mappings are not normally overwritten by dynamic name registrations unless the *migrate on* option is enabled.

The migrate on setting is best used when you have a number of non-WINS clients that you plan to subsequently upgrade to WINS clients. However, not all of your static entries will be overwritten by dynamic registrations. One example is the [1Ch] entry for a domain controller.

The UNIX Scenario The classic scenario involves a WINS client that needs to contact a UNIX server running a NetBIOS application. In order for the WINS client to establish a NetBIOS session with the UNIX server, its NetBIOS name must be resolved. The Windows client is located on a remote subnet and does not have a mapping for the UNIX host in its LMHOSTS file. The solution to this problem is to create a static mapping for the UNIX machine in the WINS database. The WINS client is then able to locate a mapping for the UNIX host and resolve its NetBIOS name to an IP address.

The only information required is the NetBIOS name, an optional scope ID, the type of mapping, and the IP address of statically mapped host. Table 8-3 defines the types of WINS mappings.

TABLE 8-3 Types of WINS Static Mappings

Type	Explanation
Unique	Configure a Unique mapping when a single IP address defines the host computer. Three NetBIOS names arise when you configure a Unique static mapping. A NetBIOS name associating the host name for the workstation service (redirector), messenger service, and server service are created. For example, NOSTROMO will have three entries in the WINS database: NOSTROMO[00h], NOSTROMO[03h], and NOSTROMO [20h].
Group	If the computer is a member of a workgroup, you can configure a Group entry for the machine. The IP address of the host is not included and Group name resolution is performed via local subnet broadcasts only. This is known as a "Normal Group."
Domain Name	A Domain Name entry creates a [1Ch] mapping in the WINS database. This mapping points to domain controllers in Windows NT environments. A WINS client queries the WINS database for [1Ch] entries for a machine to authenticate a logon.
Internet Group	Configure an Internet Group when you want to create Administrative Groups of shared resources that appear as members of the group when browsing for resources. Examples include grouping file servers and print servers into such Administrative Groups. The Group identifies itself by the shared group name with the [20h] service identifier.
Multihomed	Use the Multihomed mapping to configure multiple IP addresses for a single NetBIOS host computer. A computer may have multiple adapters or multiple IP addresses bound to a single adapter.

EXERCISE 8-8

Creating a Static Mapping

In this exercise, you will learn how to create a static mapping for a NetBIOS client in the WINS server. Do not perform this exercise on a live, production network without the permission of your network administrator.

1. Log on as Administrator.
2. Open the WINS management console.
3. Expand all nodes in the left pane and click on New Static Mapping. You should see what appears next.

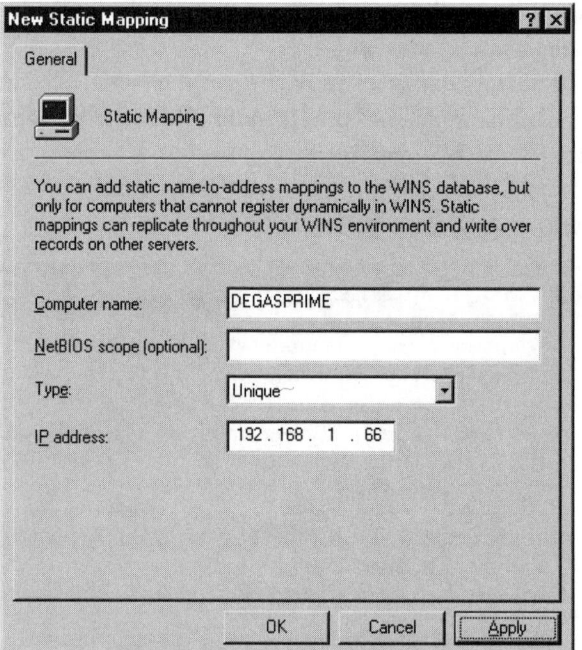

4. Type in the name of a non-WINS client in the "Computer name" text box. Type in the IP address in the text boxes provided. It will be unusual to have a scope ID, but you can enter one here as well. Individual computers will have the unique type of Static Record.
5. Click Apply, and then click OK. Close the WINS management console.

Managing the WINS Database

For the most part, the WINS database is self-tuning. However, there is a small handful of administrative tasks to insure that your WINS server is working at tip-top efficiency and reliability. The Windows 2000 WINS Server provides the new and improved WINS management console that makes these administrative tasks easier than ever.

Finding and Viewing WINS Records

If you've ever worked on a large enterprise network using Microsoft networking technologies, you know how unwieldy your WINS databases can get. In the past, if you wanted to find a record or a group of records in the WINS database, you had to sift through the list manually. Windows 2000 WINS Servers have enhanced record finding and filtering (Figure 8-7).

If you want to find all servers that begin with the letter "S," all you need to do is type the letter in the "Find names beginning with" dialog box in the WINS management console. The right pane in the WINS manager will display the results of the query, as seen in Figure 8-8.

If you want to see all the records in the database, you can type an asterisk (*) in the text box instead of a computer name string. The asterisk is the only wildcard type search supported by the WINS search mechanism.

You can also specify a search based on the owners of the WINS records. The owner is the WINS server that received the name registration from the WINS client directly, and not via replication. Figure 8-9 shows the Find by Owner dialog box.

The IP address of the server and the highest version ID number is also included on this list.

Figure 8-10 shows the contents of the Record Types tab in the Find by Owner dialog box. You can filter and view records that have specific NetBIOS service identifiers. For example, if you wanted to find all domain controllers registered in

FIGURE 8-7

The Find by Name dialog box

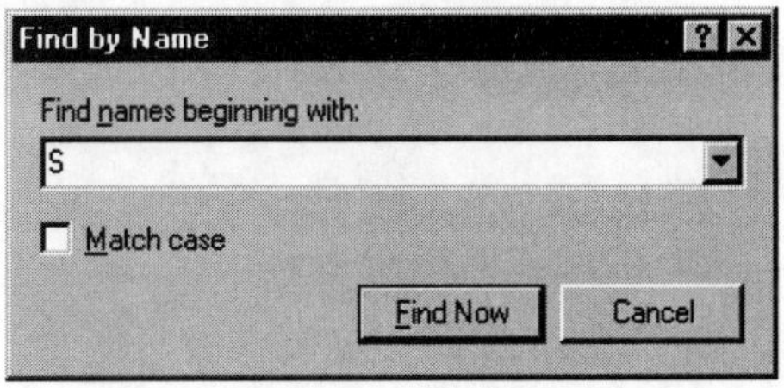

FIGURE 8-8

Results of the Find by Name query

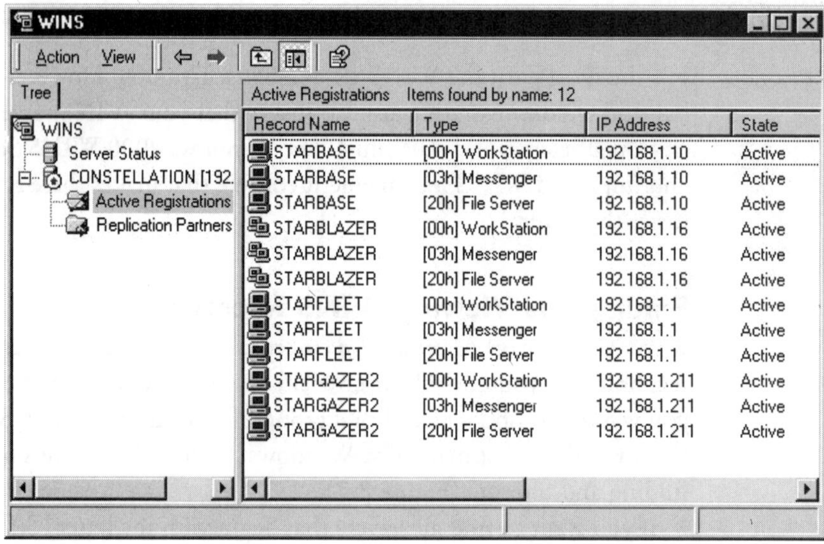

the WINS database, you could limit your search for only entries with the [1Ch] service identifier.

The find and filter features make life a lot easier for the administrator in a large enterprise environment.

FIGURE 8-9

The Find by Owner dialog box

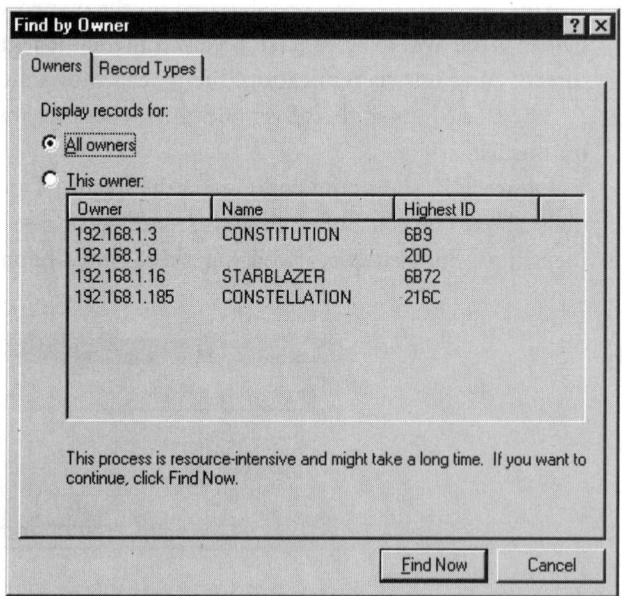

FIGURE 8-10

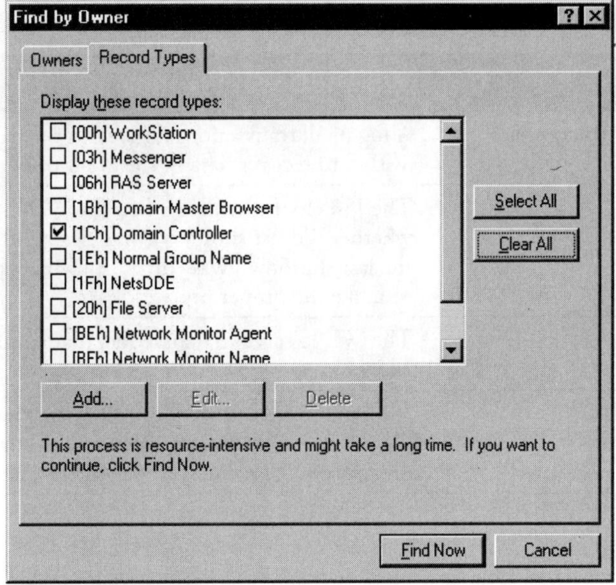

Selecting records by service identifier

Compacting the Database

The Windows 2000 WINS database uses the performance-enhanced Extensible Storage Engine, which is an updated version of the storage engine that serves both Microsoft Exchange 5.5 and Windows 2000 Active Directory.

One of the great advantages of the new WINS database structure is that there is no hard-coded limit to the number of entries it can support. The size of the WINS database grows as entries are added via NetBIOS name registrations. As entries populate the database and are removed, the amount of space taken by the scavenged entries is not immediately returned.

Like most databases, it should be compacted periodically in order to maintain optimal efficiency. In Windows 2000, WINS server database compaction occurs as an automatic background process during idle time; this is known as *online compaction.*

However, online compaction is not 100% efficient, and the database will continue to grow in size, albeit at a slower pace. To regain lost space, you will need to perform an *offline compaction* occasionally. Offline compaction requires you to take the WINS Server service offline (you do not need to shut down the computer, just stop the WINS Server service).

The WINS database files are stored in the directory:

```
%SystemRoot%\System32\Wins
```

Table 8-4 explains what the various WINS database files are and what they do.

TABLE 8-4 WINS Database Files and Their Functions

File	What It Does
J50.log and J50*xxxxx*.log	A log of all transactions done with the database. This file is used by WINS to recover data in the event of a server or service crash.
J50.chk	The J50.chk file is used when the WINS database starts up to determine whether the last shutdown was clean and all databases are consistent. If the last shutdown was "dirty," this file will determine what log file to use to make the proper updates.
Wins.mdb	The WINS server database file, that contains NetBIOS names to IP address mappings.
Winstmp.mdb	A temp file created by the WINS service. The database uses it as a swap file during index maintenance operations. It might remain in the directory %*SystemRoot*%\System32\Wins after a crash.

on the job

Do not open any of these files with a text editor or a database program such as Microsoft Access. Too many curious administrators who happened to have Microsoft Access installed on their WINS server have opened their wins.mdb file and ended up with a corrupted database. Don't do that!

CertCam 8-9

EXERCISE 8-9

Compacting the WINS Database

In this exercise, you will compact the WINS database. Do not perform this exercise on a live, production network without the permission of your network administrator.

1. Log on as Administrator.
2. Open the command prompt.
3. At the command prompt, type **net stop** WINS and press Enter.
4. Change to the %systemroot%\system32\wins directory. After changing to this directory, type:

   jetpack wins.mdb winstemp.mdb

   and then press Enter.

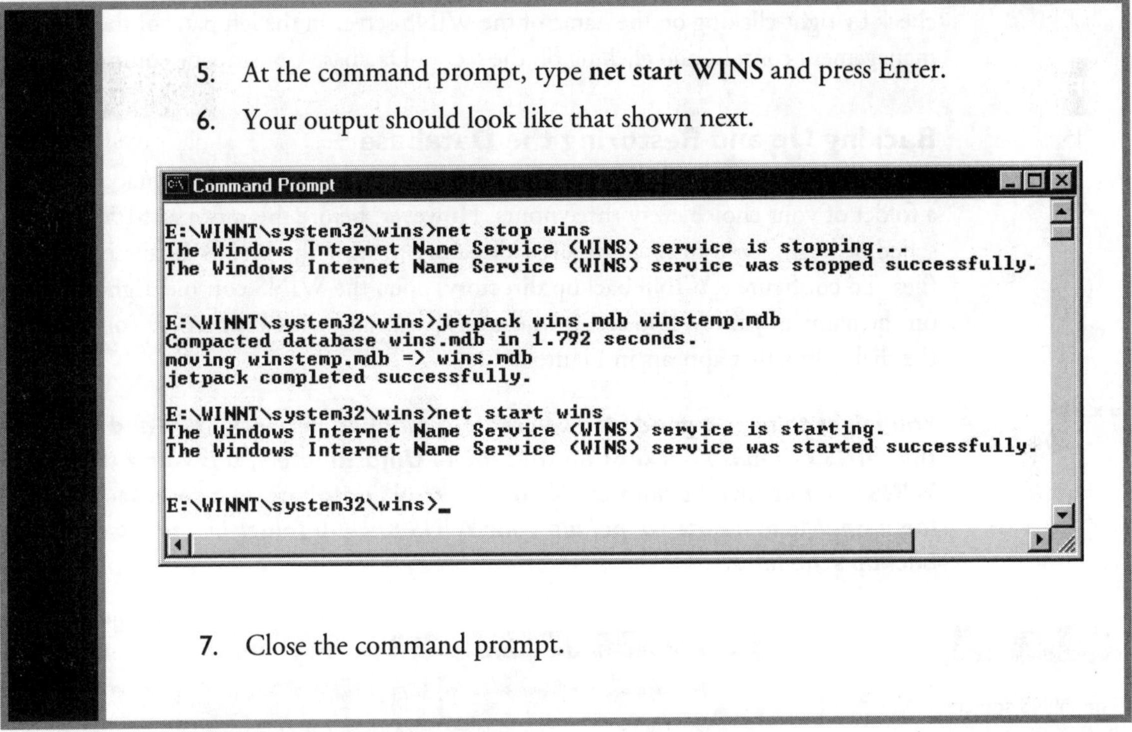

5. At the command prompt, type **net start WINS** and press Enter.
6. Your output should look like that shown next.

7. Close the command prompt.

Checking for Consistency

You can verify whether a WINS server contains correct entries in its database by performing a consistency check on the WINS database. When a WINS server verifies its database, it compares all of its entries against entries on other WINS servers that are replication partners of the WINS server you are checking. All records pulled from the other WINS servers are compared to records in the local database.

If the record in the local database is identical to the record pulled from the WINS server that owns the record, the timestamp on the local record is updated.

If the record that is pulled from the owner database has a higher version ID than the record in the local database, the pulled record is added to the local database, and the original local record is marked for deletion (tombstoned).

Depending on your replication topology, consistency checking can be a processor- and network-intensive task. It's best to wait for periods of low network utilization before undertaking a consistency check. You perform the WINS database consistency check by right-clicking on the name of the WINS server in the left pane of the WINS management console, and clicking on the Verify Database Consistency command.

Backing Up and Restoring the Database

The Windows 2000 WINS Server automatically backs up the WINS database to a folder of your choice every three hours. However, before this automated backup schedule begins, you must configure a directory to store the WINS database backup files. To configure a WINS backup directory, open the WINS console, right-click on the name of your WINS server in the left pane, and click Properties. You will see the dialog box that appears in Figure 8-11.

You might think it a good idea to create a mapped network drive and save the WINS database backups on that drive. Unfortunately, this won't work. WINS will not save backup copies of the WINS database to a remote location. Make a note to include your WINS backup folder in your routine backup schedules.

FIGURE 8-11

The WINS server Properties dialog box where the WINS backup directory is configured

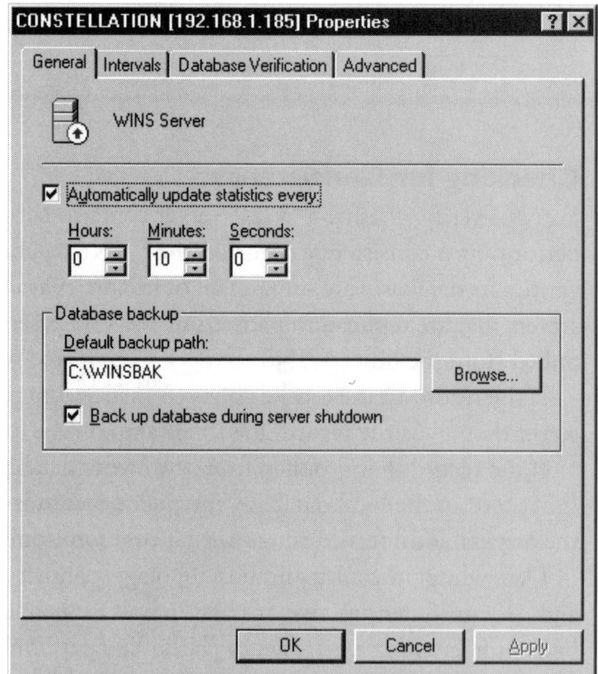

Backing Up the WINS Registry Settings If you've spent a good amount of time configuring your WINS server, you should take some time to backup the WINS server's Registry settings. These Registry settings are saved at:

```
HKLM\System\CurrentControlSet\Service\WINS
```

To save these settings, open the Registry using Regedt32. Then click the Registry menu and click Save Key. Back up the saved key to a safe place. When you need to rebuild the WINS server, open the Registry editor on the new machine, click the Registry menu, and click Restore. This will copy the saved key into the new Registry.

Restoring the WINS Database To restore the WINS database from the local backup:

1. Stop the WINS service. You can stop the WINS Server service by going to a command prompt and typing **net stop WINS,** or right-click on the WINS server name in the left pane of the WINS management console, trace to All Tasks, and then trace over and click Stop.
2. After stopping the WINS Server service, the Restore Database command appears. Click on the Restore Database.
3. The Browse for Folder dialog box appears. Select the directory housing the WINS database backup files, and click OK.

The database is restored, and the WINS Server service is restarted automatically.

CERTIFICATION OBJECTIVE 8.03

Interoperability Issues

In an all Windows 2000 network, the Windows 2000 WINS Server works flawlessly with very little management from your end. However, if you plan to integrate the WINS server with other services such as DHCP and DNS, you should be aware of some important issues.

WINS and DHCP

WINS servers and DHCP servers do not interact with one another directly. However, you can configure DHCP options that can configure the WINS client with the IP address of a WINS server, and the node type of the WINS client. Of course, you can also not configure a WINS server for DHCP clients.

If a DHCP client is configured with a WINS server, it will register with that WINS server after receiving an IP address from the DHCP server. Name registration is done via the normal mechanisms that were discussed earlier in this chapter.

WINS and DNS

All previous Microsoft operating systems are NetBIOS dependent for their networking infrastructure components. If you run a heterogeneous network that includes not only Windows 2000 computers, but also Win9*x* and Win3.*x* computers, you will need to enable NetBIOS name resolution mechanisms for those clients. Windows 2000 is not NetBIOS dependent, and the preferential method of name resolution for Windows 2000 computers is via DNS. What we need is a way for the Windows 2000 computers to use DNS and still be able to resolve the NetBIOS names of the downlevel clients that have registered with a WINS server.

The Windows 2000 DNS Server can be configured to query a WINS server for names that it cannot locate via DNS. Windows 2000 (and any other) DNS client can gain access to information in a WINS database without having to query a WINS server directly. The client communicates only with the DNS server, and the DNS server will act as a "proxy" for the DNS client in querying the WINS database.

In Windows 2000, you can configure the interoperability between WINS and DNS to enable non-WINS clients to resolve NetBIOS names by querying a DNS server. For example, if a non-WINS enabled client needs to access NetBIOS resources on another computer on the network, it can use its DNS server to resolve the name to an IP address. The DNS server then queries a WINS server, and the name is resolved and returned to the client.

How the Windows 2000 DNS Server Queries the WINS Server

When a DNS client issues a request for a NetBIOS resource to be resolved by a DNS server, the following sequence of events takes place:

1. The DNS client service on the DNS client formulates a DNS query. For example, the query is sent for a computer named FILESERVER. The query is fully qualified by appending the domain name to the NetBIOS name, and a query for FILESERVER.tacteam.net is issued to the DNS server.
2. The DNS server attempts to resolve the host name to an IP address using normal DNS mechanisms, which may include iteration.
3. If the DNS server is not able to resolve the host name to an IP address, and the DNS server is configured to query a WINS server, it will strip off the characters to the left of the leftmost period (dot) in the FQDN and issue a NetBIOS Name Query Request to the WINS server using those characters.
4. The WINS server resolves the name and replies with the IP address to the DNS server. The DNS server returns this information to the DNS client.

Interoperability with Downlevel DNS Servers When you enable WINS lookup on a Windows 2000 DNS Server, it creates resource records on the DNS server that are not compatible with downlevel DNS servers, such as the Windows NT 4.0 and UNIX-based implementations for DNS. If you plan to make a downlevel DNS server authoritative for any zone on which you have enabled WINS lookups, you need to be sure that the "Do not replicate this record" check box is checked to prevent problems with zone transfer. You configure this option in the Properties of the zone on your DNS server, as shown in Figure 8-12.

Any zone can be enabled to perform WINS lookups. However, there are a number of reasons why it is a good idea to disable WINS lookups on all populated zones (zones that have resource records in them) and create an empty WINS lookup enabled zone.

First, you would create a DNS zone without host records and enable it for WINS lookup. For example, assign the name wins.tacteam.net to the DNS zone. Then for

FIGURE 8-12

Configuring a Windows 2000 zone to not replicate the WINS forward lookup information to downlevel DNS servers

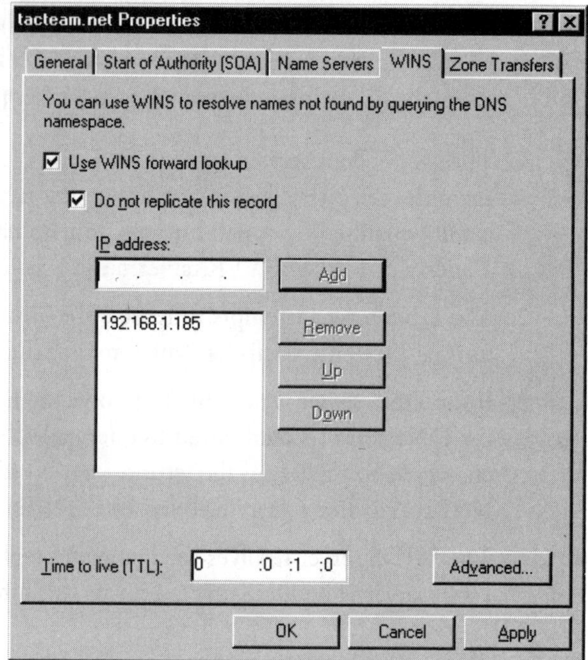

each DNS client computer, on the DNS tab of the Advanced TCP/IP Properties dialog box, add the wins.tacteam.net zone that you created to the "Append these DNS suffixes (in order)" text box.

This configuration allows for WINS lookup, and allows downlevel DNS servers to be authoritative for the domain tacteam.net.

A WINS lookup zone simplifies network administration and troubleshooting. Many network analysis and security tools use DNS to resolve host names. When the host is a NetBIOS host, the returned FQDN is dependent on the name appended to the DNS request. You can easily standardize the FQDNs returned on DNS queries for WINS clients that do not have a DNS entry by using the WINS lookup zone. Whenever you get a DNS reply that has the WINS lookup zone domain appended to it, you know the DNS server resolved the name via a WINS lookup.

EXERCISE 8-10

Configuring a DNS Service to Perform WINS Lookups

In this exercise, you will configure the Windows 2000 DNS Server service to perform a WINS lookup. You must have the DNS Server service already installed on your computer in order to perform the exercise. Do not perform this exercise on a live, production network without the permission of your network administrator.

1. Log on as Administrator.
2. Open the DNS management console from the Administrative Tools menu.
3. Expand all nodes in the left pane. Right-click on one of the existing zones and click Properties. Click the WINS tab in the zone's Properties dialog box. You should see what appears in the following illustration.

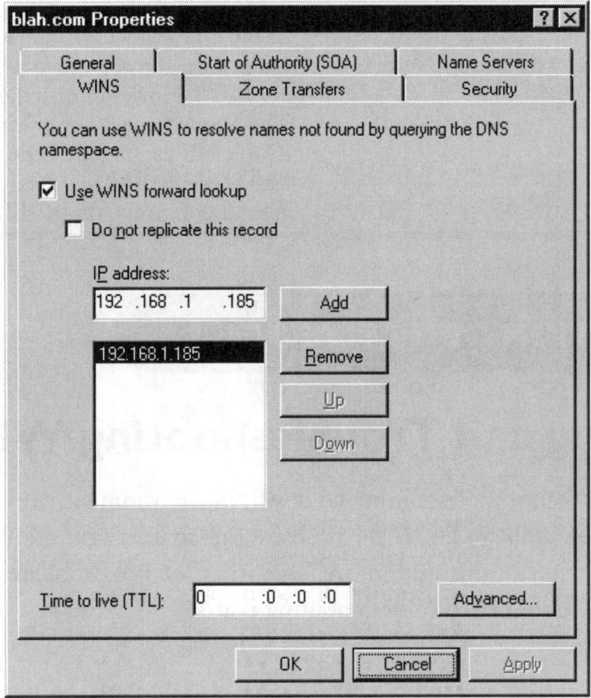

4. Place a check mark in "Use WINS forward lookup" and then type the IP address for the WINS server in the "IP address" text box. Then click Add.
5. Click Apply and then OK. Close the DNS management console.

SCENARIO & SOLUTION	
When should I create static mappings, and what is the best way to create them?	Create static mappings for computers that run NetBIOS applications but are not WINS clients. Some database applications run on UNIX or NetWare servers run as NetBIOS application servers and require NetBIOS client software. You are likely using LMHOSTS files to resolve these NetBIOS names. It is easy to import entries in LMHOSTS files to make static mapping via the WINS management console.
How long should I wait before compacting the WINS database offline?	This depends on how dynamic your NetBIOS name changes are on your network. However, a good rule of thumb is to manually compact the WINS database when it gets to be 30MB or larger.
Will my net send commands or the Alerter Service work correctly if I disable NetBIOS?	In the beta stages of Windows 2000 development, the net send command continued to work properly after disabling NetBIOS. However, with the final release version, it does not. The Alerter Service never worked after NetBIOS has been disabled. If you require either of these services, you should at least leave NetBIOS enabled on the source and destination computer running the NetBIOS applications.

CERTIFICATION OBJECTIVE 8.04

Monitoring and Troubleshooting WINS

When troubleshooting your WINS environment, you need to first consider where the problem lies. Is the problem due to errors on the WINS client or the WINS server? In this section, we'll see what sorts of problems you'll run into for common WINS-related troubleshooting issues.

Troubleshooting WINS Client-Related Problems

Problems with WINS clients are most likely to show up as failed NetBIOS name resolution requests. The following sections include some questions to ask if you are having WINS client-related problems.

Is the WINS Client Configured Correctly?

The WINS client may have the wrong IP address configured for its Primary and Secondary WINS servers. If the machine is a DHCP client, it could be that someone has manually reset the WINS server IP addresses. If a number of computers are DHCP clients and they all have problems with NetBIOS name resolution, the problem probably lies with a misconfiguration of the WINS DHCP option. Check the DHCP server to correct this situation.

Is There an Interruption in Connectivity between the WINS Client and Server?

It could be that the WINS client cannot contact the WINS server because of loss of connectivity. PING the WINS server addresses configured on the WINS client. If you don't get a response, then the problems are not with WINS or NetBIOS resolution, but with the network client or network.

Does the WINS Client Have Secondary WINS Servers Configured?

WINS clients should always have at least one Secondary WINS server configured in case the Primary server should become disabled. However, you must be aware that you can significantly slow the NetBIOS name resolution process if you enter too many WINS servers. Although the Windows 2000 WINS client can be configured with up to 12 Secondary WINS servers, this might not be a good thing.

The reason why multiple Secondaries are a double-edged sword is because it could take much longer to receive an error message regarding a failed query. If you configure 12 Secondaries for a NetBIOS name that does not exist, each one of those Secondaries must be queried in order to conclude that the name indeed does not exist, and get the error message returned.

Has NetBIOS Been Disabled?

If NetBIOS (NetBT) has been disabled on the WINS client's network adapter, it will not be able to participate in NetBIOS-dependent communications. Check to see if the user has disabled NetBIOS during an episode of "experimenting." If multiple users have the same problem, check to see if the DHCP server has been configured to deliver the Windows 2000 vendor option that disables NetBIOS on DHCP client machines.

Troubleshooting WINS Server-Related Issues

WINS server-related problems usually show up as widespread problems with NetBIOS name resolution. This is in contrast to problems you see with WINS client issues where usually a single computer or segment is having problems with name resolution.

Some questions to ask when troubleshooting WINS server-related problems are discussed in the following sections.

Is There a Problem with the WINS Database?

The WINS database can become corrupt if the system is shut down improperly or during impending disk failures. Check the Event Log to see if there have been errors reported regarding problems with the WINS database.

You can enable detailed event logging that will be reported to the Event Log by right-clicking on the name of the WINS server in the left pane of the WINS management console and clicking Properties. You will see what appears in Figure 8-13.

Is There a Static Mapping for the Name?

Static mappings can be a difficult problem to troubleshoot if you have inherited a network from another administrator that used static mappings, and then you subsequently upgraded non-WINS client to WINS-enabled systems. The upgraded systems will not automatically overwrite the static mappings. To correct this situation, enable *Migrate On* at the WINS servers.

Did the WINS Server Service Start?

A Windows 2000 Server with inadequate memory resources and a large number of services installed can easily experience "hangs" of some of the services during the boot-up process. Always check in both the Services applet and in the WINS console to see if the WINS Server service has started properly. The Event View may provide additional information regarding the nature of the failure.

Are the Network Traffic Problems on the WINS Server's Interfaces?

If the WINS server's adapter is located on a network segment that has its bandwidth saturated, queries may time out and cause a failure in NetBIOS name resolution. You may need to run a protocol analyzer such as Network Monitor on that segment to assess the percentage of network utilization.

FIGURE 8-13

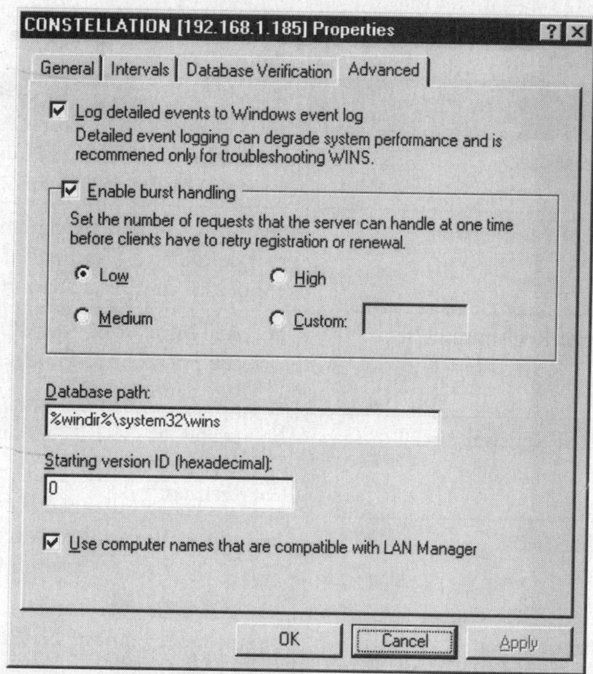

Enabling detailed event logging in the WINS server Properties dialog box

System Monitor

When you install the WINS Server service on your Windows 2000 Server computer, a number of counters are added to the System Monitor. Table 8-5 shows a list of those counters.

TABLE 8-5 Counters Added to the System Monitor After Installing the WINS Server Service

Counter	Description
Queries/sec	The number of queries per second received by the WINS server. A number that far exceeds baseline may represent a possible excessive load on the WINS server.
Releases/sec	The number of NetBIOS Name Release Requests received per second by the WINS server.
Successful Queries/sec	The number of NetBIOS Name Query Request successfully resolved by the WINS Server.

TABLE 8-5 Counters Added to the System Monitor After Installing the WINS Server Service *(continued)*

Counter	Description
Successful Releases/sec	The number of NetBIOS Name Releases successfully performed per second by the WINS server.
Total Number of Conflicts/sec	The number of NetBIOS name conflicts detected by the WINS server per second. Conflicts of both unique and group numbers are included in the calculation.
Total Number of Registrations/sec	The Total number of NetBIOS Name Registration Requests processed per second. This includes both unique and group NetBIOS names.
Total Number of Renewals/sec	The number of NetBIOS Name Renewal Requests processed by the WINS server per second. This includes both unique and Group names.
Unique Conflicts/sec	The number of conflicts in unique NetBIOS names processed by the WINS server per second. Only conflicts in unique NetBIOS names are detected.
Unique Registrations/sec	The number of unique NetBIOS names registered with the WINS server per second.
Unique Renewals/sec	The number of unique NetBIOS name registered per second.

CertCam 8-11

EXERCISE 8-11

Configuring WINS Server Startup Behavior

In this exercise, you will learn how to configure the WINS Server service startup behavior. Do not perform this exercise on a live, production network without the permission of your network administrator.

1. Log on as Administrator.
2. Open the Services applet from the Administrative Tools menu.
3. Scroll down the list of services until you find Windows Internet Name Service (WINS), and then double-click on it.
4. You should see what appears in the following illustration. Click Stop. You will see the progress bar indicating that the service is being stopped. Click Start to restart the service. Ensure that the Startup type is Automatic.

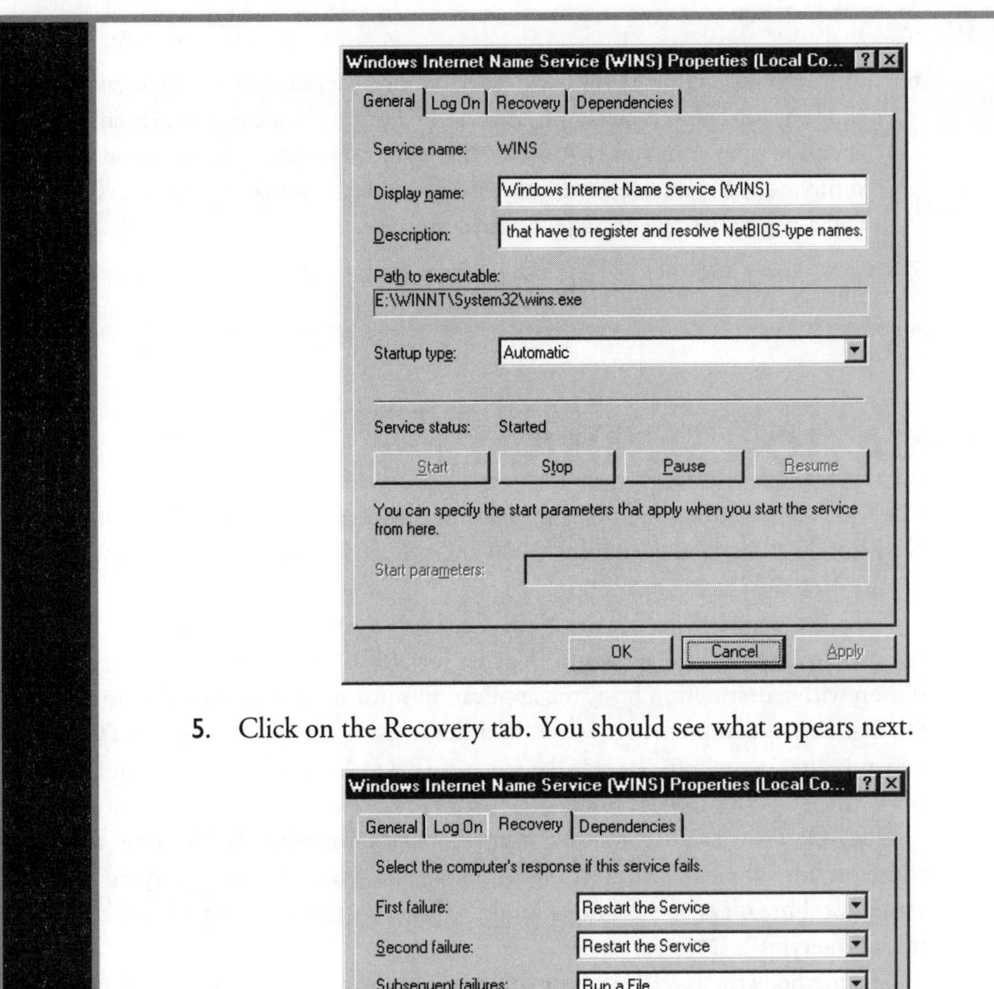

5. Click on the Recovery tab. You should see what appears next.

Windows Internet Name Service (WINS) Properties (Local Co...
General | Log On | Recovery | Dependencies
Select the computer's response if this service fails.
First failure: Restart the Service
Second failure: Restart the Service
Subsequent failures: Run a File
Reset fail count after: 0 days
Restart service after: 0 minutes
Run file
File: c:\adminmssgs\winsfailure.bat Browse...
Command line parameters:
Append fail count to end of command line (/fail=%1%)
Restart Computer Options...
OK | Cancel | Apply

6. For the "First failure" and the "Second failure," select Restart the Service. For "Subsequent failure," select the Run a File option. You can create a simple batch file to inform you that the service didn't start using the **net send** command. Or, you can configure more complex command parameters to send a pager message or SMTP e-mail message.
7. Click Apply and then OK. Close the Services console.

CERTIFICATION SUMMARY

The Microsoft Windows 2000 WINS Server provides NetBIOS name resolution for NetBIOS hosts on both Windows 2000 and other Microsoft network clients that require NetBIOS name resolution.

NetBIOS applications use the NetBIOS Session layer interface to access network resources over a TCP/IP network. In order for NetBIOS applications to create a session with a destination host, the application must use the NetBIOS name of the destination computer. However, in order to establish a session over a TCP/IP network, that name must be translated to an IP address, so the request can be passed down the TCP/IP protocol stack.

NetBIOS hosts can use a variety of methods to resolve NetBIOS names to IP addresses, including checking its NetBIOS Remote Name Cache, querying a WINS server, local broadcasts, checking a local LMHOSTS file, checking a local HOSTS file, or querying a DNS server.

The methods the NetBIOS host will use, and the order in which it will use them are dependent on the NetBIOS node type of the NetBIOS host. The basic node types are b-node, p-node, m-node, and h-node.

In order to configure a working WINS solution, you must install and configure three primary components: the WINS servers, the WINS clients, and if required, a WINS Proxy Agent. A WINS Proxy Agent can be used to provide WINS services to machines that cannot be configured as WINS clients.

The WINS server participates in four primary interactions with WINS clients: NetBIOS name resolution, NetBIOS name registration, NetBIOS name renewal, and NetBIOS name release. When WINS client machines start up, they register their names with their configured WINS servers. The WINS client must renew its name with the WINS server periodically in order to keep its name *active* in the WINS database. A WINS client will release its name in the WINS database when it no longer needs it.

WINS clients also query a WINS server to resolve NetBIOS names to IP addresses. The WINS server is essentially a database server and accepts these queries for NetBIOS name resolution.

The Windows 2000 version of WINS includes some new and improved components: the ability to maintain persistent connections between replication partners, burst handling, and easy manual tombstoning of WINS database records.

All WINS servers on your network should have the same entries in their WINS databases so that they are able to resolve the NetBIOS names to IP addresses for all the NetBIOS servers on the network. In order to assure that the WINS database is distributed correctly, you must configure WINS servers to be replication partners of one another.

WINS servers can be either *push* or *pull* replication partners. The push partner forwards the changes made in its WINS database based on how many changes have taken place. The pull partner is configured to send a pull request to its pull partner based on an interval of time. Once the interval is expired, the pull request is sent, and the pull partner's WINS database changes are sent.

Activities that you carry out when managing the WINS server include compacting the database when it becomes too large, adding static entries for non-WINS clients, backing up the database, and checking for consistency of WINS database entries.

The Windows 2000 WINS Server can interoperate with the DHCP Service and the Windows 2000 DNS Server. The Windows 2000 DNS Server can be configured to query a WINS server for name resolution.

The Windows 2000 WINS Server is reliable and mostly self-tuning. However, there may be times when you must troubleshoot and monitor the WINS server. The majority of problems with WINS server issues are related to connectivity between the WINS client and WINS server. You can use the System Monitor to monitor the health and performance of your WINS server.

✓ TWO-MINUTE DRILL

Introduction to NetBIOS Resolution

- ❑ NetBIOS applications are written to interact with the networking protocols via the NetBIOS interface. The Microsoft implementation of the NetBIOS interface for TCP/IP is called NetBIOS over TCP/IP, or NetBT.
- ❑ NetBIOS applications use the NetBIOS name as the endpoint of communication. TCP/IP uses IP addresses and port numbers. NetBIOS names must be translated to IP addresses via a process called NetBIOS Name Resolution.
- ❑ Windows 2000 can use several methods to resolve NetBIOS names, including the NetBIOS Remote Name Cache, WINS servers, Broadcasts, LMHOSTS files, HOSTS files, and DNS servers.
- ❑ The methods used to resolve NetBIOS names to IP addresses depend on the NetBIOS *node type* the NetBIOS host is using. The NetBIOS node types are b-node, p-node, m-node, and h-node. Microsoft includes a special node called the *enhanced* b-node that uses the cached entries in the LMHOSTS file.
- ❑ WINS servers register the NetBIOS name and IP addresses of WINS clients. WINS servers also respond to requests for NetBIOS name resolution.
- ❑ A WINS client is a computer that can be configured to register its NetBIOS name with a WINS server, and that can query a WINS server for the IP address of a particular NetBIOS name.
- ❑ The WINS Proxy Agent intercepts NetBIOS name resolution requests broadcasts on a local segment and forwards those to a WINS server for name resolution. They are typically used to allow NetBIOS name resolution via WINS for non-WINS clients.
- ❑ The four main interactions WINS servers and clients have are NetBIOS Name Registration, NetBIOS Name Query Request, NetBIOS Name Release, and NetBIOS Name Refresh.
- ❑ The Windows 2000 WINS Server supports *persistent connections.* These allow WINS replication partners to maintain an open channel at all times, and reduces the overhead related to establishing and tearing down sessions during each replication event.

- *Burst handling* allows the WINS server to quickly respond with a Positive Name Registration Response to WINS clients when the WINS server is overwhelmed. The TTL on the Registration is short so that the WINS client must reregister its name. This is because an entry is not added to the WINS database when the WINS client receives the response when the WINS server is in burst mode.
- A *tombstoned* record is a WINS database record that is marked for deletion. It is better to tombstone a record, because the record will not be replicated throughout the network as *active*.

Planning and Implementing a WINS Solution

- The WINS database is kept consistent throughout a WINS network via WINS database replication.
- WINS replication partners can be push partners, pull partners, or both. A push partner sends a pull notification message to its push partner after a defined number of changes have been made to the WINS database. A pull partner sends a pull request to its pull partner after a specified period of time has elapsed. WINS replication partners can be configured as both push and pull partners.
- WINS servers can find each other via a process of *Autodiscovery*. Autodiscovery is accomplished via multicast messages to the multicast address 224.0.1.24. Autoconfigured WINS replication partners are configured as push and pull partners. The pull interval is two hours.
- Entries for non-WINS clients can be entered into the WINS database via *static mappings*. Static mappings are entered manually into the WINS database and are not overwritten by dynamic registrations unless the Migrate On setting is enabled.
- You can back up the WINS database files to a local hard disk location. You cannot back up the WINS database to a mapped network drive. You must first configure a location to back up the WINS database before automatic database backups begin.

Interoperability Issues

- A DNS server can query a WINS server for NetBIOS name resolution if the DNS server does not contain an entry for the sought-after host name.
- WINS servers and DHCP servers do not communicate directly with each other. DHCP options can be used to assign WINS server IP addresses to DHCP clients, and the NetBIOS node type can also be set via DHCP options.
- Downlevel DNS servers, such as UNIX BIND DNS servers, do not support WINS Lookup. If you are using BIND Secondaries, you should disable replication of WINS lookup information.

Monitoring and Troubleshooting WINS

- You can use the Windows 2000 System Monitor to assess WINS server performance and monitor WINS server usage statistics.
- When troubleshooting WINS-related problems, try to assess whether the problem lies with the client or with the server.
- Most client-related problems are due to errors in client configuration or connectivity issues—check those first.
- The WINS Server service may "hang" on startup. Check the Services applet to insure that the service has started normally.

SELF TEST

The following questions will help you measure your understanding of the material presented in this chapter. Read all of the choices carefully, as there may be more than one correct answer. Choose all correct answers for each question.

Introduction to NetBIOS Name Resolution

1. The endpoint of communications for NetBIOS applications is/are?

A. IP address and port number

B. DNS host name

C. NetBIOS name

D. IPX address

2. You get a call from a user who complains that he cannot connect to a computer whose name shows up in the My Network Places applet. He says that every time he double-clicks on the computer name, he gets a message several seconds later that says something like the computer cannot be found on the network. You check the WINS database to confirm that the IP address of the destination computer is there and that it is correct. You check the user's computer to confirm that it has the correct WINS server in its configuration dialog boxes. The user is able to connect to other computers located on the same segment as the computer he cannot connect to. What might be the problem in this case?

A. The default gateway is incorrect on the user's computer.

B. The destination computer is not a WINS client.

C. There is an entry in the LMHOSTS file for the destination computer that is incorrect, and it has the #PRE tag appended to it.

D. The user's computer has NetBIOS disabled, and therefore is unable to connect to the destination computer using NetBIOS over TCP/IP (NetBT).

3. What tag do you use in an LMHOSTS file to denote an entry as a domain controller?

A. #BEGIN_ALTERNATE

B. #END_ALTERNATE

C. #DOM

D. #PRE

4. The REG_DWORD value for an h-node NetBIOS client is

A. 1

B. 2

C. 6

D. 8

5. You hired a new junior network administrator and have tasked him to create an LMHOSTS file for the master browsers and domain master browser on your network. Jimmy, your new network admin, calls you and says that he's done making the file, and reads the entries to you, which you confirm as correct. In order to test if the LMHOSTS file Jimmy created is working properly, you tell him to remove the WINS server's IP address from his machine, remove the DNS server's IP address, and clear both the DNS and the NetBIOS name caches. Then you tell him to PING some of the entries in the LMHOSTS file by their NetBIOS names. Jimmy PINGS each of the entries, and the only ones that work are on the local segment. What happened to Jimmy's LMHOSTS file?

A. Jimmy typed the machine names in all capital letters.

B. Jimmy saved the file in the %systemroot\system32\drivers\etc folder.

C. The machine is not the correct node type to use the LMHOSTS file.

D. Jimmy didn't put quotes around the file name when he was saving it.

6. The maximum number of WINS servers you should have on your network is

A. 5

B. 10

C. 15

D. 20

7. A single WINS server and a backup WINS server should be able to accommodate how many WINS clients?

A. 100

B. 1000

C. 10,000

D. 50,000

8. You have two subnets separated by a router: 192.168.1.0 and 192.168.2.0, both with the default Class C subnet mask. You have a WINS server on 192.168.1.0 and a WINS Proxy Agent on 192.168.2.0. You have non-WINS client UNIX servers on each subnet that runs

NetBIOS applications and need to resolve NetBIOS names to IP addresses. The UNIX machines on 192.168.2.0 have no problems resolving NetBIOS names to IP addresses, but the UNIX machines on the same subnet as the WINS server are not able to successfully resolve NetBIOS names. Why can't the UNIX machines resolve the NetBIOS names?

A. The UNIX machines on the same subnet as the WINS server must be configured with the IP address of the WINS server.

B. You must open the WINS Proxy Port UDP 140 on the router for the UNIX servers on 192.168.1.0 to communicate with the WINS Proxy Agent.

C. The WINS server does not respond to NetBIOS Name Query Request broadcast messages.

D. You must install the WINS Proxy Agent software on the UNIX NetBIOS client machines.

9. Jimmy has renamed the LMHOSTS file he created earlier and now it is not saved with the .txt file extension. When you ask him to PING the NetBIOS names in the LMHOSTS file, he gets the same results as he did before; he only gets replies from machines on the local segment. Why is Jimmy still not able to get his LMHOSTS file to work correctly?

A. All entries in the LMHOSTS file must have the #PRE tag in order to work correctly.

B. Jimmy has disabled the DNS client service on his computer.

C. Jimmy has disabled the DHCP client service on his computer.

D. The Enable LMHOSTS lookup option has not been selected in the Advanced TCP/IP Properties dialog box.

10. The first message sent to a WINS client when it tries to register a name that is already in the database but with a different IP address is called what?

A. Negative NetBIOS Name Registration Request

B. Positive NetBIOS Name Registration Request

C. Negative NetBIOS Name Query Response

D. Wait for Acknowledgement

11. Which of the following are requirements for installing the Windows 2000 WINS Server service?

A. The computer operating system must be a member of the Windows 2000 Server family of products.

B. The computer must have a static IP address.

C. The computer must have at least two network cards.

D. The computer must be a member of the same Windows 2000 domain for which it will service registration and query requests.

12. Jimmy has been working on improving NetBIOS name resolution for non-WINS clients on one of your network segments. He comes to you with a problem he's been having. He says that he's been getting a lot of calls from some of the users because the network has been "slow" and they want him to fix it. You ask him if he's made any changes lately that he hasn't told you about. Jimmy tells you that he's added four WINS Proxy Agents on one of the subnets that has a lot of UNIX workstations that must resolve NetBIOS names to access resources on other computers on the network. He tells you that since all he had to do was make a Registry entry, and didn't have to add any extra software, he thought that it was a great idea. Why is Jimmy's idea not so great?

    A. Each WINS Proxy Agent on the segment intercepts the NetBIOS Name Query Request and forwards it to the WINS server.
    B. A WINS Proxy Agent must be on the same segment as a WINS server.
    C. Multiple WINS Proxy Agents directly forward resolved queries to each other.
    D. Multiple WINS Proxy Agents detect each other's presence and deactivate each other.

13. What happens to a WINS database record if it not refreshed at one-half of the Time-to-Live it received when it registered with the WINS server?

    A. The record remains active until 87.5% of the TTL has passed.
    B. The record is marked inactive or released.
    C. The record is tombstoned.
    D. The record is removed from the WINS database via scavenging.

Planning and Implementing a WINS Solution

14. What is the multicast IP address that WINS servers listen on for automatic replication partner configuration?

    A. 224.24.0.1
    B. 224.1.0.24
    C. 224.0.1.24.
    D. 244.4.1.44

15. Your company's central office is located in Galveston, Texas. The company also has two branch offices, one located in Phoenix, Arizona, and the other in Carson City, Nevada. There are 7500 computers in Galveston, 1500 computers in Phoenix, and 500 computers in Carson City. The WAN links are 56-k Frame Relay. How many WINS servers should you place, and how should you set up the replication scheme?

A. You should place three WINS servers, one at each site. All WINS servers should be push and pull partners with each other.

B. You should place four WINS servers, two at the main office, and one each at the branch offices, and all the machines should be push and pull partners with each other.

C. You should place two WINS servers, two at the main location that will be push and pull partners for each other.

D. You should place six WINS servers, two at each location. Servers that are located at the same site should be configured as push and pull partners, and one server from each site should be configured to be a pull partner of another WINS server at a remote site.

Interoperability Issues

16. You have asked your new network administrator, Jimmy, to set up a Windows 2000 Dynamic DNS Server for your company and enable WINS lookups on the server. After completing his task successfully, Jimmy comes to you and says that he's been getting error messages related to zone transfers from the Windows 2000 DNS Server to the BIND DNS servers on the network. What could be causing the problems with the zone transfers?

A. Windows 2000 DNS Servers with WINS lookup enabled are not able to perform zone transfers.

B. Many BIND-based DNS servers do not support the WINS lookup information on a Windows 2000 DNS Server, and will not successfully perform zone transfers for zones with WINS Lookup enabled.

C. The Windows 2000 DNS Server and the Windows 2000 WINS Server have created opportunistic locks on each other's databases that prevent zone transfers to BIND Secondaries.

D. The WINS database had become corrupt; therefore, the zone transfer had failed.

17. A WINS lookup zone:

A. Sends queries directly to the WINS server for resolution when issued by a WinSock client

B. Allows a single domain name to be appended to query answers that have been answered via WINS lookups

C. Should be the first domain name to be appended to unqualified queries

D. Must be created in order for DNS servers to perform WINS lookups

Monitoring and Troubleshooting WINS

18. What utility would you use to monitor your Windows 2000 WINS Server?

A. System Monitor

B. Event Viewer

C. Network Monitor

D. View Master

19. What is the most frequent issue regarding problems with WINS clients?

A. DNS server problems

B. DHCP server problems

C. WINS server problems

D. Basic connectivity problems

LAB QUESTION

Your company is located in San Francisco, and you have branch offices in Dallas, Los Angeles, Seattle, and Laramie. The main office in San Francisco has 12,500 computers, and the branch offices have 5000–6000 computers each. How many WINS servers would you place, and where would you place them? How would you configure replication between all the WINS servers in your organization?

A

SELF TEST ANSWERS

Introduction to NetBIOS Name Resolution

1. ☑ C. NetBIOS names are used as the endpoint of communications for programs written to the NetBIOS interface.
☒ A is incorrect because the IP address and port number are used as an endpoint of communications for programs written to the WinSock interface and not the NetBIOS interface. **B** is incorrect because DNS host names are not used as an endpoint of communications for any programming interface. **D** is incorrect because IPX addresses are not used as an endpoint of communications for NetBIOS applications.

2. ☑ C. Entries in the LMHOSTS file that have the #PRE tag will be loaded in the NetBIOS remote name caching at system startup. The cache is checked before the WINS server is queried. An incorrect entry in the LMHOSTS file would lead to errors in NetBIOS name resolution.
☒ A is incorrect because the default gateway is not an issue if the user's computer can connect to another computer on the same segment as the destination computer that is having the problem. **B** is incorrect because the destination computer is located in the WINS database, regardless of its being a WINS client (it may have a static entry, and therefore would not be a WINS client, but would be located in the WINS database). **D** is incorrect because if NetBIOS had been disabled on the users computer, he would see no computer names in the My Network Places applet. This is because the My Network Places applet is populated via the browser service, and a computer without NetBIOS enabled would not be able to request the browse list from a backup browser.

3. ☑ C. The #DOM tag is used to identify an entry in the LMHOSTS file as a domain controller that can authenticate logon requests.
☒ A is incorrect because the END_ALTERNATE tag is used to mark the end of a group of INCLUDE statements in an LMHOSTS file. **B** is incorrect because the BEGIN_ALTERNATE tag is used to group multiple #INCLUDE statements that are searched for LMHOSTS files on the network. **D** is incorrect because the #PRE tag is used to load entries into the NetBIOS Remote Name Cache on system startup.

4. ☑ D. The answer is 8.
☒ **A**, **B**, and **C** are incorrect or represent other node types. There is no NetBIOS node type defined by 6.

5. ☑ **D.** If you don't put quotation marks around the file name when you save the LMHOSTS file, the file will be saved with the .txt file extension.
☒ A is incorrect because the computer name is not case sensitive in the LMHOSTS file. **B** is incorrect because that is the correct location for the LMHOSTS file. **C** is incorrect because all node types use the LMHOSTS file.

6. ☑ **D.** Microsoft recommends that you never install more than 20 WINS servers on your network. If you feel that you need more than 20 WINS servers on your network, Microsoft recommends that you install Microsoft Consulting Service for an analysis of your situation.
☒ **A**, **B**, and **C** are incorrect because you can install up to 20 WINS servers on your network.

7. ☑ **C.** Microsoft recommends a single WINS server and a backup for every 10000 WINS clients. You may want to deploy more WINS servers than this depending on the nature of the links between the organization's sites. In actual practice, it's likely that your ratio of WINS clients to servers will be higher than this, because most networks are segmented. Microsoft makes this recommendation to remind administrators and architects that often far more WINS servers are implemented than are needed.
☒ **A**, **B**, and **D** are incorrect because a single WINS server and a backup SINS server should be able to accommodate 10,000 WINS clients.

8. ☑ **C.** WINS servers will not respond to NetBIOS Name Query Requests. Since the UNIX servers are on the same subnet as the non-WINS clients, they cannot communicate with the WINS server directly and can only resolve names via broadcasts.
☒ A is incorrect because non-WINS clients cannot be configured with the IP address of a WINS server. **B** is incorrect because there is not a WINS Proxy Agent port. **D** is incorrect because there is no WINS Proxy Agent software to install on WINS clients.

9. ☑ **D.** You must enable LMHOSTS lookup in order to process entries in an LMHOSTS file. By default, this option is selected.
☒ A is incorrect because entries in the LMHOSTS file do not need the #PRE tag in order to work correctly. The #PRE tag places those entries into the NetBIOS Remote Name Cache on system startup. **B** is incorrect because disabling the DNS client service will not prevent the LMHOSTS file from working correctly. **C** is incorrect because disabling the DHCP client service will not prevent the LMHOSTS file from working correctly. The DHCP client service is responsible for allowing machines to perform dynamic updates with a dynamic DNS server.

10. ☑ **D.** A WINS server will send a WACK (Wait for Acknowledgement) to the WINS client before sending a challenge to the other computer claiming to own the NetBIOS name registration.

☒ A is incorrect because a Negative NetBIOS Name Registration Request is sent to WINS clients when a name they try to register is already in the WINS database, and the owner of the name has successfully defended the name. **B** is incorrect because a Positive NetBIOS Name Registration Request is sent to WINS clients after they have successfully registered their NetBIOS names in the WINS database. **C** is incorrect because the Negative NetBIOS Name Query Response is sent to WINS clients when the WINS server is not able to provide a mapping for the requested NetBIOS name.

11. ☑ **A, B. A** is correct because you can install Server services only on Server operating systems. The Windows 2000 WINS Server service cannot be installed on Windows 2000 Professional. **B** is correct because a WINS server must have a static IP address for WINS clients to connect to. However, it should be noted here that you can install the WINS server on the DHCP client, but it won't be of much use to you.
☒ **C** is incorrect because a WINS server does not require two network interface cards. **D** is incorrect because a WINS server does not need to be a member of the same Windows 2000 domain as the WINS clients that it services.

12. ☑ **A.** Each WINS Proxy Agent intercepts NetBIOS Name Query Requests and forwards those to the WINS server. In this example, Jimmy has added four WINS Proxy Agents. For each NetBIOS name query broadcast on the segment, four queries will be sent to the WINS server. Only a single WINS Proxy Agent is recommended per segment.
☑ **B** is incorrect because a WINS Proxy Agent does not need to be on the same segment as a WINS server. **C** is incorrect because WINS Proxy Agents do not forward NetBIOS name queries to each other. **D** is incorrect because WINS Proxy Agents do not detect each other like the Windows 2000 DHCP Servers are able to.

13. ☑ **B.** If the record is not refreshed at 50% of its TTL, it will be marked as inactive (released). An inactive record can be dynamically updated without being challenged by the WINS server.
☒ **A** is incorrect because the record doesn't remain active after 50% of the TTL unless it is refreshed. **C** is incorrect because a record is tombstoned only after the passages of the extinction interval. **D** is incorrect because the record is not removed until the extinction timeout has expired.

Planning and Implementing a WINS Solution

14. ☑ C. 224.0.1.24.
☒ **A** and **B** are incorrect because the multicast IP address that WINS servers listen on for automatic replication partner configuration is 224.0.1.24. **D** is incorrect because it is a Class E IP address, and therefore could not even be considered as a correct answer because multicast addresses belong to IP address class D.

15. ☑ **D.** You should place two WINS servers at each site: a Primary WINS server and a backup for the machines located within each site. The Primary and backup WINS servers should be push and pull partners of each other, since they are separated by fast links. A hub WINS server should be assigned to each site, and that hub server should participate in pull replication with one or more sites, depending on how you have architected your WINS network.
☒ **A, B,** and **C** are incorrect because you need to place two WINS servers at each location.

Interoperability Issues

16. ☑ **B.** The problem could result from the fact that many BIND-based DNS servers do not support the WINS lookup information on a Windows 2000 DNS Server.
☒ **A, C,** and **D** are incorrect because the problem results from the fact that many BIND-based DNS servers will not successfully perform zone transfers for zones with WINS lookup enabled because they do not support the WINS lookup information on a Windows 2000 DNS Server.

17. ☑ **B.** If you create a single empty zone that is WINS lookup enabled, and disable WINS lookups on all other zones, a single zone will be used to perform WINS lookups, and that zone will be reported as the domain name of NetBIOS host names that were resolved via WINS.
☒ **A** is incorrect because WINS-enabled zones do not send queries to the WINS server first; the WINS server is sent the query if it cannot be resolved via the DNS query process. **C** is incorrect because the WINS lookup zone domain name should be the last domain appended to unqualified queries. **D** is incorrect because you do not need to create a dedicated WINS lookup zone to successfully use WINS lookups; any zone can be enabled to perform WINS lookups.

Monitoring and Troubleshooting WINS

18. ☑ **A.** You can use the Windows 2000 System Monitor to monitor the health and performance of your WINS server.
☒ **B** is incorrect because the Event Viewer only provides information about critical failures related to the WINS server. **C** is incorrect because the Network Monitor provides information regarding the types of packets transferred between the WINS server and the WINS clients, but does not perform further analysis on this information. **D** is incorrect because a View Master was used at one time to show slides of various locations around the world.

19. ☑ **D.** The most frequent cause of WINS client problems relates to issues of connectivity and loss of the connectivity, leading to an inability to contact the WINS server.

☒ A is incorrect because DNS server related issues are not the most frequent cause of WINS client problems. **B** is incorrect because DHCP server issues are rarely the root of failures on WINS clients. C is incorrect because the WINS server itself, while important, is not the most frequent issue related to WINS client problems.

LAB ANSWER

For an organization of this size, you should have WINS servers at each site. Since each of the branch offices has fewer than 10,000 computers, a single Primary and a Secondary WINS server should be enough. The headquarters has more than 10,000 computers, but fewer than 20,000 computers, so you should have two Primary and two Secondary machines at the corporate headquarters. With four WINS servers at headquarters and two each at the branch offices, you need at least 10 WINS servers.

Replication between the WINS servers at the branch offices should be push and pull partners with each other. At the main office, since there are four WINS servers, it would be a good idea to make one of the WINS server a hub server, and have the other WINS servers serve as spoke WINS servers. Each of the spoke servers would be push and pull partners to the hub WINS server. In this way, the central hub WINS server collates the WINS database information and redistributes it to the spoke WINS servers at the corporate headquarters.

Now that you have intrasite replication configured, you need to configure intersite replication. The best way to approach this is to assign a hub server for each of the sites. You have already done so for the corporate site, so you don't need to do this again. Pick a WINS server at each of the branch sites and designate that as the hub of the site. Then, configure each of the branch office hubs to be pull partners of the corporate site hub, and configure the corporate site hub to be a pull partner to each of the branch site hubs. In this way, the corporate hub will collate WINS database information for the entire enterprise and redistribute it to all the WINS servers in the organization.

MCSE

MICROSOFT CERTIFIED SYSTEMS ENGINEER

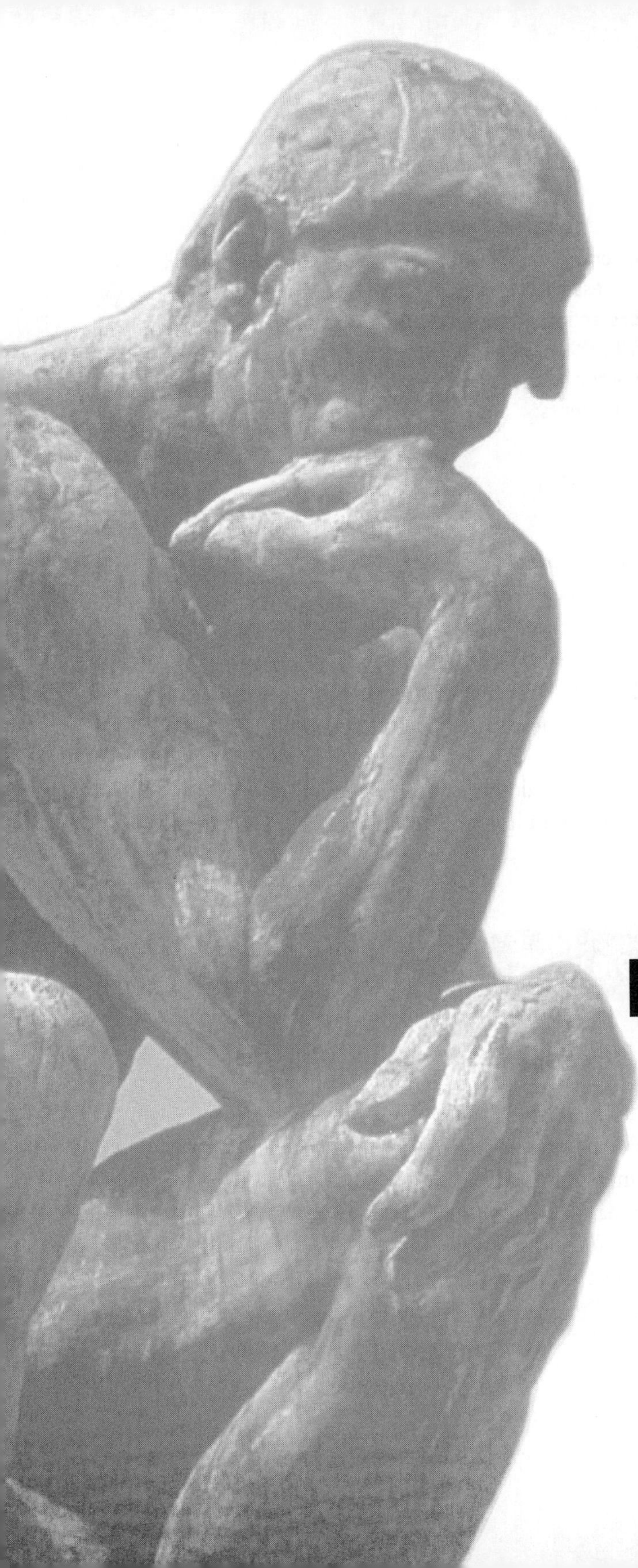

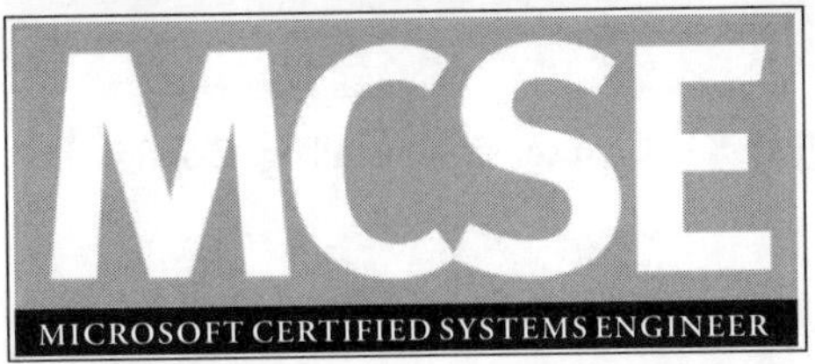

9

Installing, Configuring, Managing, Monitoring, and Troubleshooting IP Routing

CERTIFICATION OBJECTIVES

9.01	Overview of Windows 2000 IP Routing
9.02	Enabling and Configuring Windows 2000 as an IP Software Router
9.03	Implementing Routing Protocols
9.04	RIP for IP
9.05	OSFP
9.06	Demand-Dial Routing
9.07	Troubleshooting IP Routing Problems
✓	Two-Minute Drill
Q&A	Self Test

We have already seen in Chapter 5, "Configuring, Managing, Monitoring, and Troubleshooting Remote Access," how Windows 2000 Routing and Remote Access Service (RRAS) offers an integrated remote access service. Although Windows 2000 supports routing for TCP/IP, IPX, and AppleTalk, this chapter concentrates on the routing capabilities and features that comprise the Windows 2000 IP Router. Specifically, this includes support for the following components:

- IGMP
- ICMP Router Discovery
- RIP and OSFP routing protocols
- Demand-dial routing

Additionally, RRAS supports the DHCP Relay Agent and Network Address Translation (NAT). The DHCP Relay Agent is discussed in Chapters 4 and 5. You'll learn more about NAT in Chapter 10, "Installing, Configuring, and Troubleshooting NAT."

At the end of this chapter, you should have a much better understanding of how to install, configure, manage, monitor, and troubleshoot Windows 2000 as an IP router.

CERTIFICATION OBJECTIVE 9.01

Overview of Windows 2000 IP Routing

The Internet Protocol, or IP, is today's common network protocol that communicates over many different interconnected networks. The different networks can be within the same building and using the same media (e.g., Ethernet), or they can be worldwide using many different mediums such as FDDI, Frame Relay, ISDN, cable modems, analog modems, and others . Obviously, the Internet falls into the latter category, and in its simplest conceptual form, "The Internet" is merely a mesh of interconnected networks all using the same protocol suite and joined by multiple routers.

IP can span multiple networks precisely because it supports routing. Routing is the process of forwarding packets from one computer (*source host*) on one network to another computer (*destination host*) on another network. There are many different kinds of routers you can use with different routing protocols, but essentially they are all doing the same job: making decisions about forwarding traffic they receive from one network to another.

What Is a Router?

When the word *router* is used, typically people think of a physical box that is dedicated to just routing. Cisco, Bay Networks, Digital, and Cabletron Systems, for example, are just a few of the best known vendors offering this kind of technology. So how does this equate with Windows 2000 Server acting as a router? Windows 2000 Server offers a routing component tightly integrated into its operating system and network services so that it can take advantage of other Windows 2000 features (e.g., a shared GUI interface, security policies, authorization, etc.). It offers the flexibility to run additional or complementing services; for example, Remote Access is tightly integrated with the routing component.

Characteristics of a Software Routing Service

The routing service is one of many services running on the computer, and is dependent on the underlying operating system (e.g., Windows 2000).

The benefits of using Windows 2000 Server with the routing service include

- Tight integration with Windows 2000 features and benefits
- Built-in monitor and keyboard with standard Windows 2000 GUI interface for ease of use and a reduced learning curve
- Flexibility of running other applications/services on the same computer
- Potentially cheaper than a separate hardware box
- Same vendor environment as other workstations/servers

Characteristics of a Hardware Router

Hardware routers are usually configured across the network with a Telnet session or from a dial-in port on the router, so they are less "user friendly" and typically employ their own vendor-specific language for configuration. However, because they are exclusively aimed to route packets, they do offer a higher degree of control and configuration; for example, employing multiple protocols and advanced routing features. And, because their sole job is routing, they make more efficient use of their processing resources.

The benefits of using a hardware router include

- Faster, more efficient throughput
- Offers and supports a greater number of protocols and configurations

Some hybrid routers attempt to offer the best of both worlds with the basic routing functionality handled by hardware, and system configuration and routing table management done by software. ExponeNT switches from Berkeley Networks are an example of this, where the software component actually runs on Windows NT.

Routed vs. Nonrouted Networks

If we define a routed network as being one or more networks joined together by a common protocol and a router, what is a nonrouted network? A nonrouted network is one or more networks that can be physically joined together, but have no means of communicating with each other over the Network layer. This may be for a number of reasons, including:

- They do not have a common protocol (e.g., one is running TCP/IP and the other IPX).
- The protocol in use is not routable (e.g., NetBEUI or DLC).
- There is no router to forward the packets.
- The router is not configured to forward packets.

Having nonrouted networks may be desirable in certain circumstances if, for example, you don't need or want to pass packets from one network to another (for security or bandwidth reasons). Additionally, if there is no need for computers on different networks to communicate, why employ the administrative burden of installing, configuring, and monitoring a router?

However, just because one network is not routed to another doesn't preclude the passage of traffic from one network to another. This could still be accomplished higher up than the Network layer; for example, with a gateway at the Session layer, converting one protocol into another (e.g. IPX to IP). Another example is using a proxy server at the Application layer, where one computer connected to two networks proxies traffic between the two networks. Additionally, you may prefer to use NAT rather than direct routing (discussed in detail in Chapter 10).

exam Watch ***It's not just routers that allow packets to pass from one network to another; this can also be accomplished by gateways, proxy servers, and so forth.***

Routing Fundamentals

We have already said that routing is the process of forwarding packets from one computer on one network to another computer on another network. This section looks at how IP achieves this.

Static vs. Dynamic Routing

Routers make decisions of where to forward packets they receive based on the routes (paths) they know. These routes can be *static*, *dynamic*, or a mixture of both.

Static routes are paths manually specified by an administrator and do not change until they are similarly manually changed by the administrator. Dynamic routes are paths that are "learned" and updated automatically by using routing protocols designed to automate the process of forwarding packets between networks.

Dynamic routing reduces administrative overhead, since the paths are learned automatically and they are resilient to changing circumstances because they are periodically updated automatically. However, such benefits invariably come at the price of efficiency and bandwidth. As a result of the automatic updates, routers have to "talk" to other routers at specified times, which can introduce problems of reduced bandwidth, an increase in processing on the router itself, a drop in routing efficiency since large routing tables are amassed, potential security risks, and other limitations and problems (discussed later).

Static routing has a greater administrative overhead because it relies on an administrator manually entering the paths, which is an error-prone and time-consuming process. It is also vulnerable to being out of date (non-fault tolerant) when changes occur on the network (e.g., someone changes an IP address or a router is suddenly unavailable). Although it lends itself toward a more efficient and tightly secured system with minimal loss of bandwidth, the administrative overhead for static routing is prohibitive for anything but a small network.

exam Watch

Dynamic routing results in additional overhead on the routers and the network; however, one of its greatest benefits is the routers can automatically sense and recover from internetwork faults.

The Default Gateway

Historically, the terms *gateway* and *router* have been used interchangeably in the IP world. Personally, I always prefer the term *router* because, technically speaking, a gateway is higher up the seven-layer model than a router, which is why it can convert one protocol to another. However, a gateway can also "convert" an IP packet into another IP packet, and one reason why you might want to do this is to pass IP packets from one network to another, which is exactly what routing is doing!

Microsoft has always used *gateway* to mean *router* within the context of IP address assignment—this is not changed in Windows 2000. If you want to route packets from your computer to a different network, and you do not have an existing route defined, the assigned default gateway can be used for all nonlocal traffic for which there is no specific route.

exam Watch

A TCP/IP computer sends nonlocal traffic to its default gateway when there is no specific route defined for it.

Default Gateway Issues If packets destined for a different network are sent but delivery fails, there are many potential reasons for the failure, but a good starting point is to check the routing table on the sending workstation and the default gateway assignment. See if a specific route exists for that network, and if not, verify that a default gateway has been assigned. The default gateway is often assigned with the IP address; for example, this could be a DHCP setting.

Assuming there is no specific route on the workstation for the destination network, and you have verified that a default gateway is assigned, ensure that it is reachable by pinging that address. If it fails when neighboring local addresses ping successfully, you should check that the IP address of the default gateway is correct, that the router is up, and that you have the correct IP address and subnet mask assigned.

on the Job

Pay particular attention to the subnet address—remember that it's the combination of the IP address and the subnet mask that is used by the TCP/IP workstation to determine whether the packet it has to send is local or remote.

Additionally, because Microsoft's TCP/IP implementation only has a single-route table, you can only ever have *one* current default gateway per machine. Although you can configure multiple default gateways, the second gateway will only be used if the first gateway is unavailable (this is called "Dead Gateway Detection" and depends on a certain algorithm employed by the protocol). Microsoft advises that you only configure one default gateway per machine to avoid confusion. This holds true even for multihomed computers where it might appear to be a valid option to configure a default gateway on each adapter—a common misconception.

exam Watch

Each Microsoft Windows computer can only have one active default gateway. If you specify multiple gateways, the first choice will always be used unless the computer detects that it has become unavailable. Only then will it try the next default gateway defined.

Routing Interfaces

A routing interface is an entry point into a router in the form of an IP address; typically, this equates to a network card. However, because routing occurs at the Network layer and not the Physical layer, a routing interface depends on a logical IP address rather than a physical interface, although it is unusual to have more than one IP address assigned to one physical interface on a router.

For example, if you had two network adapters in your Windows 2000 Server with routing enabled, but one of these had two IP addresses assigned to it, you would have three routing interfaces, not two.

Routing Tables

Each router uses a list of known routes (static or dynamic routes, or a mixture of the two) that it amalgamates into one or more routing tables. When it receives a packet to forward, it consults its routing table to see which interface should be used to forward the packet. There may be more than one possible route, in which case the better path will also be evaluated to see which one should be used.

Having a routing table does not define a router, however. Each Microsoft client running the Microsoft TCP/IP protocol will also have its own routing table, even though it might only have one network card and is not configured with a routing

FROM THE CLASSROOM

Defining Alternative Default Gateways

Why does Microsoft advise only defining one default gateway when you can specify alternatives? Although defining alternative default gateways ensures fault tolerance for forwarding remote packets, configuring a computer for multiple default gateways presents troubleshooting complexities. For example, if your first default gateway is down and you have a second valid router specified, packets will continue to be forwarded as a result of the Dead Gateway Detection algorithm. This is great (providing the alternative router is available and correctly configured to forward these packets!), but what happens if the first router becomes available again? Because the computer has switched to using the second router, it will continue to use the second router, even though the first is now available.

Should you discover routing problems from this workstation and you check its configuration, it can be very confusing to discover that packets are being routed to a different router when the first router is actually available. It's easy to assume that because you can successfully ping the first default gateway, that is where remote packets are going, so you turn your attention to the configuration of the first router rather than the router that is actually being used.

Only by examining the current routing table or by taking a network trace would you discover that remote packets were actually being forwarded to a different router. If you want to use the fault tolerance of defining multiple default gateways, ensure they are all valid and correctly configured to route your packets. Check the routing table to determine which default gateway is actually being used.

—*Carol Bailey, MCSE+I*

service or routing protocols. This routing table on IP workstations similarly instructs the protocol as to which interface to direct packets; for example, a client workstation will have entries in its routing table for its own loopback address (127.0.0.1), its own subnet address, and its default gateway.

Host Routing vs. Router Routing When a workstation has traffic to send and consults its local routing table, the workstation is performing *host routing*, because it still has routing decisions to make and forwards packets according to its routing table. In comparison, a "real" router performs *router routing* when it receives a packet to be forwarded between routers (when the destination network is not directly attached to the router), or between a router and the destination workstation (when the destination network is directly attached). This distinction in defining these two kinds of routing is very subtle, but important.

exam Watch

Host routing occurs when a computer forwards a packet to a router, rather than sending the packet directly on its own network. Router routing occurs when a router receives a packet that is not destined for another computer, so it must send the packet to either the destination computer (if directly attached) or another router.

Even a host router has the ability to dynamically update its host routing table; for example, the *Internet Control Message Protocol (ICMP) Redirect* message sent from an IP router can inform workstations of a better route to a destination host. If the TCP/IP workstation supports ICMP Redirect (which Windows 2000 does), this better route will be added to the routing table. Another example is being able to automatically find a default gateway if one wasn't configured with its TCP/IP address assignment (discussed later in this chapter).

The structure of routing tables is discussed in more detail in a later section.

CertCam 9-1

EXERCISE 9-1

Viewing a Routing Table on a Windows TCP/IP Computer

This exercise demonstrates how every Microsoft TCP/IP computer (workstation or server) has its own routing table, even when it only has a single adapter and no default gateway assigned.

1. Find a Microsoft TCP/IP workstation that has a single adapter installed and no default gateway assigned (if it has a default gateway statically assigned, temporarily remove it for the purposes of this exercise).
2. To view the routing table on a Microsoft TCP/IP workstation, load the command prompt (Start | Run | Command on a Win9x machine; Start | Run | Cmd on a Windows NT 4.0 or Windows 2000 machine).
3. Type **route print**.

4. This should display the TCP/IP routing table similar to the following illustration, which is from a Windows 2000 Professional.

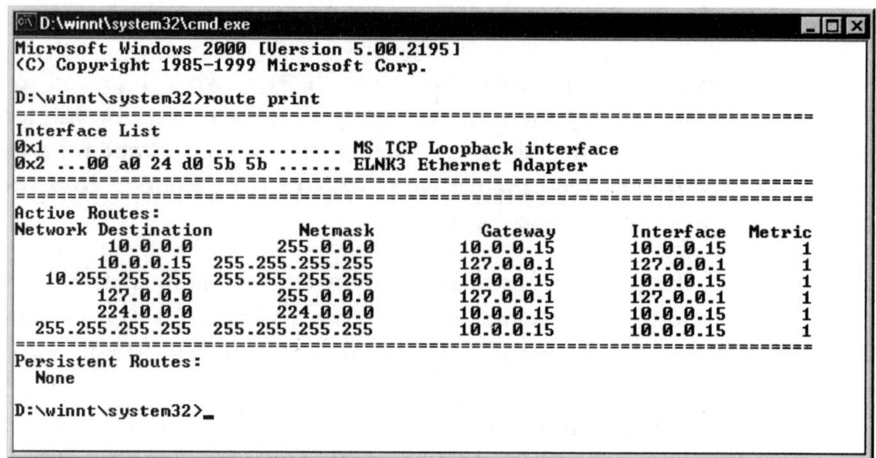

```
D:\winnt\system32\cmd.exe
Microsoft Windows 2000 [Version 5.00.2195]
(C) Copyright 1985-1999 Microsoft Corp.

D:\winnt\system32>route print
===========================================================================
Interface List
0x1 ........................... MS TCP Loopback interface
0x2 ...00 a0 24 d0 5b 5b ...... ELNK3 Ethernet Adapter
===========================================================================
===========================================================================
Active Routes:
Network Destination        Netmask          Gateway       Interface  Metric
         10.0.0.0        255.0.0.0       10.0.0.15       10.0.0.15       1
        10.0.0.15  255.255.255.255       127.0.0.1       127.0.0.1       1
   10.255.255.255  255.255.255.255       10.0.0.15       10.0.0.15       1
        127.0.0.0        255.0.0.0       127.0.0.1       127.0.0.1       1
        224.0.0.0        224.0.0.0       10.0.0.15       10.0.0.15       1
  255.255.255.255  255.255.255.255       10.0.0.15       10.0.0.15       1
===========================================================================
Persistent Routes:
  None

D:\winnt\system32>_
```

5. Even though this computer only has one IP address on one adapter with no default gateway assigned, it still has multiple entries automatically added to its routing table. We will define the routing entry fields in more detail later, but you should be able to see entries defining routes for your IP address and subnet mask, the loopback address, the broadcast address to your subnet, an address for multicasting, and a broadcast address to all hosts.

If you have access to a Microsoft multihomed computer (more than one adapter installed and configured with TCP/IP) that is routing between its adapters (e.g., Microsoft NT 4.0 server with two or more adapters and IP Forwarding enabled), type the **route print** command on it (without changing any TCP/IP parameters!) and compare the routing table. It will be longer because twice the number of adapters that can pass packets to each other will result in at least twice as big a routing table; however, it will still have the same format with the same sort of routing entries.

Single-Route Router vs. Multiple-Route Router An important difference between a hardware router (such as Cisco routers) and Microsoft's software routing component is that Windows 2000 Server, when acting as a router, only ever has one single routing table, irrespective of how many routing interfaces it has. This means that when a call comes in to the single-route router, only one routing table is used to determine the best way to direct the packet.

In comparison, a multiple-route router (most hardware routers) can usually be configured such that each interface maintains its own routing table. This obviously requires more processing, which is why hardware routers are dedicated to this sole job and can provide a faster and more efficient throughput of traffic.

exam Watch

Windows 2000 IP Routing only ever has one routing table, irrespective of how many routing interfaces or how many routing protocols it has.

FROM THE CLASSROOM

Routing and Forwarding Tables

Windows 2000 Routing and Remote Access Service (in common with many other routers) has both a *routing table* and a *forwarding table.* The routing table in Windows 2000 is maintained by the RRAS service (with the RRAS component called the Route Table Manager) and contains all the routes from all possible sources. The forwarding table, however, is maintained by the TCP/IP protocol stack and is used by the routable protocol when actually forwarding the packet. The Route Table Manager updates the IP forwarding table based on incoming route information from multiple sources. Because of the technical difference in how these two work, it is possible that the contents of the routing table and the forwarding table will differ.

—Carol Bailey, MCSE+I

Routing Table Structure Routing table information usually contains the following routing information fields:

- Destination Address (and subnet mask)
- Gateway (or sometimes termed *forwarding address*)
- Interface
- Metric
- Lifetime

It is important to understand what these fields are for both in managing and troubleshooting routing tables and in manually assigning routes (Table 9-1).

TABLE 9-1 Routing Table Attributes and Explanations

Routing Table Attribute	Explanation
Destination Address (and subnet mask)	This contains the IP network address (or name that resolves to an address) for a network route or an internetwork address for a host route.
Gateway (forwarding address)	This identifies where the packet should be forwarded (e.g., the IP address of the interface). This can be blank if the host is on the same network as one of the router interfaces.
Interface	This is the network interface to be used when forwarding packets to the destination address. It can be expressed as an IP address, as a port number, or as a logical name that refers back to an IP address.
Metric	This indicates the cost (preference) of a route, which is applicable if multiple routes exist to the same destination network. The route with the lowest metric is used. Different routing protocols use different metrics; for example, RIP uses *hops*. To reduce delays when making routing decisions, Windows 2000 never stores multiple routes when they are learned; typically, only the lowest-cost route is retained, so this value is used to determine which route should be stored in the routing table.
Lifetime	This is the "shelf-life" of a route—how long it is considered valid. Static routes automatically have an infinite lifetime, but dynamic routes have a finite lifetime and must be refreshed before the lifetime expires in order to be retained in the routing table. The timing out of dynamic routes provides fault tolerance because it allows routers to reconfigure themselves and adapt to changing circumstances such as a downed link or router. This value is typically not visible in routing tables, but is an important attribute of a routing entry.

CERTIFICATION OBJECTIVE 9.02

Enabling and Configuring Windows 2000 as an IP Software Router

Chapter 5 first introduced you to the Routing and Remote Access snap-in utility, which is unavailable under Start | Programs | Administrative Tools | Routing and Remote Access. This is a service on Windows 2000 Server that needs to be enabled rather than installed, and when it is initially enabled, it will invoke the Routing and Remote Access Server Setup Wizard. You may also remember that one of the wizard configuration options was for a Network Router, which you could select and let the wizard guide you through the rest of the setup.

If you haven't already configured RRAS for remote access, you can use the wizard to guide you through the setup of enabling routing. Or, if you are willing to forego your original RRAS configuration, you can disable RRAS and reenable it to invoke the setup wizard again.

However, if you have already set up and configured RRAS (e.g., for remote access) and now want to add support for routing, you will need to manually enable the Routing option as one of the server Properties.

Don't forget that if your server is going to route, by definition it must have two or more interfaces—so install and configure these before enabling routing!

EXERCISE 9-2

CertCam 9-2

Manually Enabling the Routing Option in RRAS

1. If not already loaded, load the RRAS snap-in located under Start | Programs | Administrative Tools | Routing and Remote Access.
2. Right-click on your server in the left pane to select Properties. It's here that you select whether to support routing and remote access.

3. Ensure the Router option is selected, and underneath specify whether this router will be used for just permanent local area connections, or for local area connections and demand-dial routing (the latter being for nonpersistent connections such as analog telephone lines and ISDN). Demand-dial routing is discussed later in this chapter.
4. If you also want to offer remote access on the same server, ensure that "Remote access server" is also selected, as shown in the following illustration.

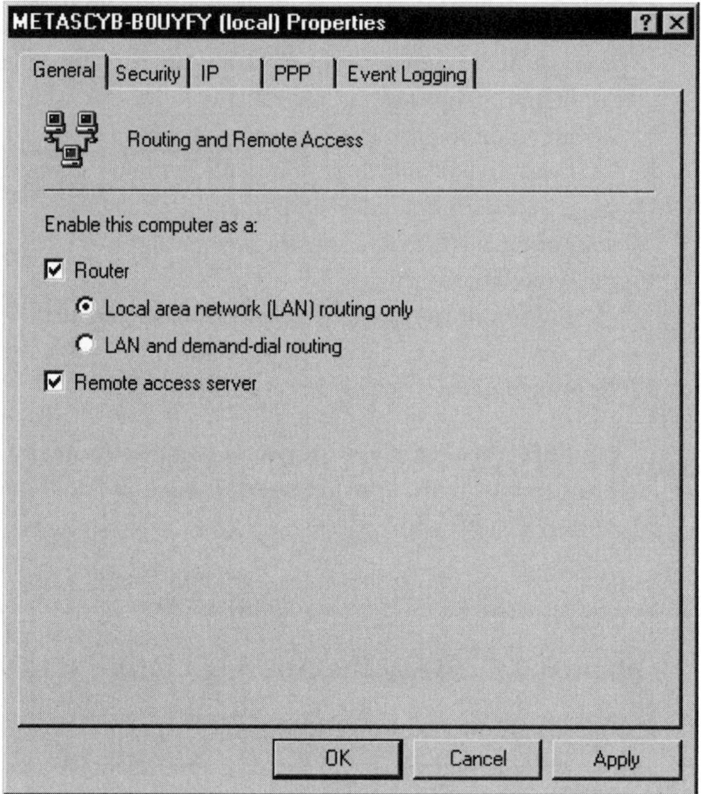

5. Click Ok. You will be prompted to restart the router in order for this configuration to take effect. Click Yes.
6. After the router has stopped and restarted, your Windows 2000 Server is now configured for IP routing.

Enabling this routing option is analogous to setting the check box for IP Forwarding as one of the TCP/IP properties on Windows NT 4.0.

Do You Need to Install Routing Protocols?

Enabling routing makes a change in the Registry to automatically forward packets between your computer's interfaces.

If this router is the only router on your network that joins all segments (two or more), and workstations are configured with one of the server's IP addresses as their default gateway (the one that is on their subnet), packets destined for another network will now be delivered by the RRAS router. There is no need to install routing protocols to achieve this.

You would only need to either define static routes or install a routing protocol if you have multiple routers in your network. This is because your router would need to know to which router it should forward packets in order to achieve successful packet delivery when it receives packets for a network that is not directly attached.

You do not need to install routing protocols to be able to route packets from one interface on your router to another interface.

Static Routes

Defining static routes is an alternative, or can be used as complementing dynamic routes. They are not mutually exclusive.

You can add a static route to Windows 2000 Server running the Routing and Remote Access Service in three ways:

- Route add command
- Netsh utility
- RRAS snap-in

Which one you decide to use will depend on your personal preferences and which is more appropriate for what you want to achieve.

Technically, you can also add static routes through an account used with demand-dial routing. Demand-dial routing is discussed later in this chapter.

Route Add Command

On Microsoft's host routers and router routers, you can use the command **route add.**

For example:

```
Route add 192.10.11.0 mask 255.255.255.0 192.10.10.1 metric 1
```

This adds a route for the network 192.10.11.0 with the subnet mask of 255.255.255.0. When a packet needs to be sent to this network, it should be directed from the router's interface with the IP address of 192.10.10.1, which is one router away.

Use the **route print** command to review your routing table to confirm the successful addition of your static route.

If you are used to defining static routes in this way, you may find it more convenient to simply add a new static route in this fashion—particularly when the need is ad-hoc.

Netsh Utility

You may remember this command shell utility mentioned in Chapter 5 that allows you to configure both local and remote RRAS components. To add a new static route, you would use the command **Netsh routing ip add persistentroute.**

For example:

```
netsh routing ip add persistentroute dest=192.10.11.0
mask 255.255.255.0
name="Internet Connection"
"
```

Use the Netsh command **Netsh routing ip show persisentroute** to confirm the successful addition of the static routes.

Using Netsh is very useful if you have a list of static routes you need to define, and for quickly adding routes onto a remote RRAS server.

The RRAS Snap-In

Using the RRAS snap-in is the easiest way to add a static route, and the new graphical user interface makes this process much less error prone. Navigate to your server, IP Routing, and right-click on Static Routes to select New Static Route.

This will display a dialog box similar to Figure 9-1 in which to enter your route details.

FIGURE 9-1

Defining a static route with the Routing and Remote Access snap-in

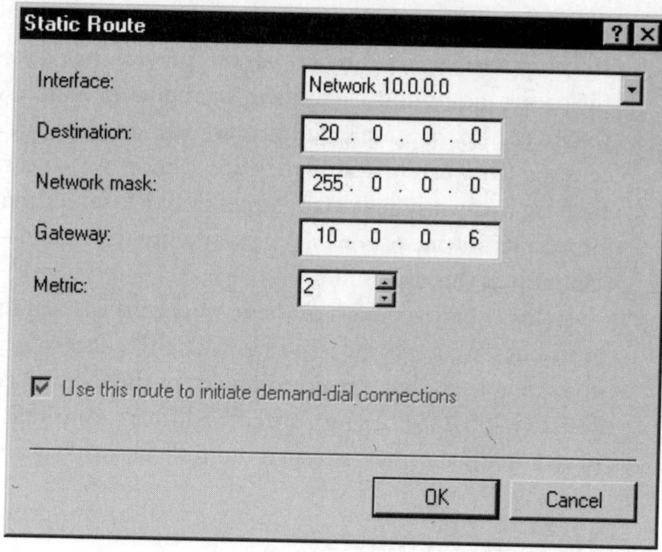

When you have finished and clicked Ok, confirm the successful addition of your static route by right-clicking on Static Routes again, this time selecting Show IP Routing Table.

Defining static routes with RRAS is easier and less error prone than command-line alternatives. However, it can become a little tedious and time-consuming if you have multiple routes to add. Using a batch file of commands instead would be quicker, and this batch file could also be reused (e.g., for backup or modified slightly for similar routers).

Configuring the Router for IGMP

Once you have enabled the Windows 2000 RRAS service, it can support other services in addition to routing data packets from one network to another. One of these is the IGMP router and IGMP proxy. IGMP stands for Internet Group Management Protocol. Multicasting is being used increasingly on TCP/IP networks and is an intrinsic component of the Windows 2000 router.

Multicasting vs. Broadcasting vs. Unicasting

Unicasting is sending a packet directly to a single TCP/IP client—it's a one-to-one relationship. *Broadcasting* is the opposite of unicasting, where multiple packets go to all TCP/IP clients. It can do this by using a broadcast address of 255.255.255.255—all computers receive this and have to process the packets even if the information in the packet means nothing to them, so it puts an unnecessary drain on each computer resource. Also, because broadcasts are sent out without checking to see if they were received (they can't because they don't know which computers should receive it), they are frequently sent many times in quick succession, which can flood a network. Broadcasts are one reason why networks are segmented—because broadcasts typically cannot pass through routers.

Halfway between both of these, *multicasting* is sending a single packet to multiple hosts but with a specific IP address. The IP address used is not a host address (which unicasting uses), but a reserved one from the Class D address range (224.0.0.0 to 239.255.255.255). Using a specific address means that packets can be acknowledged (if required), and they can span multiple networks via routers.

Multicast Members

If a TCP/IP host supports multicasting, it can register itself with a specific multicast address that lets the server that sends out the multicasts know that it wants to receive its multicast traffic. It then becomes a member of that multicast group and receives data sent to that group until it leaves the group.

A Windows 2000 router uses multicasting with its routing protocols (RIPv2 and OSPF); for example, 224.0.0.9 is used with a RIPv2 router, and 224.0.0.5 and 244.0.0.6 are used with OSPF routers. In these cases, the Internet Group Multicast members are the Windows 2000 Servers.

Multicasting Across Networks

When multicasting is used with the Windows 2000 routing protocols, there is no need to install the IGMP routing protocol, because multicasts will go directly from one interface on one router to another interface on another router on the same segment. In other words, the multicast packets are able to be delivered and received directly, rather than having to be routed.

The IGMP routing facility needs to be installed when a direct connection between an IGMP host and IGMP server is not possible, because one or more routers are in the complete route. If a client on your TCP/IP network registers with a multicast group that is on the Internet, at least one router (yours) will be in the path between IGMP host member and IGMP server. In this case, multicast packets need to be routed from the network the client is on, and then forwarded to the Internet network the server is on.

A typical example of IGMP Internet services that workstations might want to use is Internet real-time streaming audio and video. However, because of the problem of having to route multicasting traffic, not all routers on the Internet can support multicasting—only a portion of the Internet known as the MBONE (multicast backbone) currently supports multicasting. Therefore, for TCP/IP clients on your networks to be able to use multicast services on the Internet, ensure their packets are routed through your router that is enabled for IGMP routing, and ensure the server is attached to the MBONE.

exam Watch

Although IGMP is added as a protocol in Windows 2000 RRAS, this component is currently only capable of being an IGMP router or proxy rather than offering an IGMP protocol. This means that you cannot use the IGMP routing facility on your RRAS server unless it is directly connected to a multicast network. For example, to offer Internet multicasting services to workstations on your network, the RRAS server must be directly connected to the MBONE.

If your server is not directly connected to a multicast network, you can delete the IGMP interface from your RRAS server.

Enabling IGMP

Support for IGMP is enabled by installing the IGMP router and IGMP proxy services as if they were a protocol (if not already installed), and then adding to it two or more interfaces. You must add one interface that is directly connected to the multicast network; typically, this would be your Internet connection. Your other interfaces would typically be local area connections.

You then configure IGMP properties for these interfaces. The interface that is directly connected to the multicast network should be configured for IGMP *proxy mode.* Other interfaces not directly connected to the multicast network (e.g., any local area network connections) should be configured for *router mode.*

Figure 9-2 displays a typical configuration for IGMP—Proxy mode configured on the local area network connection, and Router mode configured on the Internet connection. Refer to Exercises 9-4 and 9-5 if you need more information on how to install and configure routing protocols with the RRAS snap-in.

FIGURE 9-2 Typical configuration for IGMP

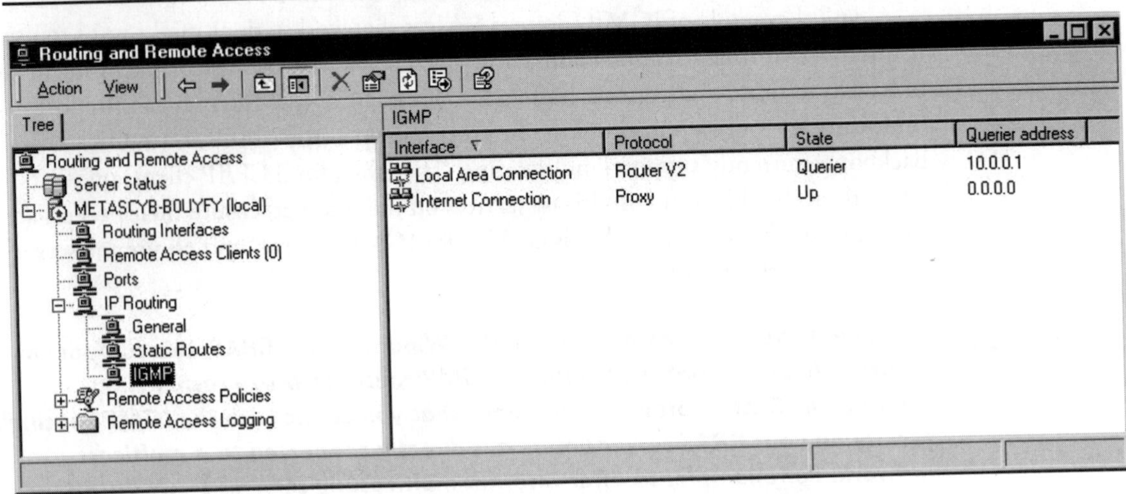

exam Watch ***To offer the benefits of Multicasting Groups on the Internet to clients on your intranet: ensure your router is connected to the MBONE on the Internet, enable IGMP on the router, add IGMP in Proxy mode on the Internet interface, and add IGMP in router mode on your local area connection interface(s).***

Configuring the Router for ICMP Router Discovery

Another service the Windows 2000 Server offers is the Internet Control Message Protocol (ICMP) Router Discovery. This means that it can automatically assign a default gateway to workstations if they don't already have one to ensure that nonlocal traffic from workstations can be routed.

What's the purpose of this if you can define the default gateway as part of the IP address? First, it is less prone to administrative error—the IP address of the default gateway is automatically sent out, so there's no need to type in any IP addresses. Second, by virtue of the fact that the router is sending out packets informing workstations about its router service, it offers service reliability that a statically assigned default gateway cannot offer. It also offers fault tolerance, because a TCP/IP workstation using this method to obtain a default gateway can automatically detect when its router is down, and therefore automatically switch to a new (available) router. In short, it ensures that TCP/IP clients can always automatically find an available router on their subnet for their nonlocal traffic.

exam Watch

Benefits of ICMP Router Discovery include offering a fault-tolerant mechanism with minimum administrative overheads for TCP/IP clients to find a default gateway to route nonlocal traffic.

Components of the ICMP Router Discovery Service

ICMP Router Discovery has two components:

- Router Advertisements (sent out by the router to advertise its availability)
- Router Solicitations (sent out by TCP/IP workstations to request router availability)

Router Advertisements When the Windows 2000 RRAS IP router is configured for ICMP Router Discovery Advertisement, it will periodically send out an ICMP Router Advertisement to the all-hosts multicast address of 224.0.0.1.

This message will also contain an *Advertisement Lifetime* and a *Preference Level.* The Advertisement Lifetime refers to the length of time between advertisements so hosts know that if this time is exceeded without a new advertisement, the route is no longer valid (the default is 30 minutes). The Preference Level is used when there are multiple routers also offering themselves as default gateways—workstations select the router with the highest preference level.

If a TCP/IP workstation has registered with this multicast address (i.e., it supports ICMP Router Discovery), it will receive the ICMP Router Discovery Advertisement from the router. If the workstation already has a default gateway statically assigned, the advertisement will be ignored. However, if it doesn't already have a default gateway assigned, it can update its routing table with the advertised default route and use it to send nonlocal traffic when there is no specific route.

exam Watch

Windows 2000 IP Router supports ICMP Router Discovery to automatically assign a default gateway to requesting workstations. It does this with multicasts to advertise a router's presence. It is not in itself a routing protocol because it doesn't route any packets; it merely advertises that capacity of the sending system to do so.

Router Solicitations When a TCP/IP host supports the ICMP multicast and it requires a default gateway (either because one has not been assigned, or because its previously discovered default gateway is down), it doesn't need to wait until the next router advertisement before it can benefit from the advertised default gateway service. Instead, it sends out a Router Solicitation ICMP message to the all-routers IP multicast address of 224.0.0.2.

Routers that have been configured for Router Advertisement will immediately respond, and the TCP/IP workstation can then choose the router with the highest preference level as its default gateway.

exam Watch

Windows 2000 and Windows 98 both support Router Solicitation to discover the default gateway if one has not been assigned, or if the previously discovered router is no longer available.

EXERCISE 9-3

Enabling ICMP Discovery Advertisements

1. In the Routing and Remote Access snap-in, select Routing | General.
2. In the right details pane, right-click on the interface onto which you want to add ICMP Router Discovery Advertisements, and select Properties.
3. In the General tab, select the option "Enable router discovery advertisements." This will enable the options listed in Table 9-2 for the ICMP Router Discovery settings.

It is usually adequate to leave the ICMP Router Discovery settings at their defaults; however, refer to Table 9-2 for a list of options you can change if required.

4. When you have finished, click OK.
5. Repeat this for other interfaces you want to enable for ICMP Discovery Advertisements.

TABLE 9-2 ICMP Router Discovery Settings—Values and Explanations

Router Discovery Settings	Description and Default Values
Level of Preference	The preference level for this router to be the default gateway if multiple routers are all sending similar advertisements. The highest preference level router is chosen as the default gateway. The default value is 0.
Advertisement Lifetime (minutes)	The time after which a workstation will consider this router to be unavailable. In other words, if this value expires before sending another advertisement, the workstation will remove this router as its default gateway. The default value is 7 minutes.
Advertisement interval minimum time (minutes)	The minimum time between advertisements. The default is 7 minutes.
Advertisement interval maximum time (minutes)	The maximum time between advertisements. Advertisements are sent at a random interval between the minimum and maximum times. The default is 10 minutes.

CERTIFICATION OBJECTIVE 9.03

Implementing Routing Protocols

If you want to use dynamic routing protocols to automatically build a routing table for networks that are not directly attached, you must install the routing protocols you want to use and then define on which interface(s) they should be used. You can configure global settings for the routing protocol, and set routing options individually for each added interface.

Installing Dynamic Routing Protocols

The two dynamic routing protocols you can install with Windows 2000 RRAS are RIP and OSPF. For RIP, the default configurations may suffice for the majority of situations, which is why RIP is such an easy routing protocol to use. However, OSPF is more complicated and must be configured correctly before your router will function correctly with this protocol.

on the Job

Dynamic routing protocols demand considerable overhead on both the server and the network. A badly configured dynamic routing protocol on the network can do much damage that is difficult to track down, so do not add and configure dynamic routing protocols unnecessarily on a live network without the knowledge of how they work and the consequences of their configuration.

The steps you perform for adding any protocol with RRAS are the same: Add the protocol, and then add to the protocol the interface(s) you want to use with the protocol. Unlike Windows NT 4.0, there is no automatic binding of protocols to adapters.

Once the protocol has been added, you can configure global options for the protocol and configure protocol options that only apply to the selected adapter. When the configuration is complete, you should then be able to exchange routing information with other routers on the network to automatically construct a local dynamic routing table. Similarly, neighboring routers will update their routing tables to include your router.

on the Job

Don't assume that because you have set a protocol option on one adapter, that option will be set for all the adapters. Also, the properties you can configure on an adapter can be specific to your configuration, so you could see some protocol configuration options on one adapter that are not available on others.

Silent RIP for IP

Silent RIP for IP is when an IP router (using the RIP routing protocol) dynamically updates its own routing table with information obtained from other RIP routers without sending out its own routing information. In this case, the routing "exchange" between the Silent RIP router and other routers is not complete because the information is one-way only—listening for routing information but not reciprocating. You can use Silent RIP on a workstation too, but this requires modifying the Registry. On a Windows 2000 RRAS router, Silent RIP is configured as one of the RIP interface properties.

exam Watch

Silent RIP allows your router to automatically construct a routing table with details of other routers, but without advertising its own routing presence on the network. This has the benefit of reducing network traffic, but the disadvantage is other routers will not be able to benefit from being able to automatically use your router.

EXERCISE 9-4

Installing Routing Protocols

1. In the RRAS snap-in, select your server and then IP Routing | General. Right-click and select New Routing Protocol.
2. In the list of available options, you will see RIP Version 2 for Internet Protocol and OSPF, which are the two dynamic routing protocols used with the Windows 2000 router.
3. Select the routing protocol you want to use, and click OK.
4. If you also want to add another routing protocol, repeat this procedure (steps 1–3).
5. Once routing protocols have been added, they should now appear under IP Routing. The following illustration shows both RIP and OSPF added to the RRAS router, but you can see that RIP has no interfaces associated with it.

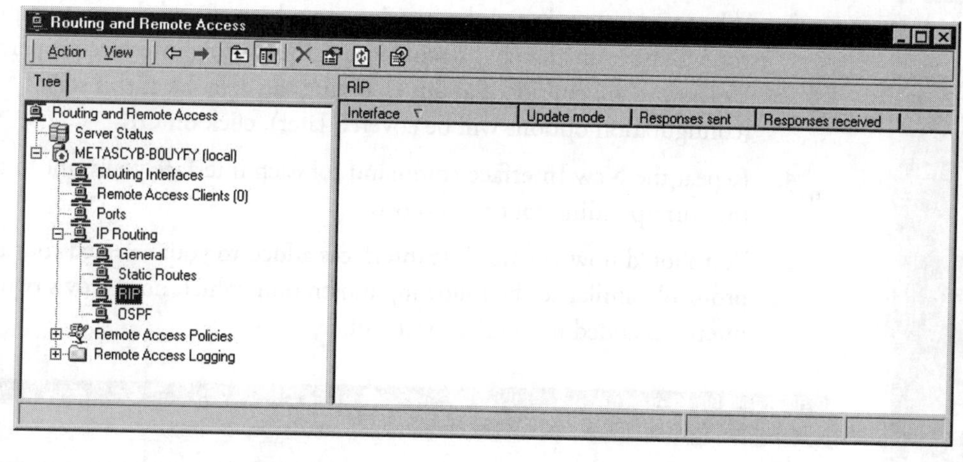

Adding Interfaces to the Routing Protocols

The next step is to add the interfaces you want to use with your dynamic routing protocol(s) (binding the protocol to the interface).

You must add at least two interfaces to the routing protocol, but if you have more than two interfaces in your router, you do not need to add all of them to the dynamic routing protocol. For example, you may be running RIP on interfaces 1 and 2, and OSPF on interfaces 3 and 4. Adding only specific interfaces to your routing protocols prevents unnecessary routing traffic that produces wasteful overhead on the network, router, and other routers.

on the Job

The "Internal" routing interface that you might see displayed in the RRAS snap-in details pane appears automatically to represent all Remote Access Services devices. All RAS clients are part of this interface—do not delete it!

EXERCISE 9-5

Adding the Dynamic Routing Protocols to Interfaces

1. Right-click on the routing protocol (RIP or OSPF) and select New Interface.
2. You will then see a list of available interfaces from which you can choose. Choose the one you want to use with the routing protocol, and click OK.
3. When you have selected the interface on which to add the routing protocol, you will be immediately presented with the routing interface properties. Unless you are confident about changing the defaults at this stage (configuration options will be covered later), click on OK.
4. Repeat the **New Interface** command for each interface you want to use with the corresponding routing protocol.
5. You should now see multiple interfaces added to your selected routing protocols similar to the following illustration, which now shows two interfaces added to the RIP protocol.

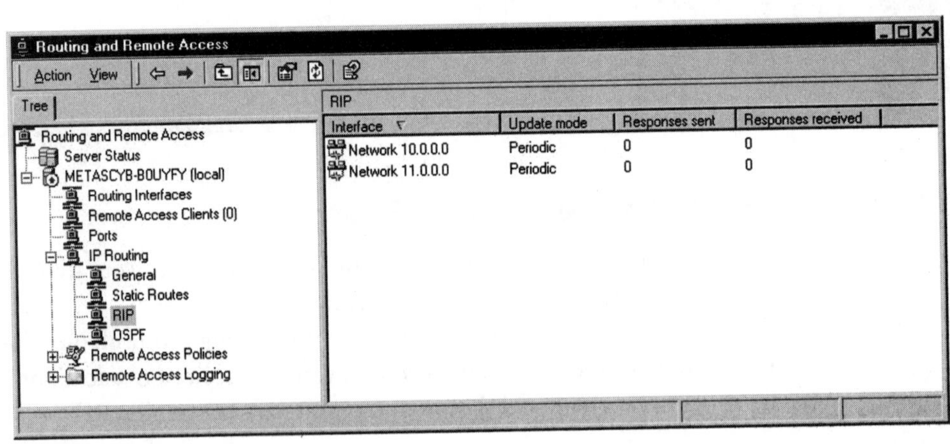

Dynamic Routing Issues

As we have seen, two dynamic routing protocols are supported in Windows 2000:

- Routing Internet Protocol (RIP) Versions 1 and 2—a distance vector routing protocol
- Open Shortest Path First (OSPF)—a link state routing protocol

Although dynamic routing protocols put additional overhead onto the router and the network, one of their most valuable assets is that they can sense and recover from internetwork problems such as a downed link or downed router. How quickly it can recover is determined by the type of fault, how it is sensed, and how the updated information is propagated throughout the internetwork.

Convergence

When all the routers on the internetwork have the correct routing information in their routing tables, the internetwork is said to have *converged.* When convergence is achieved, the internetwork is in a stable state, and all routing occurs along optimal paths.

When a link or router fails, the internetwork must reconfigure itself to reflect the new topology, and to achieve this, routing tables must be updated. Until the internetwork has converged again, routing will be vulnerable to loops and black holes. The time it takes for the internetwork to reconverge is known as the *convergence time*, and the optimal aim is for the shortest convergence time with minimum traffic.

Convergence time refers to the time it takes for all routing tables to be updated.

The main difference between distance vector and link state routing protocols centers on the following issues:

- What routing information is exchanged
- How the information is exchanged
- How quickly the internetwork can recover from an internetwork fault such as a downed router

Distance Vector vs. Link State Routing Protocols

Distance vector-based routing protocols periodically send out their known routes from their routing table, and update their routing table after receiving similar information from other routers. By "listening" to other routers, it can be determined where routers are on the network in relation to each other, so that a "hop count" can be determined. This exchange of information is unsynchronized and unacknowledged.

Link state-based routing protocols exchange link state advertisements using directed (multicast) traffic. These link state advertisements include the router's network ID (a logical number) and are sent to neighboring routers upon startup and when changes in the internetwork topology are sensed. Link state routers build a database of link state advertisements, and use this to calculate the routing table. Routing information exchanged is synchronized and acknowledged.

Features of Distance Vector Routing The advantages of a distance vector-based routing protocol are that it's simple to configure and understand in concept. This results in low administrative overhead when used in a suitable environment.

The disadvantages of a distance vector-based routing protocol include the following:

- In a large network, it produces large and unwieldy routing tables, which take time to process on the router and are difficult for an administrator to understand when troubleshooting is required.
- High bandwidth requirements, since routing information is sent out periodically even after convergence.
- Does not scale, producing large routing tables, and a single route has a limitation of 15 routers.
- High convergence time, which leaves the internetwork vulnerable to routing problems.

Features of Link State Routing Link state routing was designed specifically to overcome some of the shortcomings of the older distance vector routing protocol, which was never designed for today's wide-scale enterprise internetworks.

The advantages of a link state-based routing protocol include the following:

- Smaller routing tables which means they are quicker to process
- Lower bandwidth requirements because routing information is not exchanged unnecessarily, and traffic is directed rather than sent out indiscriminately
- Ability to scale to very large networks
- Lower convergence time

The disadvantages of a link state-based routing protocol include the following

- Complex in design and configuration from an administrator's point of view, and therefore prone to human error
- Potentially resource intensive on large networks

Even with this short introduction to distance vector-based and link state routing protocols, you should now have a good idea of which is best suited for a particular requirement.

SCENARIO & SOLUTION

Scenario	Solution
Which would be a better choice on my network—a distance vector-based routing protocol or a link state routing protocol?	Distance vector or link state routing protocol.
I have a small network with just four routers?	Distance vector is well suited for small networks.
I want the simplest to configure.	Distance vector is simple to configure and understand.
Routing reliability is more important than ease of configuring.	Link state offers a more reliable routing service, since route advertisement is directed and acknowledged.
I have a large network to manage, and require a low convergence time with minimal bandwidth loss.	Link state is more efficient in updating its routing tables, it doesn't flood the network with broadcasts, and only sends information when necessary.

Common Problems with Dynamic Routing

Before we look at RIP and OSPF, it would be helpful to identify common problems and issues that arise when using dynamic routing protocols. Once we are aware of known issues and shortcomings, you will be better able to judge which is the better routing protocol to use for your network, and how best to configure it to minimize these potential problems.

Common problems with dynamic routing include

- Rogue routers
- Routing loops
- Count to infinity
- Black holes
- Overheads of large and complex routing tables
- High network bandwidth and broadcast flooding
- Slow convergence

Rogue Routers

If routing announcements are unacknowledged, there is no way of knowing whether other routers received the information, or if a rogue router sent conflicting information such as a route redirect to divert traffic from a legitimate destination.

Authentication of routing information is one way to verify that such information is legitimate, and some routing protocols now allow you to assign a password that must be authenticated on the receiving router before updates are allowed. Alternatively, you could define exactly which routers you recognized as valid, and discard routing information from any others (however, because this is configured with IP addresses, this is still vulnerable to IP spoofing where a rogue router can send out packets with a different source IP address to its own).

Routing Loops

During routing, packets are forwarded on the optimal path as reflected in the current routing table. Providing the routing table contains only correct and current entries, everything works fine—until the information becomes out of date. This could lead to a routing loop where the packet is directed according to the routing information, but ends up being routed back to itself rather than to its desired destination. This is the perpetual "Go to" statement with all its inherent dangers, and can be very difficult to detect without network tools (e.g., network capture or tracert utility) except for high processing on routers and a slow delivery (if at all).

The Time-to-Live value (TTL) helps to prevent infinite looping because each router that handles a data packet decreases the TTL by 1, and when it reaches 0, the packet is discarded and the router sends a *Time Exceeded* message back to the sending host.

Count to Infinity

Distance vector-based routing protocols are vulnerable to this problem because of the way they send out routing announcements. It is possible for routing tables to become out of date, and routes become advertised with an increasing hop count (the count to infinity). This is one reason why the RIP maximum hop count is set to 15 to prevent an ever-increasing hop count. When a hop count reaches 16, the destination will be considered unreachable; therefore, the route will be timed out.

Black Holes

Because RIP is a distance vector-based routing protocol that uses unacknowledged delivery, data can often be lost without trace. One router could realize that its neighboring router was unavailable and send out information to broadcast this, but if the information is never received, other routers can continue to send data to the downed router in the mistaken belief it is still available. This is a "black hole" because there is nowhere for the packets to go, but the sending system hasn't realized this. Link state routing protocols that use directed and acknowledged announcements are not vulnerable to this problem.

Another example of a black hole is a *Path Maximum Transmit Unit* black hole when a router discards packets that must be fragmented, but fails to send a message to the sending system to fragment further packets. Similarly, if a host system cannot process all the packets it is receiving and fails to send out a Source Quench message to the sending system for a respite, the packets it cannot handle will be silently discarded.

Overhead of Large and Complex Routing Tables

Because vector-based routing protocols store a complete list of all the networks and all the possible ways to reach each network, the amassed routing tables in a large internetwork can become very large, which takes time to process, results in more information being exchanged, and becomes more difficult to troubleshoot.

This is one reason why some routers (which includes Windows 2000) only store a single route (typically the one with the lowest metric) for any network. However, it results in an incomplete routing table of the internetwork if all routes are not listed.

Link state-based protocols do not have this problem, as they have smaller routing tables that provide only pertinent information that is relevant to their position on the internetwork.

High Network Bandwidth and Broadcast Flooding

Distance vector-based routing protocols that announce their routes typically every 30 seconds can take up a high proportion of network bandwidth, and if using broadcasts, these messages are received by every computer on the network, which necessitates processing irrespective of whether they are also routers or even TCP/IP computers.

When available network bandwidth is low (e.g., WAN links), a high proportion of the limited bandwidth has to be given over to these periodic messages even if all routing tables are converged—leaving little bandwidth for anything else. The bigger the network, the bigger the routing tables, and the more information that has to be announced. This is certainly one reason why distance vector routing protocols do not scale well.

Using multicasts instead of broadcasts helps to alleviate this problem, and additionally, link state-based routing protocols only send out routing information when there are changes.

Slow Convergence

When a router or link fails, it can take a while for this information to be reflected in all the routing tables on the internetwork. It can take several minutes for the changes and adjustments to be propagated throughout all of the remaining routers.

RIP is particularly vulnerable to this, and it is exacerbated by the use of unacknowledged broadcasts that do not guarantee that the new routing information has been received by neighboring routers. However, you can often modify the announcement algorithms to help reduce convergence time.

Because link state routing protocols have smaller and more efficient routing tables, their convergence time is less on all but very large-scale internetworks.

Options employed to help reduce convergence time include

- Split horizon
- Split horizon with poison reverse
- Triggered updates

Split Horizon Split horizon prevents routers from advertising networks in the direction from which those networks were learned, so the only information sent in routing announcements are for those networks that are beyond the neighboring router in the opposite direction. This also helps to eliminate count-to-infinity and routing loops.

Split Horizon with Poison Reverse This announces all networks, but all networks learned in a given direction are announced with a hop count of 16 (network unreachable). This works well in a multi-path internetwork by helping to eliminate count-to-infinity and routing loops.

Triggered Updates This option allows a router to announce changes in a route's metric almost immediately, rather than waiting for the next periodic announcement. For example, if a route is unreachable, the metric will change to 16 in RIP, and it is better for other routers to know about this unavailable route as soon as possible.

Triggered updates usually have a trigger time interval so the network is not flooded with similar announcements from multiple routers.

Triggered updates help to reduce the convergence time, but require additional bandwidth.

Combining Different Routing Protocols on the Same Router

Bearing in mind that a software router only has one routing table, a Windows 2000 router with both routing protocols installed may have to decide which route is preferable (and therefore stored) if it learns of two different routes by both protocols to the same destination. Normally, if a single protocol reported multiple routes to the same network, only the one with the lowest metric would be stored. However,

RIP and OSPF use different metrics—which one should be chosen as the preferred route?

The answer lies in choosing the route from the *preferred source*, irrespective of the metric in the route. For example, a Windows 2000 RRAS configured for both RIP and OSPF adds both types of routes to its Route Table Manager (RTM) IP routing table. If OSPF is configured as the preferred source, and the router learns of two different routes to the same network (one from RIP with a metric of 2, and one from OSPF with a metric of 4), the OSPF route will be retained, and the RIP route discarded.

exam Watch

When two different routes from the same routing protocol are learned that provide paths to the same destination, the metric is used to determine which is the preferred route. When two routes from different routing protocols are learned that provide paths to the same destination, the metric is ignored, and the route that comes from the preferred source is retained.

Setting Preference Levels on the Router

Preference levels for route sources can be viewed and configured on the Preference Levels tab as an IP Routing | General Properties (Figure 9-3). You can also set a specific preference level for a static route with the Netsh command: **routing ip add rtmroute.**

Common Routing Terminology Used with Large Internetworks

These terms are used normally only in conjunction with large internetworks, and you will see them being used in OSPF contexts; however, they are not restricted to just OSPF.

AS—Autonomous System

A group of routers and networks under the same administration using a common routing protocol is referred to as an Autonomous System (AS). There is no single definition or restriction of what constitutes an AS; it could be a SOHO network, a large company spanning many buildings, and an ISP that is responsible for many Internet accounts and routes.

FIGURE 9-3 Preference levels for route sources

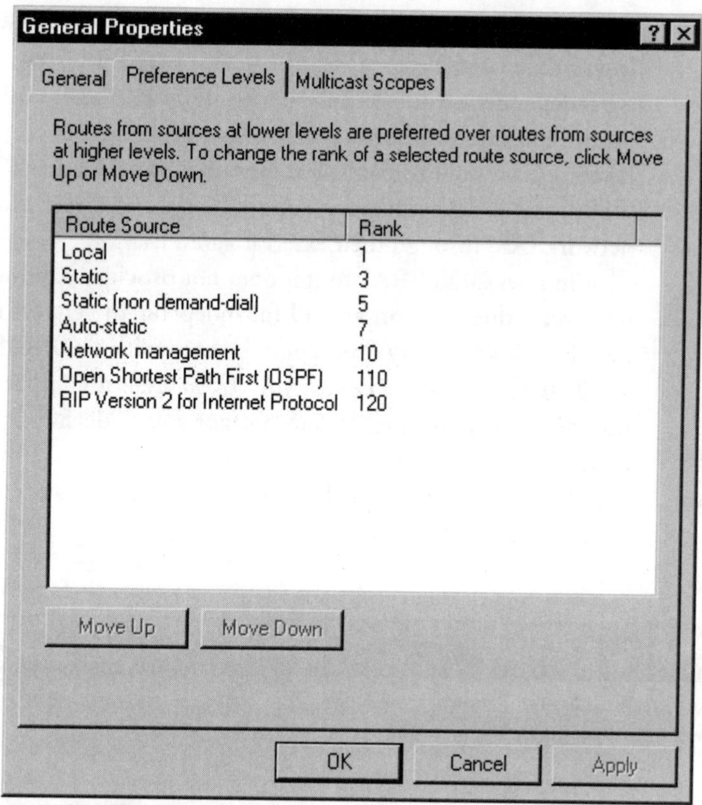

IGP—Interior Gateway Protocols

Routing protocols used within the AS are referred as *Interior Gateway Protocols* (IGP), with both RIP and OSPF being examples of IGPs. Routers that handle these protocols are known as *interior gateways,* and they handle *intra-AS routing.*

EGP—Exterior Gateway Protocols

When a routing protocol is being used to exchange routing information from one AS to another AS, it is referred to as an *Exterior Gateway Protocol*(EGP), with the Exterior Gateway Protocol (EGP) and Border Gateway Protocol (BGP) being examples of EGPs. Routers that handle these protocols are known as *exterior gateways,* and they handle *inter-AS routing.*

An important distinction is that while all interior gateways must use the same Interior Gateway Protocol within an AS, Exterior Gateway Protocols within an AS are independent from the Interior Gateway Protocols within the same AS. This means that exterior gateways can exchange routes between ASs that use different Interior Gateway Protocols. For example if one AS uses RIP, and another AS uses OSPF, the two networks can communicate and direct packets through the other network (AS) through their exterior gateways.

Windows 2000 RRAS router does not provide Exterior Gateway Protocols; however it does support an API for independent vendors to write and provide their own Exterior Gateway Protocol to be used with the RRAS router.

These terms may be new to you if you are not familiar with large routing internetwork topologies. It is important you understand them when dealing with enterprise environments, and they are essential basic terminology you will encounter with OSPF configuration. The following true and false statements will quickly test your understanding of them.

True or False?	Answer
An AS (Autonomous System) represents a large network with multiple routing protocols.	False. An AS can be any size. However, it is characterized by a single administrative system. You cannot have multiple protocols in an AS; an AS can only ever have a single protocol.
RIP is an example of an Interior Gateway Protocol (IGP), and OSPF is an example of an Exterior Gateway Protocol (EGP).	False. Both of these protocols are actually IGPs. Examples of EGPs are the Exterior Gateway Protocol and the Border Gateway Protocol.
EGPs (Exterior Gateway Protocols) are used to exchange routing information between ASs.	True. This is exactly the function of EGPs.
One AS cannot send traffic through another AS if they are not using the same Interior Gateway Protocol (IGP).	False. This is one of the main purposes of an Exterior Gateway when using an EGP.
Windows 2000 RRAS only supports Interior Routing Protocols (IGPs).	False. Although the Windows 2000 router only provides RIP and OSPF, which are both IGPs, it offers an API interface so it can support other protocols from third-party vendors, which could therefore include Exterior Gateway Protocols (EGPs) such as the well-known Border Gateway Protocol (BGP).

CERTIFICATION OBJECTIVE 9.04

RIP for IP

Windows 2000 supports both RIPv1 and RIPv2, both of which use a distance vector algorithm.

The first version of RIP (Routing Internet Protocol) was originally designed in 1988 for use in a simple local area network environment. In its day, it met its requirements very well, but in today's larger and more complex internetworks, the early version of RIP has many limitations.

RIPv2 seeks to address many of these shortcomings, and for many companies and networks now offers a more practical dynamic routing protocol that is easier to understand and manage than link state routing protocols.

Furthermore, compatibility is possible in a mixed RIP version environment. Routers that support only RIPv1 can still read and process RIPv2 packets by extracting the RIPv1 information and discarding the newer RIPv2 additional information. In addition, a RIPv2 router can send RIPv1 packets to a RIPv1 router so that redundant information is not sent—for security, this option is configurable.

Be careful when reading information on RIP; it may have been written before RIPv2 was available, and as such be relevant only to RIPv1. For example, it may assert RIP shortcomings that apply only to RIPv1 but are now addressed with RIPv2. This also applies to answering questions on the exam that might seem to assume that you have to use OSPF rather than RIP in order to support more modern features of today's internetworks.

RIPv1

As a simple distance vector-based routing protocol, RIPv1 is very easy to configure—often as simple as enabling a single option. However, it does have the following shortcomings:

- Broadcast rather than multicast announcements
- Subnet mask not announced with the route
- No protection from rogue routers

Broadcast vs. Multicast Announcements Broadcast announcements are not suitable for today's networks, because they indiscriminately put a high processing overhead on all network cards. Even if a network card is not a RIP router, it still has to process these packets.

A multicast announcement would be more efficient so that only network cards with a registered interest in RIP announcements would have to process these packets; however, RIPv1 doesn't support multicast announcements.

One advantage of broadcast announcements is when using Silent RIP; this allows a TCP/IP host to listen and act on advertised routes without having to participate. It is possible to use Silent RIP with multicasts, but not all implementations may support it.

Subnet Mask Not Announced with the Route RIPv1 was designed for class-based IP networks where the default subnet mask would always be used; therefore, there was no need to include it in routing announcements. The scarcity of IP addresses today has brought about the evolution of more complex subnet masks, where nondefault masks are used to subdivide a network, and subnetting/supernetting and variable-length subnet masks are now commonly employed.

Because RIPv1 doesn't include the subnet mask with routing announcements, routers have to try to determine the network ID based on a limited set of information. As a result, a default subnet mask may be incorrectly assumed, and a supernetted route might be interpreted as a single network rather than a range of networks.

No Protection from Rogue Routers There is no protection against a rogue RIP router announcing false or inaccurate routes, since RIPv1 announcements have no authentication mechanism.

RIPv2

The next (and current) version of RIP has the following advantages over its predecessor:

- Multicast option rather than broadcast announcements
- Subnet mask announced
- Authentication
- Route tag

Multicast Option Rather than Broadcast Announcements RIP announcements can be sent to the IP multicast address of 224.0.0.9, which means that network cards that do not wish to share RIP routing information do not have to process unnecessary packets.

However, if you are using Silent RIP, this will need to be modified to use the multicast announcement—if it is supported.

For downward compatibility, broadcast announcements can still be used.

Subnet Mask Announced Because the subnet mask is included in the routing announcements, subnetted, supernetted, and variable-length subnet masks are now fully supported.

Authentication You can now authenticate incoming RIP announcements with a predefined password. The password can be clear text or encrypted. However, Windows 2000 currently supports only clear-text passwords, which means that they are vulnerable to a network capture exposing them.

Route Tag A route tag is additional administrative information you can include with announcements on specific routes. It was designed for environments that used multiple routing protocols (e.g., RIP and another distance vector-based routing protocol such as HELLO), so that RIP-based routes could be identified from non-RIP-based routes.

on the job

Configure and use RIPv2 with greater care when it will be used with RIPv1 routers. They must have a common announcement mechanism, which means using broadcast announcements rather than multicasts, and incoming packets should be set for RIPv1 and RIPv2. Remember that while RIPv2 can support subnetted, supernetted, and variable-length subnet masks, RIPv1 may incorrectly interpret these. In particular, you should exclusively use RIPv2 if you are using variable-length subnet masks and disjointed subnets.

Windows 2000 as a RIP Router

Windows 2000 Server when configured as a router with the RIP routing protocol supports the following:

- Convergence options for split horizon, poison reverse, and triggered updates
- The ability to modify the announcement interval (default is 30 seconds)
- The ability to modify the routing table entry timeout (default is 3 minutes)

- The ability to support Silent RIP
- Peer filtering, which is the ability to accept or reject RIP announcements from specific routers (by IP address)
- Route filtering, which is the ability to accept or reject RIP announcements of specific networks or specific routers
- RIP neighbors, which is the ability to send unicast RIP announcements to specific routers that could not normally accept multicast announcements (e.g., routers over Frame Relay)
- The ability to announce or accept default routes or host routes

exam watch

Windows 2000 supports RIPv2, which means it can support many of the more desirable features heralded in OSPF. You may not have to use a complex routing protocol to benefit from some of the complex features and configurations. RIPv2 can be used with RIPv1, which offers compatibility rather than having to change an existing RIPv1 routing infrastructure.

You should now have a better understanding of when RIP can meet your routing requirements, or when your requirements are such that you should use the more complex link state routing protocol, OSPF.

SCENARIO & SOLUTION

Can I use RIP as my routing protocol if...	Choice of Routing Protocol: RIP or OSPF
I want to use multicasts rather than broadcast announcements.	RIPv2 allows you to do this, but remember it can't be used with RIPv1 routers because they must have a common announcement. The other consideration is if you have Silent RIP hosts on your network; ensure they can also support the multicast announcements.
I want protection from rogue routers.	RIPv2 allows you to do this, although Windows 2000 only supports clear-text passwords, which are not as secure as an encrypted password exchange. However, OSPF in Windows 2000 also currently does not support encrypted passwords. Cisco routers support MD5 with OSPF, which may be a better choice if this is important to you. Remember you can also specify peer and route filtering to exactly define from which routers you will accept announcements.

SCENARIO & SOLUTION

Can I use RIP as my routing protocol if...	Choice of Routing Protocol: RIP or OSPF
I want to use a variable-length subnet mask (VLSM).	RIPv2 supports this, but again, remember not to use this more modern IP facility in conjunction with RIPv1 routers.
I want to use routes that are greater than 15 hops.	For all its improvements, RIPv2 still can't handle this! Because of potential problems inherent with distance vector-based routing protocols (such as count to infinity and looping holes), it is debatable whether this value should be allowed to increase. OSPF is your only option here; it supports up to 255 routers.
I want to be able to fine-tune and optimize convergence time.	RIP allows you to do this with options for split horizon, poison reverse, and triggered updates. However, inevitably in a large internetwork, a state link routing protocol such as OSPF will have a faster convergence time.
I want to decrease the network traffic by sending fewer announcements.	This is tricky! Technically, you can decrease the network traffic by sending fewer announcements with RIP, because you can specify the periodic announcement time to be a high value. However, the higher the value, the greater the risk of being out of date. Similarly, you can disable triggered updates. Also, remember that within each announcement all the routes are announced even if there are no changes, so bandwidth is being used unnecessarily. If what you really want to do is have a lower and more efficient bandwidth utilization by only sending announcements when there are changes, and within each announcement send the minimum amount of information required to update routes, then OSPF would be the better routing protocol.

CertCam 9-6

EXERCISE 9-6

Changing RIP Interface Properties to Support RIPv2 Exclusively and with Authentication

You want the benefit of a routing protocol that supports VLSMs (Variable Length Subnet Masks), uses multicast instead of broadcast, and offers protection against rogue routers. You don't want the administrative overhead of configuring OSPF, so you update all your routers with RIPv2. On your Windows 2000 RRAS router with RIP installed and added to the interfaces you want to use, you now need to make configuration changes to support your requirements.

1. If not already loaded, load the RRAS snap-in located under Start | Programs | Administrative Tools | Routing and Remote Access.
2. Navigate to RIP under your server, right-click on the interface you want to configure, and select Properties.
3. Under the General tab, change the "Outgoing packet protocol" to "RIP version 2 multicast."
4. On the same tab, change the "Incoming packet protocol" to "RIP version 2 only."
5. On the same tab, select the "Activate authentication" box and type in the Password box the password you are going to use for all your routers.
6. Your configuration changes should look similar to the following illustration.

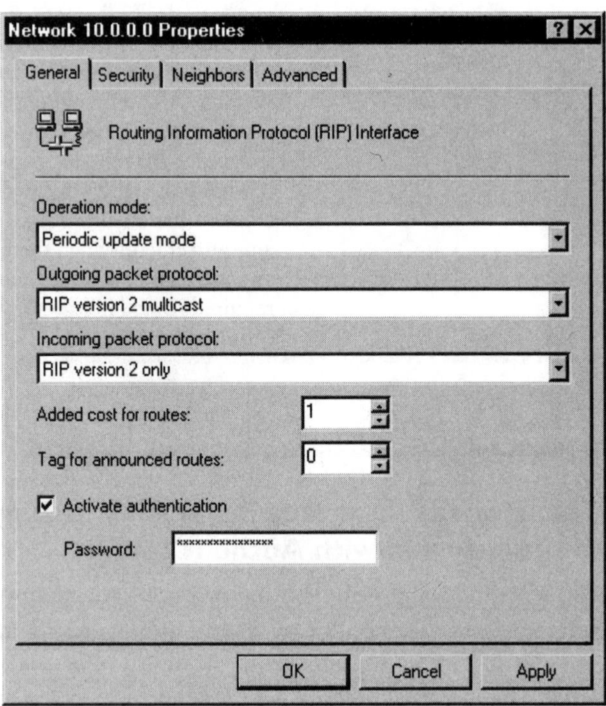

7. Click OK, and repeat this for any other interfaces on which you have added RIP.

CERTIFICATION OBJECTIVE 9.05

OSPF

Open Shortest Path First is a link state routing protocol designed for use in large-scale internetworks, and seeks to redress some of the shortcomings associated with traditional distance vector-based routing protocols.

For many of us, OSPF is a new and unfamiliar routing protocol. It is outside the scope of this chapter to give a complete and detailed description on every aspect of OSPF, but it does aim to provide the basic understanding and provide a framework of concepts and terminology to get you started. Without this, the OSPF configuration options themselves will make little sense, let alone your understanding the consequences of setting their values.

Unless you have access to many routers in a large internetwork to try out OSPF in a test environment, it is difficult to see in action all that OSPF offers. Therefore, a good grounding in the basic terminology and concepts is essential to help provide you with understanding and information about this protocol that you may not be able to gleam from experience.

Characteristics of OSPF

We have already stated some of the benefits of using a link state routing protocol such as OSPF over a distance vector routing protocol such as RIP. These include

- Efficient use of network bandwidth, by using directed (multicasts) and acknowledged information only when necessary rather than periodic announcements. This also results in faster convergence times and more reliable routing information (for example, eliminating the count to infinity problem). Because it is less bandwidth hungry, it can be used over slower WAN links.
- Only routing changes are exchanged between neighboring routers rather than whole routing tables, which considerably speeds up the routing announcements and updates.
- Routing tables are smaller and therefore more efficient, because only routes immediately adjacent are stored in the routing table rather than a complete list of every available route. This makes computing the best route much quicker and less error prone. OSPF calculated routes are always loop-free.

- It scales well for large networks, accommodating more than 15 routers (up to 255).
- Like RIPv2, it supports authenticated communication between routers as protection against rogue routers. Windows 2000 only currently supports a clear-text password rather than a more secure, encrypted password mechanism.

However, for all these benefits in comparison with RIP, OSPF is a more CPU-intensive protocol. For all the improvements you gain from using a link state routing protocol, on large networks it will become prone to routing and update delays unless the network is divided into smaller and therefore more manageable sections. When divided, obviously these sections must have a defined set of rules and mechanisms for communicating both within themselves and with each other. This is when the configuration gets complex!

OSPF Terminology and Concepts

If your previous experience of routing was limited to only RIP, you may find it difficult to separate the familiar RIP-specific terms from general routing concepts. For example, you may be used to equating a routing metric with a *hop*, and think of the two as interchangeable. However, a hop is a distance vector's implementation of a routing metric; there are no hops with a link state routing protocol, because the routing implementation works differently with a link-state implementation.

This is when it is important to understand the underlying concept before you learn a specific implementation of it. If you are familiar with RIP terminology, you may find the new OSPF terms difficult to grasp, and the plethora of new acronyms don't help! It is always difficult to "unlearn" something, redefine a familiar term with a new term, and remember that it might work differently in another implementation.

Where RIP and OSPF have different terms for an equivalent function, Table 9-3 may help.

The following sections discuss some of the terminology you will encounter when configuring OSPF, and describe how the components work and fit together.

TABLE 9-3 RIP and OSPF Terms for Equivalent Functions

RIP Term	OSPF Equivalent Term
Routing Announcement	Link State Advertisements (LSAs)
Routing Table	Link State Database (LSD)
Hop	Cost

Advertisements within an Area

The divided and manageable network sections are referred to as OSPF *areas.* Each area has a *boundary* that sets the limit on where routing announcements can go (called *Link State Advertisements,* or *LSAs* in OSPF terms). When routing announcements are sent, this is called *flooding.*

The Link State Database

All routers within a boundary contain the same routing table (called *Link State Database,* or *LSDB*) that reflects the topology of only that area. The route metric (called the *cost*) is a unitless number that indicates the preference level of that route. Entries for the routing table are calculated to determine the least-cost path to each network in the internetwork—the *Shortest Path First (SPF) Tree.*

Using multiple areas reduces the size of the routing table within each area, which therefore reduces the time and processing required for routing decisions and maintenance. Additionally, when an AS is subdivided into contiguous areas, routes within areas can be *summarized* to further minimize route table entries.

The Default Route

Each area can be configured with a *default route* (which is used when a direct route is not known) that summarizes all routes outside the AS or outside the area. This contrasts with RIP, which can only summarize subnets in a given network ID.

Identifying Areas and Routers

An ID number uniquely identifies areas in the AS, and similarly, each router is assigned a unique ID number. Although this ID number uses the same format as an IP address (32-bit dotted decimal number), it is important to remember that these IDs are not IP addresses but logical "names." However, the ID does borrow from some of the concepts used in IP address assignment in that it represents a hierarchical structure that can reflect its position to its neighbors (e.g., area 0.0.0.1 is next to area 0.0.0.2, etc.).

Although there is no direct relationship between OSPF IDs and IP addresses, it is a common industry convention to use the largest or smallest IP address assigned to the router as the Router ID, and this convention obviously closely relates the two.

The Backbone

An OSPF network must have at least one area. If an OSPF network contains more than one area, it must have a *backbone* area with the ID of 0.0.0.0. The backbone is the center, the hub of all the other areas, and is the common point of reference. All areas must report their routing information to the backbone, so the backbone can distribute this information to other ASs.

A general rule of thumb for routing efficiency in OSPF networks is to divide a network into areas when it has more than 40 routers.

Different Types of Networks

The type of network being used determines OSPF message format. When you configure an interface on an OSPF router, you must define what type of network it is going to talk to. The choices are

- Broadcast
- Point-to-Point
- Non-Broadcast Multiple Access

Broadcast Network Architectures This represents a network that can support a hardware broadcast where a single packet sent by the router is received by all routers on the network; however, an OSPF IP multicast message will be sent rather than a broadcast. Examples of broadcast networks include

- Ethernet
- Token Ring
- FDDI

OSPF sends multicasts and not broadcasts over a Broadcast network. Do not assume that OSPF will send broadcasts just because a Broadcast network type is being used. OSPF never sends broadcasts, only multicasts or unicasts.

Point-to-Point Networks This represents a network that can be connected by two routers only. An OSPF IP multicast message will be sent over this media. Examples of Point-to-Point networks include

- Leased-line WAN links (e.g., DDS)
- T1, T3, or fractional T1-Carrier links

Non-Broadcast Multiple Access (NBMA) This represents a network that can connect more than two routers, but cannot support hardware broadcasts. In this particular case, because multicasts cannot be used, OSPF must be configured to use unicast to the specific IP addresses of the routers on the NBMA network. Examples of NBMA networks include

- X.25
- Frame Relay
- ATM

The use of OSPF over nonpermanent, nonpersistent, dial-up WAN links (e.g., analog telephone lines and ISDN) is not recommended.

If your network type is NBMA, you must use unicasts, because multicasts cannot be supported. Unicasts are directed packets to a specified and known IP address. This means you have to specify these IP addresses in order to use OSPF over NBMA.

Different Types of Routing Communication

A router that sits in between areas—on the border of two or more areas—is called an *Area Border Router* (ABR), and is responsible for exchanging routing information from one area to another.

Because each area must communicate with the area's backbone, this is done either *directly* (if an area border router joins the area with the backbone) or *indirectly* with multiple border routers. When areas do not directly join to the backbone, they use *intermediate areas* and their border routers to exchange their routing information. In OSPF terms, the intermediate area is called a *transit area.*

Because these indirect connections have a virtual rather than physical link between the area and the backbone, a *virtual interface* set up in Windows 2000 RRAS is required..

Different Types of Routers

There are three classifications of OSPF routers:

- Area Border Router (ABR)
- Internal Router (IR)
- AS Border Router (ASBR)

Area Border Router (ABR) The *Area Border Router* as previously described has its interfaces in different areas and handles inter-area communication. To reduce the amount of information sent, the ABR sends only the summarized routing information (route summary) instead of individual routes.

Internal Router (IR) An *Internal Router* (IR), as its name suggests, is a router that sits in its area, and only in its area, and handles intra-area routing.

AS Border Router (ASBR) An *AS Border Router* (ASBR) is a router that connects different ASs. When the ASBR exchanges routing information with an external network, the routing information received from outside the AS is referred to as *external routes.*

How Routers Exchange Information—Forming Adjacencies with Neighbors When an OSPF router initializes, it sends out a periodic OSPF *Hello* packet that contains router configuration information, such as the router's Router ID and the list of neighboring routers that it knows about as a result of receiving similar Hello packets.

When incoming Hello packets are received, the router determines the specific router or routers with which it should communicate. This relationship is called an *Adjacency,* and should lead to the synchronization of the Link State Database (LSDB). Should adjacencies fail to establish, the internetwork will not converge successfully.

After the adjacency has been formed, each neighboring router sends periodic Hello packets according to the *Hello interval* (which defaults to 10 seconds) as confirmation that they are still there with active links. The absence of an expected Hello packet (expected within the assigned *dead interval,* which defaults to 40 seconds) signals a downed router, and the Link State Database is changed accordingly. Both of these options are found under the Advanced tab of an OSPF's interface Properties.

When these Hello packets are sent by unicast rather than multicast (such as on a nonbroadcast network), the poll interval is much longer to accommodate the different network—120 seconds by default.

Electing Routers as "Designated Routers" or "Backup Designated Routers" To minimize the amount of routing information exchanged when routers are powered on, OSPF elects a *Designated Router* (DR) on every segment except on Point-to-Point segments. All other routers in the same segment establish an adjacency with the designated router, which leads to the exchange of routing information that synchronizes the link state database with the DR. The routing information exchanged between the DR and other routers uses *multicasting* in a broadcast network, but *unicasting* in a nonbroadcast network.

If you are familiar with how Master Browsers and Backup Browsers are elected on Windows NT 4.0 networks, the following section will feel very familiar!

How does the election work? Each interface in a router has a priority that can range from 0 (lowest) to 255 (highest). The default priority is 1. These priorities, which are sent out in Hello packets, are used to elect the DR—the router with the highest priority becomes the DR.

If two or more routers have the same priority, the router with the highest router ID will become the DR.

You can "fix" the election by assigning a 0 priority to routers you don't want to become a DR (they won't participate in the election) and assign a 255 priority to the router you do want to become a DR.

For fault tolerance, a Backup Designated Router (BDR) is similarly elected so that should the DR fail, the BDR quickly and automatically becomes the DR, and a new election is held for a new BDR.

exam Watch

You must ensure that at least one router on your OSPF network (broadcast or NBMA) has a router priority configured to be 1 or greater. If all routers have this set to 0, a DR will not be elected, the Link State Database cannot be synchronized, and no transit traffic (traffic across that network) can be passed.

The Router Priority is set under the OSPF's interface's Properties | General tab as shown in Figure 9-4.

FIGURE 9-4

Router priority setting that determines whether this router will become a Designated Router or a Backup Designated Router

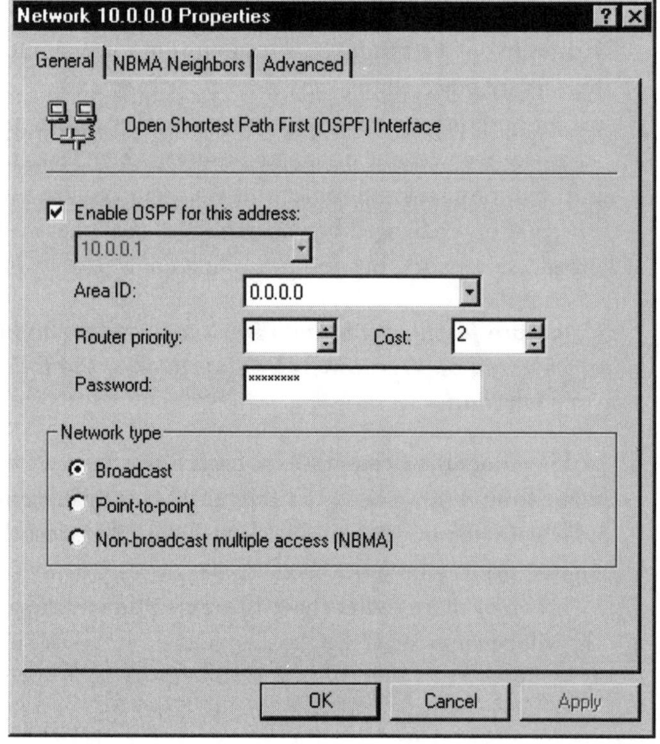

Reducing Routing Information

OSPF goals include reducing the routing information to be processed, which results in greater efficiency, and ensures the integrity of routing information. To help achieve these, two other facilities can be used

- External Route Filters
- Stub Areas

External Route Filters By default, OSPF routers acting as ASBRs import and advertise all external routes that may not be desirable from a security perspective. You may prefer to filter out external routes to protect the AS from incorrect or malicious routing information. Additionally, you may simply want to restrict the external routing information that is imported into the AS, if it is not required.

You can filter external routes on the ASBR by the external route source, or by the individual route. You can configure the ASBR to accept or ignore the routes of specified external sources; for example, certain routing protocols (e.g., RIP) or other sources (e.g., static routes or SNMP).

On an ASBR router, external filters are configured as an OSPF global property on the External Routing tab as shown in Figure 9-5. Note that you cannot configure external filters if the router is not an ASBR—this wouldn't make sense. The other two routers have no direct contact with routes outside the AS, and therefore no need to specify external filters.

Stub Areas You can import external routes into an OSPF AS with an AS Border Router, but to stop external routes from flooding into an area, you can use what is called a *stub area.*

A stub area applies the default route 0.0.0.0 to keep the topology database size small. In OSPF, you can assume that any destination that you can't reach through a designated route is reachable through the default route.

To implement a stub area, one or more of the stub area's Area Border Routers must advertise the default route 0.0.0.0 to the stub area, and the route summary.

However, a limitation of using stub areas is that you cannot use them on the backbone, and you cannot configure stub areas through virtual links.

A stub area accepts the default route and route summary, but no external routes. An extension to this is a *totally stubby area* (also known as a *stub area without a summary*), where the default route is accepted, but neither route summary nor external routes are accepted.

FIGURE 9-5

Configuring External Route filters to protect the AS from incorrect or malicious routing information

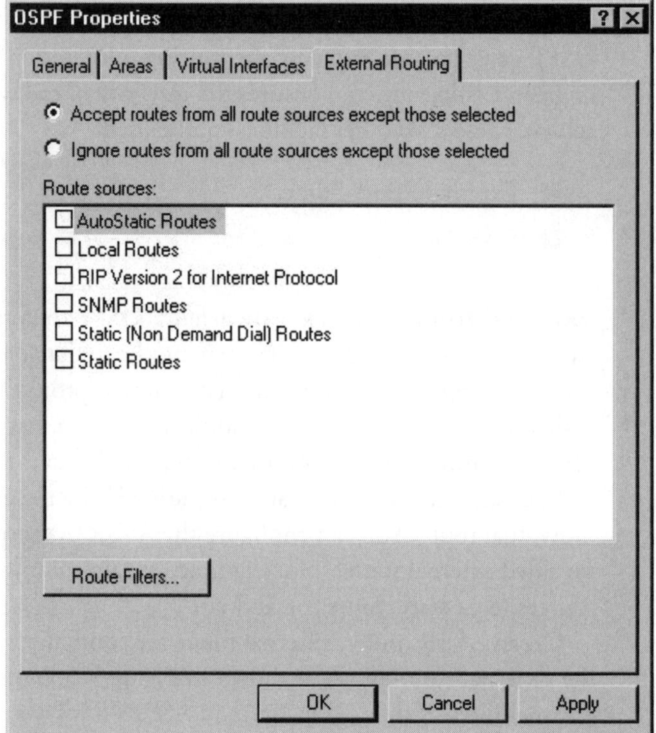

CertCam 9-7

EXERCISE 9-7

Configuring Your Router with Area Information

Your RRAS router has been configured with OSPF to be an Interior Router (IR) that will be going into a stub area with the area ID of 0.0.0.5. You need to define and configure your router accordingly.

1. If not already loaded, load the RRAS snap-in located under Start | Programs | Administrative Tools | Routing and Remote Access.
2. Ensure your server is selected in the left pane, and if you can see OSPF listed, right-click on it and select Properties. If OSPF is not listed, double-click on IP Routing, which should then expand to show OSPF.

3. Under the General tab, ensure you have configured your Router ID correctly, and that the "Enable Autonomous system boundary router" is not set.
4. Click on the Areas tab, and then click Add.
5. Under the General tab, enter your Area ID of **0.0.0.5**.
6. Still under the General tab, select the "Stub area" check box. Your dialog box should look similar to the following illustration.

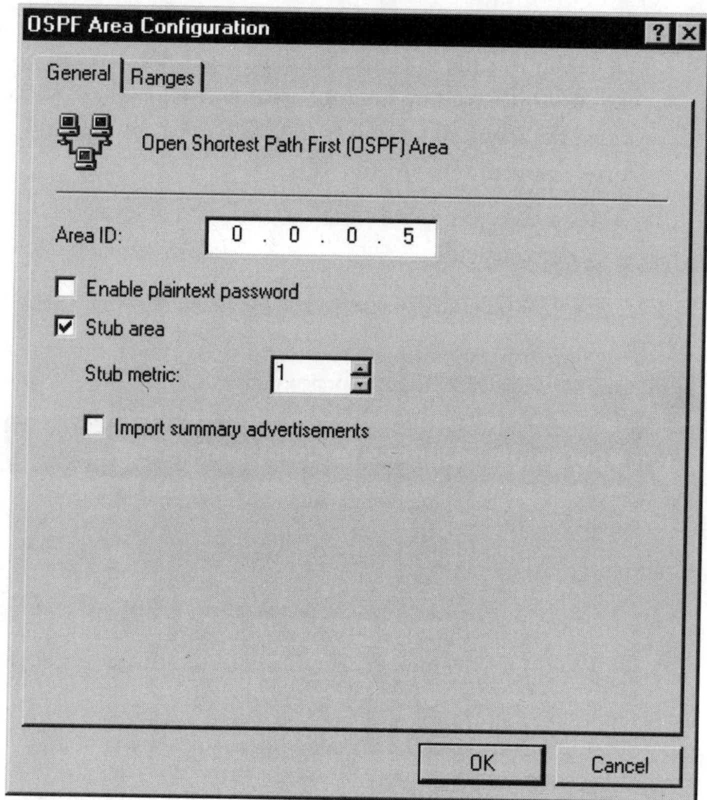

7. Click Ok.

OSPF Configuration Requirements

We have discussed the various different types of OSPF routers that can be used, and the OSPF options. The actual configuration options you must configure and that will be applicable will depend first and foremost on what kind of OSPF router you are configuring within the overall structure of the OSPF network. Because an OSPF router is highly dependent on the whole topology of its internetwork, you cannot arbitrarily change routing options and still expect routing to work!

Router Configuration

Table 9-4 lists the options that you might need to configure, depending on the role of your OSPF router. They all assume that you have successfully installed OSPF, added the required interfaces to OSPF, and configured OSPF on the router with its correct Router ID and Area IDs.

TABLE 9-4 Check List for OSPF Router Configuration

Type of OSPF Router	Options to Configure
IR	If in a stub area, enable this option.
ABR	Configure route summary (the network range) for each area this router belongs to. If in a stub area and not on a virtual link, enable the stub area option and enable the “Import summary advertisements” if in an ordinary stub area, but disable the “Import summary advertisements” if the area is a totally stubby area. If on a virtual link, you’ll need to set up the ABR’s virtual interface by linking it to the other end via a transit area.
ASBR	Configure the external routes you will accept, and which protocols will be used (e.g., RIP or static routing).

Interface Configuration

When you have configured the router, verify the OSPF configuration for each interface, which includes the following:

- Areas
- Priority for DR election
- Cost based on bandwidth
- Password for authentication (must be same as other routers in the area, and is case sensitive)
- Network type (if NBMA, must define NBMA neighboring routes)
- Values for Hello Interval, Dead Interval, and Poll Interval should to be the same as other routers in the area

CERTIFICATION OBJECTIVE 9.06

Demand-Dial Routing

When you are routing packets over a local area network or a permanent wide area network, these connections have interfaces that are always available; consequently, their interface status is always active or connected. Any packets forwarded over these types of connections do not require additional physical or logical connections to be established.

In comparison, a dial-on-demand connection does not have this permanent connection. The connection is only made when required; for example, when the dial-on-demand interface is asked to forward packets over its interface. Before the packet can be forwarded, an extra connection needs to be made (for example, a modem dialing out on an analog telephone line), which is established with an additional PPP link.

When the dial-up is completed, packets can be forwarded as if it were any other routed connection. Using the same technique on a router to forward packets on a dial-on-demand interface is referred to as *demand-dial routing*.

The PPP link is established over either a physical medium or a tunnel medium. Physical media include analog telephone lines and ISDN. Tunnel mediums include the two tunneling protocols we discussed in Chapter 5, PPTP (Point-to-Point-Tunneling Protocol) and L2TP (Layer 2 Tunneling Protocol).

Demand-dial routing can be used to connect your router to the Internet, connect together branch offices, or to implement router-to-router virtual private network (VPN) connections.

What Is Demand-Dial Routing?

Dial-on-demand connections are normally used when a permanent connection is not available, so demand-dial routing is used to connect your router to the required host or router when there is no permanent connection to do this. They can be used as a backup to a permanent connection, or if no permanent connection is possible.

Because dial-up connections are usually charged on a time basis, a demand-dial connection is an efficient method of only paying for a connection when you have data to transfer. An idle timeout value allows the connection to automatically terminate when there is no more data to transfer.

exam Watch

Demand-dial connections have the benefit of offering cost-efficient dial-up WAN links when they are configured with an idle timeout, because you only pay for the connection when there is data to transfer.

Alternatively, demand-dial routing interfaces may be used as a security precaution so that a routed connection is only made when there is data to transfer, and you are controlling the open link. Alternatively, a dial-up connection may be your only choice to connect to your destination network.

Although it is more common for a demand-dial connection to fit into the category above, there are, in fact, two types of demand-dial connections:

- On-demand
- Persistent

There are also two different ways to control and configure the demand-dial connection:

- Two-way initiated
- One-way initiated

On-Demand Demand-Dial Connections

The more common use of a demand-dial connection is to create the connection when there is data to send over the interface, and terminate it when the transfer of data is complete (the link is idle). This is an on-demand demand-dial connection.

exam watch

On-demand connections only establish a connection when traffic is forwarded, and the connection is terminated after a configured amount of idle time.

You can configure the idle timeout on either the calling router or the answering router.

Persistent Demand-Dial Connections

There is also the scenario in which you actually want a permanent connection, but do not have the infrastructure of a permanent connection (e.g., fractional T1, etc.) to support this; therefore, a dial-up connection is your only option. If the efficiency of the connection were more important than the cost of being permanently connected (for example, you had a flat-rate leased line, or your line incurs only a local charge), you would probably find a persistent demand-dial connection more beneficial.

What's the benefit of having a persistent demand-dial connection? The benefit is in efficiency and speed of connection when needed. It takes time to establish the PPP link (this is called the *connection establishment delay*), which can be anything from just a couple of seconds to more than 20 seconds. The actual delay will depend on many factors, including the type of connection; for example, a modem connection over an analog telephone line will take much longer than an ISDN connection.

This connection establishment delay could impact on the applications that are being used over a demand-dial routed connection, because an application could time out before the connection is established and therefore fail to connect.

Another factor in favor of using a persistent demand-dial connection may be cost. It may actually be cheaper to keep the same connection active than frequently establishing new connections.

Unlike the idle timeout option, which can be configured on either the calling router or the answering router, persistent demand-dial connections must be configured on both sides of the connection—on the calling router and the answering router.

exam Watch

Persistent demand-dial connections must be configured on both the calling router and the answering router.

Two-Way Initiated Demand-Dial Connections

A two-way initiated demand-dial connection is where routers can both initiate a connection when needed, and also respond to the same router calling it—over the same demand-dial interface. In other words, in a two-way initiated connection, both routers can be a calling router, or an answering router on the same interface. Use two-way initiated connections when traffic from either router can create the demand-dial connection. This offers the greatest flexibility, but also requires the greatest configuration, since not only do both routers need to be configured, but they also have to be configured similarly to ensure their configurations match.

One-Way Initiated Demand-Dial Connections

A one-way initiated connection restricts one router to being the calling router and the other to being an answering router. In many ways, this is the easiest of configurations because there is less to configure. It also offers a more secure routing environment from the perspective of the calling router, because it has complete control over when a connection is made.

exam Watch

A two-way initiated connection offers the greatest flexibility, but requires more configuration. A one-way initiated connection offers tighter control for the calling router (and therefore can be more secure), with less configuration required.

Connection Authentication

For calling routers, you must specify credentials with which to call out (which match a valid account on the answering router), and for answering routers, you must have an account that will be used to authenticate a calling router with their calling credentials.

On the answering router, the account used to authenticate the calling router must be configured with a username that matches the name of the demand-dial interface to which it corresponds. This account must also have dial-in permission and a password that never expires.

exam Watch **If the calling router supplies credentials with a username that doesn't correspond to the name of a demand-dial interface on the answering router, the calling router will be identified as a remote access user rather than a router.**

When your routers will be performing two-way demand-dial routing, the usernames and demand-dial interface names must correspond on both routers. For example, a corporate router in London that wants a demand-dial routing connection to the branch office in Brighton might call its demand-dial interface *Brighton Remote Router* (an arbitrary name, but it identifies to where it's connecting), and creates an account called *Brighton Remote Router* to authenticate incoming connections. It sets the calling credentials (username) on this demand-dial interface to be London Remote Router. To match this, the branch office in Brighton would create its demand-dial interface calling it London Remote Router, and create an account called London Remote Router to authenticate incoming connections. It sets the calling credentials (username) on this demand-dial interface to be called Brighton Remote Router. This is summarized in Table 9-5.

TABLE 9-5 Demand-dial Interfaces, Routers, and Usernames

Router	Demand-Dial Interface Name and Username on Account that Will Authenticate Incoming Connections	Username Set on the Demand-Dial Interface Credentials
Corporate office router in London	Brighton Remote Router	London Remote Router
Branch office router in Brighton	London Remote Router	Brighton Remote Router

Security on Incoming Connections

Because the demand-dial connection uses PPP, the authentication and security features for incoming connections are the same as would be used for remote access connections, which were discussed in detail in Chapter 5. These security features include

- Remote access permission
- Authentication
- Encryption
- Callback
- Caller ID
- Remote access account lockout

Remote Access Permission The calling router must specify credentials for a valid user account that the answering router can authenticate (e.g., local security database, domain security database, or RADIUS server). This account must have remote access permission in one of two ways:

- Explicitly in the dial-in account
- Implicitly through "Control access through Remote Access policy" with a matching remote access policy set to "Grant remote access"

Refer back to Chapter 5 if you require more details on configuring the remote access permission.

on the Job

If you use the Demand Dial Wizard in the RRAS snap-in and select "Add a user account so a remote router can dial in," a user account with the same name as the demand-dial interface is created in the same security accounts database being used by the router. Additionally, the remote access permission will be set to "Allow access" even if the account is in a native-mode domain or a stand-alone router where normally the default option would be "Control access through Remote Access Policy." This can cause confusion if you are otherwise using an Access by Policy administrative model, so it would probably be better to manually change this so all your user accounts are consistent. The last thing to note is that this account should have the "User must change password at next logon" cleared, and "Password never expires" selected. These should be set automatically by the Demand Dial Wizard, but it's always worth checking!

Authentication The calling router can be authenticated at the user level and the computer level.

The user level requires a username, domain, and password, using the authentication protocols previously described in Chapter 5:

- PAP
- SPAP
- CHAP
- MS-CHAPv1
- MS-CHAPv2
- EAP

The computer level is used when certificates are used with IPSec (e.g., L2TP/IPSec tunneling connection) and EAP-TLS.

Differentiation between Remote Access Clients and Routers

Remote access connects a single user to a network, whereas demand-dial routing connects together networks. However, they do both have many components in common, which is why the Routing and Remote Access service so tightly integrates the two. Common components include

- The PPP connection to negotiate and authenticate the connection
- The use of physical (e.g., modem) or logical (e.g., VPN) ports
- Use of dial-in permission
- Security (including authentication protocols and encryption)
- Use of remote access policies
- Use of authentication providers (either Windows or RADIUS)
- Use of PPP features such as Multilink, BAP, and Microsoft compression (MPPC)
- Logging, auditing, and tracing

Enabling Demand-Dial Routing

When you first enabled RRAS, one option was to select routing, and then you were asked whether you wanted to use just LAN routing or demand-dial routing.

Choosing the demand-dial option will automatically configure the router for demand-dial routing, in addition to LAN routing, and invoke the Demand Dial Interface Wizard to guide you through configuring a demand-dial interface.

Alternatively, you can manually enable demand-dial routing, and then manually add a new demand-dial interface, which will invoke the Demand Dial Interface Wizard.

The steps needed to enable demand-dial routing include

- Enabling the router for demand-dial routing in addition to LAN routing
- Enabling one or more ports for demand-dial routing
- Adding one or more demand-dial interfaces

EXERCISE 9-8

Enabling Demand-Dial Routing

This exercise takes you through the steps involved in adding a physical demand-dial interface to be both a calling and answering router.

1. If not already loaded, load the RRAS snap-in located under Start | Programs | Administrative Tools | Routing and Remote Access.
2. Right-click on your server in the left pane to select Properties. It's here that you select whether to support routing and remote access.
3. Ensure the Router option is selected, and underneath ensure you select "LAN and demand-dial routing." You must have the LAN and demand-dial routing selected in order to support demand-dial routing. Until this option is selected, you cannot add demand-dial interfaces.
4. Click OK. You will be prompted to stop and restart the router. Click OK and wait for the RRAS service to stop, restart, and initialize.
5. We need to ensure you have at least one port that can be used for demand-dial routing. To do this, right-click on Ports in the RRAS left pane and select Properties. This displays a list of available ports (e.g., modem(s),

WAN miniports (for VPNs), and Direct Parallel). If you have no modem, for the sake of this exercise you can use the Direct Parallel port. Click on the port you want to enable for demand-dial routing (e.g., your modem), click Configure, and ensure it has selected the option "Demand-dial routing connections (inbound and outbound)" similar to the following illustration. Click OK.

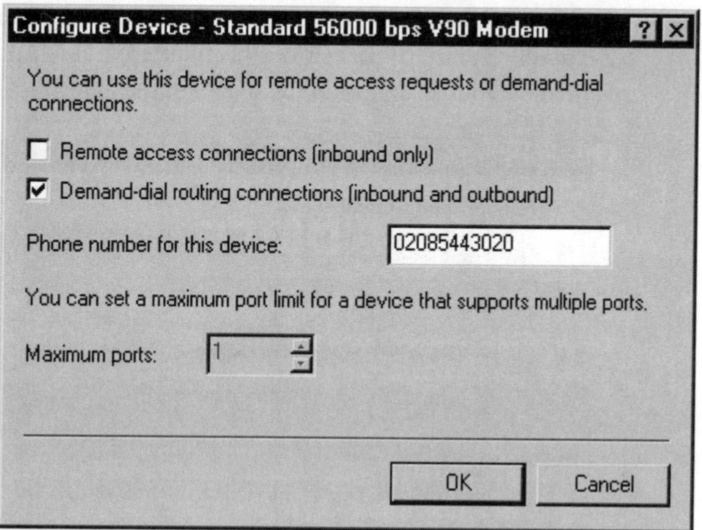

6. When you have finished enabling the ports you want to use with demand-dial routing, click OK.

Click Routing Interfaces | Properties | New Demand-Dial Interface to invoke the Demand Dial Interface Wizard. Click Next on the initial Welcome page.

7. You will then be prompted to enter a name to identify this demand-dial interface. Accept the default name of Remote Router, and click Next.
8. You will then be asked to specify the telephone number of the router you will be calling (if you selected a parallel connection, this page does not appear). Type in the calling number, and click Next.

9. The next page asks which connection type you want. Select "Connect using a modem, ISDN adapter, or other physical device," and click Next.
10. You will then be asked to select a device from the list of ports enabled for demand-dial routing. Select a modem if you have one configured for demand-dial routing, or if you have no modem and previously enabled the Direct Parallel port, select this. Click Next.
11. The next page is *important*—the Protocols and Security page. Ensure you select "Route IP packets on this interface" and "Add a user account so a remote router can dial in" as shown in the following illustration. Click Next.

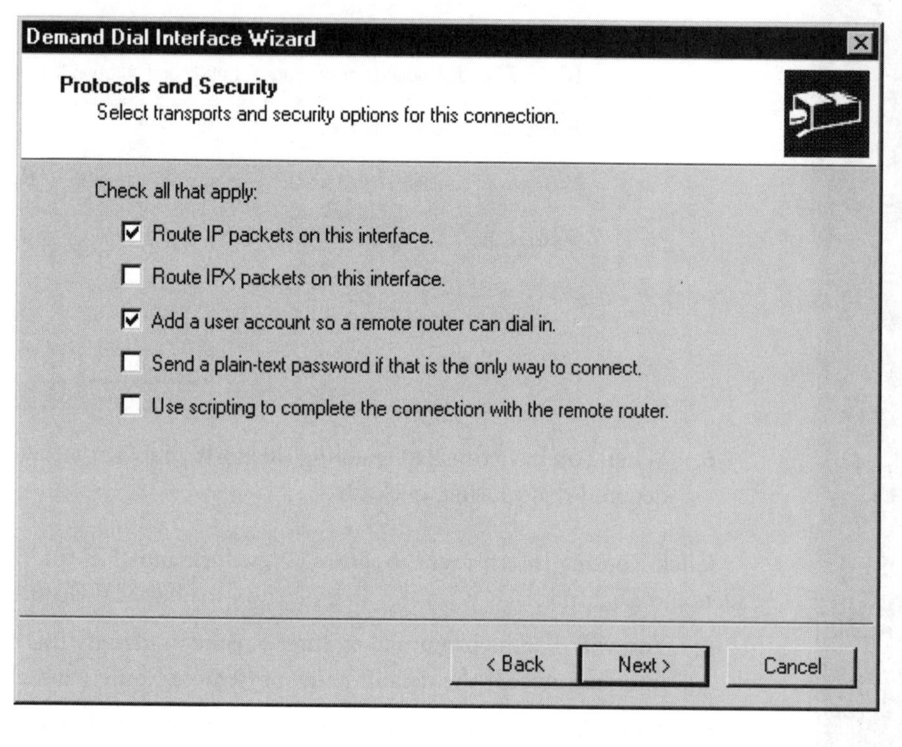

12. You will then be asked to specify Dial In Credentials that will be used to authenticate the router calling in to you. You will notice that the username has automatically been set to the same name as you chose for the demand-dial interface name. Specify a password, confirm it, and click Next.
13. You will be asked to supply the Dial Out Credentials, which need to match a valid account on the answering router. The following illustration shows this page with example credentials. When you have specified these, click Next.

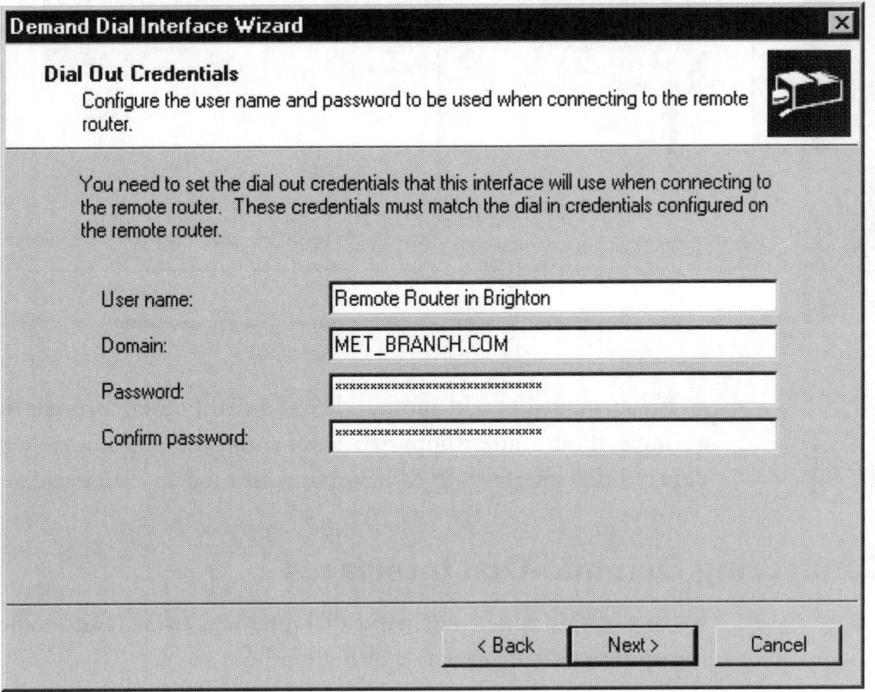

14. Next, you are told that your demand-dial interface will be installed and enabled, and that you can configure it by selecting it in the RRAS snap-in, right-clicking on it, and selecting Properties. Click Finish.

15. Your demand-dial interface should now be added and listed in the RRAS details pane with the Type of *Demand-dial,* the Status of *Enabled,* and the Connection Status of *Disconnected,* similar to the following illustration.

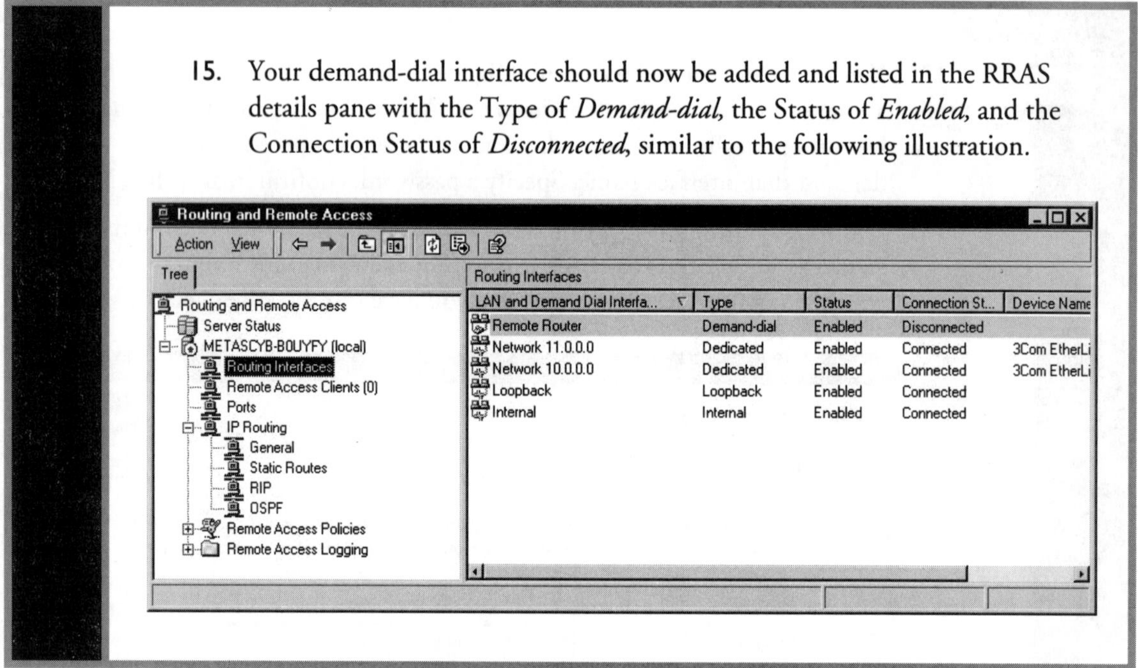

If you wanted to add another demand-dial interface, repeat this procedure. For example, if our router supported VPN connections, you may want to use some VPN demand-dial interfaces in addition to your modem demand-dial interface.

Configuring Demand-Dial Interfaces

Once you have added a demand-dial interface, select it and right-click. You will see the options that are available in Figure 9-6.

Set Credentials

This allows you view and edit the calling credentials of User name, Domain, and Password.

Connect and Disconnect

These options allow you to manually control the connection rather than, for example, relying on routing to initiate the connection, or the idle timeout to expire.

FIGURE 9-6 Options available on a demand-dial interface

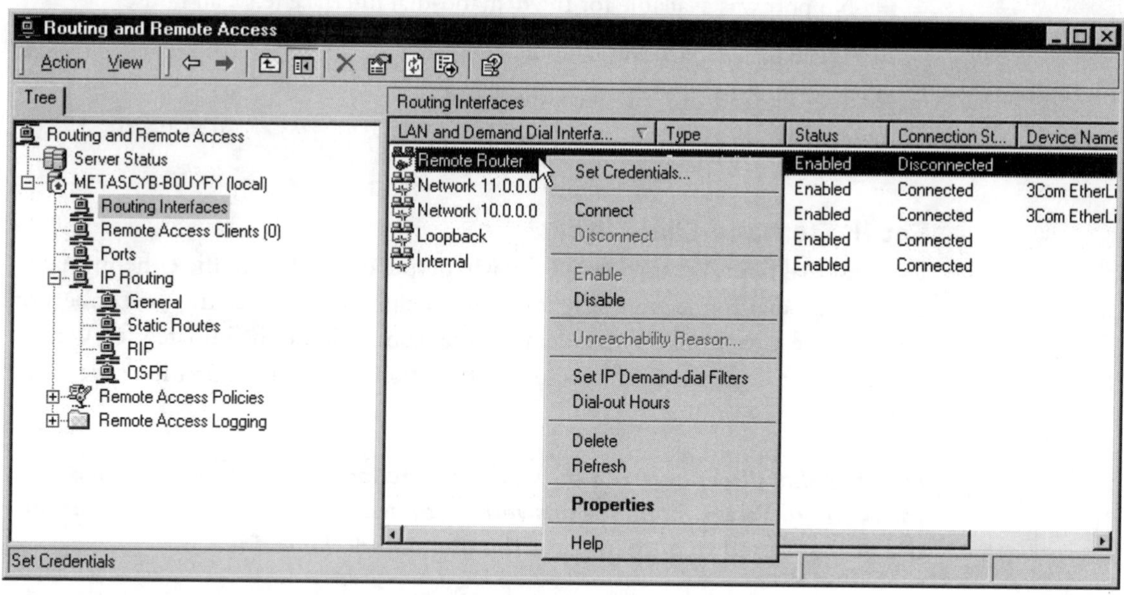

The Connect option is particularly useful for allowing you to manually test the basic connection and authentication.

Enable and Disable

This enables or disables the demand-dial interface and, for example, could be configured but disabled for security reasons until needed (e.g., permanent connection unavailable).

Unreachable Reason

This displays the last failure-to-connect error message and is useful in troubleshooting or monitoring demand-dial routing. When you manually connect the demand-dial interface and it fails to connect, you will see displayed in a dialog box the reason why the connection failed (e.g., no reply). However, when the connection is being raised automatically on demand but fails to complete the connection, this option will show the last unreachable reason recorded. Note it doesn't keep a history, just the last unreachable reason.

Potential unreachable reasons include

- No port was available for the demand-dial interface (e.g., all in use).
- The RRAS service was paused.
- The demand-dial interface was disabled.
- Dial-out hours have prevented the connection.

Set IP Demand-Dial Filters

Demand-dial filters are used to specify what types of TCP/IP traffic either initiate the demand-dial connection or ignore it for the purposes of creating the connection. For example, if you only want a demand-dial connection to be initiated for Web traffic, set the demand-dial filters so that only traffic to TCP destination port 80 can initiate the connection.

exam watch

Demand-dial filters apply to outward connections (calling), not inbound (answering). To set filters for answering connections, use remote policies on the account used to authenticate the demand-dial interface.

Demand-dial filters are only relevant for a demand-dial interface that is in a disconnected state; therefore, they will be ignored if the interface remains connected or if configured for a persistent connection. The RRAS *Dynamic Interface Manager* is responsible for checking the interface's configured demand dial filters before trying to initiate a connection.

Demand-dial filters are different from IP packet filters in that they define what traffic initiates a demand-dial connection. IP packet filters define what traffic is allowed in and out of the demand-dial interface once it is connected.

Because IP packet filters are applied after the connection is initiated, it is recommended that if you have configured IP output packet filters that prevent the flow of TCP/IP traffic on the demand-dial interface, then configure the same filters as demand-dial filters. This means that the demand-dial connection is never established for traffic that is discarded by the IP packet filters for the demand-dial interface.

exam watch

Demand-dial filters are different from IP packet filters in that they define what traffic initiates a demand-dial connection. IP packet filters define what traffic is allowed in and out of the demand-dial interface once it is connected.

Dial-Out Hours

Dial-out hours are used to specify when the demand-dial connection can be made. Similarly, the Times of Day and Week restriction in a Remote Access policy condition (it uses the same dialog box) allows you to specify the time of day and day of the week that a demand-dial connection is either allowed or denied for outbound connections.

exam Watch

Dial-out hours only apply to outward connections (calling), not inbound (answering). To set time/day restrictions for answering connections, use remote policies on the account used to authenticate the demand-dial interface.

As with the demand-dial filters, dial-out hours only apply to demand-dial interfaces that are in a disconnected state. The RRAS Dynamic Interface Manager is responsible for checking the interface's configured dial-out hours before trying to initiate a connection.

As with the similar remote access policy condition, by default all times on all days are permitted, and a connection is not automatically disconnected when it crosses the boundary from a time allowed to a time denied. The specified times denied only apply to new connections. Similar to the day and time restriction in remote access policies, the day and time taken is from the router.

Demand-Dial Interface Properties

The four property tabs are General, Options, Security and Networking.

Important demand-dial interface properties include

- The actual device being used (e.g., modem and specification), and connection details (e.g., telephone number) under the General tab.
- Connection type of Demand-dial (with idle timeout value defaulting to 5 minutes) or Persistent connection under the Options tab.
- User callback option under Callback in the Options tab.
- Required data encryption (disconnect if none) under the Security tab.
- Advanced (custom settings) under the Security tab, Settings allows you to specify exactly which authentication protocols to use (e.g., only EAP or MS-CHAP for mutual authentication).
- Device callback option under Settings in the Networking tab.
- Run Script under the Networking tab.

Using Remote Access Policies with Demand-Dial Routing

As with Remote Access, remote access policies can be used to define and control to a high degree certain conditions and settings for the account used to authenticate an answering demand-dial interface. For example, this could include only allowing a connection at restricted times, permitting only tunneled connections, enforcing strong authentication and encryption, etc.

A common implementation of remote access policies for demand-dial routing is to change the dial-in permission to control through remote policies and put all *remote router accounts* into a group. Create a policy that allows connections for the Windows-Group condition set to your remote router group and then set all common conditions and profile settings you want to use with all demand-dial routers.

Refer back to Chapter 5, which has a detailed description of remote access policies and how they are used.

Routing over Demand-Dial Interfaces

Once you have your demand-dial interface(s) configured such that your router connects over them to the answering router and is authenticated, and (if necessary) the other router can connect and authenticate with your router, you are ready to think about routing again!

How you update the routing table when using demand-dial routers depends on whether your demand-dial connection is on demand or persistent.

- If your demand-dial connection is *on-demand*, use static routing.
- If your demand-dial connection is *persistent*, use dynamic routing with routing protocols.

Static routing should be used for on-demand connections, because the periodic advertising from routing protocols can cause the connection to be permanently up if the advertising interval is less than the idle timeout.

Routing protocols can be used over persistent connections, because the periodic advertisement is not a problem if the link is always up.

on the job

When you have configured the routes for the demand-dial interfaces, test them by pinging from a workstation an address over the demand-dial interface. If routing is working correctly, you should get a reply (it may time out at first as the slower PPP connection is established), and the demand-dial interface Connection State in RRAS should change from Disconnected to Connected. If you can manually connect the demand-dial interface but not automatically connect, you have a problem with your routing setup over the demand-dial interface.

Defining Static Routes for Demand-Dial Interfaces

Add your static route for a demand-dial interface as described previously—Routing | Static Routes | New | Static Route. The important difference between defining static routes for a demand-dial interface and a standard interface is that you must specify in the Interface drop-down box that you are using a demand-dial interface. You will notice that this blanks the Gateway option because it is not relevant for a PPP connection, and you can control whether this route will initiate the demand-dial connection with the option: "Use this route to initiate demand-dial connections."

Another option for defining static routes with demand-dial routing is to specify static routes on the dial-in properties of the user account that is used to authenticate the incoming connection. When the calling router connects and is authenticated, these static routes will be amalgamated into the routing table on the answering router. If the remote network has multiple segments, the remote router should be configured for dynamic routing protocols so it can update neighboring routers with the new routes.

Auto-Static Updates An alternative to manually defining each static route if using RIP is the use of auto-static updates. When this command is initiated, it requests all known routers or services from the connecting router and adds them to its own routing table.

An auto-static update is a one-time, one-way exchange of routing information. After the routes are sent, the two routers do not periodically advertise, even if the connection remained in a connected state. The default settings for RIP already support auto-static updates—the actual options are "Auto-static update mode" and "RIP version 2 multicast" for outbound packets.

If you want to use auto-static updates with RIP, add the demand-dial interface to RIP and ensure these settings are set correctly. To perform an auto-static update, in the RRAS snap-in, double-click IP Routing | General, then select your demand-dial interface, right-click and select Update Routes.

exam Watch

Auto-static updates only transfer routing information from answering routers to the calling router, and therefore is not an exchange of routing information. For other routers to obtain routing information about the calling router, they too would have to initiate auto-static updates.

You can also schedule auto-static updates by using a netsh script to perform the auto-static update (connect, update, disconnect), and then schedule this script to be run as one of the Windows 2000 Scheduled Tasks.

When an auto-static update is performed, any existing auto-static routes for the interface are deleted before the update is requested from the other router. If there is no response from the other router, the deleted routes cannot be updated or replaced, which could obviously cause routing problems.

Using Routing Protocols over a Demand-Dial Interface

If necessary, add the routing protocol, and then add the demand-dial interface to the protocol as we did for standard interfaces (refer back to Exercises 9-4 and 9-5 if necessary).

Table 9-6 lists some configuration options that should be changed such that they are more sympathetic to a dial-up connection.

TABLE 9-6 Configuring Routing Protocols for a Persistent Demand-Dial Connection

Routing Protocol	Configuration Changes for a Persistent Demand-Dial Connection
RIP	Set the operation mode for RIP to Periodic update mode, and enable triggered updates.
OSPF	On the Advanced properties of an OSPF interface, you may want to increase the values of the transit delay, the retransmit interval, the hello interval, and the dead interval.

Routing protocols must run over a numbered connection. A numbered connection is a connection that has been assigned an IP address, which would normally happen during the PPP connection process. However, an ISP might allow connections that are unnumbered in order to preserve IP addresses—if your connection is unnumbered, the connection itself will be supported by RRAS, but the use of routing protocols over the connection will not be supported, and will not work.

CERTIFICATION OBJECTIVE 9.07

Troubleshooting IP Routing Problems

Troubleshooting IP routing is one of the most complex and challenging areas of managing TCP/IP networks. This is partly because, as we have seen, there is a lot of conceptual information to understand even before we start looking into actual implementations and configuration issues. This section cannot possibly try to cover everything you will need to troubleshoot IP routing problems, and there is no "blue print" that guarantees success. However, it will try to highlight key areas and help identify where and how you should concentrate your resources.

When Is Routing Troubleshooting Required?

So, when would you need to troubleshoot IP routing? Remember our earlier definition of routing:

Routing is the process of forwarding packets from one computer (source host) on one network to another computer (destination host) on another network, either directly if the destination host is on a network directly attached to the router, or indirectly via another router if the destination host is not on a network directly attached to the router.

First of all, if possible, ensure that you really do have a routing problem and not a hardware problem (e.g., cabling fault or adapter not working), that TCP/IP is correctly installed and configured on each end system (source computer and destination computer), and that you don't have a name resolution problem (check DNS and/or WINS functionality). All of these problems could result in a source computer failing to connect to a destination computer—but they are not routing problems. Routing problems are when IP packets fail to be correctly forwarded to their destination.

Before you troubleshoot a routing problem, ensure you do actually have a routing problem and not a problem due to hardware failure, basic TCP/IP configuration, or name resolution.

In its simplest form, you would need to troubleshoot IP routing when routing wasn't working or wasn't working well. Therefore, this usually falls into one of three categories:

- Packets sent from the source computer do not arrive at the destination computer (a total routing failure).
- Packets sent from the source computer only sometimes arrive at the destination computer (intermittent routing failure).
- Packets sent from the source computer often take a long time to arrive at the destination computer (routing efficiency problem).

These three conditions seem so simple a view of what the problem is, yet you as a network administrator know that any one and all three could be a result of many different problems. Such problems could be anything from incorrect routing tables, incorrect or inappropriate router configurations, or even signs of vulnerability to the limitations of your network capability and routing strategy. Adding to these network administration problems of trying to work out how to route between networks, why something isn't performing well or is producing errors, or even how to use the tools provided, and you could be very busy doing nothing but troubleshooting all the time!

Obstacles to Troubleshooting IP Routing

One of the taxing issues that makes IP routing difficult to troubleshoot is that it is not a single tangible service, it is a truly distributed service with many components (e.g., different hardware, different mediums, and even handled by multiple ASs), and it's constantly changing. Remember that routing tables can dynamically change even when no dynamic routing protocols are being used, and you usually have no control over when new computers and routers enter or leave the network, which means you have a constantly changing network map. So, where do you even start looking?

Of course, it always helps if the network in question is well documented, and certainly networking diagrams that identify IP networks and addresses, major servers and routers will assist in grasping the basic topology of your network. It would also help if every router were thoroughly documented with all the configuration options and why their values are so configured. However, such documentation rarely exists, and even when it does, this static information is immediately vulnerable to being out of date, inaccurate, and incomplete, simply because networks do have the capability to dynamically evolve and change very quickly. So don't rely on network documentation, but by all means use it as a "first base" and look to substantiate it with your own proof of how routing appears to be working (or not!).

Different Troubleshooting Approaches

So, where do you go next if you have no such documentation, can't find it, or the problem is too urgent for you to wade through reams of network diagrams? In my experience, I think there are actually four main typical approaches to troubleshooting IP routing problems, which divide into methodical and spontaneous.

Random Panic Mode

The first spontaneous approach is not a recommended course of action but happens far too often. Someone with little understanding of how routing works rushes about randomly checking and changing things in the desperate hope that it'll all suddenly start working. My advice to this approach is: Don't go there! The odds are against you that you'll resolve the problem, and it's much more likely you will inadvertently cause more problems (even if you are not immediately aware of them).

You are much more likely to effectively resolve problems by having a good understanding of the concepts of how routing works, in addition to understanding how it is implemented in your environment. This will allow you to deduct through logic and understanding the area(s) on which to concentrate when things go wrong. This is why this chapter has contained more theoretical than practical information in explaining the basic concepts—networks are very different, and once you understand the principles, you can then transfer the concepts to your specific implementation.

Methodically Checking Forward

The methodical approach is where someone verifies all the components until he or she finds the problem, by starting at the beginning and working forward to find the problem. So, if the source computer fails to send a packet to the destination computer on another network, the forward approach would be to check that everything was working and configured correctly on the source computer before even beginning to look at the source network, the first router, and so on.

This approach allows you to logically verify each stage of the path from source to destination until you find your failure. Conceptually, this is an easy method to follow, and more suitable if you don't have control over all the resources involved in the complete path. For example, if you have control over the source network resources, but another department (or even AS) is responsible for remote networks resources, it makes more sense to check the areas over which you have control—if only to eliminate them.

Methodically Checking Backward

This is the inverse of the previous method—verifying the destination host first, and then working backward to the source computer in order to find the break in the route link. This could be a quicker approach, particularly if other workstations on the same segment don't all have basic routing problems, which may seem to suggest it's more likely to be a remote rather than local problem. However, it is slightly more complicated to "think backwards," and you may not have control over the remote resources, which means delays in requesting additional help.

Intuition Based on Knowledge and Experience

The fourth approach is harder to precisely define; it's when someone who has a good knowledge of routing and can count on practical experience appears to bypass the methodical approaches. Instead, he or she instinctively focuses on exactly where the problem is and how to resolve it, without having to logically and methodically eliminate other possible causes. This is true networking expertise and rarely comes to novices.

When this approach works (and it won't always), it saves a lot of time and frustration. However, be aware it does take a certain amount of knowledge and experience to be able to successfully use this approach—there's a fine line between this and the first method! If the methodical approach does not appeal to you, try this, but always remember to think about the consequences of what you're doing, and be prepared to go back to a more methodical elimination approach if it isn't working.

on the job

You could argue that "common sense" could eliminate certain verification tests, which means you don't need to methodically check everything and hence will resolve the problem more quickly. However, this risks missing something because of incorrect assumptions, and could quickly result in chasing up blind alleys. For example, if your source computer can't successfully connect to your destination computer that is on another network, and you verify the default gateway is correctly assigned (e.g., with ipconfig /all), and that you can successful ping this router but not successfully ping the destination IP address, you might then turn your troubleshooting checks to the router configuration. You've forgotten that even a TCP/IP workstation is a routing host and has its own routing table, and assumed that there was no specific route defined in there for the destination network or host. If this were the case, the default gateway in this instance wouldn't be used. You might have a static route defined in there, or this workstation could have dynamically updated its routing table as a result of an ICMP Redirect message that forwarded the packet to a different IP address rather than the default gateway. If either of these were the case, checking the configuration of this first router would not be productive in resolving the actual problem.

TCP/IP Tools and Utilities

There are many different tools and utilities that you can use to help support and diagnose TCP/IP problems. For example, *ping* and *tracert* are two of the most commonly employed tools used to help troubleshoot routing problems. There are other TCP/IP troubleshooting utilities that can also be used (e.g., *netdiag, netstat* etc,) that are not covered in this section, because they are general TCP/IP troubleshooting utilities rather than ones that are most useful for specifically troubleshooting IP routing problems.

However, as with any tool, remember that they are only a tool to help you diagnose and resolve routing problems; you still have to understand when it is appropriate to use them, how to use them, and how to interpret their results. You will rarely use just one by itself, but a combination. Tools are no substitute for understanding the basic concepts and logically deducing what the problem actually is.

The following are common TCP/IP tools Microsoft provides with Windows 2000 and, with the exception of Network Monitor, can all run from the command line (which means that typing the main command followed by /help will display the correct syntax and possible parameters):

- ARP -a
- Route Print
- Ping
- Tracert
- PathPing (new in Windows 2000)
- Network Monitor or similar network capture utility

Note this list isn't extensive and doesn't include third-party products (for example, remember that the RRAS snap-in provides APIs) or SNMP (which can used to monitor and manage routers and their routing tables).

ARP -a

The Address Resolution Protocol is responsible for resolving IP addresses (logical addresses) to MAC addresses (physical addresses). Beneath the IP routing layer, a frame carrying the IP packet has to know to which MAC address it should go. If the incorrect MAC address is used, the routed IP packet will also fail.

It's unusual for an incorrect MAC address to be returned, but it is worth checking; for example, it could be incorrectly defined in an ARP table, or two computers could have the same IP address assigned (Microsoft automatically detects for duplicate IP addresses, but older systems may not).

on the Job

Swapping a network cable between two powered-on TCP/IP computers is another instance of temporarily having the incorrect MAC to IP address resolution.

You can only directly check the IP address to MAC address when the two systems are on the same segment. When you ping a remote address, because it gets routed, you will see instead the MAC address of the first router. If the address is still remote to the router, the router will find the MAC address of the next router until the host is on the same segment, and only then will the final MAC address be discovered.

Therefore, checking the ARP cache for IP to MAC address is in practice limited to verifying the MAC address of a host on the same segment or the MAC address of the first router.

To view the local ARP cache, type **ARP –a**. To ensure the IP address to MAC address is in the cache, ping the destination address first.

Route Print

We have already looked at this command, which can be used in addition to the RRAS snap-in equivalent as we saw in the section *Managing and Monitoring Routing Protocols*. Use it to view the current routing table on host computers as well as Windows 2000 routers, and don't forget that routing tables are dynamic—the output from a computer's routing table today may not be the same tomorrow, or even a few minutes later!

If you want to aim for a totally static routing table configuration, ensure no dial-up connections are made, no routing protocols are installed, and consider blocking IMCP traffic that could dynamically change the routing table. Such traffic might be ICMP type 9 and 10 (for Router Advertisement and Solicitation), and type 5 (code 1) for Redirection. However, beware of blocking all ICMP traffic—the useful *Ping, Tracert* and *PathPing* utilities will no longer work!

Ping This is every network administrator's simple and reliable friend. By sending ICMP Echo Requests to a destination address (e.g., ping 10.10.0.5), it verifies that TCP/IP is correctly installed on the source computer, and when a positive reply is returned, it confirms that the destination computer is available (a route was found to it).

It is one of the quickest and easiest troubleshooting tests you can do, and the results it yields is helped greatly if you have prior knowledge of the network topology. Ping addresses on your local subnet first, then the destination address. If a remote ping fails, try pinging another remote address—perhaps one on the same remote subnet as the previous address that failed to respond (which, if successful, may indicate a host problem rather than a routing problem to the remote network), or one that is the other side of your first router.

Don't think that successfully pinging the IP address of a router's remote interface is any proof that the router is actually routing to the remote network. Because Windows 2000 is a single-route router, there will be entries for all adapters in its routing table; therefore, pinging one of these will return a positive response. Only if you can successfully ping a computer on the remote network (e.g., beyond the interface that connects to the remote network) will you be proving that this router is actually routing (on the proviso that the packet was forwarded by this router and not a different one!).

If any of these fail, you have a break in the routing path. The next thing to check could be the current routing table on the source computer if you were troubleshooting forward, or you could try pinging another remote address if you were troubleshooting backward.

Figure 9-7 shows the results of pinging two different addresses over the Internet. The first one responds successfully, and the second fails to respond.

FIGURE 9-7 A successful ping and an unsuccessful ping to different IP addresses

```
H:\WINNT\System32\cmd.exe

C:\>ping 212.58.224.32

Pinging 212.58.224.32 with 32 bytes of data:

Reply from 212.58.224.32: bytes=32 time=30ms TTL=246
Reply from 212.58.224.32: bytes=32 time=20ms TTL=246
Reply from 212.58.224.32: bytes=32 time=20ms TTL=246
Reply from 212.58.224.32: bytes=32 time=20ms TTL=246

Ping statistics for 212.58.224.32:
    Packets: Sent = 4, Received = 4, Lost = 0 (0% loss),
Approximate round trip times in milli-seconds:
    Minimum = 20ms, Maximum =  30ms, Average =  22ms

C:\>ping 207.46.131.30

Pinging 207.46.131.30 with 32 bytes of data:

Request timed out.
Request timed out.
Request timed out.
Request timed out.

Ping statistics for 207.46.131.30:
    Packets: Sent = 4, Received = 0, Lost = 4 (100% loss),
Approximate round trip times in milli-seconds:
    Minimum = 0ms, Maximum =  0ms, Average =  0ms

C:\>
```

Even though both addresses are on the Internet, I have some prior knowledge of the network topology, which helps me to narrow down the possible problem. I know the first address is a Web server in my country (the UK), and the second is a Web server in a different country (the U.S.). Working backwards, I could try to ping an alternative IP address for the Web server (if multiple addresses are assigned, repeatedly ping the DNS name to see if round robin is being used, and if so, ping one of these alternative addresses). If an alternative IP address for the Web server is successful, I could deduce that either a different route is being used (use tracert to check), or the original destination host is down.

Another way to use ping with working backwards is to see if other addresses in the U.S. failed to respond to a ping, which would verify routing between the two countries.

Tracert Tracert can be used to determine which routers are used in a complete source to destination path, and also shows where the packet stops on the network if routing fails. The routing might fail because the last router didn't have a correct forwarding route, its forwarding address didn't respond (e.g., downed router), or because the Time-to-Live value (TTL) had expired (e.g., a bad link).

Because each router is reported in the route trace, this utility will indicate routing loops when the same router address is displayed more than once in the complete path, which indicates a router configuration problem (e.g., too slow a convergence time, or static routes incorrectly configured).

Note, however, that some routers will silently drop packets when the TTL value is expired rather than reporting that the value has expired; as such, these routers will be invisible to Tracert.

PathPing PathPing is new to Windows 2000 and combines features from both Ping and Tracert by sending packets to each router in the source to destination route, and then computing results based on the information returned from each discovered router.

It helps to indicate the degree of packet loss at each link of the route, which allows you to identify which routers or links might be causing problems in the way of packet loss and delays.

Network Monitor or Similar Network Capture Utility Capturing the actual packets from the source computer to the destination is often the only way to determine exactly what happened on the network. However, it does have its limitations in troubleshooting routing problems. First of all, because routing is usually dynamic, there are no guarantees that the captured route is typical or will be repeated in the future—it shows a historic snapshot rather than "this is what will happen" information. The only exception to this is when employing "source routing," which is when the source system (through specific programming) defines the exact destination route rather than just specifying the source address and relying on routers to dynamically determine a path. Source routing is traffic intensive and slow in comparison to dynamic routing, but sometimes used in debugging or network testing when the route needs to be predetermined.

Analyzing the captured data is more complex when it spans multiple segments, and in fact is often difficult to effectively capture when you don't know in advance which segments it will traverse. You may not be able to capture it if it includes networks outside your AS (e.g., Internet links).

However, its biggest drawback is it doesn't explain *why* a certain route was chosen (just that it was).

Verifying Each Component

Routing consists of many components, and troubleshooting routing is easier if the overall process and service can be broken down into individual components that can be verified as individual connecting links in the overall chain. In general, it is a good idea to verify basic components and configurations before homing in on specific configurations. Having said that, if you are getting a specific error message that appears to be referring to a specific configuration, it would make sense to check that first. However, when you have so many links in the chain, it is possible that a specific component failure could be as a result of something else in the chain rather than the component itself.

The following lists some of the components that should be verified:

- TCP/IP configuration on hosts (e.g., source workstations)
- Routing tables
- Router configuration
- Dynamic routing protocol configuration

TCP/IP Configuration

Starting with the basics, ensure that TCP/IP is loaded and running on the source and destination computers. If the computer is a Windows 2000 or Windows NT 4.0 computer, type **ipconfig /all** to view all TCP/IP configurations, which include IP address, subnet mask, and assigned default gateway. Verify that these are correct and you can ping your default gateway. Also verify your DNS and WINS server assignment (if any)—always remember to separate routing problems from name resolution problems (e.g., wrong DNS server assigned).

Routing Tables

Remember that routing tables are dynamic, even for hosts that aren't using dynamic routing protocols. Always check the routing tables on hosts and routers to see if a specific route exists for a destination host or network. If no specific route exists, check and verify the current default gateway. The default gateway can change; for example, if using ICMP Router Discovery, or when using remote access.

Use the **route print** command to verify the routing table entries. Additionally, on a Windows 2000 Server you can use the **netsh** command and Show IP Routing Table option in the RRAS snap-in.

When adding static routes, remember that you will probably need to specify one or more corresponding routes back on the connecting hosts/routers. Also ensure that when specifying the gateway to use, you specify an interface on your logical subnet. If you are specifying a route for a host rather than a network, either do not specify the destination subnet mask, or specify 255.255.255.255 to indicate that this is a host address and not a network address.

Verifying dynamic routes in the routing table will be more difficult simply because there could be so many of them (particularly if using RIP) and they are more difficult to verify.

Router Configuration

First, ensure that the Windows 2000 Server is correctly enabled for routing, which allows it to forward packets between its interfaces. If you intend to use demand-dial routing, ensure you have configured your port(s), dial-up adapter(s), and account information appropriately.

If you are not using dynamic routing protocols, and you have at least one other router in your network, you will need to have a mechanism for forwarding packets to the correct interface:

- Static routes defined
- Silent RIP enabled
- Dynamic routing protocols installed and added to two or more interfaces

Also check to see whether you have enabled and configured correctly any other services you need to offer, which may include

- IGMP support
- ICMP Router Discovery
- Packet filtering

Dynamic Routing Protocol Configuration

Verify the configuration of both the protocol settings that apply globally, and protocol settings on individual interfaces.

RIP Following are some common problems and issues associated with RIP configuration. In particular, pay attention to compatibility issues if you are using a mixture of RIPv1 and RIPv2 on your network. In addition:

- Remember that the limitation of RIP is that it supports a maximum of 15 routers—if your network exceeds this number, it cannot support RIP. Whenever RIP identifies more than 15 hops between source and destination host, the path will fail with a "Destination Unreachable" routing error. Sometimes hop counts are artificially changed so that slow links are allocated a higher hop number—remember, the total number of hops must not exceed 15!
- For efficiency problems such as slow convergence times, check the RIP convergence options.
- On networks with RIPv1 routers, verify that RIPv2 is configured for broadcast announcements rather than using multicasts, and verify that incoming announcements are set to RIPv1 and RIPv2.

- If you are using RIPv2 configured for multicasts, ensure Silent RIP hosts are correctly updating their routing tables. If they are not, it could be because the routers cannot support RIP2. See if you can upgrade them, or consider configuring the routers for broadcast announcements instead of multicasts.
- If you have routers on your network that use RIPv1, ensure you are not using VLSMs, disjointed subnets, or supernetting.
- If you are using RIPv2 with authentication, ensure all routers are configured similarly, all with authentication and all using the same (case-sensitive) password.
- If you are using peer filtering, verify you have the correct IP addresses for the neighboring peer RIP routers.
- If you are using RIP route filtering, verify that the ranges of network IDs for your internetwork are included (rather than being excluded).
- If you are using RIP neighbors, verify you have specified the correct IP addresses for unicast RIP announcements.
- Verify IP packet filtering is not preventing the receiving (through input filters) or sending (through output filters) of RIP announcements on the router interfaces enabled for RIP. Similarly, verify that TCP/IP filtering on the router interfaces is not preventing the receiving of RIP traffic. RIP traffic uses UDP port 520.
- If you are using demand-dial routing with auto-static updates, ensure the demand-dial interface is configured to use RIPv2 multicast announcements. Broadcasts will not work in this environment because the two systems are on different subnets.
- If you want to propagate host and/or default routes between routers, configure the nondefault setting in the Advanced tab on the RIP interface Properties.

OSPF Because of the differences between how RIP and OSPF work, configuration issues with this protocol are very different. It is important to configure each router for its assigned role and ensure it forms adjacencies with its neighbors—a failure to do so will result in incomplete routing tables.

The following configurations must be the same on neighboring routers:

- Authentication set on or off, and when it is being used, all routers must use the same (case-sensitive) password.
- The Hello interval (default 10secs).
- The Dead interval (recommendation is four times the Hello interval).
- Area ID.
- The stub setting.

To test adjacencies, use *tracert* to report the path between one router and its neighbor—there should be a direct path.

Also bear in mind the following:

- The Router ID of two neighboring routers must not match.
- Ensure you have correctly assigned multicast addresses for NBNA networks.
- There must be a Designated Router per area (the State column on the relevant OSPF interface will display "Designated Router," and for resilience you should also have a Backup Designated Router assigned). If you do not have a DR, check the Router Priority Level of your routers—one or more should be higher than 0.
- Ensure all ABRs are either physically or logically (via virtual link) connected to the backbone.

If your AS fails to route with other ASs (e.g., routes using other protocols such as RIP), check the configuration of the external routes on the ASBRs to ensure they aren't blocking these packets. ASBRs are responsible for learning and then propagating external routes, which then become integrated with the OSPF routing table (SPF) except in stub areas. If you want to increase routing efficiency when routing to other ASs, do not use stub areas so that a shortest path will have a lower cost (but at the expense of larger routing tables which results in a higher convergence time). However, if your priority is to increase routing efficiency when routing just within the AS, use stub areas to prevent external routes flooding each area—traffic to external routes will still succeed via the ASBR, but will have a higher cost.

CertCam 9-9

EXERCISE 9-9

Using PathPing to Examine Which Paths Are Used in a Route, and the Quality of Each Link

Try using PathPing yourself—to a computer on the same subnet, to a computer on a subnet the other side of your router, and to a computer over the Internet. Beware that it can take considerable time to complete this command—it is not as quick as Tracert because it has the additional information and computations to process.

What can you deduce from the results? Well, the following illustration shows the results of using PathPing from a computer in my company to a host on the Internet (www.bbc.co.uk) when I was experiencing a slow response connecting to their Web site. This slow response could have been because the Web server was busy, or because of a slow routing problem. I used PathPing against the Web server's IP address to check for routing problems.

```
H:\WINNT\System32\cmd.exe

H:\>pathping 212.58.224.32

Tracing route to 212.58.224.32 over a maximum of 30 hops

  0  metascyb-b0uyfy.metascybe-test.com [193.129.98.72]
  1  193.129.98.126
  2  158.43.206.9
  3  158.43.194.2
  4  195.66.225.25
  5  195.66.225.25
  6  212.58.255.113
  7  212.58.224.32

Computing statistics for 175 seconds...
            Source to Here   This Node/Link
Hop  RTT    Lost/Sent = Pct  Lost/Sent = Pct  Address
  0                                           metascyb-b0uyfy.metascybe-test.com
 [193.129.98.72]
                                0/ 100 =  0%   |
  1    0ms     0/ 100 =  0%     0/ 100 =  0%  193.129.98.126
                                0/ 100 =  0%   |
  2   31ms     0/ 100 =  0%     0/ 100 =  0%  158.43.206.9
                                0/ 100 =  0%   |
  3   30ms     0/ 100 =  0%     0/ 100 =  0%  158.43.194.2
                                0/ 100 =  0%   |
  4   30ms     0/ 100 =  0%     0/ 100 =  0%  195.66.225.25
                                0/ 100 =  0%   |
  5   30ms     0/ 100 =  0%     0/ 100 =  0%  195.66.225.25
                                0/ 100 =  0%   |
  6  101ms     0/ 100 =  0%     0/ 100 =  0%  212.58.255.113
                                0/ 100 =  0%   |
  7   30ms     0/ 100 =  0%     0/ 100 =  0%  212.58.224.32

Trace complete.

H:\>_
```

You can see how the command traversed eight individual routes (starting at 0 with 1 denoting the first router) to complete the source to destination path with no packet loss. Knowing a bit about the topology of the network, I can identify potentially four different ASs. There's four routers involved, with routes 0–1 being on my AS (I recognize these addresses), routers 2–3 being in my ISP's AS (again, I recognize these addresses), and 6–7 being last in the route have to be in the AS of the destination host (in this case, the BBC). Routes 5–7 are unknown intermediate routers.

Each individual route took about 30ms, with the exception of one (from route 5–6) that took 101ms. This tells us that the biggest delay in connecting to our destination host lies between routers 195.66.225.25 and 212.58.255.113. Because there is no reported packet loss, this delay is unlikely to be down to a bad link, and more likely to be a routing delay on router 195.66.225.25, or a slow link between 195.66.225.25 and 212.58.255.113.

If I were to repeat this exercise later, I might find a different route being taken, or the same route but with different responses. If the same route were taken, but the delay between 195.66.225.25 and 212.58.255.113 was considerably less, this could indicate that the initial delay was probably due to this router being too busy to route efficiently rather than a slow link.

CERTIFICATION SUMMARY

We covered a lot of material in this chapter because IP routing is such a large and complex subject! Before explaining how to install and configure Windows 2000 as an IP router, we looked at some basic definitions and concepts of what routing is, how it works, and some of the problems associated with it. This basic level of understanding is fundamental to understanding how specific implementations work and the configuration choices you have.

We then covered installing and configuring Windows 2000 as an IP router, including such components as multicasting and support for IGMP, ICMP Router Discovery, and defining static routes. We looked in some detail at installing and configuring the two routing protocols Windows 2000 supports: RIP and OSPF. You should now have a better understanding not just how each of these routing protocols work, but the advantages and disadvantages of both, so you can make a better-informed choice of which to use. Although RIP will undoubtedly remain a more popular choice for many companies, we spent more time discussing and explaining OSPF because it is a more complex routing protocol, and for many of us requires learning new terminology and new concepts before being able to understand the configuration options.

Demand-dial routing was covered next for nonpermanent links, and we saw how tightly this integrated with remote access, including components such as security and authentication, and remote access policies.

The RRAS snap-in offers a nice GUI to pull together all of the features and services the Remote Access and Routing server offers. From here you can view, monitor, log, and configure the various services and protocols installed.

Finally, we looked at some trouble-shooting methods with suggestions of how to narrow down and identify problems, and things to watch out for.

✓ TWO-MINUTE DRILL

Overview of Windows 2000 IP Routing

- ❑ The Routing and Remote Access service offers a complex and tightly integrated suite of services, including acting as a router for IPX, AppleTalk, and IP.
- ❑ Additionally, it offers Remote Access, DHCP Relay Agent, Network Address Translation, ICMP Router Discovery, and IGMP support.
- ❑ Routing is the process of forwarding packets from one computer (source host) on one network to another computer (destination host) on another network, either directly if the destination host is on a network directly attached to the router, or indirectly via another router if the destination host is not on a network directly attached to the router
- ❑ Windows 2000 offers a software routing service rather than a hardware router, which has advantages of tight integration with other Windows 2000 features and benefits, ease of use with a GUI interface, flexibility of running in conjunction with other applications/services, and is potentially cheaper than a hardware router.
- ❑ A hardware router is generally faster and more efficient at routing, because it is dedicated to this function. Additionally, a hardware router usually supports a greater number of protocols and advanced routing configuration options.
- ❑ Networks can be routed or nonrouted. There may be genuine reasons why you don't want to route between two connected networks (e.g., security, bandwidth control).
- ❑ Routes can be static or dynamic, and are stored in a routing table. All Windows 2000 TCP/IP computers only have one routing table for all routes and all protocols.
- ❑ Dynamic routing protocols such as RIP and OSPF reduce administrative overheads, since routes are learned automatically.

- ❑ Dynamic routing results in additional overhead on the router and the network, but one of its greatest benefits is that it can automatically sense and recover from internetwork faults.
- ❑ A TCP/IP computer sends nonlocal traffic to its default gateway when there is no specific route defined for it.
- ❑ Routing table entries include a Destination Address, Gateway Address, Interface, Metric – and Lifetime (although the Lifetime doesn't display in the routing table).

Enabling and Configuring Windows 2000 as an IP Software Router

- ❑ Enabling the Router option in the RRAS snap-in automatically allows packets to pass between each of its interfaces.
- ❑ You do not need to install routing protocols to be able to route packets from one interface on your router to another interface.
- ❑ You can add static routes with the Route Add command, Netsh utility, and with the RRAS snap-in.
- ❑ Multicasting makes much more efficient use of network bandwidth by sending a single message to multiple hosts through one IP address. Multicasting can be used to facilitate automatic discovery of network services and is the mechanism by which RIPv2 and OSPF routers communicate with their neighboring routers. However, there is no need to install the IGMP Routing Protocol on the RRAS server unless you need to route IGMP between your intranet and the multicast backbone on the Internet (e.g., for audio-streaming data).
- ❑ Through multicasts, Windows 2000 Router supports ICMP Router Discovery to automatically assign a valid default gateway to TCP/IP hosts that don't already have one.
- ❑ TCP/IP hosts that support ICMP Router Discovery send out *router solicitations* to discover routers on their networks, and they choose the router with the highest preference level in its response.
- ❑ Routers offering ICMP Router Discovery send out *router advertisements* both in response to router solicitations and periodically to notify hosts on the network that the router is still available.

Implementing Routing Protocols

- To use dynamic routing protocols, you first add them via RRAS, and then add to them the interfaces you want to use.
- Two dynamic routing protocols offered by Windows 2000 are RIP (a distance vector-based routing protocol) and OSPF (a link state-based routing protocol).
- Convergence time is very important in dynamic routing, and refers to the time it takes for all routing tables to be updated so that all network routes are known and valid. It is desirable that this is done quickly and with the minimum amount of information.
- Advantages of a distance vector-based protocol such as RIP include its simple configuration with low administrative overhead.
- Disadvantages of a distance vector-based protocol such as RIP include potentially large routing tables, high bandwidth requirements, lack of scalability, and a high convergence time.
- Advantages of a link state-based routing protocol such as OSPF include smaller routing tables, lower bandwidth requirements, ability to scale, and a lower convergence time.
- Disadvantages of a link state-based routing protocol such as OSPF include complexity in design and configuration, and potentially resource intensive on large networks.
- Common problems with dynamic routing include rogue routers, routing loops, count-to-infinity, black holes, overhead of large and complex routing tables, high network bandwidth, and slow convergence. RIP is particularly vulnerable to these, and many of its configuration options are aimed at addressing or minimizing these problems.
- When a Windows 2000 router learns of two different routes to the same destination, the metric is used to determine which is the preferred route, and only that route is stored in the routing table.
- When a Windows 2000 router learns of two different routes by two different protocols to the same destination, the metric is ignored; instead, it's the route that comes from the Preferred Source, which is stored in the routing table. Preference levels are configured under IP Routing | General | Preferences | Preferences tab.

- ❑ Common routing terminology you will hear with large internetworks include AS (Autonomous System), IGP (Interior Gateway Protocol), and EGP (Exterior Gateway Protocol).
- ❑ RIP and OSPF are both examples of IGPs; Windows 2000 supports EGPs through APIs, but does not provide any EGPs "out of the box."

RIP for IP

- ❑ RIP for IP supports both RIPv1 and RIPv2. RIPv1 can only work with broadcasts, has no protection from rogue routers, and does not announce the subnet mask. RIPv2 can use multicasts as well as broadcasts, offers authentication as protection against rogue routers, supports a route tag, and does announce the subnet mask (which means nondefault masks such as VLSMs are supported).
- ❑ You can configure a Windows 2000 router for RIPv1 compatibility if you have other RIPv1 routers on your network.
- ❑ RIPv2 supports many of the newer and more desirable features found in OSPF, but with lower administrative costs. This makes it a suitable choice in all but very large networks (it can still only support paths of up to 15 routers).
- ❑ Windows 2000 with RIP offers the ability to modify the following: convergence options, announcement intervals, and the routing table entry timeout. It supports the following: Silent RIP, peer filtering, route filtering, RIP neighbors, and announce or accept default routes or host routes.

OSPF

- ❑ Benefits of using this routing protocol include the following: more efficient use of network bandwidth, uses only multicasts with acknowledgments, lower convergence times, smaller routing tables, routing information is only announced when there are changes rather than periodically, scales well (up to 255 routers), and offers protection against rogue routers with authentication.
- ❑ OSPF's terminology includes areas, boundaries, Link State Advertisements (LSAs), flooding, Link state Database (LSDB), cost, and default route.
- ❑ Areas and routers are uniquely identified by logical names that have the same format as IP addresses—32-bit dotted decimal number.

- An OSPF network must have at least one area; if more than one area, it must have a backbone area with ID 0.0.0.0 that all other areas report to.
- You must configure an OSPF router for a particular network type. Choices are Broadcast, Point-to-Point, and Non-Broadcast Multiple Access (NBMA). The packets it sends over these are multicasts or unicasts—*never* broadcasts!
- An OSPF router must be defined as an Area Border Router (ABR), Internal Router (IR), or an AS Border Router (ASBR).
- OSPF routers must form adjacencies with their neighbors, which is achieved with Hello packets.
- Within each area, routers choose a Designated Router (DR) and a Backup Designated Router (BDR) through an election process—the router with the highest priority wins.
- An OSPF's router's default priority is 1, which can be changed under OSPF's interface properties, General tab. Set it to 0 if you don't want your router to enter the election, and set it to 255 if you want it to be the DR. You must have at least one router on your OSPF network that is capable of being a DR, or the LSDB will fail to synchronize.
- Routing information can be further controlled and reduced with the use of external route filters and stub areas.
- OSPF must be correctly configured to work; unlike RIP, it is not a "point and click" implementation! Depending on the role of your router, certain configurations must be set.

Demand-Dial Routing

- A dial-on demand routing connection does not have a permanent connection—the connection is only made when required (for example, when the dial-on-demand interface is asked to forward packets over its interface).
- All connections use PPP over either a physical medium (e.g., modem or ISDN) or tunnel medium (e.g., PPTP or L2TP).
- Demand-dial routing allows you to connect to the Internet, to connect branch offices, or to implement router-to-router VPNs.

- Demand-dial connections have the benefit of offering cost-efficient dial-up WAN links when they are configured with an idle timeout, because you only pay for the connection when there is data to transfer.
- The two types of demand-dial connections are *on-demand* and *persistent,* both of which can be either *two-way initiated* or *one-way initiated.*
- Security for demand-dial connections use the same security features as remote access connections, which include remote access permission, authentication, encryption, callback, Caller ID, and remote access account lockout.
- Although remote access and demand-dial routing have many components in common, the primary difference is that remote access connects a single user to a remote access network, whereas demand-dial routing connects two networks.
- Common components between remote access and demand-dial routing include the PPP connection negotiation, the use of physical or logical ports, use of remote access permission, authentication and encryption, remote access policies, use of authentication providers, and PPP features such as multilink, BAP, compression, and logging/auditing/tracing.
- The configuration of demand-dial routing includes installing and configuring the demand-dial interface, configuring the authentication at both ends of the connection, and defining static routes where necessary. Optionally, you can configure demand-dial filters and demand-dial hours for the calling router, which apply if the demand-dial interface is in a disconnected state.
- Remote access policies can be used with demand-dial routing to define and control conditions and settings on the answering router.
- Only use dynamic routing protocols over a demand-dial route if it is a persistent connection, and consider changing some of the routing configurations to be sympathetic to a slower link.

Troubleshooting IP Routing Problems

- Before troubleshooting an IP routing problem, ensure it is a routing problem and not a problem with hardware, basic TCP/IP configuration, or name resolution.

- Troubleshooting IP routing problems is difficult and complex because routing is a distributed and dynamic service.
- One of the most reliable and recommended approaches to troubleshooting routing is to methodically check forward from the source computer to the final destination computer until you find the break in the complete route.
- Don't dive into changing routing options without an understanding of how routing works and appreciating the potential consequences of your changes.
- Troubleshooting tools include ARP –a to check the MAC to IP address, Route Print to check the current routing table, Ping to check reachability of a host, Tracert to check the route a packet travels, Pathping to both trace the route taken and compute response times on each link, and a network monitor to capture the traffic.
- Verify the following: TCP/IP configuration on hosts, routing tables, router configuration, and dynamic routing protocol configuration.
- Remember that routing tables aren't static, even when not using dynamic routing protocols.
- Check configuration on the router of the following if enabled: IGMP, ICMP Router Discovery, and packet filtering.
- If using RIP, check configuration options and pay particular attention to compatibility issues between RIPv1 and RIPv2.
- If using OSPF, check configuration options and pay particular attention to forming adjacencies (certain values must have the same settings on neighboring routers).

SELF TEST

The following questions will help you measure your understanding of the material presented in this chapter. Read all of the choices carefully, as there may be more than one correct answer. Choose all correct answers for each question.

Overview of Windows 2000 IP Routing

1. What are some of the true differences between a hardware router and RRAS in Windows 2000 acting as a software router? (Select all that apply.)

A. Hardware routers usually don't have a GUI interface, attached monitor, and keyboard—Windows 2000 offers all of these.

B. Windows 2000 has the benefit of tight integration with other Windows 2000 features that hardware routers wouldn't normally be able to offer.

C. Hardware routers can be configured to route multiple protocols, whereas Windows 2000 can only route with one protocol at a time (either RIP or OSPF).

D. Hardware routers have more configuration options, and are therefore slower at routing.

2. You have three network adapters in your Windows 2000 Server and have assigned to your computer three separate IP addresses. You plan to use two different routing protocols. How many default gateways should you define on this computer?

A. One

B. Two

C. Three

D. Six

Enabling and Configuring Windows 2000 as an IP Software Router

3. When wouldn't you need to install routing protocols? (Select all that apply.)

A. When you only have two segments in your network.

B. When you have multiple segments in your network, but your Windows 2000 RRAS Server is attached to all of them through multiple interfaces.

C. When you prefer to define static routes for greater control and security.

D. When you want your router to be a Silent RIP router that doesn't advertise its presence on the network, but can still automatically add routes from other routers.

4. You have been asked to only use multicasts on your Windows 2000 RRAS Server and not broadcasts. Which of the following are valid reasons for installing IGMP (Internet Group Multicast Protocol) to ensure you comply with this request? (Select all that apply.)

A. When you want to use OSPF routing

B. When you want to use RIPv1 routing

C. When you want to use RIPv2 routing

D. When you want to provide workstations with multicast services from the Internet

5. You are responsible for a completely Windows 2000 network with RRAS routers and DHCP servers on your multisegmented TCP/IP network. What's the best way of ensuring your Windows 2000 Professionals always have a valid default gateway to ensure nonlocal traffic is routed? (Select all that apply.)

A. Configure multiple DHCP servers for resilience, and on these configure different default gateways with the TCP/IP assignment.

B. Do not configure your DHCP servers to assign a default gateway.

C. Configure one of your Windows 2000 RRAS Servers for ICMP Router Discovery.

D. Configure all of your Windows 2000 Professionals for Router Solicitation, so they can accept a default gateway through ICMP Router Discovery.

E. Configure all of your Windows 2000 RRAS Servers for ICMP Router Discovery.

Implementing Routing Protocols

6. Which of the following are disadvantages of a distance vector-based routing protocol such as RIP? (Select all that apply.)

A. Large routing tables

B. High bandwidth requirements

C. Low convergence times

D. Inability to scale up

7. Your router has four interfaces with RIP on interfaces one and two, and OSPF on interfaces three and four. When it learns of two different routes to the same destination, which does it use? The two different routes are RIP with a routing metric of 1, and OSPF with a routing metric of 3.

A. The RIP route, because it has the lower routing metric.

B. The OSPF route, because it has the higher routing metric.

C. The OSPF route, because OSPF is a more efficient routing protocol than RIP.

D. There's not enough information to determine which route will be used.

RIP for IP

8. If you upgraded your IP routers to support RIPv2, what advantages would this provide? (Select all that apply.)

   A. You could use VLSMs.

   B. You could have some protection from rogue routers by configuring authentication between routers.

   C. Routing tables would be smaller.

   D. You could have more than 15 routers in your network.

9. Increasingly, people have been reporting slow connection times, and a network trace and analysis has showed that a large percentage of available network bandwidth is being taken up by routing exchanges. Which of the following would help to decrease this traffic? (Select all that apply.)

   A. Change from broadcasts to multicasts (upgrading to RIPv2 if necessary).

   B. Increase the announcement interval.

   C. Use triggered updates.

   D. Enable the split horizon convergence option.

OSFP

10. What are some of the advantages of using OSPF rather than RIP on your Windows 2000 RRAS Server? (Select all that apply.)

    A. You can use multicasts rather than broadcasts.

    B. You can have protection from rogue routers with an encrypted password.

    C. Routing tables are smaller; therefore, convergence time is lower.

    D. It can support more than 15 routers.

11. If your OSPF router is capable of communicating with routers that are configured for RIP, what sort of OSPF router do you have?

    A. ABR

    B. IR

C. AR

D. ASBR

12. Which of the following are valid configuration options you could use to reduce the routing information stored and processed on an ASBR? (Select all that apply.)

A. Enable the Stub option.

B. Disable the Import summary advertisements.

C. Define which protocols (e.g., RIPv2, SNMP routes) you will accept.

D. Define which routes you will accept or reject.

Demand-Dial Routing

13. Which of the following are valid reasons to use demand-dial routing? (Select all that apply.)

A. When you don't want a permanent connection for security reasons.

B. When you can't have a permanent connection.

C. When you want a backup connection to your permanent connection.

D. It's more cost efficient because the link is only up when there is data to transfer.

14. Which of the following can be used for a demand-dial interface? (Select all that apply.)

A. A modem

B. A WAN Miniport (used with VPNs)

C. LPT1

D. An Ethernet adapter

15. You have been asked to restrict routing on your one-way initiated demand-dial router that allows users to connect to a Web server on a branch network. It's to be used only for Web traffic and during office hours only. How do you configure this? (Select all that apply.)

A. You configure the dial-out hours on the demand-dial interface for Monday–Friday, 8 A.M.–6 P.M.

B. You configure IP demand-dial filters and IP packet filters to only allow packets that are TCP port 80.

C. You change the remote access policy to allow connections only between Monday–Friday, 8 A.M.–6 P.M.

D. You change the remote access policy to only allow packets that are TCP port 80.

Troubleshooting IP Routing Problems

16. You ping a remote IP address and it comes back as "Request timed out." What could this mean? (Select all that apply.)

A. TCP is correctly installed and configured on the source machine.

B. The destination host is down.

C. Your default gateway is down.

D. There's a router down between you and the host.

17. A failure to form adjacencies is one of the most common problems with OSPF routing. Which of the following must have the same value on OSPF neighboring routers? (Select all that apply.)

A. The Hello interval

B. The Area ID

C. The Router ID

D. The stub setting

LAB QUESTION

Connecting to distributed company resources has become a bit of a problem in your company. In the past, RIP routers were added piecemeal as more subnets were added to the IP network. Now that more people want to access more resources, routing problems are increasing with slow connections and intermittent failures. The network is being slowly migrated over to a Windows 2000 native–domain network with predominantly Windows 2000 computers throughout. The question of using Windows 2000 RRAS as additional or replacement routers has been raised. You have been asked to assess this and put forward your recommendations to address both immediate problems and future requirements within the next five years.

On the strength of your recommendations, Management may be prepared to upgrade both hardware and software if you can make a good case for proposed changes. You need to present your recommendations in the form of a written report. What things would you consider before coming to any conclusions?

SELF TEST ANSWERS

Overview of Windows 2000 IP Routing

1. ☑ A, B. Hardware routers usually don't have a GUI interface, attached monitor, and keyboard, whereas Windows 2000 offers all of these. Additionally, Windows 2000 has the benefit of integrating with other Windows 2000 features such as Active Directory, IPSec, remote access polices, and so forth.
   ☒ C is incorrect because Windows 2000 RRAS can use both RIP and OSPF simultaneously, and also simultaneously support third-party protocols if written to the RRAS API. **D** is incorrect because although hardware routers often have more configuration options, these are usually to optimize routing efficiency rather than to decrease efficiency. When hardware routers are dedicated to routing and nothing else, they are more likely to route more efficiently than any software router, including Windows 2000 RRAS.

2. ☑ A. You should assign just one default gateway or none at all to your computer, even though it has three adapters and you want to run different IP routing protocols over them. This is because Windows 2000 only ever has a single routing table, and as such can only ever have one current default gateway.
   ☒ B, C, and D are incorrect because unlike a hardware router, which may have different routing tables per interface or protocol, Windows 2000 only ever has one single routing table per computer. Grasping this concept is fundamental to understanding how routing works on Windows 2000 computers, and is one of the major differences between a software router and a hardware router.

Enabling and Configuring Windows 2000 as an IP Software Router

3. ☑ A, B, C. When your server is directly attached to the other segments of your network, there is no need to install routing protocols to forward packets from one segment to the other—this happens automatically after enabling the routing option. Workstations should put as their default gateway the IP address of the adapter that is on their subnet, and then they will be able to send packets via the router to the rest of the network. **C** is also correct because you may prefer to use only static routes for greater control and security; for example, you will reduce processing required on the server and have a higher network bandwidth for the actual data packets. However, static routes are vulnerable to human error and being out of date (non fault tolerant if a router or link is down).

☒ D is incorrect because if you want your router to be a Silent RIP router, you will still need to install RIP and then configure it for Silent RIP. This will result in your router being able to benefit from learning other RIP routes without advertising its own presence on the network.

4. ☑ D. You would only need to install IGMP when you want to provide multicast services from another network. Typically, this would be to deliver video and audio streaming from the Internet to a workstation on your local area network; however, your router would have to be connected to the MBONE.
☒ A, B, and C are all incorrect reasons for installing and configuring IGMP. It is not needed for routing OSPF or RIP because the multicast packets are not being routed; the data packets are being routed. For example, one router with an interface configured for OSPF sends multicast packets to the next router with an interface configured for OSPF, so there is a direct link between the two interfaces. To ensure your router doesn't use broadcasts, you simply have to configure RIP for multicasts—OSPF uses multicasts only.

5. ☑ B, E. Do not assign a default gateway with a DHCP server. If you do, and this router becomes unavailable, workstations will not be able to benefit from ICMP Router Discovery because they will already have a default gateway assigned (although it's down, they have no way of knowing this). Configure all routers with ICMP Router Discovery, so that if one router goes down that was the default gateway, the workstations will detect this and can choose another default gateway from the other routers.
☒ A would offer DHCP resilience, but not resilience from the assigned default gateway being unavailable. C will automatically provide a default gateway from the router offering the service, but offers no fault tolerance if this router were to be unavailable. If you have multiple routers that are capable of offering this service, it is easier and offers immediate fault tolerance to configure all of them for ICMP Router Discovery—you can artificially determine the order of preference by setting the preference level if required. **D** is unnecessary—Windows 2000 and Windows 98 computers automatically can benefit from ICMP Router Discovery. There's no need to configure anything on the client side. Be aware, however, that Windows NT 4.0 and Windows 95 do not automatically register for Router Solicitations, so do not use this feature when your network includes these down-level clients.

Implementing Routing Protocols

6. ☑ A, B, and D are all potential problems with a distance vector-based routing protocol, and as such are disadvantages of choosing this over a link state-based routing protocol. The higher the number of routers, the larger the routing table, since RIP must record all routes to all routers. High bandwidth requirements are another disadvantage, even if using multicasts rather than broadcasts, because routing information is periodically exchanged even if no changes have occurred. RIP can only support 15 routers; when 16 routes are detected, this is interpreted as an unreachable route. This safety net number helps to guard against impossibly large routing tables and problems such as looping routes and count-to-infinity.

☒ C is not a disadvantage of a distance vector routing protocol. Convergence refers to the time taken for a routing table to be updated with new and correct routes, so the quicker this can be achieved, the better. However, because of the large amount of information that a distance vector routing protocol exchanges, it is vulnerable to a high convergence time, which can lead to high processing and wrong decisions being made about forwarding packets.

7. ☑ **D.** When two routes are learned from the same protocol to the same destination, the one with the lower routing metric will be used. However, because routing metrics are not comparable between RIP and OSPF (one is a hop, the other a cost), which one is preferred will depend on the configured preference level on the router. If OSPF had a higher preference level than RIP, the OSPF route would be used, even though it has a higher routing metric than the RIP route.

☒ **A** is incorrect because the metric is only taken into account when the routing protocol is the same for the same route; in other words, the routing metric is a like-for-like comparison. Then the lowest routing metric would be used. **B** is incorrect because even if the routing metric were being taken into account, it is always the lowest value that wins the day. **C** is incorrect; this is expressing an opinion rather than a technical reason! You may think OSPF is more efficient than RIP and configure the preference level on the router to reflect this, but the decision on which route to use will ultimately depend on the preference level configuration.

RIP for IP

8. ☑ **A, B.** Because RIPv2 advertises the subnet mask, you could use VLSMs without fear that they would be incorrectly interpreted. You could also configure a password to be used between routers, which would offer some protection against rogue routers. However, Windows 2000 offers only a clear-text password rather than an encrypted password, which means it can be captured and read from a network trace.

☒ C is incorrect. Whichever version of RIP you use, it will still be a distance vector routing protocol, which means all routes are stored on all routers. On large networks, that leads to large routing tables, and RIPv2 does nothing to combat this because it is an inherent disadvantage of a distance vector routing protocol. **D** is also incorrect. This is a set limitation of RIP and a safety net for the routing problems it is vulnerable to, such as routing loops. If your network has more than 15 routers, you cannot use RIP.

9. ☑ **A, B.** Changing to mulitcasts will mean fewer packets, because packets are directed. Increasing the announcement interval will mean that routers exchange their routing information less often; however, this could be at the expense of having out-of-date information.
☒ C is incorrect. Using triggered updates will actually increase network traffic, because every time a change to a route is learned, it is announced immediately rather than waiting for the next announcement interval. However, using a longer announcement interval together with triggered updates might be a better overall solution and a good compromise between less routing traffic and having out-of-date information. **D** is also incorrect. The split horizon convergence option is useful for shortening convergence time (how long it takes for all routing tables to be up to date), but will have little impact on the actual routing traffic on the network.

OSFP

10. ☑ **C, D.** Routing tables are smaller because each router only stores information about its neighboring router and not all routers in the network. OSPF can support up to 255 routers, whereas RIP is limited to 15.
☒ A is incorrect. Using multicasts rather than broadcasts is not an advantage of OSPF alone—RIPv2 can also be configured to use multicasts. **B** is incorrect because both RIP and OSPF offer protection with authentication. However, both implementations in Windows 2000 only offer a clear-text password rather than an encrypted password.

11. ☑ **D.** ASBR, which stands for an Autonomous System Border Router, would be the type of OSPF router that would communicate with a router configured with RIP. Each AS can only have one protocol, so by definition, if a router is exposed to two different protocols, it must be on the border between two ASs.
☒ A is incorrect. ABR stands for Area Border Router, and cannot talk to RIP routers. These routers handle traffic between OSPF areas within the AS, and you can only have a single protocol in an AS. **B** is incorrect. IR stands for Internal Router and indicates a router that sits in its own OSPF area. As such, it cannot interact with other ASs, and you can only have a single protocol in an AS. **C** is incorrect. There are many OSPF acronyms to learn, but AR isn't one of them!

12. ☑ **C, D.** Defining protocols and routes are valid configuration options you could use to reduce the routing information stored on an ASBR router.
☒ A is not a valid option for an ASBR router; it would only be valid for an IR (Internal Router) or an ABR (Area Border Router). **B** is also not a valid option for an ASBR router. It would only be valid on an ABR (Area Border Router).

Demand-Dial Routing

13. ☑ A, B, C, D. These could all be valid reasons to use demand-dial routing, but would all require some qualifying, depending on your circumstances. For example, if your priority when routing is security rather than any other need to use demand-dial routing, you may be better off configuring security on a standard interface. For example, you can configure packet filtering on an interface without having to use dial-out filters or remote access policy filters. However, if you are calling out, only a demand-dial interface allows you to restrict the days of the week and times of the day the link can be initiated. As such, this offers greater security than if you had a standard interface for routing. B. A perfect example of when and why demand-dial routing is used is when you can't have a permanent connection. C. Another classic example of when demand-dial routing is configured is when you want a backup connection to your permanent connection. However, your backup doesn't have to be demand-dial; it's usually chosen when a standard interface can't be used as a backup, or the different medium is considered to add resilience. D. It's more cost efficient because the link is only up when there is data to transfer could be true if you are using on-demand demand-dialing where either router will drop the link after a specified idle timeout. However, this should only be used when this type of connection is more cost effective than a persistent line; for example, a dedicated leased line or a line that incurred only local charges. You may find that if you are frequently using this demand-dial router, the costs of constantly setting up a new connection could be more expensive overall than the cost of a persistent link.

14. ☑ A, B, C. These are all examples of ports that can be used for a demand-dial interface. Ports don't have a permanent connection, but must make a temporary connection over PPP, with examples of ports being a modem, a WAN Miniport, and a parallel port. To use these with demand-dial routing, you must configure them for demand-dial routing, enable the router for demand-dial routing, and then add the demand-dial interface(s).

☒ D is incorrect. An Ethernet adapter cannot be used as a demand-dial adapter because it has a permanent connection without having to use PPP to establish a temporary connection.

15. ☑ A, B. You would set the dial-out hours on the demand-dial interface, and then set the IP demand-dial filters. However, because the dial-out filters only apply when the interface is disconnected, it would be a wise precaution to also configure IP packets for those times when the interface is already connected.

☒ C and D are incorrect. You would only make changes to the remote access policy for an incoming connection—your router is one-way initiated, and your router is calling out. If these restrictions were required on the answering router, then the remote policies on the remote router should be set to accommodate them.

Troubleshooting IP Routing Problems

16. ☑ **B, C, D.** These could all be possible reasons why you might get a Request Timed Out when pinging a remote address. The destination host could be down, your default gateway could be down (if the packet was being routed via the default gateway), or one or more routers could be down in the complete path between you and the destination host.
☒ A is incorrect because although it confirms you have TCP/IP configured, it does not confirm that it is correctly configured. For example, you may have the wrong subnet address, which means that the remote address is being interpreted as a local address and never gets sent to the default gateway. Additionally, you may not have a default gateway assigned. Be careful not to make assumptions with the results of a ping command!

17. ☑ **A, B, D.** The Hello interval, the Area ID, and the stub setting must all have the same value on neighboring OSPF routers, or adjacencies will not be formed.
☒ C is incorrect. The Router ID must be unique for each router in that area.

LAB ANSWER

- Current topology of the network to obtain better understanding of the various subnets, workstations, server and routers with projected growth. Remember, the larger the network, the less suitable a distance vector routing protocol becomes, and the more vulnerable it becomes to certain problems. Decide on the pay-off between controlling these problems with better configuration, or cutting your losses and advocating a state link-based protocol that is more suited to a large network but more difficult to configure.
- Efficiency of current routers, looking to see if they could be better configured.
- Some network statistics to highlight common patterns, problems, and delays.
- If currently using RIPv1, advantages and disadvantages of upgrading to RIPv2.
- If currently using RIP, advantages and disadvantages of migrating to OSPF.
- Outline of routing configurations to use (which ones are applicable to your network).
- Advantages and disadvantages of hardware routers vs. software routers.
- Plans for monitoring and managing.
- Plans for resilience and fault tolerance.
- Resources required for any changes, including retraining for network administrators and potential testing time and downtime.

MCSE

MICROSOFT CERTIFIED SYSTEMS ENGINEER

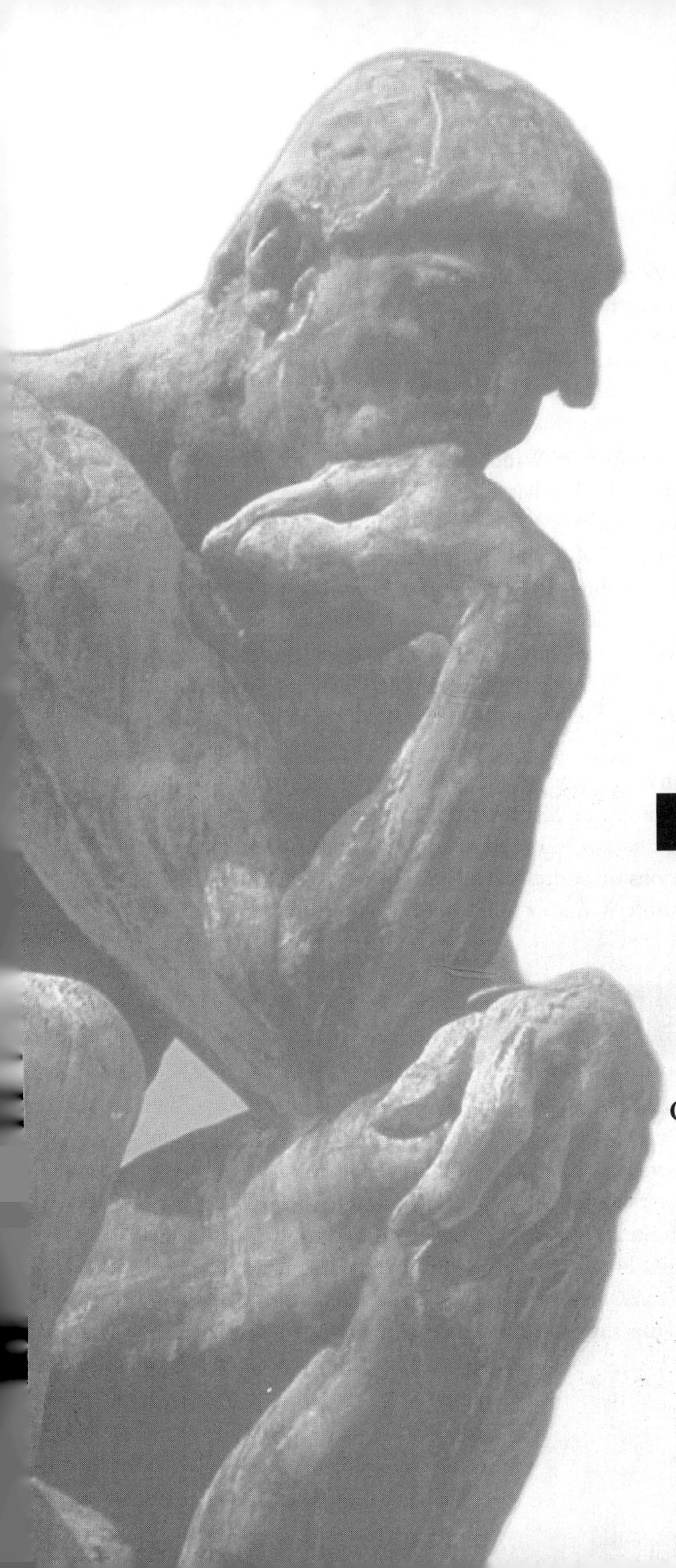

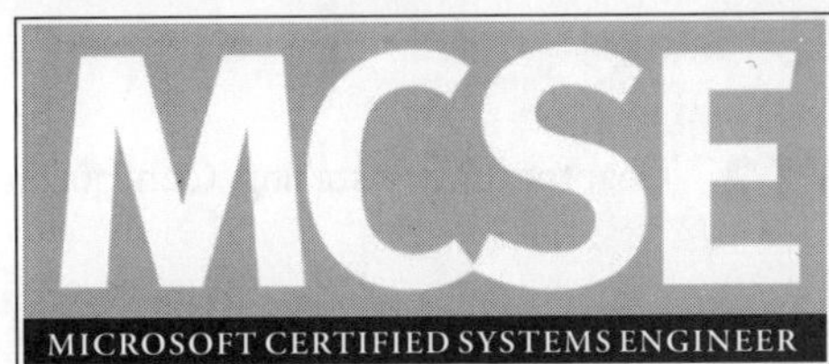

10

Installing, Configuring, and Troubleshooting NAT

CERTIFICATION OBJECTIVES

10.01	Overview of ICS and NAT
10.02	Internet Connection Sharing
10.03	Network Address Translation
10.04	Troubleshooting ICS and NAT
✓	Two-Minute Drill
Q&A	Self Test

Many of the new features in Windows 2000 are aimed at the large enterprise environment, so it comes as rather a surprise to see new features specifically aimed at the smallest of networks. However, Windows 2000 is very Internet oriented, and this does relate directly with network address translation (NAT), which is the topic of this chapter.

NAT is a very useful new feature in Windows 2000 from which many people can immediately benefit, and as such it has received a lot of media attention and is being heralded as one of the Windows 2000 benefits. Also, since address translation was not available in Windows NT 4.0 (only in Windows 98 Second Edition), you can be sure it will be covered in the Microsoft exams. Unless you had Windows 98 Second Edition, the previous choices for connecting a Microsoft network to the Internet were to use a directly routed connection, Proxy Server, or a third-party product—so you can see how NAT fills a critical gap in Microsoft networking services. Networking services are the core of Windows 2000, and as such, NAT claims an important role.

This chapter describes in detail exactly what Network Address Translation is, how it works, how to configure it in Windows 2000, when to use it, and its limitations. It contains information you need to know for live implementations as well as for answering questions on address translation in the exam "Implementing and Administering a Microsoft Windows 2000 Network Infrastructure (70-216)."

CERTIFICATION OBJECTIVE 10.01

Overview of ICS and NAT

Windows 2000 Internet Connection Sharing (ICS) and the Network Address Translation (NAT) protocol both offer a relatively simple and inexpensive way for small networks to benefit from an Internet network connection. As such, you will see the abbreviations ICS and NAT in close proximity to another acronym: SOHO, which stands for *Small Office/Home Office* and is the environment perceived as the most likely to benefit from this simple method of connecting to the Internet.

A SOHO network typically has the following characteristics:
- A single segment network
- Peer-to-peer networking
- A single protocol: TCP/IP
- A demand-dial or dedicated link connection to the Internet via an ISP

A user on a SOHO network frequently needs to use more than one computer, and also needs to be able to share resources, such as files, applications, and printers, from one computer to another.

However, despite these typical characteristics that define SOHO, bear in mind this is only a theoretical definition. In reality the clear textbook definitions can blur into less distinct categories. For example, SOHO may include workstations with multiple protocols and servers for DHCP, WINS, and DNS. And it may have more than one segment. Additionally, although ICS and NAT are envisaged as being suited to SOHO, it may also have a place in the corporate network. So be prepared to be flexible in your perceptions of how and when these services could be deployed. They could even be mixed; for example, a small branch office could be defined as a SOHO network that connects via the Internet to your corporate network. Using VPNs in a SOHO environment will be covered in a later section.

When you connect a workstation on a private network to the Internet, your connection will be either *routed* or *translated.* Routing was covered in Chapter 9, "Installing, Configuring, Managing, Monitoring, and Troubleshooting IP Routing," with an explanation of how to connect networks together and direct packets from one network to another. The theory of connecting together two private networks still holds for when you want to connect your private network to the public Internet. However, in this scenario, you have the administrative overhead of more carefully managing and configuring network traffic and security, because you don't want to expose your internal networks and resources to unlawful access or unwanted traffic.

A translated connection transparently transfers packets between one network (such as your internal company network) and another (such as an external network like the Internet). One computer connected to both networks converts packets from your internal network (with private addresses) to packets to the Internet (with public addresses), and vice versa. The benefit of this is that internal addresses are completely hidden from the Internet, because all traffic appears to come from the one computer. This is the opposite of a routed connection, where the source and destination IP addresses remain the same irrespective of how many hops(routers) the packets have to traverse before reaching their final destination. With a translated connection, the source and destination addresses of the computers on the internal network are converted into the address of the one computer running the translation service—which is how the IP addresses of computers remain "hidden."

on the job

Masquerading is another term used when hiding the true IP address of the sending/receiving client workstation, and Address Aggregation is another term you might hear to describe many private workstations connecting over one public (or a few) Internet addresses.

Why Share an Internet Connection?

As outlined earlier, security is one of the automatic advantages of having a translated connection—and both ICS and NAT use translation rather than routing. A translated connection is easier to secure than a routed connection, because hosts on the Internet will not know the true identity of your workstations (which, for example, will significantly reduce the risk of Denial of Service attacks).

Simplicity is another reason to share an Internet connection—it is easier to set up, configure, and share one single Internet connection than to correctly set up and configure multiple connections for each computer on your network that needs Internet access. You can allow multiple computers on your network to have Internet access without adding additional client software or reconfiguring them.

Cost is anther factor when considering whether to share an Internet connection. It is obviously cheaper to have just one Internet connection with its single associated hardware and ISP costs and share it among multiple computers than have an Internet connection on each computer. Also, the administrative overheads of managing and configuring just one connection rather than multiple connections will be lower.

However, some limitations of a translated connection determine whether ICS and/or the NAT protocol are suitable. These limitations will be discussed later.

exam watch

Benefits of ICS and NAT include low cost and low administrative overhead.

What's the Difference between ICS and NAT?

Internet Connection Sharing and NAT both work by offering to workstations on small networks:

- Address translation
- Address assignment
- Name resolution

So what's the difference between ICS and NAT?

Although similar in purpose, the NAT protocol offers more functions and greater flexibility than ICS—ICS is a cut-down, simplified version of NAT. This doesn't necessarily denigrate the status of ICS, because in the simplest environments, ICS may be a better choice over NAT. As a network administrator, it is your responsibility to know the differences between them, and what each offers before making an informed choice as to which is better to implement.

Features of ICS

First, protocols are distinguished by how and where you configure them. ICS is a feature of the Network and Dial-Up Connections, while NAT is presented as a routing protocol to be added and configured through the Routing and Remote Access snap-in.

ICS in Windows 2000 offers the simplest Internet connection service, and can be configured on either a computer running Windows 2000 Professional or on a Windows 2000 Server. The ICS computer must have two network connections—one to your internal network with a private address, and the other to the Internet, which will use a publicly assigned IP address. Typically, the connection to the Internet would be a dial-up modem or ISDN adapter, but you could also use a dedicated connection such as cable modem, DSL, or even a fractional T1 line. Your ISP could statically assign your public IP address to you, or it could be dynamically assigned when you connect.

To configure ICS on Windows 2000 Professional/Server, you use the Make New Connection Wizard to create your Internet connection just as we saw in Chapter 5, "Configuring, Managing, Monitoring, and Troubleshooting Remote Access," selecting the "Dial-up to the Internet" option and specifying the adapter to use with a number to connect to the Internet (e.g., as supplied by your ISP). ICS is then enabled when you select the option "Enable Internet Connection Sharing for this connection" in the

Internet Connection Sharing dialog box. If you have already configured your Internet connection, this option is under the connection's Properties | Sharing tab.

This option will configure automatic IP address assignment for the workstations on the private network so that all workstations on the private network use the same (private) network address, and it automatically assigns the IP address of 192.168.0.1 to the internally connected adapter.

ICS is suitable for a single segmented private network with up to 254 workstations, where all workstations are configured to automatically receive an IP address. It allows you to share one public IP address among these workstations, providing there are no other servers on the same segment offering DNS or DHCP services. In such a configuration it automatically resolves Internet DNS names, but it doesn't offer WINS resolution for your internal workstations. The only configuration is for defining static mappings (discussed later). There may be some applications and services that will not translate correctly (this will be discussed later), which may limit what applications you can use through an ICS connection.

exam Watch

To configure Internet Connection Sharing, you must be a member of the Administrators group.

NAT Features

NAT can only be run on a Windows 2000 Server through the Routing and Remote Access snap-in, as a routing protocol. You'll need to add at least two interfaces to the new NAT component (minimum of one connected to the Internet and one connected to your private network), but you can use multiple adapters, which allows you to use multiple subnets on your private network. The Internet-connected interface would typically be a dedicated connection such as a fractional T1 line, DSL, or cable modem, but you can also use it with a demand-dial adapter/modem.

NAT configuration options include settings for dynamic mappings, static mappings, address assignment, and name resolution (all discussed later). These options include allowing your internal clients to automatically receive IP addresses from this server or from a standard DHCP server (or use static addresses), and whether you want the NAT server to resolve DNS names for connecting clients. As with ICS, there may be some applications and services that will not translate correctly (this will be discussed later), which may limit what applications you can use through a NAT connection.

Multiple Public Addresses on the NAT Server An importance difference with NAT is that you can use more than one public IP address on the server, which provides scalability since your internal workstations can be mapped to a pool of public Internet addresses to take advantage of better throughput and availability. Or you can more finely control access by assigning certain services or machines to specific Internet IP addresses—this being one way of offering secure reverse proxying where a machine on your internal network is dedicated to offering, for example, an Internet Web server without revealing its real (private) address. Similarly, you can use special port mappings where, for example, the default http port 80 is advertised for your company Web server but the Web server on your private network is actually hosting this service on port 1234.

exam Watch

You cannot use more than one Internet IP address with ICS—only NAT allows you to do this with either multiple Internet adapters and/or Internet address pools.

You should now be able to answer which of the two solutions would be more suitable in given circumstances.

What's the Difference Between an Address Translation Service and a Proxy Server Service?

Microsoft and third-party vendors offer both NAT and Proxy server solutions for connecting private networks to the Internet. In either case, there are two interfaces as described above. Proxy servers also use a form of address translation to convert private addresses to a single public address. However, proxy translation may not comply with RFC 1631 (NAT specifications), and proxies provide additional features such as sophisticated filtering and web caching.

The "easy" and theoretical answer to this is that Microsoft's Proxy Server is aimed at large and complex corporate networks, NAT at the medium-small sized networks, and ICS at the smallest and simplest of networks. However, it's more useful to know why these generalizations apply by looking into what services they offer and their limitations.

Application Layer vs. Network Layer

For a start, a proxy server works at the Session or Application layer, and NAT at the Network layer. While this may seem to be a theoretical difference only, in practice this means that additional software and/or reconfiguration is needed on the client workstations in order to use the proxy server's services. For example in a Microsoft Proxy Server environment, a workstation running Windows 2000 Professional on a

SCENARIO & SOLUTION

Which Should I Use If...	ICS or NAT
I want the easiest solution to set up and configure?	ICS is the easiest solution to set up and configure; it's simply a check box as one of your Dial-up connection properties. NAT is more complicated to set up and configure because it offers more of a flexible service.
I want to use Windows 2000 Professional rather than Windows 2000 Server?	ICS can be set up on either Windows 2000 Professional or Windows 2000 Server, but NAT can only be set up on a Windows 2000 Server with Routing and Remote Access enabled.
I want to take advantage of a pool of public Internet addresses for better availability, or reserve an Internet address just for an Internet Web server on my private network?	Only NAT allows you to have more than one Internet address on your single connection.
I want to host Internet services on my internal workstations with a fractional T1 line?	Both ICS and NAT allow you do this.
I want my workstations to get IP addresses and other DHCP options from a standard DHCP server, rather than from the computer hosting the Internet connection?	Only NAT allows you to do this.
I want a choice over how DNS names are resolved?	Only NAT gives you this choice.
I want to configure settings for static mappings?	Both ICS and NAT allow you do this.
I want to configure settings for dynamic mappings?	Only NAT gives you this choice.

private network that wants to connect a telnet session to an Internet host must have the WinSock Proxy Client software installed.

Additionally, because the conversion is processed higher up the stack, additional processing is needed at the workstation and/or the server. Microsoft's Proxy Server actually offers three services: Web Proxy, WinSock Proxy, and Socks Proxy. Together, these three services offer just about any and every Internet application and service a workstation could need (including IPX clients and non-Microsoft workstations such as UNIX and Macintoshes).

For Web access and FTP, Internet Explorer 5 can be automatically configured to use proxy servers. However, for other connections such as Telnet, NNTP, POP3, NFS, and IRC, and for IPX clients, you will have to install and configure the WinSock Proxy

Client software. Paradoxically, for larger organizations the additional overhead of configuring the client workstations could be less important than it might be for smaller networks, because larger organizations are usually more adept at deploying workstation configuration (e.g., use of SMS and/or specialist deployment teams).

Administrative Overhead

For the additional overhead in configuring a more complex service, as well as additional computer resources required, a proxy server may be a more expensive solution for a SOHO environment. In a larger network, Microsoft's Proxy Server offers better security and greater flexibility than ICS or NAT. For example, you can define which services can be used by users and groups, ban access to specified

SCENARIO & SOLUTION

Will ICS or NAT Suffice, or Should I Use Microsoft's Proxy Server?	
If I have just one connection to the Internet and want to hide my private addresses?	ICS and NAT fulfill this requirement.
If I want to use reverse proxying to offer an Internet Web service on one of my internal workstations?	ICS and NAT fulfill this requirement.
If I want to connect workstations running just IPX to the Internet?	Only Proxy Server can do this.
If I want to set up packet filtering on the Internet adapter for security reasons?	NAT allows you to do this.
If I want to set up packet filtering alerts, so I'm e-mailed if certain packets come in from the Internet?	Only Proxy Server can do this.
If I want to restrict users accessing certain sites?	Only Proxy Server can do this.
If I want to specify by users or groups certain Internet services that can be used?	Only Proxy Server can do this.
If I want to centrally cache Web pages to make better use of Internet bandwidth and availability?	Only Proxy Server can do this.
If I want to have built-in redundancy for multiple servers, such that if one is unavailable, users can still access Internet Web sites and FTP servers?	Only Proxy Server can be configured as an array to offer redundancy for these services.
If I want the simplest service to configure and maintain for all workstations?	We recommend ICS and/or NAT over Proxy Server.

domains and IP addresses, and set up alerts on packet filtering. IP address assignment is not a component of Microsoft's Proxy Server, which allows greater flexibility for configuring workstations on different subnets—which is obviously more suited to enterprise environments.

Also, Microsoft's Proxy Server supports Windows clients that don't use TCP/IP (workstations running IPX can use the proxy server to access Internet Web servers). Proxy servers can also centrally cache Web pages to make better use of Internet bandwidth, and when you have multiple proxy servers, they can be grouped together in an array to offer better throughput and availability.

In short, although NAT and proxy servers appear to do the same job, they differ in how they technically achieve this, the flexibility they offer, and the ease of configuration. If ICS or NAT cannot meet your requirements, it is possible that the better choice is to use a proxy server irrespective of the size of your network.

Using VPNs in a SOHO Environment

Chapter 5 explained the benefits of using a VPN connection to securely connect over the Internet to your corporate network. Normally, VPN users would have to dial up to their ISP first and then initiate the VPN connection. Using ICS or NAT in Windows 2000 means each SOHO workstation could create its own VPN connection, but use the shared Internet connection for the underlying connection. This would allow each user to securely connect to a corporate network without the need for additional modems/adapters or individual ISP accounts for his or her own IP address.

As with any VPN connection, each user must have a valid user account to authenticate him or her on the VPN server, which could be a local account on the VPN server, an account in the Active Directory, or a RADIUS account.

exam Watch

The VPN connections must be created on the workstations and not on the computer that is actually connected to the Internet. Additionally, the computer connected to the Internet must have a dedicated link or demand-dial enabled.

on the Job

If you did create the VPN connection on the computer running ICS/NAT, and shared that rather than the Internet connection, not only will packets intended for the Internet not get through, but all nonlocal traffic from the private workstations would go over the VPN connection rather than the Internet, using the credentials of the user who originally logged on to the VPN server!

The only limitation of tunneling with NAT is that the tunneling protocol used would have to be PPTP rather than L2TP/IPSec (because IPSec is one of the protocols that NAT cannot translate). If you are running Windows 2000 Professional, the default setting for a VPN connection is to try L2TP/IPSec first and then PPTP. To decrease your initial VPN connection time, change the Properties of your VPN connection so the Server Type is set to PPTP.

How Address Translation Works

Network address translation works by translating a private address to a public address, and vice versa. For example, if a workstation on your private network had the IP address of 10.0.0.2 and it wanted to connect to a Web site on the Internet with an address of 207.46.131.137 (one of Microsoft's addresses), it would send its packet to the Internet via the computer offering the Internet connection. This computer would have one connection to the private network (e.g., address 10.0.0.1) and one connection to the Internet (e.g., dial-up modem with assigned IP address of 162.1.2.3). The translation would keep the destination address of 207.46.131.137, but would change the source address to 162.1.2.3. When the reply came back from the Web site (for example, the data for its homepage), it would send this packet to 162.1.2.3, but the translation service would know that this maps to the original IP address of 10.0.0.2 and send it to that computer with its 10.0.0.1 interface.

These are the basics of how the translation service works, but for full Internet services to function, it works in conjunction with other components such as address assignment and name resolution. Therefore, the three elements of a network address translation service are

- Translation
- Addressing assignment
- Name resolution

Translation

We have already discussed how one address is translated into another. The NAT component translates packets that contain IP addresses, TCP port and UDP port information in the IP, TCP, and UDP headers. If the application contains any of these in the *application header* instead of the *IP header*, NAT is unable to directly translate these packets. In other words, for NAT to directly translate packets between a private network and a public network, the following must be true:

- Packets have an IP address in the IP header.

One of the following must also be true:

- Packets have TCP port numbers in the TCP header.

or

- Packets have UDP port numbers in the UDP header.

Some protocols do not fulfill these requirements. For example, PPTP packets cannot be directly translated, because PPTP doesn't use a TCP or UDP header—you may remember from Chapter 5 that PPTP uses a Generic Routing Protocol header and, in fact, the tunnel ID in the GRE header identifies the data. Similarly, FTP stores the IP addresses in the FTP header in the port command rather than in the IP header.

NAT Editors However, these protocols and some others that do not directly translate will work through Windows 2000 ICS and NAT because of the addition of *NAT editors*. Both ICS and the NAT routing protocol include built-in NAT editors for FTP, ICMP (e.g., ping packets), and PPTP (for VPN support), so these can be used with address translation. Examples of protocols that do not directly translate and for which there are no NAT editors include IPSec and Kerberos. This means you cannot use IPSec or Kerberos authentication through ICS/NAT, which is one of the major limitations of these services.

exam Watch

Neither ICS nor NAT support IPSec or Kerberos. The addition of NAT editors means that when packets pass through the NAT service, it examines their format. When the format is recognized as one requiring additional processing because it will not directly translate (e.g., FTP packets), it passes those packets to the appropriate NAT editor to modify so the packets can be translated correctly. After the packets have been modified by the NAT editor, they are returned to the NAT service to complete its translation task of passing them onto the Internet.

Additionally, Windows 2000 NAT includes proxy software for the following protocols:

- H.323 (for voice and video)
- DirectPlay (for multiplayer gaming)

- LDAP-based ILS registration
- RPC

This means that for those protocols, the computer running ICS or the NAT routing protocol will send out these protocols directly to the Internet from its public address on behalf of the client workstation, rather than translating them.

on the job

When you install NAT, you will see errors in the Event Log (IDs 33001 and 34001) that relate to DirectPlay Proxy. This is a known event error and will appear even if you select to disable NAT event logging. DirectPlay will only support one client at a time on your private network when using ICS/NAT.

Addressing Assignment

The addressing component refers to how client workstations obtain an IP address and other related configurations, including the subnet mask, default gateway, and IP address of a DNS/WINS server. This configuration is important because it defines how these clients communicate with each other, the computer offering the shared Internet services, and ultimately with Internet resources.

When the computer offering the shared Internet service assigns IP addresses, it acts as a simplified DHCP server. This works well in a small network, since computers running Windows 2000, Windows NT, and Windows 9*x* configured with TCP/IP have a default configuration to be a DHCP client.

The DHCP Allocator For ICS, you have no choice over this component. When you enable ICS, you automatically invoke what is referred to as the *DHCP allocator*. A DHCP allocator is a simplified DHCP service without the database or configurable options. Invoking the DHCP allocator means that the computer will automatically assign IP addresses to other workstations on the same subnet using a private address range, and it will assign the default gateway and the DNS server to be the same IP address as the computer running ICS. Note there is no WINS server allocation.

When using the NAT routing protocol, you have a choice of whether to use the built-in DHCP allocator. If you don't use the DHCP allocator, you can instead use a standard DHCP server that has been installed on your network, or use static addresses. If you are using the DHCP allocator, you can define what address range you want to use, and exclude addresses that are already in use on your private network. It would be a wise precaution to add the server's static IP address as one of the reserved addresses, on this server if running the DHCP allocator, and/or on other DHCP servers.

If you choose to use the DHCP allocator on the NAT server, it will assign clients an IP address in the range specified (you can choose the range) and exclude addresses you have defined. It will also assign the default gateway, and the DNS server to be the same IP address as the internal interface on the NAT server. Additionally, if the NAT server is configured with a WINS server on the internal interface, requests for NetBIOS name resolution from clients will be sent to that WINS server.

If you already have a DHCP server on your network, you should use that rather than using the NAT DHCP allocator—you can't run the two together on the same subnet. In fact, using a standard DHCP server allows greater flexibility because you can more precisely define and configure IP address assignment to include DHCP Class options and the choice of which DNS/WINS server to use.

exam Watch

The DHCP allocator component in ICS and NAT acts as a simplified DHCP server. It is not the same as running a full DHCP Server, and you cannot disable the DHCP allocator in ICS.

When you are using the DHCP allocator, it will use the predefined settings listed in Table 10-1.

on the Job

Despite NAT being able to support multiple private interfaces, remember that the DHCP allocator can only support a single scope of IP addresses (although you can choose which scope to use). If you want to use a different scope for each private interface, you should use a standard DHCP server, or use static addresses.

TABLE 10-1 DHCP Allocator's Predefined DHCP Options that Cannot Be Changed

DHCP Option Number	Description	Option Value
1	Subnet mask	255.255.255.0
3	Default gateway	IP address of private interface
6	DNS server (providing name resolution is set in NAT)	IP address of private interface
58	Renewal time	5 minutes
59	Rebinding time	5 days
51	IP address lease time	7 days
15	DNS domain	Primary domain name of computer

Host Name Resolution

When using the DHCP allocator, both ICS and NAT assign to clients the DNS server as being the IP address of the internal interface on the computer offering the Internet connection. This allows both local and remote DNS names to be resolved. For Internet name resolution, this means that *DNS proxying* will be used to resolve Internet names to IP addresses.

For example, workstation A on your private network wants to connect to a Web server www.microsoft.com. Before a connection can be made, it needs to resolve the name to an IP address—so it uses its DNS server to find the answer. The DNS server in this case is the IP address of the computer offering the Internet connection, so when the DNS request for www.microsoft.com comes in, it queries its own DNS server specified on the Internet interface (e.g., your ISP's DNS server), and when the response comes back, it passes this back to workstation A.

You can disable DNS resolution for clients on the NAT server, but you can't disable this for ICS.

Another solution would be to use your own local DNS server, which would resolve local names and then forward unresolved names to the Internet. This is only possible with NAT, not with ICS, because you can specify not to use IP name resolution and also disable the DHCP allocator. Instead, workstations could use a local DHCP server that assigns to clients a local DNS server rather than the IP address of the NAT server.

NetBIOS Name Resolution

Resolving NetBIOS names works slightly differently. There is no WINS server assignment with ICS, which means that if clients wanted to connect to shares on each other in the form of \\computer_name\share, this would be resolved by broadcast. On a single segment and small network this NetBIOS name resolution should not be a problem, but you may prefer to use an LMHOSTS file to keep such broadcasts to a minimum.

NAT as WINS Proxy With NAT configured to use the DHCP allocator, the NAT server acts as a *WINS proxy* in much the same way as the DNS proxying works, except that requests would go to the server's local WINS server rather than out to the Internet. When a NetBIOS name needs to be resolved to an IP address, the NAT server will query the WINS server on behalf of the private workstations and return the IP address to name resolution. However, it doesn't register the clients in the WINS database or check for duplicate names.

In practice, this means that if workstation A wanted to connect to workstation B in the form of a share name, and both received their IP address assignment from the NAT server, the name could be resolved. However, if you had another workstation that didn't receive its IP address assignment from the NAT server so it was configured to use the WINS server directly, the name resolution by WINS would fail, and the resolution would only succeed if a broadcast was successful (not possible if on a different subnet) or if an LMHOSTS file was in place.

You can see how in all but the simplest of network configurations, using a full DHCP server rather than the built-in DHCP allocator on the NAT server allows you to assign specific DNS and WINS servers to your workstations, which in turn offers greater flexibility in name resolution.

Now that you understand how name resolution works with ICS and NAT, you should be able to select which is an appropriate solution depending on your name resolution requirements.

Dynamic vs. Static Mapping

So far, in our discussion of how address translation works, we have mainly concentrated on outbound connections from a private network to the Internet. We have seen how a

SCENARIO & SOLUTION

Should I Use ICS or NAT if...	
I have just a few workstations on my single segment network with no other servers?	Both ICS and NAT would work in this situation, but ICS would the simplest to configure.
I already have a DHCP server on my network?	NAT, because you can disable the DHCP allocator, and with the full DHCP server assign specific DNS/WINS servers—you can't do this with ICS.
I want to resolve DNS names?	Both ICS and NAT allow you do this, but only NAT allows you to disable this option.
I want to resolve local NetBIOS names?	Both ICS and NAT allow you to resolve local NetBIOS names, but NAT allows greater flexibility. ICS does not assign a WINS server to clients, so names have to be resolved by broadcast or preconfigured LMHOSTS files. In NAT, the DHCP allocator invokes WINS proxying. However, you may prefer to disable the DHCP allocator, and through a standard DHCP server assign a local WINS server to clients so they can directly register with the WINS server.

mapping occurs where a private address is dynamically translated into a public address. It's dynamic because the ICS computer or NAT server handles the translation automatically, keeping track of which addresses/ports are mapped in a mapping table that it periodically refreshes. If these mappings are not refreshed by users reusing the connection, the mappings are removed from the table after a set time. For TCP connections, this time period is 24 hours; for UDP connections, this time period is 1 minute. You can change these default timeouts in NAT, but you cannot change them in ICS.

Dynamic Mappings

For dynamic mappings, the default setting is to translate not just the address, but also the source port. So, for example, your client workstation initiates a TCP/IP connection with a source port of 1024, but after translation this goes out as port 5001. This is necessary when you have more private addresses than public addresses, in order to ensure the same source port is not used again.

For example, client workstation A initiates a TCP/IP connection with source port 1024 and so does workstation B—the translation of the source port in addition to the address would be necessary; otherwise, the ICS/NAT computer would attempt to use duplicate source ports, which is not allowed. Source ports must be unique to the computer sending out the connection request. There is no problem sending out the same destination port from the same computer, and by default, the destination port number is not translated.

Static Mappings

If you wanted to define in advance how the addresses and/or ports should be mapped rather than letting the ICS/NAT computer make this decision, you would have to define *a static mapping.* The most common reason for defining a static mapping is if you wanted to host an Internet resource on one of your client workstations, because the ICS/NAT computer would need to know where to direct the incoming connection.

At the simplest level, you could define a static mapping so that the public IP address Internet users call of 162.1.2.3 with TCP port 80 should map to your internal IP address of 192.168.0.2, port 80. However, you may also want to change the internal port number for added security, or if the Web server may be hosting different sites based on different port numbers.

If you have multiple Internet addresses, it would be wise to reserve one for an incoming connection service such as your company Web server or FTP server, and use the others for dynamic outbound sessions. You can do this with NAT because it allows you to use more than one Internet address, but with ICS you can only use one Internet address. However, ICS does allow you to define static mappings for both incoming and outbound connections.

In ICS, static mappings are configured with the Application Settings button in the Sharing tab. In NAT, outbound static mappings are part of the NAT global properties, and inbound static mappings are part of the Internet interface properties. Later sections will cover how to configure these for both services.

exam Watch

Static mapping is a requirement if you want to host Internet services on your private network.

Mappings for Outbound Internet Traffic

When ICS or NAT receives connection requests for the Internet from the private network, it assesses whether a mapping already exists. This could be either a static mapping you have defined, or a dynamic mapping that is still in memory (the mapping table). If a mapping already exists, that is used. If a mapping does not already exist, a new dynamic mapping is created in one of the following ways:

- If NAT is being used with multiple Internet addresses, and one of these is free, it maps the private address of the originating workstation to its own public address, and passes through the source port number unchanged. When the last Internet address is available, it behaves as if it only had one Internet address.
- If NAT is being used with only one Internet address, or if ICS is being used, it maps the private address of the originating workstation to its public address, AND it maps the original source port number (e.g., 1024) to a new source port number (e.g., 5000).

After the mapping is complete, it will look to see if a NAT editor is needed, and modify the packet as necessary before sending it out onto the Internet.

Mappings for Inbound Internet Traffic

When ICS or NAT receives connection requests from the Internet (which will happen, for example, if you are hosting your own FTP server on the private network for Internet users), it assesses whether a mapping exists for the destination address and port number. If a mapping exists, it will redirect the connection accordingly to the workstation on the private network (IP address or workstation name, and port number). If a mapping does not exist, the connection request is discarded.

Additionally, after the mapping is complete, it will look to see if a NAT editor is needed, and modify the packet as necessary before sending it to the workstation on the private network.

NAT automatically offers security against malicious Internet connections, because dynamic mappings are only used for outbound connections; static mappings have to exist for inbound connections.

Private vs. Public IP Addresses

The connection protocol of the Internet is IP, and for computers to communicate with each other over the Internet, they need a valid IP address that has been allocated by the Internet Network Information Center (InterNIC). These addresses are known as public addresses, and typically an ISP will have a limited range of public addresses available for customers who want Internet access. A small business or home office will usually be granted one or more such public addresses, and the scarcity of these addresses is one reason why Internet connection sharing is so attractive.

Private Address Ranges

Because there is a very real limit on the number of available public addresses, the InterNIC provided an address reuse scheme by reserving certain network IDs for private networks:

- 10.0.0.0 with the subnet mask 255.0.0.0
- 172.16.0.0 with the subnet mask 255.240.0.0
- 192.168.0.0 with the subnet mask 255.255.0.0

Private addresses cannot receive traffic directly from Internet locations. This has several implications for a network that requires an Internet connection. The first is that you must convert a private address to a public address before you can connect to the Internet. This is because routers on the Internet will not route addresses from the private address range. The second is that if private addressing is being used, this offers immediate security for your workstations, because traffic can only pass from the Internet to your network via a network translation service or a routed service. This will be on designated points on your network (e.g., your NAT server) rather than having to configure and maintain each workstation's connection integrity.

IP Addressing Issues on the Internal Network It is highly recommended that you use private addresses on your network even if you initially have no plans to connect to the Internet, because changing your IP address scheme if you later decide to connect to the Internet is not a quick or easy conversion once connectivity patterns have been established.

If you continue to use IP addresses that are valid public addresses but haven't been allocated to you by the InterNIC or an ISP, you will probably be using the same addresses as another organization on the Internet. This is called *illegal* or *overlapping IP addressing*. Not only do you run the higher risk of unwanted Internet traffic coming into your private network, but you will also not be able to connect to the legal IP network, because connections that should be remote will appear as local and never leave your company network.

EXERCISE 10-1

Walkthrough of Address Translation in Action

This exercise is a theoretical run-through of what happens when address translation is being used for both the source address and source port, either when using ICS or NAT.

1. Workstation A is a SOHO workstation with a single network adapter, configured to automatically receive TCP/IP address assignment, and as such receives the following:

   IP address: 192.168.0.2

   Subnet mask: 255.255.255.0

   Default gateway: 192.168.0.1

   DNS server: 192.168.0.1

2. Workstation B is another SOHO workstation, but also has a connection to the Internet that is shared. As such, it has two interfaces:

   SOHO interface (for private network)

   IP address: 192.168.0.1

   Subnet mask: 255.255.255.0

   Internet interface (for public network—these values assigned by an ISP)

IP address: 130.100.1.2

Subnet mask: 255.255.0.0

Default gateway: 130.100.100.222 (ISP's router)

DNS server: 200.100.100.243 (ISP's DNS server)

3. When workstation A running Internet Explorer tries to connect to the Web site www.microsoft.com, it first needs to resolve this DNS name to IP address. It sends out the DNS query to its DNS server, which is the computer running the Internet sharing connection. This machine sees the DNS query, and on behalf of the client, it queries its own DNS server (on the Internet). When the reply comes back that www.microsoft.com resolves to the IP address 207.46.130.45, it passes this information back to workstation A.
4. Workstation A knows that address 207.46.130.45 is not on its local subnet, so it sends the http request via its default gateway. The default gateway is the internal IP address of the computer hosting the Internet sharing.
5. Workstation B receives the packet and passes it to the Internet via its Internet connected interface (IP address 130.100.1.2), but before it sends it out, it changes the source address from 192.168.0.2 to 130.100.1.2. It also changes the source port number from 1026 to 5001. As far as the host on the Internet is concerned, the call is initiated by the machine with address 130.100.1.2 and source port 5001—and has no knowledge of workstation A with address 192.168.0.2, source port 1026.
6. When the reply comes back from the Internet host, it sets the destination address to be 130.100.1.2 and destination port to be 5001. When the computer running the Internet sharing receives the packet, it looks in its translation mapping table, finds that this packet is really destined for workstation A, and changes the destination address from 130.100.1.2 to 192.168.0.2, and changes the destination port from 5001 to 1026.
7. Further exchange of packets between workstation A and the Microsoft Web site continue in this manner, with the mapping table directing packets until workstation A no longer needs to communicate with this Internet host. The mapping remains in the mapping table for the default timeout period of 24 hours, and then is discarded. After this time, any new connection from workstation A to the same host would have to set up a new dynamic mapping.

Private addresses are assumed when using Internet sharing. With ICS, you have no choice over the internal addresses—they will be in the 192.168.x.x range. With NAT, you do have the choice of which IP address range to use, both when configuring the DHCP allocator on the NAT server itself and when using a full DHCP server. However, it is strongly recommended you keep to the practice of using addresses from the private address range.

CERTIFICATION OBJECTIVE 10.02

Internet Connection Sharing

Now that we have looked at how Internet connection sharing works in theory, let's look at how to put this into practice for a machine running ICS.

Creating and Sharing a Dial-Up Connection

You must already have installed and configured the hardware to connect your computer to the Internet (e.g., modem or ISDN adapter), and have a network connection specified to the Internet that uses this interface (for example, specify your ISP's details).

Then sharing this connection is simply a matter of selecting its Properties, then the Sharing tab, and selecting the check box "Enable Internet connection sharing for this connection." If your Internet connection is dial-up rather than dedicated, you will also need to check the option "Enable on-demand dialing."

At this point, if you only require dynamic mappings so SOHO workstations can connect to Internet resources, your job is finished for configuring ICS. However, there may be two circumstances in which you need to specify static mappings, which you do with the Settings button on the same Sharing dialog box. This displays two tabs, one for Applications and one for Services.

Application-Specific Mappings

The Applications tab allows you to specify static mappings for outbound connections. You would not normally need to do this, but it may be required if the application requires particular port numbers (rather than letting ICS dynamically choose a number) and/or additional associated connections. For example, some firewalls are configured to allow through only a certain range of source port numbers, so if you were connecting over the Internet with this restriction, you would have to configure a static mapping to ensure the connection went out with the source port number that was required. Another example is when using multiuser applications over the Internet (e.g., games) that require one or more additional inbound connections.

Service-Specific Mappings

The Services tab allows you specify static mappings for inbound connections; for example, if you want to offer Internet services (e.g., a Web server, FTP server, mail or NNTP server) on your SOHO workstations for other Internet users. Because these connections will be initiated by other people on the Internet rather than users on your internal network, the computer running ICS will need to know the workstation details to which it should map the connection.

The Services tab displays a list of well-known Internet services, such as FTP Server, POP3, and SMTP. For those not listed, click Add to specify your own reference name to identify the service (e.g., "company Web server"), the port number the remote client will be calling (e.g., TCP port 80 for Web services), and then identify to which workstation it should be mapped. Then when a connection comes in from the Internet, ICS will look up its static mapping and direct the call to the correct workstation on the internal network.

FROM THE CLASSROOM

Identifying the Workstation

How can you know what IP address the workstation will have if it's using DHCP? In theory, you may immediately think that these two are mutually exclusive— if a workstation is using DHCP, you cannot guarantee what IP address it will have, and therefore, it is better to specify the workstation name, which remains constant. However, if you are running a full-time service, the SOHO workstation will remain up and running and therefore be able to renew its initially obtained IP address (viewed with ipconfig or winipcfg). Despite this, you may prefer to identify the workstation by its constant host name.

—Carol Bailey, MCSE+I

EXERCISE 10-2

Enabling Internet Connection Sharing for Dynamic Mapping

1. Ensure you are logged on with Administrative privileges and click on Start | Settings | Network and Dial-up Connections.
2. Right-click the Internet connection you want to share (e.g., your dial-up to your ISP) and select Properties | Sharing. Select the check box "Enable Internet connection sharing for this connection."
3. If your Internet connection uses a dial-up connection rather than a dedicated link, also select the check box "Enable on-demand dialing."
4. When you Click OK you will see the dialog box, shown as follows, warning you that your internal IP address will be changed for one supported by ICS.

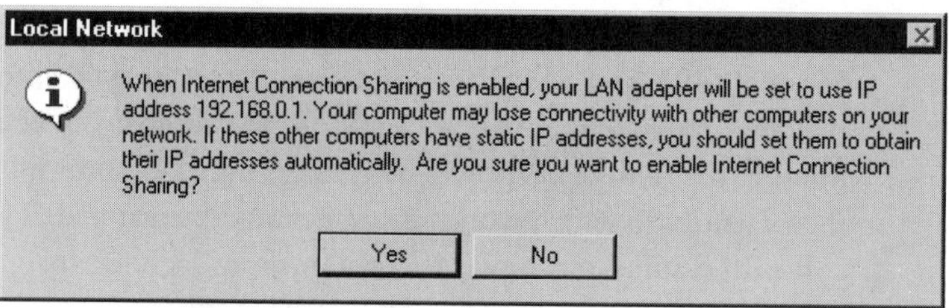

5. Click Yes.
6. That's it! Ensure you have no other DHCP servers on your network, and reboot your SOHO client workstations with DHCP configuration enabled so that they receive their new automatic IP address assignment from the ICS computer.

You must have a dedicated Internet connection to offer incoming Internet services (such as FTP servers or Web servers) to Internet users.

Configuring Connection Sharing on the Clients

You will need to configure Internet Explorer on the client workstations to use Internet sharing, which means a local area connection rather than a direct Internet connection. Additionally, Internet Connection Sharing is *not* using a proxy server or automatically detecting settings, so options for these should be cleared.

EXERCISE 10-3

Enabling Internet Connection Sharing for a Static Mapping

The most likely time you will want to do this is if you want to host an Internet resource (e.g., Web Server) on your private network. Ensure you have a dedicated link to the Internet and have completed the previous exercise. The workstation on your private network that will be hosting the Web server is called WRKST1-WEB, and uses the default TCP port of 80. To configure access to this Web server from the Internet, complete the following:

1. On the Sharing tab, click Settings, and select the Services tab.
2. In the "Name of service," type in a name for your reference, such as Company Web Server.
3. In the "Service port number," type in **80** and keep the default selection of TCP rather than UDP.
4. Under the "Name or address of server computer on the private network," type in **WRKST1-WEB.**

Your dialog box should look similar to the following illustration.

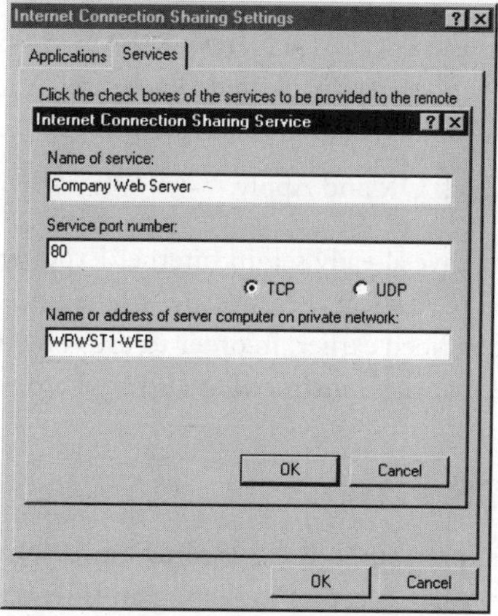

5. Click OK three times to save all your ICS settings.

The first time Internet Explorer is started on a particular machine, you will need to complete the following steps for Internet Explorer 5 on a Windows 2000 Professional computer.

1. Start | Programs | Internet Explorer.
2. When prompted, select "I want to set up my Internet connection manually, or I want to connect through a local area network (LAN)," and click Next.
3. Clear the option "Automatic discovery of proxy server [recommended]"—NAT was not available when IE5 was released! Then click Next.
4. You will then be prompted to configure mail options; either supply these if known, or click No (you can supply them later). Then click Finish.

If you have already set up Internet Explorer for a direct Internet connection and need to reconfigure it to use your Internet Connection Sharing service, you will need to complete the following steps for Internet Explorer 5 on a Windows 2000 Professional.

1. Start | Programs | Internet Explorer.
2. From Tools | Internet Options | Connections, click "Never dial a connection," and then click LAN Settings.
3. In the Local Area Network (LAN) Settings dialog box, ensure that all three check boxes are cleared. These are "Automatically detect settings," "Use automatic configuration script," and "Use a proxy server."
4. Click OK and Apply.

If you have already set up Internet Explorer for a Proxy Server connection, you will need to deselect these settings in the Local Area Network (LAN) Settings dialog box as described earlier, in order to use your Internet Connection Sharing service.

Note that these instructions also apply to workstations if connecting via NAT.

Limitations of ICS

As stated previously, ICS has some limitations in comparison with the NAT routing protocol when it comes to sharing an Internet connection. If these limitations are relevant to your network and/or requirements, you should consider using NAT instead if that is able to fulfill your requirements.

- ICS cannot disable the DHCP allocator service, so the full range of DHCP options are not available to SOHO clients, such as your choice of local DNS and/or WINS server.
- ICS is restricted to using just one Internet address, so you cannot make use of better throughput and availability, cannot disable dynamic port mappings, and cannot reserve a single Internet address for an inbound connection (e.g., Web server).
- ICS cannot be used on a network already using network services such as DHCP, DHCP Relay, domain controllers, routers, etc.
- You cannot scale ICS by running it on two computers within the same segment. You can do this with NAT if you disable the DHCP allocator, which also provides some (not automatic) backup should one computer/connection fail.
- You cannot mix static and dynamic IP addresses on the client workstations.
- You cannot exclude addresses from the DHCP allocator.
- ICS can only work in a single segmented network.
- There is no WINS proxying with ICS, so either use broadcasts to resolve NetBIOS names or configure and implement an LMHOSTS file for each workstation.
- You cannot as easily monitor ICS. There is no desktop utility or command to see what addresses have been allocated, what DNS names have been resolved and what mappings are in memory. The System Event Log is the only indication of what ICS is doing, and the information passed to this is limited.

CERTIFICATION OBJECTIVE 10.03

Network Address Translation

You may prefer to use Windows 2000 Server and install a NAT routing protocol to overcome some of ICS' limitations. However, NAT does require more configuration, which will be covered in the following sections.

Enabling RRAS with NAT on the Server

Chapter 5 first introduced you to the Routing and Remote Access snap-in utility, which is unavailable under Start | Programs | Administrative Tools | Routing and Remote Access. This is a service on Windows 2000 Server that needs to be enabled rather than installed, and when it is initially enabled it will invoke the Routing and Remote Access Server Setup Wizard. You may also remember that one of the wizard configuration options was to enable NAT, which when selected will ask whether you wanted to use ICS or NAT.

If you haven't already configured RRAS for remote access and/or routing, you can use the wizard to guide you through setting up NAT. Or, if you are willing to forego your original RRAS configuration, you can disable RRAS and reenable it to invoke the Setup Wizard again.

If you have already set up and configured RRAS (e.g., for remote access) and now want to add support for NAT, you will need to ensure that your RRAS server supports routing, and then add NAT as a routing protocol. The next step is to add the NAT protocol to the interfaces you want to use, and review and, if necessary, configure properties to ensure you have the best setup for your workstations.

The NAT server uses Internet Control Messages (ICMP) Router Solicitation and DHCP Discover packets to detect if there are competing DHCP servers or routers on your network. If it gets a positive response, it will attempt to shut down or disable its own services. Ensure these are not running before installing the NAT protocol.

Ensuring RRAS is Configured for Routing

You may not have to complete this step if your server is already configured for routing. If it isn't or you want to check this, select your server under the Routing and Remote Access snap-in, and select Properties. Here you can select whether to support routing and remote access. You must have the Router option selected in order for NAT to work. If you also want to offer remote access on the same server, ensure the "Remote access server" check box is also selected, as shown in Figure 10-1.

Installing the NAT Protocol

If the Routing and Remote Access snap-in is already opened with the RRAS service enabled, but no NAT support, you need to add NAT as if it were a routing protocol.

FIGURE 10-1

This RRAS server is configured to allow routing (for NAT) and remote access

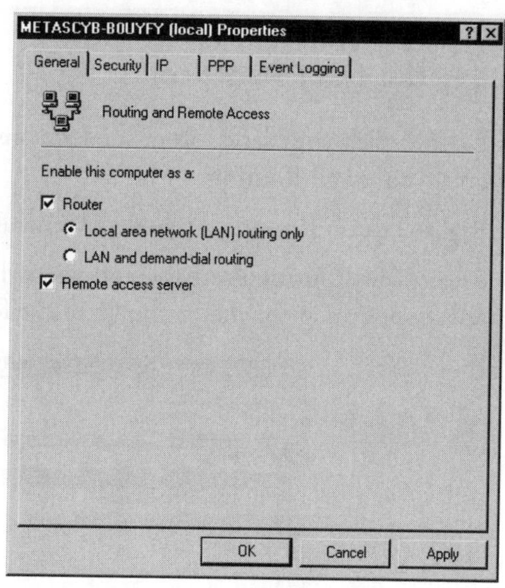

Configuring Global NAT Properties

Now that NAT is installed, you will need to review its default global properties and change these if necessary. Right-click on the new NAT routing protocol, and select Properties. This displays the global properties with four tabs as shown in Figure 10-2.

FIGURE 10-2

Global Properties for the NAT routing protocol

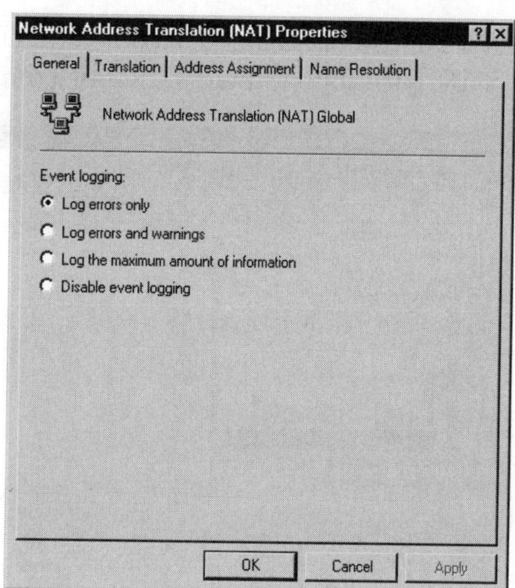

EXERCISE 10-4

Installing the NAT Protocol

1. Double-click your server from the left console pane to expand its contends, until you see IP Routing.
2. Right-click on Routing, and select General.
3. Select New Routing Protocol, and you will see a list of routing protocols for selection, similar to what is shown in the following illustration.

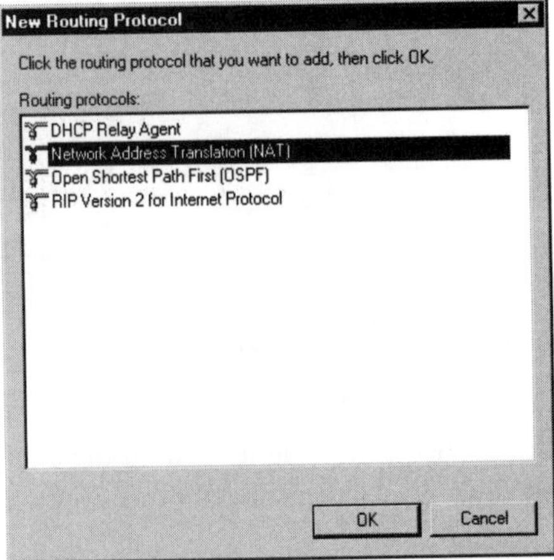

4. Select Network Address Translation (NAT), and Click OK. It should appear in the main console under IP Routing similar to what is shown next.

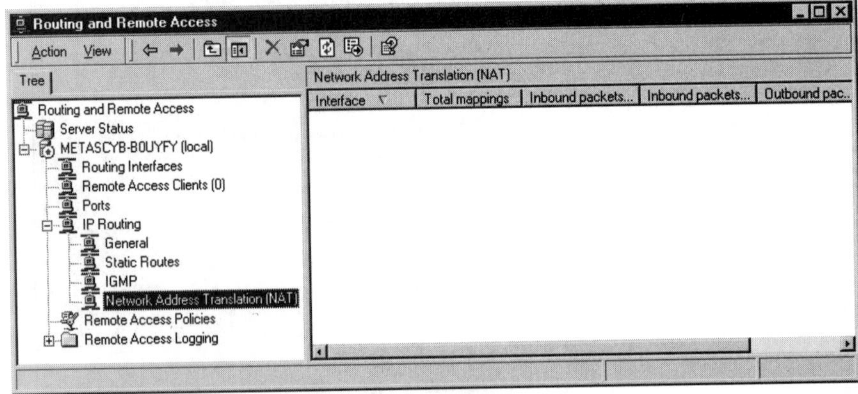

The first tab, General, is fairly self-explanatory, and is similar to other components under the RRAS snap-in, which provides various levels of logging in the System Event Log.

The Translation tab deals with both dynamic and static mappings. "Remove TCP mapping after (minutes):" and "Remove UDP mapping after (minutes)" govern how long a dynamic mapping remains in memory. The defaults should suffice for most applications (the 1440 minutes for TCP is 24 hours). Clicking Applications on the same tab allows you to create static mappings for outbound connections similar to the Applications tab option in ICS, allowing you to statically map both IP addresses and ports if needed.

The Address Assignment tab allows you to specify whether the DHCP allocator should be used (this is the "Automatically assign IP addresses by using DHCP" check box), and allows you to specify the private address range that should be used for connecting workstations. If you are using a static address on your internal interface, an appropriate range will be suggested from this setting. Otherwise, the default of 192.168.0.0 with subnet mask of 255.255.255.0 is suggested, but unlike ICS, you can actually change this here. You can also exclude addresses from this range by clicking Exclude. If you want to use a standard DHCP server to take advantage of a different WINS server or some of the advanced DHCP options you get with Windows 2000 DHCP Server, uncheck "Automatically assign IP addresses by using DHCP."

exam Watch

"Automatically assign IP addresses by using DHCP" refers to the DHCP allocator, a cut-down version of the Windows 2000 DHCP service. If this is unchecked and you do not have a standard DHCP server on your network, NAT will not work.

on the Job

If you change the default address range, don't forget to also change the IP address of the private interface. It is recommended that you change it to be the first IP address in the configured range, and then exclude this (by clicking Exclude).

The Name Resolution tab allows you to specify whether the NAT server should resolve DNS names to IP addresses for connecting clients. If your Internet DNS server is available only over a dial-up connection, you can additionally specify here which dial-up connection to use. Note that this tab has nothing to do with NetBIOS name resolution.

Configuring NAT Interface Properties

Now that NAT is installed and configured, you need to tell it which interfaces to use, and configure their properties.

Adding the Interfaces to NAT

It's not enough to just install NAT, you must tell it which interfaces to use—it won't automatically use NAT on all interfaces as you might expect.

You must add at least two interfaces (for example, one adapter on your private network and another on your Internet modem/adapter). To add interfaces to NAT, select the NAT routing protocol you have just added, right-click and select Add. You will be able to select your interface connections from the next dialog box.

When you have selected your interface, you will immediately be presented with its General Properties options. For your internal connection, select the "Private interface connected to private network" option. For your external connection, select the "Public interface connected to the Internet" and also the check box for "Translate TCP/UDP headers (recommended)."

When you configure your Internet interface as your Public interface connected to the Internet, you will then see two more Properties tabs: Address Pool and Special Ports.

Configuring IP Address Ranges

The Address Pool tab is where you specify multiple public addresses if these have been allocated by your ISP and you wish to use more than one public IP address on this one

FROM THE CLASSROOM

Translating TCP/UDP Headers

When wouldn't you want to translate TCP/UDP headers? The only time this setting is applicable is if you have a range of Internet addresses on the NAT server, and this number was greater or equal to the number of workstations on the private network that needed Internet connections. If it was important to keep the same source port number for outbound connections, and you didn't want to configure static mappings, you could deselect the option to translate TCP/UDP headers.

—Carol Bailey, MCSE+I

server. Click Add to specify your start and end range, or if your address range is a power of 2, you can define your range with one address and a subnet mask.

You can also reserve specific IP addresses with the Reservations button, which may be applicable if for example you want to keep one address separate for an Internet service you want to host on one of the workstations.

Configuring Interface Special Ports

The Special Ports tab allows you to specify static mappings for inbound connections. It corresponds to the Services tab in ICS where you can specify ports and addresses to which packets should be sent when they come into the server from the Internet - to either the server's Internet address or to one of the reserved addresses in the address pool.

Monitoring NAT

When NAT is installed and configured, it should now look similar to Figure 10-3, which shows one internal adapter for the private interface and one external adapter for the Internet connection.

As you can see, you can monitor the NAT service from the Routing and Remote Access snap-in by viewing statistics for each NAT interface. The details pane on the right has columns for the number of mappings, inbound/outbound packets translated or rejected, and so forth, and when NAT is being used, you will see mappings dynamically update here.

Additionally the current mappings table can be viewed for each interface—select your Internet interface, then right click on Show Mappings to see exactly what protocols, ports, and addresses are mapped in memory.

FIGURE 10-3

NAT installed and configured for two interfaces, and working

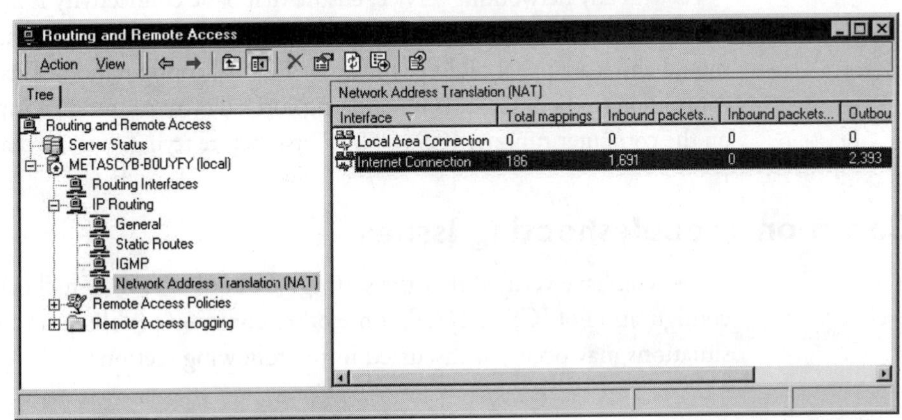

If you right-click on the Network Address Translation (NAT) you can select Show DHCP Allocator Information and Show DNS Proxy Information to display statistics on these components. Another way to see the DHCP Allocator Information would be to use Netsh with the **routing ip autodhcp show global** command.

CERTIFICATION OBJECTIVE 10.04

Troubleshooting ICS and NAT

The whole of this chapter has included troubleshooting information by describing how these services work and what their configuration options are. If you have problems when using ICS and NAT, rather than blindly running through a list of possible problems and solutions, think about how these services work so you can better define what is going wrong and at what stage.

For example, first check that you're not asking ICS and NAT to do something that is outside their limitations. For example you can't run ICS and NAT together on the same computer, and since these services were designed for the simplest networks you cannot expect them to run correctly if in competition with other network services (such as domain controllers, routers, DHCP servers, etc).

Both of these services will only work with the TCP/IP protocol – so ensure it is installed and particularly for ICS ensure that a DHCP client component is also installed (this will be automatic for later Windows computers such as Windows 9x, Windows NT and Windows 2000).

As with any networking service, ensure that basic connectivity is not the problem (for example, ping the computer running ICS or NAT from a workstation, which should check adapters, cabling, and basic TCP/IP configuration). Ensure that your connection to the Internet is functioning correctly (try running an Internet application on the computer running ICS or NAT first, before trying to share that connection).

Common Troubleshooting Issues

When you have verified that the settings are correct and then checked your configuration of ICS or NAT, some other common problems and likely problem situations may occur, as discussed in the following sections.

Address Assignment

These relate to connectivity issues—between the client workstation and the ICS/NAT computer, and the ICS/NAT computer and the Internet resource:

- For ICS, ensure the Enable Internet Connection Sharing option is set under the Sharing tab. For NAT, ensure that the server supports routing, and the NAT routing protocol is installed with at least one internal interface (for your private network connection) and one external interface (for your Internet connection) added to the NAT protocol.
- The default private address range can be changed for NAT, but not for ICS. If you change this, ensure that the private addresses assigned to the clients are in the same network address range as the IP address on the private network interface on the NAT computer. If they are not, your connections will fail.
- Verify that clients have received the correct TCP/IP configuration by typing on the client computers **ipconfig /all** (or **winipcfg** for Win9*x*). The default TCP/IP address assignment will be an address in the 192.168.x.x range (although you can change this with NAT). Additionally, verify that the Default Gateway IP address corresponds to the IP address on the internal interface of the ICS/NAT computer.
- If clients do not receive correct IP address settings for NAT, and you have no standard DHCP server on your network, ensure you have "Automatically assign IP addresses by using DHCP" set as a global NAT option. There is no equivalent setting for ICS, because you cannot disable this in ICS.
- If you have changed the addressing information on the NAT server so it is not using the default of 192.168.x.x, but you are using the DHCP allocator ("Automatically assign IP addresses by using DHCP"), verify that you are using instead one of the other private address ranges (10.0.0.0 with a subnet mask of 255.0.0.0, or 172.16.0.0 with a subnet mask of 255.240.0.0).
- If you have a standard DHCP server on your network and you wish to use this rather than the DHCP allocator with NAT, uncheck "Automatically assign IP addresses by using DHCP," and ensure that your DHCP server is available and configured correctly to offer clients an IP address in the same network range as the internal network adapter on the NAT server. Also ensure that other DHCP options are set correctly; for example, setting your

local WINS server if you have one, and the IP address of your local DNS server if it is configured to forward to the Internet.

- Verify that you have entered the correct IP address, subnet mask, default gateway, and DNS server on the Internet interface—these would normally be supplied by your ISP. If you have been given more than one public IP address to use with NAT (you cannot use more than one with ICS), ensure that you have entered these correctly in the Address Pool tab of the NAT Internet Interface properties. If you enter an invalid public address for outbound connections, you will not be able to use that address, and the translation will fail because the connection will fail. If you enter an invalid public address for inbound connections (e.g., you are hosting a Web server for Internet access on one of your client workstations), your Web server will be inaccessible to other people on the Internet.

Network Address Translation

This applies to how applications work through a translated connection:

- If you have specific programs that do not seem to work correctly through ICS or NAT, but standard programs (e.g., Web access) are okay, check whether this program can be translated. If the program runs from the computer with the direct connection to the Internet, but not from a workstation on the private network, chances are the application uses packets that may not be translatable. However, before giving up on it, check with the vendor about how their application works in a translated environment, because it may just need a certain static mapping defined to work correctly (multiuser Internet games fall into this category).
- For incoming connections (e.g., if you want to host your own Web server on the Internet), ensure that you have a permanent connection to the Internet, your ICS or NAT computer is not turned off, you have defined a correct static mapping for the internal workstation, and the workstation is left switched on with the service running.
- Unless you specifically need a one-to-one mapping of source ports (only possible with NAT if you have multiple public IP addresses), verify that the "Translate TCP/UDP headers (recommended)" check box on the General tab of the properties of the public interface is selected.

Internet Name Resolution

This applies to how "friendly" Internet names are resolved to IP addresses; for example, if a client workstation can connect by an IP address (e.g., http://207.46.130.45) but not through the DNS name (e.g., http://www.microsoft.com):

- Verify that DNS name resolution is enabled; for ICS, this should be automatic. Use ipconfig (or winipcfg on Win9*x* computers) to view the assigned DNS server—it should correspond to the same IP address as the internal interface on the NAT server or ICS computer. If you want to use your own DNS server, you must assign this with a standard DHCP server and disable the name resolution on the NAT server. Also ensure that your DNS server can forward to the Internet for nonlocal names.

Other Configuration Issues

This applies to general configuration issues for applications, the NAT computer, and the network:

- Ensure that client applications (e.g., Internet Explorer) are configured correctly for ICS or NAT, rather than directly connecting to the Internet or via a proxy server.
- On the NAT server, check the status of both interfaces in the RRAS snap-in. Under IP Routing | General, the two interfaces should show their correct IP address and that they are Operational.
- Check that packet filtering on the interface, server, or a firewall/router isn't blocking valid packets (packet filtering was discussed in Chapter 5). You can easily check whether packet filtering has been enabled on your NAT interfaces by checking under the Filters column under the relevant interface in RRAS under IP Routing | General | <interface connection>.

Miscellaneous

Finally, this applies to help in identifying or eliminating problems:

- Check the System Event Log for any errors or warnings (for example, if it detects any configuration errors or conflicting services). If problems still persist with NAT, try setting logging to the maximum, stop and restart

EXERCISE 10-5

Detecting a Conflicting DHCP Server

How would you know if there was a conflicting DHCP server on your network? Suppose your NAT server had been running fine for about a month, and suddenly you came in one day to discover that some people couldn't access the Internet from their workstations. The reason for this is that someone installed a DHCP server without your knowledge that is allocating a different network address—which means that workstations will get new IP address assignment from the DHCP server rather than from your NAT server. Because the new address range is different from the one on your NAT server, the new leases when obtained will result in workstations being unable to access your NAT server, and hence be unable to access the Internet.

If you can, simulate this by installing a DHCP server on your network, and configure it to use a different address range (if it has the same address range, NAT will continue to work). This exercise steps through some of the troubleshooting steps you might go through in a similar situation.

1. Ensure that your NAT server is up and functional—connect one of your workstations to the Internet to verify the NAT connection.
2. Install a DHCP server that assigns a different range of IP addresses than your NAT server's range, and activate the scope.
3. Stop and restart the RRAS service on the NAT server.
4. On one of your workstation clients, release and renew your IP address (e.g., ipconfig /release and then ipconfig/renew).
5. Try to connect your browser to the Internet with Internet Explorer. You should receive a "The page cannot be displayed" message if your connection fails.
6. Check that the NAT server is running and available—the interfaces both say they are operational, so you know it's not an interface failure problem (e.g., modem not functioning).
7. Check that you can access the Internet resource from the NAT server directly, so you know it's not a basic Internet connectivity problem (e.g., ISP link down or Internet resource not available).
8. Check the System Event Log on the NAT server; you should see an entry similar to the one shown in the following illustration that explains the

problem. The DHCP allocator (on IP address 10.10.0.1) was disabled in favor of a standard DHCP server with address 192.168.0.1.

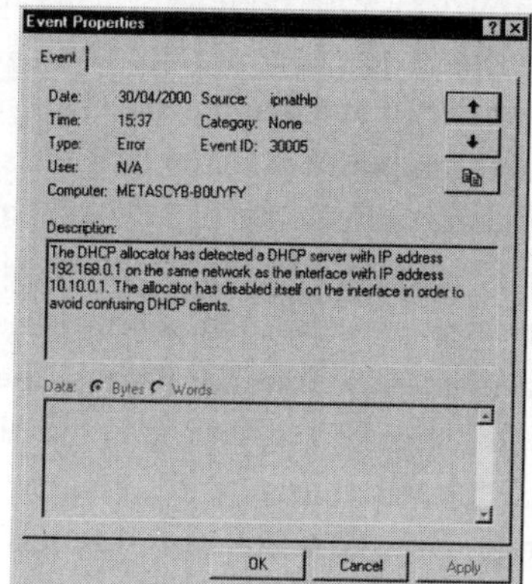

9. You confirm this is the problem on the workstation by viewing the IP address details (e.g., by typing **ipconfig /all**). Your choice now is to either stop the DHCP server if it is not needed, or use the same address range so workstations can connect to the NAT server.

RRAS, and then check the System Event Log again (set maximum logging under NAT properties, General tab).

- Use Network Monitor or an equivalent to capture and analyze the packets as they travel from the workstation to the ICS/NAT computer, and from the ICS/NAT computer to the Internet (if possible). Now you have a good understanding of how ICS and NAT works, you should be able to verify the packets, or identify where the problems lie.

If such a conflict occurs with ICS, you do not get any errors in the System Event Log—ICS simply won't work.

CERTIFICATION SUMMARY

To provide a good understanding of network address translation, this chapter has detailed how it works, with both its benefits and limitations. In Windows 2000, Microsoft offers network address translation in two different forms: ICS and NAT. Which one you use (if at all) will depend on your requirements. Both have advantages as well as limitations, and it is better to understand thoroughly how they both work rather than make assumptions. You may instinctively feel that ICS should only be used when a server is not available and NAT is always the better choice, but that may not always be the case. To make such assumptions may cost you in the exam when you are asked how each technically works, because they both share many components in common—it is dangerous to dismiss ICS as the "poor relation!"

We looked at how to install and configure both ICS and NAT, and finally offered suggestions on how to troubleshoot these services, should you have problems.

TWO-MINUTE DRILL

Overview of ICS and NAT

- ❑ Network Address Translation is aimed at small, not large networks.
- ❑ Network Address Translation was not available in Windows NT 4.0.
- ❑ The introduction of Network Address Translation has been perceived and pushed as one of the immediate benefits to be gained from using Windows 2000.
- ❑ Internet Connection Sharing and Network Address Translation are two Windows 2000 services that offer an easy-to-configure and simple Internet connection typically suited to a SOHO environment.
- ❑ A SOHO (Small Office or Home Office) network is typically a single-segment network with a few peer-to-peer workstations running TCP/IP, where just one computer has an Internet connection with demand dial-up or a dedicated link.
- ❑ Connections to the Internet are either routed or translated; a translated connection hides the IP addresses on the private network from the Internet.
- ❑ Translated connections are easier to set up and secure in comparison to routed connections; as such, they have low administrative overheads.
- ❑ ICS is less flexible in configuration than NAT, but can be run on Windows 2000 Professional as well as Windows 2000 Server.
- ❑ ICS is configured through Dial-up Network Connections on the Sharing tab; NAT is configured as a routing protocol in the RRAS snap-in.
- ❑ Not all applications are suitable for translation; some will only work with the addition of NAT editors and proxying.
- ❑ Although Microsoft's Proxy Server is usually aimed at medium-sized to large networks, it may be a better choice than ICS/NAT in certain circumstances; for example, it offers better security, central caching facilities, and Internet connectivity for IPX clients.
- ❑ Address translation has the following components: translation, addressing assignment, and name resolution.

- Automatic address assignment is handled by the DHCP allocator, which is a simplified version of a standard DHCP server.
- Address translation uses either dynamic or static mappings—you must have a static mapping for incoming connections such as Web hosting, and you must have a dedicated Internet connection.
- Private addresses cannot directly send or receive packets to or from the Internet, which is why you need a routed or translated connection for Internet access. InterNIC reserved three ranges of addresses for private networks to cater for Class A, B, and C networks; ICS and NAT default to the Class C range of 192.168.0.0.

Internet Connection Sharing

- Configuration could be as simple as a check box in the Sharing tab: "Enable Internet sharing for this connection."
- You cannot disable the DHCP allocator, and the private address range will be 192.168.0.0 with a subnet mask of 255.255.255.0.
- Static mappings are set by clicking Applications on the Sharing tab—specify outbound static mappings with the Applications tab, and inbound static mappings with the Services tab.
- Although using a dial-up modem is the more common setup with ICS, there is no reason why you cannot use a faster, dedicated connection to the Internet.

Network Address Translation

- With RRAS configured for routing, you install NAT as a routing protocol with the RRAS snap-in.
- You have to add at least two interfaces to the NAT protocol: one that is connected to the Internet, and the other that is connected to the private network.
- Global NAT properties include Event logging levels, defining address assignments, outbound mappings, and DNS name resolution.
- Inbound static mappings are defined on the external (Internet) interface properties with the Special Ports tab.

Troubleshooting ICS and NAT

- ❑ Verify basic network connectivity from client to computer running ICS or NAT.
- ❑ Verify that the application works directly from the computer hosting ICS or NAT—that should verify your Internet connection configuration details and hardware.
- ❑ Verify that the application supports a translation connection; check with the vendor if in doubt, or in case it needs static mappings to work correctly.
- ❑ Break down the various elements that make up the ICS/NAT service so that you can identify which element is causing the problem. This will enable you to more effectively concentrate your troubleshooting efforts.
- ❑ Verify that NAT is not in competition with other network services, such as a standard DHCP server, DHCP Relay, or routers. Check the System Event Log for automatic detection.

SELF TEST

The following questions will help you measure your understanding of the material presented in this chapter. Read all of the choices carefully, as there may be more than one correct answer. Choose all correct answers for each question.

Overview of ICS and NAT

1. Which of the following best defines a typical SOHO environment where ICS or NAT could be employed?

   A. A small network with all workstations running Windows 2000 Professional with a Windows 2000 Server domain controller.

   B. A small network with a mixture of workstations operating systems running TCP/IP or IPX.

   C. A branch network of computers running Windows NT 4.0 with one Windows 2000 Server (stand-alone).

   D. Two small networks connected together, with a Windows 2000 Server (stand-alone) acting as a router.

2. Which of the following are benefits of address translation? (Select all that apply.)

   A. Cost savings in that only one ISP account is required with just one Internet address.

   B. It offers better security, because you can block connections from specific sites.

   C. It is easier to set up, configure, and maintain than routing or having multiple Internet connections.

   D. All Internet access is transparently handled—there is no configuration for applications to work over the Internet.

3. You have been asked to set up and configure address translation on your network so all workstations can share the ISDN connection on the Windows 2000 Server. Which of the following requirements would ICS fulfill? (Select all that apply.)

   A. Only a single connection to the Internet is needed without having to reconfigure anything on the workstations, which are a mixture of Windows 98 and Windows NT 4.0, all running TCP/IP.

   B. You want to host a Web server on one of your Windows 98 computers running Personal Web Server.

   C. You want to connect to shares on other workstations without using broadcasts.

D. You want workstations to be able to use DNS names on the Internet so they can use "friendly names" instead of IP addresses.

4. If you needed a shared Internet connection for your small network, which of the following would the NAT routing protocol support? (Select all that apply.)

   A. Support for multiple Internet addresses on a single interface
   B. Support for VPN connections using L2TP/IPSec
   C. Support for more than one subnet
   D. Support for local DNS resolution

5. You're considering using Microsoft's ICS or NAT rather than Microsoft's Proxy Server. Which of the following would be supported by ICS/NAT? (Select all that apply.)

   A. Just one Internet connection that hides your internal IP addresses
   B. Reverse proxying, so you could host Internet services on internal workstations
   C. Choice of who could use the Internet connection
   D. Restrict certain sites from Internet access

6. Which of the following protocols/applications *cannot* be used with ICS/NAT? (Select all that apply.)

   A. FTP
   B. LDAP
   C. IPSec
   D. Telnet

Internet Connection Sharing

7. If you're using a modem rather than a dedicated link to the Internet, which option must you select?

   A. ICS automatic dial-up
   B. Enable automatic Internet connection
   C. Enable on-demand dialing
   D. Automatically dial

8. When you configure ICS, what IP address will be used on your private interface?

A. 10.0.0.0

B. 10.0.0.1

C. 192.168.0.0

D. 192.168.0.1

9. If you wanted to share a multiuser Internet game for workstations on your private network, where would you configure this?

   A. On the application running on each client workstation

   B. As an application with the Settings button on the Sharing tab

   C. As a service with the Settings button on the Sharing tab

   D. ICS doesn't support this kind of application

10. When would it be applicable to use NAT rather than ICS? (Select all that apply.)

    A. When you want to use static mappings

    B. When you want to reserve an IP address for your company Web server

    C. When you want to use the single subnet address of 10.0.0.0

    D. When you want the minimum of configuration on the client side

Network Address Translation

11. If you have two segments to your SOHO network and want to keep different subnet addresses for them, how would you do this with NAT? (Select all that apply.)

    A. Add both internal interfaces to the NAT routing protocol.

    B. Disable the DHCP allocator.

    C. Define two static address pools with the subnet addresses you wanted to use.

    D. Manually assign IP addresses to your server's two internal interfaces.

12. You want to use a standard DHCP server on your network rather than the built-in DHCP allocator in NAT. Where do you set the option in NAT that allows you to do this?

    A. Select the NAT protocol, Properties, and under the Address Assignment tab, set the option "Automatically assign IP addresses by using DHCP."

    B. Select the NAT protocol, Properties, and under the Address Assignment tab, deselect the option "Automatically assign IP addresses by using DHCP."

C. Select the internal interface/s, Properties, and under the Address Pool tab, set the option "Automatically assign IP addresses by using DHCP."

D. Select the internal interface/s, Properties, and under the Address Pool tab, deselect the option "Automatically assign IP addresses by using DHCP."

13. How can you monitor the NAT DHCP allocator? (Select all that apply.)

A. Right-click on the Network Address Translation (NAT) in the left pane of the RRAS snap-in, and choose Show DHCP Allocator Information.

B. Right-click on the internal interface under Address Translation (NAT) in the RRAS snap-in and choose Show DHCP Allocator Information.

C. Expand the Network Address Translation (NAT) in the left pane of the RRAS snap-in, and the details pane will show DHCP information.

D. Use Netsh.

Troubleshooting ICS and NAT

14. Somebody complains that an application that connects over the Internet isn't working. What's one of the first things to check?

A. That the application is translatable

B. That the application is configured with the correct static ports

C. That nobody's installed any conflicting services such as a DHCP server

D. That you can run the application directly from the machine running ICS or NAT

15. You've been told that your Web site isn't always available. You're using ICS and have configured the workstation details and port number under the Service tab. You have a dedicated Internet connection. What could be wrong?

A. You must use NAT rather than ICS to do this.

B. Somebody's turning off the workstation hosting the Web service.

C. Because DHCP is being used, the IP address of the workstation keeps changing, so you need to specify the workstation name rather than IP address in the Services tab.

D. You need to configure ports under the Applications tab.

16. You know that you can't run ICS and/or NAT with a DHCP server on the same segment. How would you know if a DHCP server had been installed on your network? (Choose all that apply.)

A. You work in a small office, so you know your colleagues would tell you.

B. ICS/NAT connections would stop working.

C. An error message about DHCP detection and a conflict would be logged on the machine running ICS/NAT.

D. An error message about DHCP detection and a conflict would be displayed on the workstation when users tried to connect to the Internet.

17. Your company sometimes uses the services of a small independent company that has six employees all using Windows 2000 Professional. These are networked for sharing files and printers, and one has an ISDN link for Internet access. Every so often they need to connect to your network so they can use your company resources. Your company is running a native mode Windows 2000 network that includes an RRAS server, so you create user accounts in your Active Directory for these six users and put them into an group called "Outsource." What's the best way to achieve this with just the one Internet connection?

    A. Configure ICS on the workstation with the ISDN link so users can create a dial-up connection to your company RAS server and authenticate with their AD account.

    B. Configure ICS on the workstation with the ISDN link, and then create and share on the ICS workstation one VPN connection to your company VPN server so all workstations can use this.

    C. Configure ICS on the workstation with the ISDN link, and then create on each workstation a VPN connection with default settings to your company VPN server.

    D. Configure ICS on the workstation with the ISDN link, and then create on each workstation a VPN connection to your company VPN server. Because they are using Windows 2000, they can take advantage of the higher-security L2TP/IPSec offers, so they configure their Server Type to use L2TP/Ipsec.

LAB QUESTION

You've been given five Internet addresses from your ISP, and you want to use a shared Internet connection on your small network that has a DHCP server but no domain controller or routers. You want to reserve one of these addresses for your company Web server. What steps should you go through to implement a solution using network translation?

SELF TEST ANSWERS

Overview of ICS and NAT

1. ☑ C. A branch network of computers running Windows NT 4.0 with one Windows 2000 Server (stand-alone) describes the best answer for what constitutes a Small Office/Home Office that could benefit from ICS and/or NAT. It doesn't matter that the workstation clients are not Windows 2000, as long as the computer connected to the Internet is able to run ICS and/or NAT (i.e., Windows 2000, or ICS on Windows 98 Second Edition).
   ☒ A would not offer a good environment for ICS or NAT, because SOHO is aimed at peer-to-peer workstations. Connecting clients do not need to be Windows 2000 as long as they are running TCP/IP and, in the case of ICS, can be configured as DHCP clients so they can use address translation on the Windows 2000 Server. **B** is incorrect because address translation requires the TCP/IP protocol on all client workstations. Microsoft's Proxy Server would be a better choice here if you needed a single Internet connection for your IPX clients. **D** is incorrect because address translation cannot run in conjunction with routing services on the same subnet.

2. ☑ **A, C.** Cost savings are a benefit with address translation in that only one ISP account is required with just one Internet address, and it is easier to set up, configure and maintain than routing or having multiple Internet connections.
   ☒ **B** is incorrect because although NAT uses a private address that is hidden and therefore offers better security, NAT cannot block specific sites—only proxy servers or firewalls can do this. **D** is not entirely true, because although this may be true for the majority of outbound connections, you must configure static mappings for inbound connections such as a Web server, mail server, or FTP server. Additionally, some applications are not suited to address translation and will not work (e.g., IPSec, Kerberos).

3. ☑ **A, B, C, D. A** is correct. Only a single connection to the Internet is needed without having to reconfigure anything on the workstations which are a mixture of Windows 98 and Windows NT 4.0 all running TCP/IP. **B** is correct. Hosting a Web server on one of your Windows 98 computers running Personal Web Server is fulfilled by configuring a static mapping under the Services tab. **C** is correct. Connecting to shares on other workstations without using broadcasts can be achieved (although not automatically as would be possible with NAT) by configuring a local LMHOSTS file. **D** is also correct. Configuring workstations to be able to use DNS names on the Internet so they can use "friendly names" instead of IP addresses is fulfilled by the automatic DNS proxying that ICS uses.

4. ☑ **A, C, D.** **A** is correct. Support for multiple Internet addresses on a single interface is supported by NAT but not by ICS—you define your address pool on the Internet interface properties. **C** is correct. Support for more than one subnet is supported by NAT if you disable the DHCP allocator and either use a standard DHCP server or static addresses. **D** is also correct. Support for local DNS resolution is supported on both ICS and NAT, although you can disable this in NAT in the Name Resolution tab as one of the NAT global properties.
   ☒ **B.** Support for VPN connections using L2TP/IPSec, is not supported by NAT because IPSec cannot be translated. If you wanted to use a VPN connection with NAT, you could instead use PPTP if your VPN server supported this alternative tunneling protocol.

5. ☑ **A, B.** Both ICS and NAT require just one Internet connection that hides all internal IP addresses, and both can use reverse proxying, so you could host Internet services on internal workstations.
   ☒ **C** is incorrect; you can only do this with Proxy Server. **D** is also incorrect; you can only do this with Proxy Server.

6. ☑ **C.** IPSec is only protocol here that cannot be used with ICS/NAT.
   ☒ **A** is incorrect. FTP can be used with ICS/NAT, because although it does not translate directly, it can be used because of the built-in NAT editors. **B** is incorrect. LDAP can be used with ICS/NAT, because although it does not translate directly, it is proxied by the computer running ICS/NAT. **D** is also incorrect. Telnet can be used with ICS/NAT, and in fact is directly translatable—there is no need to use an editor or proxy.

Internet Connection Sharing

7. ☑ **C.** Enable on-demand dialing is the correct option under the Sharing tab of your Internet connection properties. If this option is not set, other users will only be able to connect to the Internet through ICS when you manually connect to the Internet.
   ☒ **A, B,** and **D** are all incorrect options and do not exist under the Sharing tab of your Internet connection properties.

8. ☑ **D.** 192.168.0.1 is the IP address that will be automatically assigned to your private interface. The private address range 192.168.x.x will be used, and the first available host address from this range is 192.168.0.1, which is assigned to the computer.
   ☒ **A** is incorrect because this reflects the incorrect private address range, and it is not a valid host address. **B** is incorrect because although this is a valid host address, it is using the wrong private address range for ICS. **C** is incorrect, because although using the correct private address range, it is not a valid host address.

9. ☑ **B.** If an outbound application needs to have a static mapping defined, it should be configured with the Settings button and then the Application tab.
☒ A is incorrect. One of the advantages of ICS and NAT is that client reconfiguration is not necessary. C is incorrect because this is where you would specify static mappings for inbound connections. D is incorrect because ICS allows you to specify static mappings for both outbound and inbound connections.

10. ☑ **B, C.** B is correct because you would need to use NAT rather than ICS if you wanted to reserve an IP address for your company Web server because you cannot use more than one Internet address with ICS. C is correct because ICS will only use the network address of 192.168.0.0.
☒ A is incorrect; you can do this with both ICS and NAT. D is also incorrect because both ICS and NAT require the minimum of configuration on the client side; the greater configuration for NAT is on the server, not the clients.

Network Address Translation

11. ☑ **A, B, D.** You should add both interfaces to the NAT protocol, disable the DHCP allocator (or clients will receive the same subnet address), and then manually assign IP addresses to each interface from the subnet ranges you want to use. Additionally, you will have to manually assign IP addresses to your clients, unless you had a DHCP server on your network that could automatically assign the correct addresses to clients.
☒ C is incorrect because this would not guarantee which address pool would be used for your internal interfaces. Typically, the first address pool would be used first, irrespective of which interface clients connected from.

12. ☑ **B.** To use a full DHCP server with NAT, you must disable the DHCP allocator, which is identified by the option "Automatically assign IP addresses by using DHCP." This is a global NAT option; you cannot set this for just one interface.
☒ A is incorrect; it is the opposite of what you're trying to achieve. It's a rather confusing option label, so don't be caught selecting the opposite of what you actually want! C and D are both incorrect because this option is global to NAT; therefore, you wouldn't be setting it on a single interface. Additionally, the internal interface does not have multiple property tabs—only the external interface has multiple tabs, and the Address Pool here is for defining multiple Internet addresses.

13. ☑ **A, D.** If you right-click on the Network Address Translation (NAT) in the left pane of the RRAS snap-in and choose Show DHCP Allocator Information, this displays a dialog box with

DHCP statistics. You can also use the **netsh routing ip autodhcp show global** command.
☒ **B** is incorrect. DHCP is global to NAT, which is why this option would not be under a specific interface. **C** is incorrect; this will show the inbound and outbound mappings.

Troubleshooting ICS and NAT

14. ☑ **D.** You don't know at this point whether other applications over the Internet work, or whether it's just one application that is having a problem. Check the basic, obvious problems such as modem problems, ISP problems, etc., by trying to run the application directly yourself. Checking the basics first can save a lot of time.
☒ **A** is a good idea if somebody reports an application isn't working through ICS/NAT, but it's not the first thing to check if you don't know whether standard applications are working. Not much point checking whether the application is translatable if you have no Internet connection! Similarly, **B** may be something to check after you have established that basic connectivity is working with other applications. If you can run the application directly but not from workstations when other applications work, check the application's documentation and/or the vendor to see if it is translatable and/or requires special port configuration. **C** is valid by looking in the Event Viewer for confliction messages; however, verifying basic Internet connectivity first should be your top priority.

15. ☑ **B.** What time of day are people complaining they can't access your Web site? If you want to offer a 24/7 service, ensure that the workstation hosting the service isn't switched off!
☒ **A** is incorrect. There's absolutely no reason why you couldn't offer a Web service like this with ICS. **C** is unlikely to be the problem; first, a workstation hosting a Web service shouldn't normally be switched off, and therefore should keep and renew its IP address. Second, "isn't always available," is not the same as "used to be available but now isn't," so it's an intermittent problem rather than a reconfiguration issue. This would not tie in with the reported problem if the Web site is sometimes available, but other times not. **D** is incorrect because not only do standard Web services not require additional port settings, but this tab is for outbound ports rather than inbound ports—which is what would be used when hosting your own Web service.

16. ☑ **B, C.** ICS and NAT cannot work in conjunction with a DHCP server, so these services would be automatically disabled and an error logged in their Event Logs.
☒ **A** is incorrect. Although you might work in a small office where you think everybody talks to each other, don't rely on colleagues supplying vital information! First, they may not realize the consequences of installing DHCP, so they see no reason to mention it; and second, they may simply forget to mention it. **D** is incorrect. The only error displayed on the workstation

would be when the Internet connection failed (e.g., host not found). Because the workstation is unaware that Internet connections are actually going via ICS/NAT, you can't expect the workstation to log an ICS/NAT error! Instead, you must look to the machine actually hosting the ICS/NAT service for any errors.

17. ☑ C. For shared VPN connections in a SOHO environment, you should create the VPN connection on each workstation rather than on the computer with the Internet connection. The default VPN Server Type is Automatic, which will try LT2P/IPSec first (which will fail because IPSec is not translatable), and then PPTP (which is translatable with the help of a NAT editor). Initial connections would be quicker if the Server Type were set to PPTP rather than Automatic.

☒ A is incorrect because you should not directly join a SOHO network when using ICS/NAT—the SOHO network would then be subject to packets from all your company network services such as domain controllers, routers, etc., which do not work with NAT. Also, Kerberos will be used to authenticate the users, and this protocol is not translatable. **B** is not the correct way to use a VPN connection over a shared link. If you do this, no Internet traffic from other users on the SOHO network will work, because all nonlocal traffic will be automatically routed to the company network. **D** will fail because IPSec is not translatable.

LAB ANSWER

The steps you should take include the following:

1. Configure NAT on a Windows 2000 Server—if you want to use a DHCP server, you must disable the DHCP allocator, which you can't do with ICS. Additionally, only NAT allows you to use more than one public address.
2. If not already done so, configure your Internet connection so you can successfully connect to the Internet from this machine.
3. If not already done so, enable RRAS with routing support.
4. Add the NAT routing protocol, and then add it to the internal interface and the external interface.
5. Disable the DHCP allocator under the NAT global properties by deselecting the option "Automatically assign IP addresses by using DHCP."

6. On the external interface, specify your Internet addresses under the Address Pools, and with the Reservations button, specify the Internet IP address that will be used for your company Web server.

7. On the external interface, specify under the Special Ports tab the workstation IP address or name that will be hosting the Web server, and the port it will be using.

MCSE

MICROSOFT CERTIFIED SYSTEMS ENGINEER

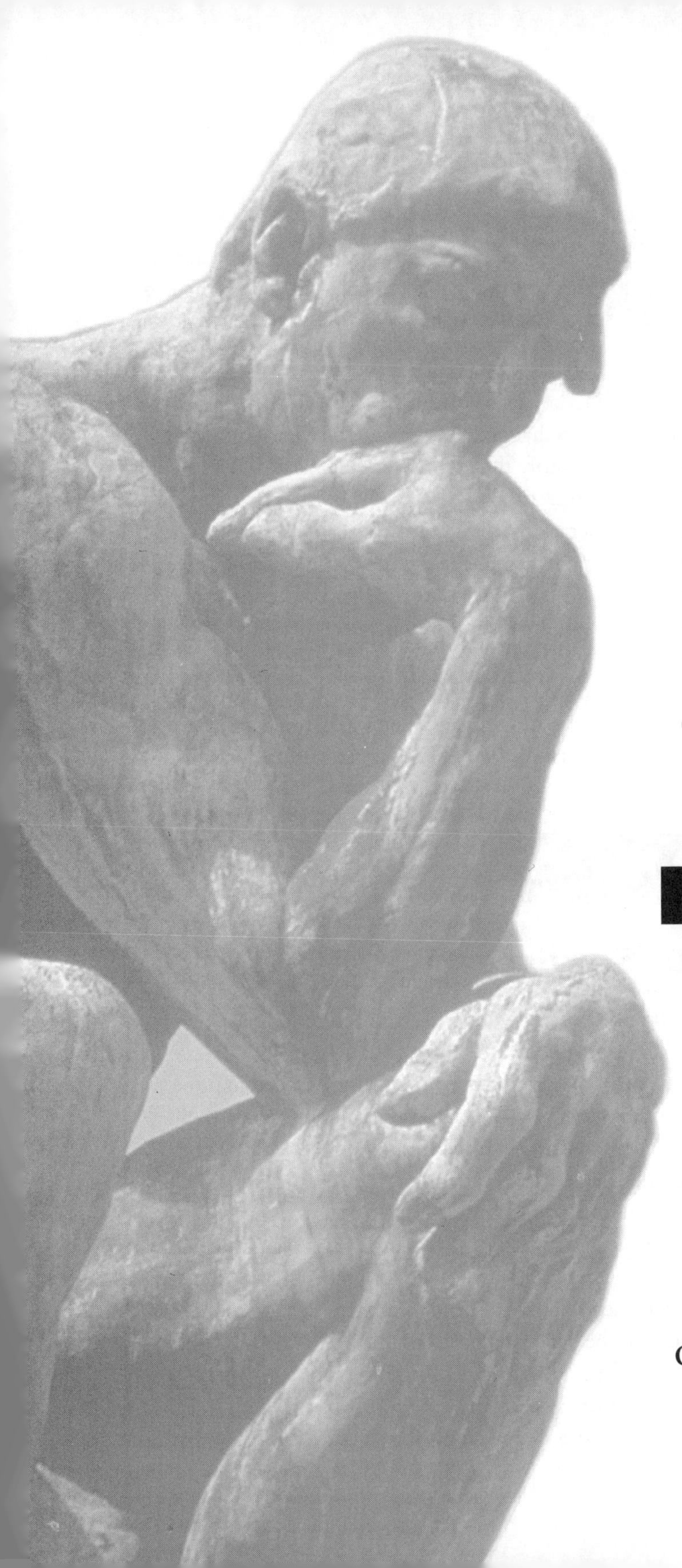

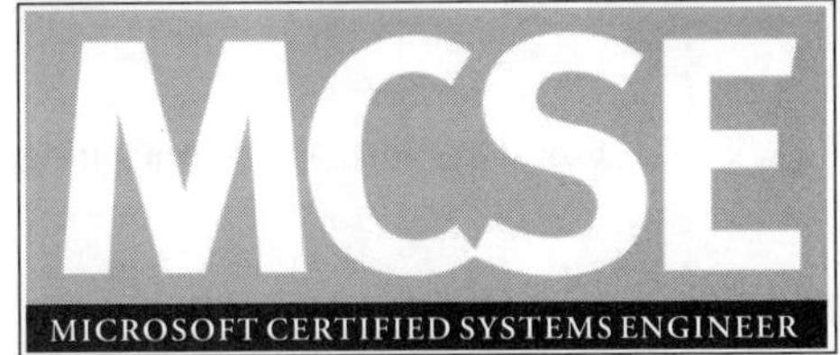

11

Installing, Configuring, Managing, Monitoring, and Troubleshooting Certificate Services

CERTIFICATION OBJECTIVES

11.01	Overview of Certificate Services
11.02	Management and Administration of Certificates
11.03	Creating and Issuing Certificates in Windows 2000
11.04	Certificate-Based Authentication
11.05	Encrypting File System (EFS) Recovery Keys
11.06	Troubleshooting Certificates
✓	Two-Minute Drill
Q&A	Self Test

Windows 2000 incorporates many industry-standard (as well as industrial-strength) security features to protect data. Microsoft has included Public Key Infrastructure (PKI) based technology in the form of Certificate Services to ensure that critical data remains secure.

Originally, certificates and public key encryption were an Internet-based phenomenon. Encryption keys were exchanged between Web servers and clients via certificates or cookies, and used to verify the identity of each party and authenticate transactions carried out between them.

Microsoft Certificate Servers generate X.509 certificates that are used by clients and other servers to establish their identity and the identity of the issuing server. Certificates are commonly used on Web sites to accurately verify the identities of individuals accessing the site and to secure data passed between the Web browser and the Web server.

In this chapter, we look at Windows 2000 Certificate Services, and how certificate-based authentication and the Encrypting File System (EFS) are used to further extend security past the limits of the NTFS file permissions used in Windows NT.

CERTIFICATION OBJECTIVE 11.01

Overview of Certificate Services

To gain a good understanding of Certificate Services, we need to look at the underlying technology that drives it: Public Key Infrastructure, or PKI.

Public Key Infrastructure is one of the cryptography methods developed to protect data exchanged between computer systems. PKI was developed to overcome the limitations of network size on client and server authentication processes. PKI uses cryptography algorithms, the most widely used of which is the Rivest-Shamir-Adleman (RSA) algorithm, to scramble and unscramble data. The system uses a pair of keys, a public encryption key and a private encryption key, to perform cryptographic functions on data. Each key can be used to encrypt or decrypt data passed between two systems. For example, if the public key is used to encrypt some data, then the corresponding private key can be used to decrypt the data, and vice versa.

The public encryption key is freely distributed by the system that owns it, while the private key is kept securely on the system and never distributed. The reason public key encryption works is because even though the keys are created in pairs, unlike encryption keys used in other cryptography systems, they are distinctly different from each other. Public encryption keys are digitally signed by the issuer of the public key to guarantee authenticity. This digital signature is essential when the owner of the private key intends to send encrypted data to another computer that possesses the public key. The computer verifies the identity of the sender by using the public key to check the digital signature. Digital signatures are unique to each system, so there is no mistaking who the owner of the certificate is. PKI basically works using the following method, shown in Figure 11-1:

1. System A contacts System B, requesting a secure connection.
2. System B gives its public encryption key to System A.
3. System A uses System B's public encryption key to encrypt the data it wishes to exchange with System B and submits the encrypted data.
4. System B receives the data, verifies the signature on the public encryption key, and uses its private encryption key to decrypt the data. If System B needs to pass any data back to System A, it also uses the private encryption key to encrypt that data.

Windows 2000 Certificate Services is Microsoft's implementation of PKI technology. Certificate Services was introduced with Microsoft Internet Information Server 4.0 in the Windows NT Option Pack as a component of Internet Information Server. Microsoft has taken the original intention of Public Key Infrastructure a step further, by incorporating Certificate Services as another level of security and authentication on private networks as well as on the Internet.

Certificates along with the Encrypting File System (EFS) help further secure data by applying a public encryption key to it, rendering it undecipherable to anyone without the corresponding private encryption key.

Encryption keys are created in pairs: a private encryption key, that stays protected on the server, and a public key that is freely distributed by the server to clients requesting a connection to the server. The client uses the public encryption key

FIGURE 11-1 Two systems exchanging secure data via PKI

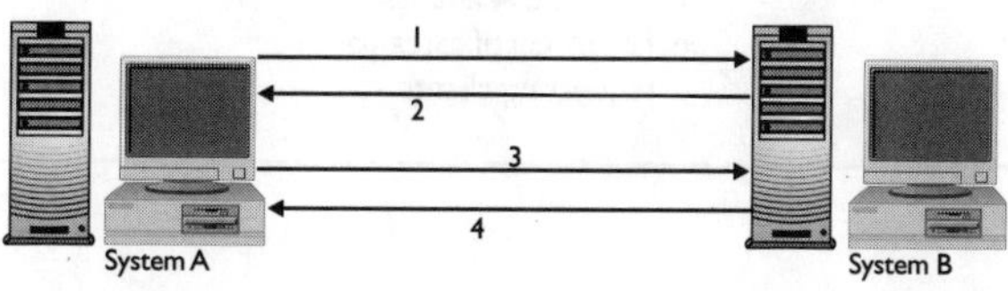

issued it by the server to encrypt data it intends to send to the server. The server then uses its corresponding private encryption key to decrypt the data received.

Certificates are typically either created by a well-known Certificate Authority company such as VeriSign, or are created by a certificate server owned and operated by the company running the Web site. Certificate Services servers allow systems to exchange information securely both on the Internet and within private networks. Certificate Services employs a hierarchical structure (see Figure 11-2) with the main server, called the Certification Authority, or CA, as the root of the hierarchy. A CA is a trusted server responsible for generating, issuing, and signing certificates. The original server certificates stay on the CA, but the public key certificates are issued to subordinate certificate servers that rely on the root CA. These subordinate certificate servers in turn issue public key user certificates to clients that request secure communications.

FIGURE 11-2 Certificate Services servers

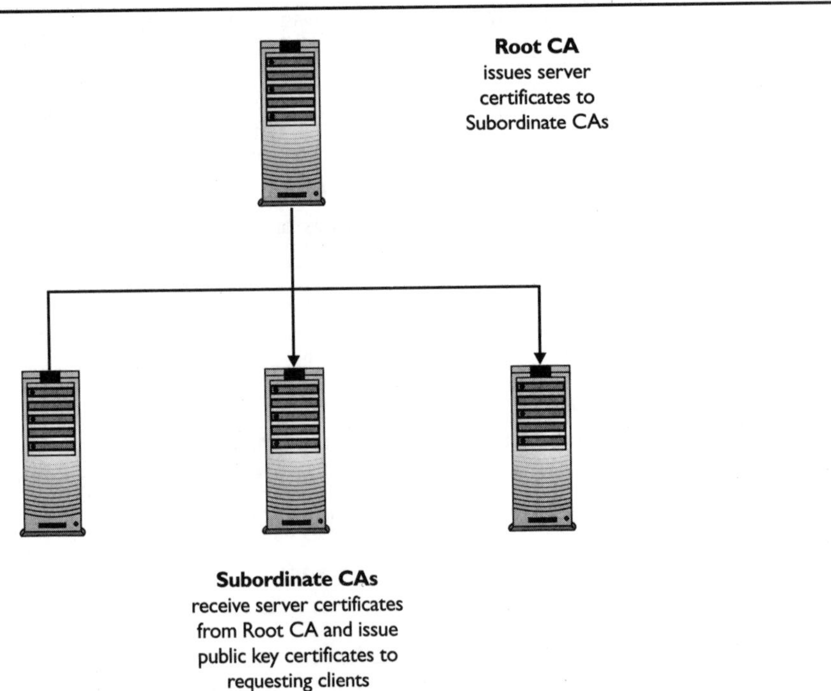
Root CA
issues server
certificates to
Subordinate CAs
Subordinate CAs
receive server certificates
from Root CA and issue
public key certificates to
requesting clients

EXERCISE 11-1

Installing Certificate Services

1. Click Start | Settings | Control Panel.
2. Double-click Add/ Remove Programs.
3. Click Add/Remove Windows Components.
4. Select Certificate Services, as shown in the following illustration.

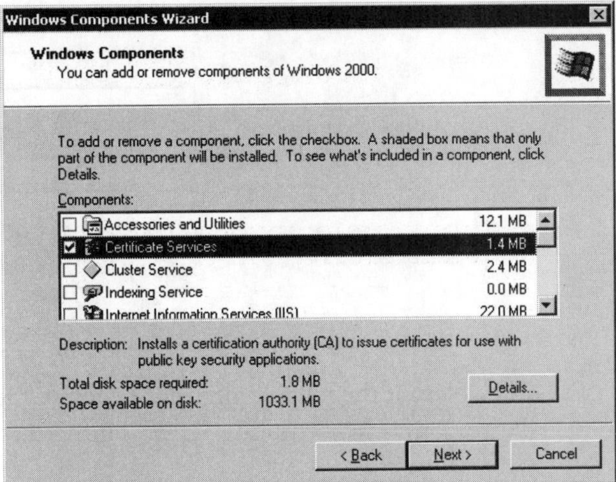

5. Select the type of server you wish to install, and click Next. For our purposes, a Stand-alone root CA will do, as shown in the following illustration.

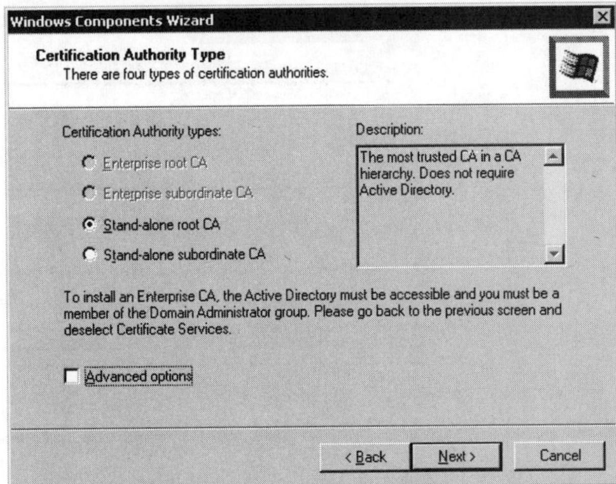

6. Enter your information in the next window, shown in the following illustration, and click Next.

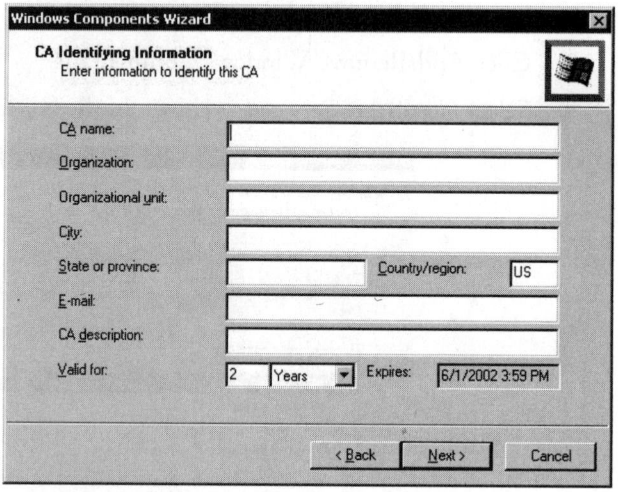

7. Click Next at the following screens to accept the defaults (see the following illustration). The Certificate Server is installed.

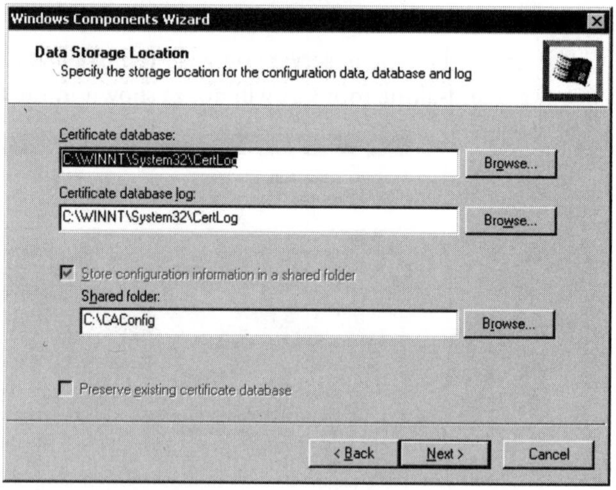

exam watch

An Organizational Unit (OU) is similar to a corporate division or User Group, and is a common term associated with directory services like X.500 and Active Directory.

on the job

You cannot change the name of the server that you install Certificate Server on. You will find that the option for changing the name of the server is not available. If you wish to change the name of the server, you will need to remove certificate services.

exam watch

Enterprise Certificate Servers should only be installed in domains using Active Directory. Stand-alone servers can exist in domains with or without Active Directory, but they are not "visible" unless included in an Active Directory tree.

What Is a Public Key Certificate?

A Public Key Certificate is a security token that is passed between two computer systems that allows data exchanged between the two to be encrypted. A public encryption key included in the public key certificate is responsible for encoding the data. As mentioned before, only the corresponding private encryption key can decrypt the encrypted data exchanged between the client and the server. Certificates can be either single use (e.g., secure e-mail [S/MIME] only) or multiuse (e.g., secure e-mail [S/MIME], Encrypting File System, and client authentication). So, we can easily see that the certificates can be applied in various scenarios.

Uses of Certificates

A public key certificate exchanged between a client and a server identifies the server to the client as the correct entity with which to communicate. Public key certificates are popular on e-commerce Web sites or secure sites that offer file downloads. Users need to know that they can trust the site with which they exchange data. For example, as a result of the high security provided by certificates, it is common practice now for people to do their banking over the Internet—even in cases where the bank doesn't even have a physical premises. Users with accounts at the bank can trust that their financial transactions and data will remain secure even though they are accessing them over the public Internet, because the CA at the bank issued a public key certificate bearing the bank's identity in it.

Certificates are a good way to verify identity without having to do any time-consuming, manual checking, or having to create a user account for each user that contacts a site. Some popular e-mail applications like MS Outlook and Lotus Notes use certificates to encrypt e-mail, thus ensuring that only the intended recipient can read the message. Apart from Web security, using certificates is also an excellent way to authenticate users and protect data via the Encrypting File System (EFS) on the LAN. This is evident via the advent of corporate extranets, where companies conduct business and share sensitive data with each other and with their customers. We examine this aspect later in the chapter.

Information Contained in Certificates

Certificates usually contain the following information, as shown in Figure 11-3:

- The public or private encryption key value
- The name and digital signature of the certificate bearer, which may be either a user or a service
- The length of time the certificate is valid
- The identity of the Certificate Authority

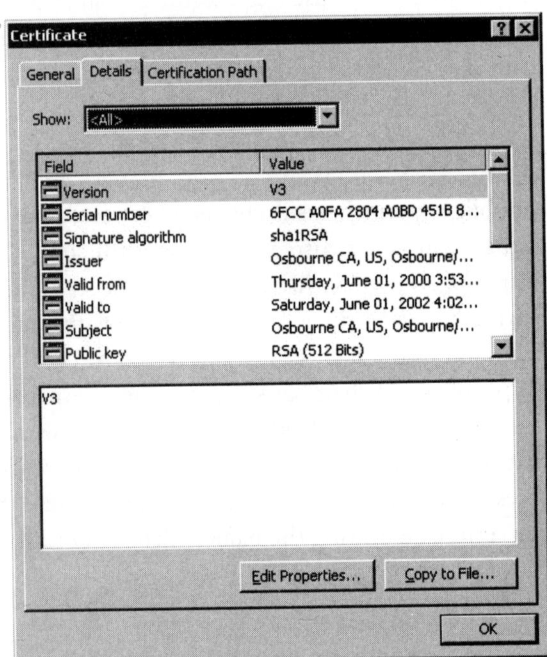

FIGURE 11-3

Information contained in a certificate

The public and private encryption key values are used in the encryption/decryption process. The name and digital signature serve as proof of identity for the client. Certificates have life spans, after which they cannot be used to encrypt or decrypt data and need to be reissued. The receiving computer uses the length of time information to note how long it can use the certificate. The identity of the CA verifies that the issuing CA is valid and trusted.

The Certification Hierarchy

Certificate hierarchies pretty much resemble DNS hierarchies in that they are structured in a top-down fashion (see Figure 11-4). This hierarchical structure results in a flexible infrastructure that is scalable and easy to administer. The certification hierarchy is one of the characteristics of PKI that makes it such an effective security model. The certification path is also another feature of the hierarchy that makes management easier. A certificate's certification path is what is used to verify the authenticity and validity of a certificate. The path tracks the

FIGURE 11-4 Certification Authority hierarchy

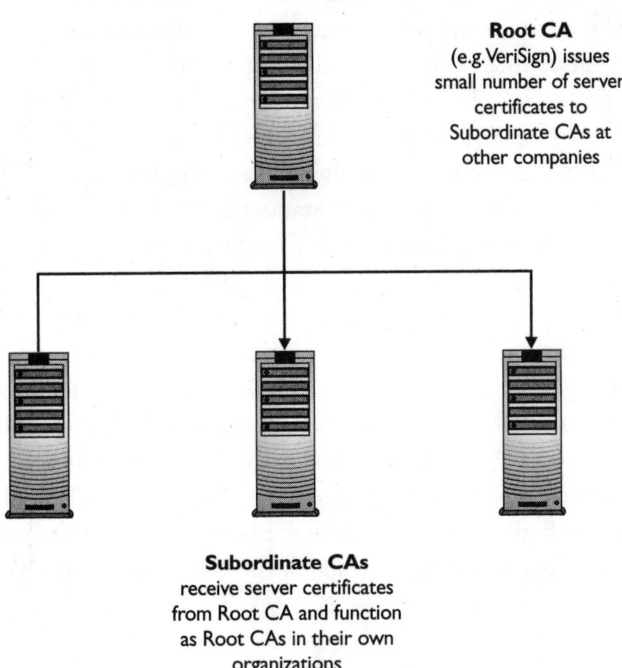
Root CA
(e.g.VeriSign) issues
small number of server
certificates to
Subordinate CAs at
other companies
Subordinate CAs
receive server certificates
from Root CA and function
as Root CAs in their own
organizations

certifiers of a certificate back to the original root CA that issued the certificate in the first place. As mentioned previously, this is usually a well-known, respected CA company.

Certification Authorities

A Certification Authority (CA) is a trusted server responsible for generating, issuing, and signing certificates. The CA handles all certificate requests. There are two main types of Certification Authority in a certification hierarchy: the root CA and the subordinate CA, as shown in Figure 11-4.

Root Authorities

A Root Authority is the supreme CA. Root CAs are responsible for issuing certificates to subordinate CAs. Much like root DNS servers only know a small number of other DNS servers, root CAs only sign a small number of certificates. These certificates are issued to subordinate CAs, as shown in Figure 11-4.

Subordinate Certification Authorities

Subordinate Certification Authorities are servers that rely on the root CA. These subordinate certificate servers receive certificates from root CAs and, in turn, issue public key certificates to clients that request secure communications.

During installation of Certificate Services, the administrator can select the level of CA to create. Subordinate CAs receive signed server certificates from the root CA, which they use to service clients. In a Windows 2000 domain, CAs come in two flavors: Enterprise CAs and Stand-alone CAs. Enterprise CAs require and use the Active Directory. Stand-alone CAs do not require the Active Directory, but will use it if the CA is installed on a domain controller.

Certificate hierarchies should typically mimic the domain administration hierarchy. This guarantees their security and availability, and makes management simpler. A Subordinate CA can exist in the same Windows 2000 domain as its root CA, in a child domain, or even in a domain in a separate Windows 2000 forest. Management of subordinate CAs can be delegated to the local administrators where the server resides.

Certificate management in the hierarchy is effected through group policies. The policies are basically a set of rules for issuing, verifying, and signing certificates. The policies differ depending on whether the CA enforcing the policy is an Enterprise root CA or a Stand-alone root CA. Enterprise CAs rely on Active Directory and the Windows 2000 security model to recognize and authenticate certificates, whereas Stand-alone CAs rely on direct administrator action to verify client requests.

Well-known, commercial CA organizations possess root CA servers that issue certificates to subordinate CAs in other companies (for a fee, of course!). These subordinate CAs function as root CAs in their own organization and issue certificates to clients requesting secure communication and authentication.

exam Watch

Certificate Services uses templates that are stored in Active Directory to define and enforce policies.

The Certificate Store

The Certificate Store is a database created during the installation of a CA. If Certificate Services is installed on an Enterprise root CA, the store resides in the Active Directory. If it is installed on a Stand-alone root CA, the store resides on the server itself. The certificate store is a repository for supporting or verifying certificates issued by that particular CA. A single certificate store can support up to 250,000 certificates.

Now that we've covered the basics of Certificate Services, here are some possible scenario questions and their answers:

SCENARIO & SOLUTION	
I am installing a root Enterprise Certification Authority…	Your domain should be running Active Directory.
How do I know that my certificate is authentic?	The Digital Signature on the certificate proves the identity of the issuer.
Can I use Certificate Services to secure my mail?	Yes, certificates can be used to secure mail as well as data.
Can users on my Web site access my private encryption key?	No, private encryption keys are kept secret.

CERTIFICATION OBJECTIVE 11.02

Management and Administration of Certificates

As you no doubt already know, the Microsoft Management Console (MMC) is used to manage and administer many configurable services in Windows 2000. These services are accessed via snap-ins, modules that contain the objects that control settings for the services.

Using the Certificates MMC

Certificate management and administration is done via the Certificates or Certificate Authority Management MMC snap-in. Certification Authority management is done in the same snap-in, but administrator privilege is required.

EXERCISE 11-2

Using the MMC Certificates/Certificate Authority Snap-In

1. Start the Microsoft Management Console, by clicking Start | Run, and typing **mmc** in the Open: field.
2. In the MMC, click Console, and select Add/Remove Snap-in.
3. In the Add/Remove Snap-in window, click Add, as shown in the following illustration.

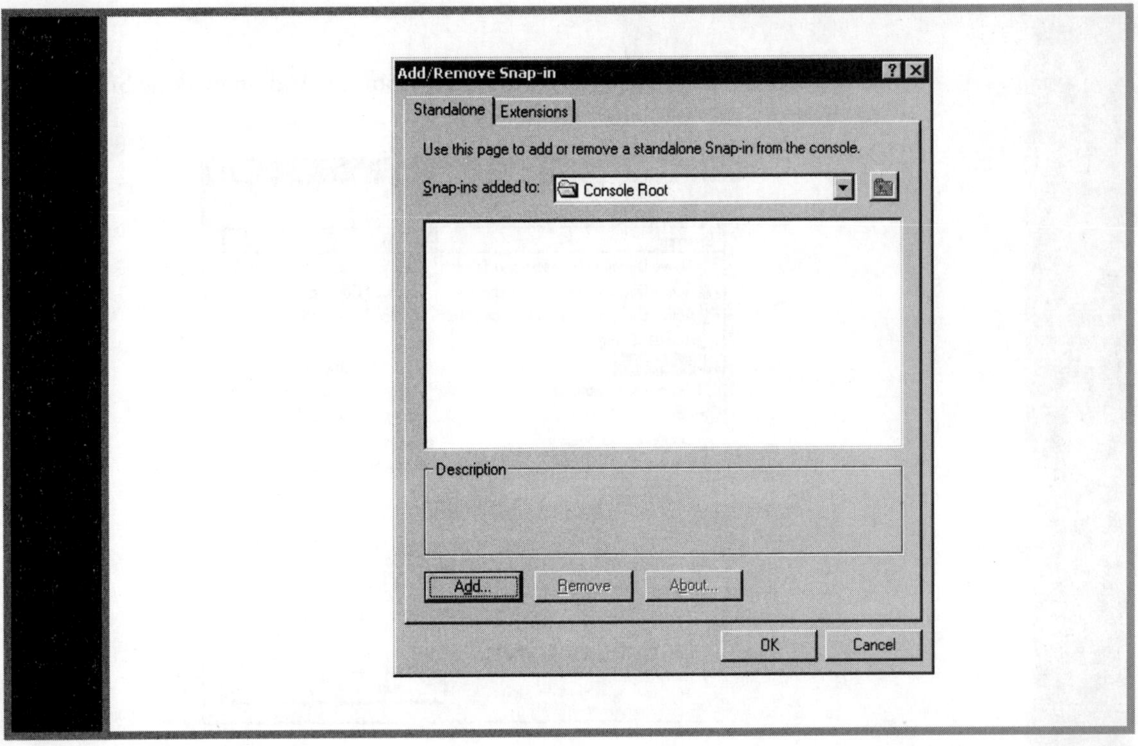
Add/Remove Snap-in
Standalone
Extensions
Use this page to add or remove a standalone Snap-in from the console.
Snap-ins added to:
Console Root
Description
Add...
Remove
About...
OK
Cancel

4. Select Certificates or Certificate Authority from the Add Standalone Snap-in list shown in the following illustration.

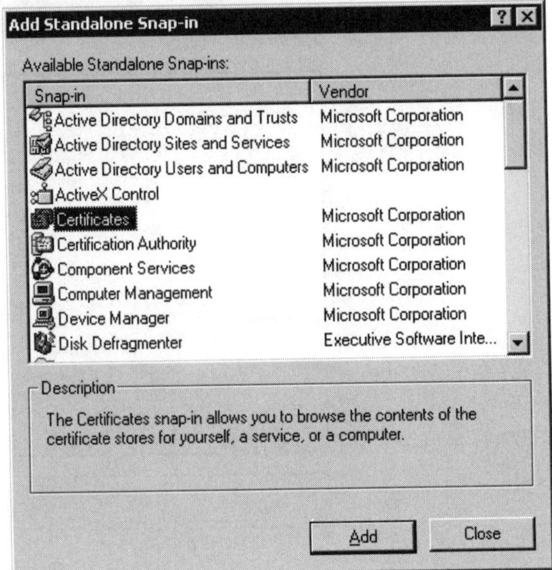

5. Double-click Certificates/Certificate Authority to view the list of certificates and CAs available.

Publishing Certificates to Active Directory

When Certificate Services is installed on an Enterprise CA, certificate information is automatically published in different objects in Active Directory. The following information is published in Active Directory:

- **User Certificates** Used for data exchange applications; e.g., Encrypting File System
- **CA Certificates** Used for building certification paths to trusted root CAs
- **Certificate Revocation Lists (CRL)** To facilitate checking of certificate validity status

Active Directory has three directories for specific types of data, only two of which are pertinent to this topic. The Domain Data directory contains all of the objects in the Active Directory for one particular domain. User certificates are published in the User object in the Domain Data directory. CA certificates are published on a "CertificationAuthority" object, and CRLs (Certificate Revocation Lists) are published in CRLDistrbutionPoint object in the Configuration Data directory.

Certificates from a Stand-alone CA can also be published in Active Directory, but this must be done by an administrator.

A common security practice at root CA sites is to take the server running Certificate Services off the network and physically store the server in a vault to prevent tampering.

Certificate Formats

Windows 2000 Certificate Services supports four standard certificate formats.

Personal Information Exchange

The Personal Information Exchange format, also known as the Public Key Cryptography Standards #12 (PKCS #12) format, is an industry standard format that facilitates backup and restoration of a certificate and its private key. This vendor-independent certificate format enables certificates and their corresponding private keys to be transferred from one computer to another, or from a computer to removable media. Personal Information Exchange format is the only format used by Windows 2000 when exporting certificates and private keys because it avoids exposing the keys to unintended parties. Certain conditions must exist for the format to be used

- The Cryptographic Service Provider (CSP) must recognize the certificate and keys as exportable.
- The certificate is for EFS or EFS recovery.
- The certificate is requested via the Advanced Certificate Request certification authority Web page with the "Mark keys as exportable" check box checked.

Cryptographic Message Syntax Standard

Better known as PKCS #7, this format enables the transfer of a certificate and all other certificates in its certification path either from one computer to another, or from a computer to removable media. PKCS #7 files use the .p7b file extension.

DER Encoded Binary X.509

This is the format used for non-Windows 2000 certification authorities. Since the Internet is still dominated by non-Windows servers, it is supported for interoperability. DER certificate files use the .cer file extension.

Base64 Encoded X.509

This format is also used by non-Windows certificate servers, and therefore supports interoperability. Base64 Encoded X.509 certificate files also use the .cer file extension.

Importing and Exporting Certificates

The usefulness of certificates is again seen in the ability to pass certificates between organizations. Certificates can be imported from other sources, be it a CA external to your organization or simply another computer. Certificates can also be exported from your organization to another, or simply to media as with a PKCS #12 certificate. The Certificates/Certificate Authority MMC snap-in is used to import and export PKCS #12, PKCS #7, and DER encoded binary X.509 certificate files.

When a certificate is imported, it is copied from a certificate file that uses one of the standard certificate storage formats introduced earlier to a certificate store for a user or computer account. Certificates may be imported in order to:

- Install a certificate that was sent in a file by another user, computer, or CA
- Restore a damaged or lost certificate that was previously backed up
- Install a certificate and its associated private key from a computer that the certificate holder was previously using

Certificates are exported by copying the certificate from its certificate store to a file that uses one of the standard certificate storage formats. Certificates may be exported in order to:

- Back up a certificate
- Back up a certificate and its associated private key
- Copy a certificate so it can be used on another computer
- Remove a certificate and its private key from the current certificate holder for installation on another computer

EXERCISE 11-3

Importing a Certificate

Now that we have discussed importing and exporting certificates, let's try importing a certificate. Windows 2000 employs a wizard-driven method to accomplish this.

1. Launch the MMC by clicking Start | Run, and then typing **mmc**.
2. In the console, expand the Certificates node. Then expand Personal.
3. Right-click the Certificates folder, point to All Tasks, and then click Import. The Certificate Import Wizard launches, as shown in the following illustration. Click Next.

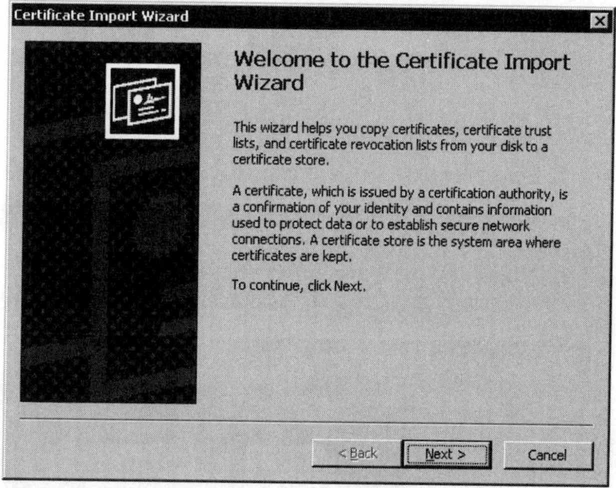

4. Click Browse to select the CA certificate you would like to import. After you've selected the file, click Next.

5. Click the "Automatically select certificate store based on the type of certificate" option, as shown in the following illustration. Click Next.

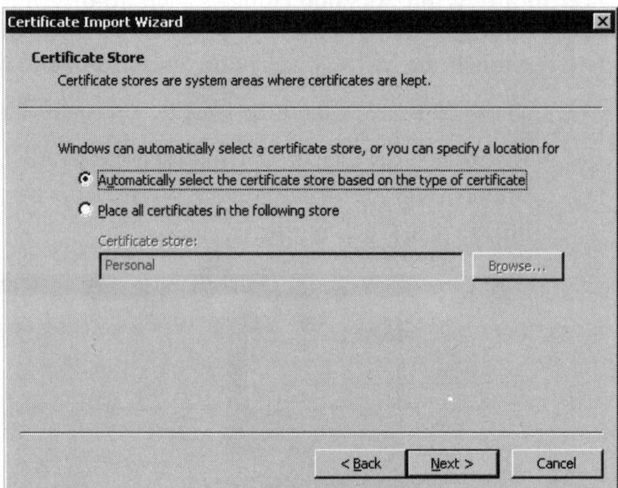

6. Read the information in the Completing the Certificate Import Wizard window shown in the following illustration, and then click Finish. The CA certificate is now installed.

7. To verify this, scroll through the list of certificates in the right pane to find the one you have just installed, as shown in the following illustration.

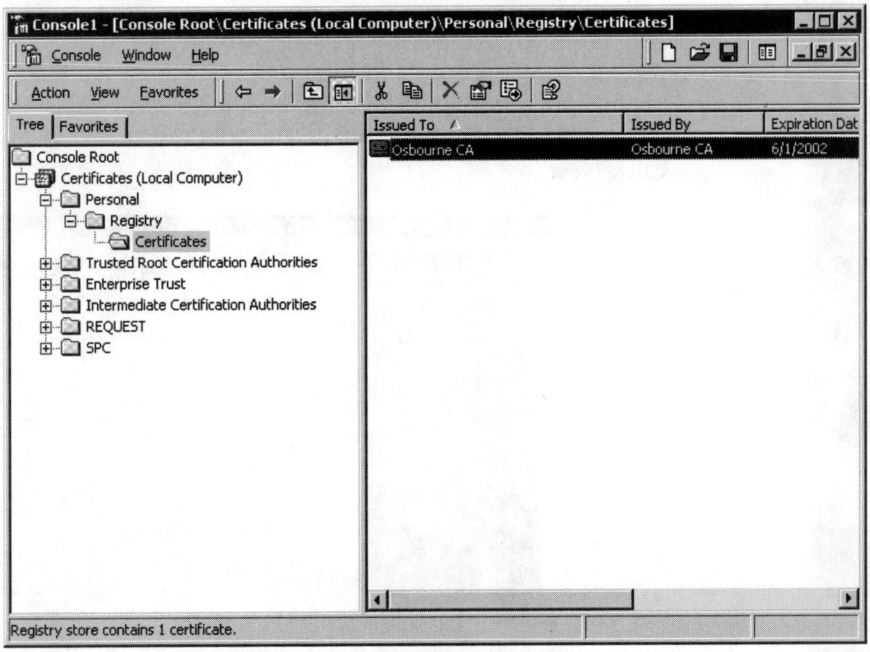

EXERCISE 11-4

Exporting a Certificate

Since we are still in the Certificates console, let's export a certificate file. There is also a wizard-driven tool utility for this procedure.

1. Right-click the certificate(s) you want to export.
2. Point to All Tasks on the Context menu, and click Export to launch the Certificate Export Wizard, as shown in the following illustration. Click Next.

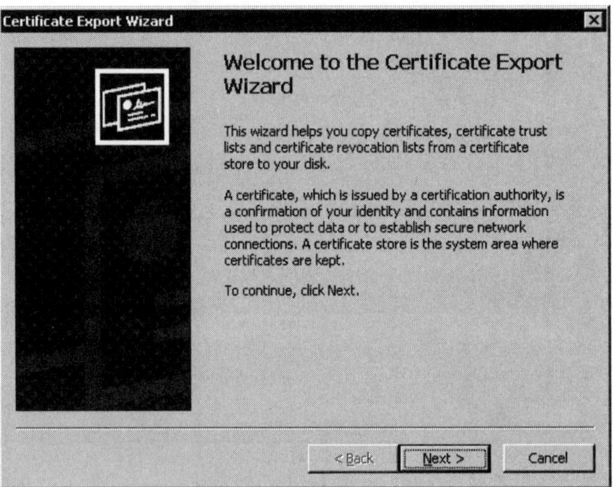

3. Select, "No, do not export the private key," as shown in the following illustration. Click Next.

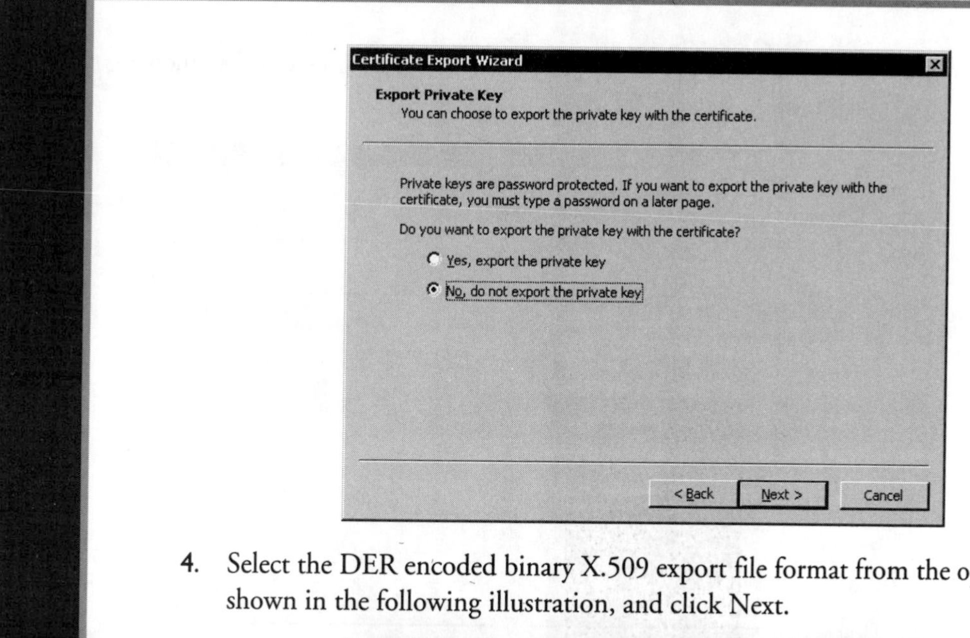

4. Select the DER encoded binary X.509 export file format from the options, as shown in the following illustration, and click Next.

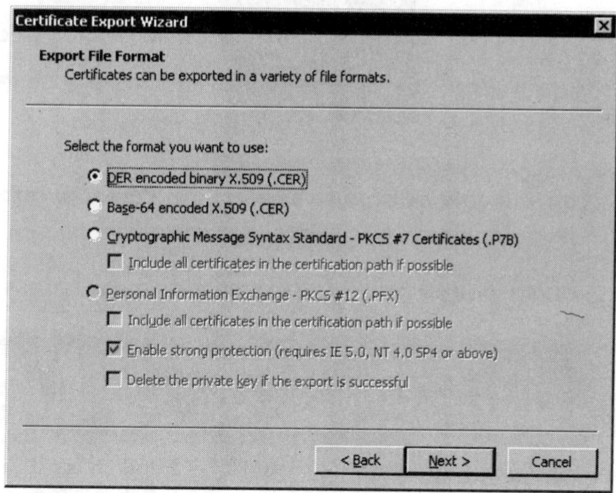

5. Enter the name of the file you want to export (shown in the following illustration). Click Next.

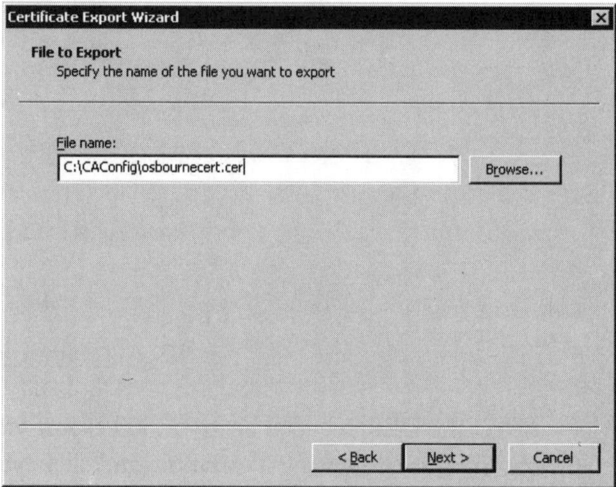

6. Verify the choices you have made in the wizard. Click Finish to export to the file.

You will only be able to export to a Personal Information Exchange PKCS#12 file if you want to export the private key.

Let's look at this grid with scenarios and solutions on certificate management.

SCENARIO & SOLUTION	
I want to access information from another company's secure Web site…	Import a certificate from the other company's root CA that grants access to the site, and issue it to yourself.
How do I manage the certificates I do have?	Certificates are managed in the Certification Authority/Certificates MMC snap-in.
I want to publish certificates in Active Directory…	Install your Enterprise root CA on a domain controller.
I need to export a certificate to a non-Windows host…	Export the certificate in either the DER Binary encoded, or the Base64 encoded format.

CERTIFICATION OBJECTIVE 11.03

Creating and Issuing Certificates in Windows 2000

Every client of a CA receives its own public key certificate. The next section discusses the process of creating and issuing these certificates to clients. This process is also referred to as X.509 certificate enrollment.

Generating Encryption Keys and Certificate Requests

PKI standards dictate the process for generating encryption keys and certificate requests. PKI allows the use of multiple methods of requesting and receiving certificates, some of which are Web-based enrollment, and policy-based auto-enrollment. Web-based enrollment is commonly seen when a user visits a site and requests a certificate, whereas policy-based auto-enrollment can be configured to occur when a user logs on to a Windows 2000 domain. In Windows 2000, this process is handled by Microsoft's X.509 certificate enrollment control.

The enrollment control either identifies or generates the user's key, builds the certificate request, and signs it. The certificate request is generated as a standard PKCS #10 certificate request and is submitted to the issuing certificate server. The PKCS #10 certificate request is comprised of:

- A version value
- The subject name and subject public key
- The signature algorithm and the digital signature of the requesting user
- Additional optional attributes

The Certificate Services server processes the requests and returns PKCS # 7 X.509 certificates to the client.

CryptoAPI

CryptoAPI is a software component that allows management of cryptographic functionality to be added to certificates. During certificate generation, CryptoAPI introduces cryptographic hardware or software modules called Cryptographic Service Providers (CSP) to the private key.

The CSP

A Cryptographic Service Provider, or CSP, is a hardware or software module used to perform a variety of cryptographic operations. CSPs are responsible for creating and destroying keys, as well as using the keys to perform a variety of cryptographic functions within the certificate.

Microsoft uses a base CSP that employs the RSA cryptographic algorithms; however, additional CSPs are available from third-party vendors like smart-card manufacturers. Traditionally, hardware-based CSPs are used because they offer better performance and significantly reduce the risk of tampering. Each CSP uses a different implementation of the CryptoAPI.

Processing Certificate Requests

Once a certificate request is submitted to the Certificate server, the request is processed and a certificate is returned to the requesting client. Let's look at this as a step-by-step process shown in Figure 11-5.

FIGURE 11-5 How certificate requests are processed

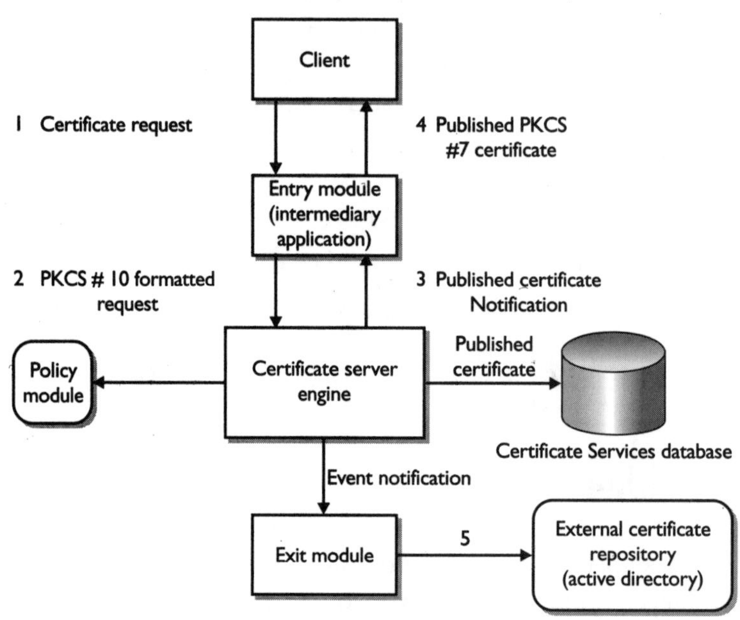

Request Reception

1. A client sends a certificate request to the server via an intermediary application, sometimes known as an Entry Module. The application interprets the request, formats it into a PKCS #10 type request, and submits it to the Certificate server engine.
2. The Certificate server engine queues the request and passes it to the Policy module, which queries the request properties to determine if the request is authorized. The module also adds any extra information asked for in the request to the certificate.

Request Approval

3. If the request is approved, the Certificate server engine takes the request and builds a complete certificate. The engine also logs the certificate creation. If the request is denied, the log will also record the revoked request.

Certificate Formation

4. The Certificate server engine stores completed certificates in the Certificate Services database and notifies the Entry Module of the status of the request. The Entry Module retrieves the certificate from the server engine and passes it back to the requesting client.

Certificate Publication

5. The server engine also notifies an Exit Module that publishes the certificate to an external repository such as the Active Directory.

EXERCISE 11-5

Requesting a Certificate via the Web-Based Request Form

Because we installed a Stand-alone root CA, we will have to request a certificate using the Web-based enrollment form.

1. Launch Internet Explorer.
2. Type in the URL for the Web-based certificate request form (http://servername/Certsrv).
3. Select "Request a certificate," as shown in the following illustration, and click Next.

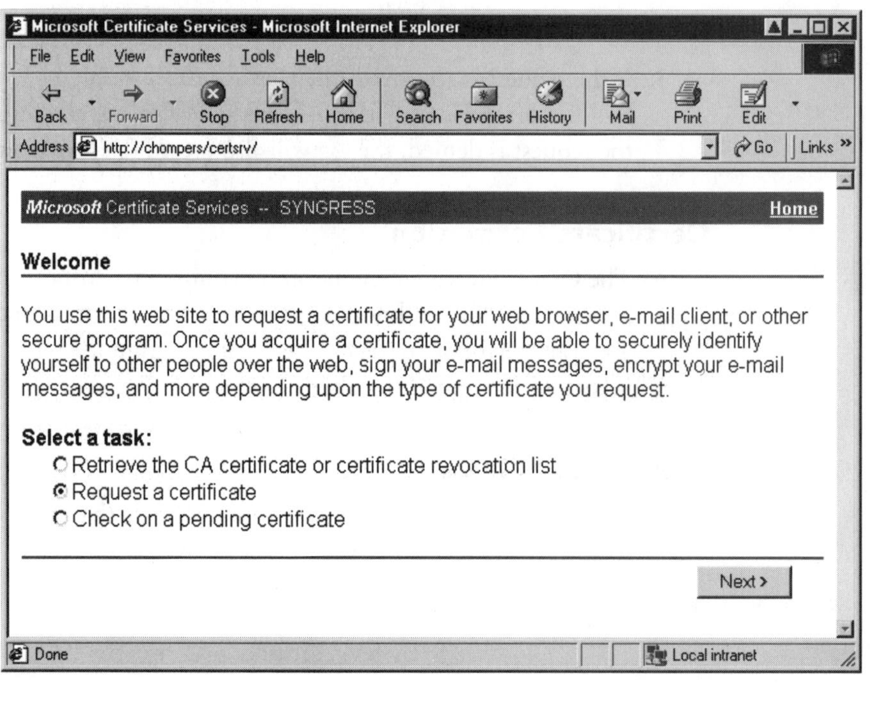

4. Select Web Browser Certificate type, as shown in the following illustration, and click Next.

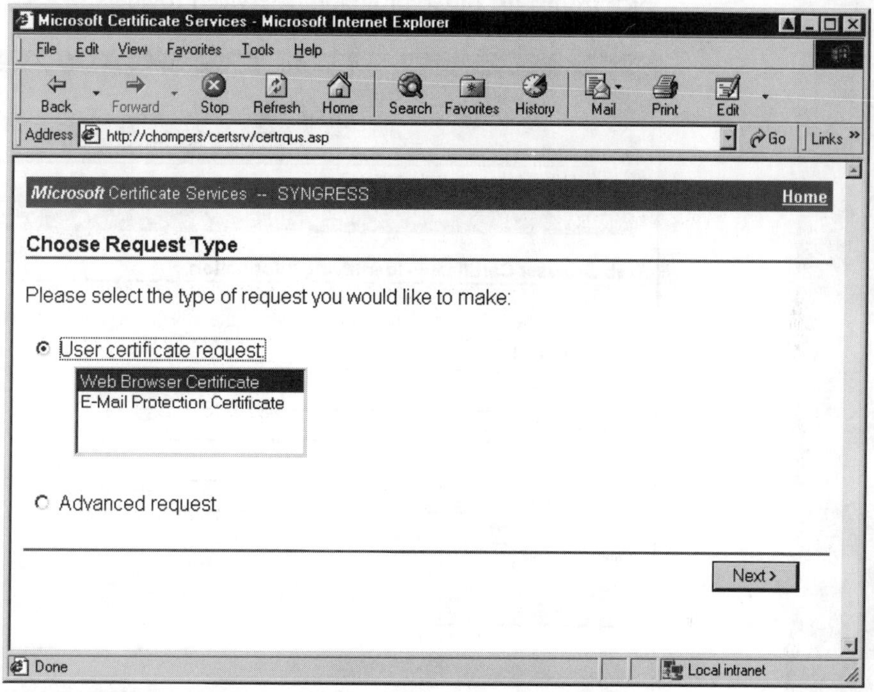

Microsoft Certificate Services - Microsoft Internet Explorer

File Edit View Favorites Tools Help

Back Forward Stop Refresh Home Search Favorites History Mail Print Edit

Address http://chompers/certsrv/certrqus.asp Go Links

Microsoft Certificate Services -- SYNGRESS Home

Choose Request Type

Please select the type of request you would like to make:

User certificate request:

Web Browser Certificate
E-Mail Protection Certificate

Advanced request

Next >

Done Local intranet

5. Enter your personal information in the fields shown in the following illustration, and click Submit. Clicking More Options allows you to pick from a list of Cryptographic Service Providers.

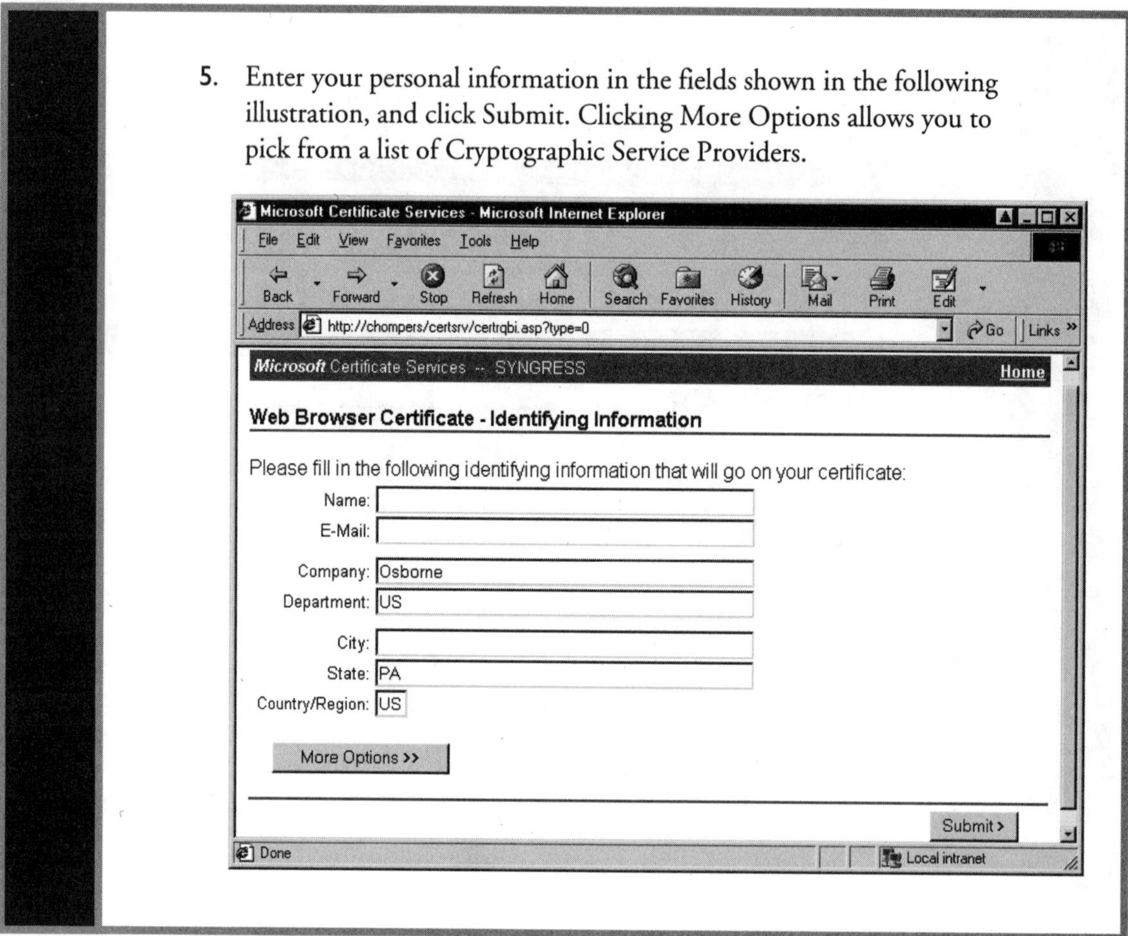

Revoking Certificates

Certificates or certificate requests can be revoked either automatically by using a Certificate Revocation List (CRL), or manually by an administrator.

Internet Information Services for Windows 2000 supports real-time Certificate Revocation List checking. A Certificate Revocation List is a list of certificates that are denied access to a Web server or Web site. CRLs are built using the Certificate Authority MMC snap-in. Real-time CRL checking allows the Web server to enforce access control on the fly. An administrator can also manually revoke certificates.

EXERCISE 11-6

Revoking a Certificate

1. Select the Issued Certificates folder in the Certificate Authority snap-in.
2. Right-click the certificate to be revoked.
3. Click All Tasks.
4. Select Revoke Certificate.
5. Select the reason for revocation from the drop-down box (see the following illustration).

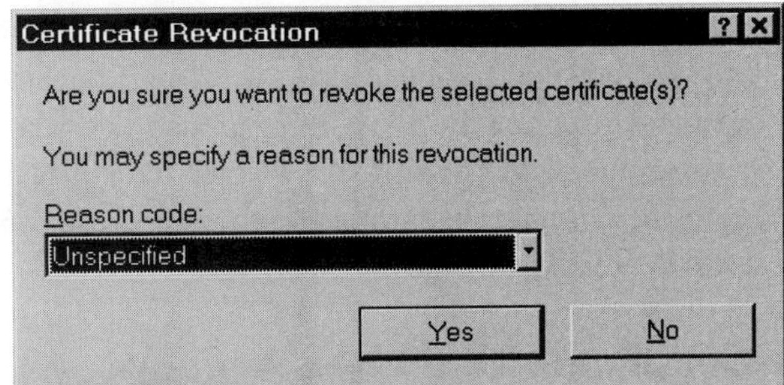

6. Click OK.

Revoked certificates can be re-signed and reissued by a Domain Administrator.

CERTIFICATION OBJECTIVE 11.04

Certificate-Based Authentication

Certificate-based authentication occurs in two ways:

- **User domain authentication** When a user in a Windows 2000 domain requests a certificate, Active Directory identifies the user to the CA, which in turn uses the user's security context to generate certificates with the correct user rights.

- **Computer auto-enrollment** Here, domain authentication is used to identify the computer account in the Windows 2000 domain. Group policies define the certificate the computer is eligible to receive. If the computer does not have a certificate corresponding to each of its eligible templates, the computer automatically enrolls with an Enterprise CA to receive the missing certificate.

External Users

Users who are not part of a Windows 2000 domain are handled differently. This scenario commonly occurs on the Internet. Users visit a Web site, supply personal information (e.g., name, address, credit card number), and request a secure connection to the site. The Web server returns a public key certificate to the client browser, which is used to encrypt the data submitted to the site by the browser. The encrypted information is passed to the server where the private key is used to decrypt the data. Once users visit a site, and receive a public key certificate, they can return to the site and use the certificate to create secure connections over and over again until the certificate expires.

Mapping a Certificate to a User Account

Mapping certificates to user accounts provides a way to seamlessly authenticate users and grant access to resources both on and off the Internet. Two types of certificate mapping are used, one-to-one mapping and many-to-many mapping. Let's look at these types of mapping more closely.

User Principle Name Mapping

This is a special kind of one-to-one mapping only available through the Active Directory. An Enterprise CA inserts an entry called a User Principle Name (UPN) into each of its certificates. UPNs are unique to each user's account within a Windows 2000 domain, and they are of the format *user@domain.* The UPN is used to locate the user account in Active Directory, and that account is logged on. This only occurs if the following conditions are met:

- The mapped certificate contains a UPN.
- The Windows 2000 domain is in the hierarchy of the Active Directory.
- The CA that issued the certificate is trusted to insert UPNs into the certificate.

If all of these conditions are not met, the user account can't be retrieved, and the Active Directory is searched for a mapping set by an administrator.

One-to-One Certificate Mapping

This type of mapping simply involves mapping a single user certificate to a single Windows 2000 user account. Certificates may be issued from your own Enterprise CA or from a trusted CA. These certificates are then manually mapped to their respective user accounts.

Many-to-One Certificate Mapping

This involves mapping many certificates to a single user account. This is particularly convenient when organizations need to share specific information with each other. An administrator must install the root CA certificates of all the desired CAs as trusted root CAs in his or her enterprise. The administrator can then set a rule that maps all certificates installed by the trusted CAs to a single Windows 2000 account. Users using these mapped certificates possess access rights defined by the rights set on the mapped account.

FROM THE CLASSROOM

Launching the Web Server Certificate Wizard

Your Web server should already have a server certificate for the following exercise to work. Please remember to request a certificate using the certificate request method described in Exercise 11-5 in the section *Creating and Issuing Certificates ion Windows 2000.* Clicking Server Certificate launches the Web Server Certificate Wizard, which you use to process and install the certificate.

—Chris O. Broomes, MCSE, MCP+I, MCT, CCDA

EXERCISE 11-7

Mapping a Certificate to a User Account

Certificate mapping is done via the Internet Service Manager on an IIS server. We will now attempt to map a certificate to a user account.

1. Click Start | Programs | Administrative Tools | Internet Services manager, as shown in the following illustration.

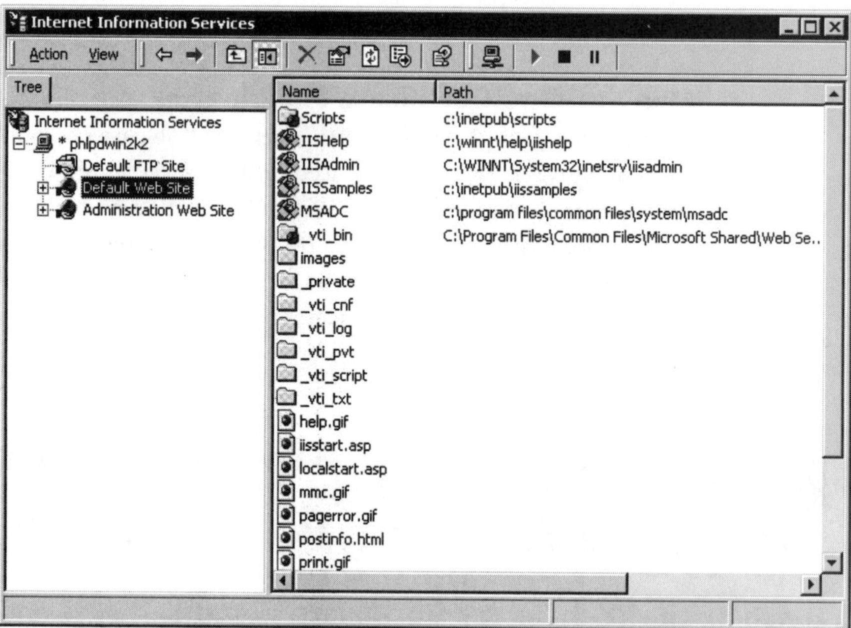

2. Expand the computer name folder. Right-click the Default Web Site folder, and click Properties on the submenu.
3. Click the Directory Security tab on the Default Web Site Properties dialog box, as shown in the following illustration.

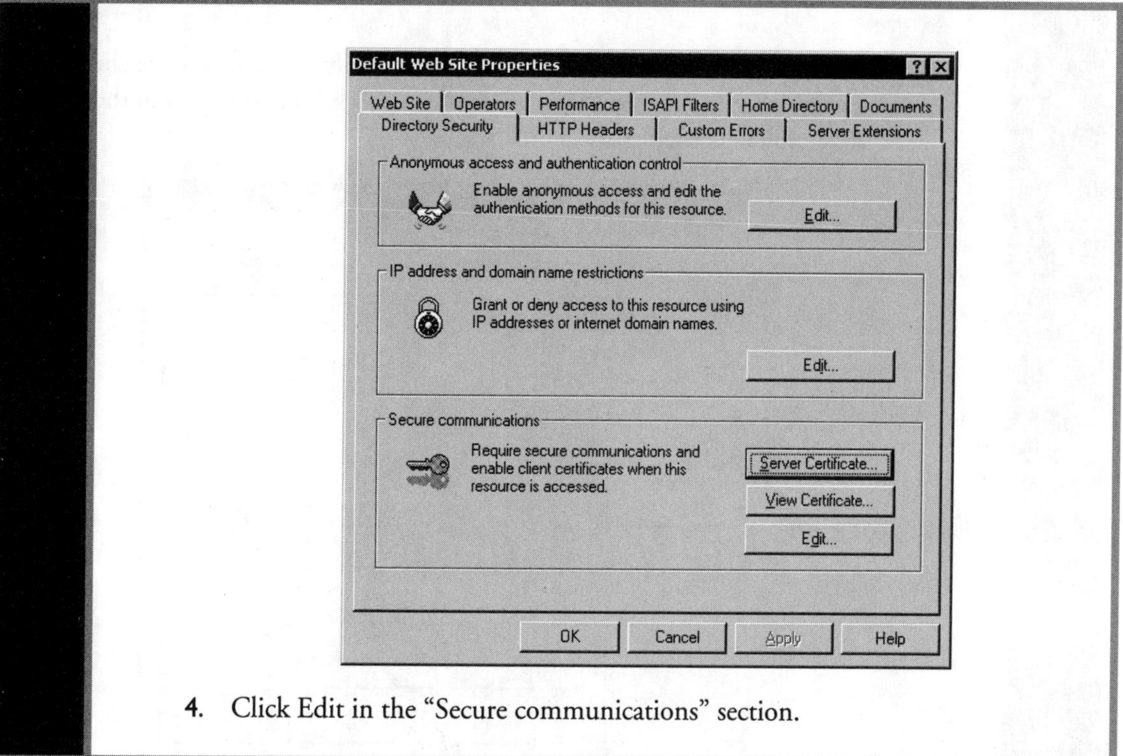

4. Click Edit in the "Secure communications" section.

5. In the Secure Communications dialog box, verify that the "Enable client certificate mapping" option is selected, and click Edit, as shown in the following illustration.

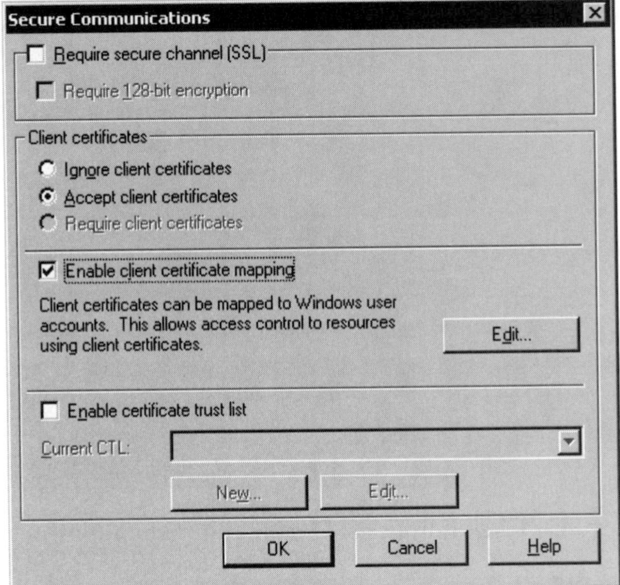

6. On the Account Mappings page, click the 1-to-1 tab, and click Add, as shown in the following illustration.

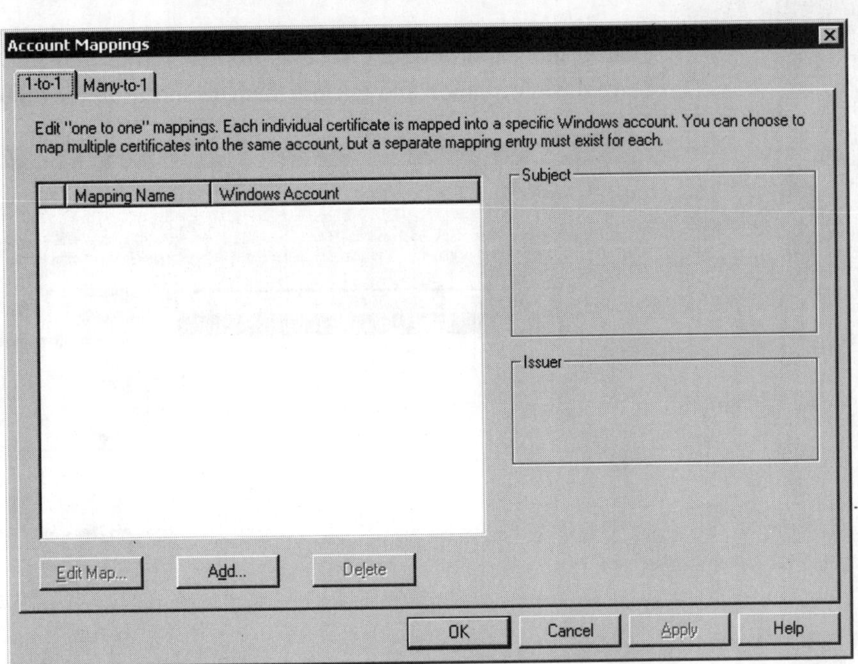

7. Select the user's certificate from the list, and click Open. For IIS, this certificate must be Base64-encoded and cannot be a binary certificate. Although Windows 2000 works with both types, IIS can only process Base64-encoded files,.
8. The Map to Account dialog opens, as shown in the following illustration. Click Browse to select the desired account. Enter the password, and click OK.

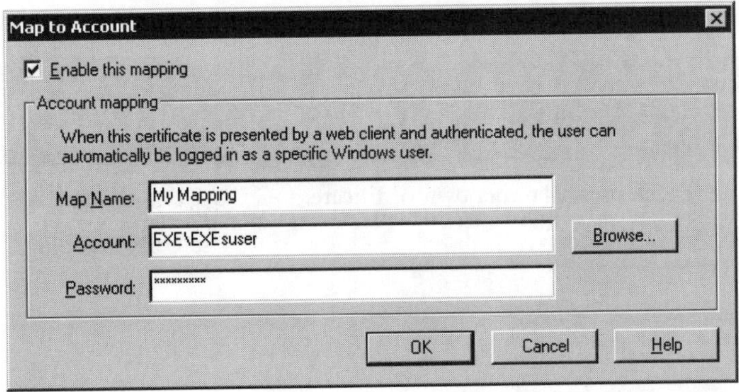

9. Click Apply and/or click OK, as appropriate, in the remaining dialog boxes to save the information and to close them, as shown in the following illustration.

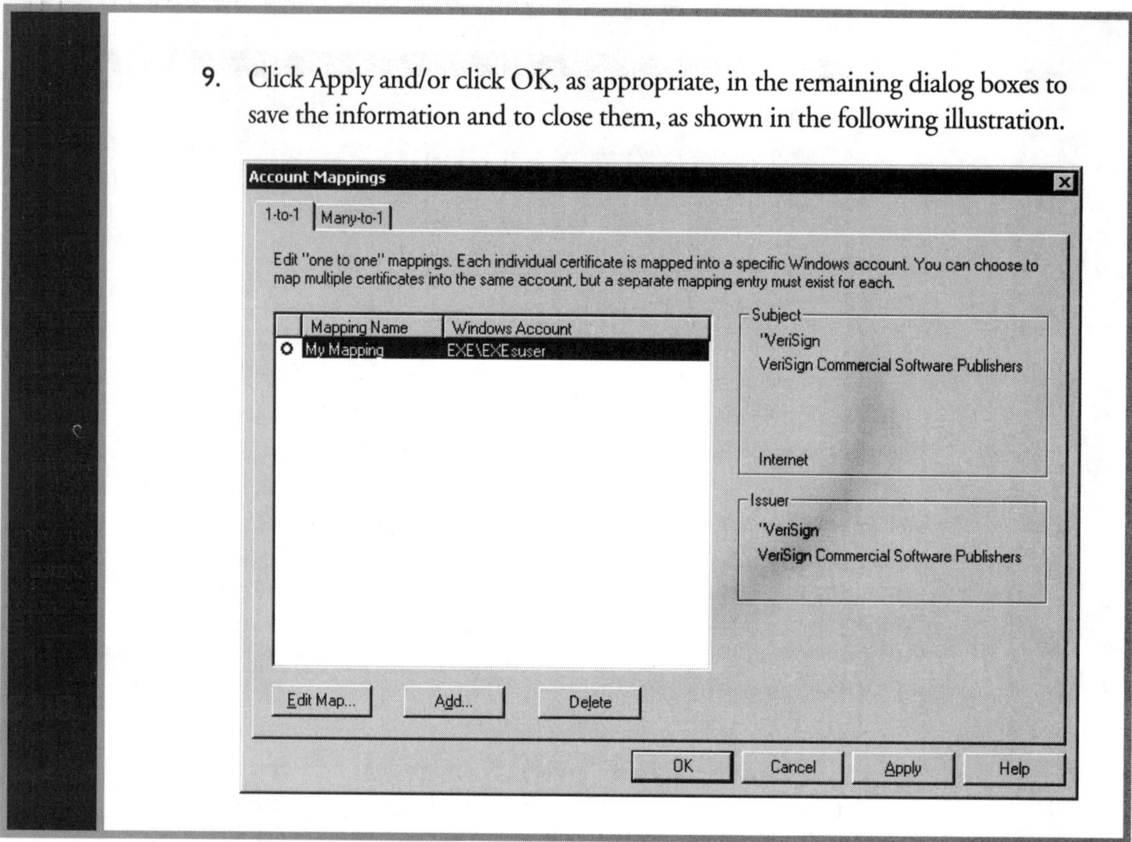

Now that you have a better idea of certificate mapping, here are some possible scenario questions and their answers:

SCENARIO & SOLUTION	
I want to give each user his or her own certificate…	Use one-to-one mapping.
I am using Active Directory…	Use UPN mapping.

CERTIFICATION OBJECTIVE 11.05

Encrypting File System (EFS) Recovery Keys

Encrypting File System (EFS) uses PKI-based security to encrypt and decrypt data on a computer. Combining the data in them with their public encryption key value contained in their public key certificate encrypts files. Only the private encryption key of the user who encrypted it can decrypt the data. This way, no one can access this data except the user who encrypted it and the Recovery Agent. The Recovery Agent is the Domain Administrator by default.

When the "Encrypt contents" check box is selected in a file's properties, Windows 2000 creates a private encryption key for the file that it uses to encode the data contained within the file. A public encryption key is then created to protect the private encryption key. This is commonly referred to as *lock-box security.* A further step is taken to create a spare private encryption key that is capable of decrypting the data, and to map that key to a trusted account (e.g., the Domain Administrator). This is the EFS recovery key. All the EFS recovery keys in a domain are mapped to the Domain Administrator account.

It is a good practice to make a backup copy of the recovery key and certificate on a diskette, store it some place safe, and delete the copy of the key on the server. This way, if an intruder does break into the Recovery Agent account, he or she can't decrypt any files.

EXERCISE 11-8

Removing the EFS Recovery Key

Removing the EFS recovery key allows an administrator to have even more control over the access of sensitive data. Removing the key prevents anyone, even someone with the administrator password, from accessing the data unless he or she has the recovery key. Exercise 11.8 walks you through removing and securing the recovery key. You must be logged on with the local Administrator account to perform this exercise.

1. Click Start | Settings | Control Panel, and double-click Administrative Tools.
2. Double-click Local Security Policy. The Security Policy console appears, as shown in the following illustration.

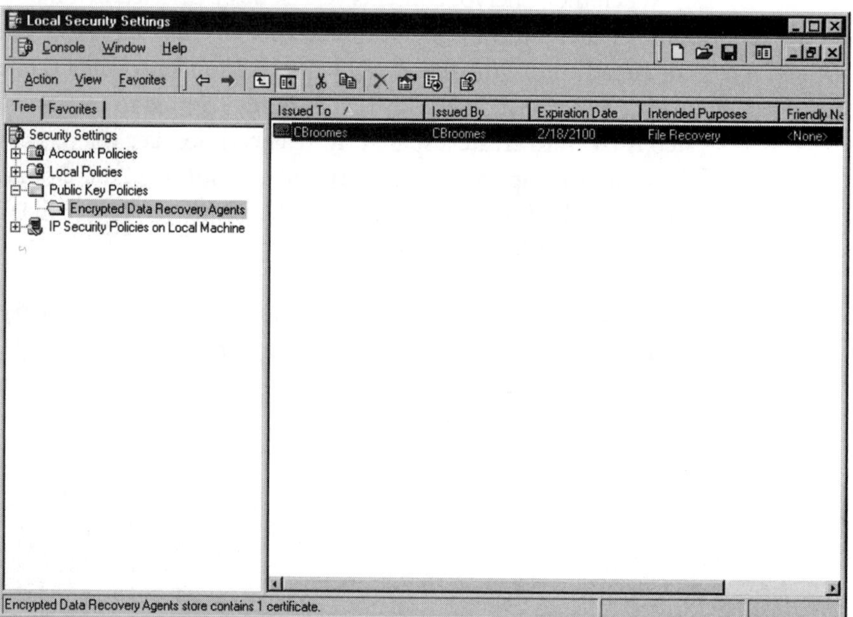

3. Click the Public Key Policies folder and then the Encrypted Data Recovery Agents folder to display all the recovery keys (see the previous illustration).
4. Right-click each Agent, select All Tasks, and then select Export. The Certificate Export Wizard launches. Follow the instructions for exporting certificates to floppy. After you have exported all the recovery keys, move on to Step 5.
5. Right-click the file recovery agent and select Delete to remove the recovery keys (see the following illustration).

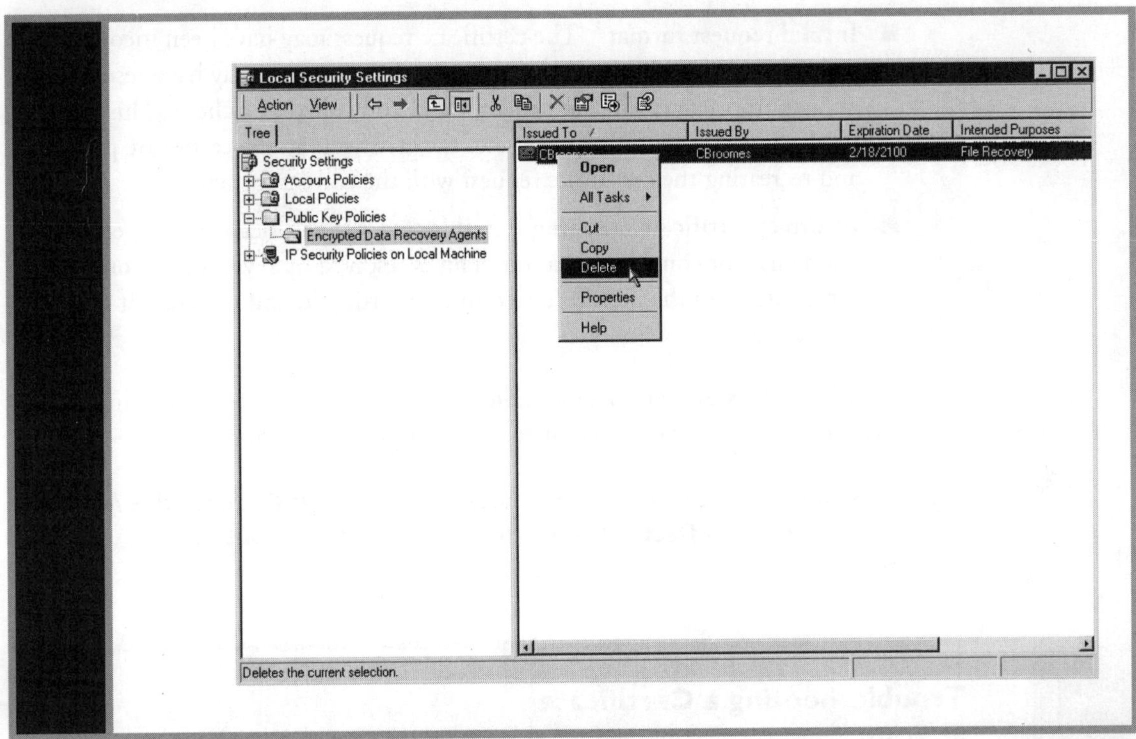

exam watch ***Administrators can designate backup EFS Recovery Agents to decrypt data if the default agents have been removed.***

CERTIFICATION OBJECTIVE 11.06

Troubleshooting Certificates

Nonfunctional certificates may come about as a result of a number of factors. Troubleshooting and resolving problems with certificates requires understanding how certificates are requested, created, and issued, as well as familiarity with the contents of certificates. Some common sources of problems with certificates include

- **Data corruption** This usually manifests itself as an invalid password or account error message. Troubleshooting this entails checking the password on the referenced account, and ensuring that the certificate content is properly formatted.

- **Invalid request format** The certificate request may have been incorrectly processed as a result of an invalid request format. This may have resulted in an inappropriate certificate being created and issued to a client. This may be resolved by checking the purpose of the certificate in the certificate properties and recreating the certificate request with the correct format.
- **Incorrect certificate mapping** In this case, the certificate is mapped to the wrong user or computer account. This is resolved by revoking the original certificate from the incorrect account, importing it, and mapping it to the correct account.

Apart from the scenarios just mentioned, regular performance monitoring on your certificate servers is essential to ensure their proper function.

As with monitoring any server or service with Windows Performance Monitor, monitoring is most effectively done from a separate computer.

EXERCISE 11-9

Troubleshooting a Certificate

The following exercise involves using what we just learned about troubleshooting certificates to solve a problem with a certificate.

You set up a secure intranet site for Human Resources so that the staff can access employee information via a Web browser. You sent an e-mail to the HR staff instructing them to request a certificate for access to this site via a certificate request Web page. One of the staff members calls and says that he gets a "page not available" error message when he tries to access the site. You and other employees in HR can access the site. You suspect that it is a problem with his certificate. Now let's troubleshoot it.

1. Click Start | Run, and type **mmc.**
2. Load the Certificates console, and then go to the Personal folder.
3. Select the Certificates folder to view the problem certificate. Look at the Intended Purpose field to see what the certificate is used for. In this case, the Intended purpose is Secure Email, (see the following illustration), not Web browser as it should be.

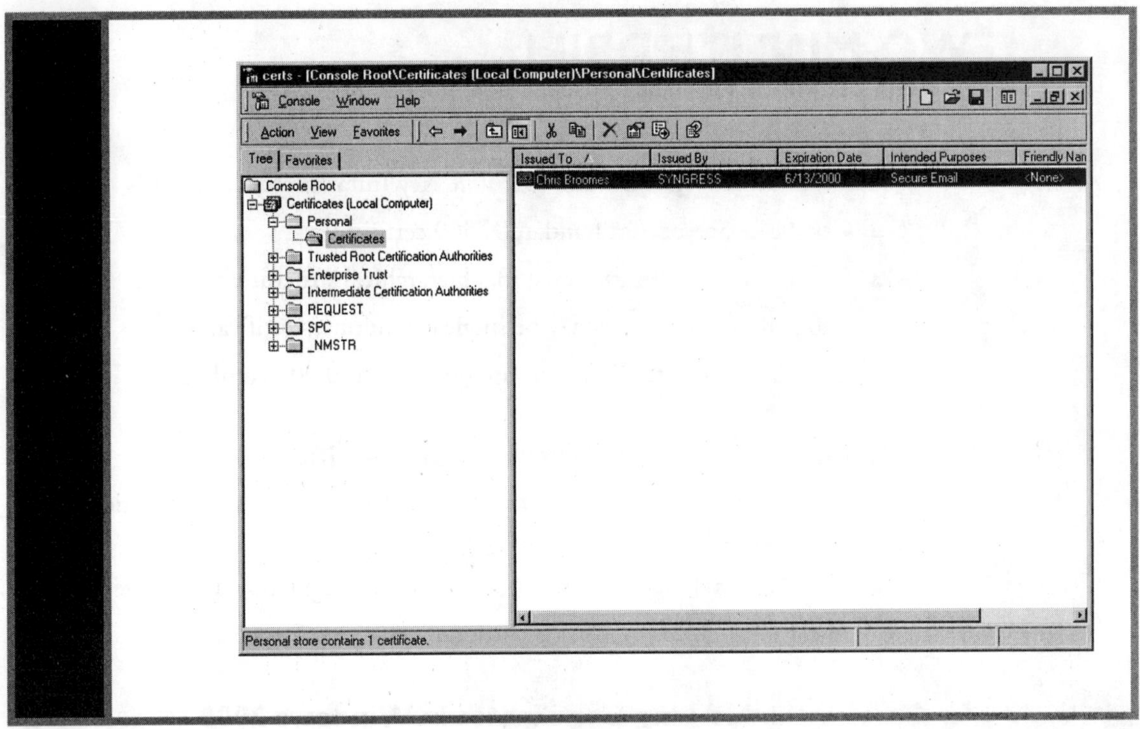

CERTIFICATION SUMMARY

In this chapter, we discussed Windows 2000 Certificate Services. We talked about Public Key Infrastructure and outlined how it works. We learned how to install and configure a root Certification Authority server and how to manage certificates. We looked at the elements that make up a certificate, and we saw how a certificate is created. We've talked about the hierarchical structure of Certificate Authorities (CA), and about distributing certificates between enterprises.

Some of the applications of certificates and Certificate Services were covered, as well as some possible problems that may occur, and how to troubleshoot and resolve them.

TWO-MINUTE DRILL

Overview of Certificate Services

- Certificate Services is built on Public Key Infrastructure standards.
- Certificate Server uses standard X.509 certificates.
- Certification Authorities exist in a hierarchical structure.
- Public Key Certificates may be single or multiuse certificates.
- A single Certificate Store can support up to 250,000 certificates.

Management and Administration of Certificates

- Certificate Management is performed in the Certificates/Certification Authority MMC snap-in.
- If the CA is a domain controller, its certificates are published in Active Directory.
- Windows 2000 supports four standard certificate formats.

Creating and Issuing Certificates in Windows 2000

- Windows 2000 Certificate Services generates PKCS #10 certificate requests.
- Cryptographic Service Providers are hardware or software devices used to perform encryption tasks on certificates.
- Certificates can be manually revoked or revoked via a Certificate Revocation List.

Certificate-Based Authentication

- There are two main types of certificate-based authentication: one-to-one mapping and many-to-one mapping.
- A User Principle Name (UPN) is a user identifier used by Active Directory to locate a user account.

Encrypting File System (EFS) Recovery Keys

- ❑ Encrypting File System creates a private encryption key to encode data.
- ❑ The default Recovery Agent is used to recover encrypted files in the Domain Administrator account.

Troubleshooting Certificates

- ❑ Common certificate problems involve data corruption, incorrect mapping, or server performance issues.

SELF TEST

The following questions will help you measure your understanding of the material presented in this chapter. Read all of the choices carefully, as there may be more than one correct answer. Choose all correct answers for each question.

Overview of Certificate Services

1. PKI stands for:

   A. Public Key Infrastructure

   B. Pretty well-Known Infrastructure

   C. Packaged Key Information

   D. Publicly Known Infrastructure

2. Certificate Services uses:

   A. X.25 certificates

   B. H.232 certificates

   C. X.509 certificates

   D. PKCS # 10 certificates

3. A Subordinate CA can exist: (Select all that apply.)

   A. On the same server as the root CA

   B. In another domain in a Windows 2000 forest

   C. In the same domain as the root CA

   D. Anywhere, as long as it was certified by an Enterprise Root CA

4. You are a consultant brought in to assist with a Windows 2000 upgrade at Acme Publishing Co. The company has decided to implement Certificate Services, and although they have upgraded their Windows NT 4.0 Servers to Windows 2000 and installed a CA, clients cannot request certificates. When users attempt to request a certificate from the Certificates MMC snap-in, they get an error message stating that a Certificate Server cannot be located on the network. How would you troubleshoot and rectify this problem?

   A. Check to make sure that an Enterprise CA is installed and operational on the network.

   B. Make sure that Active Directory is being used, then install and configure an Enterprise CA on the network.

C. Enter the name of the CA in the certificate request on the client computer.

D. Make sure that the clients are in the same domain as the CA.

5. Which of the following are contents of a certificate? (Select all that apply.)

A. The public or private encryption key value

B. The length of time the certificate is valid

C. The name of the server the certificate is on

D. The name of the user requesting the certificate

Management and Administration of Certificates

6. You have successfully installed a CA hierarchy in your enterprise. You wish to secure the CA certificate to prevent loss. How would you go about doing so to ensure that the private encryption key is secured as well?

A. Run the Windows 2000 Backup utility to back up the system files.

B. Export the CA certificate using the Certificate Export Wizard to copy the certificate to a file on another directory on the system.

C. Copy the entire contents of the CAConfig folder.

D. Export the CA certificate in PKCS #12 format to a floppy disk using the Certificate Export Wizard.

7. Acme Kitchen Products has decided to open a Web storefront for its major customers. The CIO has read that Certificate Services can provide the security that Acme needs on the Internet for the storefront, so he instructs you to come up with a solution using Certificate Services for the project. He needs to make sure that the ordering and purchasing transactions conducted between Acme and its customers are secure. He also wants to ensure that their customers trust the security that Acme is using on the storefront. What is the best solution to fulfill both of these criteria?

A. Install a root CA at Acme to handle certificate management so customers are offered a certificate when they access the storefront.

B. Install a root CA at Acme and purchase a CA certificate from a well-known security provider like VeriSign. Install the VeriSign CA certificate on the Acme CA via the Certificate Import Wizard. The customers can then see that a certificate was issued from VeriSign and trust it.

C. Install an Enterprise root CA and a Subordinate CA at Acme. Then the customers know that the certificates offered come from Acme Kitchen Products.

D. Give the customers' logon accounts to the Web server running the Web storefront.

Creating and Issuing Certificates in Windows 2000

8. Smart cards are an example of:

A. A logon device

B. A certificate decoding device

C. A Cryptographic Service Provider

D. A security provider

9. You find out that a former employee has been getting access to company data. You check his domain user account and see that it has been disabled. You remember, however, that his department uses a secure Web site that they access using certificates mapped to a user account on that Web server. You discover that he is using a copy of his certificate that he copied to diskette before leaving the company. What is the best way to prevent the intruder from gaining further access without disrupting access to the site?

A. Disable the user account on the Web server.

B. Delete all the mappings between the certificate and the user account.

C. Add the employee's certificate to a Certificate Revocation List.

D. Deny access to the site from all network addresses other than your own.

10. Which of these are included in a PKCS # 10 certificate request? (Select all that apply.)

A. The subject public key

B. The signature algorithm

C. The digital signature of the issuing server

D. The name of the certificate

Certificate-Based Authentication

11. A UPN mapping uses the format:

A. Firstname_lastname@microsoft.com

B. User@domain

C. User@domain.com

D. server.domain

12. What are the two types of certificate-based authentication?

A. User Domain Authentication

B. Challenge Handshake Authentication

C. Microsoft Encrypted Authentication

D. Computer auto-enrollment

13. One of the managers in your organization comes to you complaining that he cannot access a secure part of your corporate Web site. He mentions to you that his user account was accidentally deleted by one of the junior administrators and had to be recreated. He has not been able to access his home directory either since then. What could be the problem?

A. He may not have had all his user rights and account settings properly restored.

B. He may not be logging on to the correct domain.

C. He may not have typed in the correct URL for the site.

D. His certificate may have expired.

Encrypting File System (EFS) Recovery Keys

14. The CIO of your company has asked that you secure a computer with sensitive data belonging to the CEO and CFO to be accessible only to them. How would you accomplish this? (Select all that apply.)

A. Select the "Encrypt contents to secure data" check box in the Advanced Options window on the directories with data.

B. Take the computer off the network and lock it in a secure room.

C. Backup the EFS recovery keys to floppy and then delete them from the system.

D. All of the above.

15. What is the default EFS Recovery Agent?

A. The user certificate of the file owner

B. The Domain Administrator

C. The public encryption key used to protect the private encryption key

D. The Local Administrator account of the computer

Troubleshooting Certificates

16. You are the network administrator at Carry-All Luggage Company. You receive complaints from a few employees using the company intranet site. They report that they receive an "Incorrect password" error message when they try to access their personal pages on the site. You check the site and it seems to work properly. What would you do next to troubleshoot the problem?

    A. Check their certificate mappings on the site to make sure that the appropriate user accounts are mapped to certificates granting access to the pages. Check the encryption key value and compare it with a saved copy of the key for any spaces or any other characters that should not be there.

    B. Check the certificate mappings, since there is no way you could decipher the encryption key value anyway.

    C. Have the users log off and then log on again to see if they are allowed into the site again.

    D. Stop and restart the Web server, since it may be the problem.

17. You are the new network administrator for Haystacks Clothing, Inc. The Sales department calls and says that one of their largest customers can no longer access their extranet site that the client uses to order clothing materials from Haystacks. You attempt to troubleshoot the problem and suspect that the problem may be the result of an expired certificate. How do you determine this? How would you fix this problem?

    A. Call the customer and ask them to send you a list of error messages they receive when they try to access the site. Reboot the Web server.

    B. Check the "Valid to" field on the Certificate details tab of the certificate issued to the customer. Renew the expired certificate and reissue it to the customer.

    C. Check the date that the CA issuing certificates was brought online.

    D. Check the expiration date of the CA certificate and create a renewal request if it has expired.

LAB QUESTION

You are the administrator at Money Bags Bank, and you need to set up secure access to accounts for your customers as well as for your internal auditing staff. You decide to use Certificate Services because you are on a Windows 2000 network with Active Directory running. What steps would you take to create a secure Web site that both your customers and the staff can access?

SELF TEST ANSWERS

Overview of Certificate Services

1. ☑ A. Public Key Infrastructure is the security method used in Certificate Services.
☒ B, C, and D are incorrect because these terms don't exist.

2. ☑ C. RFC 2459 defines X.509 v3 certificates for use in PKI.
☒ A is incorrect because X.25 is actually a networking topology and not a certificate format. **B** is incorrect because H.232 is an hardware interface specification. **D** is incorrect because PKCS #10 is a certificate request format and not an actual certificate format.

3. ☑ **B, C, D. B** and **C** are correct because a subordinate CA can exist anywhere in a Windows 2000 forest, as long as it can contact the root CA. **D** is correct because an Enterprise CA belonging to another company on a different network can certify a subordinate CA.
☒ **A** is incorrect because a root and subordinate CA cannot exist on the same server.

4. ☑ **B.** An Enterprise CA in a Windows 2000 domain running Active Directory is necessary for clients to request certificates using the MMC snap-in. Remember, an Enterprise CA's certificate store is stored in Active Directory, which is where clients look when a certificate request is made via the MMC snap-in.
☒ **A** is only partly correct. An Enterprise CA is needed, but Active Directory is necessary in order to install it. **C** is incorrect because you do not need to enter the name of the CA anywhere when requesting a certificate. **D** is incorrect because clients don't necessarily need to be in the same domain as the CA.

5. ☑ **A, B.** The contents of a certificate are the public or private encryption key value and the length of time the certificate is valid.
☒ **C** and **D** are incorrect because neither the name of the server nor the name of the user are included in a certificate. *(see the section, Information Contained in Certificates).*

Management and Administration of Certificates

6. ☑ **D.** You cannot export a certificate's private key unless you use the PKCS #12 format when exporting. Also, it is recommended that you store the certificate off the server to avoid access and tempering.

☒ A, B, and C are incorrect because using Windows 2000 Backup and Recovery Tools is not the prudent or recommended method for backing up certificates. The certificate must be exported in PKCS #12 format in order to get the private key. The CAConfig folder does not contain the CA certificate.

7. ☑ **B.** Importing the certificate allows you to use it when issuing certificates. Getting a certificate from a familiar and trusted provider like VeriSign ensures that customers know that they are interacting with a proven secure solution.
☒ **A** and **C** are incorrect; customers may not accept a certificate from Acme because it is not a recognized security provider. **D** would not be the best solution because you would be required to create accounts every time Acme added a new customer.

Creating and Issuing Certificates in Windows 2000

8. ☑ **C.** A smart card is a type of hardware Cryptographic Service Provider.
☒ **A**, **B**, and **D** are all incorrect because they don't correctly identify a smart card.

9. ☑ **C.** Adding the employee's certificate to a Certificate Revocation List allows you to disable a particular user's access to the site.
☒ **A** and **B** are incorrect because they disable all access to the Web site. **D** is incorrect because it denies access from outside your local area network. Employees in that department may also exist in other sites with a different network address.

10. ☑ **A, B.** PKCS #10 certificate requests contain both a subject name and a subject public key. They also contain a signature algorithm.
☒ **C** and **D** are incorrect because even though the requests contain digital signatures, they are signatures from the requesting user, not the issuing server. Also, the certificate name doesn't exist in the request.

Certificate-Based Authentication

11. ☑ **B.** User Principle Name mapping uses the format user@domain to locate the user account in Active Directory. This user account is used to log the user on to access the desired resources.
☒ **A**, **C**, and **D** are all incorrect because they use the wrong format.

12. ☑ **A, D.** The two types of certificate-based authentication are User Domain Authentication and computer auto-enrollment.
☒ **B** and **C** are incorrect because Challenge-Handshake Authentication and Microsoft Encrypted Authentication are noncertificate-based methods of authentication used in the Windows logon process.

13. ☑ A. The fact that the user could not access other objects on the network besides the secure site hints that there is a problem with his user account rights and settings. Remember that in User Domain authentication the CA issues certificates that grant access based on the user's access rights.
☒ B may have also been an alternative answer, but it ignores the clue that his account was deleted and recreated. C and D are incorrect because they don't explain why he can't access his home directory as well.

Encrypting File System (EFS) Recovery Keys

14. ☑ D. Performing only one of these actions does not guarantee the security of the data. Carrying out all of these options ensures that the machine is physically tamper proof and not accessible over the network.

15. ☑ D. The default EFS Recovery Agent is the Local Administrator account of the computer.
☒ Although **B** is also correct, it is not so in every case. The local Administrator account is always the EFS Recovery Agent. **A** is incorrect because the certificate is what the Agent uses to encrypt the file. **C** is also incorrect because the public encryption key is not used in both the encryption and decryption process.

Troubleshooting Certificates

16. ☑ A. As mentioned in the section, *Troubleshooting Certificates*, the problems associated with certificates usually involve incorrect mappings or corrupt encryption key values. These areas should be among the first checked.
☒ **B** is incorrect, because even though you cannot decipher the data, you should be able to compare the syntax of the value to a saved copy of the certificate. **C** is incorrect because a problem with the user account would manifest itself elsewhere on the network (printing, logon, etc.) before it did on the intranet site. **D** is incorrect because no one would be able to access the intranet site at all.

17. ☑ B. The "Valid to" field on the details tab tells you the date that the certificate will expire. Expired certificates can be renewed and reissued at the CA.
☒ **A** and **C** are incorrect because they don't directly address the problem of the expired certificate. The date that a CA comes online doesn't necessarily have anything to do with the expiration date of its certificates. **D** is incorrect because even though an expired CA certificate could affect the validity of user certificates, other customers were able to access their sites.

LAB ANSWER

The steps include the following:

1. Install an Enterprise CA for your organization.
2. Purchase a secure Web access (SSL) certificate from a trusted security provider, like Entrust or VeriSign, and install it on your CA. This will be used for your customers.
3. Have your customers then go to the secure Web page and receive a user certificate by entering some personal information that identifies them to the bank.
4. Create and issue a certificate for the auditing staff, and map the certificate to each of their user accounts. This enables them to access their accounts via a Web browser. Their access is limited to the level of access their user accounts have to the data.

A

About the CD

This CD-ROM contains the CertTrainer software. CertTrainer comes complete with ExamSim, Skill Assessment tests, CertCam movie clips, the e-book (electronic version of the book), and Drive Time. CertTrainer is easy to install on any Windows 98/NT/2000 computer and must be installed to access these features. You may, however, browse the e-book directly from the CD without installation.

Installing CertTrainer

If your computer CD-ROM drive is configured to autorun, the CD-ROM will automatically start up upon inserting the disk. From the opening screen you may either browse the e-book or install CertTrainer by pressing the *Install Now* button. This will begin the installation process and create a program group named "CertTrainer." To run CertTrainer use START | PROGRAMS | CERTTRAINER.

System Requirements

CertTrainer requires Windows 98 or higher and Internet Explorer 4.0 or above and 600 MB of hard disk space for full installation.

CertTrainer

CertTrainer provides a complete review of each exam objective, organized by chapter. You should read each objective summary and make certain that you understand it before proceeding to the SkillAssessor. If you still need more practice on the concepts of any objective, use the "In Depth" button to link to the corresponding section from the Study Guide or use the CertCam button to view a short .AVI clip illustrating various exercises from within the chapter.

Once you have completed the review(s) and feel comfortable with the material, launch the SkillAssessor quiz to test your grasp of each objective. Once you complete the quiz, you will be presented with your score for that chapter.

ExamSim

As its name implies, ExamSim provides you with a simulation of the actual exam. The number of questions, the type of questions, and the time allowed are intended to be an accurate representation of the exam environment. Figure A-1 shows you the screen you will see when you are ready to begin ExamSim.

FIGURE A-1 The ExamSim opening page

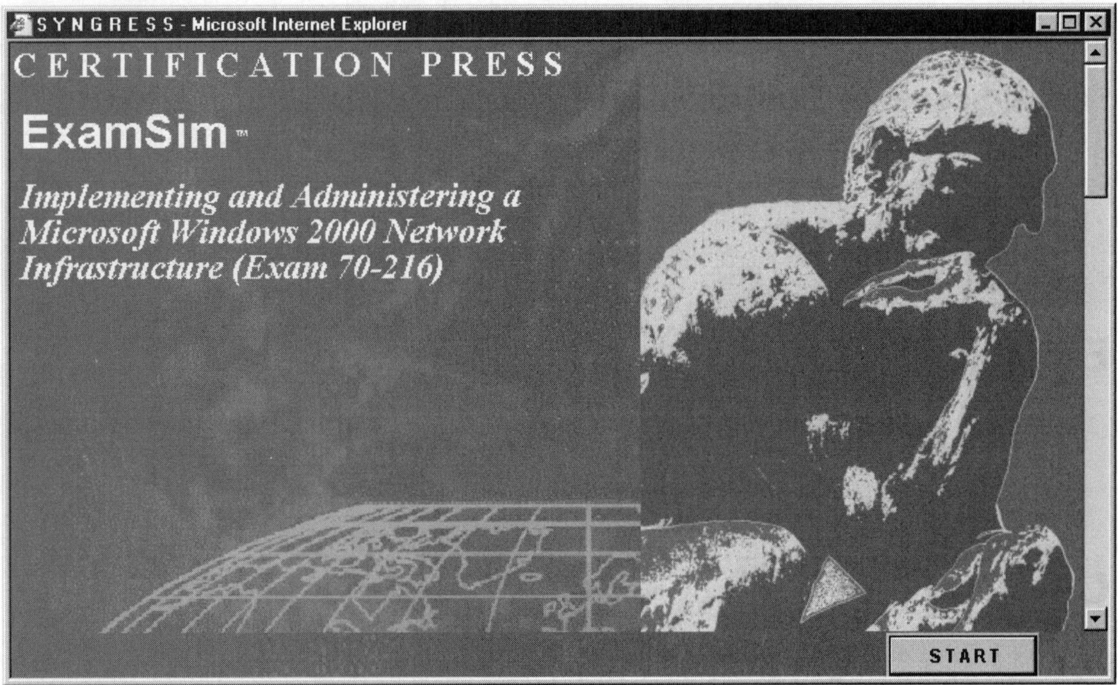

When you launch ExamSim, a digital clock display will appear in the upper left-hand corner of your screen. The clock will continue to count down to zero unless you choose to end the exam before the time expires.

There are three types of questions on the exam:

- **Multiple Choice** These questions have a single correct answer that you indicate by selecting the appropriate check box.
- **Multiple-Multiple Choice** These questions require more than one correct answer. Indicate each correct answer by selecting the appropriate check boxes.
- Simulations These questions simulate actual Windows 2000 menus and dialog boxes. After reading the question, you are required to select the appropriate settings to most accurately meet the objectives for that question.

Saving Scores as Cookies

Your ExamSim score is stored as a browser cookie. If you've configured your browser to accept cookies, your score will be stored in a file named *History*. If your browser is not configured to accept cookies, you cannot permanently save your scores. If you delete this History cookie, the scores will be deleted permanently.

E-Book

The entire contents of the Study Guide are provided in HTML form, as shown in Figure A-2. Although the files are optimized for Internet Explorer, they can also be viewed with other browsers including Netscape.

CertCam

CertCam .AVI clips provide detailed examples of key certification objectives. These clips walk you step by step through various system configurations and are narrated by Thomas Shinder, M.D., MCSE, MCT. You can access the clips directly from the CertCam table of contents (shown in Figure A-3) or through the CertTrainer objectives.

The CertCam .AVI clips are recorded and produced using TechSmith's Camtasia Producer. Since .AVI clips can be very large, ExamSim uses TechSmith's special AVI

FIGURE A-2 Study Guide contents in HTML format

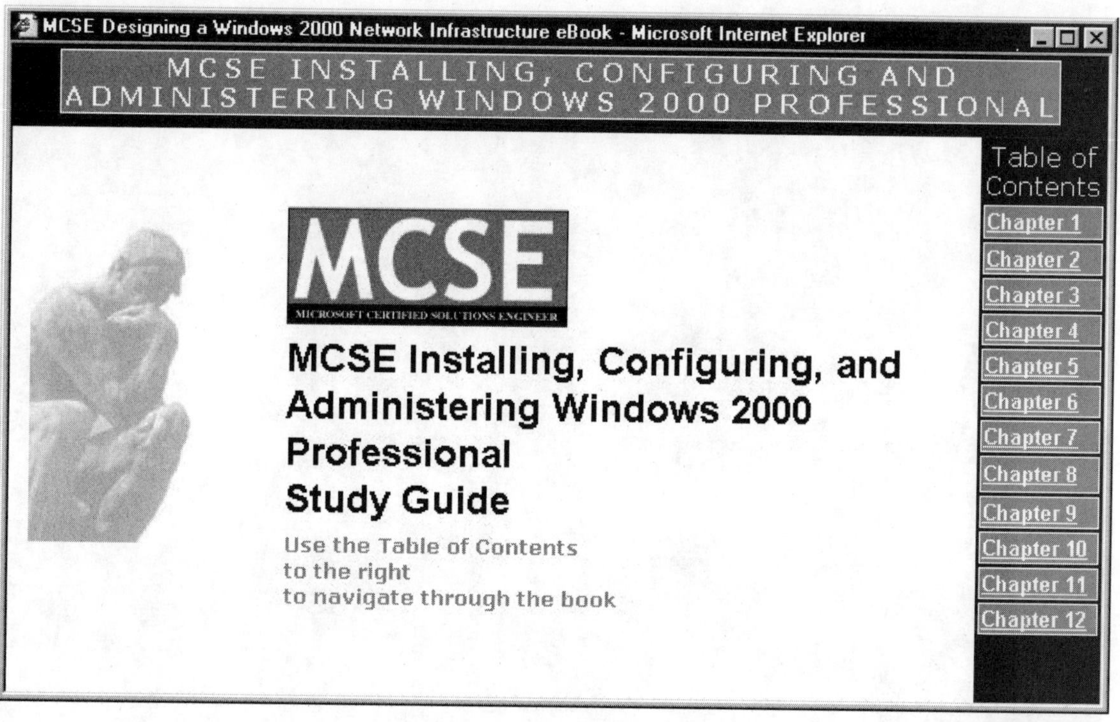

Codec to compress the clips. The file named **tsccvid.dll** is copied to your Windows\System folder when you install CertTrainer. If the .AVI clip runs with audio but no video, you may need to reinstall the file from the CD-ROM. Browse to the "bin" folder, and run TSCC.EXE.

DriveTime

DriveTime audio tracks will automatically play when you insert the CD-ROM into a standard CD-ROM player, such as the one in you car or stereo. There is one track for each chapter. These tracks provide you with certification summaries for each chapter and are the perfect way to study while commuting.

FIGURE A-3 The CertCam Table of Contents

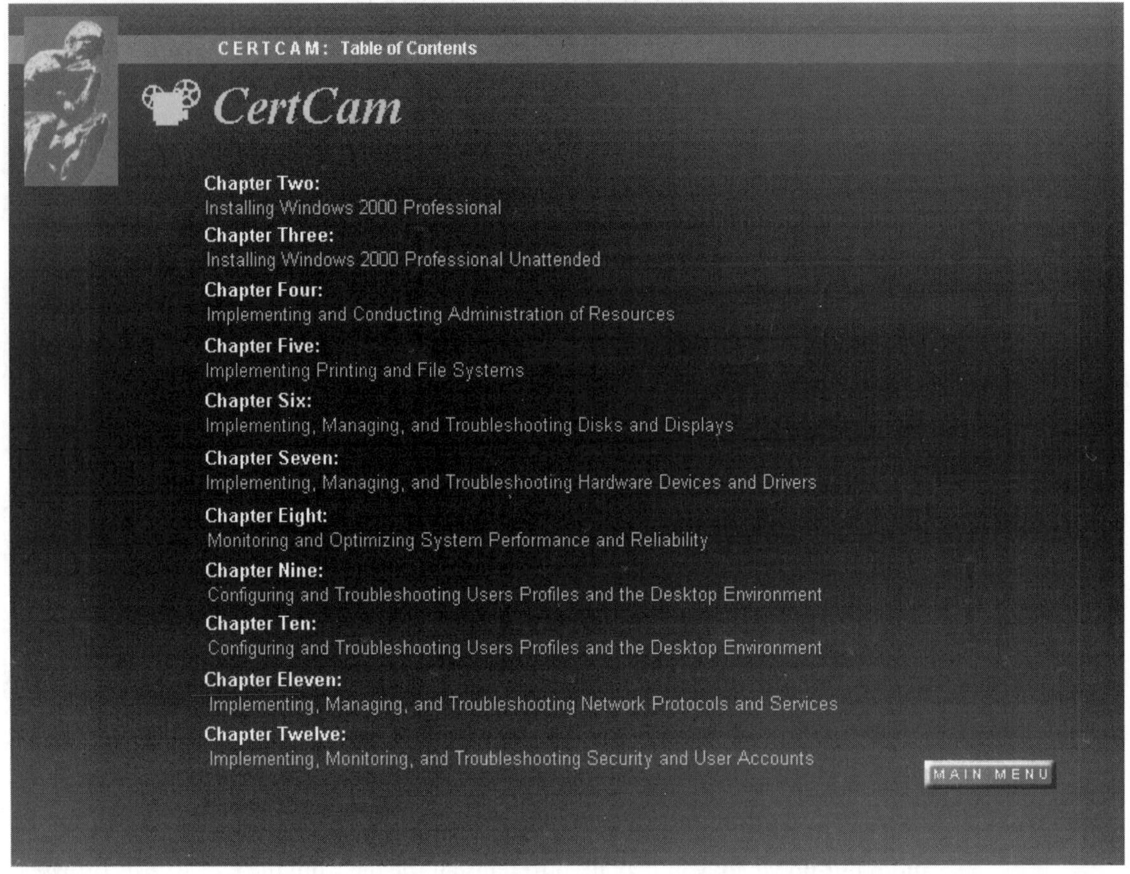

Help

A help file is provided through a help button on the main CertTrainer screen in the lower right-hand corner.

Upgrading

A button is provided on the main ExamSim screen for upgrades. This button will take you to www.syngress.com, where you can download any available upgrades.

B

About the Web Site

At Access.Globalknowledge, the premier online information source for IT professionals (http://access.globalknowledge.com), you'll enter a Global Knowledge information portal designed to inform, educate, and update visitors on issues regarding IT and IT education.

Get *What* You Want *When* You Want It

At the Access.Globalknowledge site, you can:

- Choose personalized technology articles related to your interests. Access a news article, a review, or a tutorial, customized to what you want to see, regularly throughout the week.
- Continue your education, in between Global courses, by taking advantage of chat sessions with other users or instructors. Get the tips, tricks, and advice that you need today!
- Make your point in the Access.Globalknowledge community by participating in threaded discussion groups related to technologies and certification.
- Get instant course information at your fingertips. Customized course calendars show you the courses you want, and when and where you want them.
- Obtain the resources you need with online tools, trivia, skills assessment, and more!

All this and more is available now on the Web at http://access.globalknowledge.com. Visit today!

Glossary

Account Lockout Policy The Account Lockout Policy dictates the behavior for locking and unlocking user accounts. There are three configurable parameters: Account lockout threshold determines how many times users can attempt to log on before their accounts are locked. This can range from low (five attempts) to high (one or two attempts). The Account lockout duration parameter controls how long an account is locked after the Account lockout threshold parameter is triggered.

ACPI *See* Advanced Configuration and Power Interface.

Active Directory The Active Directory is implemented on Windows 2000 domain controllers, and the directory can be accessed from Windows 2000 Professional as an Active Directory client. The Active Directory arranges objects—including computer information, user and group information, shared folders, printers, and other resources—in a hierarchical structure, in which domains can be joined into trees (groups of domains that share a contiguous namespace). Trees can be joined into forests (groups of domain trees that share a common schema, configuration, and global catalog).

Active Directory Service This service provides the means for locating the Remote Installation Service (RIS) servers and the client computers on the network. The RIS server must have access to the Active Directory.

Administration The word *administer* is generally used as a synonym for *manage,* which in turn means to exert control. One of the many enhancements to Windows 2000—both the Professional and Server incarnations—is the ability Microsoft has given administrators to apply the degree of control desired, in a flexible and granular manner.

Add Printer Wizard All clients running a version of the Windows operating system (Windows 2000, Windows NT, Windows 98, and Windows 95) can use the Add Printer Wizard to create a printer entry on the client. This Add Printer Wizard can create and share a printer on a print server. The Windows 2000 version of the Add Printer Wizard has more options than the wizard in other versions of Windows, but many of the same methods can be used to get the printer set up on the client.

Address Resolution Protocol (ARP) The Address Resolution Protocol (ARP) is used to resolve Internet Protocol (IP) logical addresses to Media Access Control (MAC) physical hardware addresses. ARP uses broadcasts to discover the hardware addresses, and stores the information in its arp cache.

Advanced Configuration and Power Interface (ACPI) ACPI combines Plug and Play (PnP) capability with Power Management, and places these functions under complete control of the operating system.

Advanced Power Management (APM) An Intel/Microsoft application programming interface (API) allowing programs to indicate their requirements for power to regulate the speed of components.

Alerts Alerts allow some action to be performed when a performance counter reaches a particular threshold. A common action is to log the event in the application event log. You can also send a network message to a specified computer. You can have the alert start a performance log to start logging when the alert occurs. And finally, you can configure the alert to start a program.

Algorithm A procedure or formula used to solve a problem.

Analysis Analysis is the process of comparison, contrast, diagnosis, diagramming, discrimination, and/or drawing conclusions.

Answer file An answer file is a file containing the information you would normally have to key in during the setup process. Answer files help automate the installation process as all the queries presented to you during installation are answered by the answer files. With careful planning, you can prepare answers that eliminate the possibility of incorrect answers typed in by the person performing the installation, thus reducing the chances of setup failure. You can use the Setup Manager wizard to create a customized answer file. This technique minimizes the chances of committing syntax-related errors while manually creating or editing the sample answer files.

APIPA *See* Automatic Private Internet Protocol Addressing.

APM *See* Advanced Power Management.

AppleTalk The AppleTalk protocol suite was developed by Apple Computer for use in its Macintosh line of personal computers, and is a local area networking system. AppleTalk networks can run over a variety of networks that include Ethernet, FDDI, and Token Ring as well as Apple's proprietary media system LocalTalk. Macintosh computers are very popular in the education and art industries, so familiarity with the way they communicate using their native protocol is very useful.

AppleTalk printing device Another type of remote printer is the AppleTalk printing device. Like a Transmission Control Protocol/Internet Protocol (TCP/IP) printer, an AppleTalk printer can be connected directly to an AppleTalk network or shared across the network through an AppleShare print server. Like the TCP/IP printers, a large number of modern, high-capacity PostScript printers can be configured to communicate with an AppleTalk network as well as a TCP/IP network. In fact, many Hewlett-Packard LaserJet printers have JetDirect cards that will speak TCP/IP and AppleTalk at the same time.

Application Software A program designed to perform a specific function directly for the user or for another application program. An application would be, for example, word processors, database programs, graphics/drawing programs, Web browsers, and e-mail programs.

Application The process of choice, demonstration, performing a procedure, solving, plotting, calculation, changing, interpretation, and operation.

Application Service Provider (ASP) ASPs are companies that manage applications and provide organizations with application-hosting services. Analysts expect the ASP market will be a six billion dollar industry by the year 2001. The application-hosting model offers organizations the option of outsourcing application support and maintenance.

Application System Border Router (ASBR) An AS Border Router is a router that connects together different ASs. When the ASBR exchanges routing information with an external network, the routing information received from outside the AS is referred to as external routes.

ARP *See* Address Resolution Protocol.

ARPAnet ARPAnet, the predecessor of the Internet was begun by the U.S. Department of Defense (DoD), in conjunction with major universities. The DoD developed the nation-wide system (which then was extended throughout the world) to provide highly reliable, redundant communications links that could withstand even a nuclear war.

ASBR *See* Application System Border Router.

ASP *See* Application Service Provider.

Asymmetric algorithm A cryptographic algorithm that utilizes a different key for encrypting data from the one used to decrypt the data.

Asynchronous Transfer Mode over Asymmetric Digital Subscriber Line (ATM over ADSL) ADSL offers a new technology aimed at small businesses and residential customers. It offers a higher throughput than Public Switched Telephone Network (PSTN) and Integrated Services Digital Network (ISDN) connections, but the bit rate is higher downstream than upstream—typically 384 Kbps when going out and 384 Kbps–1.544 Mbps when coming in (this usually suits Internet traffic usage where users download a much higher percentage of data than they upload). ADSL equipment can appear to a Windows 2000 Server as one of two interfaces—Ethernet or dial-up. When seen as an Ethernet interface, the ASDL behaves in the same way as a standard network adapter connected to the Internet. When seen as a dial-up interface, ADSL provides the physical connection for ATM traffic.

Auditing Windows 2000 gives the ability to audit security-related events, track access to objects and use of user rights, and detect attempted and successful access (authorized and unauthorized) to the network. Auditing is not enabled by default, but once enabled, a security log is generated that provides information in regard to specific activities performed on the computer.

Authenticated data exchange The only problem with confidential data exchange is that there is no assurance that the person who used your public key to encrypt and send you a message is really who he or she claims to be. How can we ensure that? What if the sender encrypted the message using his or her private key, and then you decrypted it using his or her public key? What would this accomplish? We get the same confidentiality of the data as with the first method, but since presumably only the sender has the private key, we can be confident of his identity. Now we have an authenticated data exchange.

Authentication Authentication is when a user is identified (usually by means of a username and password). If this is done in an encrypted form, an authentication protocol is used. A successful authentication proves that users are who they say they are, but has nothing to do with what resources they can access.

Authentication Header (AH) The Authentication Header ensures data integrity and authentication. The AH does not encrypt data, and therefore provides no confidentiality, but does protect the data from modification. When the AH protocol is applied in transport mode, the Authentication Header is inserted between the original Internet Protocol (IP) header and the Transmission Control Protocol (TCP) or User Datagram Protocol (UDP) header.

Authorization Authorization is when it is determined whether users can have access to requested resources based on their identity. By definition, this can only happen after a successful authentication. In the context of Routing and Remote Access (RRAS), remote users' connection attempts can be authenticated (because they have proved who they are), but their connection can still be denied because their authorization failed if they did not have permission to dial in, for example.

Automatic Partner Discovery You can configure your Windows Internet Name Server (WINS) servers to find other WINS servers on the network and create a replication partnership with them automatically. When you enable Automatic Partner Discovery, WINS servers use the multicast address 224.0.1.24 to discover or find other WINS servers.

Automatic Private Internet Protocol Addressing (APIPA) APIPA, or Automatic Client Configuration, is a new feature initially available in Windows 98. The feature has been extended to Windows 2000 and allows Dynamic Host Control Protocol (DHCP) client computers to self-configure their IP addressing information in the event a DHCP server is not available when the computer issues a DHCPDISCOVER message. It also allows self-configuration when it senses that it has been moved from a previous network via Windows 2000 media sensing capabilities.

Backup Domain Controller (BDC) A backup file or copy of the Primary Domain Controller (PDC). Periodically, the BDC is synchronized with the PDC.

Backup Logs Windows Backup generates a backup log file for every backup job. These files are the best place to review the backup process in case some problem is encountered by the program. The backup log is a text file that records all the events during the backup process.

BACP *See* Bandwidth Allocation Control Protocol.

Bandwidth Allocation Control Protocol (BACP) BACP polices multiple peers using Multilink Point-to-Point Protocol (MP)—for example, it elects a favored peer when more than one PPP peer requests to add or remove a connection at the same time. The sole job of this protocol is to elect a favored peer when necessary. If both peers of an MP- and BAP-enabled connection send a BAP Call Request or BAP Link Drop Query Request message at the same time, only one request can succeed, and it is the responsibility of this protocol to elect which peer wins.

Bandwidth Allocation Protocol (BAP) BAP is a Point-to-Point Protocol (PPP) that is used to dynamically add or remove additional links to an MP connection.

BAP *See* Bandwidth Allocation Protocol.

Basic Input/Output System (BIOS) A set of programs encoded in ROM on IBM PC–compatible computers programs handle startup operations such as Power

On Self Test (POST) and low-level control for hardware such as disk drives, keyboards, etc.

BDC *See* Backup Domain Controller.

BIOS *See* Basic Input/Output System.

Black holes Because the Routing Information Protocol (RIP) is a distance vector-based routing protocol that uses unacknowledged delivery, data can often be lost without trace. One router could realize that its neighboring router was unavailable and send out information to broadcast this, but if the information is never received, other routers can continue to send data to the downed router in the mistaken belief it is still available. This is a "black hole" because there is nowhere for the packets to go but the sending system hasn't realized this. Link state routing protocols that use directed and acknowledged announcements are not vulnerable to this problem.

B-Node A b-node (broadcast node) client uses broadcasts instead of a WINS server. A Windows NetBIOS client computer without a configured WINS server is a b-node client.

Boot The process of loading an operating system into the computer's memory (RAM) so those applications can be run on it.

Boot ROM A boot ROM is a chip on the network adapter that helps the computer boot from the network. Such a computer need not have a previously installed operating system. The BIOS of the computer that has a PXE-based boot ROM must be configured to boot from the network. Windows 2000 Server RIS supports PXE ROM versions 99 or later.

BOOTP *See* Bootstrap Protocol.

Bootstrap Protocol (BOOTP) Bootstrap Protocol (BOOTP) is the predecessor to DHCP. It was originally designed to provide IP address configuration to diskless workstations, which not only received IP addressing information from a BOOTP server, but also received information regarding where to download its operating system image. DHCP was developed to improve on the host configuration services offered by BOOTP, and address some of the problems encountered in using it.

Bottleneck A bottleneck is a component of the system as a whole that restricts the system from operating at its peak. When a bottleneck occurs, the component that is a bottleneck will have a high rate of usage and other components will have a low rate of usage. A lack of memory is a common cause of bottleneck when your computer doesn't have enough memory for the applications and services that are running.

Burst mode When the Windows Internet Name Server (WINS) server is in burst mode, any name registration requests received over a predefined number receive immediate acknowledgement. However, the WINS server does not check the NetBIOS against the WINS database; it does not issue a challenge against duplicate names, and it does not write an entry to the WINS database.

CA *See* Certificate Authority.

Caching resolver The caching resolver not only caches queries that have been answered positively, but also caches negative results as well. When a Domain Name System (DNS) query fails, this failed result is placed in cache for five minutes, by default. If the machines issues a DNS query for the same object within five minutes, no query will be sent, and a failure message will be retrieved from cache. This can significantly reduce the overall DNS query traffic on a large network.

Caching-only DNS server The caching-only Domain Name System (DNS) server does not contain any zone information; it only stores (caches) the results of previous queries it has issued. You might want to place a caching-only server on the other side of a slow Wide Area Network (WAN) link, since they do not generate zone transfer traffic.

Caching-only server All Domain Name System (DNS) servers cache results of queries they have resolved. The caching-only DNS server does not contain zone information or a zone file. The caching-only server builds its database of host name and domain mappings over time from successful DNS queries it has resolved for DNS clients.

CAL *See* Client Access License.

Callback Callback is when the remote user dials in and requests the server to call back, so the connection cost of the remote access session is charged to the server's line and not the user.

Canonical Name (CNAME) This is an alias for a computer with an existing A Address record. For example, if you have a computer called "bigserver" that is going to be your Web server, you could create a CNAME for it, such as "www". It is important to note that you must have an A record for the host that you intend to create the alias for, since the CNAME record requests that you include the host name of the computer for which you wish to create the alias.

CAPI *See* CryptoAPI.

Capture filter A capture filter works somewhat like a database query; you can use it to specify the types of network information you want to monitor. For example, you can capture packets based on the protocol or based on the addresses of two computers whose interactions you wish to monitor. When a capture filter is applied, all packets are examined and compared to the filter's parameters; those that do not fulfill the filter requirements are dropped. This can be a processor-intensive activity during periods of moderate or high network utilization when the network card is placed in promiscuous mode.

Centralized model This model consolidates administrative control of group policies. A single team of administrators is responsible for managing all Group Policy Objects (GPOs) no matter where they are. This is usually applied by giving all the top-level Organizational Unit (OU) administrators full control to all GPOs no matter where they are located. They give each second-level OU administrator Read permission only to each GPO. You can also decentralize other resources or keep all resources centralized, depending on the environment.

Certificate A message that contains the digital signature of a trusted third party, called a certificate authority, which ensures that a specific public key belongs to a specific user or device.

Certificate Authority (CA) An authority/organization that produces digital certificates with its available public key. A Certificate Authority (CA) is a public key certificate issuer (for example, Verisign). To use a public key certificate, you must trust the issuer (CA). This means that you have faith in the CA's authentication policies. The CA is used for doing things such as authorizing certification authenticity, revoking expired certificates, and responding to certification requests. Windows 2000 offers an alternative to a third-party CA. You can become a CA within your own Intranet. Thus you can manage your own certificates rather than relying on a third-party Certification Authority.

Certificate service Provides security and authentication support, including secure e-mail, Web-based authentication, and smart card authentication.

Challenge Handshake Authentication Protocol (CHAP) A protocol (Point-to-Point Protocol or PPP) in which a password is required to begin a connection as well as during the connection. If the password fails any of these requirements, the system breaks the connection.

Change Permission You can use this permission to allow users the ability to change permissions on files and folders without giving them the Full Control permission. You can use this permission to give a user or group access to modify permissions on file or folder objects without giving them the ability to have complete control over the object.

CHAP *See* Challenge Handshake Authentication Protocol.

Cipher This process turns readable text data into ciphertext, which is encrypted data that must be deciphered before it is readable.

Cipher Block Chaining (CBC) Because the blocks of data are encrypted in 64-bit chunks, there must be a way to "chain" these blocks together. The chaining algorithm will define how the combination of the unencrypted text, the secret key, and the encrypted text (also known as ciphertext) will be combined to send to the destination host. Data Encryption Standard (DES) can be combined with Cipher Block Chaining (CBC) to prevent identical messages from looking the same. This

DES-CBC algorithm will make each ciphertext message appear different by using a different "initialization vector" (IV).

Cipher command The cipher command is another way to encrypt and decrypt data. You can use it from the command line and it has many switches, so that you can define exactly what you want to have done. The **Cipher.exe** command syntax is simply CIPHER, followed by the switches that you would like to use, followed by the path and directory/file name. The most common switches are the /E switch (encrypts the specified directories) and the /D switch (decrypts the specified directories). You can also use wildcards with the **cipher** command. For example, C:\>cipher /e /s *win* will encrypt all files and folders with "win" in the name and all files within them.

CIW *See* Client Installation Wizard.

Class A Addresses Class A addresses are for the "large size" networks, those that have a tremendous number of computers, and thus a need for many host addresses. Class A addresses always begin with a 0 in the first octet (also called the W octet). This will be the first bit on the left. This leaves seven bits for the individual network ID, and 24 bits to identify the host computers. When we convert to decimal, we see that this means a Class A address will have a decimal value in the first octet of 127 or less. Class A addresses, because they use only the first octet to identify the network, are limited in number. However, each Class A network can have a huge number of host computers, over 16 million. The Class A network numbers were all used up some time ago; they have been assigned to very large organizations such as IBM, MIT, and General Electric.

Class B Addresses Class B networks are the "medium size" networks. Class B networks use the first two octets (the 16 leftmost bits) to identify the network, and the last two octets (or the 16 rightmost bits) to identify the host computers. This means there can be far more Class B networks than Class As (more than 16,000), but each can have fewer hosts ("only" 65,535 each). Class B addresses always begin with a 10 for the two leftmost bits in the W octet, and the network is defined by the first two octets, which translates to decimal values of 128 through 191 for the first octet. 16 bits identify the Network ID, and the remaining 16 bits identify the Host ID. Microsoft's network is an example of a Class B network.

Class C Addresses The smallest-sized block of addresses designated by a class is the Class C network, each of which can have only 254 hosts. However, there can be more than 2 million Class C networks. A Class C network always has 110 as its first three bits. This leaves 24 bits to identify the network, with only 8 bits to use for host IDs. A Class C network, in decimal notation, will have a first octet decimal value of 192 through 223.

Class D Addresses Class D addresses, whose four high order (leftmost) bits in the W octet are 1110, are used for multicasting. This is a method of sending a message to multiple computers simultaneously.

Class E Addresses Class E addresses, with four high order bits of 1111, are reserved to be used for experimental and testing purposes.

Classless Addressing (CIDR) The use of address classes is the traditional way of working with Internet Protocol (IP) addressing and subnetting. A more recent development is called Classless InterDomain Routing (CIDR). CIDR networks are referred to as "slash x" networks, with the "x" representing the number of bits assigned originally as the network ID (before subnetting). Think of this as the number of bits that don't "belong" to you. With CIDR, the subnet mask actually becomes part of the routing tables. CIDR allows us to break networks into subnets and combine networks into supernets.

Client Access License (CAL) The CAL allows clients to access the Windows 2000's network services, shared folders, and printers. There are two types of CAL modes: Per Seat and Per Server. It important to understand the difference between the two modes: Per Seat and Per Server. When you use the Per Seat mode, each computer that accesses the server must have a CAL. The Per Server mode requires a CAL for each connection to the server. This is a subtle but significant difference. In addition, the CAL allows clients to access the Windows 2000 Server's network services, shared folders, and printers. The licensing modes are the same as under Windows NT 4.0.

Client impersonation This is when somebody takes over an existing authenticated connection by obtaining connection parameters from a successfully authenticated client, disconnecting the client, and then taking control of the original connection.

Client Installation Wizard (CIW) When a client computer boots using either the Remote Boot Disk or the PXE-based Boot ROM, it tries to establish a connection to the Remote Installation Service (RIS) server. If the RIS server is preconfigured to service the RIS clients, it helps the client get an Internet Protocol (IP) address from the Dynamic Host Control Protocol (DHCP) service. The CIW is then downloaded from the RIS server. This wizard has four installation options. The options that are presented to the user depend on the group policy set in the Active Directory. A user may get all four options, or may not get any of the options starting an automatic setup.

Client reservations Client reservations allow you to manage virtually the entirety of your Internet Protocol (IP) addresses space centrally, with the exception being your Dynamic Host Control Protocol (DHCP) servers.

Cloning *See* Disk imaging/cloning.

CNAME *See* Canonical Name.

Comprehension The process of distinguishing between situations, discussing, estimating, explaining, indicating, paraphrasing, and giving examples.

Computer account A computer account is an account that is created by a domain administrator and uniquely identifies the computer on the domain. A newly created account is used so that a computer may be brought into a Windows 2000 Domain.

Confidential data exchange Think of the method used to secure safety deposit boxes at banks. When you rent a box, you have a key to it—but your key alone won't unlock it. The bank officer also has a key, but again, that key by itself isn't of much value. When both keys are used, however, the authorized person can access the box. Likewise, with public key encryption technologies, it takes two keys to tango. One is the public key, which is made available to those who want to send you an encrypted message. They can all use that public key to encrypt their messages, but they cannot use it to decrypt them—only your private key, which you keep secret, can do that. This is called a confidential data exchange.

Configuration Configuration of an operating system involves specifying settings that will govern how the system behaves.

Container Object Container objects can contain other objects. A special type of container object you can create in the Active Directory is the Organizational Unit (OU).

Containers Containers are used to describe any group of related items, whether they are objects, containers, domains, or an entire network.

Control Panel Accessibility Options These are options that include StickyKeys, FilterKeys, ToggleKeys, SoundSentry, ShowSounds, High Contrast, MouseKeys, and SerialKeys.

Convergence When all the routers on the internetwork have the correct routing information in their routing tables, the internetwork is said to have converged. When convergence is achieved, the internetwork is in a stable state and all routing occurs along optimal paths. When a link or router fails, the internetwork must reconfigure itself to reflect the new topology and to achieve this, routing tables must be updated. Until the internetwork has converged once again, routing will be vulnerable to loops and black holes. The time it takes for the internetwork to reconverge is known as the convergence time and the optimal aim is for the shortest convergence time with minimum traffic.

Cooperative multitasking An environment in which application relinquishes its use of the computer's Central Processing Unit (CPU) so that another application could use the CPU.

Copy backup This type of backup simply copies the selected files. It neither looks for any markers set on the files nor clears them. The Copy backup does not affect the other Incremental or Differential backup jobs and can be performed along with the other types of backup jobs.

Counter logs Counter logs are maintained in a similar fashion as they were in Windows NT 4.0, but the procedure for configuring the Counter logs is a bit different. Trace logs are much easier to configure in Windows 2000 because you now can set them up from the console, rather than having to edit the registry as you had to do in Windows NT 4.0.

CryptoAPI (CAPI) CryptoAPI (CAPI) architecture is a collection of tasks that permit applications to digitally sign or encrypt data while providing security for the user's private key data.

Cryptography The science of encrypting and decrypting data. The science (and art) of breaking cryptographic code is called cryptanalysis.

Daily backup This type of backup does not use any markers to back up selected files and folders. The files that have changed during the day are backed up every day at a specified time. This backup will not affect other backup schedules.

Data Backup A backup and disaster protection plan is an essential part of a network administrator's duties. Windows 2000 provides a built-in Backup utility used to back up data to tape or file, or to create an Emergency Repair Disk (ERD). An ERD can be used to repair a computer with damaged system files.

Data compression Windows 2000 offers the capability of compressing data on a file-level basis, as long as the files and folders are located on an NT File System (NTFS) formatted partition or volume. Compression saves disk space; however, NTFS compression cannot be used in conjunction with file encryption.

Data Encryption Standard (DES) The most commonly used encryption algorithm used with Internet Protocol Security (IPSec) is the Data Encryption Standard (DES) algorithm. The widely used Data Encryption Standard (DES) uses secret key algorithms. Standard DES operates on 64-bit blocks of data, and uses a series of complex steps (even more complex than our Bible-assisted method) to transform the original input bits to encoded output bits. DES is the current U.S. government standard for encryption. The DES algorithm is an example of a symmetric encryption algorithm.

Data Link Control (DLC) DLC is a nonroutable protocol used for connecting to IBM mainframes and some network-connected laser printers.

Debugging Mode This is the most advanced startup option of all. To use this option you will need to connect another computer to the problematic computer through a serial cable. With proper configuration, the debug information is sent to the second computer.

Decentralized model This model is appropriate for companies that rely on delegated levels of administration. They decentralize the management of Group Policy Objects (GPOs), which distributes the workload to a number of domains. To apply this model, simply give all Organizational Unit (OU) administrators full control of their respective GPOs.

Dedicated Server A dedicated printer server is a Windows 2000 server whose only role is to provide printing services. The server does not provide directory space for users other than storage for spooled print jobs. It does not provide authentication services, does not host database services, does not act as a Domain Name System (DNS) server, and so on. A dedicated print server can host several hundred printers and print queues, however. Though it may not be obvious, the printing process does have an impact on the performance of the server providing the printing services. An environment with a large number of printers or print jobs should strongly consider using at least one dedicated print server.

Defragmentation The task of finding fragmented files and moving them into contiguous space is called defragmentation.

Demand-dial routing Dial-on demand connections are normally used when a permanent connection is not available, so demand-dial routing is used to connect your router to the required host or router when there is no permanent connection to do this. They can be used as a backup to a permanent connection or if no permanent connection is possible. Because dial-up connections are usually charged on a time basis, a demand-dial connection is an efficient method of only paying for a connection when you have data to transfer. An idle timeout value allows the connection to automatically terminate when there is no more data to transfer.

Deny Permissions Unlike the Allow permission, the Deny permission overrides all other permissions set for a file or folder. If a user is a member of one group with a Deny Write permission for a folder and is a member of another group with a Allow Full Control permission, the user will be unable to perform any of the Write permission tasks allowed because it has been denied. The Deny permission should be used with extreme caution, as it can actually lock out all users, even administrators, from a file or folder. The proper way to remove a permission from a user or group on a file or folder is to uncheck the Allow permission for that user or group, not to check the Deny permission.

DER Encoded Binary X.509 This is the format used for non-Windows 2000 certification authorities. Since the Internet is still dominated by non-Windows servers, it is supported for interoperability. DER certificate files use the .cer file extension.

DES *See* Data Encryption Standard.

Dfs *See* Distributed File System.

DHCP *See* Dynamic Host Control Protocol.

Dictionary attack Dictionary attack is when a malicious user attempts to gain access by "cracking" a password by automatically trying a list of words or commonly used phrases.

Differential backup The Differential backup checks and performs a backup of only those files that are marked. It does not clear the markers after the backup, which means that any consecutive differential backups will backup the marked files again. When you need to restore from a differential backup, you will need the most current full backup and the differential backup performed after that.

Diffie-Hellman key exchange Provides a method for two parties to construct a shared secret (key) that is known only to the two of them, even though they are communicating via an insecure channel.

Digital signature A string of bits that is added to a message (an encrypted hash), which provides for data integrity and authentication.

Digital Subscriber Line (DSL) There are many variants of digital subscriber line (xDSL). All versions utilize the existing copper loop between a home and the local telco's Central Office (CO). Doing so allows them to be deployed rapidly and inexpensively. However, all DSL variants suffer from attenuation, and speeds drop as the loop length increases. Asymmetrical DSL (ADSL) and Symmetrical DSL (SDSL) may be deployed only within 17,500 feet of a CO, and Integrated Services Digital Network emulation over DSL (IDSL) will work only up to 30,500 feet. All DSL variants use Asynchronous Transfer Mode (ATM) as the data-link layer.

Direct Memory Access (DMA) DMA is a microprocessor capable of transferring data between memory units without the aid of the Central Processing Unit (CPU). Occasionally, built-in circuitry can do this same function.

Directory A directory is a database that contains information about objects and their attributes.

Directory service The directory service is the component that organizes the objects into a logical and accessible structure, and provides for a means of searching and locating objects within the directory. The directory service includes the entire directory and the method of storing it on the network.

Directory Services Restore Mode This startup mode is available on Windows 2000 Server domain controller computers only. This mode can be used to restore the SYSVOL directory and Active Directory on the domain controller.

Discover A Dynamic Host Control Protocol (DHCP) client begins the lease process with a DHCPDISCOVER message. The client broadcasts this message after loading a minimal Transmission Control Protocol/Internet Protocol (TCP/IP) environment. The client does not know the address of the DHCP server, so it sends the message using a TCP/IP broadcast, with 0.0.0.0 as the source address and 255.255.255.255 as the destination address. The DHCPDISCOVER message contains the client's network hardware address, its computer name, a list of DHCP options the client supports, and a message ID that will be used in all messages between the client and server to identify the particular request.

Disk compression This compression allows you to compress folders, subfolders, and files to increase the amount of file storage, but slows down access to the files.

Disk Defragmenter Disk Defragmenter can analyze your volumes and make a recommendation as to whether or not you should defragment it. It will also give you a graphical display showing you the fragmented files, contiguous files, system files and free space. Disk Defragmenter does not always completely defragment free space; instead, it often moves it into just a few contiguous areas of the disk, which will still improve performance. Making the free space one contiguous space would have little added benefit.

Disk imaging/cloning The deployment of a new operating system is one of the most challenging and time-consuming tasks that a network administrator has to perform. The disk duplication methods are particularly useful when you need to deploy Windows 2000 Professional on a large number of computers. This is also known as disk imaging or cloning. These tools make the rollout fast and easy.

Disk quota Windows 2000 comes with a disk quota feature that allows you to control users' disk consumption on a per user/per partition basis. To begin setting disk quotas for your users, right-click any partition in either Windows Explorer or the My Computer object. Click Properties and then click the Quota tab. Also, a disk quota allows you to limit the amount of disk space used by each user.

Distance vector protocol Routing Information Protocol (RIP) is known as a distance vector protocol. This means that it has a maximum path length of 15 hops. If a packet must pass through more than 15 routers (gateways) to reach its destination, RIP considers the destination "unreachable."

Distinguished Name (DN)) DN, in Active Directory parlance, is a Lightweight Directory Access Protocol (LDAP) way of uniquely identifying an object.

Distributed File System (Dfs) The Windows 2000 Distributed File System provides you a method to centralize the organization of the shared resources on your network. In the past, shared resources were most often accessed via the Network Neighborhood applet, and users would have to wade through a number of domains and servers in order to access the shared folder or printer that they sought. Network users also had to remember where the obscure bit of information was stored, including both a cryptic server name and share name. The Distributed File System (Dfs) allows you to simplify the organization of your network resources by placing them in central shares accessed via a single server. Also, the Dfs allows you to create a central share point for shared resources located throughout the organization on a number of different servers.

Distribution Server This is a server on which the Windows 2000 installation files reside. When you install the operating system over the network, the client machine does not need a CD-ROM drive. The first requirement for network installation is a distribution server that contains the installation files. The distribution server can be any computer on the network to which the clients have access.

DLC *See* Data Link Control.

DMA *See* Direct Memory Access.

DN *See* Distinguished Name.

DNM *See* Domain Naming Master.

DNS *See* Domain Name System.

Domain A collection of connected areas. Routing domains provide full connectivity to all end systems within them. Also, a domain is a collection of accounts and network resources that are grouped together using a single domain name and security boundary.

Domain controller Domain controllers validate logons, participate in replication of logon scripts and policies, and synchronize the user account database.

This means that domain controllers have an extra amount of work to perform. Since the Terminal Server already requires such heavy resources, it is not a good idea to burden a Terminal Server with the extra work of being a domain controller. Also, all user accounts, permissions, and other network details are all stored in a centralized database on the domain controllers.

Domain Local Groups Domain Local Groups are used for granting access rights to resources such as file systems or printers that are located on any computer in the domain where common access permissions are required. The advantage of Domain Local Groups being used to protect resources is that a member of the Domain Local Group can come from both inside the same domain and from outside as well.

Domain Name System (DNS) Because the actual unique Internet Protocol (IP) address of a web server is in the form of a number difficult for humans to work with, text labels separated by dots (domain names) are used instead. DNS is responsible for mapping these domain names to the actual Internet Protocol (IP) numbers in a process called resolution. Sometimes called a Domain Name Server.

Domain Naming Master (DNM) A Domain Naming Master is one of the operations masters roles played by domain controllers in a Windows 2000 network.

Domain restructure Domain restructure, or domain consolidation, is the method of changing the structure of your domains. Restructuring your domains can allow you to take advantage of the new features of Windows 2000, such as greater scalability. Windows 2000 does not have the same limitation as the Security Accounts Manager (SAM) account database in Windows NT. Without this limitation, you can merge domains into one larger domain. Using Windows 2000 Organizational Units (OUs), you have finer granularity in delegating administrative tasks.

Domain Tree A domain tree is a hierarchical collection of the child and parent domains within a network. The domains in a domain tree have contiguous namespaces. Domain trees in a domain forest do not share common security rights, but can access one another through the global catalog.

Downlevel clients Downlevel clients with static Internet Protocol (IP) addresses are not able to communicate directly with the Dynamic Domain Name System (DDNS) server. DDNS entries for these clients must be manually reconfigured at the DDNS server.

Driver signing One of the most frustrating things about Windows operating systems is that any software vendors can overwrite critical system level files with their own versions. Sometimes the vendor's version of a system level file is buggy or flawed, and it prevents the operating system from functioning correctly, or in the worst case, prevents it from starting at all. Windows 2000 uses a procedure called Driver Signing that allows the operating system to recognize functional, high-quality files approved by Microsoft. With this seal of approval, you should be confident that installing applications containing signed files will not disable your computer. Windows 98 was the first Microsoft operating system to use digital signatures, but Windows 2000 marks the first Microsoft operating system based on NT technology to do this.

DSL *See* Digital Subscriber Line.

Dynamic compulsory tunnels Dynamic compulsory tunnels are where a connection is dynamically assessed and the tunnel directed accordingly. For example, based on certain criteria, the same user may be directed to different Virtual Private Network (VPN) servers depending on what time of day the connection is made. Or, realms can be further divided into usernames, departments, the telephone number being used, and so forth. In this way, dynamic compulsory tunnels offer the highest degree of flexibility and granularity. An additional advantage for the owner of the Network Access Server is that it can simultaneously support both tunneling and nontunneling connections.

Dynamic disks Dynamic disks introduce conceptual as well as technical changes from traditional basic disk structure. Partitions are now called volumes, and these can be created or changed without losing existing data on the disk. Recall that when using basic disks, you must first create primary partitions (up to a maximum of four), then extended partitions (a maximum of one) with logical drives. Dynamic disks allow you to create volume after volume, with no limit on the number or type that can exist on a single disk; you are limited only by the capacity of the disk itself.

Dynamic Host Configuration Protocol (DHCP) A software utility that is designed to assign Internet Protocol (IP) addresses to clients and their stations logging onto a Transmission Control Protocol/Internet Protocol (TCP/IP) and eliminates manual IP address assignments.

Dynamic Host Control Protocol (DHCP) allocator A Dynamic Host Control Protocol (DHCP) allocator is a simplified DHCP service without the database or configurable options. Invoking the DHCP allocator means that the computer will automatically assign Internet Protocol (IP) addresses to other workstations on the same subnet using a private address range, and it will assign the default gateway and the DNS server to be the same IP address as the computer running Internet Connection Sharing (ICS). Note there is no Windows Internet Name Server (WINS) server allocation.

Dynamic routing Dynamic routing uses routing protocols such as the Routing Information Protocol (RIP) or Open Shortest Path First (OSPF) to allow routers to communicate with one another and automatically, dynamically update their routing tables without human intervention.

EAP *See* Extensible Authentication Protocol.

EFS *See* Encrypting File System.

Encapsulating Security Payload (ESP) A header used by Internet Protocol Security (IPSec) when encrypting the contents of a packet.

Encrypting File System (EFS) Unlike Windows NT 4.0, Windows 2000 provides the Encrypting File System (EFS) that allows you to encrypt and decrypt data on a file-by-file basis without the need for third-party software, as long as it is stored on an NTFS formatted partition or volume.

Encryption Scrambling of data so as to be unreadable; therefore, an unauthorized person cannot decipher the data.

ESP *See* Encapsulating Security Payload.

Ethernet A networking protocol and shared media (or switched) Local Area Network (LAN) access method linking up to 1K nodes in a bus topology.

Evaluation Evaluation is the process of assessing, summarizing, weighing, deciding, and applying standards.

Event Viewer The Windows 2000 Event Viewer has a dedicated log for DNS-specific information. The Event Viewer can provide you information on when zone transfers have taken place, if there was a problem with a zone transfer, when changes have taken place within the zone, or even report that an excessive number of changes have occurred to the zone for a specific period of time.

Extended Partitions Although extended partitions cannot be used to host operating systems, they can store other types of data and provide an excellent way to create more drives above the four-partition limit. Extended partitions do not represent one drive; rather, they can be subdivided into as many logical drives as there are letters in the alphabet. Therefore, one extended partition can contain several logical drives, each of which appears as a separate drive letter to the user.

Extensible Authentication Protocol (EAP) The Extensible Authentication Protocol is an extension to Point-to-Point Protocol (PPP) that allows for arbitrary authentication mechanisms to be used to validate a PPP connection. Its design is such that it allows authentication plug-in modules at both the client and server. One example is using security token cards ("smart cards"), where the remote access server queries the client for a name, PIN, and card token value. Another example is using biometrics; for example, a retina scan or finger print match to uniquely identify an individual. Once the connection authentication phase is reached, the client negotiates which EAP authentication it wants to use, which is known as the EAP type. Once the EAP type is agreed upon, the server can issue multiple authentication requests to the client (as in the client name, then PIN, then card token value).

Fast Transfer The Windows 2000 Domain Name System (DNS) Server supports a method of zone transfer that allows multiple records to be included in a single message. This compressed form of zone file transfer is referred to as a fast transfer. Not all DNS servers support the fast transfer mode, although most of the popular ones do. One popular DNS server that does not support fast transfers is Berkeley Internet Name Domain (BIND) versions before 4.9.4. Subsequent versions of BIND do support the fast transfer mode. If you do maintain BIND versions lower than 4.9.4, you can use the Advanced Options in the DNS server to indicate you have BIND Secondaries, and this disables the fast transfer mode.

FAT *See* File Allocation Table.

Fault tolerance Fault tolerance is high-system availability with enough resources to accommodate unexpected failure. Fault tolerance is also the design of a computer to maintain its system's performance when some internal hardware problems occur. This is done through the use of back-up systems.

FEK *See* File Encryption Key.

File Allocation Table (FAT) A FAT is an area on a disk that indicates the arrangement of files in the sectors. Because of the multi-user nature of Terminal Server, it is strongly recommended that the NTFS file system be used rather than the FAT file system. FAT does not offer file and directory security, whereas with NTFS you can limit access to subdirectories and files to certain users or groups of users.

File Allocation Table 16 (FAT16) The earlier version of the FAT file system implemented in MS-DOS is known as FAT16, to differentiate it from the improved FAT32.

File Allocation Table 32 (FAT32) FAT32 is the default file system for Windows 95 OSR2 and Windows 98. The FAT32 file system was first implemented in Windows 95 OSR2, and was supported by Windows 98 and now Windows 2000. While FAT16 cannot support partitions larger than 4GB in Windows 2000, FAT32 can support partitions up to 2TB (Terabytes) in size. However, for performance reasons, the creation of FAT32 partitions is limited to 32GB in Windows 2000. The second major benefit of FAT32 in comparison to FAT16 is that it supports a significantly smaller cluster size—as low as 4K for partitions up to 8GB. This results in more efficient use of disk space, with a 15 to 30 percent utilization improvement in comparison to FAT16.

File Encryption Key (FEK) A random key called a file encryption key (FEK) is used to encrypt each file and is then itself encrypted using the user's public key. At least two FEKs are created for every encrypted file. One FEK is created with the user's public key, and one is created with the public key of each recovery agent. There could be more than one recovery agent certificate used to encrypt each file, resulting in more than two FEKs. The user's public key can decrypt FEKs created with the public key.

File Transfer Protocol (FTP) Transfers files to and from a computer running an FTP server service (sometimes called a daemon).

Filter Actions Filter actions define the type of security and the methods in which security is established. The primary methods are: Permit, Block, and Negotiate security.

FireWire Also known as IEEE 1394. An Apple/Texas Instruments high-speed serial bus allowing up to 63 devices to connect; this bus supports hot swapping and isochronous data transfer.

Forest A forest is a grouping of one or more domain trees that do not share a common namespace but do share a common schema, configuration, and global catalog; in fact, it forms a noncontiguous (or discontiguous) namespace. The users in one tree do not have global access to resources in other trees, but trusts can be created that allow users to access resources in another tree.

Forward Lookup Query A forward lookup query occurs when a computer needs to get the Internet Protocol (IP) address for a computer with an Internet name. The local computer sends a query to a local Domain Name System (DNS) name server, which resolves the name or passes the request on to another server for resolution.

Forward lookup zones Forward lookup zones are used to provide a mechanism to resolve host names to IP addresses for DNS clients. A forward lookup zone will contain what are known as resource records. These resource records contain the actual information about the resources available in the zone.

Forwarder A DNS forwarder accepts requests to resolve host names from another DNS server. A forwarder can be used to protect your internal DNS server from access by Internet users.

FQDN *See* Fully Qualified Domain Name.

FTP *See* File Transfer Protocol.

Fully Qualified Domain Name (FQDN) A full site name of a system rather than just its host name. The FQDN of each child domain is made up of the combination of its own name and the FQDN of the parent domain. The FQDN includes the host name and the domain membership of that computer.

Gateway In networking, gateway refers to a router or a computer functioning as one, the "way out" of the network or subnet, to get to another network. You also use gateways for software that connects a system using one protocol to a system using a different protocol, such as the Systems Network Architecture (SNA) software (allows a Local Area Network (LAN) to connect to an IBM mainframe). You can also use Gateway Services for NetWare used to provide a way for Microsoft clients to go through a Windows NT or Windows 2000 server to access files on a Novell file server.

Global Groups Global Groups are used for combining users who share a common access profile based on job function or business role. Typically organizations use Global Groups for all groups in which membership is expected to change frequently. These groups can have as members only user accounts defined in the same domain as the Global Group.

Globally Unique IDentifier (GUID) The Globally Unique IDentifier (GUID) is a unique numerical identification created at the time the object is created. An analogy would be a person's social security number, which is assigned once and never changes, even if the person changes his or her name, or moves.

Glue record The Host (A) Address record is referred to as a glue record. It is called a glue record because it associates the host name in the Name Server (NS) record with an Internet Protocol (IP) address of the machine noted in the NS record. It glues together the name server's host name and IP address in this way.

GPC *See* Group Policy Container.

GPO *See* Group Policy Object.

GPT *See* Group Policy Template.

Graphical User Interface (GUI) An overall and consistent system for the interactive and visual program that interacts (or interfaces) with the user. GUI can involve pull-down menus, dialog boxes, on-screen graphics, and a variety of icons.

Group policy Group Policy provides for change management and desktop control on the Windows 2000 platform. You are familiar with the control you had in Windows NT 4.0 using System Policies. Group Policy is similar to System Policies but allows you a much higher level of granular configuration management over your network. Some of the confusion comes from the change of names applied to different groups in Windows 2000. You can apply Group Policy to sites, domains, and organizational units. Each of these represents a group of objects, so Group Policy is applied to the group of objects contained in each of these entities. Group Policy cannot be directly applied to Security Groups that are similar to the groups you are used to working with in Windows NT 4.0. However, by using Group Policy Filtering, you can successfully apply Group Policy to individual Security Groups.

Group Policy Container (GPC) The Active Directory object Group Policy Containers (GPCs) store the information for the Folder Redirection snap-in and the Software Deployment snap-in. GPCs do not apply to local group policies. They contain component lists and status information, which indicate whether Group Policy Objects (GPOs) are enabled or disabled. They also contain version information, which insures that the information is synchronized with the Group Policy Template (GPT) information. GPCs also contain the class store in which GPO group policy extensions have settings.

Group Policy Object (GPO) After you create a group policy, it is stored in a Group Policy Object (GPO) and applied to the site, domain, or Organizational Unit (OU). GPOs are used to keep the group policy information; essentially, it is a collection of policies. You can apply single or multiple GPOs to each site, domain or OU. Group policies are not inherited across domains, and users must have Read permission for the GPO that you want to have applied to them. This way, you can filter the scope of GPOs by adjusting who has read access to each GPO.

Group Policy Template (GPT) The subset of folders created on each domain controller that store Group Policy Object (GPO) information for specific GPOs are called Group Policy Templates (GPTs). GPTs are stored in the SysVol (System Volume) folder, on the domain controller. GPTs store data for Software Policies, Scripts, Desktop File and Folder Management, Software Deployment, and Security settings. GPTs can be defined in computer or user configurations. Consequently, they take effect either when the computer starts or when the user logs on.

GUI *See* Graphical User Interface.

GUID *See* Globally Unique IDentifier.

HAL *See* Hardware Abstraction Layer.

Hardware Abstraction Layer (HAL) Windows NT's translation layer existing between the hardware, kernel, and input/output (I/O) system.

Hardware Compatibility List (HCL) The Hardware Compatibility List is published by Microsoft for each of its operating systems, and is updated on a monthly basis. There is a copy of the HCL on the Windows 2000 Professional CD, located in the Support folder and named Hcl.txt.

Hardware profile A hardware profile is a set of instructions that tells your computer how to boot the system properly, based on the setup of your hardware. Hardware profiles are most commonly used with laptops. This is because laptops are frequently used in at least two different settings: stand-alone and in a docking station on a network. For example, when the laptop is being used at a docking station, it requires a network adapter. However, when the laptop is used away from the network, it does not. The hardware profile dialog manages these configuration changes. If a profile is created for each situation, the user will automatically be presented these choices on Windows startup.

Hash function A mathematical calculation that produces a fixed-length string of bits, which cannot be reverse-engineered to produce the original.

HCL *See* Hardware Compatibility List.

HINFO *See* Host Information.

HKEY_CLASSES_ROOT Contains information used for software configuration and object linking and embedding (OLE), as well as file association information.

HKEY_CURRENT_CONFIG Holds data about the current hardware profile that is in use.

HKEY_CURRENT_USER Has information about the user who is currently logged on.

HKEY_LOCAL_MACHINE Stores information about the hardware, software, system devices, and security information for the local computer.

HKEY_USERS Holds information and settings for the environments of all users of the computer.

H-Node H-node (hybrid node) Windows Internet Name Server (WINS) clients are similar to M-node, but use WINS NetBIOS name resolution first, before initiating a NetBIOS broadcast message.

Host Information (HINFO) HINFO records provide information about the Domain Name System (DNS) server itself. Information about the CPU and operating system on the host can be included in the HINFO record. This information is used by application protocols such as File Transfer Protocol (FTP) that can use special procedures when communicating between computers of the same CPU and OS type (RFC 1035).

Host routing Host routing occurs when a computer forwards a packet to a router rather than sending the packet directly on its own network.

Host-to-host layer This layer is basically the same as the Transport layer in the OSI model. It is responsible for flow control, acknowledgments, sequencing (ordering) of packets, and establishment of end-to-end communications. Transmission Control Protocol (TCP) and the User Datagram Protocol (UDP) operate at this level.

HTML *See* HyperText Markup Language.

HTTP *See* HyperText Transfer Protocol.

HyperText Markup Language (HTML) The format used to create documents viewed on the World Wide Web (WWW) by the use of tags (codes) embedded within the text.

HyperText Transfer Protocol (HTTP) HTTP is an Internet standard supporting World Wide Web (WWW) exchanges. By creating the definitions of Universal Resource Locators (URLs) and their retrieval usage throughout the Internet.

IAS *See* Internet Authentication Services.

ICS *See* Internet Connection Sharing.

IDE *See* Integrated Drive Electronics.

IIS *See* Internet Information Service.

IKE *See* Internet Key Exchange.

in-addr.arpa domain The in-addr.arpa domain indexes host names based on Network IDs and makes reverse lookups much more efficient and speedy.

Incremental backup This backup process is similar to the Differential backup, but it clears the markers from the selected files after the process. Because it clears the markers, an incremental backup will not back up any files that have not changed since the last incremental backup. This type of backup is fast during the backup but is very slow while restoring the files. You will need the last full backup and all of the subsequent incremental backups to fully restore data. The positive side of this backup type is that it is fast and consumes very little media space.

Indexing service Provides indexing functions for documents stored on disk, allowing users to search for specific document text or properties.

Industry Standard Architecture (ISA) A PC's expansion bus used for peripherals' plug-in boards.

Infrastructure Infrastructure of a computer network consists of the basic components upon which it is built.

Initialization Vector (IV) The IV is a random block of encrypted data that begins each chain. In this fashion, we are able to make each message's ciphertext appear different, even if we were to send the exact same message a hundred times.

Integrated Drive Electronics (IDE) drive An IDE drive is a hard disk drive for processors containing most controller circuitry within the drive. IDE drives combine Enhanced System Device Interface (ESDI) speed with Small Computer System Interface (SCSI) hard drive interface intelligence.

Integrated Services Digital Network (ISDN) Integrated Services indicates the provider offers voice and data services over the same medium. Digital Network is a reminder that ISDN was born out of the digital nature of the intercarrier and intracarrier networks. ISDN runs across the same copper wiring that carries regular telephone service. Because attenuation and noise cause the signal to be unintelligible, an ISDN circuit can run a maximum of 18,000 feet. A repeater doubles this distance to 36,000 feet.

Internal Router (IR) An Internal Router as its name suggests, is a router that sits in its area, and only in its area and handles intra-area routing.

Internet Authentication Services (IAS) IAS performs authentication, authorization, and accounting of dial-up and Virtual Private Networking (VPN) users. IAS supports the Remote Access Dial-In User Service (RADIUS) protocol.

Internet Connection Sharing (ICS) ICS can be thought of as a less robust version of Network Address Translation (NAT lite). ICS uses the same address translation technology. ICS is a simpler version of NAT, useful for connecting a few computers on a small Local Area Network (LAN) to the Internet or useful for a remote server through a single phone line and account.

Internet Control Message Protocol (ICMP) The Internet Control Message Protocol (ICMP) is a Transmission Control Protocol/Internet Protocol (TCP/IP) standard that allows hosts and routers that use IP communication to report errors and exchange limited control and status information. The PING utility works by sending an ICMP echo request message and recording the response of echo replies.

Internet Group Management Protocol (IGMP) The Internet Group Management Protocol is used for multicasting, which is a method of sending a message to multiple hosts but only addressing it to a single address. Members of a multicast group can be defined, and then when a message is sent to the group address, only those computers that belong to the group will receive it. IGMP is used to exchange membership status information between IP routers that support multicasting and members of multicast groups.

Internet Information Service (IIS) Windows NT web browser software that supports Secure Sockets Layer (SSL) security protocol from Netscape. IIS provides support for Web site creation, configuration, and management, along with Network News Transfer Protocol (NNTP), File Transfer Protocol (FTP), and Simple Mail Transfer Protocol (SMTP).

Internet Key Exchange (IKE) Automated Key Management uses a combination of the Internet Security Association Key Management Protocol and the Oakley Protocol (ISAKMP/Oakley). This combination of protocols is often referred to collectively as the Internet Key Exchange (IKE). The IKE is responsible for exchange of "key material" (groups of numbers that will form the basis of a new key), session keys, SA negotiation, and authentication of peers participating in an Internet Protocol Security (IPSec) interaction. During this exchange, the Oakley protocol protects the identities of the negotiating parties.

Internet Packet eXchange (IPX) Novell NetWare's built-in networking protocol for Local Area Network (LAN) communication derived from the Xerox Network System protocol. IPX moves data between a server and/or workstation programs from different network nodes. Sometimes called an Internetwork Packet eXchange.

Internet Protocol Security (IPSec) IPSec is a new feature included in Windows 2000 and provides for encryption of data as it travels between two computers, protecting it from modification and interpretation if anyone were to see it on the network.

Internet Security Association and Key Management Protocol (ISAKMP) An Internet Protocol Security (IPSec) protocol required as part of the IPSec implementation, which provides a framework for Internet key management.

Internet Service Provider (ISP) The organization allowing users to connect to its computers and then to the Internet. ISPs provide the software to connect and sometimes a portal site and/or internal browsing capability.

Internetwork layer This layer matches the Network layer in the OSI model. The Internet Protocol (IP) works here to route and deliver packets to the correct destination address. Other protocols that operate at this layer include the Address Resolution Protocol (ARP), Reverse Address Resolution Protocol (RARP), and the Internet Control Message Protocol (ICMP).

Interrupt ReQuest (IRQ) An electronic signal that is sent to the computer's processor requiring the processor's attention. Also, a computer instruction designed to interrupt a program for an Input/Output (I/O).

IPCONFIG command-line utility IPCONFIG is used to gather information about the Transmission Control Protocol/Internet Protocol (TCP/IP) configuration on the computer. Typing IPCONFIG at the command line will display the computer's Internet Protocol (IP) address, subnet mask, and default gateway. Adding the /all switch will display additional information such as the host name, Media Access Control (MAC) address, node type, and much more. IPCONFIG includes new switches that increase its usefulness beyond a great tool for getting IP addressing information about your machines.

IPSec *See* Internet Protocol Security.

IPX *See* Internet Packet eXchange.

IR *See* Internal Router.

IRQ *See* Interrupt ReQuest.

ISA *See* Industry Standard Architecture.

ISDN *See* Integrated Services Digital Network.

ISP *See* Internet Service Provider.

Iterative query Iterative queries allow the Domain Name System (DNS) server responding to the request to make a best-effort attempt at resolving the DNS query.

If the DNS server receiving an iterative query is not authoritative for the domain included in the query, it can return a Referral response.

JetBEUI Microsoft had intended NetBEUI to become even more robust, and even routable. They were working on a networking protocol dubbed "JetBEUI" that would have been a routable implementation of NetBEUI.

Kerberos Kerberos guards against username and password safety vulnerability by using tickets (temporary electronic credentials) to authenticate. Tickets have a limited life span and can be used in place of usernames and passwords (if the software supports this). Kerberos encrypts the password into the ticket. It uses a trusted server called the Key Distribution Center (KDC) to handle authentication requests. Kerberos speeds up network processes by integrating security and rights across network domains and also eliminates workstations' need to authenticate themselves repeatedly at every domain they access. Kerberos security also makes maneuvering around networks using multiple platforms such as UNIX or NetWare easier.

Knowledge Knowledge is the very lowest level of learning. It is, of course, important that a network administrator have this knowledge. Knowledge involves the processes of defining, location, recall, recognition, stating, matching, labeling, and identification.

L2TP *See* Layer-Two Tunneling Protocol.

Last Known Good Configuration This mode starts the system using the configuration that was saved in the registry during the last system shutdown. This startup option is useful when you have changed some configuration parameters and the system fails to boot. When you use this mode to start the system, all changes that were made after the last successful logon are lost. Use this option when you suspect that some incorrect configuration changes are causing the system startup failure. This mode does not help if any of the installed drivers have been corrupted or any driver files are deleted by mistake.

Layer Two Tunneling Protocol (L2TP) L2TP offers better security through the use of IPSec and creates Virtual Private Networks (VPNs). Windows 2000 uses

L2TP to provide tunneling services over Internet Protocol Security (IPSec)-based communications. L2TP tunnels can be set up to traverse data across intervening networks that are not part of the VPN being created. L2TP is used to send information across intervening and nonsecure networks.

LDAP *See* Lightweight Directory Access Protocol.

Lease A lease is an agreement to let someone use something for a defined length of time. The Dynamic Host Control Protocol (DHCP) client leases Internet Protocol (IP) addressing information from the DHCP server. The DHCP client does not own this information, and does not get to keep it forever.

Legend The legend displays information about the counters that are being measured. It is the set of columns at the bottom of System Monitor.

Lifetime This is the "shelf-life" of a route – how long it is considered valid. Static routes automatically have an infinite lifetime but dynamic routes have a finite lifetime and the route must be refreshed before the lifetime expires in order to be retained in the routing table.

Lightweight Directory Access Protocol (LDAP) A simplified Directory Access Protocol (DAP) accessing a computer's directory listing. LDAP is able to access to X.500 directories.

Line Printer Daemon (LPD) LPD is the server process that advertises printer queues and accepts incoming print submissions, which are then routed to the print device.

Line Printer Remote (LPR) LPR is a process that spools a print job to a remote print spool that is advertised by the Line Printer Daemon (LPD).

Link State Routing Link state routing was designed specifically to overcome some of the shortcomings of the older distance vector routing protocol, which was never designed for today's wide-scale enterprise internetworks.

LMHOSTS An LMHOSTS file is a plain-text file that contains NetBIOS names to IP address mappings. LMHOSTS can be useful as a backup method of resolving names of especially important computers when other methods fail.

Load balancing The fine tuning process of a system (computer, network, etc.) to allow the data to be distributed more efficiently and evenly. Load balancing is an add-on feature of MetaFrame that must be purchased separately from the base product. Load balancing allows the administrator to group servers in a server farm which can act as a single point of access for clients accessing published applications.

Local policy A group policy stored locally on a Windows 2000 Member Server or a Windows 2000 Professional computer is called a local policy. The local policy is used to set up the configuration settings for each computer and for each user. Local policies are stored in the \%systemroot%\system32\grouppolicy folder on the local computer. Local policies include the auditing policy, user rights and privilege assignment, and various security options.

Local printer A print device that is directly attached, via a parallel or serial cable, to the computer that is providing the printing services. For a Windows 2000 Professional workstation, a local printer is one that is connected to the workstation. For a Windows 2000 Server, a local printer is one that is connected to the server. Drivers for the print device must reside on the computer that connects to the printer.

Local user profiles (local profiles) Local user profiles are kept on one local computer hard drive. When a user initially logs on to a computer, a local profile is created for them in the \%systemdrive%\Documents and Settings\<username> folder. When users log off the computer, the changes that they made while they were logged on will be saved to their local profile on that client computer. This way, subsequent logons to that computer will bring up their personal settings. When users log on to a different computer, they will not receive these settings, as they are local to the computer in which they made the changes. Therefore, each user that logs on to that computer receives individual desktop settings. Local profiles are ideal for users who only use one computer. For users that require access to multiple computers, the Roaming profile would be the better choice.

Logical infrastructure Logical infrastructure is the networking protocols, the Domain Name System (DNS) namespace and services, the Internet Protocol (IP) addressing scheme and Dynamic Host Control Protocol (DHCP) strategy, the remote access services, and security protocols. Components of the logical infrastructure include Network Protocols, IP Addressing Schemes, Name Resolution Services, Remote Access, Routing and Network Address Translation, and Security Infrastructure (Certificate Services).

LogicalDisk object The LogicalDisk object measures the transfer of data for a logical drive (i.e., C: or D:) or storage volumes. You can use the PhysicalDisk object to determine which hard disk is causing the bottleneck. Then, to narrow the cause of the bottleneck, you can use the LogicalDisk object to determine which, if any, partition is the specific cause of the bottleneck. By default, the PhysicalDisk object is enabled and the LogicalDisk object is disabled on Windows 2000 Server.

LPD *See* Line Printer Daemon.

LPR *See* Line Printer Remote.

MAC *See* Media Access Control; Message Authentication Code.

Mail eXchanger (MX) Identifies the preferred mail servers on the network. If you have several mail servers, an order of precedence will be run. Note that the MX record has similar requirements to the Canonical Name (CNAME) record. You must have an existing A record for the machine that you wish to create a MX record for.

Mandatory Roaming profiles Mandatory roaming profiles are mandatory user profiles the user cannot change. They are usually created to define desktop configuration settings for groups of users in order to simplify administration and support. Users can make changes to their desktop settings while they are logged on, but these changes will not be saved to the profile, as Mandatory profiles are read-only. The next time they log on, their desktop will be set back to the original Mandatory profile settings.

Many-to-One Certificate Mapping This involves mapping many certificates to a single user account. This is particularly convenient when organizations need to share specific information with each other. An administrator must install the Root Certificate Authority (CA) certificates of all the desired CAs as trusted Root CAs in their enterprise. The administrator can then set a rule that maps all certificates installed by the trusted CAs to a single Windows 2000 account. Users using these mapped certificates possess access rights defined by the rights set on the mapped account.

Master File Table (MFT) The MFT stores the information needed by the operating system to retrieve files from the volume. Part of the MFT is stored at the beginning of the volume and cannot be moved. Also, if the volume contains a large number of directories, it can prevent the free space from being defragmented.

Master image After configuring one computer with the operating system and all the applications, Sysprep is run to create an image of the hard disk. This computer serves as the master or model computer that will have the complete setup of the operating system, application software, and any service packs. This hard disk image is the master image and is copied to a CD or put on a network share for distribution to many computers. Any third-party disk-imaging tool can then be used to replicate the image to other identical computers.

MCSE *See* Microsoft Certified Systems Engineer.

Media Access Control (MAC) A sublayer in the Open System Interconnection (OSI) data link layer that controls access, control, procedures, and format for a Local Area Network (LAN), for example, Institute of Electronic and Electrical Engineers (IEEE) 802.3, 802.5, and 802.5 standards.

Message Authentication Code (MAC) A cryptographically generated fixed-length code associated with a message in order to ensure the authenticity of the message (a digital signature is a public key MAC).

Message queuing service Provides a communication infrastructure and a development tool for creating distributed messaging applications. Such applications can communicate across heterogeneous networks and with computers that might be offline. Message queuing provides guaranteed message delivery, efficient routing, security, transactional support, and priority-based messaging.

Metric A metric is the cost of using a particular route from one destination to another. Generally this will be the number of hops to the Internet Protocol (IP) destination. Anything on the local subnet is one hop, and every time a router is crossed, this adds 1 to the hop count. The value of this is that it lets Windows 2000 select the route with the lowest metric if there are multiple routes to the same destination.

MFT *See* Master File Table.

Microsoft Certified Systems Engineer (MCSE) An engineer who is a technical specialist in advanced Microsoft products, specifically NT Server and NT Workstation.

Microsoft Challenge Handshake Authentication Protocol (MS-CHAP) This is Microsoft's version of the Challenge Handshake Authentication Protocol, and offers the same features as CHAP with some additional advantages. It is supported on all versions of Windows, and as such, makes a suitable default authentication protocol. However, where you have the choice, you should instead use the later version, MS-CHAPv2, which is a more secure protocol that protects against server impersonation. If mutual authentication (where both sides can verify they are who they say they are) is important to your security policies, then you should ensure that Microsoft clients have the latest MS-CHAPv2 and disable MS-CHAP on the server.

Microsoft Management Console (MMC) The MMC provides a standardized interface for using administrative tools and utilities. The management applications contained in an MMC are called Snap-ins, and custom MMCs hold the Snap-ins required to perform specific tasks. Custom consoles can be saved as files with the .msc file extension. The MMC was first introduced with NT Option Pack. Using the MMC leverages the familiarity you have with the other snap-ins available within MMC, such as SQL Server 7 and Internet Information Server 4. With the MMC, all your administrative tasks can be done in one place.

Mini-Setup Wizard The purpose of this wizard is to add some user-specific parameters on the destination computer. These parameters include: End-user license agreement (EULA); Product key (serial number); Username, company name, and administrator password; Network configuration; Domain or workgroup name; and, Date and time zone selection.

Mirror Set In a mirror set, all data on a selected partition or drive are automatically duplicated onto another physical disk. The main purpose of a mirror set is to provide fault tolerance in the event of missing or corrupt data. If one disk fails or contains corrupt files, the data is simply retrieved and rebuilt from the other disk.

Mirrored Volume Like basic disks, dynamic disks can also be mirrored, and are called mirrored volumes. A continuous and automatic backup of all data in a mirrored volume is saved to a separate disk to provide fault tolerance in the event of a disk failure or corrupt file. Note that you cannot mirror a spanned or striped volume.

Mirroring Also called RAID 1. RAID 1 consists of two drives that are identical matches, or mirrors, of each other. If one drive fails, you have another drive to boot up and keep the server going.

Mixed-Mode When in Mixed-Mode, the domain still uses master replication with a Windows 2000 DC. The Windows NT Backup Domain Controllers (BDCs) replicate from the Windows 2000 Server, as did the Windows NT Primary Domain Controller (PDC). When you are operating in Mixed-Mode, some Windows 2000 functionality will not be available. You will not be able to use group nesting or transitive trusts. Mixed-Mode is the default mode.

MMC *See* Microsoft Management Console.

M-Node M-node (mixed node) Windows Internet Name Server (WINS) clients use both broadcasts and WINS servers to resolve NetBIOS names to Internet Protocol (IP) addresses. The mixed-node client preferentially uses broadcasts before querying a WINS server.

MP *See* Multilink Point-to-Point Protocol.

MSCHAP *See* Microsoft Challenge Handshake Authentication Protocol.

MX *See* Mail eXchanger.

Multilink Point-to-Point Protocol (MP) MP allows multiple physical links to appear as a single local link over which data can be sent and received at a higher throughput than if going over a single physical link.

Name collision When a machine tries to update its name in the zone database, and finds that its name is already there with a different IP address, it has experienced a name collision. The default behavior of the DNS client is to overwrite the existing record with its own information.

Name Server (NS) An NS record lists the Domain Name System (DNS) servers that can return authoritative answers for the domain. This includes the Primary DNS server for the zone, and any other DNS servers to which you delegate authority for the zone. The NS record is also used to direct DNS client requests to other DNS servers when the server is not authoritative for a zone. For example, when you issue a query for the microsoft.com domain, the .com domain DNS server is not authoritative for the microsoft.com domain. However, an NS record is contained on the .com DNS server that can return a referral answer to the requesting client, which will direct it to the microsoft.com DNS server.

NAT *See* Network Address Translation.

Native-Mode Native-Mode allows only Windows 2000 domain controllers to operate in the domain. When all domain controllers for the domain are upgraded to Windows 2000 Server, you can switch to Native-Mode. This allows you to use transitive trusts and the group-nesting features of Windows 2000. When switching to Native-Mode, ensure you no longer need to operate in Mixed-Mode, because you cannot switch back to Mixed-Mode once you are in Native-Mode.

NBMA *See* Non-Broadcast Multiple Access.

NBNS *See* NETwork Basic Input/Output System Name Server.

NBTSTAT NBTSTAT is used to display the local NetBIOS name table, a table of NetBIOS names registered by local applications, and the NetBIOS name cache, a local cache listing of NetBIOS computer names that have been resolved to IP addresses.

NDS *See* NetWare Directory Service.

Net Shell (Netsh) Net Shell (Netsh) is a command-line and scripting tool for both local and remote Windows 2000 Servers running Routing and Remote Access. It can be used in conjunction with remote access settings, but is also for routing, Dynamic Host Control Protocol (DHCP) Relay, and Network Address Translation (NAT).

NetBEUI *See* NETwork Basic Input/Output System Extended User Interface.

NetBIOS *See* Network Basic Input/Output System.

NETDIAG The Resource Kit for Windows 2000 Professional includes the NETDIAG utility. This is a command-line diagnostic tool that helps isolate networking and connectivity problems. It does this by performing a series of tests designed to determine the state of the network client software, and ascertain whether it is functional. This tool does not require that parameters or switches be specified, which means support personnel and network administrators can focus on analyzing the output, rather than training users on how to use the tool.

NETSTAT command-line utility NETSTAT is used to display protocol statistics and current TCP/IP network connections.

NetWare Directory Service (NDS) NDS (created by Novell) has a hierarchical information database allowing the user to log on to a network with NDS capable of calculating the user's access rights.

Network Two or more computers connected together by cable or wireless media for the purpose of sharing data, hardware peripherals, and other resources.

Network Address Translation (NAT) With NAT, you can allow internal users to have access to important external resources while still preventing unauthorized access from the outside world.

NETwork Basic Input/Output System (NetBIOS) A program in Microsoft's operating system that links personal computers to a Local Area Network (LAN).

NETwork Basic Input/Output System Extended User Interface (NetBEUI) The transport layer for the Disk Operating System (DOS) networking protocol called Network Basic Input/Output System (NetBIOS).

NETwork Basic Input/Output System Name Server A NetBIOS Name Server (NBNS) is a machine that runs server software dedicated to resolving NetBIOS names to IP addresses. The NBNS contains a database file that can accept dynamic NetBIOS name registrations and answer queries for NetBIOS name resolution.

Network Interface Card (NIC) A board with encoding and decoding circuitry and a receptacle for a network cable connection that, bypassing the serial ports and operating through the internal bus, allows computers to be connected at higher speeds to media for communications between stations.

Network interface layer This bottom layer of the U.S. Department of Defense (DoD) model corresponds to both the Data Link and Physical layers of OSI. It provides the interface between the network architecture (Ethernet, Token Ring, AppleTalk, etc.) and the upper layers, as well as the physical (hardware) issues.

Network News Transfer Protocol (NNTP) The Network News Transfer Protocol is used for managing messages posted to private and public newsgroups. NNTP servers provide for storage of newsgroup posts that can be downloaded by client software called a newsreader. Windows 2000 Server includes an NNTP server with IIS, and Outlook Explorer version 5, which is part of the Internet Explorer software included with Windows 2000, provides both an e-mail client and a newsreader.

Network protocol Network protocol usually refers to the network and transport layer protocols (often part of a protocol "stack" or "suite") used for communication over a Local Area Network (LAN).

Network printer A print device that has a built-in network interface or connects directly to a dedicated network interface. Both workstations and servers can be configured to print directly to the network printer, and the network printer controls its own printer queue, determining which jobs from which clients will print in which order. Printing clients have no direct control over the printer queue and cannot see other print jobs being submitted to the printer. Administration of a network printer is difficult. Drivers for the print device must reside on the computer that connects to the printer.

NIC *See* Network Interface Card.

NNTP *See* Network News Transfer Protocol.

Non-Broadcast Multiple Access (NBMA) This represents a network that can connect more than two routers, but which cannot support hardware broadcasts. In this particular case, because multicasts cannot be used, Open Shortest Path First (OSPF) must be configured to use unicast to the specific IP addresses of the routers on the NBMA network.

Nondedicated server A nondedicated print server is a Windows 2000 Server that hosts printing services in addition to other services. A domain controller, database server, or Domain Name System (DNS) server can provide printing services as well, but should be used only for a smaller number of printers or for printers that are not heavily used. Anyone setting up a nondedicated print server should monitor the performance of the printing process and the other tasks running on the server and be prepared to modify the server configuration if the performance drops below acceptable levels.

Nonmandatory Roaming profiles Roaming user profiles are stored on the network file server and are the perfect solution for users who have access to multiple computers. This way their profile is accessible no matter where they log on in the domain. When users log on to a computer within their domain, their Roaming profile will be copied from the network server to the client computer and the settings will be applied to the computer while they are logged on. Subsequent logons will compare the Roaming profile files to the local profile files. The file server then copies only any files that have been altered since the user last logged on locally, significantly decreasing the time required to logon. When the user logs off, any changes that the user made on the local computer will be copied back to the profile on the network file server.

Normal backup This is the most common type and is also known as a full backup. The Normal backup operation backs up all files and folders that are selected irrespective of the archive attributes of the files. This provides the easiest way to restore the files and folders but is expensive in terms of the time it takes to complete the backup job and the storage space it consumes. The restore process from a Normal backup is less complex because you do not have to use multiple tape sets to restore data completely.

NS *See* Name Server.

NSLOOKUP command-line utility NSLOOKUP is used to check records, domain host aliases, domain host services, and operating system information by querying Domain Name System (DNS) servers. NSLOOKUP works in two modes: interactive mode and command mode. Command mode is used when you only want to do a single query.

NT File System (NTFS) The NT File System (with file names up to 255 characters) is a system created to aid the computer and its components in recovering from hard disk crashes.

NTFS *See* NT File System.

NWLink IPX/SPX/NetBIOS Compatible Transport Protocol (NWLink) Microsoft's implementation of Novell's Internet Packet eXchange/Sequenced Packet eXchange (IPX/SPX) protocol stack, required for connecting to NetWare servers prior to version 5. NWLink can also be used on small networks that use only Windows 2000 and other Microsoft client software. NWLink is a Network Driver Interface Specification (NDIS) compliant, native 32-bit protocol. The NWLink protocol supports Windows sockets and NetBIOS.

ODBC *See* Open DataBase Connectivity.

Offer After the Dynamic Host Control Protocol (DHCP) server receives the DHCPDISCOVER message, it looks at the request to see if the client configuration request is valid. If so, it sends back a DHCPOFFER message with the client's network hardware address, an IP address, a subnet mask, the length of time the lease is valid, and the IP address of the server that provided the DHCP information. This message is also a Transmission Control Protocol/Internet Protocol (TCP/IP) broadcast, as the client does not yet have an Internet Protocol (IP) address. The server then reserves the address it sent to the client so that it is not offered to another client making a request. If there are more than one DHCP server on the network, all servers respond to the DHCPDISCOVER message with a DHCPOFFER message.

Off-Subnet Addressing When the Dynamic Host Control Protocol (DHCP) server allocates an Internet Protocol (IP) address that is on a different subnet to the remote access server itself; this is called off-subnet addressing.

One-to-One Certificate Mapping This type of mapping simply involves mapping a single user certificate to a single Windows 2000 user account. Certificates may be issued from your own Enterprise CA or from a trusted CA. These certificates are then manually mapped to their respective user accounts.

One-way initiated demand-dial connections A one-way initiated connection restricts one router to being the calling router and the other to being an answering router. In many ways, this is the easiest of configurations because there is less to configure. It also offers a more secure routing environment from the perspective of the calling router because it has complete control over when a connection is made.

On-Subnet Addressing When the allocated addresses are on the same subnet as the remote access server, this is called on-subnet addressing and is by far the more common setup.

Open DataBase Connectivity (ODBC) A database programming interface that allows applications a way to access network databases.

Open Shortest Path First (OSPF) Open Shortest Path First is a link-state routing protocol designed for use in large scale internetworks and seeks to redress some of the shortcomings associated with traditional distance vector-based routing protocols.

Open Systems Interconnection (OSI) model This is a model of breaking networking tasks into layers. Each layer is responsible for a specific set of functionality. There are performance objects available in System Monitor for analyzing network performance.

Organizational Units (OUs) OUs in Windows 2000 are objects that are containers for other objects, such as users, groups, or other organizational units. Objects cannot be placed in another domain's OUs. The whole purpose of an OU is to have a hierarchical structure to organize your network objects. You can assign a group policy to an OU. Generally, the OU will follow a structure from your company. It may be a location, if you have multiple locations. It can even be a department-level organization. Also, OUs are units used to organize objects within a domain. These objects can include user accounts, groups, computers, printers, and even other OUs. The hierarchy of OUs is independent of other domains.

OSI *See* Open Systems Interconnection.

OSPF *See* Open Shortest Path First.

OU *See* Organizational Unit.

Paging When enough memory is not available for the running applications, pages of memory can be swapped from physical memory to the hard disk and slow the system down. This is known as paging because pages of memory are swapped at a time. Windows 2000 separates memory into 4KB pages of memory to help prevent fragmentation of memory. Swapping can even get bad enough that you can hear your hard disk running constantly.

Paging file A file on the hard disk (or spanning multiple disks) that stores some of the program code that is normally in the computer's RAM. This is called virtual memory, and allows the programs to function as if the computer had more memory than is physically installed.

PAP *See* Password Authentication Protocol.

Password Authentication Protocol (PAP) The Password Authentication Protocol is the least secure of the authentication protocols provided using a simple, plain-text authentication. It offers no protection against replay attacks, client impersonation, or server impersonation. However, it is offered in Windows 2000 Routing and Remote Access for downward compatibility for older clients and non-Microsoft clients that cannot support a stronger authentication protocol.

Password policy A password policy regulates how your users must establish and manage their passwords. This includes password complexity requirements and how often passwords must change. There are several settings that can be used to implement a successful password policy. You can enforce password uniqueness so those users cannot simply switch back and forth between a few easy to remember passwords. This can be set to low, medium, or high security. With low security, the system remembers the user's last 1–8 passwords (it is your choice as administrator to decide how many); with medium, it remembers the last 9–16 passwords; with high, it remembers the last 17–24 passwords.

PathPing This is new to Windows 2000 and combines features from both Ping and Tracert by sending packets to each router in the source to destination route, and then computing results based on the information returned from each discovered router. It helps to indicate the degree of packet loss at each link of the route, which allows you to identify, which routers or links might be causing problems in the way of packet loss and delays.

PATHPING command-line utility PATHPING is used to verify configurations and test IP connectivity by name or IP address. PATHPING combines features of PING and TRACERT with added functionality, and is used to trace the route a packet takes to a destination and display information on packet losses for each router in the path. PATHPING can also be used to troubleshoot Quality of Service (QoS) connectivity.

PCMCIA *See* Personal Computer Memory Card Interface Adapter.

PDC *See* Primary Domain Controller.

Peer-to-peer network A workgroup is also referred to as a peer-to-peer network, because all the computers connected together and communicating with one another are created equal. That is, there is no central computer that manages security and controls access to the network.

Performance logging Performance logging has many features. The data collected are stored in a comma-delimited or tab-delimited format, which allows for exportation to spreadsheet and database applications for a variety of tasks such as charting and reports. The data can also be viewed as collected. You can configure the logging by specifying start and stop times, the name of the log files and the maximum size of the log. You can start and stop the logging of data manually or create a schedule for logging. You can even specify a program to run automatically when logging stops. You can also create trace logs. Trace logs track events that occur rather than measuring performance counters.

Permissions Inheritance By default, all permissions set for a folder are inherited by the files in the folder, the subfolders in the folder, and the contents of the subfolders. When the permissions on a folder are viewed in the Security tab of the file or folder Permissions window, inherited permissions are indicated with a gray check box.

Personal Computer Memory Card Interface Adapter (PCMCIA) An interface standard for plug-in cards for portable computers; devices meeting the standard (for example, fax cards, modems) are theoretically interchangeable.

Personal Information Exchange The Personal Information Exchange format is an industry format that facilitates backup and restoration of a certificate and its private key. This vendor-independent certificate format enables certificates and their corresponding private keys to be transferred from one computer to another or from a computer to removable media. Personal Information Exchange format is the only format used by Windows 2000 when exporting certificates and private keys because it avoids exposing the keys to unintended parties.

Physical infrastructure Physical infrastructure is the machines themselves along with the cables and network interface cards, and hubs and routers.

Physical layer protocols Physical layer protocols consist of specifications or standards governing the hardware components.

Physical memory Physical memory is the actual Random Access Memory (RAM) on the computer. When the physical memory becomes full, the operating system can also use space on the hard disk as virtual memory. When memory becomes full, rather than locking up the computer, the operating system stores unused data on the hard disk in a page file (also called paging or swap file). Data are swapped back and forth between the hard disk and physical memory as needed for running applications. If memory is needed that is in virtual memory, it is swapped back into physical memory.

PhysicalDisk object The PhysicalDisk object measures the transfer of data for the entire hard disk. You can use the PhysicalDisk object to determine which hard disk is causing the bottleneck. By default, the PhysicalDisk object is enabled and the LogicalDisk object is disabled on Windows 2000 Server.

PKI *See* Public Key Infrastructure.

Plug and Play (PnP) A standard requiring add-in hardware to carry the software to configure itself in a given way supported by Microsoft Windows 95. Plug and Play can make peripheral configuration software, jumper settings, and Dual In-line Package (DIP) switches unnecessary. PnP allows the operating system to load device drivers automatically and assign system resources dynamically to computer components and peripherals. Windows 2000 moves away from this older technology with its use of Kernel-mode and User-mode PnP architecture. PnP autodetects, configures, and installs the necessary drivers in order to minimize user interaction with hardware configuration. Users no longer have to tinker with IRQ and I/O settings.

P-Node A p-node (peer node) Windows Internet Name Server (WINS) client uses a WINS server and does not issue broadcasts. When a WINS client is configured as a p-node WINS client, it will *not* broadcast to resolve a NetBIOS name to an IP address. The advantage of configuring WINS clients as p-nodes is that there is no possibility of NetBIOS broadcast traffic using up valuable network bandwidth. On the other hand, if the p-node client is not able to access a WINS server, it will have to use alternate methods to resolve the NetBIOS name to an IP address, even if the destination host is local. This can lead to strange things, like the p-node client accessing a remote Domain Name System (DNS) server to resolve the Internet Protocol (IP) address of a host on the local segment.

PnP *See* Plug and Play.

Pointer record (PTR) The Pointer record is created to allow for reverse lookups. Reverse lookups are valuable when doing security analysis and checking authenticity of source domains for e-mail.

Point-to-Point Protocol (PPP) A serial communication protocol most commonly used to connect a personal computer to an Internet Service Provider (ISP). PPP is the successor to Serial Line Internet Protocol (SLIP) and may be used over both synchronous and asynchronous circuits. Also, PPP is a full-duplex, connectionless protocol that supports many different types of links. The advantages of PPP made it de facto standard for dial-up connections.

Point-to-Point Tunneling Protocol (PPTP) One of two standards for dial-up telephone connection of computers to the Internet, with better data negotiation, compression, and error corrections than the other Serial Line Internet Protocol (SLIP), but costing more to transmit data and unnecessary when both sending and receiving modems can handle some of the procedures.

Policy Inheritance Group policies have an order of inheritance in which the policies are applied. Local policies are applied first, then group policies are applied to the site, then the domain, and finally the Organizational Unit (OU). Policies applied first are overwritten by policies applied later. Therefore, group policies applied to a site overwrite the local policies and so on. When there are multiple Group Policy Objects (GPOs) for a site, domain, or OU, the order in which they appear in the Properties list applies. This policy inheritance order works well for small companies, but a more complex inheritance strategy may be essential for larger corporations.

Ports A channel of a device that can support single point-to-point connections is known as a port. Devices can be single port, as in a modem.

Power options Power options are dependent on the particular hardware. Power options include Standby and Hibernation modes. Standby mode turns off the monitor and hard disks to save power. Hibernation mode turns off the monitor and disks, saves everything in memory to disk, turns off the computer, and then restores the desktop to the state in which you left it when the computer is turned on.

PPP *See* Point-to-Point Protocol.

PPTP *See* Point-to-Point Tunneling Protocol.

Preboot eXecution Environment (PXE) The PXE is a new Dynamic Host Control Protocol (DHCP)-based technology used to help client computers boot from the network. The Windows 2000 Remote Installation Service (RIS) uses the PXE technology along with the existing Transmission Control Protocol/Internet Protocol (TCP/IP) network infrastructure to implement the RIS-based deployment of Windows 2000 Professional. The client computer that has the PXE-based ROM uses its Basic Input/Output System (BIOS) to contact an existing RIS server and get an Internet Protocol (IP) address from the DHCP server running on the network. The RIS server then initializes the installation process on the client computer.

Preemptive multitasking An environment in which timesharing controls the programs in use by exploiting a scheduled time usage of the computer's Central Processing Unit (CPU).

Preshared keys A preshared key is a secret key agreed upon previously by two users conducting the transaction. This method, like the public key certificate, has the advantage of working with computers that are not running Kerberos v5. The disadvantage is that Internet Protocol Security (IPSec) must be configured, on both sides, to use the specified preshared key. However, this simple method is also appropriate for non-Windows 2000 computers, and works well in cases where only authentication protection is required.

Primary Domain Controller (PDC) An NT security management for its local domain. The PDC is periodically synchronized to its copy, the Backup Domain Controller (BDC). Only one PDC can exist in a domain. In an NT 4.0 single domain model, any user having a valid domain user account and password in the user accounts database of the PDC has the ability to log onto any computer that is a member of the domain, including MetaFrame servers.

Primary Domain Name System (DNS) Server The Primary DNS server maintains the master copy of the DNS database for the zone. This copy of the database is the only one that can be modified, and any changes made to its database are distributed to secondary servers in the zone during a zone transfer process. The server can cache resolution requests locally so a lookup query does not have to be sent across the network for a duplicate request. The primary server contains the address mappings for the Internet root DNS servers. Primary servers can also act as secondary servers for other zones, as described below.

Primary Partitions Primary partitions are typically used to create bootable drives. Each primary partition represents one drive letter, up to a maximum of four on a single hard disk. One primary partition must be marked as active in order to boot the system, and most operating systems must be loaded on a primary partition to work.

Print Device The hardware that actually does the printing. A print device is one of two types as defined in Windows 2000: local or network-interface. A local print device connects directly to the print server with a serial or parallel interface. A network-interface print device connects to the printer across the network and must have its own network interface or be connected to an external network adapter.

Print Driver A software program used by Windows 2000 and other computer programs to connect with printers and plotters. It translates information sent to it into commands that the print device can understand.

Print Server A print server is a computer that manages printing on the network. A print server can be a dedicated computer hosting multiple printers, or it can run as one of many processes on a nondedicated computer.

Printer permissions Printer permissions are established through the Security tab in the printer's Properties dialog. The security settings for printer objects are similar to the security settings for folder shares.

Private key A digital code used to decrypt data, which is kept secret and works in conjunction with a published public key.

Protocol stack A protocol stack consists of two or more protocols working together to accomplish a purpose (communication with another computer across a network). Transmission Control Protocol (TCP) and Internet Protocol (IP) make up the stack, which handles the most important tasks of communication such as handling addressing and routing issues, error checking, and flow control.

Protocol suite A protocol suite is a more elaborate collection of communication protocols, utilities, tools, and applications. The suite includes a large number of additional protocols, used in various situations and for different purposes. Different vendors may include different tools and utilities in their implementations of the Transmission Control Protocol/Internet Protocol (TCP/IP) suite.

Protocols Protocols are sets of rules that computers use to communicate with one another. Protocols usually work together in stacks, so called because in a layered networking model, they operate at different layers or levels. These protocols govern the logic, formatting, and timing of information exchange between layers.

Proxy autodiscovery Proxy autodiscovery is used only by clients that have Internet Explorer 5.0. This option informs the client of the location of the Internet Explorer 5.0 automatic configuration file.

PSTN *See* Public Switched Telephone Network.

PTR *See* Pointer record.

Public key A digital code used to encrypt or decrypt data, which is published and made available to the public, used in conjunction with a secret private key.

Public Key Certificate A Public Key Certificate is a security token that is passed between a certificate server and a client that causes data exchanged between the two to be encrypted. Public encryption keys include the public key certificates are responsible for encoding the data. Certificates can be either single use (e.g. secure e-mail (S/MIME) only) or multi-use (e.g. secure e-mail (S/MIME), Encrypting File System, and client authentication). So, we can easily see the certificates can be applied in various scenarios.

Public Key Infrastructure (PKI) A key and certificate management system that is trusted.

Public Switched Telephone Network (PSTN) Also known as POTS (Plain Old Telephone Service), this is the analog telephone system originally designed to transfer human voice. The dial-up equipment consists of an analog modem at the client and at the server. The maximum bit rate is low.

Publishing resources Resources, such as folders and printers, which are available to be shared on the network, can be published to the Active Directory. The resources are published to the directory and can be located by users, who can query the directory based on the resource's properties (for example, to locate all color printers).

Push replication Push replication causes the push partner to send changes based on the number of changes made in the Windows Internet Name Server (WINS) database. After the minimum number of changes have been made, the push partner sends a pull notification to the WINS server to request the changes. Windows 2000 WINS Servers are able to maintain persistent connections, which allow push partners to push changes as soon as they take place.

PXE *See* Preboot eXecution Environment.

QoS *See* Quality of Service.

Quality of Service (QoS) Admission Control Admission control allows you to control how applications are allotted network bandwidth. You can give important applications more bandwidth, less important applications less bandwidth.

RADIUS *See* Remote Access Dial-In User Service.

RAID *See* Redundant Array of Inexpensive Disks.

RARP *See* Reverse Address Resolution Protocol.

RAS *See* Remote Access Service.

RDP *See* Remote Desktop Protocol.

Realm-based tunneling Realm-based tunneling is where the access concentrator makes decisions on the tunnel's final destination (Virtual Private Network—VPN—server) based on additional group information about the user (referred to as the realm).

Rebinding Time Value The Rebinding Time Value represents 87.5 percent of the lease period. If the lease period is eight days, then the rebinding interval is 168 hours. The client will attempt to rebind its IP address at this time only if it was not able to renew its lease at the Renewal Time (T1). The client broadcasts a DHCPREQUEST message. If the server that granted the Internet Protocol (IP) address does not respond, the client will enter the Rebinding State and begin the DHCPDISCOVER process, attempting to renew its IP address with any Dynamic Host Control Protocol (DHCP) server. If it cannot renew its IP address, it will try to receive a new one from any responding DHCP server. If unsuccessful, TCP/IP services are shut down on that computer.

Recovery agent The recovery agent restores the encrypted file on a secure computer with its private recovery keys. The agent decrypts it using the cipher command line and then returns the plain text file to the user. The recovery agent goes to the computer with the encrypted file, loads the recovery certificate and private key, and performs the recovery.

Recovery Console The Recovery Console is a new command-line interpreter program feature in Windows 2000 that helps in system maintenance activities and resolving system problems. This program is separate from the Windows 2000 command prompt.

Recursive query The Domain Name System (DNS) client most often will send a recursive query. When a recursive query is sent to the client's Preferred DNS server, the server must respond to the query either positively or negatively. A positive response returns the Internet Protocol (IP) address; a negative response returns a "host not found" or similar error. A recursive query is one that requires a definitive response, either affirmative or negative.

Redundant Array of Inexpensive Disks (RAID) Although mirroring and duplexing are forms of RAID, most people think of RAID as involving more than two drives. The most common form of RAID is RAID-5, which is the striping of data across three or more drives, providing fault tolerance if one drive fails. For the best disk performance, consider using a SCSI RAID (Redundant Array of Independent Disks) controller. RAID controllers automatically place data on multiple disk drives and can increase disk performance. Using the software implementation of RAID provided by

NT would increase performance if designed properly, but the best performance is always realized through hardware RAID controllers.

Redundant Array of Inexpensive Disks 5 (RAID-5) Volume A RAID-5 volume on a dynamic drive provides disk striping with parity, and is similar to a basic stripe set with parity. This disk configuration provides both increased storage capacity and fault tolerance. Data in a dynamic RAID-5 volume are interleaved across three or more disks (up to 32 disks), and parity information is included to rebuild lost data in the event of an individual disk failure. Like a spanned or striped volume, a RAID-5 volume cannot be mirrored.

Referral response The Referral response contains the Internet Protocol (IP) address of another Domain Name System (DNS) server that may be able to service the query. The Referral is based on information contained in delegations (NS records) on the DNS server being queried.

Registry The Registry is the hierarchical database that stores operating system and application configuration information. It was introduced in Windows 9*x* and NT and replaced much of the functionality of the old initialization, system, and command files used in the early versions of Windows (.ini, .sys, and .com extensions). The registry is also a Microsoft Windows program allowing the user to choose options for configuration and applications to set them; it replaces confusing text-based .Ini files.

Remote The word "remote" can take on a number of different meanings depending on the context. In the case of an individual computer, the computer you are sitting in front of is sometimes referred to as being "local" while any other computer is considered "remote." In this context, any machine but your own is considered a remote computer. In discussions related to network configuration and design, "remote" may refer to segments and machines that are on the far side of a router. In this context, all machines on your physical segment are considered "local" and machines located on other physical segments are referred to as remote.

Remote access Remote access is when a workstation connects to a remote network so that remote resources can be transparently accessed. All applications are still run on the workstation—the only processing done on the remote access server involves the connection process (e.g., routing, authentication, encryption) rather than running any applications for the remote client.

Remote Access Dial-In User Service (RADIUS) RADIUS is an industry-standard protocol providing what's often referred to as the three "A"s—Authentication, Authorization, and Accounting services for distributed dial-up networking. RADIUS is actually a client/server protocol. In the context of Windows 2000 Routing and Remote Access, the RAS server is actually the RADIUS client because although it physically accepts the incoming connections, it passes all connection requests and information about the connections to the RADIUS server. That RADIUS server is usually devoted to running a large user account database against which it can identify remote users.

Remote Access Policy Remote access policies allow you to create demand-dial connections to use specific authentication and encryption methods. In Windows NT versions 3.5*x* and Windows NT 4.0, authorization was much simpler. The administrator simply granted dial-in permission to the user. The callback options were configured on a per-user basis.

Remote Access Service (RAS) Remote Access Service is a built-in feature of the Microsoft NT operating system. It allows users to establish a connection to an NT network over a standard phone line. Remote Access allows users to access files on a network or transfer files from a remote PC, over a Dial-Up Networking connection. The performance of transferring files over a dial-up connection is very similar to the performance you would get if you were downloading a file from the Internet.

Remote control Remote control is when a workstation shares (controls) a remote machine's resources (screen, keyboard, mouse, processor) over a remote link. This means that the remote machine can run applications for the client workstation because the CPU is shared. In this case, the workstation effectively becomes a dumb terminal, because it is not running applications itself but using the CPU on the remote machine.

Remote Desktop Protocol (RDP) Remote Desktop Protocol (RDP) is the application protocol between the client and the server. It informs the server of the keystrokes and mouse movements of the client and returns to the client the Windows

2000 graphical display from the server. RDP is a multi-channel, standard protocol that provides various levels of compression so that it can adapt to different connection speeds and encryption levels from 40 to 128 bit. Transmission Control Protocol/ Internet Protocol (TCP/IP) carries the messages, and RDP is the language in which the messages are written. Both are needed to use Microsoft's implementation of Terminal Services.

Remote Installation Preparation (RIPrep) RIPrep is a disk duplication tool included with Windows 2000 Server. It is an ideal tool for creating images of fully prepared client computers. These images are the customized images made from the base operating system, local installation of applications such as Microsoft Office, and customized configurations.

Remote Installation Preparation (RIPrep) Wizard The RIPrep wizard enables the network administrator to distribute to a large number of client computers a standard desktop configuration that includes the operating system and the applications. This not only helps in maintaining a uniform standard across the enterprise; it also cuts the costs and time involved in a large-scale rollout of Windows 2000 Professional.

Remote Installation Service (RIS) The RIS, part of Windows 2000 Server, allows client computers to install Windows 2000 Professional from a Windows 2000 Server with the service installed. The Remote Installation Service (RIS) facilitates installation of Windows 2000 Professional remotely on a large number of computers with similar or dissimilar hardware configurations. This not only reduces the installation time but also helps keep deployment costs low. Also, the Windows 2000 Remote Installation Service allows you a way to create an image of Windows 2000 Professional you can use to install Windows 2000 Professional on your network client systems. This image actually consists of the installation files from the Windows 2000 Professional CD-ROM.

Remote local printer A remote local printer is a print device that is connected directly to a print server but accessed by another print server or by workstations. The queue for the print device exists on the server, and the print server controls job priority, print order, and queue administration. Client computers submit print jobs to the server and can observe the queue to monitor the printing process on the server. Drivers for the print device are loaded onto the client computer from the print server.

Remote network printer A remote network printer is a network printer connected to a print server that is accessed by client workstations or other print servers. Like the remote local printer, the printer queue is controlled by the print server, meaning that the client computers submit their print jobs to the print server, rather than to the print device directly. This allows for server administration and monitoring of the printer queues. Drivers for the print device are loaded onto the client computers from the print server.

Renewal Time Value The Renewal Time Value represents 50 percent of the lease period. If the lease period were eight days, then the Renewal Time Value (T1) would be four days. At T1, the DHCP client will attempt to renew its IP address by broadcasting a DHCPREQUEST message containing its current Internet Protocol (IP) address. If the Dynamic Host Control Protocol (DHCP) server that granted the IP address is available, it will renew the IP address for the period specified in the renewed lease. If the DHCP server is not available, the client will continue to use its lease, since it still has 50 percent of the lease period remaining.

Replay attack This is when somebody captures the packets of a successful connection attempt and then later replays the same packets in an attempt to obtain an authenticated connection.

Request After the client receives the DHCPOFFER message and accepts the Internet Protocol (IP) address, it sends a DHCPREQUEST message out to all Dynamic Host Control Protocol (DHCP) servers indicating that it has accepted an offer. The message contains the IP address of the DHCP server that made the accepted offer, and all other DHCP servers release the addresses they had offered back into their available address pool.

Reserved client A reserved client is a Dynamic Host Control Protocol (DHCP) client that you configure to always receive the same Internet Protocol (IP) address. Creating reserved clients allows you to assign functionally static IP addresses to computers that require these, such as Windows Internet Name Service (WINS) and DNS servers. DHCP servers also require a static IP address. However, the DHCP server itself cannot be a DHCP client, so creating a client reservation for them would be a waste of IP addresses.

Resolver software Resolver software on the Domain Name System (DNS) client formulates and issues query statements sent to the DNS server. Resolver software can be included in the WinSock application, or in the case of Windows 2000, be a component of the operating system. The Windows 2000 operating system has a system-wide caching resolver. Examples of WinSock programs that make use of resolver software include: Web browsers (such as Microsoft Internet Explorer), File Transfer Protocol (FTP) clients (such as the command-line FTP program found in Windows 2000), Telnet clients, and DNS servers.

Resource record The resource record contains data about the resources contained in the domain. The resource record that you will use most is the A, or Host Address, record. This record contains the host name to Internet Protocol (IP) address mappings that most Domain Name System (DNS) clients will ask for when seeking to resolve a host name to an IP address.

Retry Interval The Retry Interval defines the period of time the Secondary should wait until sending another pull request message. The Secondary will continue to retry the zone transfer until it is successful in contacting the Primary for its zone.

Reverse Address Resolution Protocol (RARP) RARP does the same thing as the Address Resolution Protocol (ARP) in reverse; that is, it takes a physical address and resolves it to an IP address. The **arp –a** command can be used to view the current entries in the ARP cache.

Reverse lookup The process of resolving a known Internet Protocol (IP) address to a host name is called a reverse lookup, in contrast to the forward lookup where a host name is resolved to an IP address. Reverse lookups query reverse lookup zones.

Reverse Lookup Query A reverse lookup query resolves an Internet Protocol (IP) address to a Domain Name System (DNS) name, and can be used for a variety of reasons. The process is different, though, because it makes use of a special domain called in-addr.arpa. This domain is also hierarchical, but is based on IP addresses and not names. The sub-domains are organized by the *reverse* order of the IP address. For instance, the domain 16.254.169.in-addr.arpa contains the addresses in the 169.254.16.* range; the 120.129.in-addr.arpa domain contains the addresses for the 129.120.*.* range.

Reverse lookup zones While forward lookup zones allow Domain Name System (DNS) clients to resolve a host name to an IP address, a reverse lookup zone allows the DNS client to do the opposite: resolve an IP address to a host name. Reverse lookup zones are especially helpful if your organization is using inventory or security software that depends on reverse lookups to identify the host names of the Internet Protocol (IP) addresses they discover.

RIPrep *See* Remote Installation Preparation.

Rogue DHCP server A rogue Dynamic Host Control Protocol (DHCP) server (a DHCP server that has not been approved by the IT department) is likely to contain invalid scopes and DHCP options. Rogue DHCP servers can assign inaccurate IP addressing information to DHCP clients, which may disrupt network communications for these hapless clients.

Rollback Strategy As with any upgrade, problems can sometimes require going back to the previous state. This possibility also applies to upgrading your domain to Windows 2000. You need to create a plan to roll back your network to its previous state if the upgrade to Windows 2000 fails. When upgrading the domain controllers, do not upgrade the Backup Domain Controller (BDC) that has the current directory database. Make sure the BDC is synchronized with the Primary Domain Controller (PDC), and then take it offline. Leave the BDC as is until the upgrade is successful. If you run into problems during the upgrade, you can bring the BDC back online, promote it to the PDC, and recover the Windows NT state. Once the upgrade is successful, you can upgrade the BDC to Windows 2000.

ROUTE command-line utility ROUTE is used to display or make modifications to the local routing table.

Router When the word "router" is used, typically people think of a physical box which is dedicated to just routing – Cisco, Bay Networks, Digital and Cabletron

Systems for example are just a few of the best known vendors offering this kind of technology.

Router routing Router routing occurs when a router receives a packet that is not destined for another computer so it must send the packet to either the destination computer (if directly attached) or another router.

Routing and Remote Access Service (RRAS) Within Windows NT, PRAS is a software routing and remote access service with the capability of combining packet filtering, Open Shortest Path First (OSPF) support, etc.

Routing Tables Each router uses a list of known routes (either static routes or dynamic routes or a mixture of the two) which it amalgamates into one or more routing tables. When it receives a packet to forward, it consults its routing table to see which interface should be used to forward the packet. There may be more than one possible route, in which case the various paths will also be evaluated to see which one should be used.

RRAS *See* Routing and Remote Access.

Safe Mode Safe Mode starts Windows 2000 using only some basic files and device drivers. These devices include monitor, keyboard, mouse, basic VGA video, CD-ROM, and mass storage devices. The system starts only those system services that are necessary to load the operating system. Networking is not started in this mode. The Windows background screen is black in this mode, and the screen resolution is 640 by 480 pixels with 16 colors.

Safe Mode with Command Prompt This option starts the operating system in a safe mode using some basic files only. The Windows 2000 command prompt is shown instead of the usual Windows desktop.

Safe Mode with Networking This mode is similar to the Safe Mode, but networking devices, drivers, and protocols are loaded. You may choose this mode when you are sure that the problem in the system is not due to any networking component.

SA *See* Security Association.

SAM *See* Security Accounts Manager.

Scavenging Scavenging is the process of removing stale entries from the zone. The default setting is not to allow scavenging from the Domain Name System (DNS) database. Scavenging can be set on a per-server or per-zone basis.

Scope A scope is a collection or pool of Internet Protocol (IP) addresses. A single scope includes all the IP addresses that you wish to make available to Dynamic Host Control Protocol (DHCP) clients on a single subnet. Only one scope can be created for each subnet. A single DHCP server can manage several scopes.

Scope options Scope options allow you to specify Dynamic Host Control Protocol (DHCP) options that apply to a single scope. A good example of when you want to set scope options is when you automatically want to configure the Internet Protocol (IP) address of the default gateway for the DHCP clients. Each subnet must have a different default gateway, since the default gateway must be local to each subnet. It wouldn't make much sense to assign the same default gateway to all the scopes. Therefore, you configure a scope option for the default gateway for each scope that has a different default gateway.

Scripted method This method for Windows 2000 Professional installation uses an answer file to specify various configuration parameters. This is used to eliminate user interaction during installation, thereby automating the installation process. Answers to most of the questions asked by the setup process are specified in the answer file. Besides this, the scripted method can be used for clean installations and upgrades.

SCSI *See* Small Computer System Interface.

Secondary Domain Name System (DNS) Server Secondary DNS servers provide fault tolerance and load balancing for DNS zones. Secondary servers contain a read-only copy of the zone database that it receives from the primary server during a zone transfer. A secondary server will respond to a DNS request if the primary server fails to respond because of an error or a heavy load. Since secondary servers can resolve DNS queries, they are also considered authoritative within a domain, and can help with load balancing on the network. Secondary servers can be placed in remote locations on the network and configured to respond to DNS queries from local computers, potentially reducing query traffic across longer network distances. While there can be only one primary server in a zone, multiple secondary servers can be set up for redundancy and load balancing.

Secondary server The server receiving the zone files can be called either a Slave server or a Secondary server. It is preferred to refer to the machine receiving the zone file as a secondary, because the term Slave DNS server has another meaning that refers to an inability to perform recursion for DNS clients.

Second-level domain name The second-level domain name distinguishes your organization from all others on the Internet. Examples of second-level domains are microsoft.com, osborne.com, and syngress.com.

Secret key Also called a shared secret, a digital code shared between two parties and used for both encrypting and decrypting data.

Secure callback This is when the remote access server calls back the remote client after a successful authentication, and is used particularly when the connection charge should be the responsibility of the server rather than the client. Either the client can specify the number that should be called back (greatest flexibility so they can dial in from anywhere), or this feature can be restricted for security to only call back on a specific number (secure callback).

Security Accounts Manager (SAM) The Security Accounts Manager (SAM) is the portion of the Windows NT Server registry that stores user account information and group membership. Attributes that are specific to Terminal Server can be added to user accounts. This adds a small amount of information to each user's entry in the domain's SAM.

Security Association (SA) Security Associations (SAs) define Internet Protocol Security (IPSec) secured links. One of the tasks of IPSec is to establish a Security Association between the two computers desiring to communicate with one another securely. This could include: communications between remote nodes and the network; communications between two networks; and communications between two computers on a Local Area Network (LAN).

Security Groups The Windows 2000 Security Groups allow you to assign the same security permissions to large numbers of users in one operation. This ensures consistent security permissions across all members of a group. Using Security Groups to assign permissions means the access control on resources remains fairly static and easy to control and audit. Users who need access are added or removed from the appropriate security groups as needed, and the access control lists change infrequently.

Security Negotiation Security negotiation ensures that the authentication and encryption methods used by the sending and receiving computers are the same. If they are not, reliable communication cannot take place. To provide for compatibility between the security systems being used, there must be protocols in place to negotiate the security methods. Internet Protocol Security (IPSec) uses ISAKMP and IKE to define the way in which security associations are negotiated.

Security Parameters Index A Security Parameters Index (SPI) tracks each Security Association (SA). The SPI uniquely identifies each SA as separate and distinct from any other Internet Protocol Security (IPSec) connections current on a particular machine. The index itself is derived from the destination host's IP address and a randomly assigned number. When a computer communicates with another computer via IPSec, it checks its database for an applicable SA. It then applies the appropriate algorithms, protocols, and keys, and inserts the SPI into the IPSec header.

Security Templates Windows 2000 comes with several predefined Security Templates. These templates address several security scenarios. Security Templates come in two basic categories: Default and Incremental. The Default or Basic templates are applied by the operating system when a clean install has been performed. They are not applied if an upgrade installation has been done. The incremental templates should be applied after the Basic Security Templates have been applied. There are four types of incremental templates: Compatible, Secure, High Secure, and Dedicated Domain Controller.

Segment In discussions of Transmission Control Protocol/Internet Protocol (TCP/IP), segment often refers to the group of computers located on one side of a router, or sometimes a group of computers within the same collision domain. In TCP/IP terminology, "segment" can also be used to describe the chunk of data sent by TCP over the network (roughly equivalent to the usage of "packet" or "frame"). In discussions of the physical networking infrastructure, "segment" usually refers to a length of cable, or the portion of the network connected to a length of backbone between repeaters.

Sequenced Packet eXchange (SPX) The communications protocol (from NetWare) used to control network message transport.

Serial Line Interface Protocol (SLIP) The SLIP is an older Wide Area Network (WAN) link protocol that does not support encryption or compression, and requires a manually configured static Internet Protocol (IP) address. It can be used only on the Windows 2000 RAS client, and is used now primarily to connect to remote servers running the UNIX operating system.

Server The word "server" can take on a variety of different meanings. A server can be a physical computer. Such as "Check out that Server over in the Accounting Department". A server can also represent a particular software package. For example, Microsoft Exchange 2000 is a mail and groupware Server application. Often server applications are just referred to as "servers," as in "Check out what the problem is with the mail server." The term "server" is also used to refer to any computer that is currently sharing its resources on the network. In this context, all computers, whether Windows 3*x* or Windows 2000, can be servers on a network.

Server impersonation This is when a bogus server appears to be a valid server so that it can capture credentials of a remote user trying to connect so it can use these to connect to the valid server.

Server options Server options apply to all scopes configured on a single DHCP server. Server options were known as global options on the Windows NT 4.0 DHCP Server.

Service Identifiers A computer running the TCP/IP NetBIOS interface actually has several NetBIOS names. Each name is used by a service to "advertise" that the service is running on that particular computer. It's like putting a sign on the door saying "these people live here." For example, if a Windows 2000 machine is running both the Server service and the Workstation (Microsoft Redirector) service, it will register two NetBIOS names, one for each of the services running. This is a way for the NetBIOS applications to let other machines know that they are running and available.

Service pack A service pack typically contains bug fixes, security fixes, systems administration tools, drivers, and additional components. Microsoft recommends installing the latest service packs as they are released. In addition, as a new feature in Windows 2000, you do not have to reinstall components after installing a service pack, as you did with Windows NT. You can also see what service pack is currently installed on a computer by running the WINVER utility program. WINVER brings up the About Windows dialog box. It displays the version of Windows and the version of the service pack you are running.

Service record (SRV) The SRV record provides information about available services on a particular host. This is similar to the "service identifier" (the hidden 16th character) in NetBIOS environments. If a particular host is looking for a server to authenticate against, it will check for an SRV record to find an authenticating host. SRV records are particularly important in Windows 2000 domains. Since the DNS server is now the primary domain locator for Windows 2000 clients, the appropriate SRV records must be contained on the DNS server to inform Windows 2000 clients of the location of a Windows 2000 domain controller that can authenticate a logon request.

Setup Manager The Setup Manager is the best tool to use when you have no idea of the answer file syntax or when you do not want to get into the time-consuming task of creating or modifying the sample answer file. When you choose to use the Setup Manager for unattended installations, you need to do a lot of planning beforehand. It is understood that you will not be using Setup Manager for automating installations on one or two computers; that would be a waste of effort. Setup Manager is useful for mass deployments only.

SETUPACT.LOG The Action log file contains details about the files that are copied during setup.

SETUPAPI.LOG This log file contains details about the device driver files that were copied during setup. This log can be used to facilitate troubleshooting device installations. The file contains errors and warnings along with a time stamp for each issue.

SETUPCL.EXE The function of the SETUPCL.EXE file is to run the Mini-Setup wizard and to regenerate the security IDs on the master and destination computers. The Mini-Setup wizard starts on the master computer when it is booted for the first time after running SysPrep.

SETUPERR.LOG The Error log file contains details about errors that occurred during setup.

SETUPLOG.TXT This log file contains additional information about the device driver files that were copied during setup.

Shared Folders Sharing folders so that other users can access their contents across the network is easy in Windows 2000, as easy as right-clicking on the folder name in Windows Explorer, selecting the Sharing tab, and choosing Share This Folder. An entire drive and all the folders on that drive can be shared in the same way.

Shared Folders Permissions As only folders, not files, can be shared, shared folder permissions are a small subset of standard NT File System (NTFS) permissions for a folder. However, securing access to a folder through share permissions can be more restrictive or more liberal than standard NTFS folder permissions. Shared folder permissions are applied in the same manner as NTFS permissions.

Shared Printers The process for sharing a printer attached to your local computer is similar to that for sharing a folder or drive. If the users who will access your printer will do so from machines that don't run the Windows 2000 operating system, you will need to install drivers for the other operating system(s).

Shared resource A shared resource is a device, data, or program that is made available to network users. This can include folders, files, printers, and even Internet connections.

Shiva Password Authentication Protocol (SPAP) The Shiva Password Authentication Protocol is a reversible encryption mechanism used by Shiva remote access servers. Although a remote access client might use SPAP to authenticate on a Windows 2000 Routing and Remote Access server, this protocol is more likely to be used by clients who need to connect to a Shiva remote access client. This protocol is more secure than Password Authentication Protocol (PAP), but less secure than the other protocols, and offers no protection against server impersonation. It is unlikely you would need it on a server running Windows 2000 Routing and Remote Access Service.

Silent Routing Information Protocol for Internet Protocol (Silent RIP for IP) Silent RIP for IP is when an IP router (using the RIP routing protocol) dynamically updates its own routing table with information obtained from other RIP routers without sending out its own routing information. In this case, the routing "exchange" between the Silent RIP router and other routers is not complete because the information is one-way only. You can use Silent RIP on a workstation too, but this requires modifying the registry. On a Windows 2000 RRAS router, it is configured as one of the RIP interface properties.

Simple Mail Transfer Protocol (SMTP) The Simple Mail Transfer Protocol is used for sending e-mail on the Internet. SMTP is a simple ASCII protocol and is non-vendor specific.

Simple Network Management Protocol (SNMP) The Simple Network Management Protocol provides a way to gather statistical information. An SNMP management system makes requests of an SNMP agent, and the information is stored in a Management Information Base (MIB).

Simple volume A simple volume is a volume created on a dynamic disk that is not fault tolerant, and includes space from only one physical disk. A simple volume is just that—it is a single volume that does not span more than one physical disk, and does not provide improved drive performance, extra capacity, or fault tolerance.

One physical disk can contain a single, large simple volume, or several smaller ones. Each simple volume is assigned a separate drive letter. The number of simple volumes on a disk is limited only by the capacity of the disk and the number of available letters in the alphabet.

Single-Instance-Store (SIS) Volume When you have more than one image on the Remote Installation Service (RIS) server, each holding Windows 2000 Professional files, there will be duplicate copies of hundreds of files. This may consume a significant hard drive space on the RIS server. To overcome this problem, Microsoft introduced a new feature called the Single-Instance-Store, which helps in deleting all the duplicate files, thus saving on hard drive space.

SIS *See* Single-Instance-Store.

Site Server Internet Locator Server (ILS) Service This service supports Internet Protocol (IP) telephony applications. It publishes IP multicast conferences on a network, and can also publish user IP address mappings for H.323 IP telephony. Telephony applications, such as NetMeeting and Phone Dialer in Windows Accessories, use Site Server ILS Service to display user names and conferences with published addresses. Site Server ILS Service depends on Internet Information Services (IIS).

Slave server Slave servers are a special type of forwarder, which is configured not to attempt to resolve the host name on its own. The server receiving the zone files can be called either a Slave server or a Secondary server. It is preferred to refer to the machine receiving the zone file as a secondary, because the term Slave Domain Name System (DNS) server has another meaning that refers to an inability to perform recursion for DNS clients.

Slave server/caching-only forwarder The slave server/caching-only forwarder combination is very helpful in protecting your intranet zone data from Internet intruders. We can use this combination to prevent users on the other side of a firewall from having access to information on our Internal Domain Name System (DNS) server.

SLIP *See* Serial Line Interface Protocol.

Small Computer System Interface (SCSI) A complete expansion bus interface that accepts such devices as a hard disk, CD-ROM, disk drivers, printers, or scanners.

Small Office/Home Office (SOHO) A SOHO network typically has the following characteristics: a single segment network; peer-to-peer networking; a single protocol (e.g., TCP/IP); and a demand-dial or dedicated link connection to the Internet via an Internet Service Provider (ISP). A user on a SOHO network frequently needs to use more than one computer, and also needs to be able to share resources from one computer to another, such as files, applications, and printers.

SMP *See* Symmetric Multiprocessing.

SMS *See* Systems Management Server.

SMTP *See* Simple Mail Transfer Protocol.

SNA *See* Systems Network Architecture.

SNMP *See* Simple Network Management Protocol.

SOA *See* Start of Authority.

SOHO *See* Small Office/Home Office.

Spanned volume A spanned volume is similar to a volume set in NT 4.0. It contains space from multiple disks (up to 32), and provides a way to combine small "chunks" of disk space into one unit, seen by the operating system as a single volume. It is not fault tolerant. When a dynamic volume includes the space on more than one physical hard drive, it is called a spanned volume. Spanned volumes can be used to increase drive capacity, or to make use of the leftover space on up to 32 existing disks. Like those in a basic storage volume set, the portions of a spanned volume are all linked together and share a single drive letter.

SPAP *See* Shiva Password Authentication Protocol.

SPI *See* Security Parameters Index.

SPX *See* Sequenced Packet eXchange.

SQL *See* Structured Query Language.

SRV *See* Service record.

Stack A data structure in which the first items inserted are the last ones removed, unlike control structure programs that use the Last In First Out (LIFO) structure.

Start of Authority (SOA) The SOA identifies which Domain Name System (DNS) server is authoritative for the data within a domain. The first record in any zone file is the SOA.

Static Internet Protocol (IP) address A static IP address allows users to use a domain name that can be translated into an IP address. The static IP address allows the server to always have the same IP address, so the domain name always translates to the correct IP address. If the address was assigned dynamically and occasionally changed, users might not be able to access the server across the Internet using the domain name.

Stripe Set The term "striping" refers to the interleaving of data across separate physical disks. Each file is broken into small blocks, and each block is evenly and alternately saved to the disks in the stripe set. In a two-disk stripe set, the first block of data is saved to the first disk, the second block is saved to the second disk, and the third block is saved to the first disk, and so on. The two disks are treated as a single drive, and are given a single drive letter.

Stripe Set with Parity A stripe set with parity requires at least three hard disks, and provides both increased storage capacity and fault tolerance. In a stripe set with parity, data is interleaved across three or more disks, and includes parity (error checking) information about the data. As long as only one disk in the set fails, the parity information can be used to reconstruct the lost data. If the parity information itself is lost, it can be reconstructed from the original data.

Striped volume Like a stripe set in NT 4.0, a striped volume is the dynamic storage equivalent of a basic stripe set and combines free space from up to 32 physical disks into one volume by writing data across the disks in stripes. This increases performance but does not provide fault tolerance. A striped volume improves drive performance and increases drive capacity. Because each data block is written only once, striped volumes do not provide fault tolerance.

Striping Striping is when the data are striped across the drives and there is parity information along with the data. The parity information is based on a mathematical formula that comes up with the parity based on the data on the other drives.

Structured Query Language (SQL) SQL is a concise IBM query language (only 30 commands) structured like English, which is widely used in database management applications for mainframes and minicomputers.

Stub Areas You can import external routes into an Open Shortest Path First (OSPF) AS with an AS Border Router, but to stop external routes from flooding into an area you can use what is called a Stub Area. A stub area applies the default route 0.0.0.0 to keep the topology database size small. In OSPF, you can assume that any destination that you can't reach through a designated route is reachable through the default route. To implement a stub area, one or more of the stub area's Area Border Routers must advertise the default route 0.0.0.0 to the stub area, and the route summary.

Subnetting Using several data paths to reduce traffic on a network and avoid problems if a single path should fail is called subnetting. It is usually configured as a dedicated Ethernet subnetwork between two systems based on two Network Interface Cards (NICs).

Supernetting Supernetting is a way of combining several small networks into a larger one. For example, a company may need a Class B network, but because those have all been assigned, it can't get one. However, Class C networks *are* available, so the company can be assigned multiple Class C networks with contiguous addresses.

By "stealing" bits again, but in the opposite direction (sort of like taking from the poor and giving to the rich instead of vice versa), you can use some of the bits that originally represented the network ID to represent host IDs, reducing the number of networks but increasing the number of hosts available per network.

Superscope A superscope is a Windows 2000 Dynamic Host Control Protocol (DHCP) feature that lets you use more than one scope for a subnet. The superscope contains multiple "child" scopes, grouped together under one name and manageable as one entity. The situations in which superscopes should be used include: when many DHCP clients are added to a network, so that it has more than were originally planned for; when the Internet Protocol (IP) addresses on a network must be renumbered; and when two (or more) DHCP servers are on the same subnet for fault tolerance purposes.

Symmetric algorithm A cryptographic algorithm that uses the same key to both encrypt and decrypt, also called a secret key algorithm.

Symmetric Multiprocessing (SMP) SMP is a system in which all processors are treated as equals, and any thread can be run on any available processor. Windows 2000 also supports processor affinity, in which a process or thread can specify which set of processors it should run on. Application Programming Interfaces (APIs) must be defined in the application.

Synthesis The process of design, formulation, integration, prediction, proposal, generalization, and show relationships.

SYSPREP.INF SYSPREP.INF is an answer file. When you want to automate the Mini-Setup wizard by providing predetermined answers to all setup questions, you must use this file. This file needs to be placed in the %Systemroot%\Sysprep folder or on a floppy disk. When the Mini-Setup wizard is run on the computer on which the image is being distributed, it takes answers from the SYSPREP.INF file without prompting the user for any input.

System Preparation (Sysprep) SysPrep provides an excellent means of saving installation time and reducing installation costs. Sysprep is the best tool to copy the image of a computer to other computers that have identical hardware configurations. It is also helpful in standardizing the desktop environment throughout the organization. Since one Sysprep image cannot be used on computers with identical hardware and software applications, you can create multiple images when you have more than one standard. It is still the best option where the number of computers is in hundreds or thousands and you wish to implement uniform policies in the organization.

System Monitor The System Monitor is part of the Administrative Tools utility, and allows you to collect and view data about current memory usage, disk, processor utilization, network activity and other system activity. The System Monitor replaces the Performance Monitor used in Windows NT. System Monitor allows you to collect information about your hardware's performance as well as network utilization. System Monitor can be used to measure different aspects of a computer's performance. It can be used on your own computer or other computers on the network.

System policy Group policies have mostly replace system policies since group policies extend the functionality of system policies. A few situations still exist in which system policies are valuable. The system policy editor is used to provide user and computer configuration settings in the Windows NT registry database. The system policy editor is still used for the management of Windows 9*x* and Windows NT server and workstations and stand-alone computers using Windows 2000.

Systems Management Server (SMS) This Windows NT software analyzes and monitors network usage and various network functions.

Systems Network Architecture (SNA) Systems Network Architecture (SNA) was developed by IBM in the mainframe computer era (1974, to be precise) as a way of getting its various products to communicate with each other for distributed processing. SNA is a line of products designed to make other products cooperate. In your career of designing network solutions, you should expect to run into SNA from time to time because many of the bigger companies (i.e., banks, healthcare institutions, government offices) bought IBM equipment and will be reluctant to part with their investment. SNA is a proprietary protocol that runs over SDLC exclusively, although it may be transported within other protocols, such as

X.25 and Token Ring. It is designed as a hierarchy and consists of a collection of machines called nodes.

Take Ownership Permission This permission can be given to allow a user to take ownership of a file or folder object. Every file and folder on an NT File System (NTFS) drive has an owner, usually the account that created the object. However, there are times when ownership of a file needs to be changed, perhaps because of a change in team membership or a set of new responsibilities for a user.

Task-based model This model is appropriate for companies in which administrative duties are functionally divided. This means that this model divides the management of Group Policy Objects (GPOs) by certain tasks. To apply this model, the administrators that handle security-related tasks will also be responsible for managing all policy objects that affect security. The second set of administrators that normally deploy the companies' business applications will be responsible for all the GPOs that affect installation and maintenance.

TCP/IP *See* Transmission Control Protocol/Internet Protocol.

Telnet Telnet is a Transmission Control Protocol/Internet Protocol (TCP/IP-based) service that allows users to log on to, run character-mode applications on, and view files on a remote computer. Windows 2000 Server includes both Telnet server and Telnet client software.

Terminal Services In application server mode, Terminal Services provides the ability to run client applications on the server, while "thin client" software acts as a terminal emulator on the client. Each user sees an individual session, displayed as a Windows 2000 desktop. The server manages each session, independent of any other client session. If you install Terminal Services as an application server, you must also install Terminal Services Licensing (not necessarily on the same computer). However, temporary licenses can be issued for clients that allow you to use Terminal servers for up to 90 days. In remote administration mode, you can use Terminal Services to log on remotely and manage Windows 2000 systems from virtually anywhere on your network (instead of being limited to working locally on a server). Remote administration mode allows for two concurrent connections from a given server and minimizes impact on server performance. Remote administration mode does not require you to install Terminal Services Licensing.

TFTP *See* Trivial File Transfer Protocol.

TKEY The TKEY resource record is used to transfer security tokens between the DNS client and server. It allows for the establishment of the shared secret key that will be used with the TSIG resource record.

Token Ring A Local Area Network (LAN) specification that was developed by IBM in the 1980s for PC-based networks and classified by the IEEE (Institute of Electrical and Electronics Engineers) as 802.5. It specifies a star topology physically and a ring topology logically. It runs at either four Mbps or 16 Mbps, but all nodes on the ring must run at the same speed.

Tombstoning Windows 2000 allows you to manually mark a record to eventually be deleted. This is called tombstoning. The tombstone state of the record replicates to other Windows Internet Name Service (WINS) servers, and this prevents any replicated copies of the deleted records from reappearing at the same server where they were originally deleted.

Top-level domain names Top-level domain names include .com, .net, .org, and .edu. Organizations that seek to have an Internet presence will obtain a domain name that is a member of one of the top-level domain names.

Trace log The Windows 2000 DNS Server allows you to enable trace logging via the Graphical User Interface (GUI) interface if you require extremely detailed information about the Domain Name System (DNS) server's activities. The information gathered in the trace is saved to a text file on the local hard disk. A trace log can track all queries received and answered by the DNS server.

TRACERT command-line utility TRACERT is used to trace the route a packet takes to a destination.

Transmission Control Protocol/Internet Protocol (TCP/IP) A set of communications standards created by the U.S. Department of Defense (DoD) in the 1970s that has now become an accepted way to connect different types of computers in networks because the standards now support so many programs.

Transport Mode When Internet Protocol Security (IPSec) is used to protect communications between two clients (for example, two computers on the same Local Area Network or LAN), the machines can utilize IPSec in what is known as transport mode.

Trees Trees are groups of domains that share a contiguous namespace. It allows you to create a hierarchical grouping of domains that share a common contiguous namespace. This hierarchy allows global sharing of resources among domains in the tree. All the domains in a tree share information and resources with a single directory, and there is only one directory per tree. However, each domain manages its own subset of the directory that contains the user accounts for that domain. So, when a user logs into a domain, the user has global access to all resources that are part of the tree, providing the user has the proper permissions.

Trivial File Transfer Protocol (TFTP) A simplified version of the File Transfer Protocol (FTP), associated with the Transmission Control Protocol/Internet Protocol (TCP/IP) family, that does not provide password protection or a user directory.

Trust The users in one tree do not have global access to resources in other trees, but trusts can be created that allow users to access resources in another tree. A trust allows all the trees to share resources and have common administrative functions. Such sharing capability allows the trees to operate independently of each other, with separate namespaces, yet still be able to communicate and share resources through trusts.

Trust relationship A trust relationship is a connection between domains in which users who have accounts in and log on to one domain can then access resources in other domains, provided they have proper access permissions.

TSIG The TSIG resource record is used to send and verify messages that have been signed with a hash algorithm.

Tunnel Mode This communication mode is a gateway-to-gateway solution. Internet Protocol Security (IPSec) protects information that travels through a transit network (such as the Internet). Packets are protected as they leave the exit gateway, and then decrypted or authenticated at the destination network's gateway. When gateways represent the endpoints of the secure communication, IPSec is operating in tunnel mode. A tunnel is created between the gateways, and client-to-client communications are encapsulated in the tunnel protocol headers.

Two-way initiated demand-dial connections A two-way initiated demand-dial connection is where routers can both initiate a connection when needed, and also respond to the same routers calling them over the same demand-dial interface. In other words, in a two-way initiated connection, both routers can be a calling router, or an answering router on the same interface. Use two-way initiated connections when traffic from either router can create the demand-dial connection. This offers the greatest flexibility but also requires the greatest configuration since not only do both routers need to be configured, but they also have to be configured similarly to ensure their configurations match.

UDF *See* Unique Database File.

UDP *See* User Datagram Protocol.

Unattended method The unattended method for Windows 2000 Server installation uses the answer file to specify various configuration parameters. This method eliminates user interaction during installation, thereby automating the installation process and reducing the chances of input errors. Answers to most of the questions asked by the setup process are specified in the answer file. In addition, the scripted method can be used for clean installations and upgrades.

UNATTEND.TXT file The creation of customized UNATTEND.TXT answer files is the simplest form of providing answers to setup queries and unattended installation of Windows 2000. This can either be done using the Setup Manager or by editing the sample UNATTEND.TXT file using Notepad or the

MS-DOS text editor. The UNATTEND.TXT file does not provide any means of creating an image of the computer.

UNATTEND.UDF This file is the Uniqueness Database File, which provides customized settings for each computer using the automated installation.

UNC *See* Universal Naming Convention.

UNICODE UNICODE is a 16-bit character encoding standard developed by the Unicode Consortium between 1988 and 1991 that uses two bytes to represent each character and enables almost all of the written languages of the world to be represented using a single character set.

Uninterruptible Power Supply (UPS) A battery that can supply power to a computer system if the power fails. It charges while the computer is on and, if the power fails, provides power for a certain amount of time allowing the user to shut down the computer properly to preserve data.

Unique Database File (UDF) When you use the WINNT32.EXE command with the /unattend option, you can also specify a Unique Database File (UDF), which has a .UDB extension. This file forces Setup to use certain values from the UDF file, thus overriding the values given in the answer file. This is particularly useful when you want to specify multiple users during the setup.

Universal Groups Universal Groups are used in larger, multi-domain organizations, in which there is a need to grant access to similar groups of accounts defined in multiple domains. It is better to use Global Groups as members of Universal Groups to reduce overall replication traffic from changes to Universal Group membership. Users can be added and removed from the corresponding Global Groups with their account domains, and a small number of Global Groups are the direct members of the Universal Group. Universal Groups are used only in multiple domain trees or forests. A Windows 2000 domain must be in native-mode to use Universal Groups.

Universal Serial Bus (USB) A low-speed hardware interface (supports MPEG video) with a maximum bandwidth up to 1.5 MBytes per second.

Universal Naming Convention (UNC) A UNC is an identification standard of servers and other network resources.

UPS *See* Uninterruptible Power Supply.

USB *See* Universal Serial Bus.

User account The information that defines a particular user on a network, which includes the username, password, group memberships, and rights and permissions assigned to the user.

User classes User classes allow Dynamic Host Control Protocol (DHCP) clients to identify their class membership to a DHCP server. The server can return to the client a specific set of options relevant to the class. The process is the same as when vendor class options are requested by the client and sent by the DHCP server.

User Datagram Protocol (UDP) A Transmission Control Protocol/Internet Protocol (TCP/IP) normally bundled with an Internet Protocol (IP) layer software that describes how messages received reached application programs within the destination computer.

User Principle Name Mapping This is a special kind of one-to-one mapping only available through the Active Directory. Enterprise CAs insert an entry called a User Principle Name (UPN) into each of its certificates. UPNs are unique to each user's account within a Windows 2000 Domain, and they are of the format ***user@domain.*** The UPN is used to locate the user account in Active Directory and that account is logged on.

Value Bar The value bar is positioned below the graph area. It displays data for the selected sample, the last sample value, the average of the counter samples, the maximum and minimum of the samples, and the duration of time the samples have been taken over.

Vendor class options RFCs 2131 and 2132 define Dynamic Host Control Protocol (DHCP) vendor class options, which allow hardware and software vendors to add their own options to the DHCP server. These options are additions to the list of standard DHCP options included with the Windows 2000 DHCP Server.

Virtual Private Networking (VPN) VPNs reduce service costs and long distance/usage fees, lighten infrastructure investments, and simplify Wide Area Network (WAN) operations over time. To determine just how cost-effective a VPN solution could be in connecting remote offices, use the VPN Calculator located on Cisco's Web site at www.cisco.com.

Volume Set The term "volume" indicates a single drive letter. One physical hard disk can contain several volumes, one for each primary partition or logical drive. However, the opposite is also true. You can create a single volume that spans more than one physical disk. This is a good option when you require a volume that exceeds the capacity of a single physical disk. You can also create a volume set when you want to make use of leftover space on several disks by piecing them together as one volume.

VPN *See* Virtual Private Networking.

WDM *See* Windows32 Drive Model.

Windows 3x Windows 3 changed everything. It was a 16-bit operating system with a user interface that resembled the look and feel of IBM's (at that time not yet released) OS/2, with 3D buttons and the ability to run multiple programs simultaneously, using a method called cooperative multitasking. Windows 3 also provided virtual memory, the ability to use hard disk space to "fool" the applications into behaving as if they had more RAM than was physically installed in the machine.

Windows 9x In August of 1995, Microsoft released its long-awaited upgrade of Windows, Windows 95. For the first time, Windows could be installed on a machine that didn't already have MS-DOS installed. Many improvements were made: the new 32-bit functionality (although still retaining some 16-bit code for backward compatibility); preemptive multitasking (a more efficient way to run multiple programs in which the operating system controls use of the processor and the crash of one application does not bring down the others that are currently running); and support for filenames longer than the DOS-based eight-character limit.

Windows32 Driver Model (WDM) The Win32 Driver Model (WDM) provides a standard for device drivers that will work across Windows platforms (specifically Windows 98 and 2000), so that you can use the same drivers with the consumer and business versions of the Windows operating system.

Windows 2000 Microsoft's latest incarnation of the corporate operating system was originally called NT 5, but the name was changed to Windows 2000 between the second and third beta versions—perhaps to underscore the fact that this is truly a *new* version of the operating system, not merely an upgrade to NT.

Windows 2000 Control Panel The Control Panel in Windows 2000 functions similarly to the Control Panel in Windows 9*x* and NT, except that "under the hood" there are now two locations in which information is stored, which are modified by the Control Panel applets. The Control Panel in previous operating systems was a graphical interface for editing Registry information.

Windows Backup Windows Backup is a built-in Backup and Restore utility, which has many more features than the backup tool provided in Windows NT 4.0. It supports all five types of backup: Normal, Copy, Differential, Incremental, and Daily. Windows Backup allows you to perform the backup operation manually or you may schedule it to run at a later time in unattended mode. Included with the operating system, it is a tool that is flexible and easy to use.

Windows Internet Name Service (WINS) WINS provides name resolution for clients running Windows NT and earlier versions of Microsoft operating systems. With name resolution, users can access servers by name, instead of having to use Internet Protocol (IP) addresses that are difficult to recognize and remember. WINS is used to map NetBIOS computer names to IP addresses. This allows users to access other computers on the network by computer name. WINS servers should be assigned a static IP address, which allows clients to be able to find the WINS servers. Clients cannot find a WINS server by name because they need to know where the WINS server is in order to translate the name into an IP address.

Windows Internet Name Service (WINS) Name Registration Each WINS client has one or more WINS servers identified in the network configuration on the computer, either through static assignment or through DHCP configuration. When the client boots and connects to the network, it registers its name and IP address with the WINS server by sending a registration request directly to the server. This is not a broadcast message, since the client has the address of the server. If the server is available and the name is not already registered, the server responds with a successful registration message, which contains the amount of time the name will be registered to the client, the Time To Live (TTL). Then the server stores the name and address combination in its local database.

Windows Internet Name Service (WINS) Name Release When a WINS client shuts down properly, it will send a name release request to the WINS server. This releases the name from the WINS server's database so that another client can use the name, if necessary. The release request contains the WINS name and address of the client. If the server cannot find the name, it sends a negative release response to the client. If the server finds the matching name and address in its database, it releases the name and marks the record as inactive. If the name is found but the address does not match, the server ignores the request.

Windows Internet Name Service (WINS) Name Renewal As with Dynamic Host Control Protocol (DHCP), WINS name registrations are temporary and must be renewed to continue to be valid. The client will attempt to renew its registration when half (50 percent) of the Time To Live (TTL) has elapsed. If the WINS server does not respond, the client repeatedly attempts to renew its lease at ten-minute intervals for an hour. If the client still receives no response, it restarts the process with the secondary WINS server, if one is defined. The client will continue attempting to renew its lease in this manner until it receives a response from a server. At that time, the server sends a new TTL to the client and the process starts over.

Windows Internet Name Server (WINS) Proxy Agent The WINS Proxy Agent has a single purpose: to resolve NetBIOS names for non-WINS clients. The non-WINS clients can be UNIX servers, or even Windows computers that are configured as b-node clients. Keep in mind that the WINS Proxy Agent resolves NetBIOS names, it does not register them. When a non-WINS client starts up, it may broadcast its name to the local segment, but the WINS Proxy Agent on that segment does not register the non-WINS client name in the WINS database. The WINS Proxy Agent solves the problem of NetBIOS name resolution for non-WINS clients. The other side of the coin is resolving the NetBIOS name of a non-WINS client. A non-WINS client does not register its name in the WINS database. If a WINS client tries to resolve the name of a non-WINS client, the attempt fails, because there is no entry in the WINS database for the non-WINS client. The solution to this problem is to add a *static entry* into the WINS database for the non-WINS client.

Windows Internet Name Service (WINS) Referral Zone A WINS Referral Zone is usually a forward lookup zone that has no resource records in it. After creating the WINS Referral Zone, you disable WINS Referral for all other zones. After you have done this, any queries that are resolved via WINS are returned with the Fully Qualified Domain Name (FQDN) that contains the NetBIOS name returned from the WINS server with the WINS Referral Zone's domain name appended to it. In this way, it is easy to identify what queries have been resolved via WINS lookups.

Windows Internet Name Service (WINS) Snap-in With the snap-in, you can view the active WINS entries under the Active Registrations folder. In addition, you can supply static mappings for non-WINS clients on the network through the snap-in. To configure a static mapping, select the Active Registrations folder and the Select New Static Mapping from the Action menu. Once a static mapping is entered into the WINS database, it cannot be edited. If you need to make changes to a static mapping, you must delete and recreate the entry.

Windows NT The NT kernel (the core or nucleus of the operating system, which provides basic services for all other parts of the operating system) is built on a completely different architecture from consumer Windows. In fact, NT was based on the 32-bit preemptive multitasking operating system that originated as a joint project of Microsoft and IBM before their parting of the ways, OS/2. NT provided the stability and security features that the "other Windows" lacked, albeit at a price, and not only a monetary one; NT was much pickier in terms of hardware support, did not run all of the programs that ran on Windows 9*x* (especially DOS programs that accessed the hardware directly), and required more resources, especially memory, to run properly.

WINNT.EXE program The WINNT.EXE program is used for network installations that use an MS-DOS network client. The WINNT32.EXE program is used to customize the process for upgrading existing installations. The WINNT32.EXE program is used for installing Windows 2000 from a computer that is currently running Windows 95/98 or Windows NT.

WINS *See* Windows Internet Name Service.

Workgroup A workgroup is a logical grouping of resources on a network. It is generally used in peer-to-peer networks. This means that each computer is responsible for access to its resources. Each computer has its own account database and is administered separately. Security is not shared between computers, and administration is more difficult than in a centralized domain.

X25 X25 uses an international standard for sending data across public packet-switching networks. The Windows 2000 Routing and Remote Access server will only support direct connections to X25 networks by using an X25 smart card.

Zone delegation Zone delegation provides a way for you to distribute responsibility for zone database management, and provides a measure of load balancing for Domain Name System (DNS) servers. When you create a delegation for a zone, you are "passing the buck" to another DNS server to answer DNS queries for a particular zone. Zones can be delegated to Secondary DNS Servers or Primaries.

Zone transfer The zone transfer process can be considered a "pull" operation. This is because the Secondary Domain Name System (DNS) server initiates the zone transfer process. The Secondary DNS server will initiate a zone transfer when a Primary DNS server sends a "notify" message to the Secondary DNS server, informing it that there has been a change to the zone database.

Zones of Authority The Domain Name System (DNS) name space is divided into zones, and each zone must have one name server that is the authority for the name mapping for the zone. Depending on the size of the name space, a zone may be subdivided into multiple zones, each with its own authority, or there may be a single authority for the entire zone. For instance, a small company with only 200-300 computers could have one DNS server handle the entire namespace.

INDEX

A

B

C

D

E

F

G

H

I

J

K

L

M

N

O

Q

R

S

T

U

V

W

X

Z

Custom Corporate Network Training

Train on Cutting Edge Technology We can bring the best in skill-based training to your facility to create a real-world hands-on training experience. Global Knowledge has invested millions of dollars in network hardware and software to train our students on the same equipment they will work with on the job. Our relationships with vendors allow us to incorporate the latest equipment and platforms into your on-site labs.

Maximize Your Training Budget Global Knowledge provides experienced instructors, comprehensive course materials, and all the networking equipment needed to deliver high quality training. You provide the students; we provide the knowledge.

Avoid Travel Expenses On-site courses allow you to schedule technical training at your convenience, saving time, expense, and the opportunity cost of travel away from the workplace.

Discuss Confidential Topics Private on-site training permits the open discussion of sensitive issues such as security, access, and network design. We can work with your existing network's proprietary files while demonstrating the latest technologies.

Customize Course Content Global Knowledge can tailor your courses to include the technologies and the topics which have the greatest impact on your business. We can complement your internal training efforts or provide a total solution to your training needs.

Corporate Pass The Corporate Pass Discount Program rewards our best network training customers with preferred pricing on public courses, discounts on multimedia training packages, and an array of career planning services.

Global Knowledge Training Lifecycle Supporting the Dynamic and Specialized Training Requirements of Information Technology Professionals

- Define Profile
- Assess Skills
- Design Training
- Deliver Training
- Test Knowledge
- Update Profile
- Use New Skills

College Credit Recommendation Program The American Council on Education's CREDIT program recommends 53 Global Knowledge courses for college credit. Now our network training can help you earn your college degree while you learn the technical skills needed for your job. When you attend an ACE-certified Global Knowledge course and pass the associated exam, you earn college credit recommendations for that course. Global Knowledge can establish a transcript record for you with ACE, which you can use to gain credit at a college or as a written record of your professional training that you can attach to your resume.

Registration Information

COURSE FEE: The fee covers course tuition, refreshments, and all course materials. Any parking expenses that may be incurred are not included. Payment or government training form must be received six business days prior to the course date. We will also accept Visa/ MasterCard and American Express. For non-U.S. credit card users, charges will be in U.S. funds and will be converted by your credit card company. Checks drawn on Canadian banks in Canadian funds are acceptable.

COURSE SCHEDULE: Registration is at 8:00 a.m. on the first day. The program begins at 8:30 a.m. and concludes at 4:30 p.m. each day.

CANCELLATION POLICY: Cancellation and full refund will be allowed if written cancellation is received in our office at least six business days prior to the course start date. Registrants who do not attend the course or do not cancel more than six business days in advance are responsible for the full registration fee; you may transfer to a later date provided the course fee has been paid in full. Substitutions may be made at any time. If Global Knowledge must cancel a course for any reason, liability is limited to the registration fee only.

GLOBAL KNOWLEDGE: Global Knowledge programs are developed and presented by industry professionals with "real-world" experience. Designed to help professionals meet today's interconnectivity and interoperability challenges, most of our programs feature hands-on labs that incorporate state-of-the-art communication components and equipment.

ON-SITE TEAM TRAINING: Bring Global Knowledge's powerful training programs to your company. At Global Knowledge, we will custom design courses to meet your specific network requirements. Call 1 (919) 461-8686 for more information.

YOUR GUARANTEE: Global Knowledge believes its courses offer the best possible training in this field. If during the first day you are not satisfied and wish to withdraw from the course, simply notify the instructor, return all course materials, and receive a 100% refund.

In the US:

CALL: 1 (888) 762-4442

FAX: 1 (919) 469-7070

VISIT OUR WEBSITE:

www.globalknowledge.com

MAIL CHECK AND THIS FORM TO:

Global Knowledge
Suite 200
114 Edinburgh South
P.O. Box 1187
Cary, NC 27512

In Canada:

CALL: 1 (800) 465-2226

FAX: 1 (613) 567-3899

VISIT OUR WEBSITE:

www.globalknowledge.com.ca

MAIL CHECK AND THIS FORM TO:

Global Knowledge
Suite 1601
393 University Ave.
Toronto, ON M5G 1E6

REGISTRATION INFORMATION:

Course title ____________________

Course location ____________________ Course date __________

Name/title ____________________ Company __________

Name/title ____________________ Company __________

Name/title ____________________ Company __________

Address ____________________ Telephone __________ Fax __________

City ____________________ State/Province __________ Zip/Postal Code __________

Credit card __________ Card # ____________________ Expiration date __________

Signature ____________________

LICENSE AGREEMENT

THIS PRODUCT (THE "PRODUCT") CONTAINS PROPRIETARY SOFTWARE, DATA AND INFORMATION (INCLUDING DOCUMENTATION) OWNED BY THE McGRAW-HILL COMPANIES, INC. ("McGRAW-HILL") AND ITS LICENSORS. YOUR RIGHT TO USE THE PRODUCT IS GOVERNED BY THE TERMS AND CONDITIONS OF THIS AGREEMENT.

LICENSE: Throughout this License Agreement, "you" shall mean either the individual or the entity whose agent opens this package. You are granted a non-exclusive and non-transferable license to use the Product subject to the following terms:

(i) If you have licensed a single user version of the Product, the Product may only be used on a single computer (i.e., a single CPU). If you licensed and paid the fee applicable to a local area network or wide area network version of the Product, you are subject to the terms of the following subparagraph (ii).

(ii) If you have licensed a local area network version, you may use the Product on unlimited workstations located in one single building selected by you that is served by such local area network. If you have licensed a wide area network version, you may use the Product on unlimited workstations located in multiple buildings on the same site selected by you that is served by such wide area network; provided, however, that any building will not be considered located in the same site if it is more than five (5) miles away from any building included in such site. In addition, you may only use a local area or wide area network version of the Product on one single server. If you wish to use the Product on more than one server, you must obtain written authorization from McGraw-Hill and pay additional fees.

(iii) You may make one copy of the Product for back-up purposes only and you must maintain an accurate record as to the location of the back-up at all times.

COPYRIGHT; RESTRICTIONS ON USE AND TRANSFER: All rights (including copyright) in and to the Product are owned by McGraw-Hill and its licensors. You are the owner of the enclosed disc on which the Product is recorded. You may not use, copy, decompile, disassemble, reverse engineer, modify, reproduce, create derivative works, transmit, distribute, sublicense, store in a database or retrieval system of any kind, rent or transfer the Product, or any portion thereof, in any form or by any means (including electronically or otherwise) except as expressly provided for in this License Agreement. You must reproduce the copyright notices, trademark notices, legends and logos of McGraw-Hill and its licensors that appear on the Product on the back-up copy of the Product which you are permitted to make hereunder. All rights in the Product not expressly granted herein are reserved by McGraw-Hill and its licensors.

TERM: This License Agreement is effective until terminated. It will terminate if you fail to comply with any term or condition of this License Agreement. Upon termination, you are obligated to return to McGraw-Hill the Product together with all copies thereof and to purge all copies of the Product included in any and all servers and computer facilities.

DISCLAIMER OF WARRANTY: THE PRODUCT AND THE BACK-UP COPY OF THE PRODUCT ARE LICENSED "AS IS." McGRAW-HILL, ITS LICENSORS AND THE AUTHORS MAKE NO WARRANTIES, EXPRESS OR IMPLIED, AS TO RESULTS TO BE OBTAINED BY ANY PERSON OR ENTITY FROM USE OF THE PRODUCT AND/OR ANY INFORMATION OR DATA INCLUDED THEREIN. McGRAW-HILL, ITS LICENSORS, AND THE AUTHORS MAKE NO GUARANTEE THAT YOU WILL PASS ANY CERTIFICATION EXAM BY USING THIS PRODUCT. McGRAW-HILL, ITS LICENSORS AND THE AUTHORS MAKE NO EXPRESS OR IMPLIED WARRANTIES OF MERCHANTABILITY OR FITNESS FOR A PARTICULAR PURPOSE OR USE WITH RESPECT TO THE PRODUCT. NEITHER McGRAW-HILL, ANY OF ITS LICENSORS, NOR THE AUTHORS WARRANT THAT THE FUNCTIONS CONTAINED IN THE PRODUCT WILL MEET YOUR REQUIREMENTS OR THAT THE OPERATION OF THE PRODUCT WILL BE UNINTERRUPTED OR ERROR FREE. YOU ASSUME THE ENTIRE RISK WITH RESPECT TO THE QUALITY AND PERFORMANCE OF THE PRODUCT.

LIMITED WARRANTY FOR DISC: To the original licensee only, McGraw-Hill warrants that the enclosed disc on which the Product is recorded is free from defects in materials and workmanship under normal use and service for a period of ninety (90) days from the date of purchase. In the event of a defect in the disc covered by the foregoing warranty, McGraw-Hill will replace the disc.

LIMITATION OF LIABILITY: NEITHER McGRAW-HILL, ITS LICENSORS NOR THE AUTHORS SHALL BE LIABLE FOR ANY INDIRECT, SPECIAL OR CONSEQUENTIAL DAMAGES, SUCH AS BUT NOT LIMITED TO, LOSS OF ANTICIPATED PROFITS OR BENEFITS, RESULTING FROM THE USE OR INABILITY TO USE THE PRODUCT EVEN IF ANY OF THEM HAS BEEN ADVISED OF THE POSSIBILITY OF SUCH DAMAGES. THIS LIMITATION OF LIABILITY SHALL APPLY TO ANY CLAIM OR CAUSE WHATSOEVER WHETHER SUCH CLAIM OR CAUSE ARISES IN CONTRACT, TORT, OR OTHERWISE. Some states do not allow the exclusion or limitation of indirect, special or consequential damages, so the above limitation may not apply to you.

U.S. GOVERNMENT RESTRICTED RIGHTS: Any software included in the Product is provided with restricted rights subject to subparagraphs (c), (1) and (2) of the Commercial Computer Software-Restricted Rights clause at 48 C.F.R. 52.227-19. The terms of this Agreement applicable to the use of the data in the Product are those under which the data are generally made available to the general public by McGraw-Hill. Except as provided herein, no reproduction, use, or disclosure rights are granted with respect to the data included in the Product and no right to modify or create derivative works from any such data is hereby granted.

GENERAL: This License Agreement constitutes the entire agreement between the parties relating to the Product. The terms of any Purchase Order shall have no effect on the terms of this License Agreement. Failure of McGraw-Hill to insist at any time on strict compliance with this License Agreement shall not constitute a waiver of any rights under this License Agreement. This License Agreement shall be construed and governed in accordance with the laws of the State of New York. If any provision of this License Agreement is held to be contrary to law, that provision will be enforced to the maximum extent permissible and the remaining provisions will remain in full force and effect.